Xtra! for Managerial Accounting

Free when bundled with a new text, Xtra! provides access to **additional multi-media learning tools** including:

- E-Lectures that review core accounting topics
- Crossword Puzzles to review vocabulary
- Topical and multiple choice quizzes to test understanding of the content
- Spanish Dictionary of Accounting Terms

Personal Trainer® 3.0

Personal Trainer 3.0 helps students complete their homework from the text as well as grade homework for the instructor! Available for sale separately or included in WebTutor Advantage, new Personal Trainer 3.0 upgrades include:

1. Enhanced Hints:
   - Up to 3 hints plus an additional hint that the instructor can add
   - Hints can include not only text but PowerPoint® slides as well

2. Enhanced Questions:
   - Now includes all end-of-chapter exercises and problems
   - Students can spell check their answers before submitting

3. Enhanced Instructor Capabilities:
   - Questions can be assigned as "required" or "excluded"
   - Grades can be captured on demand or preset
   - A more flexible gradebook that can display and download any combination of data

4. Enhanced Look-and-Feel:
   - New graphic design
   - Greater ease-of-use

Study Tools for Students

Visit **http://albright.swlearning.com** to access the following FREE student learning resources:

- Quizzes with feedback
- Hotlinks to the Web sites listed in the text
- PowerPoint® presentation slides for review of chapter coverage
- Check figures to selected assignments
- Learning objectives from the chapter

4 TH EDITION

MANAGERIAL ACCOUNTING
Information for Decisions

Thomas L. Albright
University of Alabama

Robert W. Ingram
University of Alabama

John W. Hill
Indiana University

THOMSON

SOUTH-WESTERN

Australia · Canada · Mexico · Singapore · Spain · United Kingdom · United States

THOMSON

SOUTH-WESTERN

Managerial Accounting: Information for Decisions, 4e

Thomas L. Albright, Robert W. Ingram, and John W. Hill

VP/Editorial Director:
Jack W. Calhoun

Publisher
Rob Dewey

Acquisitions Editor:
Sharon Oblinger

Developmental Editor:
Allison Rolfes

Marketing Manager:
Keith Chassé

Production Editor:
Chris Sears

Manufacturing Coordinator:
Doug Wilke

Technology Project Editor:
Robin Browning

Web Coordinator:
Kelly Reid

Compositor
GGS Information Services, Inc.

Production House:
Litten Editing and Production, Inc.

Art Director:
Michelle Kunkler

Cover and Internal Designer:
Grannan Graphic Design
Cincinnati, OH

Cover Image:
© Digital Vision

Photo Researcher:
Darren Wright

Printer:
Transcontinental
Beauceville, Quebec

BRIEF CONTENTS

MANAGERIAL ACCOUNTING

iii

CONTENTS

iv

STUDENT PREFACE

How to Do Well in This Course

We are going to let you in on some trade secrets instructors seldom tell students. That's why this section is labeled "For Students Only." If instructors find out we have revealed these secrets, we'll probably get a lot of mail.

Getting good grades is not a matter of luck. That's not the secret. Also, it is no secret that doing assignments (on time), going to class (regularly), getting enough sleep and exercise, eating properly, and studying throughout the semester (instead of just at exam time) will improve your grades. But this is hard work. So, what you want is a way to get good grades and not work so hard, right? Well, pay attention—the secret is to work smarter! That's not the same as being smarter, which is a matter of luck. Here's how you work smarter.

Step 1: Determine why this course is important for you. First, figure out why you're taking this class. What are your goals for the class? Do you care about this course? Do you have a strong motivation to learn about accounting? Perhaps being an accountant comes on your list of career options just below sweeping up at McDonalds'. Maybe your goal is to make lots of money. Or maybe you're just in college to have a good time until you inherit the family fortune. In any case, this course is designed for you. One of the surest ways to have a million dollars is to start with ten million and not know anything about accounting and business management. If you don't inherit wealth, you're not likely to get it without speaking the language of business. Accounting is the language! Maybe you just want to get a good job but you're pretty sure you don't want to be an accountant. Fine! This course isn't going to make an accountant out of you. It will help you understand some of the "mystical rituals" of accounting that nonaccountants often find confusing. Whatever type of management position you have in any organization, you can count on having to work with accountants and with accounting information. You should know they can have a major effect on your life. Many organizations use accounting information to evaluate their employees for salary and promotion decisions. You should understand how to interpret this information. You may even learn accounting isn't what you think. Whether you grow to love or hate accounting, decide what you can get out of this course that will be useful to you.

Step 2: Find out what your instructors expect of you in this course. Next, check out your instructor. If you're lucky, your instructor is sensitive, warm, caring, has a good sense of humor, is witty, loves teaching, and wants you to do well in the course. If instead your instructor is more normal (and less perfect), remember, the instructor is still the instructor. And as the instructor, she has power over your life. So, find out what she expects from you. What are her goals for the course? What does she want you to know or be able to do once you complete the course? Perhaps she will tell you (good sign), but if not, ask. You should say: "Professor Whatever-Your-Name-Is (it would be wise to use the right name), what's the lowdown on the layout for this course?" This is education jargon for "what are your goals for this course?" This may catch her off guard, so give her a minute or two to think. You may even have to wait until the next class meeting to get your answer. Make sure you and your instructor understand each other's goals

Step 3: Find out how you will be graded. How does the instructor test? Is he one of the picky types: "What is the third word on the fifth line on page 211?" Or, does he go for the broader, thought-provoking questions: "How was accounting instrumental in negotiating the third treaty of Versailles in 1623." Does he go for multiple guess, or are short answers his cup of tea? Whatever the method, you need to know what is expected of you and how these expectations translate into grades. Occasionally, you'll find an instructor whose stated expectations don't agree with how he tests and grades. That's why you need to find out about both expectations and grades. If they don't seem to be consistent, you'll have to determine what the instructor really expects.

Step 4: Emphasize learning what's important. Figure out what you need to do to accomplish your goals and meet the instructor's expectations. A major lesson you should learn, if you haven't already, is "what you take from a course (and almost anything else) depends on what you bring to it." Your attitude is important. If you decide something is worth learning, you'll probably find a way to learn it . . . not because you're supposed to learn it, but because you want to. "Wanting to" is the biggest part of working smarter. Wanting to learn will go a long way toward helping you get a good grade. Unfortunately, it may not be enough unless what you want to learn is also what your instructor wants you to learn. Therefore, you need to make sure you and your instructor are on the same wavelength. If you're not, talk it over. Find out why the instructor has a different outlook. You may change your opinion about what's important. Determine how to focus your efforts. Not everything in this book or course is equally important. Focus on what's most important to you and to your instructor.

Step 5: Communicate with your instructor. Try to remember your instructor is a person. Even the authors of this book are people. We have wives, children, and pets. Most instructors really want to see you do well, but we need your help. Instructors don't know everything. In particular, we can't read your mind. You need to let your instructor know if you're having problems understanding the material you're expected to learn, figuring out what the instructor expects of you, or figuring out how to prepare for tests and other assignments. Talk with your instructor about problems you're having with the class. Remember, your instructor *is* human.

This is your class. You paid for it. OK, maybe it was your parents, or somebody else who put out cold, hard cash for you to take this course. Don't let anybody keep you from getting your money's worth. Working smarter means determining what's important and focusing your attention and efforts on these things. Then, don't be distracted from your goals. If you run into problems, deal with them. If you don't understand something in class or in the book, ask questions. If you're afraid of asking dumb questions in class, remember: looking dumb in class is better than looking dumb on an exam. If you think you may be missing key points, talk with your instructor. If you want to learn, you can.

That's it. Give it a try. We think you'll find the course more enjoyable and the experience more rewarding. Of course, you might also try doing assignments, going to class, getting enough sleep and exercise, eating properly, and studying throughout the semester. These things usually help, even though they are hard work.

Best wishes to you, not only in this course, but throughout life.

Tom Albright
Rob Ingram
John Hill

A side note. To aid you in the learning process, the following icons appear throughout the text.

SPREADSHEET

Excel activities are integrated throughout the text. At the end of the text, you will find an appendix titled "A Short Introduction to Excel" that will help you get started. Throughout the text, specific assignments that you may choose to complete using spreadsheet software are identified with this icon. Problems titled "Excel in Action," which contain more assistance with using this very helpful tool, create a continuing managerial accounting case that unfolds throughout each half of the book.

http://albright.
swlearning.com

In addition to providing helpful links to specific resources, as indicated with the icon in the text, this Web site contains many helpful learning aids. You will find Projects on the Web, quiz questions with feedback, PowerPoint® presentation slides for review of chapter coverage, check figures to selected assignments, learning objectives from the chapter to help you focus on the core goals, and updates for the latest information about changes in GAAP and any new, important information related to the text. In addition, this icon lets you know there's a related Internet hotlink connected to the text's Web site.

INSTRUCTOR PREFACE

Prepare Your Students for Success

The business world no longer views accountants as "bean counters." Within companies, large and small, the managerial accountant has an integral role in core decision making. Accounting has transformed from its traditional role of collecting data and creating information to interpreting information and participating with the rest of the management team in developing company strategy.

Your students may or may not have much knowledge of the internal accounting concerns of companies that determine pricing, manage costs, communicate data, etc. Some of your students will choose accounting as their major area. All of your students should gain the knowledge of how managerial accounting is significant to all businesses. This fourth edition of *Managerial Accounting: Information for Decisions* will serve as a carefully crafted tool to assist you in preparing your students for success as they move toward becoming the business decision makers of tomorrow.

Develop Understanding with Quality Content

As future managers and business professionals, students need a clear understanding of how accounting will help them analyze and interpret critical information. Their ability to make smart decisions is a valuable skill as they strive for success in today's competitive business environment. *Managerial Accounting: Information for Decisions* vividly illustrates how accounting contributes to the activities and accomplishments of the entire organization.

To assist you, the instructor, in educating your students, we have integrated strong pedagogical elements throughout the text. These elements put managerial accounting topics in context to help students visualize their role in the "real world." Highlighted below are some of the most significant learning aids.

REVISED! Young Design, Inc.—Looking Inside a Company
This simple, yet realistic case of a small, startup company unfolds throughout the text and provides students with an easy-to-understand example of the purpose of accounting, its process, and its importance in decision making. As students move from chapter to chapter, they learn how the owners of the company tackle basic business decisions using accounting information and how their accounting system develops over time.

Chapter-Opening Question—Focusing on the Main Issues
Each chapter opens with a question, which is followed by a stage-setting paragraph about Young Design, Inc. This feature helps students focus on the "bigger picture" as they study the chapter.

COST CATEGORIES AND FLOWS

M2

How can accounting classifications help us understand costs?

Erin and Seth believe they have designed a product that customers will want to buy. Seth understands how to make the product, and Erin has developed a marketing plan. In order to make a profit, Erin and Seth must control their costs so the revenue they receive from selling their products is greater than the costs of producing and selling them. Therefore, the next problem Erin and Seth must address involves understanding costs.

From page M29

Food for Thought—Stepping Inside the Company
As your students read about Young Design, Inc., they are asked to put themselves in a role within the company and think about what decisions they would make. This challenge brings home how accounting information is essential for decision making.

FOOD FOR THOUGHT

Put yourself in the role of Seth and Erin. What would you like to know about costs? Would you want to understand how the cost of making the product differs from the cost of selling the product and administering the business? Let's join Erin and Seth as they discuss the accounting information they will need to make pricing decisions.

From page M29

Dialogue—Hearing Business Concerns
Each scenario concludes with a discussion between the owners (Erin and Seth) and, when needed, with the company's accountant (Roberta). These meetings highlight issues and concerns that may arise within companies.

Seth: *I've been thinking about how to distinguish between costs incurred to make products and those incurred to generate sales. I think we should classify all costs that result from production activities as product costs.*

Erin: *That makes sense because all of these costs can be traced to the products we make. For example, we can identify materials such as lumber and hardware used in making each product. Also, we can trace the labor of production employees to the products.*

Seth: *You're right. But I haven't figured out what to do with the costs of a lot of miscellaneous items such as*

From page M29

Thinking Beyond the Question—Reaching Higher

The chapter-opening question is revisited in the end-of-chapter section. Students are asked a challenge question that requires them to think beyond what has been presented in the chapter.

Thinking Beyond the Question

How can accounting classifications help us understand costs?

In the opening scenario, Erin and Seth were considering ways to classify costs and to use their accounting reports. Can managers use cost reports based on past activities to help control future costs?

From page M43

NEW! Computerized Manufacturing Systems—Visualizing AIS

New Chapter M6 examines *computerized manufacturing systems*. A goal of this chapter is to help students see *accounting as a dynamic, technological process*. Students sometimes get the impression that accounting is a clerical process without much technological sophistication. Modern accounting systems require a basic understanding of computer networks and database management systems. The world in which accountants work is not one of traditional journals and ledgers. It is one in which computer systems are essential to processing and analyzing business information. The chapter includes an *illustration of a simple accounting database system*. By working through this project, students learn how basic accounting functions are automated and how computers facilitate the accounting process. The database file that ties to the project is provided on the Student CD-ROM and on the text's Web site (http://albright.swlearning.com).

Exhibit 1 Components of an Accounting Information System

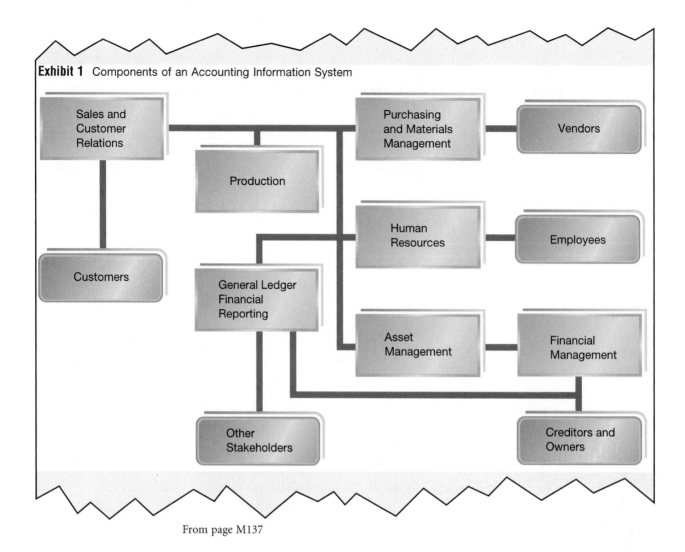

From page M137

REVISED! Organization—Moving Smoothly Through the Topics
Several chapters have been revised, reorganized, and enhanced. The changes have created a more focused presentation of job order and process costing, among other important refinements. Like-topics have been clustered to increase clarity and continuity for students.

- **Accounting and Management Decisions.** Chapter M1 has been *simplified* and includes an *explanation of the scope of managerial accounting* in business organizations.
- **Cost Categories and Flows.** Chapter M2 has been *streamlined* and contains an *increased focus on how managerial accounting systems support decision making.*
- **Job-Order Costing and Process Costing.** This coverage is *significantly revised* and covered individually in *two separate chapters* (Chapters M3 and M4).
- **Cost Allocation and ABC.** Chapter M5 provides *all new coverage* of this important topic.
- **Analyzing Cost Behavior.** Chapter M7 is a *significant revision* of cost behavior coverage that had been presented primarily in Chapter M4 of the prior edition.
- **Budgeting.** Now in Chapter M8, this content is *substantially revised* with more visuals for understanding *the relationships of the budgets* and where they fit in the business organization.

ENHANCED! Coverage of Ethics—Mentoring High Standards
The importance of ethics is reinforced in many places throughout the text.

P2-1 **Ethics—Product versus Period Classification**
Obj. 1
Assume management intentionally misclassified a period expense as a product cost in order to meet analysts' earnings expectations. The fraud later was discovered during the annual audit.

Required Explain how the misclassification enabled management to boost the company's earnings.

From page M46

REVISED! Case In Point Boxes—Providing a Glimpse into the Business World
The content presented in these boxes provides students with a variety of enrichment information, some featuring the business community in general while others focus on specific examples of company practices.

Case In Point

http://albright.
swlearning.com
....
**Learn more about
target costing.**

Target Costing at Hewlett-Packard

The Vancouver Division of **Hewlett-Packard** (HP) uses target costing to work with its suppliers to manage the cost of making the desk jet printer. The facility recently has changed its strategy from producing low-volume, high-margin industrial products to high-volume, low-margin consumer products. HP reports achieving substantial price decreases as a result of their target costing program. In addition, the company uses target costing to support continuous improvement efforts and to identify various activities that cause costs within the value chain.

Source: Anonymous. 2000. Target costing gives HP better control over supply costs. New York: Supplier and Management Report.

From page M40

ENHANCED! Assignment Material—Reinforcing Understanding
New exercises and problems have been added. Many problems have been revised as well as updated for real-company information.

NEW! Student CD-ROM—Providing More Opportunities
In response to requests from instructors for more assignment material, we have added this new resource, bundled without charge with new texts. It contains alternative exercises, problems, and cases that provide more choices to instructors who may use this as "set B" and a greater opportunity for students who want more practice.

TIMELY! Managerial Topics—Teaching Current Topics
Current topics, such as quality management, are featured along with the important traditional ones.

- **Strategic Focus.** The book's strategic focus demonstrates how businesses and organizations use managerial accounting to achieve operating and organizational objectives.
- **Contemporary vs. Traditional Approaches.** Contemporary, as well as traditional, management accounting philosophies and methods are covered. The benefits and drawbacks of the different approaches are explained in a simple, straightforward manner.
- **Service Industry Coverage.** Managerial accounting issues are related to service companies within each managerial chapter and in the end-of-chapter material to provide a broader view of the business environment.

PROVEN! Pedagogical Features—Shaping Understanding with Confidence

- **Learning Objectives.** Learning objectives serve as ongoing reminders to students as to what is key in each part of the chapter and provide a basis for review. These objectives, which are written as measurable goals, are partnered with the assignments so instructors can easily select applicable coverage.
- **Learning Notes.** These notes highlight issues that frequently are troublesome for students or that enrich student understanding.
- **Self-Study Problems.** These problems provide opportunity for students to test themselves as they progress throughout the chapter.
- **Introducing Students to Excel as a Helpful Tool.** For students with little or no Excel experience and those needing a reference, we have included A Short Introduction to Excel in an appendix at the end of the text. Experience with using spreadsheets as a helpful tool in managerial accounting continues throughout the text in the *Excel in Action* problems.

APPENDIX B

A Short Introduction to Excel™

SPREADSHEET

This introduction summarizes some of the primary operations and functions of a spreadsheet. It is intended to get you started if you have not had previous experience with Excel. There are many operations and functions in addition to those mentioned here.

Identifying and Selecting Cells

A spreadsheet consists of rows and columns. Rows are identified by numbers, and columns are identified by letters. An intersection of a row and column is a cell. A cell is identified by the column letter and row number that intersect at that cell.

From page B1 *(continued)*

From page B1

- **Review of Important Concepts.** This section provides a summary in outline form of each chapter's important concepts.
- **Key Concepts and Terms.** This section lists, with page references, the concepts and terms that are defined in the chapter.
- **Solutions to Self-Study Problems.** These solutions give students the answers to the chapter Self-Study Problems as a way of reinforcing their understanding of the material.
- **Questions.** These questions are designed specifically to stimulate in-class discussion of each chapter's most important concepts.
- **Exercises.** These are short assignments that focus on computations and are excellent for in-class demonstration and discussion.
- **Problems.** These provide for a more complex learning experience, taking student learning further by focusing on analysis of information. Each chapter contains a problem set of multiple-choice questions, which many instructors like to use as an in-class quiz. A spreadsheet icon identifies assignments that work well with Excel.
- **Cases.** Cases are more challenging than problems and encourage thinking and analytical skills.

SPREADSHEET

Bring Content Alive Through the Technology

ENHANCED! Technology—Making Learning Easier

Personal Trainer® 3.0. (0-324-29135-3) Students can complete textbook end-of-chapter exercises and problems online and receive immediate feedback with Personal Trainer! Additionally, student results instantaneously flow into your gradebook! Each assignment begins with a warmup, to get students started in the right direction; then, hints are provided that offer additional assistance, if needed, once students receive the feedback on their work. This new, dynamic version of Personal Trainer offers many other helpful ways to assist both instructors and students.

WebTUTOR Advantage   **WebTutor® Advantage with Personal Trainer.** Available in either WebCT™ (0-324-29137-X) or Blackboard® (0-324-29138-8) platforms, this rich course management product is a specially designed extension of the classroom experience that enlivens the course by leveraging the power of the Internet with comprehensive educational content. WebTutor Advantage on WebCT or Blackboard® includes Personal Trainer to provide both students and instructors an unprecedented real-time, guided, self-correcting study outside the classroom. Instructors or students can use these resources along with those on the Product Web Site to supplement the classroom experience. Use this effective resource as an integrated solution for your distance learning or web-enhanced course! This powerful, turnkey solution provides the following content customized for this edition:

- **E-Lectures.** PowerPoint® slides of the key topical coverage accompanied by audio explanations that provide additional learning support.
- **Interactive Quizzes.** Multiple-choice questions that test the knowledge of the chapter content and provide immediate feedback on the accuracy of the response. These quizzes help students pinpoint areas needing more study.
- **Practice Exercises.** Short exercises with feedback to provide extra practice tied to chapter content.
- **Problem Demonstrations.** Selected Self-Study Problems with an audio step-by-step explanation of the solution to guide student understanding.
- **Video Clips.** Short, high-interest segments that focus on chapter-related topics to provide application of concepts to the real world.
- **Chapter Review.** Comprehensive chapter reviews that reinforce important concepts from each chapter.
- **Flashcards.** A terminology quiz that helps students gain a complete understanding of the key terms from the chapter.
- **Spanish Dictionary of Accounting Terminology.** An aid for Spanish-speaking students.
- **Crossword Puzzles.** Interactive puzzles that provide an alternative tool for students to test their understanding of terminology.
- **Quiz Bowl Game.** A fun online game similar to Jeopardy!® that reinforces chapter content.
- **Personal Trainer.** An Internet-based homework tutor for students and instructors. See description in the preceding section.

Access certificates for WebTutor® Advantage with Personal Trainer® can be bundled with the textbook or sold separately. **For more information, including a demo, visit** http://webtutor.swcollege.com. **To adopt the course in either WebCT or Blackboard, contact your sales representative or sign up at** http://webtutor.thomsonlearning.com.

Xtra! This enrichment resource provides topic reinforcement resources and interactive quizzes so students can test their understanding of the content of the fourth edition. **Free** when bundled with a new text, students receive an access code so that they can receive Xtra! reinforcement in accounting.

http://albright.
swlearning.com
....

Text Web Site. (http://albright.swlearning.com) The Web site for the fourth edition offers you and your student many resources for teaching and learning.

Among the many elements available to *Students* are:

- *Quizzes with feedback.*
- *Hotlinks* to many resources on the Web, including all of the Web sites listed in the text; this provides a quick connection to key information.
- *PowerPoint® presentation slides* for review of chapter coverage.
- *Internet Research and Other Projects* link text content to today's business environment. These assignments challenge students to expand their knowledge, apply what they have learned, and think critically.
- *Projects on the Web* for expanded learning through this helpful resource.
- *Check figures* to selected assignments.
- *Learning objectives* from the chapter are repeated as a study aid to keep clear focus on the core goals.
- *Updates* for the latest information about changes in GAAP and any new, important information related to the text.

For Instructors, in addition to full access to the student resources listed above, a password-protected section of the Web site contains a number of resource files, including:

- *Solutions Manual* in Microsoft® Word.
- *Cooperative Learning and Instructor's Resource Guide* in Microsoft® Word.
- *Solutions to Excel templates* for the *Excel in Action* and other assignments identified by the spreadsheet icon in the text.

- *Solution transparency file* in Microsoft® Word.
- Additional *updates* pertinent to instructors.

ENHANCED! Additional Support Material—Providing More Learning Experience

FOR STUDENTS

- **Student CD-ROM** (0-324-22242-4). Automatically packaged free with new texts, this new set of alternative exercises, problems, and cases has been created by Scott Colvin, Naugatuck Valley Community College, to provide instructors an extensive list to choose from and to provide students with more opportunities to practice. Many instructors like to use one version of assignments in class for demonstration and discussion and the other set for homework. Others like to alternate sets from semester to semester. Also included on the CD are the accounting information system database files for the Kwiki Oil Company illustration, which appears in Chapter M6.
- **Study Guide and Forms** (0-324-22248-3). This guide reinforces and enhances student understanding of the topics covered in the text. It is a thorough, value-adding book, prepared by Stephen Senge (Simmons Graduate School of Management) and George Sanders (Western Washington University). Included are working paper forms for selected text assignments.

FOR INSTRUCTORS

- **Cooperative Learning and Instructor's Resource Guide** (0-324-22235-1). Contained in this supporting item are chapters, prepared by Philip Cottell, Jr. of Miami University, explaining cooperative learning techniques for use in the classroom and matrices that suggest application of techniques to specific end-of-chapter items. In addition, there are outlines of each chapter, teaching notes, and descriptions of the exercises, problems, and cases to assist in class preparation. This guide's content is also available in electronic form on the Instructor's Resource CD-ROM and (restricted) on the product support Web site.
- **Solutions Manual (0-324-22236-X).** Author-prepared and carefully verified solutions to all exercises, problems, and cases are presented in this manual.
- **Test Bank** (0-324-22238-6). A complete and plentiful set of newly revised test items in print form; also available in electronic form (using ExamView® software, provided) on the Instructor's Resource CD-ROM.
- **Instructor's Resource CD-ROM with ExamView®** (0-324-29134-5). This IRCD contains the files for key instructor's ancillaries (the Cooperative Learning and Instructor's Resource Guide, the solutions manual, and the PowerPoint® Presentation slides). This gives instructors the ultimate tool for customizing lectures and presentations. The presentation slides reinforce chapter content and provide a rich tool for in-class lectures and out-of-class reviewing. The test bank files on the CD-ROM are provided in ExamView® format. This program is an easy-to-use test creation software compatible with Microsoft® Windows. Instructors can add or edit questions, instructions, and answers, and select questions (randomly or numerically) by previewing them on the screen. Instructors can also create and administer quizzes online, whether over the Internet, a local area network (LAN), or a wide area network (WAN).
- **Solution Transparencies** (0-324-22237-8). Acetate transparencies of the numerical solutions to the exercises, problems, and cases are available to adopters.

Add Enrichment with Other Accounting Resources

Business & Professional Ethics for Directors, Executives, and Accountants, 3e (0-324-20066-8). Leonard J. Brooks of the University of Toronto has extensively revised his text to include the latest ethical concerns in today's business environment. Cases, readings, and textual material are blended to provide accounting and business students with a concise, practical understanding of how to behave ethically in a post-Enron world. This text includes a complete business and professional ethics guide to working in the age of accounting scandals. Issues and cases in this new edition cover: Enron and Enron-triggered changes in governance for corporations and the accounting profession; increased ethical sensitivity to ethical issues; calls for increased accountability to stakeholders, ethical decision making and behavior; and the development of ethical organization cultures domestically and internationally.

Accounting Ethics in the Post-Enron Age, 1e (0-324-19193-6) (by Iris Stuart and Bruce Stuart of California State University—Fullerton). With the Enron/Andersen debacle, ethics is becoming an increasingly important (and interesting) part of accounting education. Ethics coverage is also required by the AACSB for accreditation purposes. Most texts include some limited ethics coverage, but many instructors would like to see more. This timely supplement contains ethics cases based on real and hypothetical situations in the business world. Examples include cases tied to Enron, Global Crossing, and Boston Chicken. Identifying ethical dilemmas and projecting their resolution will allow students to develop essential skills for success in their future careers. In each section of the textbook, the problems will be labeled according to subject matter (e.g., bad debt expense, revenue recognition). This allows the instructor to select problems consistent with the needs of the course.

California Car Company: An Active Learning Costing Case, 2e (0-324-18450-6) (by Steven J. Adams and LeRoy J. Pryor, both of California State University, Chico). This award-winning project forms the foundation of much of the management material. Using interlocking-block cars, students learn about the manufacturing process and managerial accounting by creating their own production line. Also available is a supporting instructor's manual.

An Introduction to Accounting, Business Processes, and ERP (0-324-19161-8) (by Phil Reckers, Julie Smith David, and Harriet Maccracken, all of Arizona State University). Utilizing JD Edwards software demos, an industry leading ERP company, your students will learn an overview of the use of ERP software for accounting and business processes. Unlike any other product on the market, they will not only learn the advantages of technology in accessing business information but will also learn to apply it in three different business models. After each module, student learning is reinforced by quizzing. Equip your students with this class-tested and easy-to-use experience to help them meet the ever-changing challenges of business and technology!

InfoTrac® College Edition. With this resource, your students can receive anytime, anywhere online access to a database of full-text articles from hundreds of popular and scholarly periodicals, such as *Newsweek, Fortune, Entrepreneur, Journal of Accountancy,* and *Nation's Business,* among others. Students can use its fast and easy search tools to find relevant news and analytical information among the tens of thousands of articles in the database-updated daily and going back as far as five years—all at a single Web site. InfoTrac is a great way to expose students to online research techniques, with the security that the content is academically based and reliable. An InfoTrac College Edition subscription card is packaged free with new copies of our financial accounting texts. For more information, visit http://www.swlearning.com/infotrac/infotrac.html.

INTACCT Managerial Accounting (by D. V. Rama and K. Raghunandan, both of Florida International University). These Internet-based tutorials at http://rama.swlearning.com are designed for use in an introductory accounting course or in any course where a review of the key accounting concepts and terminology is needed. The program offers a visual, user-friendly way to reinforce accounting principles and includes tutorials, demonstration problems, exercises, and an interactive glossary. Users will receive an access certificate that will allow them to do the online tutorial over the full term of a course.

Acknowledgments

Throughout the writing and development of the four editions of our text, many colleagues have contributed creative, helpful suggestions through reviews, focus groups, surveys, etc. We have considered all of the feedback carefully as each edition has been prepared and will continue to do so in the future. Therefore, in appreciation, we thank the following contributors:

Judy Beebe, Western Oregon University
Scott Colvin, Naugatuck Valley Community College
Elizabeth Davis, Baylor University
Patricia A. Doherty, Boston University
William H. Dresnack, SUNY College at Brockport
Stephen L. Duncan, Navarro College
Rafik Z. Elias, Cameron University
Kel-Ann Eyler, Brenau University
Benjamin Foster, University of Louisville
Roger Gee, San Diego Mesa College

Sheri L. Henson, Western Kentucky University
Candace Leuck, University of North Carolina—Charlotte
Cathy Lumbattis, Southern Illinois University
Kevin McNelis, New Mexico State University
Stephen G. Morrissette, University of St. Francis
Carol Nemec, Southern Oregon University
Alfonso R. Oddo, Niagara University

In addition, we wish to thank all who worked diligently to provide the carefully crafted content of this edition's supporting materials.

Tom Albright
Rob Ingram
John Hill

ABOUT THE AUTHORS

Thomas L. Albright   Thomas L. Albright is the J. Reese Phifer Faculty Fellow in the Culverhouse School of Accountancy at the University of Alabama. He teaches courses at the undergraduate and graduate levels in financial and managerial accounting. Professor Albright has received the Professor of the Year award numerous times in relation to his work with the MBA and Executive MBA students.

Professor Albright is a Certified Public Accountant (California) and holds a Ph.D. from the University of Tennessee. He has received the Certificate of Merit from the Institute of Management Accountants (IMA) for his work in the area of quality costs. Dr. Albright is actively involved with manufacturing companies in both the United States and Mexico. His work is used to help companies determine more accurate product costs and to develop better performance measures to achieve manufacturing excellence.

Professor Albright lives with his wife, Debby, and their two children, Michael and Jenny. He enjoys scuba diving, underwater photography, and sailing.

Robert W. Ingram   Robert W. Ingram is the Ross-Culverhouse Chair and Associate Dean in the Culverhouse College of Business at The University of Alabama. He teaches courses in financial accounting and has been actively involved in course curriculum development. He has served as Director of Education for the American Accounting Association, as a member of the Accounting Education Change Commission, and as editor of *Issues in Accounting Education*, a journal dedicated to accounting education research.

Professor Ingram is a Certified Public Accountant and holds a Ph.D. from Texas Tech University. Prior to joining the faculty at the University of Alabama, he held positions at the University of South Carolina and the University of Iowa and a visiting appointment at the University of Chicago. His research, which examines financial reporting and accounting education, has been published widely in accounting and business journals. He is the recipient of the National Alumni Association Outstanding Commitment to Teaching Award and the Burlington Northern Foundation Faculty Achievement in Research Award at The University of Alabama. He has also received the Notable Contribution to Literature Award of the Government and Nonprofit Section of the American Accounting Association and the Award for Excellence and Professional Contributions of the Alabama Association for Higher Education in Business.

Professor Ingram and his wife, Chris, enjoy sports, travel, reading, music, and art. They live contentedly in Tuscaloosa, Alabama.

John W. Hill   John W. Hill is Associate Dean, Research and Operations, and Professor of Accounting at the Kelley School of Business, Indiana University, where he teaches courses in financial analysis, firm valuation, strategic cost management, and mergers and acquisitions. Professor Hill also serves as Chairman of the Board, Kelley Executive Partners, and is affiliated with the CPA/consulting firm of Clifton Gunderson, LLP as Senior Advisor engaged in business valuation consulting. He has served on several editorial boards and is the recipient of 16 teaching and research awards including the President's Award for Distinguished Teaching at Indiana University, the Deloitte &

Touche/American Accounting Association Wildman Medal, the Silver and Bronze Lybrand Medals, and three Certificates of Merit from the Institute of Management Accountants.

Professor Hill is a member of the Georgia Bar Association and holds a Ph.D. from the University of Iowa. Prior to becoming an academic, he was the chief financial and administrative officer of a bank. Professor Hill has conducted executive education for firms such as Baxter Healthcare, Graco, and John Deere and is engaged in various international executive education and consutling programs. He has consulted with the Hungarian Telecommunications company Matav and taught at the Borsa Italiano (Italian Stock Exchange), the Catholic University of Milan (Italy), University of Lubjyana (Solvenia), and the Ryazan State Pedagogical University (Russia). He currently is actively working on a three-year teaching/consulting engagement involving Vietnamese banks.

Professor Hill is a retired Major General, U.S. Marine Corps Reserve, and formerly Vice Commander, Marine Forces Atlantic, Europe, and South. He and his wife alternate living between Bloomington, Indiana, a log cabin in the hills of Brown County, Indiana, and Perdido Key, Florida.

Systems for Product Costing and Decision Making

ACCOUNTING AND MANAGEMENT DECISIONS

What basic financial information do we need to run a business?

Erin Stein and Seth Phillips have been friends for many years. Both share a common hobby of designing and making furniture. Recently, Erin and Seth decided to launch a new business, Young Designs, Inc., making children's furniture such as bunk beds. They hope to use their carpentry talents to create a new line of furniture that will be unique and distinctive and to sell the furniture to retail firms such as furniture and department stores. Erin and Seth have begun their business planning. One issue that has arisen is what type of information they will need to properly manage the business. Neither Erin nor Seth has a background in accounting. They decide to visit a local CPA and ask for her advice on how to set up an accounting information system that can provide the right information for management decision making.

FOOD FOR THOUGHT

Imagine yourself in the role of a business adviser. How might you advise Erin and Seth? First, consider what basic activities will be required to establish and run the business. Second, identify what types of business decisions Erin and Seth will need to make that will require the use of financial information. Third, think about what basic types of financial information will be needed to make these decisions. Now, let's join the conversation Erin and Seth are having with their accountant, Roberta Hernandez.

Roberta: *First, to establish the business, you will need to decide what pieces of furniture you intend to produce and project how much of each piece you will sell. Then, you will need to decide what types of equipment and how many employees will be needed to manufacture the furniture.*

Erin: *Seth and I have already discussed our planned sales by product and the equipment we will need. Our projections allow for substantial growth in both types of products and sales for the first few years of the business. We will also need information about the cost of operating and maintaining this equipment, the cost of raw materials used to make the furniture, and the cost of the labor to produce it.*

Roberta: *Excellent. You will likely need information about the cost of making the furniture to determine how to price your products and whether your profit margins are acceptable. Also, have you thought about how much cash you will need?*

Seth: *I assumed we could collect enough cash from our customers to meet our needs.*

Roberta: *You will have to purchase raw materials and labor to make the furniture and then pay for these resources before you collect from the customers. Consequently, you need enough cash to take care of obligations for materials and labor until you are paid by customers. Also, your cash requirements will likely grow as the business grows, so you will need to plan on growth in cash along with growth in sales.*

Erin: *That's fine for starting up the business, but what about once it is up and running?*

Roberta: *Periodically, perhaps once a month, you will need to have information about how well the business is doing in terms of sales, cost of manufacturing, costs of selling and administration, and profitability. This will enable you to better manage sales and costs. You will also want to know the financial condition of your business in terms of assets and liabilities and cash flows. I suggest both monthly and annual budgets. That way, each period you can compare how well your business is actually performing to how well you expected it to perform when you created the budget.*

OBJECTIVES

Once you have completed this chapter, you should be able to:

1 Explain the purpose of managerial accounting and why it is important.

2 Explain the role of managerial accounting in planning and control decisions.

3 Discuss ways in which managerial accounting interacts with marketing and operations.

4 Explain the scope of managerial accounting.

INTRODUCTION TO MANAGERIAL ACCOUNTING

OBJECTIVE 1

Explain the purpose of managerial accounting and why it is important.

Managerial accounting **is the process of preparing, reporting, and interpreting accounting information for use by an organization's internal decision makers.** Different management functions within a company, such as marketing and operations, require types of accounting information for decision making that differ from the needs of external decision makers and from those of other managers. For example, marketing managers consider the cost per unit of a product when they determine a price for that product. On the other hand, operations managers may be interested in the cost of the labor, materials, and overhead required to make the product. Thus, the needs for managerial accounting information differ depending on the types of decisions being made.

Also, new demands for information arise as the business environment changes. For instance, as the profit earned on a line of products begins to shrink, accurate information about the cost of manufacturing the product becomes critical if the product is to remain profitable. A shrinking profit may indicate a shift in consumer preferences and a need to change the way a company competes. In that instance, the company may need to become a low-cost producer rather than competing on the basis of product features or quality.

Changes in companies' strategies have taken place in recent years because of intense foreign competition and the growing complexity of business. These changes have increased demand for accurate, high-quality managerial accounting information. However, systems that produce high-quality information often are expensive. The more detailed and accurate the information, the more it costs to produce. This cost includes the cost of the accounting systems that produce information and the cost of the services of the employees who design and manage these systems. Therefore, companies must balance the level of detail and accuracy they demand from their accounting systems in order to make good business decisions with what is affordable.

Corporate Structure and Accounting Information Needs

As companies grow, they divide managerial responsibilities among a larger number of people. Businesses frequently are organized according to functions to assist in decision making and control. For example, a company might be structured around the functions of accounting, finance, information systems, marketing, and production. Middle managers report to the company's top managers. Top managers develop company goals and the plans to achieve these goals. Top management also is responsible for reporting to stockholders, creditors, and other external decision makers. As illustrated in Exhibit 1, the types of information that different decision makers need depend on their positions in an organization's structure. Those at the top of the structure require less detailed and timely information about the ongoing operations of a company than those at the bottom of the structure.

Each function in a business usually has subdivisions, resulting in an organization with several layers of management. Typically, the higher managers are in the structure,

Exhibit 1
Types of Users and
Information Needs

Users	Accounting Information Needs
External Users Stockholders, creditors	Summary information about performance for a period of time (financial accounting)
Top Management Board of directors Chief executive officer	Information for evaluating performance, for establishing goals, and for devising plans to meet goals (financial and managerial accounting)
Functional and Division Managers Accounting Finance Information systems Marketing Operations Product and territory sales managers Plant managers	Timely and detailed information for evaluating performance and implementing plans (primarily managerial accounting)
Middle Managers Sales representatives Production managers Purchasing managers Service managers	Very timely and detailed information for day-to-day decisions to achieve company goals (managerial accounting)

the more responsibility they have for results and the more authority they have to make decisions. These decisions often require information that is more timely and detailed than the information required by external decision makers. Therefore, in markets where the prices and costs of products change frequently, marketing managers may need continuous information about product costs to make profitable sales.

Some of the accounting information used for internal decision making is the same as that reported to external decision makers. For example, the product cost information used for internal decisions also may be used in valuing inventories for a company's financial statements. Top managers often examine financial accounting information to evaluate a company's overall performance. However, the managerial accounting information provided to decision makers within the organization differs in many respects from the information reported externally. These differences will be considered in this and future chapters.

Financial accounting provides information that conforms with generally accepted accounting principles (GAAP). GAAP help to ensure that information is consistent from period to period and is comparable across companies. This information is valuable particularly to stakeholders, such as stockholders and creditors, who have limited access to information about companies.

An accountant who produces managerial accounting information for a specific company is referred to as a *management accountant*. Because managerial accounting information is used only within a company, it does not have to conform to GAAP. Rather, it is produced in a variety of formats that meet the particular information needs of a company's managers. Thus, the type, format, amount of detail, and timeliness of the information differ between financial and managerial accounting.

The Changing Needs of Business

Prior to World War II, the United States produced about one-fourth of the world's total goods and services. After World War II, all of the world's major economies except the United States had been severely damaged by the war. In contrast, the United States emerged with a huge productive capacity, greatly increased by the war effort, and a labor force swollen by returning veterans. As a result, following the war, the United States produced about one-half of the world's total goods and services. Most products consumed in the United States were produced in this country. In this type of environment, U.S. businesses could survive using less than optimal business practices. The situation began to change, however, with the growth of economies in Western Europe and Asia during the 1960s and 1970s. Foreign competitors seriously challenged U.S. companies with high-quality, technologically sophisticated products. U.S. companies had to change if they were to remain competitive in a global economy.

In recent years, changes in the ways companies market and produce their goods and services have led to changes in managers' needs for accounting information. For example, increased foreign competition has led U.S. firms to place more emphasis on the quality of the goods and services they produce. This emphasis on quality and the increasing complexity of business have increased the demand for timely and accurate information, thereby changing the role of managerial accounting.

Competition is driving many manufacturing and service companies to redesign their marketing and operations to meet the demands of a changing marketplace. Examples of such changes are just-in-time manufacturing, time-based competition, and total quality management, which are described later in this chapter. Managerial accounting systems are being redesigned to meet the changing information needs caused by these changes in the way products and services are created and delivered.

Today, many U.S. businesses are changing their management philosophies to become more competitive. These changes frequently involve:

- New marketing strategies directed at global markets
- Emphasis on customer satisfaction, including a focus on product quality and variety
- Large investments in new production technologies, including increased reliance on robotics and computerized manufacturing
- New relationships between management and labor that emphasize a greater role for labor in many decisions
- Creation of management teams to make key business decisions with representatives from the various functional areas of business, including accounting
- Development of real-time (immediate) business information systems, including use of the Internet to facilitate communication within a company and between a company and its stakeholders

These changes have created a new business environment, which has brought a high degree of product and service complexity, a greater number of parts that go into products, and new types of business transactions.

Managerial accounting must change in two ways if businesses are to compete successfully in this new competitive environment. First, management accountants must become involved in making decisions about a company's products and the processes used to create, market, and deliver these products. Through this involvement, management accountants can identify the critical accounting information needs of other decision makers. Second, decision makers throughout a company must be able to use accounting information properly. This means that decision makers must have a knowledge of managerial accounting concepts and techniques. It also means that they must be aware of the potential inaccuracies in accounting information. Companies that fail to make these changes in their managerial accounting systems are likely to receive inadequate information that leads to poor decisions.

The Quality of Accounting Information

The quality of information must be weighed against its cost. To be useful, information must have the potential to affect decisions and influence behavior. If a company is to perform well, information must be accurate enough to lead to the right decisions and behaviors. Accounting information often is not as accurate as many decision makers believe, however.

Accountants and managers select the methods used to produce accounting information. GAAP permit choices among methods of measuring certain business activities and reporting them to external decision makers, such as the choice of inventory and depreciation methods. Estimation also is used in preparing accounting information, such as estimation of the expected useful lives of depreciable assets. When accounting information is prepared for *internal purposes*, a company is not restricted to any particular accounting method. Nevertheless, companies often use the same accounting methods for internal purposes that they use for external purposes. Unfortunately, accounting systems and methods designed for external reporting are not always well suited for internal use. For example, GAAP require the use of historical costs in accounting for plant assets. Using historical costs in plant replacement decisions, however, may lead to poor decisions.

The decision about using financial accounting systems for internal purposes usually involves weighing the increased accuracy that comes from a separate management accounting system against the costs of maintaining two systems. Greater accuracy in accounting information is costly, because greater accuracy frequently involves more extensive data collection. Thus, a company must decide how much accuracy it needs and how much it is willing to pay for this accuracy. Further, **a particular accounting system that is adequate for one company may be inadequate for another because of differences in strategies, markets, production and delivery systems, and controls.**

All accounting systems rely on assumptions and choices, such as the choice of LIFO or FIFO to estimate inventory and cost of goods sold. The usefulness of an accounting system depends largely on how well these assumptions fit the intended purpose of the information. For example, if products are sold separately, accurate costs for each individual product are needed, but the accuracy of individual product costs may not be as important if products are sold only as a bundle. Therefore, the following are important questions when assessing the adequacy of managerial accounting systems:

- What is the intended use of the information produced by a system?
- How accurate does the information need to be?
- Is greater accuracy worth the additional cost?

1 SELF-STUDY PROBLEM

Miko Song is chief executive officer of a manufacturing company that produces paper products. Lars Dalton is head of one of the company's manufacturing plants. Deborah Styles is in charge of scheduling production in one of the plant's production processes that converts paperboard into containers.

Required Explain why the accounting information needs of the three managers are different and briefly describe the type of information needed by each.

The solution to Self-Study Problem 1 appears at the end of the chapter.

THE ROLE OF MANAGERIAL ACCOUNTING IN PLANNING AND CONTROL

OBJECTIVE 2

Explain the role of managerial accounting in planning and control decisions.

Managerial accounting traditionally has been viewed as providing information needed for two management functions, planning and control. Planning and control are important for business success. Managerial accounting information is very important to planning and control.

Recall the issues faced by Erin and Seth in the scenario at the beginning of the chapter. They were deciding what types of financial information are needed for their new business. This decision really revolves around planning and control. Exhibit 2 illustrates the planning and control process. Managers **(a) develop goals,** such as a target return on assets, which are major outcomes desired by top management. Next, managers **(b) set specific objectives,** such as target income for each division of the company, and **(c) develop plans** for achieving these objectives. Then management **(d) implements**

Exhibit 2
The Planning and
Control Process

the plans and controls the actions of employees to ensure proper execution of the plans. Managers (e) **evaluate the performance of products, services, activities, and people** who are responsible for them. As feedback about how well plans are being met is received, adjustments are made. This means that management (f) **modifies its goals** or changes its plans or procedures for meeting these goals. The process then is repeated. Managerial accounting provides financial numbers used in making these planning and control decisions.

As an illustration, consider the process of purchasing various types of synthetic fiber used to make carpet at Charles Robert Carpets (CRC), a manufacturer of carpet for automobiles, recreational vehicles, and boats. Before the beginning of the year, management sets a goal to maintain production costs at a specific level (a). It establishes a specific objective by identifying a planned cost for each type of synthetic fiber used in its products (b). The purchasing department, which is responsible for purchasing all raw materials used in production, is held accountable for meeting this objective. It creates a plan to meet the objective by identifying sources of materials and negotiating costs with suppliers (c). The purchasing department buys the materials at the agreed-upon costs (d). After the year begins, the vice president of operations, who is responsible for the purchasing department, receives periodic reports identifying the actual cost of various types of fiber and comparing these costs to planned costs (e). If the actual costs exceed the planned costs, the differences are investigated to determine their cause. The production cost goal may have to be adjusted, or a new source of materials may be sought in order to achieve the existing goal (f).

Planning

Planning involves creating a map for achieving corporate goals and objectives. Planning can be strategic or operational. **Strategic planning involves identifying a company's long-run goals and developing plans for achieving these goals.** Strategic plans often involve large investments. Strategic decisions include starting a new line of products, building a new plant, or entering a foreign market for the first time. In Erin and Seth's case, they have to decide what types of furniture Young Designs, Inc., will make. This illustrates a strategic decision since it will impact the long-term activities and success of the business.

An example of strategic planning at CRC is a long-term plan for financing a new line of boat carpets. Strategic planning almost always involves top management because of its importance to a company's long-run success. CRC's chief executive, marketing, operations, and financial officers probably would participate in a decision to expand into a new product line.

Operational planning **involves identifying objectives for day-to-day activities.** For example, CRC will need to plan the types and amounts of carpet to be produced each day to meet sales requirements for the boat line. Except in small companies, operational plans often are made by middle management with input from top management. In planning CRC's daily production requirements, the production manager will work with managers in marketing, purchasing, and accounting to plan production and to ensure that sufficient materials are available to meet production goals.

Operational planning also involves setting performance objectives, **which are standards for the desired performance of various divisions of a company**. Every department is expected to meet specific performance objectives. The marketing department has sales quotas, and the production department has production quantity and quality expectations. Performance standards are a major part of operational planning and are used to evaluate performance.

Managerial accounting is important in strategic and operational planning. An important part of strategic planning is long-range financial planning. Companies often develop strategic, long-range financial plans that set target financial results several years into the future. These plans are supported by operational plans that forecast the monthly or quarterly financial results necessary to achieve the company's long-range financial plans. **The master budget is a one-year financial plan for a company.** As shown in Exhibit 3, the master budget ties together long-range financial plans and day-to-day financial objectives for the company's divisions and departments. It is developed from other operational plans for specific activities, such as sales, production costs, and operating expenses. The master budget identifies required investment in new plant assets and expected cash flows. It also describes expected profits for a company's product lines and major divisions.

Exhibit 3 Levels of Planning

Type of Plan	Planning Time Horizon	Nature of Planning
Strategic financial plan	Several years in the future	Sets major financial goals, such as long-range profitability, targeted stock price, and market share.
Master budget	Annual	Provides a one-year financial master plan linking long-range planning with operational planning. Developed from operational budgets such as projected sales, production, operating expenses, and cash flows.
Operational budgets	Monthly to quarterly	Provide specific inputs to the master budget. Often developed at the divisional and departmental levels as well as for the company as a whole.

Operational planning often involves departmental budgeting, analysis of budgeted versus actual revenues and costs, and evaluation of departmental performance. Inadequate and inaccurate data can result in budgets that provide poor plans. Imagine what would happen if CRC's budget greatly overstated the profits that could be generated by a new product line. CRC would invest in new plant assets and market its new line, only to discover that its profits were much lower than expected.

Decision making during the planning process often involves choosing among alternatives. For example, management may need to decide whether to use available cash (1) to offer a new line of products or (2) to invest in new equipment that will improve the quality of existing products. Once a plan is adopted, however, management must continue to make decisions in order to implement the plan. Management accountants become involved in several types of ongoing decisions. Examples include decisions:

- to continue producing a product or to drop it from a product line,
- to retain or close a branch or plant facility,
- to accept or reject a special product order from a customer,
- to complete a product or sell it partially completed at a lower price,
- to produce more of one product or more of another, and
- to keep, reduce, or eliminate certain costs.

Control

Once a plan is in place, it is necessary to monitor the performance of a company and its members. In all but the smallest companies, monitoring usually means assigning the responsibility for achieving certain objectives to specific managers and evaluating their success. Control involves identifying and rewarding behavior that encourages desired outcomes and detecting and correcting behavior that does not. It is concerned with controlling people's behavior so that desired outcomes are achieved. A company identifies performance characteristics useful for evaluating results. Measurement of these characteristics can be objective or subjective, formal or informal, but in any case it is tied to some form of incentive system. Identification and detection can be accomplished using three methods:

- Directly observing behavior to assess the quantity and quality of effort
- Measuring the outcomes of behavior
- Establishing informal work environment habits (corporate culture) that guide behavior

Many businesses use some combination of all three methods of control. For example, **Schofield Electronic Instruments, Inc.,** uses direct **observation of behavior** by office managers to control the quality and efficiency of clerical personnel in the telephone sales department. These employees perform tasks such as answering incoming calls, returning customers' calls, taking orders, and processing order forms. Their work is observable by the department manager, who can control behavior and take corrective action. For example, if telephones are unanswered after several rings, an office manager can temporarily reassign people to telephone duty to correct the situation. In this environment, performance measurement tends to be subjective and is based on effort.

Control of outside sales personnel is a different matter. Because outside sales representatives frequently travel alone, their behavior is not directly observable. Therefore, Schofield **measures** sales **outcomes** to control behavior. Representatives are assigned sales dollar quotas and are evaluated on whether they meet these quotas. A large portion of a sales representative's compensation is determined by sales outcomes.

Laboratory workers responsible for the research and development (R&D) of new products are governed in the short run mainly by yet another form of control. Because of the highly creative nature of their work, and their tendency to work in informal teams, R&D workers' behavior is not easy to observe directly. Schofield does not use short-term outcome measures, such as the number of new products developed, to evaluate R&D personnel because it is better to develop one outstanding new product than several poor ones. Instead, Schofield uses **cultural controls** for R&D personnel. Its culture emphasizes using R&D time and funds carefully to improve upon competitors' products and to develop ways to manufacture similar products at a lower cost than competitors. Researchers are guided by Schofield's culture, which defines the type and extent of risks the company is willing to take in the R&D area.

Incentives are important to the control process. **Incentives** are the rewards, monetary and nonmonetary, used to encourage employees to make decisions that are consistent with company goals. Examples of incentives are salaries, bonuses, special benefits, such as the use of a company car, and awards, such as recognition for outstanding performance.

Exhibit 4 shows the role of incentives in the corporate planning and control process. Planning influences measurement because plans establish measurable performance targets.

Exhibit 4

Role of Incentives, Evaluation, and Rewards in Corporate Planning and Control

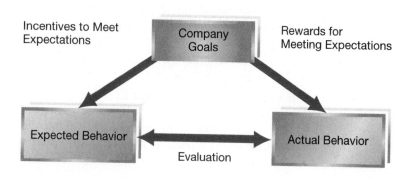

Measurement aids in controlling performance. Measures provide a means of comparing planned performance results (expected behavior) with actual results. Measurement, in turn, is linked to financial and nonfinancial incentives. These incentives are based on achievement of planned results (meeting goals) and motivate the company's members to accomplish corporate objectives.

Accounting usually is important when outcomes are measured and evaluated. Some accounting measures are collected specifically for the purpose of measuring performance. Such was the case suggested in the scenario at the beginning of the chapter. Erin and Seth were advised by Roberta to develop a monthly budget that could be compared with each month's actual results. In this way, budgets are used expressly to help measure and control performance. Other measures are collected for other reasons and are used to measure performance as a matter of convenience. Incentives and measurement do not always lead to the desired behavior or outcomes, however, as explained in the following section.

http://albright.
swlearning.com
....
**Learn more about the
IMA and the CMA
certification.**

Ethics and Control

Ethics involves standards of conduct for members of organizations. Well-designed managerial accounting systems encourage ethical behavior on the part of employees. Management should try to eliminate features of managerial accounting systems that inadvertently encourage unethical behavior. For example, many companies consider it improper for an employee to record transactions associated with one period in another period in order to make performance appear better than it really is. Senior management should make it clear that this type of behavior is considered unethical. Senior management should also be careful to design managerial accounting systems with safeguards that limit employees' ability to engage in this kind of behavior.

The Institute of Management Accountants (IMA) has created ethical standards for management accounting. Certified Management Accountants (CMAs) are accountants who have received professional certification by the IMA. CMAs are expected to adhere to the ethical standards set forth by the IMA. Throughout this text you are challenged to think about ethics.

LEARNING NOTE

People who are evaluated on the basis of managerial accounting reports sometimes will try to make their performance look better by manipulating the numbers in the reports. If in doing this they take actions that are not in the company's best interests, the company will suffer in the long run. Managers responsible for designing managerial accounting systems need to consider the possibility of this kind of behavior when creating these systems.

INTERACTIONS AMONG ACCOUNTING, MARKETING, AND OPERATIONS

OBJECTIVE 3

Discuss ways in which managerial accounting interacts with marketing and operations.

Marketing and operations managers use accounting information extensively in day-to-day decisions. Pricing and production activities depend heavily on accounting measurement. Consequently, as shown in Exhibit 5, a close relationship among accounting, marketing, and operations managers is needed in most companies, both to facilitate day-to-day decisions and to formulate marketing and production strategy.

Managerial Accounting and Marketing

Why is accounting information so important in marketing decisions? The marketing function involves the activities required in order to advertise, promote, and sell products. Marketing is essential for the success of a company because it drives sales revenue. If a company cannot market its products, it has little need for other functions such as production and accounting. Marketing strategy also affects a company's plant investment and manufacturing strategies. Recall how Roberta informed Erin and Seth about the need to first determine what products would be sold and in what quantities to help

Exhibit 5 Examples of Ways Accounting, Marketing, and Operations Work Together

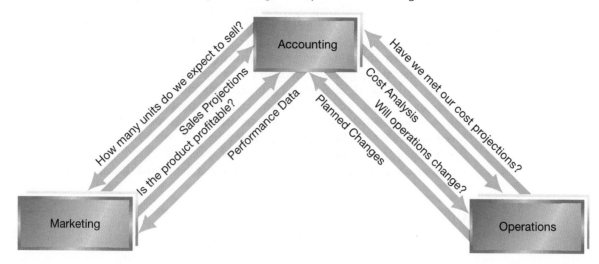

determine their needs for plant assets and cash. Without knowing the firm's marketing decisions, it is virtually impossible to determine the types and quantities of products to produce. This information, in turn, is necessary to make decisions about the type and amount of labor, materials, and equipment necessary for production.

For companies to be competitive in the new business environment, they require accurate and timely information to support their marketing efforts. As customers have demanded faster response times, companies have given their sales forces more authority to make decisions. The sales forces, in turn, rely on up-to-date accounting information to monitor and control sales activity. A company must price its products competitively and meet profit objectives. Manufacturing cost per unit of product frequently affects the product price. For example, a manufacturer may set the price of a product at some percentage above cost to achieve a target profit. Using inaccurate unit costs to set prices can have serious adverse consequences. Further, many companies allocate resources to divisions based on their profitability. If profit data are inaccurate, poor resource allocation decisions can result. These decisions, in turn, can lead to reduced profits and lower company value.

As noted earlier, sales representatives are often compensated on the basis of sales results. The commissions they are paid may be based on profits rather than on unit or dollar sales. Accounting information can help representatives negotiate prices with customers. Also, it can help them to identify products that produce high profits so that they can encourage sales of these products.

Organizations usually compete as either (1) low-cost producers of products and services or (2) providers of products and services that are differentiated in terms of quality and performance, or both. A company's accounting system should provide information that is consistent with the company's marketing strategy. For example, detailed and timely reporting of production costs to marketing is likely to be more important for success with a low-cost strategy than with a product-differentiation strategy. Thus, accounting information should meet the needs of a company's marketing managers.

Managerial Accounting and Operations

Operations refers to the actions necessary to create and deliver products or services. Operations decisions also rely on accounting information. For example, production is concerned with manufacturing or acquiring the products that a company sells, including obtaining the raw materials necessary for the production process. This means that production managers need information about the costs of production, such as labor and materials. Production managers often compare the actual cost of production to costs that were forecast during the company's budgeting process to determine whether production costs are being properly controlled.

Traditional production methods sometimes have failed to produce quality products that can compete in a global market. As a result, production managers in many companies have changed to new manufacturing methods, such as just-in-time and flexible manufacturing. Just-in-time manufacturing improves product quality and speeds up delivery times. Flexible manufacturing helps meet customer demands for a wider variety of products. At the same time, production managers have reduced inventory costs and reduced the time required to manufacture products by using automated processes. This need for faster production has led to efforts to compress product-development and production cycles. These changes affect production managers' information needs and require adjustments in managerial accounting systems.

Other Effects on Marketing and Operations

Developing a marketing plan is one area in which marketing and accounting interact at the strategic level. In addition to being concerned about unit costs, marketing personnel are concerned about such strategic issues as competitors' costs and marketing strategies, and the cost and profit implications of changes in product mix. At the operational planning level, accounting and marketing managers work together to make decisions about pricing individual products and monitoring competitors' responses to this pricing, tracking sales force time and costs, accounting for advertising and promotion costs for individual products, and monitoring marketing and distribution expenditures. For example, at the operational level, financial measures of quality, such as warranty cost, can be linked to nonfinancial measures of quality, such as defective parts per thousand. This linkage provides information about which parts generate the most warranty costs and helps focus management's attention on those areas where quality improvement can be most effective in reducing costs.

At the strategic planning level of operations, accounting can play an important role in providing information about the costs and benefits of alternative strategies to improve quality, delivery, and service. For example, information about a company's share of the market for a product line and about the profitability of that product line can be combined. This allows the company to weigh lowering prices to increase sales against maintaining prices in order to make a higher profit on each unit of product sold.

Though manufacturing companies have been the focus of much of this discussion, service companies face similar issues. In these companies, pricing and resource allocation decisions are sometimes more troublesome than in manufacturing companies because measuring service costs and profits is more difficult. Consider the difficulties a bank faces in determining the cost of checking accounts. Transactions involving checking accounts are performed by many different departments within the bank. Examples are check cashing, check processing, electronic funds transfers, and new customer services. Because these departments handle many other types of transactions as well as checking, it is difficult to determine the portion of each department's costs that is associated with checking accounts. In some service businesses, a lack of accurate cost data has led to poor decisions because managers have little guidance as to which services are profitable and which are not.

Because of the role that product cost data play in strategic marketing and production decisions, it is difficult to overestimate the importance of accounting to business strategy. Companies often focus on the operational aspects of accounting information and forget the strategic aspects. However, they ignore the strategic implications of managerial accounting information at their peril. There are numerous examples of businesses that made poor strategic decisions, or even failed, because of inaccurate accounting data.

Case in Point

The Importance of Accounting Information for Operating Decisions

Managerial accounting information showed a division of a major manufacturer to be losing money. The company decided to put the division up for sale. A group of employees in the division purchased it. Under the new ownership, the division immediately became profitable. A major reason was that when the division was part of the major manufacturer, it was charged for costs incurred by the manufacturer's other divisions. When it became a separate company, it was no longer charged for these costs. Errors in the managerial accounting system led the manufacturer's management to believe that the division was unprofitable when, in fact, it was profitable. The result was a bad business decision.

2 SELF-STUDY PROBLEM

An automobile parts manufacturer was concerned about the company's poor financial performance and complaints from customers about late deliveries and low product quality. The company was plagued by overproduction of some products and underproduction of others. The company's marketing department often promoted products on which it earned a small profit instead of products on which it earned a higher profit.

Required How could the company's problems be reduced by better communication among accounting, marketing, and operations?

The solution to Self-Study Problem 2 appears at the end of the chapter.

THE SCOPE OF MANAGERIAL ACCOUNTING

OBJECTIVE 4

Explain the scope of managerial accounting.

Managerial accounting relates to your course in financial accounting, but is different in many important aspects. Exhibit 6 illustrates the role of managerial accounting in business organizations. Managerial accounting systems capture the results of business activities and report these results to decision makers using financial and operational reporting systems. You are already familiar with financial reporting systems from your financial accounting course. Based on a general ledger, these systems capture information used to prepare a company's financial statements. Both external and internal decision makers use this information. Later chapters demonstrate how management accountants trace manufacturing costs through the general ledger to determine ending balances of various inventory accounts and cost of goods sold.

Exhibit 6 The Role of Managerial Accounting in Business Organizations

Managerial accounting systems capture the dynamics of a manufacturing process. Some accounting systems are designed to capture costs associated with a variety of unique products, such as custom-built homes. Other accounting systems capture manufacturing costs associated with producing homogeneous products, such as gasoline or synthetic fiber. Managers need accurate cost information to support a variety of cost-related decisions. For example, managers often make pricing decisions to ensure their products are competitive in the market.

Managers rely on operational reporting systems to understand certain dynamics of their processes. Operational reporting systems capture nonfinancial information such as the number of units produced, time required for production, and defect rates. Managers use information from both systems to justify capital investments in new property, plant, and equipment and other innovations to help their companies remain competitive. Thus, managerial accounting extends the financial reporting view of traditional accounting.

Much of the traditional accounting system involves measuring and reporting business activities in terms of the dollar values associated with these activities. Financial statements express business activities in terms of the dollar amounts of assets, liabilities, owners' equity, revenues, expenses, and cash flows associated with a company's activities for a fiscal period or at the end of a fiscal period. Accounting, especially managerial accounting, does not focus exclusively on financial data, however. Accounting measurement, especially in the contemporary business environment, includes quantitative and qualitative data about the effectiveness and efficiency of business activities. These measures are necessary to meet information needs of managers who are concerned with creating value in their organizations.

Nonfinancial Performance Measures

Financial results are affected by how effectively and efficiently an organization runs. Understanding the factors that affect effectiveness and efficiency, measuring these factors, and evaluating the measures are important management tasks. Nonfinancial measures often are needed for many of these factors.

Operations managers can reduce product costs by eliminating waste, scrap, and spoilage in the production process; product defects; and activities that do not add value to a company's products. Activity measures, such as the amount of materials used to produce each unit of product, are useful for determining efficiency in the manufacturing process. Quality measures also are important. The number of defects and customer satisfaction measures, for example, can help a company determine how well its production process is working. These measures help managers evaluate their processes so that costs associated with warranties, product returns, and reworking defective products, as well as lost revenues, can be reduced.

Many companies have attempted to reduce inventory costs by only producing those goods that are needed to meet customer orders and by placing materials into production as soon as they are received. These processes reduce storage costs and the amount of cash necessary to acquire materials and maintain inventory. For this type of production process to work, receiving, production, and delivery schedules must be carefully coordinated. Information about the time required to complete products, materials required to complete orders, and constraints that limit the ability of a company to meet its production demands are critical for the success of this type of operation.

Highly competitive markets often require companies to develop, produce, and deliver products quickly. Measuring the time required to bring products to market and structuring the production process to create flexible and efficient production schedules are critical to many companies. Companies operating in these environments need to eliminate idle time in the production process, eliminate unnecessary operations or activities, and deliver completed products to customers quickly. Production processes must be designed that can be converted quickly from the production of one product to the production of another. Investments in technology and computer-controlled machinery often are needed to support these activities. Benefits of acquiring this type of equipment and modifying production processes are important to measure, along with the costs of these acquisitions and changes. Benefits may be intangible, such as improved customer relations and larger sales potential, as well as tangible, such as short-run sales dollars.

Costs are clearly important for management decisions. However, cost data often are not sufficient for making informed decisions. Managers need information about *cost drivers*—**those activities that create costs.** Attempting to reduce costs without changing the activities that create the costs can be dysfunctional. For example, managers may reduce repair and maintenance costs by postponing these activities. The result, however, is likely to be inefficient operations and higher costs to replace and repair equipment in the future. Focusing strictly on costs can lead to short-run improvements in profits that are detrimental to long-term success. Incentive and reward systems should be developed that lead to long-run profits as a result of continuously improving product quality.

Quality is a major factor in determining the success of most business organizations. Short-term cost reductions that jeopardize the quality of a company's goods and services or the interaction between the company and its customers or suppliers can lead to lower company value. Consequently, costs must be considered in the context of the broader scope of a company's goals. A broad set of measures for evaluating company performance generally leads to better results than a narrow focus on current-period costs.

Because of the additional information needs of managers in modern business organizations, management accountants have become essential players in upper- and middle-level management decisions. Accountants work with other managers in teams to make strategic and operating decisions. By working together, these management teams can examine short-run and long-run implications of decisions and consider financial and nonfinancial consequences of decisions.

Service Companies

As the United States economy has matured, it has changed from being principally a manufacturing economy to being a service economy. This means that more companies are providing services than goods. This change has implications for the use of managerial accounting. The production of tangible products makes tracing costs to products somewhat different in manufacturing companies than in service companies. For example, manufacturing companies have inventories of materials and finished goods, whereas service companies do not.

Like manufacturing companies, service companies require relevant, timely, and accurate accounting information in order to make sound decisions. However, service companies have often been slower to use managerial accounting than manufacturing companies, perhaps partly because many service companies, such as airlines, railroads, and banks, have been regulated. Regulation may have made service companies less cost conscious than manufacturing companies because it often limited the services that companies could provide and fixed the prices that they could charge.

In recent years, many service industries have been deregulated. Examples are the airline and banking industries. Deregulation means that these companies will be operating in a more competitive environment. As competition increases, so does the need for better accounting information. Companies need to know the costs of their services with more accuracy. They need to be able to predict the financial results of changes in marketing and operations. Without relevant, timely, and accurate managerial accounting information, it is unlikely that service companies can prosper.

3 | **SELF-STUDY PROBLEM** A division of a major corporation that manufactures transmissions for trucks and other heavy vehicles installed a new manufacturing system. Parts made by many departments must be assembled to form the transmission. Under the new manufacturing system, the parts should arrive at the point in production where they are ready at the time they are needed. The division spent a great deal of time training its production personnel in the new system. Despite these efforts, however, the results were disappointing. Departments continued to manufacture more parts than were needed, and quality did not improve as much as had been expected.

Management was disappointed. The firm had spent a great deal of time and effort implementing the new manufacturing system, with poor results. They began to look at the managerial accounting system that was used to measure departmental performance and discovered some problems. The division had long used an accounting system that emphasized producing as many parts as possible as fast as possible. Because labor was paid by the hour, the more component parts a department could make in a day, the lower its labor cost per unit. Consequently, department managers pressed for higher production volume despite the change in production philosophy.

Required Why did the information provided by the accounting system lead to the wrong results? What types of information might the accounting system provide that would be useful for achieving management's objectives?

The solution to Self-Study Problem 3 appears at the end of the chapter.

REVIEW

SUMMARY of IMPORTANT CONCEPTS

1. Managerial accounting refers to accounting information developed for use by decision makers inside the company.
   a. Managerial accounting is different from financial accounting.
   b. Managerial accounting is not governed by GAAP.
   c. The information produced by managerial accounting systems is important to many business decisions, especially marketing and operations decisions.

2. Managerial accounting interacts with decisions by other functions, notably marketing and operations.
   a. Marketing decisions often are based on the cost of manufacturing a product.
   b. Operations decisions frequently require cost and other accounting data for purposes of cost control and quality assurance.

3. Businesses' needs for accounting information are changing.
   a. Global competition and the need for higher quality are driving U.S. businesses to control costs and produce higher-quality products, creating new accounting information needs.
   b. Management accountants need to be involved in business functions like marketing and operations to ensure that the information they produce is timely and accurate enough and appropriate to the decisions being made.

4. The traditional view of managerial accounting needs to be changed to fit the new business environment.
   a. Managerial accounting has been traditionally viewed in the context of planning and control at the operational level.
   b. This view has been expanded to include a more strategic focus and the demands made by the new business environment.

5. Managerial accounting involves nonfinancial as well as financial measures of business activities.
   a. Measures of activity, such as material usage and defect rates, are useful for understanding and reducing production costs.
   b. Measures of time required for production and delivery are important for reducing inventory requirements and increasing efficiency.
   c. Global competition requires many companies to produce products quickly. Determining the benefits of investments in modern technology are important for operating in this environment.
   d. Managers need to understand cost drivers, the activities that create costs, in order to control costs. Focusing on cost reduction in the short run may not lead to long-term success.
   e. Companies often need to focus their efforts on improving the quality of their products and activities. A broad set of measures for evaluating company performance is needed for these efforts.

       f. Accountants work in teams with other managers to make strategic and operating decisions.

       g. Managerial accounting is important for service companies as well as manufacturing and retail companies.

DEFINE

TERMS and CONCEPTS DEFINED in this CHAPTER

cost drivers (M15)   managerial accounting (M3)

management accountant (M4)   operational planning (M7)

SELF-STUDY PROBLEM SOLUTIONS

SSP1-1   The kinds of decisions made by the three managers differ; therefore, the information they need differs. Miko needs information for making and evaluating strategic decisions. Lars needs information for planning and controlling the ongoing operations of the plant. Deborah needs information for efficient planning of production in the process she runs.

        As chief executive officer, Miko needs summary information about the company's performance. She needs to know general operating information, such as the amount of sales and net income for a period, and company-wide performance measures, such as return on assets. Comparative information about the company's plants and products would be used to evaluate performance and to make strategic decisions about whether to retain the plants or products.

        A plant manager needs information specific to the plant. This information can be used to evaluate plant efficiency and effectiveness. Information about production costs, plant profitability, and production delays can help Lars assess whether the plant is meeting expected performance objectives. If objectives are not being met, Lars needs information to help determine causes for the failures.

        Deborah needs specific information about production needs on a day-to-day basis. She needs to know which products need to be produced and the quantities demanded. She needs to be able to evaluate costs associated with the production process to eliminate unnecessary costs and to provide production cost information to other decision makers.

SSP1-2   Poor financial performance often is a symptom of poor communication within an organization. If accounting and marketing communicated about product costs and profits, the marketing department could focus on the products that are the most profitable. Without good cost information, the marketing department can only guess about which products should be promoted. If it had this information, it could focus its advertising and sales efforts on more profitable products. It could offer discounts and other incentives on these products if doing so would increase sales volume and create higher overall profits.

        If accounting and operations communicated, the operations department would have better information about which products were being sold and when the orders were needed. Information about operating costs could help operations schedule production more efficiently to meet demand and avoid costly delays or hurried production. Hurried production often results in poor quality of output.

SSP1-3   The basic problem in this situation was that division management failed to take its management accounting system into consideration when it implemented a new manufacturing system. The division wanted to minimize the costs associated with the inventory of component parts used to manufacture the transmissions, in the belief that this would lower the overall costs of production. Parts were not to arrive at the place where they were needed until just before they were actually used in production. Only the exact number of parts that were needed at the time were to be manufactured.

        Problems arose when the division attempted to operate the new manufacturing system in conjunction with the old managerial accounting system. The old accounting system was ill suited to the new manufacturing system because the way in which it measured departmental performance was not aligned with the desired performance under the new manufacturing system.

        The old accounting system had measured the efficiency of each individual department in making the individual parts of the transmissions, not the overall cost of making the transmissions. Efficiency was defined as the number of parts made per labor hour used. Under the old system, departments were evaluated in terms of cost per component manufactured, with lower being considered better. Each department therefore had an incentive to make as many parts as possible during a given period of time. The result was that some departments made parts faster than they could be used in manufacturing. Thus, excess parts often accumulated at various stages in the production process. This resulted in a costly buildup of inventory awaiting further processing.

Despite the training on the goals of the new manufacturing system, the department managers continued to act as they had under the old system, making as many parts as possible. This meant that the expected savings in inventory costs were not realized. Only after management recognized the problem and changed the managerial accounting system to one that recognized the reduction in inventory cost achieved by making only what was needed at the time did the managers' behavior become aligned with the division's goals. Perhaps the most important lesson to learn from this situation is that human beings respond to the way they are measured. Even though the department managers knew that they were supposed to reduce production to the level required for current needs, they continued to produce as much as possible to make their accounting reports look better. It is important to ensure that accounting systems used to measure human performance are aligned with corporate goals and objectives.

Thinking Beyond the Question

What basic financial information do we need to run a business?

In the opening scenario, you learned about some of the information needs identified by Erin and Seth. What role could a management accounting information system play in changing management's behavior? How can changing the way a business activity is measured also change decisions about that activity? Refer back to the scenario at the beginning of the chapter. For example, what are the implications of Erin and Seth measuring production efficiency versus the quality of their products? Is there a tradeoff in this decision?

QUESTIONS

Q1-1
Obj. 1
Managerial accounting is useful only to profit-oriented manufacturing companies. Do you agree? Why or why not?

Q1-2
Obj. 1
Rita Patterson went into the marketing field because she "hated accounting." Rita has been working for a large multinational company and is being promoted to assistant product manager. In her new job, Rita will prepare sales quotes for various large clients. Should Rita expect to use managerial accounting techniques in her new job? Why or why not?

Q1-3
Obj. 1
James and Hanna are senior accounting students at the state university. James plans to find a job in financial accounting, whereas Hanna wants to work in managerial accounting. What is the difference between these two types of accounting?

Q1-4
Obj. 1
If managerial accounting is primarily concerned with costs of business activities, why are both financial and nonfinancial measures of business activities important?

Q1-5
Obj. 1
Managerial accounting is important for all forms of business. How is managerial accounting different for retail, manufacturing, and service companies?

Q1-6
Obj. 1
It is important for middle- and upper-level managers throughout an organization to understand accounting information. Do you agree or disagree? Why?

Q1-7
Obj. 1
An accounting classmate notes that adherence to GAAP is not required for managerial accounting reports. She observes, "If it's so darned important for financial accounting, it seems reasonable that it would also be useful for managerial reporting." Do you agree or disagree? Why? Explain to her why it's more important that financial accounting reports adhere to GAAP than it is for managerial accounting reports to do so.

Q1-8
Objs. 1, 2
Why does the accounting system used for financial statement preparation not always provide the information that managers need for decision-making purposes?

Q1-9
Obj. 2
Tri-States Manufacturing produces a line of electric fans. Over the past several years, the company has seen its profit margin on fans decline from 12% to 8%. How has the decrease in profit margin affected the company's need for managerial accounting information?

Q1-10
Obj. 2
In order to meet increasing demand for its product, Hathaway Industries is considering an expansion of its manufacturing facilities. What sort of planning does this decision represent, strategic or operational? Explain your answer.

Q1-11
Obj. 2
Webco Products manufactures a line of small ice chests. The production department has experienced problems working with some of the raw materials used in the production process. The company is considering a change in materials that would increase the cost of an ice chest by 5%. What sort of planning does this decision represent, strategic or operational? Explain your answer.

Q1-12
Obj. 2
Advent Technologies, Inc., has developed a detailed planning and budgeting program that involves almost every layer of management. Tina Riser, plant manager, made this comment: "I don't know why we put so much effort into these budgets; after we complete them, we never see them again until the end of the year." If it is true that managers are not held accountable to budgets, does this represent a weakness in planning or in control? Explain your answer.

Q1-13
Obj. 2
Why is accounting important for planning and control decisions?

Q1-14
Obj. 3
Why must marketing and production managers have accounting information to make decisions? Are there any other managers needing accounting information?

Q1-15
Obj. 3
If marketing and operations managers need information for decision making, why don't they collect and keep the information themselves instead of relying on the accounting department to provide the needed information?

Q1-16
Obj. 4
Virgil Cartwright is a medical doctor with a small family practice. Each time a patient visits the doctor, certain medical and administrative costs are incurred. Would you agree that patients are a cost driver for the doctor? Explain your answer.

EXERCISES

If your instructor is using Personal Trainer® in this course, you may complete your assignments online.

E1-1
Write a short definition for each of the terms listed in the *Terms and Concepts Defined in this Chapter* section.

E1-2
Complete each of the following sentences with the proper term or terms.

1. Managerial accounting information is used primarily by _____ decision makers.
2. An accountant who produces information for use within a specific company is referred to as a(n) _____.
3. _____ involves the identification of long-run goals and plans to achieve these goals.
4. _____ involves the identification of objectives for day-to-day activities.
5. A financial plan that summarizes operational activities for the coming year is known as the _____.
6. Managerial accounting exists primarily to assist in the management functions of _____ and _____.

E1-3
Obj. 1

Alberta Enterprises is being audited by a local public accounting firm. The management of Alberta hired an independent accountant to prepare financial statements in good form for presentation to the board of directors. The financial statements will contain an auditor's report stating that the financial statements have been prepared in accordance with generally accepted accounting principles.

Brent Haskill, production manager at Alberta, reviewed the financial statements prepared by the independent accountant and noted that the reported inventory value was higher than that contained in the company's monthly operating report. Brent asked the company's accountant to explain the difference. The accountant explained that the auditors adjusted inventory to a LIFO basis in accordance with GAAP, whereas the company does not reflect LIFO calculations in the monthly operating report.

a. Does managerial accounting prescribe specific methods that must be followed? Since the inventory value was adjusted by the independent accountant, would the company's inventory valuation be worthless to its managers? Why or why not?
b. Must accounting information be calculated in accordance with generally accepted accounting principles to be useful to managers? Why or why not?

E1-4
Obj. 1

Dream Easy, a manufacturer of mattresses, sells 10 different models of mattresses. Each model generates $4,000,000 in sales each year. Dream Easy currently does not have the resources to be able to determine the profitability of each product line. Steve, the company president, has a hunch that one of the models is not profitable, and estimates a loss of $400,000 each year. He suggests installing a new managerial accounting information system at a cost of $120,000 per year. This system would determine the profitability of each product line, so Dream Easy could stop manufacturing unprofitable models.

Assuming Steve's assumption is correct, should Dream Easy install the new system? Explain.

E1-5
Obj. 1

An advertising firm has 100 clients, each generating $500,000 in sales. It currently generates profitability reports only by office. One office president suggests that the firm produce profitability reports for each individual client. He estimates that 30 clients are running at a net loss of 20% on their sales. A new client reporting system could be installed for $1,000,000. This system would identify the clients that are losing money, so the advertising firm could drop those clients or develop a plan to make them profitable.

Assuming the office president's assumptions are correct, should the advertising firm install the new system? Explain.

E1-6
Obj. 2

During the planning process, a company identifies its goals, its objectives, and its plans for reaching those goals. To ensure these plans are implemented, managers must control employees' behavior. One method of control is measuring the outcomes of behavior. Managerial accountants develop accurate and timely measurements of these outcomes.

Match the measurements with the decisions that managers must make.

Measurements:
i. Data that show how reduction in costs will impact revenues
ii. Data that show how a product's elimination will affect the company's total profitability
iii. Data that show the profitability per unit for each product line and the investments needed to increase production and sales
iv. Data that show the costs and revenues of a custom ordered product
v. Data that show the costs and revenues for completing a partially completed product

Decisions:
a. To continue producing a product or to drop it from a product line
b. To accept or reject a special product order from a customer
c. To complete a product or sell it partially completed at a lower price
d. To produce more of one product or more of another
e. To keep, reduce, or eliminate certain costs

E1-7
Obj. 2

Identify each of the following as a planning or control decision:

a. Decision to buy new production machinery.
b. Decision to change the mix in a chemical compound used to produce a synthetic fiber to reduce the cost of the product.

    c. Decision to replace a factory that is no longer efficient.

    d. Decision to retrain workers to enhance long-run productivity.

    e. Decision to open retail stores in a foreign country.

    f. Decision to count goods for sale to verify inventory records.

    g. Decision to sell a production plant that is no longer profitable.

    h. Decision to survey customers to determine their satisfaction with a company's products.

E1-8
Objs. 2, 3

Ally's Bowling produces bowling balls. The company focuses on making high-end, custom balls. Ally's decides to enter a new highly competitive market, in which it will focus on a low-cost strategy. Describe Ally's changes in information needs with the new product line.

E1-9
Objs. 2, 3

Unisco Products manufactures a line of children's toys that are painted in bright, colorful tones. One of the most popular toy colors is yellow oxide. The company has become aware, however, that the yellow oxide paint it is using is possibly toxic. Accordingly, the company has sought a replacement paint of the same color that is guaranteed safe. The only feasible replacement it has found will cost three times as much as the paint currently being used. Switching to this paint would require a substantial increase in the toy's sales price to cover the added cost.

    Rosemary Terry, marketing manager, insists that sales of this toy will decline significantly if the price is increased to cover the additional paint cost.

    a. Does paint add value to the product? Why or why not?

    b. How does managerial accounting create an ethical concern for managers at Unisco? Explain your answer.

E1-10
Obj. 3

A manufacturer of printers is considering making a new high-end laser printer. Market research estimates your company could sell 2,000 of these printers per year at $3,000 each, without reducing the sales of any other product. The marketing manager asks you, a managerial accountant, to determine if the company should make this printer. What information would you need to make this decision?

E1-11
Obj. 3

The vice president of marketing is struggling at determining the selling price of a new toaster oven. He estimates that the company could sell 20,000 units if the price is set at $30 each, but if the price is dropped to $25 each, he estimates sales would rise to 23,500 units. What managerial accounting information could you provide him to assist in the pricing decision?

PROBLEMS

If your instructor is using Personal Trainer® in this course, you may complete your assignments online.

P1-1
Obj. 1

http://albright.
swlearning.com

Learn more about
UTC's ethics code.

Ethics and Managerial Accounting

Many business organizations have adopted codes of ethics that describe expected behavior for managers with respect to other stakeholders. For example, **United Technologies Corporation** publishes an extensive Code of Ethics that describes the relationships between the company and other parties. Excerpts from the code follow:

Our Customers
We are committed to providing high quality and value, fair prices and honest transactions to those who use our products and services. We will deal both lawfully and ethically with all our customers.

Our Employees
We are committed to treating one another fairly and to maintaining employment practices based on equal opportunity for all employees. We will respect each other's privacy and treat each other with dignity and respect irrespective of age, race, color, sex, religion, or nationality. We are committed to providing safe and healthy working conditions and an atmosphere of open communication for all our employees.

Our Suppliers
We are committed to dealing fairly with our suppliers. We will emphasize fair competition, without discrimination or deception, in a manner consistent with long-lasting business relationships.

(Continued)

Required Why is ethical behavior important for managerial accounting? How does ethical behavior in accounting affect the relationship between a company and its customers, employees, and suppliers?

P1-2 Managerial Accounting and Performance Measures

Objs. 1, 2

An-Hour Foto provides film processing at a single store location. The store has a policy that film will be developed in 24 hours, or the processing is free. It also has a policy that it will refund customers' money for any pictures that were poorly developed.

In order to improve income without raising prices, the company must find ways to reduce costs. To this end, the company has experimented with a new chemical used in its film processing. Management has determined that the new chemical takes longer to process film and is more sensitive to improper handling than the old chemical. While the new chemical is less expensive than the old chemical, the amount of free processing and photo returns have increased since the company switched to this chemical. Accordingly, management must decide whether to continue using the new chemical or return to the old chemical.

Required

A. How can managerial accounting be used to assist the company in determining whether to continue using the new chemical?
B. What are some of the nonfinancial measures provided by managerial accounting to assist managers in the decision-making process?

P1-3 Accounting Information and Business Decisions

Objs. 1–3

Ned Bonapart is purchasing manager for a clothing store. On April 12, Ned received the following weekly report for men's suits purchased from one of the company's suppliers. Ned immediately ordered another 12 wool suits and another 20 cotton suits from the manufacturer.

Merchandise Report
April 12

Fabric Type	Usual Order Quantity	Unit Cost	Last Order Date	Actual Number on Hand	Desired Number on Hand
Wool	12	$120	Feb. 15	5	10
Cotton	20	80	Mar. 2	8	15
Synthetic	25	75	Mar. 10	20	15

Required

A. What information did Ned consider in making his decision?
B. How does the merchandise report assist him with the decision? Does this report appear to meet his information needs for the decision he made?
C. What effect does the information in the report and Ned's decision have on the future of the company?

P1-4 Strategic and Operational Planning

Obj. 2

Rebecca owns several successful coffeehouses. Each one has its own manager and is operated independently of the others. Rebecca meets with the manager of each location each month to review operating results. During this meeting, the manager must present a projection of operations for the coming month. Rebecca reviews the sales projections and any promotional campaigns and entertainment that the manager is planning to use.

Based on the success of her current coffeehouses, Rebecca is considering opening three new facilities. She has found three locations where long-term leases can be obtained. All locations are in high traffic areas near a mall or shopping center. Rebecca has determined the cost to furnish the shops with equipment and has obtained approval from a bank that will assist in the required financing.

Required

A. In what ways do the coffeehouses utilize managerial accounting in the operational planning process?
B. Explain how Rebecca utilizes strategic planning.

P1-5 Strategic and Operational Planning

Obj. 2

Workout Enterprises owns a chain of successful fitness centers. The founder and CEO, Sally, sets a company-wide return on assets goal of 30%. In order to meet this objective Sally determines that she will need to open three new fitness centers in the next year. Sally looks at 30 potential sites for her new stores and determines the three that will maximize her return. In setting the master budget, Sally meets with the general manager of each store to predict the sales for their store and to review their performance from the previous year.

Required

A. How does Sally utilize managerial accounting information in the strategic planning process?
B. How does Sally utilize managerial accounting information in the operational planning process?
C. Why does Sally review the previous year's performance with each manager?

P1-6 Accounting and Planning Decisions

Obj. 2

Myrla Rhyman is planning to start a new business as a systems consultant. She has saved $7,000 to invest in the business. She expects to receive $3,800 each month, on average, from sales to customers. She expects that she will need cash to pay the following items each month, on average: rent, $900; supplies, $500; utilities, $100; other, $250. She will need to purchase $13,000 of equipment to start the business; in addition, she will need $3,000 to cover initial operating costs. A local bank has agreed to consider a loan to help Myrla start her business and has asked her to develop a plan that describes her expected cash receipts and payments for the first year. The plan should show how much cash she will need for the business, how much she will need to borrow, and how she expects to pay back the loan. Monthly payments will be required to pay off the loan and interest. The bank will charge $10 per year in interest for each $100 borrowed until the loan is repaid at the end of the year. Myrla has asked you to prepare a plan for her to submit to the bank.

Required Prepare a plan for Myrla. Describe any assumptions you make.

P1-7 Planning and Control Decisions

Obj. 2

Joyce Mercer is manager of the Long-Term Care Division of the Olin County Health Department. The division has a $100 million budget and is responsible for providing long-term care services (often in nursing homes) to the elderly and physically disabled. The division contracts with providers for nursing home care, adult day care, in-home visiting nurses, and a variety of other long-term care services. As manager, Joyce makes a variety of planning and control decisions on a daily basis. On a recent Tuesday morning, Joyce sat at her desk with the following issues and decisions needing attention:

1. Two months ago, the family of a nursing home patient filed a complaint alleging mistreatment of the patient. An investigation revealed substance to the complaint, and several remedial actions have been developed. Joyce must decide which actions to require of the nursing home.
2. For nearly a year, a task force in Joyce's department has been developing an experimental alternative to nursing home care. It will require a waiver of the federal Medicaid rules, but it has the potential to provide better-quality care at a lower cost to taxpayers. Joyce must decide whether to proceed with this initiative via a formal request to Washington, DC.
3. Budget problems caused the state legislature to reduce funding for a certain program. A citizens committee has recommended priorities to Joyce for trimming the program. Joyce must make and announce the final decision today.
4. Joyce is contemplating engagement of a consultant to conduct an evaluation of her division. Such an evaluation would judge whether the goals and objectives of her unit are being carried out in an effective and efficient manner.
5. Joyce's immediate superior has proposed moving a service unit currently located in another division to the Long-Term Care Division. The unit is not operating effectively because of a variety of problems within the unit. Joyce must provide a written recommendation to her supervisor by tomorrow about how this new unit could be integrated into the work of her division.

(Continued)

Required

A. Describe the differences between a planning decision and a control decision.
B. Specify whether each issue described previously is primarily a planning decision or primarily a control decision. Briefly justify your answer. If an issue involves elements of both planning and control, indicate why you believe this is true.

P1-8 Planning and Business Decisions

Obj. 2

(All of the knowledge required to solve this problem is not contained in this chapter. The problem is based on material covered in financial accounting and is included here to prompt thinking about accounting problems, accounting processes, and decisions.) Van Gogh is considering a business opportunity selling artificial flowers, especially irises and lilies. He needs $25,000 in financing to begin operations. He has $15,000 in savings that he can invest. He has spoken with a local bank about borrowing the additional $10,000 he needs. The bank has indicated that it will consider the loan but has asked for a set of financial statements that describes what Van believes the company's financial condition will look like at the end of the first three months of operations. Van has asked for your assistance in preparing the financial statements. He has provided you with the following expectations:

1. Plant assets costing $22,500 will be needed.
2. Inventory of $5,000 will be purchased for the first month. The inventory will be paid for in the month following purchase. The amount of inventory purchased each month will equal the amount sold in the prior month.
3. Average monthly sales should be about $7,500. Two-thirds of the sales will be for cash each month, and one-third will be for credit. Credit sales will be collected in the month following sale.
4. The cost of the inventory sold will be $4,000 each month.
5. The interest on the loan will require a payment of $125 at the end of each month. An additional $100 will be paid to the bank each month to repay the loan.
6. Operating expenses, other than depreciation, each month should be $1,000. These will be paid in cash. Depreciation should be $200 each month.
7. Van expects to withdraw $1,000 from the business each month for living expenses.

In addition, he has provided the following work sheet, completed for the first month of operations:

	First Month	Second Month	Third Month
Sales revenues	$ 7,500		
Cost of goods sold	(4,000)		
Gross profit	3,500		
Depreciation	(200)		
Other operating expenses	(1,000)		
Income from operations	2,300		
Interest expense	(125)		
Net income	$ 2,175		
Cash	$ 5,275		
Accounts receivable	2,500		
Inventory	1,000		
Plant assets, net of depreciation	22,300		
Total assets	$31,075		
Accounts payable	$ 5,000		
Notes payable	9,900		
Investment by owner	15,000		
Retained earnings	1,175		
Total liabilities & owners' equity	$31,075		

Required Complete the work sheet for the second and third months.

P1-9 **Cost Management**

Objs. 2, 3

UniversEd employs faculty from various universities on a part-time basis for specific education and consulting jobs. These professors come from many disciplines including accounting, economics, finance, information systems, marketing, operations, and strategic planning.

UniversEd has two different lines of business, providing customized financial education to corporate executives from large firms and providing financial consulting services to small firms. In its executive education line of business, UniversEd educates international executives from various firms in the United States, Europe, and the Far East in such financial topics as analyzing firm performance and controlling financial risks. In its consulting line of business, UniversEd uses cost management concepts to work with businesses to improve their financial performance and provide economic value added through better utilization of assets and cost control. In both lines, client satisfaction is very important to firm performance but can be measured in different ways.

Recently, UniversEd undertook a consulting job for a small parts manufacturer, AAA, that sells alternators to large automobile manufacturers and auto parts companies. AAA makes over 600 different types of alternators, some of which management suspects are not profitable to make in the small quantities demanded by AAA's customers. AAA's current management accounting system does not permit AAA's management to tell which products are profitable and which are not. UniversEd's task is to help management develop a management accounting system that will improve the manufacturer's performance and add economic value for its investors.

Required

A. Why does UniversEd sometimes employ faculty with expertise in disciplines such as marketing and operations when delivering financial executive education and consulting services?

B. Why might UniversEd's two lines of business require different performance measures to evaluate success? What measures might be good indicators of whether or not UniversEd is performing well in each of its two lines of business?

C. What things should AAA's new management accounting do to help AAA's management create value for its shareholders? Give an example of possible performance measures for AAA's delivery and accounting departments.

P1-10 **Planning for Marketing Decisions**

Objs. 2, 3

(All of the knowledge required to solve this problem is not contained in this chapter. The problem is based on material covered in financial accounting and is included here to prompt thinking about accounting problems, accounting processes, and decisions.) You are working as an assistant to the vice president for marketing at Long Life Incorporated, a startup manufacturer of a healthy, minimally refined breakfast cereal. Since little processing will be done, much of the cost of the product will be in the premium ingredients. The company will be investing $3 million in processing and packaging facilities to produce a maximum of 15,000 cases of cereal per month. It will advertise and market only in a restricted regional area in the foreseeable future, although expansion is possible in the long run. Fixed costs for operating the facility will be approximately $85,000 per month. Variable costs, primarily for ingredients and labor, are expected to be approximately $17 per case.

In the past, most cereals of this sort have been sold at specialty stores for high prices. However, in recent years, some have moved into supermarkets at prices that are competitive with those of traditional cereals. A marketing research study has given you estimated results after the first year for three possible scenarios:

1. Sell to supermarkets for $29 per case, spend $25,000 per month on advertising, and sell approximately 11,000 cases per month. The average price grocery stores pay competitors for a case of this size is $30, and $25,000 is a minimal monthly budget for advertising in the local area.

2. Sell to supermarkets for $31 per case, spend $40,000 per month on advertising, and sell approximately 12,000 cases per month.

3. Sell to specialty stores for $34 per case, spend only $7,000 per month advertising in health food periodicals, and sell approximately 7,500 cases per month.

(Continued)

Required

A. Prepare a schedule that shows the expected profit from each scenario.
B. Write a report for your company president and vice presidents in which you analyze each of the strategies and make a recommendation concerning which one to choose.
C. Include discussion of any long-term trends and other outside factors that you feel should be considered in making this strategic decision.

P1-11   Excel in Action

SPREADSHEET

Music Makers produces compact disks for various software and music companies. Music Makers receives a master version of the software or music from a customer in computer form. The company copies the master version of the data to blank CDs, packages the CDs, and ships the completed product to the customer.

Because its product is generic, Music Makers relies on being a low-cost producer of CDs in order to remain competitive. It also relies on a quality production process to ensure customer satisfaction. The company is considering upgrading some of its production equipment to include faster copying capability and to automate some parts of the packing process that are now done manually.

Currently, the cost of producing a CD for Music Makers, including materials and labor, is $1.10 per CD. In addition, depreciation on equipment, utilities, and other period costs are $324,000 per month. The company currently is producing 500,000 CDs each month. If it upgrades its equipment, Music Makers' production costs will decrease to $1.06 per unit, but its period costs will increase to $340,000 per month.

Required Use a spreadsheet to prepare a cost comparison for Music Makers. Your spreadsheet should appear similar to the following example. Use the formatting instructions that follow the example for this purpose.

	A	B	C
1		**Current**	**Upgraded**
2	Production cost per unit		
3	Monthly volume		
4			
5	Production cost		
6	Period cost		
7	Total cost		

The spreadsheet should automatically calculate the total production and total cost for each option. Enter =B2*B3 in cell B4 to calculate the balance that appears in this cell, for example. The contents of cell B3 can be copied to cell C4. Use the Comma button ❟ to format columns B and C beginning with row 2 to display two decimal places and include commas to separate thousands from hundreds. Draw a line to separate totals from other amounts. Also, use a double line beneath the amounts in the Total cost rows to indicate totals. Select the appropriate cells and click on the borders button. ▦ ▾ Use the drop-down arrow to select the line style from the options provided. Align text on the left-hand side of each column and align numbers on the right-hand side by selecting the appropriate cells and clicking on the alignment buttons. ≣ ≣ ≣ You may use dollar signs for dollar amounts in your spreadsheet by selecting on the appropriate cell and clicking on the dollar button. $ Captions in row 1 should be centered and in bold type.

Your spreadsheet can be modified as needed by inserting or deleting rows, columns, or cells. To insert a row, column, or cell, select the row above the row to be added, the column to the left of the column to be added, or the cell(s) where you want the new cell(s) to appear. Click on the Insert menu and select the appropriate item. To delete a row, column, or cell, select that row, column, or cell(s) and click on the Edit menu. Then click on Delete.

It is important to **save your work on a regular basis.** Save your work before you make any major changes so that mistakes will not require you to redo a lot of work.

Which options provide the lower cost for Music Makers? Assume that production volume decreased to 300,000 units per month. Which option would produce the lower cost?

P1-12 Multiple-Choice Overview of the Chapter

1. Management accounting is concerned primarily with providing:
   a. information in accordance with generally accepted accounting principles.
   b. information to stockholders, creditors, and others outside the organization.
   c. information to managers inside the organization.
   d. information to regulatory agencies.
2. The managerial functions of planning, control, and decision making typically are:
   a. approached in precisely the same way in every organization.
   b. carried out simultaneously, with decision making being an inseparable part of the other functions.
   c. carried out independently of one another, so that a function may be omitted without negative effects.
   d. conducted only by the managers of manufacturing entities.
3. In decision making, a manager uses:
   a. financial accounting information exclusively.
   b. information from his or her department only, ignoring other departments' costs and activities.
   c. information that must conform to generally accepted accounting principles.
   d. information that is relevant to the decision even if the information does not conform to generally accepted accounting principles.
4. Daley is a stockholder of Public Company, Inc. In his role as a stockholder, Daley would most likely use:
   a. managerial accounting information developed by the organization.
   b. financial information contained in Public's annual report.
   c. accounting information obtained directly from Public's computer system.
   d. no accounting information about Public, since it is not available to outsiders.
5. Budgets are:
   a. a form of planning for an organization's operating and financial matters.
   b. concerned only with the company's cash position.
   c. typically not prepared on an annual basis.
   d. usually prepared for an organization as a whole, not for individual departments.
6. Management accounting in the beginning of the 21st century would be most accurately described as a:
   a. branch of financial accounting.
   b. form of accounting that is concerned mainly with production-related managerial decisions.
   c. form of accounting that is necessary if a business is to successfully compete in a global business environment.
   d. branch of industrial technology.
7. The primary difference between a planning decision and a control decision is that:
   a. investors make planning decisions, while management makes control decisions.
   b. planning decisions involve dollars, while control decisions involve qualitative factors.
   c. planning decisions involve revenues, while control decisions involve expenses.
   d. planning decisions are developmental, while control decisions are corrective.
8. A difference between the information needs of top management and those of middle managers of a business is that:
   a. top managers make planning decisions, while middle managers make control decisions.
   b. top managers are concerned with profits, while middle managers are concerned with costs.
   c. middle managers require more timely and detailed information than top managers.
   d. middle managers require less accurate information than top managers.
9. Which of the following is a control decision?
   a. Developing goals
   b. Determining strategic objectives
   c. Determining operational objectives
   d. Measuring outcomes
10. The use of managerial accounting in service organizations:
    a. is pointless, since service organizations produce no tangible product.
    b. provides timely, relevant, and accurate information to managers.
    c. occurs more than the use of managerial accounting in manufacturing companies.
    d. is required by regulatory agencies.

CASE

C1-1   Cost Management in a University

Objs. 1–4

Most states now require five years of education for accounting graduates to sit for the Certified Public Accountant (CPA) examination. Many accounting jobs, however, do not require a CPA license, so some students still seek only four-year degrees. The Business School at Cassidy University offers three degrees in accounting: (1) Bachelor of Science (BS) in Accounting, (2) Master of Professional Accountancy (MPA), and (3) Master of Business Administration in Accounting (MBA). Tuition for a semester of graduate study costs approximately twice as much as a semester of undergraduate study. Undergraduate students who meet certain academic requirements are normally admitted to the BS program at the end of their sophomore year after taking a series of prerequisite courses. The school operates undergraduate and graduate placement services to assist students in finding employment. The school also operates an Accounting Graduate Programs office with a staff to administer the accounting graduate programs. The programs office has an annual budget that sets targets for tuition revenues, teaching costs, administrative costs, and merit-based financial aid provided to students. The school is adding a new building to accommodate its graduate programs.

The BS degree is a four-year degree with a curriculum similar to other four-year accounting programs. Each year the school graduates about 275 students with this degree. Some graduates of the BS program are employed as management accountants by corporations or governments. Others are employed by CPA firms and expect to complete a fifth year of education later. Undergraduate tuition costs are similar to those at other universities.

The MBA is a two-year degree in which high-performing students can convert to graduate student status at the end of their junior year in the BS program and continue their education for two more years. Upon graduation, these students receive both BS and MBA degrees. In the first year of the MBA program, students take graduate courses in a broad variety of disciplines such as accounting, economics, finance, information systems, marketing, and quantitative methods. Using a series of intensive business simulations the students learn how to integrate six basic business processes to achieve business success. In the second year of the MBA, accounting students take one of four accounting tracks: consulting, assurance, taxation, or information systems. In addition to an accounting track, the students also take a complementary, nonaccounting concentration of advanced graduate courses in areas such as finance, marketing, operations, or tax law. Finally, the students receive instruction in leadership, cognitive development, oral and written communications, and self-assessment skills throughout the two years of graduate study. The school expects to graduate about 60–120 students each year from the MBA program. Recently, graduates of the MBA program received starting salaries approximately 33% higher than graduates of the BS program.

The MPA is a one-year degree with a BS degree as a prerequisite for entry. Admitted students have grade point averages and standardized test scores similar to students admitted to the MBA program. The curriculum in the one year of graduate study is similar to that of the second year of the MBA program. The school expects to graduate about 80 students each year from the MPA program. Most students entering the MPA program come from undergraduate programs at other schools. Recently, graduates of the MPA program received starting salaries approximately 20% higher than graduates of the BS program.

Required

A. Describe how the Business School adds value and who receives this value.
B. How must the school manage the economic and quality aspects of its activities to be successful?
C. What are the major cost drivers involved in the school's educational process? How do you think the school might attempt to control costs?

COST CATEGORIES AND FLOWS

How can accounting classifications help us understand costs?

Erin and Seth believe they have designed a product that customers will want to buy. Seth understands how to make the product, and Erin has developed a marketing plan. In order to make a profit, Erin and Seth must control their costs so the revenue they receive from selling their products is greater than the costs of producing and selling them. Therefore, the next problem Erin and Seth must address involves understanding costs.

FOOD FOR THOUGHT

Put yourself in the role of Seth and Erin. What would you like to know about costs? Would you want to understand how the cost of making the product differs from the cost of selling the product and administering the business? Let's join Erin and Seth as they discuss the accounting information they will need to make pricing decisions.

Seth: *I've been thinking about how to distinguish between costs incurred to make products and those incurred to generate sales. I think we should classify all costs that result from production activities as product costs.*

Erin: *That makes sense because all of these costs can be traced to the products we make. For example, we can identify materials such as lumber and hardware used in making each product. Also, we can trace the labor of production employees to the products.*

Seth: *You're right. But I haven't figured out what to do with the costs of a lot of miscellaneous items such as factory insurance, glue, sandpaper, and varnish. The managers where I worked previously talked about overhead costs. These must be the kinds of costs they were talking about.*

Erin: *What about the other costs of administering our business and selling products? For example, we will have consulting charges from Roberta and travel expenses as I visit potential customers. These costs shouldn't be part of the product cost.*

Seth: *I think you're right. But, after we have classified our costs, what then? Isn't the purpose of an accounting system to help us make better decisions? How do we use all of this information?*

OBJECTIVES

Once you have completed this chapter, you should be able to:

1 Differentiate between product costs and period expenses.

2 Explain how direct material, direct labor, and manufacturing overhead costs flow through an accounting system.

3 Discuss methods for proactively managing inventory levels and manufacturing costs.

PINE BELT FURNITURE COMPANY: MARKETS AND MANUFACTURING PROCESSES

OBJECTIVE 1

Differentiate between product costs and period expenses.

Pine Belt Furniture Company manufactures and sells mid-priced pine furniture to retailers. The company's product line consists primarily of bedroom sets. Pine Belt markets its products to cost-conscious buyers who want quality products but cannot afford furniture constructed of expensive wood, such as maple, oak, or mahogany. Marketing studies indicate the company's typical customer is under 30 years old, recently married, and has an annual family income of less than $50,000. Pine Belt recognizes the needs of cost-conscious buyers and has developed marketing and manufacturing strategies to meet those needs.

The designs for new products at Pine Belt begin with the engineering department. There the product and the manufacturing process are designed at the same time, minimizing manufacturing costs. Once product design and manufacturing processes are complete, raw materials (lumber and hardware) are ordered from suppliers and placed into raw materials inventory. Pine Belt works closely with its suppliers to minimize variation in the quality of the materials it buys. In addition, as materials are delivered and placed into inventory, quality control engineers select random samples for inspection and testing. Working with customers' orders, production schedulers at Pine Belt try to group similar products so that they can be manufactured at the same time. The manufacturing process involves cutting the lumber into components, assembling the components, and finishing the assembled product.

When an order is received on the manufacturing floor, an equipment operator removes raw materials from the storage area and places them into production. Processing steps involve cutting lumber to meet specifications, cutting square edges of the lumber at appropriate points to produce curves or other geometric designs, cutting dovetail joints where two pieces of lumber will be attached, and drilling holes to accommodate hardware. In the assembly department, the wooden components are assembled and hardware is attached. Here the pieces of lumber are glued, clamped, and screwed together. In the finishing stage, the assembled products are sanded and stained to darken the wood and to accent the grain. Next a polyurethane finish is applied to the surface to protect against scratching and other damage during use. Pine Belt applies five coats of polyurethane to each product. Workers lightly buff the surface with steel wool between each coat. When the last coat of polyurethane has dried, the product is boxed and shipped to retail furniture stores. Exhibit 1 illustrates Pine Belt's production process.

Many of Pine Belt's activities involve selling and administration. For example, the company employs salespersons who visit furniture retailers to promote the product line. In addition, the company employs a variety of people who serve in an administrative capacity. For example, Pine Belt Furniture has accounting, marketing, and human resources departments. Individuals employed in these functions support the manufacturing efforts of the company, but are not directly involved in making the company's products. Pine Belt incurs expenses for other types of selling and administrative activities. For example, the company contracts with a trucking company

Exhibit 1 Production Process at Pine Belt

A. Cutting

Raw materials inventory

Transportation

Workcenter

Lumber is cut to required dimensions per engineering specifications

Square edges are rounded

Dovetail joints are cut into wood to make strong joints

Holes are drilled

B. Assembly

Carpenter's GLUE

Cut lumber from the cutting department

Drawer knobs

Assembled chest

C. Finishing

Sand Paper   Stain   Polyurethane   Steel wool between coats   Finished chest

to transport its finished products to retail stores. Pine Belt incurs many of the costs that are familiar to you from studying retail organizations in your financial accounting course. The company incurs costs for utilities, insurance, legal services, building rent, office supplies, and depreciation on office equipment. In the next section, we consider why accountants separate manufacturing costs from selling and administrative expenses.

Product Costs versus Period Expense

Erin and Seth, who own a manufacturing company, discussed the importance of understanding their production and selling costs in order to control them and to earn a profit. Before managers can use cost accounting information to make decisions, they must understand how that information is gathered. In your study of financial accounting you learned that most expenses are classified as either operating expenses or cost of goods (or services) sold. Period expenses are the costs of selling and administrative activities. Examples of period expenses include rent, interest, taxes, losses on equipment sales, and administrative salaries. These expenses are recognized on the income statement during the fiscal period in which they are incurred.

For a manufacturing company, cost of goods sold represents resources consumed in producing the goods that were sold during a fiscal period. Unsold goods are reported as assets on the balance sheet. Thus, product costs do not become expenses until the products are sold. Accountants classify resources consumed during production as direct materials, direct labor, and manufacturing overhead.

Direct Material Costs. The costs of significant raw materials from which a product is manufactured are classified as *direct material costs.* For example, Pine Belt uses lumber to construct its product line. The cost of lumber is a direct material cost. The company also classifies the costs of the wooden knobs or brass drawer pulls that workers attach to furniture as direct material costs.

Direct Labor Costs. *Direct labor costs* **are the wages of workers who add value to a product through their direct involvement in the production process.** For example, Pine Belt's direct labor costs include wages of the saw operators who cut parts from the lumber. Wages of those who assemble parts and apply stain and polyurethane finish also are classified as direct labor costs.

Manufacturing Overhead Costs. In the discussion at the beginning of this chapter, Seth recalled hearing managers speak of overhead costs. He seemed to have a vague idea about the kinds of costs that are classified as manufacturing overhead. As a general rule, manufacturing overhead costs are not as easily associated with products as are direct materials and direct labor costs. *Manufacturing overhead costs* **result from activities that support a manufacturing process but often are not directly related to any specific product.** Thus, overhead costs often are classified as indirect manufacturing costs. While examples of direct materials and direct labor at Pine Belt have been identified, certain types of materials and labor are classified as indirect. For instance, the salary of the quality inspector and wages of workers who maintain equipment and clean the manufacturing area are considered indirect labor costs.

The cost of indirect materials is a manufacturing overhead cost. At Pine Belt, those costs include the costs of saw blades in the cutting department, glue and screws in the assembly department, and steel wool in the finishing department. How do accountants decide whether to treat glue and screws as direct materials or indirect materials? Generally they use a cost/benefit rule. If the cost of tracking an item exceeds the benefit or value of that information, the cost of the item should be assigned to an overhead category and later allocated to products in a logical manner. For example, the cost of glue (about $0.03 per unit) is not worth measuring separately as a direct material cost. We consider overhead allocation in Chapter M3.

In addition to indirect labor and indirect materials, Pine Belt incurs other overhead costs in the production process as follows:

- Electricity for the manufacturing equipment
- Fire insurance on factory assets
- Supplies (cleaning rags, solvents, brooms, safety glasses, ear plugs, and dust masks) for equipment operators
- Depreciation on factory buildings and manufacturing equipment

Associating overhead costs with individual products is one of the most challenging and interesting aspects of management accounting. We further explore these issues in Chapter M5.

1 SELF-STUDY PROBLEM

WebTUTOR Advantage

Greencut Manufacturing produces energy-efficient lawn mowers for homeowners. Workers at Greencut manufacture the mower bodies from steel sheets and then attach a gasoline-powered engine, a blade, a handle, and four wheels to each unit.

The following events took place during the month of January:

1. Greencut bought steel sheets (cost, $5,000) for constructing mower bodies.
2. Steel sheets (cost, $2,000) were removed from raw materials inventory and delivered by forklift operators (total January wages, $5,000) to a metal-press machine operator (total January wages, $3,000), who pressed the flat sheets of steel into mower housings. Forklift operators delivered the mower housings to an automated painting booth. There, workers (total January wages, $2,000) placed the housings onto overhead conveyor hooks that moved through a booth containing robotic paint sprayers. All surfaces of the mower housing were sprayed with paint (total paint cost, $1,000). The painted housings moved along the conveyor belt into a dryer that was heated with propane gas (total January gas cost, $1,000).
3. After drying, forklift operators transported the painted housings to the assembly area. At the same time, engines, blades, handles, and wheels were removed from the inventory of "purchased parts" (total cost of parts removed from inventory, $20,000) and delivered by forklift to the assembly area. Finally, workers installed a motor, a blade, a handle, and four wheels to each housing (total January wages of assemblers, $6,000).
4. Greencut estimates depreciation costs on plant equipment to be $24,000 for the month of January.
5. Following assembly, the completed mowers were crated and shipped to retail stores throughout the world.

Required Classify each of Greencut's costs in January as direct material, direct labor, or overhead.

The solution to Self-Study Problem 1 appears at the end of the chapter.

HOW MANUFACTURING COSTS FLOW THROUGH AN ACCOUNTING SYSTEM

OBJECTIVE 2

Explain how direct material, direct labor, and manufacturing overhead costs flow through an accounting system.

Your financial accounting course addressed inventory reporting issues for retail and manufacturing organizations. Recall that retail organizations purchase completed goods from suppliers, add a markup, and sell the finished goods to their customers. Thus, a retail organization typically reports one type of inventory (finished goods) on its balance sheet. On the other hand, manufacturing organizations purchase raw materials from suppliers and convert them into finished goods during the manufacturing process.

Most manufacturing companies report three types of inventory on their balance sheets, raw materials, partially completed goods known as work-in-process (WIP), and finished goods. When retail and manufacturing organizations sell finished goods, the unit cost is reported on the income statement as cost of goods sold.

Companies use accounting systems to help them keep track of the various types of inventory and cost of goods sold. Exhibit 2 illustrates the flow of product costs through an accounting system. When materials are removed from raw materials inventory and placed into production, the work-in-process inventory account is increased. Accordingly, the raw materials inventory balance is reduced by the same amount, representing the cost of raw materials placed into production. As direct labor is used to convert the direct materials in the production area, these costs also are added to work-in-process inventory. Finally, various types of overhead costs are incurred during production and are added to the work-in-process inventory.

Exhibit 2 Cost Flows Through the Accounting System of a Manufacturing Company

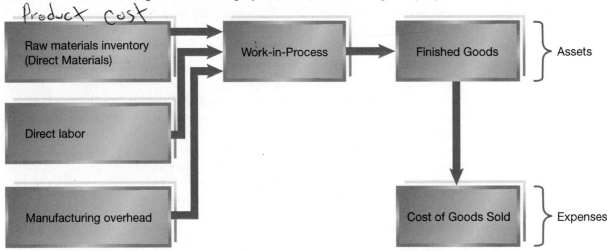

When goods are completed and moved from the production facility to the completed goods warehouse, accountants must adjust the work-in-process and finished goods inventory values. The cost of the completed products is added to the finished goods inventory account and removed from the work-in-process account. As shown in Exhibit 2, the final step involves transferring costs from the finished goods inventory to cost of goods sold. The accounting system records this transfer when the products are sold. Raw materials, work-in-process, and finished goods inventory appear on the balance sheet as assets. Their production costs appear as cost of goods sold on the income statement when the products are sold.

Exhibit 2 provides a general model of cost flows through an accounting system. Let's look at some actual transactions and see how the system keeps track of manufacturing costs. Assume the following activities took place at Pine Belt during January:

(a) Purchased raw materials (lumber, knobs, hardware) costing $50,000.
(b) Placed raw materials costing $20,000 into production.
(c) Incurred labor costs of $8,000 for cutting, assembling, and finishing activities.
(d) Purchased and consumed manufacturing supplies, such as sandpaper, stain, varnish, glue, and screws, costing $300.
(e) Incurred depreciation in the amount of $1,000 on manufacturing equipment.
(f) Incurred other overhead costs (including fire insurance, supervisors' salaries, and various utilities) in the amount of $5,000.
(g) Completed furniture costing $40,200.
(h) Sold furniture that cost $45,000 to produce.
(i) Paid 10% sales commissions on the furniture sold in transaction (h).

In addition to transactions (a)–(i), Pine Belt reported the following inventory balances at January 1:

Raw materials inventory	$10,000
Work-in-process inventory	40,000
Finished goods inventory	15,000

We use Exhibit 3 to illustrate cost flows through Pine Belt's accounting system. The columns in Exhibit 3 represent raw materials inventory, work-in-process inventory, finished goods inventory, and cost of goods sold. Without preparing journal entries, we may trace costs through our simple accounting system using plusses and minuses to indicate increases and decreases as resources flow through Pine Belt's accounting system.

Exhibit 3 Cost Flows Through Pine Belt's Accounting System

	Inventory			
	Raw Materials	**Work-in-Process**	**Finished Goods**	**Cost of Goods Sold**
Beginning balance	$10,000	$40,000	$15,000	
	+50,000 (a)			
	−20,000 (b)	+20,000 (b)		
Ending balance	$40,000	+8,000 (c)		
		+300 (d)		
		+1,000 (e)		
		+5,000 (f)		
		−40,200 (g)	+40,200 (g)	
	Ending balance	$34,100	−45,000 (h)	+45,000 (h)
		Ending balance	$10,200	Ending balance $45,000

As shown in Exhibit 3, the beginning balances of raw materials inventory, work-in-process inventory, and finished goods inventory are $10,000, $40,000, and $15,000, respectively. We add or subtract transaction values from these balances as resources are placed into production, converted, completed, and sold. For example, a raw materials purchase of $50,000 increases the raw materials inventory account as shown by transaction (a). When raw materials costing $20,000 are placed in production, work-in-process inventory increases by $20,000 and raw materials inventory decreases by $20,000, as shown by transaction (b). Transaction (c) indicates Pine Belt incurred direct labor costs of $8,000 while manufacturing its products. These costs also are added to the work-in-process account in Exhibit 3.

In Chapter M3 we learn more about applying overhead to products. For now, let's put all overhead costs directly into work-in-process inventory as these costs are incurred. Transactions (d), (e), and (f) represent various types of overhead costs consumed during the production process. Each of these costs is added to work-in-process inventory.

Transaction (g) tells us Pine Belt completed furniture costing $40,200. As these goods are moved from the production area to the finished goods warehouse, the accounting system increases the finished goods inventory account by $40,200 and reduces the work-in-process inventory account by $40,200.

Transaction (h) indicates goods costing $45,000 were sold. The transaction to record cost of goods sold and reduce finished goods inventory is identical for a retail store and a manufacturing company. In each case, finished goods inventory is reduced and cost of goods sold is increased.

Transaction (i) is not shown in Exhibit 3. Sales commissions are period expenses rather than product costs. Thus, we omit the transaction from our product cost model.

Having recorded transactions (a)–(h), we may sum the columns to calculate the ending balances for each account. Exhibit 3 reports ending balances for raw materials, work-in-process, and finished goods inventory of $40,000, $34,100, and $10,200, respectively. In addition, cost of goods sold for the period is $45,000.

Here are several key points to remember about the way costs flow through the accounting system of a manufacturing company. First, when materials are placed into production, their costs become part of work-in-process inventory. In addition, direct labor and overhead costs become part of work-in-process inventory as labor and overhead are used to convert raw materials to products. Accountants often refer to direct labor and overhead costs as conversion costs. *Conversion costs* **are the costs of activities required to convert materials into products.** Imagine a product with hooks on it. As it moves through the factory, direct labor and overhead costs are attached to the hooks. When the product is finished, all of the costs that have "hooked on" to the product during manufacturing become part of finished goods inventory and, ultimately, the cost of goods sold.

Companies typically provide details of their inventory values in the notes to the financial statements. Exhibit 4 is from the **Vulcan Materials Company** 2002 annual report and illustrates the financial statement disclosure of various types of inventory. Included are finished products, raw materials, products (work) in process, and operating supplies and other inventories.

Exhibit 4

Excerpt from the Vulcan Materials Company 2002 Annual Report—Inventory Note Disclosure

Note 2 Inventories Inventories at December 31 were as follows (in thousands of dollars):			
	2002	**2001**	**2000**
Finished products	$189,378	$176,940	$155,258
Raw materials	10,191	13,284	15,578
Products in process	486	564	1,020
Operating supplies and other	39,531	37,627	27,188
Total inventories	$239,586	$228,415	$199,044

2 SELF-STUDY PROBLEM

WebTUTOR Advantage

To solve this problem, use the information in Self-Study Problem 1. In addition, assume Greencut does not carry work-in-process or finished goods inventory. All units are completed and sold during the month. Salespersons earned commissions of $10,000 in January.

Required

A. Prepare an exhibit similar to Exhibit 3 that shows the effects of January's activities on the company's raw materials inventory, purchased parts inventory, work-in-process inventory, finished goods inventory, and cost of goods sold. Assume that all beginning balances on January 1 were zero, except for purchased parts inventory, which had a beginning balance of $25,000.
B. What was the company's cost of goods sold for January?
C. What was the value of Greencut's raw materials and purchased parts inventories at the end of January?

The solution to Self-Study Problem 2 appears at the end of the chapter.

MANAGERIAL ACCOUNTING SYSTEMS TO SUPPORT DECISION MAKING

Previous sections of this chapter considered how to classify production costs and administrative expenses. We also addressed production cost flows through an accounting

OBJECTIVE 3

Discuss methods for proactively managing inventory levels and manufacturing costs.

system to determine values for inventory and cost of goods sold. However, the purpose of understanding these costs, and the activities that drive them, is to help managers make better decisions. Thus, recording, summarizing, and reporting inventory costs are just part of the inventory picture. Management uses accounting information to coordinate activities with suppliers and customers. Suppliers that provide raw materials or components used in assembling a product are an integral part of a company's ability to profitably deliver goods to its customers. Reliable delivery of quality material and components from suppliers is necessary for a business to meet obligations to its customers. These interrelationships are known as a value chain. **The** *value chain* **is the set of value-creating activities that extends from the production of raw materials, to the sale of finished goods, to servicing customers after the sale.** The value chain includes activities both inside and outside a company. Managing the value chain requires a company to look beyond its own operations to those of its customers and suppliers. For example, to eliminate or reduce cost-creating activities, companies develop close relationships with customers and suppliers to reduce costs of excess inventories of raw materials and finished products.

Value chain analysis permits management to identify when a company has a competitive advantage by understanding the value added at each stage in the chain. When value chain analysis is applied at an operational level, non-value-adding activities within a company's production and delivery processes are eliminated or reduced. Identifying product costs helps managers identify and reduce the costs of making and handling inventory. Many companies use an inventory system called just in time (JIT) to make their manufacturing operations more efficient.

Just-in-time manufacturing (JIT) **is a manufacturing philosophy that attempts to improve efficiency by reducing inventory levels.** Under JIT, no product or component is manufactured until it is needed. JIT seeks to reduce the amount of time spent creating products, minimize inventories, improve quality, and reduce costs. Inventories of raw materials, component parts, and finished products held just in case they might be needed are eliminated. Managerial accounting can support JIT by supplying information that identifies sources of delay, error, and waste in the manufacturing system.

A goal of JIT systems is to reduce the length of time it takes to manufacture and deliver a product. JIT concepts require processing small batches that match demand, and to maximize time spent adding value to products. Examples include:

- Reducing the time required to respond to customer demands such as cashing checks at banks,
- Moving finished products faster to reduce inventory, and
- Reducing distribution time once products leave the factory.

Thus, value chain and JIT concepts permit managers to examine relationships among themselves, their suppliers, and customers. These concepts are important to managers when proactively controlling costs.

Proactively Controlling Costs Using Target Costing

Target costing begins by understanding customer expectations for product cost, quality, and functionality. Managers then design a product that meets their customers' expectations. Targets are established for product costs that permit the company to meet specific profits levels. Suppliers are involved to ensure raw materials meet cost and quality targets. In addition, delivery terms often are consistent with JIT concepts. We illustrate the integrative nature of target costing using Pine Belt Furniture Company.

Assume that the managers at Pine Belt have made the strategic decision to expand the product line to offer a product that can compete with those offered by high-quality furniture manufacturers. The first piece in the new line is a bedroom chest of drawers constructed from clear (knot-free) pine and solid brass drawer pulls.

Pine Belt's managers have invested resources in engineering drawings, product prototypes, and studies of manufacturing processes before implementing full-scale production of the chest. Naturally they want to recover their investment and earn a profit on the sale of the new product. To determine the price of the chest, managers first estimated the per-unit costs of producing it.

Pine Belt's management offered the following explanation of the unit costs:

Direct materials. The chest differs from other products in the line because expensive, knot-free wood and solid brass are used in its construction.

Direct labor. Managers predict the direct labor costs of the chest in the cutting department will be identical to that of other products in the line. However, they expect direct labor costs to go up in the assembly and finishing departments because the process of assembling and finishing the chest is more complex and time-consuming than for other products in the line.

Manufacturing overhead. Management expects an increase in the manufacturing costs per unit due to additional engineering time and new equipment purchased solely to assemble and finish the product.

The total estimated materials, labor, and overhead cost per unit is $475. Pine Belt generally adds a 30 percent markup to the unit cost when it quotes prices to customers. The markup is calculated as follows:

Unit manufacturing cost × Markup percentage = Markup
$475.00   ×   0.30   = $142.50

The managers at Pine Belt calculate the selling price to a furniture store as follows:

Unit manufacturing cost + Markup = Selling price
$475.00   + $142.50 = $617.50

Using costs to help them determine a selling price, Pine Belt's managers set the wholesale price of the chest at $618. After applying their own markup, retailers must sell the chest for approximately $1,000. Unfortunately, after producing a new catalog and price list, as well as floor models of the chest for display in retailers' showrooms, the managers at Pine Belt hear some disappointing news. Retailers are not interested in carrying the line because consumers are not willing to pay $1,000 retail for pine furniture, even when that furniture is constructed of knot-free lumber and solid brass pulls. How could this happen? The management of Pine Belt carefully studied the components of product cost, yet found the flagship of its product line sank! What went wrong?

This situation illustrates a traditional cost-based pricing policy in which the following steps occur:

1. A product and manufacturing process are designed.
2. The product is manufactured.
3. Manufacturing costs are accumulated.
4. The unit cost plus markup determines the selling price.
5. The company tries to sell the product.

Pine Belt failed to analyze the market before developing its new product. Although the new chest seemed to meet consumers' demands for quality and functionality, it did not meet their price demands. By adding a markup to its manufacturing costs, Pine Belt's managers overpriced the chest.

Target costing changes the focus of product pricing. Instead of production costs determining the selling price, the selling price determines the production costs. The purpose of a target costing system is to provide quality and functionality at a cost that achieves long-term profit objectives. The process of calculating a target cost is as follows:

1. Determine the quality and functionality consumers want in a new product and the price they are willing to pay for that product.

2. Subtract the manufacturer's required profit margin from the price to determine what the manufacturer can spend to produce the product.

3. Study the feasibility of the new product. Can the company produce a product consumers want at a price the market will accept?

The target cost calculation involves an understanding of the relationships among three variables: the selling price, the targeted manufacturing cost (cost), and the required profit margin. The relationship among the variables is defined as follows:

Selling price − Required profit margin = Target cost

Suppose market research sets the wholesale price of the chest at $400. Management has determined a margin of 23 percent on sales is required for long-term profitability. The company's required margin and target cost are calculated as follows:

$$
\begin{aligned}
\text{Margin} &= \text{Selling price} \times 0.23 \\
&= \$400 \qquad\quad \times 0.23 \\
&= \$92
\end{aligned}
$$

The target cost information for Pine Belt can be summarized as follows:

Selling price	$400
Less required margin	−92
Target cost	$308

Determining the cost at which Pine Belt must deliver the chest is the first step in using target costing for strategic purposes. Clearly the managers at Pine Belt have a problem: To market the new chest successfully, they must reduce the unit cost of producing the chest from $475 to $308.

One way companies begin to address a cost problem is by forming a multidisciplinary team, a team whose members are drawn from different functions such as marketing, accounting, finance, production, purchasing, and engineering. The team looks for ways to save costs and to eliminate inefficiencies.

Pine Belt's team would evaluate major production costs. Managers would discuss redesigning the manufacturing process and reconsidering the types of materials used. Using value chain concepts, they would examine ways to reduce suppliers' costs. They would study the sources of overhead costs and methods of reducing those costs. However, if the team determines that they cannot produce the chest for $308, Pine Belt should not produce the product. Exhibit 5 compares the cost-plus philosophy with the target costing philosophy.

Exhibit 5

Cost-Plus and Target Costing Philosophies

Cost-plus philosophy

Cost + Markup = Selling price

Implications:
- Cost is the starting point (given)
- Markup is added (given)
- The firm puts the product on the market and hopes the selling price is accepted

Target costing philosophy

Selling price − Required margin = Target cost

Implications:
- Markets determine prices (given)
- Required margins must be sustained for survival (given)
- Target cost is the residual, the variable to be managed

Case In Point

http://albright.
swlearning.com

Learn more about
target costing.

Target Costing at Hewlett-Packard

The Vancouver Division of **Hewlett-Packard** (HP) uses target costing to work with its suppliers to manage the cost of making the desk jet printer. The facility recently has changed its strategy from producing low-volume, high-margin industrial products to high-volume, low-margin consumer products. HP reports achieving substantial price decreases as a result of their target costing program. In addition, the company uses target costing to support continuous improvement efforts and to identify various activities that cause costs within the value chain.

Source: Anonymous. 2000. Target costing gives HP better control over supply costs. New York: Supplier and Management Report.

Cost Information for Service Organizations

In service organizations, costs attach to services in much the same way as they do in manufacturing organizations; only the nature of the product is different. For example, a hospital doesn't produce a tangible product, such as furniture. Its product is an intangible service, patient health care. When a patient leaves the health-care system, the costs of providing care become part of the cost of services provided, the service organization's equivalent to cost of goods sold. This section describes cost categories and cost control in a service environment. As you will see, many similarities exist between a service and manufacturing organization.

Cost Categories

Hospitals, like manufacturers, classify costs as direct and indirect. The costs of nurses' salaries, drugs, and X-rays are all direct costs of delivering care to patients. Like direct costs in manufacturing, direct costs in a hospital are easily associated with a patient. Hospitals and most other service organizations generally have a large proportion of indirect costs that must be assigned to individual patients or customer services in some manner. Among a hospital's indirect costs are salaries of administrators, admission and discharge personnel, and insurance specialists.

Cost Control

In today's economy, all businesses are taking steps to control production costs. Health-care providers face a special challenge. At one time, hospitals were reimbursed by insurance companies (or the federal government in the case of Medicare) based on their costs of treating patients. Today, insurance companies are applying pressure by limiting the fees they pay for each type of treatment. Because their revenue largely is determined by insurance providers, hospitals can operate profitably only if they manage costs effectively.

Manufacturing companies use target costing to help provide products desired by customers at costs that ensure profitability. Hospitals use a similar technique called critical path. They identify the steps necessary for each procedure from pre-admission to discharge. By standardizing procedures, health-care providers often find ways to reduce inefficiency and costs. The critical path helps service organizations control costs in a similar way that target costing helps manufacturing companies control costs.

3 SELF-STUDY PROBLEM

webTUTOR Advantage

Greencut is considering adding a mulching lawn mower to its product line. The new mower cuts grass clippings into fine particles, eliminating raking, bagging, and disposing of lawn wastes. The new product is intended to meet the needs of urban and environmentally conscious homeowners.

Greencut wants to conduct a target costing exercise to determine the cost at which the new product must be produced. Market surveys indicate that retailers typically pay $300 and sell for $500 products with similar features. Thus, the company expects the wholesale price for the new mower to be $300. Greencut's required margin on sales is 26 percent.

Required Calculate the target cost of the new mower and Greencut's required markup.

The solution to Self-Study Problem 3 appears at the end of the chapter.

REVIEW

SUMMARY of IMPORTANT CONCEPTS

1. Costs may be classified according to a number of categories including:
   a. Product cost versus period expense.
   b. Direct materials, direct labor, or overhead.

2. Manufacturing costs flow through an accounting system as products physically move through the factory.
   a. When raw materials are acquired, their value is added to raw materials inventory.
   b. When raw materials are placed into production, their costs, along with the costs of labor and overhead, are added to work-in-process inventory.
   c. The cost of completed goods is transferred to finished goods inventory.
   d. The costs in finished goods inventory are transferred to cost of goods sold when the units are sold.

3. Managers use cost information to help them make better decisions.
   a. Understanding the value chain enables managers to work with their customers and suppliers to minimize costs and to provide high-quality products or services.
   b. Just-in-time inventory practices help companies reduce inventory levels and the time required to produce and deliver a product.
   c. Target costing helps managers in the introduction of new products.

4. Organizations that produce services instead of tangible products also incur production costs.
   a. The costs of services are classified as direct or indirect.
   b. Service organizations often implement cost control procedures to identify and eliminate waste.

DEFINE

TERMS and CONCEPTS DEFINED in this CHAPTER

conversion costs   (M36)
direct labor costs   (M32)
direct material costs   (M32)

just-in-time manufacturing (JIT)   (M37)
manufacturing overhead costs   (M32)
value chain   (M37)

SELF-STUDY PROBLEM SOLUTIONS

SSP2-1   The costs identified by Greencut included the following:

Direct material
Steel
Paint
Wheels, motors, handles, and blades

Direct labor
Metal-press machine operator
Spray-booth workers
Assembly area workers

Overhead
Indirect materials:
    Propane gas
Indirect labor:
    Forklift operators' wages
Other manufacturing overhead costs:
    Depreciation on the plant equipment

SSP2-2   A.

Inventory

	Raw Materials	Purchased Parts	Work-in-Process	Finished Goods	Cost of Goods Sold
Beg. bal.	$ 0	$25,000	$ 0	$ 0	$ 0
	+5,000 (a)	−20,000 (h)	+2,000 (b)	+64,000 (k)	+64,000 (l)
	−2,000 (b)	End. $ 5,000	+5,000 (c)	−64,000 (l)	End. $64,000
	End. $3,000		+3,000 (d)	End. $ 0	
			+2,000 (e)		
			+1,000 (f)		
			+1,000 (g)		
			+20,000 (h)		
			+6,000 (i)		
			+24,000 (j)		
			−64,000 (k)		
			End. $ 0		

Key to cost flows:
(a) Greencut purchased steel sheets that were placed into raw materials inventory.
(b) Steel was removed from inventory and placed into production as work-in-process inventory.
(c) Overhead for the forklift operators' wages was incurred.
(d) Direct labor costs of $3,000 for the metal-press operator were incurred.
(e) Direct labor wages for paint booth/conveyor operators were incurred.
(f) Direct materials cost of $1,000 for paint was incurred.
(g) Overhead cost (indirect materials) for the propane gas was consumed.
(h) Purchased parts (direct materials) were transferred from inventory to production.
(i) Direct labor costs ($6,000) for workers in the assembly area were incurred.
(j) Depreciation on manufacturing assets was estimated to be $24,000 during the month.
(k) Completed mowers were transferred to the finished goods inventory.
(l) Finished mowers costing $64,000 were sold.

Note: Sales commissions are not part of product costs or the cost of goods sold. Sales commissions are a period expense and are reported on the income statement below gross profit.

B. Cost of goods sold in January was $64,000.

C. The balance in raw materials inventory was $3,000, and the balance in purchased parts inventory was $5,000.

SSP2-3   Required margin = Required percentage × Sales price
                              = 0.26 × $300
                              = $78

The target cost information for Greencut may be summarized as follows:

Selling price (wholesale)	$300
Less required margin	−78
Target cost	$222

Thinking Beyond the Question

How can accounting classifications help us understand costs?

In the opening scenario, Erin and Seth were considering ways to classify costs and to use their accounting reports. Can managers use cost reports based on past activities to help control future costs?

QUESTIONS

Q2-1
Obj. 1
Your textbook is manufactured from a number of materials including paper, ink, and glue. Typically, publishing company accountants consider paper and ink direct materials; however, they consider glue an indirect material. How do accountants make these distinctions?

Q2-2
Obj. 1
Wendell Fromm Company manufactures hand tools that are used in many factory applications. The company manufactures tools from metal alloys and incurs labor and overhead costs during the manufacturing process. What costs should Wendell Fromm include in the cost of goods sold section of its income statement? Why?

Q2-3
Obj. 1
Carlton Industries manufactures orthopedic devices, such as hips and joints, from specialty metals. Each device is produced individually based on the dimensions of a specific patient. The company ships the devices to surgeons as soon as production is completed. Define and explain the different types of inventory accounts that Carlton would use in its manufacturing environment. What costs are associated with each of these accounts?

Q2-4
Obj. 1
The nurses on the fourth floor of Western Medical Center care for and administer drugs to patients who have undergone orthopedic surgery. Also located on the fourth floor is a mobile X-ray station that Western recently purchased for $250,000. How would you classify the costs of nursing care and drugs? How would you classify the depreciation costs associated with the X-ray machine? Explain your answer.

Q2-5
Obj. 1
If product costs eventually become expenses when a product is sold, why are accountants so careful when making product cost and period expense classifications?

Q2-6
Obj. 1
Can service organizations, such as legal and accounting firms, report work-in-process and finished goods inventories on their balance sheets?

Q2-7
Obj. 1
How are direct labor costs different from indirect labor costs?

Q2-8
Obj. 2
Why do manufacturing companies typically report three kinds of inventory on the balance sheet, while merchandising companies typically report only one kind of inventory?

Q2-9
Obj. 2
What is meant by the term "conversion costs"? What kinds of costs would you classify as a conversion cost?

Q2-10
Obj. 3
How does the target costing approach to new product introduction differ from the traditional cost-plus approach? Are these differences important? Why or why not?

Q2-11
Obj. 3
Discuss how JIT and supply chain concepts are related.

Q2-12
Obj. 3
What steps are required to develop a target cost? How are these steps different from the cost-plus approach?

| EXERCISES | *If your instructor is using Personal Trainer® in this course, you may complete your assignments online.* |

E2-1 Write a short definition for each of the terms listed in the *Terms and Concepts Defined in this Chapter* section.

E2-2
Obj. 1
Westco, Inc., has the following costs and expenses. Complete the schedule provided. Indicate the classification of each item listed. The first one is done for you.

	Period Expense	Product Cost Direct	Product Cost Indirect
a. Factory depreciation			X
b. Packaging materials			
c. President's salary			
d. Sales commissions			
e. Machine lubricants			
f. Magazine subscriptions, factory break room			
g. Insurance on finished goods			
h. Workers' wages in assembly department			
i. Salary of payroll clerk			
j. Grounds upkeep			
k. Shop rags			
l. Training program, factory workers			
m. Ink used in textbook production			
n. Health insurance, factory workers			
o. Glue used in production of wooden chairs			
p. Life insurance on executives			
q. Raw steel, toolbox production			
r. Gas for salesperson's car			
s. Sales travel expenses			
t. Disposal of machine coolants			

E2-3
Objs. 1–3

a. The costs of significant raw materials from which a product is manufactured are classified as _____.

b. _____ are the costs of activities required to convert materials into products.

c. _____ result from activities that support a process but often are not directly related to any specific product.

d. The _____ is the set of value-creating activities that extends from the production of raw materials, to the sale of finished goods, to servicing customers after the sale.

e. _____ are the wages of workers who add value to a product through their direct involvement in the production process.

f. _____ is a manufacturing philosophy that attempts to improve efficiency by reducing inventory levels.

E2-4
Obj. 1
Classify each of the following costs as either a product cost or a period expense. Briefly justify your answers.

a. Wages for factory maintenance workers
b. Direct materials
c. Sales salaries and commissions
d. Depreciation expense, office equipment
e. Machinery repairs and maintenance
f. Advertising
g. Property taxes, factory building
h. Indirect materials
i. Accounting fees
j. Warehousing costs for finished goods
k. Production supervisor's salary
l. Utilities for plant
m. Rent on factory buildings

E2-5
Obj. 1
Matt Holgren is the marketing manager for a small manufacturing firm. The salespersons in his division are paid commissions of 29% of the gross margin of each product sold. Because a salesperson complained that gross margin was calculated improperly when preparing a commission check, Matt is auditing the commission report that follows:

Item #531

Sales price:		$1,300
Costs:		
Raw materials	$375	
Raw material transportation	110	
Direct labor	90	
Manufacturing overhead	200	
Finished goods transportation	150	
Administrative costs	60	
Total		985
Gross margin		$ 315

Commission: $315 \times 0.29 = $91.35

   a. If gross margin is computed according to GAAP, does the salesperson have a valid complaint? Explain.

   b. What type of behavior is management attempting to promote by basing commissions on gross margin rather than on total sales dollars? Explain.

E2-6
Obj. 1
For all costs you identified as product costs in E2-4, indicate whether each should be classified as a direct material, direct labor, or manufacturing overhead cost. Justify your answer.

E2-7
Obj. 1
Exercise 2-5 identifies two forms of transportation cost: raw material transportation and finished goods transportation. Explain why GAAP require two different accounting treatments for transportation costs.

E2-8
Obj. 2
The partial information that follows pertains to the operations of Good Time Clock Company for 2004:

Raw materials inventory, January 1, 2004	$ 5,000
Raw materials inventory, December 31, 2004	2,000
Direct labor charged to production during 2004	18,000
Factory overhead costs incurred during 2004	15,000
Cost of goods manufactured for the year 2004	45,000
Work-in-process inventory, January 1, 2004	5,000
Work-in-process inventory, December 31, 2004	15,000
Finished goods inventory, January 1, 2004	15,000
Cost of goods sold	40,000

     Determine (a) the cost of materials purchased, (b) the cost of raw materials used during the year, and (c) the balance in the finished goods inventory account on December 31, 2004.

E2-9
Obj. 2
Wendy Minor is the plant controller at Medical Supply Company. She is reviewing year-end balances of raw materials, work in process, and finished goods. In attempting to control inventory carrying costs, management has established programs designed to minimize inventory levels throughout the organization. Relevant data are presented as follows:

	Raw Materials	Work in Process	Finished Goods
January 1, 2004	$550,000	$900,000	$650,000
Data for year ended December 31, 2004			
Raw material purchases			$1,350,000
Raw material issued to production			1,150,000
Direct labor costs incurred			2,250,000
Manufacturing overhead costs incurred			3,000,000
Goods completed and transferred to finished goods inventory			6,050,000
Cost of goods sold			6,550,000

(Continued)

  a. Compute the ending balances of each inventory account.
  b. Has the company been successful in reducing inventory balances? Explain.
  c. What types of costs may be associated with high levels of inventory?

E2-10 Rowflex manufactures exercise equipment that is sold through major retail chain stores. The
Obj. 3 company has developed a new exercise bench. Based on the company's market research, the
selling price should not exceed $450. If Rowflex requires a margin of $75, determine the target cost and explain why the cost is important to the company's planning process.

E2-11 Calico has the following products. Complete the schedule below. The first one has been done
Obj. 3 for you.

Item Description	Target Unit Cost	Target Margin	Target Margin %	Selling Price
Item A	$15	$ 5	25%	$20
Item B	$72	?	?	$84
Item C	?	?	15%	$70
Item D	$42	$ 6	?	?
Item E	?	$12	?	$96

Note: Target margin is expressed as a percentage of selling price.

E2-12 April Incorporated is developing a product that will sell for $160 per unit. The unit cost of
Obj. 3 the product is expected to include direct materials ($70), direct labor ($35), and manufacturing overhead ($15). What is the margin as a percentage of sales?

E2-13 Refer to the information in E2-12. If April requires a margin on sales of 30%, how much cost
Obj. 3 must be eliminated from the product to reach this margin if there is no change in the sales price?

PROBLEMS

If your instructor is using Personal Trainer® in this course, you may complete your assignments online.

P2-1   Ethics—Product versus Period Classification

Obj. 1 Assume management intentionally misclassified a period expense as a product cost in order to meet analysts' earnings expectations. The fraud later was discovered during the annual audit.

Required Explain how the misclassification enabled management to boost the company's earnings.

P2-2   Accounting Irregularities at WorldCom

Obj. 1 In a widely publicized accounting scandal, management at **WorldCom** was accused of recording $11 billion of operating expenses as long-term assets on its balance sheet. The action significantly increased the company's reported earnings.

Required
  A. Explain how misclassifying expenses allowed the company's management to overstate earnings.
  B. Does the WorldCom case represent an ethical issue?

P2-3   Cost Classification

Obj. 1 Tim Ricker lives in Atlanta. He is a toolmaker for Georgia Industries, a manufacturer of heavy equipment such as backhoes, graders, and earthmoving equipment. Tim makes specialty tools and jigs that are used on different machines in the plant. His annual salary is $35,000. Ann Thompson also works for Georgia Industries. She is an independent sales representative who lives in El Paso, Texas. She is paid a straight salary of $25,000 but also earns a 5% commission on sales. Ann is responsible for accounts in the west Texas area, works out of an office in her home, and is reimbursed by Georgia Industries for her travel expenses. The company provides Ann with a leased vehicle and a gasoline credit card.

Required

A. Is Tim's salary a manufacturing or nonmanufacturing expense? If manufacturing, would it be classified as direct labor? Explain your answer.
B. Is Ann's salary a manufacturing or nonmanufacturing expense? Are the commissions she earns manufacturing or nonmanufacturing? Explain your answer.

P2-4 Cost Flows in an Accounting System

Obj. 2

Bama Company showed the following balances in its inventory accounts as of January 1, 2004:

Raw materials inventory	$10,000
Work-in-process inventory	20,000
Finished goods inventory	10,000

The following transactions took place during 2004:

1. Manufacturing overhead costs of $96,000 were incurred and placed into work-in-process.
2. Raw material purchases totaled $34,000.
3. Direct labor charges in the amount of $119,000 were paid.
4. The cost of goods sold was determined to be $225,000.
5. Raw materials in the amount of $34,000 were placed into production.
6. The ending finished goods inventory balance was $14,000.

Required

A. Prepare a schedule that shows the raw materials, work-in-process, finished goods, and cost of goods sold accounts. Determine the year-end balance for each account.
B. A variety of individuals may find these balances useful. For example, bank loan officers, production managers, and sales managers may make decisions using comparative account balances. Describe how each of these individuals might use the data.
C. What trends do you observe in the raw materials, work-in-process, and finished goods inventory accounts?
D. If the marketing department forecasts flat or slightly declining sales for the coming year, what recommendations might you make to the company about managing inventory levels?

P2-5 Cost Flows through an Accounting System

Obj. 2

Clearview Glass Company purchases sand and various chemicals to be melted in the company's glass furnace. The molten glass flows along a conveyor system that defines sheet thickness and width and cools the molten glass. At the end of the process, workers cut the sheets of glass to a variety of dimensions and package them for delivery to their customers. During the month, Clearview purchased sand and chemicals totaling $190,000 and placed $175,000 of the amount purchased into production. Natural gas consumed in the melting process equaled $200,000. The manufacturing process is machine-intensive, thus depreciation on the furnace and conveyor systems totaled $300,000. Direct labor totaled $80,000. Supplies purchased and consumed in cutting and packaging equaled $65,000. The company's beginning sand and chemical inventory was valued at $18,000, while the beginning work-in-process inventory was valued at $75,000. Ending work-in-process inventory was valued at $60,000. During the month Clearview sold goods costing $795,000 for $1,330,000. The beginning inventory of finished goods was reported on the company's balance sheet at $90,000. General, selling, and administrative costs were recorded at $400,000.

Required

A. Prepare a schedule similar to Exhibit 3 to illustrate how costs flow through Clearview's accounting system.
B. Calculate the cost of goods manufactured.
C. Determine the balance in the raw materials and finished goods inventory accounts.
D. Having determined production costs, a manager might use this information to support decision making in a variety of ways. How might a production manager use cost and profitability information? How might a marketing manager use cost and profitability information?

SPREADSHEET

P2-6   Decision Making—Inventory and Cost of Goods Sold

Obj. 2

The accounting firm of Lawton and Smith provides tax preparation services for its clients. Secretaries typically contact the client to schedule an appointment. When a client arrives at the firm's office, a partner conducts an interview and collects documentation supporting the information for the tax return. A staff accountant is given the interview notes and supporting documents, such as Form W-2 and cancelled checks, and enters the data into a computer program. The partner is responsible for reviewing the accuracy of the return before a secretary duplicates and packages it.

During the month of March, Lawton and Smith incurred revenue and costs as follows:

Revenues	$95,000
Product costs	
Secretarial salaries	$ 4,000
Partner salaries	15,000
Various overhead accounts	5,000
Professional accountant salaries	30,000
Computer supplies purchased and consumed	2,000
Period expenses	
Building rent (administrative portion)	3,000
Utilities (administrative portion)	700
Depreciation on furniture (administrative portion)	7,000

The company maintained insignificant balances of supplies that can be ignored, but reported work-in-process and finished services inventories on March 1 as $20,000 and $5,000, respectively. On March 31, the company reported work-in-process and finished services inventories as $15,000, and $7,000, respectively.

Required

A. Identify each product cost as direct materials, direct labor, or overhead.
B. Calculate the cost of services provided (cost of goods sold) during March.
C. Calculate cost of services sold percentage and the gross margin percentage as a percentage of revenues.
D. How might your analysis support partners in decisions concerning the firm?

P2-7   Accounting for Inventory at Ford Motor Company

Obj. 2

Ford Motor Company reported the following information in the notes of its 2002 annual report:

Note 5. INVENTORIES—AUTOMOTIVE SECTOR
Inventories at December 31 were as follows (in millions):

	2002	2001
Raw materials, work-in-process and supplies	$3,174	$2,430
Finished products	4,763	4,602
Total inventories	7,937	7,032
Less adjustment	(957)	(905)
Total inventories	$6,980	$6,127

Required

A. Speculate on the types of raw materials Ford Motor Company reported in its annual report.
B. What is an example of work-in-process for Ford Motor Company? Have inventories increased or decreased during the reporting period? What might explain the increase or decrease?

P2-8   Manufacturing Cost Flows

Objs. 2, 3

O'Neill Company began the year with $870,000 of raw materials inventory, $1,390,000 of work-in-process inventory, and $620,000 of finished goods inventory. During the year, the company purchased $3,550,000 of raw material and used $3,720,000 of raw materials in production. Labor used in production for the year was $2,490,000. Overhead was $1,380,000. Work-in-process completed and transferred to finished goods inventory was $7,410,000. Cost of goods sold for the year was $7,500,000.

Required

A. Determine the ending balance in the raw materials, work in process, and finished goods inventory accounts.
B. Assume O'Neill practices JIT inventory management. Its goal is to reduce inventory levels, improve quality, and reduce costs. Comment on O'Neill's success in reducing inventory levels.

P2-9

Obj. 3

Target Cost Calculation and Use

Go-yo is a company that designs, manufactures, and markets the world's best competition yo-yos. The company's engineers have designed a new product to be manufactured using a titanium bearing. Such a design will permit the user to accomplish more sophisticated tricks resulting from the yo-yo's ability to "sleep" for longer periods of time. Market research has determined that customers will pay $225 for such a product. A margin of 30% (based on the selling price) is required.

Required

A. Calculate the target cost for Go-yo's new yo-yo.
B. If the estimated cost to produce the product exceeds the target cost, what options are available to Go-yo's management?

P2-10

Obj. 3

Target Costing and Managerial Action

SPREADSHEET

Surgery Corporation has developed a surgical instrument that permits less invasive surgical procedures, resulting in less scarring and quicker rehabilitation. Management believes demand for the instrument will come primarily from sports medicine clinics that specialize in athletic-related injuries. Because health-care providers are under intense pressure from insurance companies to control costs, Surgery understands the new instrument must be priced to permit clinics to earn a reasonable return from surgical procedures.

Surgery's marketing department conducted numerous interviews and surveys with potential customers to determine a price that would be attractive to buyers. In addition, the interviews revealed numerous ideas for product enhancement. Based on these efforts, the marketing vice president recommended a target price of $270,000. Surgery intends to finance the development of the new instrument by issuing bonds. The vice president of finance estimates the margin on sales must be approximately 15% to provide an adequate rate of return to investors.

Required

A. Determine the target cost for the new surgical instrument.
B. Explain why understanding cost behavior is crucial for estimating cost reductions associated with the target costing process.
C. What actions might managers consider if a cost study results in an estimated cost of $240,000 to produce the new surgical instrument? Elaborate.
D. Identify the functional areas of those who would be selected to evaluate the problem. Explain your reasoning.

P2-11

Obj. 3

Just-in-Time Manufacturing

Happy PC makes personal computers for home consumers. The company decides to switch to a just-in-time manufacturing system. Since Happy PC's manufacturing processes have changed, the managerial accounting information measured must change.

Required

A. What accounting information is needed to evaluate the just-in-time manufacturing process?
B. How detailed should the information be?

P2-12
Obj. 3

Managerial Accounting and Value Chain Analysis

Jenny Smith, the owner of Blasto Walkmans, analyzed the high warranty costs the company was incurring. She determined one of the major defects was the result of a low-priced battery device provided by a supplier.

Required

A. How can managerial accounting be used to assist Jenny in determining whether she should install a more expensive, higher-quality battery device?
B. How could Jenny use value chain analysis to provide better information in making this decision?

P2-13

Excel in Action

SPREADSHEET

Music Makers copies software and music to CDs and packages these products for customers. The company's production process includes two departments. The first department copies the software to blank CDs. The second department places the CDs in plastic containers, places printed title pages in the CDs, wraps the containers in cellophane, and transfers the boxes to shipping.

During March, Music Makers started and completed 500,000 units. There were no beginning work-in-process or finished goods inventories. Material costs per unit were:

Blank CDs	$0.70
Plastic containers	0.09
Printed material	0.06
Cellophane	0.01

Labor costs were $40,000 in the copying department and $60,000 in the packaging department. Manufacturing overhead was $20,000 in the copying department and $6,000 in the packaging department.

The company's inventory at the beginning of March included $8,000 of blank CDs, $1,800 of plastic containers, and $2,500 of cellophane. Printed materials are not inventoried. They are received from printers as needed for the products. During March, Music Makers purchased blank CDs costing $355,000, plastic containers costing $60,000, and cellophane costing $3,000. By the end of the month, the company had shipped goods costing $520,000 to customers. The remaining goods were in the finished goods inventory.

Required Use a spreadsheet to calculate inventory balances and manufacturing costs for Music Makers for March. The following partial spreadsheet is illustrated as an example:

	A	B	C	D	E	F	G	H	I
1		CD Inventory	Container Inventory	Cellophane Inventory		Copying WIP	Packaging WIP	Finished Goods	Cost of Goods Sold
2	Beginning	8,000	1,800	2,500	Beginning	–	–	–	–
3	Purchases				Materials				
4	To production				Labor				
5	Ending				Overhead				
6					Transferred in				
7					Transferred out				
8					Ending				

Use the Format menu to adjust cell formats as needed to wrap text for long titles. Use the comma button to format dollar amounts. See instructions from the appendix, *A Short Introduction to Excel*, if you need help with formatting.

Materials costs include the costs of materials used in the department during March. These should be calculated by multiplying unit costs times the number of units produced. Use references to other cells in your calculations where possible. For example, the material costs in the copying department (column F) are equal to the CD inventory costs transferred out of raw materials (column B). Transferred-in costs are those from a preceding process. Consequently, the costs transferred in to packaging are those transferred out (total costs) from copying, and the costs transferred in to finished goods are those transferred out from packaging. Transferred-in costs should be positive and transferred-out costs should be negative. Multiply the amount in a cell by (21) to make it negative. For example, 5100*(21) will result in 2100.

Format cells so that totals are separated from other cells by single underlines and cells containing totals contain double underlines. Use the Borders button ⊞ ▾ for this purpose.

P2-14 Multiple-Choice Overview of the Chapter

1. During May 2003, Bennett Manufacturing Company purchased $43,000 of raw materials. The company's manufacturing overhead for the month totaled $27,000 and the total manufacturing costs were $106,000. Assuming a beginning inventory of raw materials of $8,000 and an ending inventory of raw materials of $6,000, direct labor must have totaled:
   a. $34,000.
   b. $38,000.
   c. $36,000.
   d. $45,000.

2. The wages of the maintenance personnel in a manufacturing plant are an example of:

	Indirect Labor Costs	Manufacturing Overhead Costs
a.	No	Yes
b.	Yes	No
c.	Yes	Yes
d.	No	No

3. The distinction between indirect and direct costs depends on:
   a. whether the costs are product costs or period expenses.
   b. whether the company has paid for the resource consumed.
   c. whether the costs can be easily traced to specific units of production.
   d. the manager responsible for controlling the cost.

4. The Rockin Roller Company manufactures rocking chairs. The following costs have been identified with rocking chairs produced during the current month:

   - $100,000 of springs were purchased and used. Each chair requires 2 springs at a cost of $10 per spring.
   - $1,700 of glue was used from one-gallon containers.
   - $500 of stain was used to touch up spots on the chairs.

   The total amount of indirect materials for the month would be:
   a. $102,200.
   b. $500.
   c. $2,200.
   d. $1,700.

5. Product costs appear on the balance sheet only:
   a. if goods are partially complete at the end of the period.
   b. if goods are unsold at the end of the period.
   c. if raw materials used to make the goods have been paid for.
   d. Both a and b are correct.

6. The value chain for a given product or service:
   a. reflects all activities associated with providing the particular product or service.
   b. identifies non-value-adding activities that should be eliminated or reduced.
   c. includes activities both inside and outside the company.
   d. All of the above are correct.

7. Costs flow through an accounting system as follows:
   a. raw materials, work in process, cost of goods sold, finished goods.
   b. finished goods, cost of goods sold, work in process, raw materials.
   c. raw materials, work in process, finished goods, cost of goods sold.
   d. raw materials, finished goods, cost of goods sold.

8. Target costing begins with a:
   a. target cost to which a markup is added.
   b. selling price from which a required margin is subtracted.
   c. required margin that is added to a target cost.
   d. selling price to which a markup is added.

9. The target cost calculation involves understanding the relationship among three variables:
   a. target cost, required profit margin, and selling price.
   b. selling price, target cost, and gross profit.
   c. gross profit, selling price, and cost of goods sold.
   d. target cost, selling price, and dividends.

10. Service organizations are different from manufacturing companies.
    a. Thus, product costing techniques are not relevant to them.
    b. Service costs are reported as a cost of services provided.
    c. Service organizations classify their costs as direct and indirect.
    d. Both b and c are correct.

CASE

C2-1 The Supply Chain at General Mills

Obj. 3

The 2002 **General Mills** annual report disclosed the following information:

Part A.

TO OUR SHAREHOLDERS:

For General Mills, fiscal 2002 was a year of significant change. On Oct. 31, 2001, we completed our long-anticipated acquisition of Pillsbury. Overnight our annualized revenues nearly doubled, our workforce more than doubled, and our portfolio of leading brands expanded to include the *Pillsbury Doughboy, Progresso, Totino's, Green Giant, Old El Paso,* and more. Over the next seven months, we rapidly integrated work teams and activities. By year-end, much of the hard work to create one sales force, one supply chain organization and one unified marketing plan for our businesses was completed. As a result, we entered 2003 more confident than ever that the combination of General Mills and Pillsbury creates a powerful consumer foods company with excellent prospects for delivering superior long-term growth and returns.

The strategies that will drive our growth in 2003—and beyond—are the same ones that have guided General Mills in the past:

The first key is product innovation...

Our second growth strategy is channel expansion. Today's consumers are picking up groceries in lots of new places, from general merchandise chains to convenience stores. In addition, sales for food eaten away from home are expected to grow faster than at-home food sales over the long term. Our Bakeries and Foodservice business is focused on expanding sales of our products with foodservice distributors and operators, bakeries, convenience stores and vending companies. Adding Pillsbury quadrupled the size of this business for General Mills, and we are already generating new volume by selling General Mills product lines to established Pillsbury customers and vice versa.

Our final key strategy is margin expansion... And beyond (efficiencies resulting by combining Pillsbury and General Mills) we expect our larger supply chain to create opportunities for ongoing productivity savings as we (realize cost savings resulting from our larger size after the acquisition).

Part B.

The following information appears in the notes to consolidated financial statements.

6. INVENTORIES

The components of inventories are as follows:

In Millions

	May 26, 2002	May 27, 2001
Raw materials, work in process and supplies	$ 234	$129
Finished goods	753	326
Grain	99	94
Other	(31)	(30)
Total inventories	$1,055	$519

Required

A. In general, describe General Mills' supply chain.
B. Discuss how the acquisition of Pillsbury radically altered General Mills' supply chain.
C. Evaluate the various types of inventory reported at May 26, 2002, and May 27, 2001. What kinds of products are included in the first three categories shown in note 6?

PRODUCING GOODS AND SERVICES: BATCH PROCESSING

How do we assign overhead costs to our products?

Erin and Seth now understand the importance of product costs and realize they need the monthly financial reports to show the costs of manufacturing each type of product their company manufactures. Erin and Seth manufacture products when they are ordered, and frequently the job requires specific modifications to meet customer needs. Seth is particularly concerned about accurately assigning manufacturing costs to products. There is still confusion about how to assign overhead to each product. Erin has suggested tracking the direct costs, such as the cost of wood and labor to make the furniture, to each order. Next, a portion of overhead costs, such as insurance, electricity, and glue, would be assigned to each job.

FOOD FOR THOUGHT

If you were advising Seth and Erin, what would be your recommendation for assigning overhead costs to the furniture they manufacture? Let's join Erin, Seth, and Roberta again as they discuss the situation.

Erin: We've been trying to decide how to assign overhead costs to our products. If we divide the month's total overhead costs by the month's total direct labor hours, we'll have an average overhead cost for each labor hour. Then, we can assign overhead to our products by multiplying the overhead cost per hour by the number of labor hours worked on a particular job.

Seth: But I see a problem with assigning costs. Unlike materials and labor, we do not receive the bill for some overhead costs until weeks later. We probably won't know our actual total overhead costs when we complete a job or even at the end of the month. I guess we would have to assign some amount of estimated overhead.

Roberta: You are correct; we need a way to estimate overhead and assign it to units of product. Let's discuss the details of how we go about this.

OBJECTIVES

Once you have completed this chapter, you should be able to:

1 Explain the importance of unit costs to managerial decision making.

2 Apply overhead costs to products using a predetermined overhead rate.

3 Determine unit cost using job-order costing.

THE IMPORTANCE OF UNIT COSTS

OBJECTIVE 1

Explain the importance of unit costs to managerial decision making.

Retail organizations purchase completed goods from suppliers, add a markup, and sell the finished goods to their customers. Thus, a retail organization typically reports one type of inventory (finished goods) on its balance sheet. On the other hand, manufacturing organizations purchase raw materials from suppliers and convert them into finished goods during the manufacturing process. **The *unit cost* of an individual product is the total manufacturing cost for a period divided by the number of units produced in that period.** As we saw in Chapter M2, most manufacturing companies report three types of inventory on their balance sheets, raw materials, work-in-process (partially completed goods), and finished goods. When retail and manufacturing organizations sell finished goods, the product's unit cost is reported on the income statement as cost of goods sold.

Unit costs also play an important role in the strategic and operational decisions of marketing and operations managers. For example, unit costs assist in determining whether to market a product as a high-priced specialty product or a low-priced commodity. Unit costs also help managers determine whether to discontinue a product if profit margins are too small (or even negative). Managers also use unit costs to help determine the selling price of a product. Production managers use unit cost information to control costs. Service organizations use unit costs to determine the cost of services and to analyze whether costs are in line with strategic plans. Because unit costs are used extensively in managerial decisions in both manufacturing and service organizations, it is important to know how to develop those costs and how to assess their accuracy.

Managers are concerned about determining the most accurate unit costs and using that information effectively. To develop unit costs, a company must measure total production costs and then assign these costs to individual units. Typically, labor and materials costs are easily traced to products. However, overhead costs must be allocated in some manner. This chapter describes two methods, actual costing and normal costing, for assigning overhead costs to products. Most companies use one of these methods. The chapter also describes job-order costing systems used to keep track of materials, labor, and overhead costs incurred by individual jobs, or batches, of product. In choosing methods for measuring and assigning costs, unit cost not only is a basis for managerial decision making, it also is an outcome of the decision-making process.

Unit costs play an essential role in establishing the value of a company's inventories, and they also are a key element in the decisions managers make about products. For example, managers use product cost information to answer questions such as:

- How should we price a particular product? (Product pricing)
- Should we continue to offer a particular product? (Marketing strategy and Product life cycle)
- What is the best way to allocate our limited production resources? (Allocating resources)
- On which products should marketing focus its efforts to maximize profits? (Unit profit margin)

Product Pricing

Choosing the right selling price for its products is extremely important to the success of a company. A company that does not make an adequate profit on its products cannot survive over the long term. Pricing decisions often are based on unit cost, the prices competitors charge for similar products, and market research on how customers will respond to different prices. Knowing the cost to make a product is important when there is no competitive market for a product. In this case, the unit cost of the product may be the only information available to guide management in setting the price. Managers must set selling prices above product costs in order to earn a profit. The importance of unit cost to a pricing decision often depends on the company's marketing strategy.

Marketing Strategy

Some companies choose to compete by marketing their products at low prices. For example, **Hyundai** offers cars priced far below those offered by **Mercedes**. Likewise, **Timex** offers watches at prices far below those of **Rolex**. On the other hand, Mercedes and Rolex differentiate their products on a quality dimension that Hyundai and Timex do not attempt to match. A company's need for accounting information depends on its marketing strategy. Companies that use a low-price strategy have a greater need for accurate cost information than those that differentiate their products and sell them at higher prices. Profit margins (price minus total manufacturing cost) usually are lower on low-priced products; therefore, controlling costs is very important to these companies. Accurate information about manufacturing costs is required for careful cost control. Companies that differentiate their products tend to have higher profit margins. Thus, tight cost controls generally are less critical to the profitability of their products than are product quality and brand image.

Product Life Cycle

Product life cycle also plays an important role in determining the need for accurate unit costs. As shown in Exhibit 1, products tend to have finite lives characterized by growth, followed by stability, and then decline. Although the lengths of various products' life cycles may vary, a product's life cycle generally is characterized as follows:

(a) A company introduces a new product (growth stage).
(b) The company builds market share in anticipation of future profits (growth stage).
(c) The company focuses on holding the market share of the mature product (hold stage).
(d) The company maximizes the available return as sales of the product decline (harvest stage).
(e) When profits are no longer adequate, the company eliminates the product (divest stage).

Exhibit 1
A Product Life Cycle

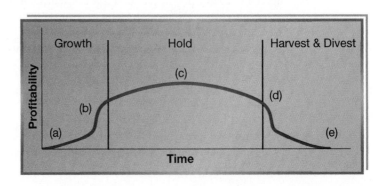

In the growth stage after a product has been introduced (a), the producer normally is interested in building market share. *Market share* **is the portion of sales captured by a particular product relative to total sales of all similar products.** For example, assume total sales of all brands of soft drinks are $45 billion per year. If **Coca-Cola Company's** sales are $20 billion, the company has a 44 percent ($20/$45) market share. During the growth phase, a company often is willing to sacrifice profits to encourage new customers to buy its product. For example, when cellular phone companies give away phones, they are trying to encourage prospective customers to subscribe to their services. In the building phase (b), a company may not be concerned about maintaining tight cost control. It is willing to spend money on product improvements and marketing to build market share. As products mature (c), a company is less willing to spend money on further product and market development. Instead, it concentrates on maintaining market share and profits. As the emphasis shifts to profits, cost control and accuracy of unit costs become more important because of greater emphasis on profitability. In the harvest stage (d), the company's focus is on earning as much profit as possible from the product until, finally, the product is eliminated (e).

Allocating Resources

Unit costs help managers decide how to allocate limited production and marketing resources. When a company's production resources prevent the company from making enough products to meet the demand for those products, managers must decide how much of each product to make. The question here is "What mix of products will provide the greatest profit for the company?" Similarly, when a company's marketing budget does not allow advertising to emphasize all of its products, managers must decide which products to promote. Unit costs help managers make these kinds of decisions by allowing managers to compare profit margins across their product line. Generally, they decide to produce a mix of products that maximizes net income.

Unit Profit Margin

Unit costs also play a role in the decision to continue to offer a product. *Unit profit margin* **is the difference between the selling price per unit of a product and the unit cost.** If the unit profit margin is too low to meet the company's profit goals for that product, the company may discontinue it. A company estimates its profit margin on a particular product by multiplying the unit profit margin times the number of units it expects to sell.

1 SELF-STUDY PROBLEM Jeff Arnold recently graduated from a business school and joined the family business as a production manager. At his first management meeting with marketing, production, accounting and administrative personnel, a great deal of attention was focused on the unit cost of products.

Required What are four kinds of decisions managers make that draw on unit cost information? Why is the unit cost information an important factor in these decisions?

The solution to Self-Study Problem 1 appears at the end of the chapter.

MEASURING COSTS

The first step in calculating product costs is determining which costs should be included. As we saw in Chapter M2, direct materials, direct labor, and manufacturing overhead traditionally have been included in product cost calculations. This is because generally

OBJECTIVE 2

Apply overhead costs to products using a predetermined overhead rate.

accepted accounting principles (GAAP) require companies to include the full costs of production in inventory costs reported in their financial statements. Many companies use their financial accounting systems to provide internal information for management decisions. However, management accounting information is not required to conform to GAAP. Accountants may accumulate product costs differently from those reported in the financial statements. We further explore different ways to calculate unit costs for internal purposes in Chapter M7.

Two basic methods, actual costing and normal costing, are used to measure product costs. *Actual costing* **measures product costs based on the actual costs of direct materials, direct labor, and overhead incurred in producing the products.** *Normal costing* **measures product costs by adding the actual costs of direct materials and direct labor to an estimated overhead cost incurred in producing the products.** The difference between the two methods is whether actual or estimated overhead costs are used in determining a product's cost.

When a company uses actual costing, it assigns direct materials, direct labor, and manufacturing overhead costs to work-in-process inventory as those costs are incurred. Chapter M2 illustrated the use of an actual cost system. Measuring the costs of direct materials and direct labor usually is not difficult. Measuring manufacturing overhead, however, can be a problem. The company often does not know the actual cost of overhead until after a product is produced or even sold. The total actual overhead cost is not known with certainty until the bills arrive. Thus, many companies rely on estimates of overhead to measure unit costs.

As in actual costing, normal costing measures actual direct materials and direct labor costs incurred in producing a product. However, normal costing uses estimates of manufacturing overhead to assign overhead to products. These overhead cost estimates are applied to products using a predetermined overhead rate.

A *predetermined overhead rate* **is an estimate of the amount of overhead assigned to a product for each unit of activity.** To establish a predetermined rate, a company first must choose an activity base. **An** *activity base* **is a production activity (such as direct labor hours or machine hours) or a measure of the cost of production activity (such as direct labor cost).** A company selects a particular activity base because management believes overhead costs increase in proportion to the activity base. For example, if accountants think overhead cost varies according to the number of machine hours, they would select machine hours as the activity base. If more machine hours are used, we might expect to consume greater amounts of electricity, water, chemicals, natural gas, and supplies. If fewer machines hours are used, fewer resources should be consumed. Thus, accountants look for a relationship between overhead costs and an activity base. At the beginning of its fiscal year, a company divides the total overhead it expects to incur during that year by the amount of the activity base expected for that period. Then, as products are manufactured, the company multiplies the amount of the activity base used during the period by the predetermined overhead rate. The result is the estimated overhead cost for the products manufactured.

Any cost allocation method relies on the use of estimates. The use of estimates in accounting is not uncommon. As you saw in your financial accounting course, accountants often rely on estimates when preparing financial statements. For example, they estimate depreciation expense for fixed assets and an allowance for uncollectible accounts. Accountants also use estimates to prepare a company's internal reports.

Iron Mountain Gear: The Product and Manufacturing Process

Examples in this chapter are based on the manufacturing operations of Iron Mountain Gear (IMG), a company that makes backpacks for outdoor enthusiasts. The manufacturing process begins after purchasing fabric, aluminum, and a variety of other materials from suppliers. Using computer-controlled machinery, fabric is cut into various components whose dimensions are determined from engineering specifications. Next, the fabric components and zippers and various closures are sewn together by operators using industrial-grade sewing machines. Aluminum tubing, purchased from suppliers, is used to construct the backpack frame that is joined to the fabric backpack. Finally, shoulder straps provided by suppliers are attached to complete the backpack.

IMG uses normal costing to measure its product costs. The company's accountant expects to incur manufacturing overhead costs totaling $250,000 in the coming year. Direct labor hours is used as the activity base to allocate these overhead costs to products. Based on expected sales and production levels, the company should use 5,000 hours of direct labor in the coming year. Using direct labor hours as an allocation base, the predetermined overhead rate for the coming year is calculated at $50 per hour as follows:

Predetermined overhead rate = Estimated overhead costs ÷ Estimated activity base
= $250,000 ÷ 5,000 direct labor hours
= $50 _or machine or overhead_

Thus, for each direct labor hour actually worked, the company will add $50 of overhead to the work-in-process inventory. Overhead is traced to individual products in a similar manner. For example, assume IMG produces a backpack that requires 6/10 of a machine hour for the cutting and sewing operations. Overhead cost applied to the backpack would be $30 ($50 × 6/10 = $30). Materials and labor costs would be added to overhead to determine the total unit cost of a backpack. Later in this chapter we explore systems that allow managers to record the amount of materials, labor, and overhead costs associated with each batch of product.

Exhibit 2 illustrates transactions that affect IMG's various inventory and cost of goods sold accounts during an accounting period. The cost flows do not illustrate all accounts affected by a transaction. For example, when raw materials are purchased on credit, Accounts Payable and Raw Materials Inventory are both increased. However, Exhibit 2 illustrates only the flow of product costs and the effect on inventory and cost of goods sold.

Exhibit 2 Cost Flows Through Iron Mountain Gear's Accounting System

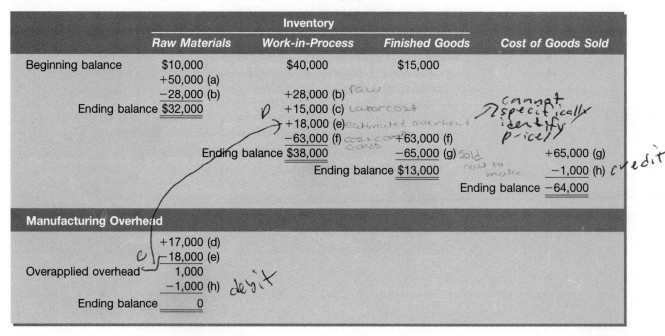

The beginning balances of the raw materials, work-in-process, and finished goods inventories are $10,000, $40,000, and $15,000, respectively. Transaction (a) records the purchase of $50,000 of raw materials. When raw materials costing $28,000 are removed from inventory and placed into production in transaction (b), the raw materials inventory and work-in-process inventory accounts are decreased and increased, respectively. IMG incurred direct labor costs of $15,000 in transaction (c). Recall from Chapter M2 that direct materials and direct labor are placed into the work-in-process inventory as materials and labor are added to the manufacturing process.

Exhibit 2 introduces a new account, known as Manufacturing Overhead. Actual overhead costs increase the manufacturing overhead account balance, while the application of manufacturing overhead to work-in-process reduces the manufacturing overhead account balance. Actual overhead costs of $17,000 are accumulated in the manufacturing overhead account as shown in transaction (d). However, overhead is applied using a predetermined overhead rate of $50 per direct labor hour. In January, assume the company used 360 direct labor hours in manufacturing operations. In transaction (e), the estimated cost of overhead of $18,000 (360 hours $\times$ $50) is recorded in the work-in-process inventory account.

Transaction (f) records the transfer of completed goods costing $63,000 to manufacture. Thus, work-in-process inventory is reduced and finished goods inventory is increased by $63,000. Goods costing $65,000 were sold. Transaction (g) records the effect on the finished goods inventory and cost of goods sold accounts.

Because normal costing uses estimates of overhead costs, the amount of overhead costs allocated to work-in-process inventory often differs from actual overhead incurred. In comparing transactions (d) and (e) in Exhibit 2, we see the company overapplied its overhead costs. The amount of overhead costs applied to inventory ($18,000) was $1,000 more than the actual overhead costs ($17,000) incurred during the period. Transaction (h) transfers the underapplied overhead to the cost of goods sold account. At the end of an accounting period, the manufacturing overhead account always is adjusted to a zero balance. Any overapplied or underapplied overhead is transferred to the cost of goods sold account. If the actual overhead costs had been more than the amount of overhead recorded in the work-in-process inventory account, the company would have underapplied its overhead costs. Often companies investigate the underapplied or overapplied overhead, known as a variance, to learn why it occurred. We further explore overhead variances in Chapter M9. Exhibit 3 summarizes the steps for applying overhead in a normal costing system.

Exhibit 3

Application of Overhead Costs in a Normal Costing System

Establishing the predetermined overhead rate
At the beginning of the fiscal year:
1. Estimate total manufacturing overhead costs for the period.
2. Choose a relevant activity base and estimate the activity level for the year.
3. Calculate the predetermined overhead rate by dividing the estimate of total manufacturing overhead costs by the estimated activity base.

Assigning (or applying) overhead costs using the predetermined overhead rate
At the end of each accounting period:
1. Determine the actual activity level during the period.
2. Multiply the actual activity level by the predetermined overhead rate.
3. Transfer any remaining balance in the manufacturing overhead account to the cost of goods sold account.

2 SELF-STUDY PROBLEM

Russell Lumber Company uses an actual costing system. The company's controller has been wondering what would be the effect of using a normal costing system to assign overhead. She has determined that under the normal costing approach the predetermined overhead rate would be calculated based on machine hours. Russell Lumber Co. expects to use 50,000 machine hours during the year. Overhead is expected to be approximately $750,000 for the year. The company used 4,500 machine hours during March. Russell Lumber reported the following events:

(a) Raw lumber was purchased for $110,000.
(b) $100,000 in raw lumber was used in production.
(c) $40,000 in direct labor was incurred.
(d) $60,000 in overhead was incurred.

Required Compute the work-in-process inventory using both actual and normal costing for the month of March. Explain why the numbers are different. Assume all of the products produced in March were sold in that month. What would be the amount of the adjustment to the cost of goods sold account for the overapplied or underapplied overhead? Would cost of goods sold increase or decrease as a result of this adjustment? Why?

The solution to Self-Study Problem 2 appears at the end of the chapter.

JOB-ORDER COSTING

OBJECTIVE 3

Determine unit cost using job-order costing.

Companies that produce a variety of products or services typically use job-order costing. *Job-order costing* **identifies and assigns production costs to a particular job.** Accounting systems help managers keep track of production costs. For example, a *job cost sheet* **is used to identify each job and to accumulate the costs of manufacturing associated with that job.** Job cost sheets can be either a sheet of paper or a record in a computer file. Both forms allow space to record all the costs of direct materials, direct labor, and manufacturing overhead associated with a job. The job cost sheet functions like a work-in-process inventory account. If a company uses only job-order costing, the total of all of its job cost sheets should equal the total work-in-process inventory account. Exhibit 4 provides an example of a job cost sheet used by IMG for a production run, or batch, of backpacks.

Exhibit 4 A Job Cost Sheet

Job Number	225P					Date	6-12-04	
Product	High Forest Backpack					By	Linda Smith	
Units	40					Ship	6-30-04	
Materials		**Direct Labor**				**Overhead**		
Requistion Number	Amount	Employee Number	Hours	Rate	Amount	Hours	Rate	Amount
X2134	$100.00	59	6	$9.35	$56.10	24	$50.00	$1,200.00
X2147	$420.00	107	18	$13.55	$243.90			
Total Materials	$520.00	Total Direct Labor			$300.00	Total Overhead		$1,200.00
Total Job Cost								$2,020.00

In the job cost sheet illustrated in Exhibit 4, job 225P was completed on June 12, 2004, resulting in forty backpacks produced. Materials were issued twice in the amounts of $100 and $420, respectively, as shown by requisitions X2134 and X2147. Thus, total material costs for the job were $520.

Two employees worked on the job. Employee 59 worked 6 hours and was paid $9.35 an hour, and employee 107 worked 18 hours at a rate of $13.55 per hour. Total direct labor cost for the job was $300.00 [(6 × $9.35) + (18 × $13.55)]. The job sheet also shows the amount of overhead that has been applied to the job. In this example, the activity base is direct labor hours and the predetermined overhead rate is $50 per hour. Because 24 (6 + 18) labor hours were charged to job 225P, a total of $1,200 (24 × $50) of overhead was applied.

The total cost of job 225P was $2,020, the sum of direct materials, direct labor, and overhead applied ($520 + $300 + $1,200). The cost per product for the 40 products produced in this job was $50.50 ($2,020 ÷ 40 products). Once the job was completed, the costs of the 40 products were transferred to finished goods inventory at $50.50 per product. When the products are sold, the $50.50 product cost will be used to determine the amount that appears on the income statement as cost of goods sold.

Materials are ordered for individual jobs using a materials requisition form as shown in Exhibit 5. According to the materials requisition form, 100 pounds of aluminum tubing were used in job 225P. Each pound of material cost $1. The total materials cost assigned to job 225P was $100. The document identifies the specific type and quantity of materials that have been drawn from the storeroom and the job to which the materials should be charged. The form is a means of controlling raw materials inventories because each requisition must be signed by the employee issuing and the employee receiving the materials. The form also is used as a source document for recording the actual materials used on a particular job.

Exhibit 5
A Materials Requisition Form

Materials Requisition Number	X2134	Date	June 11, 2004	
Job Number	225P			
Item Description	Quantity		Unit Cost	Total Cost
Aluminum tubing	100 lbs.		$1.00	$100.00
Issued by Murry Roberts				
Received by Frank Jones				

Case In Point

Job Order Costing at Ki-Tek

Ki-Tek manufactures kites. The company uses a job system to record the cost of producing its products. Ki-Tek replaced its error-prone manual data entry system with hand-held data collection terminals that read bar coding. Management estimates the new system has reduced product costing errors by 50 percent.

Source: Automatic I.D. News. Cleveland, May 1997. Vol. 13, Issue 6, page 33.

Costs in the Service Sector

Companies in the service sector also use unit costs to set prices and manage costs. Those companies can use job-order or process costing systems. For example, **MCI** provides telephone services. MCI can use a process costing system to account for costs because the unit of product (one minute of telephone connect time) is like all of the other units; each unit of product consumes a similar amount of costs. The average cost of a minute of connect time gives MCI's managers information they need to decide how much they must charge to make a profit. MCI must set its price low enough to be competitive with other phone companies such as **AT&T**. If the unit cost of telephone connect time at MCI is too high for the company to earn a reasonable profit, the company must look for ways to lower its costs. It cannot simply raise prices to earn higher profits without losing customers to competitors.

Service organizations also can use job-order costing. For example, public accounting firms audit their clients' financial statements. The primary cost to those firms in providing this service is employee wages. Auditors track the time each individual spends on each task they perform in the audit. The times of all employees who work on the audit of a particular client are multiplied by a price per hour to assign costs to each audit.

3 SELF-STUDY PROBLEM

WebTUTOR Advantage

Robotool Corporation is a machine shop that manufactures replacement parts for industrial machinery. Production at Robotool is characterized by small lot sizes and precision manufacturing. A recent production run of five gears, Job 2B38, required the following activities and costs:

Raw materials requisitioned:
10 pounds of brass at $11.65 a pound

Labor	Hours	Rate
Cutting and forming	3	$ 9.75
Lathe and milling	4	11.50
Finishing	1	10.00

Robotool applies overhead to jobs on the basis of direct labor hours using a predetermined rate of $25 an hour.

Required Calculate the total cost of Job 2B38 and the average cost per unit produced.

The solution to Self-Study Problem 3 appears at the end of the chapter.

REVIEW

SUMMARY of IMPORTANT CONCEPTS

1. Unit costs have two primary functions.
   a. Accountants use unit costs to determine the value of ending inventory and cost of goods sold.
   b. Managers use unit costs as the basis of decisions about pricing products, continuing a product line, allocating limited resources, and establishing marketing strategies.

2. According to GAAP, unit costs must reflect the costs of direct materials, direct labor, and manufacturing overhead.

3. Most companies use one of two methods for measuring costs.
   a. Actual costing bases unit costs on actual costs incurred for direct materials, direct labor, and manufacturing overhead.
   b. Normal costing bases unit costs on actual costs incurred for direct materials and direct labor and an estimate of manufacturing overhead.
   c. Estimated overhead costs are the product of the actual activity base multiplied by the predetermined overhead rate.
      (1) At the end of the accounting period, the company adjusts the manufacturing overhead account as necessary to make the estimated overhead equal the actual overhead.

4. Job-order costing yields the unit cost of a particular job or batch of output.
   a. Job-order costing is most effective when a company produces a variety of products (or services) that incur different costs during production.
   b. Companies that use job-order costing track job costs with job cost sheets.

DEFINE	*TERMS and CONCEPTS DEFINED in this CHAPTER*

activity base (M58)

actual costing (M58)

job cost sheet (M61)

job-order costing (M61)

market share (M57)

normal costing (M58)

predetermined overhead rate (M58)

unit cost (M55)

unit profit margin (M57)

SELF-STUDY PROBLEM SOLUTIONS

SSP3-1 Managers need unit cost information for various decision-making purposes, including pricing products, deciding whether to drop a product, and allocating production and marketing resources. Unit cost information is also used for valuing inventory, preparing financial statements, and determining net income. Both the accuracy of unit cost information and what managers choose to include in unit cost can greatly affect the decisions that are made.

SSP3-2 Under the actual costing system, work-in-process inventory would contain the following costs: raw materials ($100,000), direct labor ($40,000), and actual overhead ($60,000) for a total of $200,000. Under the normal costing system, the account would contain: raw material ($100,000), direct labor ($40,000), and applied overhead ($67,500) for a total of $207,500. Thus, the difference between the two approaches would be $7,500.

  Note: To assign overhead under the normal costing system, it is necessary to calculate the predetermined overhead rate. For Russell Lumber the rate would be $750,000 expected annual overhead costs ÷ $50,000 expected annual machine hours = $15 per machine hour. Therefore, for March, the amount of overhead applied would be $15 × 4,500 actual machine hours for the month = $67,500.

  The difference of $7,500 is the overapplied overhead. More overhead was assigned to work-in-process inventory than was actually incurred. This means manufacturing overhead contains a positive balance of $7,500 and must be reduced to zero. Cost of goods sold is decreased by that amount also.

SSP3-3 The cost of job 2B38 includes total direct materials, direct labor, and manufacturing overhead that has been applied as follows:

Direct materials (10 pounds × $11.65)		$116.50
Direct labor:		
Cutting and forming (3 × $9.75)	$29.25	
Lathe and mill (4 × $11.50)	46.00	
Finishing (1 × $10.00)	10.00	
Total labor		85.25
Overhead applied (8 labor hours × $25.00)		200.00
Total costs for job 2B38		$401.75

The average cost per gear is $80.35 = $401.75 ÷ 5 gears produced.

Thinking Beyond the Question

How do we assign overhead costs to our products?

In this chapter Erin and Seth were introduced to overhead allocation. We discussed using a predetermined overhead rate to assign overhead costs to products using allocation bases such as direct labor hours, machine hours, and direct labor costs. To accurately assign overhead costs to products, allocation bases should capture the manner in which products consume resources. Do allocation bases such as the number of labor hours or the number of machine hours explain how products consume all types of overhead costs?

QUESTIONS

Q3-1
Obj. 1
Gloves to Go manufactures one product, a low-priced, no-frills winter glove. The company has been offering this product for 15 years, and has recently experienced a large decline in market share. Describe the likely importance of unit cost information to this company, and explain your reasoning.

Q3-2
Obj. 1
Explain the importance of unit costs at various stages of a product's life cycle.

Q3-3
Obj. 2
Rene Manzor plans to use a recent inheritance to buy a small factory that produces travel bags. Rene has done a great deal of reading about managing a business and realizes that she must establish a costing system to accumulate the costs of producing the bags. In her reading, she learned about two methods of accumulating product costs, actual and normal. Rene has no experience in accounting and is confused about the difference between the two methods. How would you explain the difference in cost accumulation between actual costing and normal costing?

Q3-4
Obj. 2
Hoy Heating and Air Conditioning Company repairs heating and cooling equipment. Each time a service technician completes a job, a time sheet is turned in and the job cost is computed. The company calculates the cost of each job by adding the cost of any materials used on the job, the labor cost of the service technician, and an overhead charge to cover administrative and support expenses. Hoy uses an estimated cost of support expenses in its calculation. Why do you think the company uses predetermined rates rather than actual costs in computing the costs of each service call?

Q3-5
Obj. 2
Assume fuel oil represents a significant overhead cost for a manufacturing company. Because of unexpected price increases in the cost per barrel, the company underapplied its overhead cost for the year. How might management have adapted to the change in prices to prevent a large amount of underapplied overhead?

Q3-6
Obj. 3
The accounting system of Gardner and Associates, a manufacturer of kitchen utensils and accessories, has an account called "Over- or Underapplied Overhead." How would you explain this account to management? How will Gardner's accountant adjust the over- or underapplied overhead account before preparing the company's financial statements?

Q3-7
Obj. 3
Engineers at Rose Company recently designed a new badminton racket for the company's sporting goods line. The technical drawings were sent to the production department, and the first lot of 1,000 rackets has been manufactured. Management at Rose is anxious to see the cost sheet for this job. What information does the job cost sheet contain that would generate such management interest?

Q3-8
Obj. 3
Danny Fitchen is the warehouse clerk for Big Chairs Limited. A production apprentice has asked Danny for a batch of raw materials, but he refuses to release the goods without the appropriate paperwork. What form is needed as supporting documentation for materials used in production? What are the essential parts of that form?

Q3-9
Obj. 3
Assume a service organization, such as an accounting firm, uses job-order costing to keep track of work performed for clients. Of the three types of product (service) costs—direct materials, direct labor, and overhead—which would be the most important for a service firm?

Q3-10
Obj. 3
Job-order costing also is used by service organizations. Why might a walk-in medical clinic use job-order costing to understand the cost of treating their patients?

EXERCISES

If your instructor is using Personal Trainer® in this course, you may complete your assignments online.

E3-1 Write a short definition for each of the terms listed in the *Terms and Concepts Defined in this Chapter* section.

E3-2

Objs. 1, 2

Rollo Enterprises recorded the following activity in work-in-process inventory for September:

Direct labor	$15,000
Direct materials	10,000
Factory supervisor's salary, September	3,000
Indirect materials	7,000
Factory utilities	500

1,000 units were started and completed during the month.

a. Compute the amount of manufacturing overhead incurred for the month.
b. Assume all costs are actual. Using actual costing, calculate the cost of one unit.

E3-3

Objs. 1, 2

The M & S Company uses normal costing. The following information pertains to a recent production period:

Estimated manufacturing overhead	$70,000
Actual manufacturing overhead	$82,000
Machine hours	14,000
Actual machine hours	14,500
Estimated direct labor hours	2,000
Actual direct labor hours	2,300

a. Determine the predetermined overhead rate if the company uses machine hours as the activity base.
b. Determine the predetermined overhead rate if the company uses direct labor hours as the activity base.
c. If machine hours is used as the activity base, how much manufacturing overhead would be applied for the period?

E3-4

Objs. 1, 2

DuraPlastics Inc. recorded the following activity in work-in-process inventory during July:

Direct labor (300 hours)	$3,000
Direct materials	5,000
Manufacturing overhead applied	2,400

DuraPlastics uses normal costing. The activity base used to apply manufacturing overhead is direct labor hours.

a. What was the predetermined overhead rate used by DuraPlastics?
b. Assume 800 units were produced during July. What was the cost of one unit?

E3-5

Objs. 1, 2

Montclair Products prepared the following estimates for 2005:

Manufacturing overhead	$400,000
Direct labor cost	500,000

Actual information recorded at the end of the year is as follows:

Manufacturing overhead	$420,000
Direct labor cost	$475,000
Direct materials cost	$220,000
Units produced	5,000

a. Assume Montclair uses actual costing. What was the cost of one unit produced during 2005? For parts (b) and (c), assume instead that Montclair uses normal costing, with direct labor dollars as the activity base.
b. What was the predetermined overhead rate used by Montclair in 2005?
c. Was manufacturing overhead over- or underapplied for the year, and by how much?

E3-6
Objs. 1, 2

Harold Gordon operates a manufacturing company that uses a job-order costing system. The following activity was recorded in work-in-process inventory for August:

Direct materials	$ 150,000
Direct labor	80,000
Manufacturing overhead applied	120,000
Completed production	(322,000)

Harold charges overhead to work-in-process on the basis of direct labor dollars. There were no jobs in process as of August 1. At the end of August, only one job was still in process (Job 75). This job had incurred labor charges of $6,000 during the month.

a. Compute the predetermined overhead rate that Gordon used in August.
b. Compute the amount of manufacturing overhead and direct materials costs that were incurred in Job 75.

E3-7
Obj. 2

Tortolla Company is a manufacturing firm that uses a job-order costing system. The company uses machine hours to apply overhead to work-in-process. On January 1, Tortolla's management estimated that it would incur $700,000 in manufacturing overhead costs and 56,000 machine hours over the coming year.

a. Compute the company's predetermined overhead rate for the year.
b. Assume that the company uses only 54,000 machine hours over the year and incurs the following manufacturing costs:

Maintenance	$ 56,000
Depreciation	206,000
Indirect materials	76,000
Utilities	164,000
Insurance	94,000
Indirect labor	64,000

Compute the amount of overhead that was applied to production and the amount of over- or underapplied overhead for the period.

E3-8
Obj. 2

Tom Brooks, production manager for Clarion Manufacturing, was told that product overhead costs were too high, and the amount of overhead applied to inventory is less than the actual costs incurred over the last few months. Tom responds that he doesn't understand what "applied" means when dealing with inventory costs. Explain to Tom what is meant by the statement overhead is *applied* to units of product. Must the actual amount of overhead costs incurred always equal the amount of overhead applied to inventory?

E3-9
Objs. 2, 3

Trackers Inc. is a manufacturer of various specially designed radar devices. During May, Trackers completed Job 66 and began work on Job 67. Partial information concerning the two jobs is as follows:

Job 66		**Job 67**	
Direct labor (30 hours)	$600	Direct labor (10 hours)	$200
Direct materials	$900	Direct materials	$450
Manufacturing overhead	??	Manufacturing overhead	??

Total manufacturing overhead applied to both jobs was $1,400. Trackers uses normal costing and assigns manufacturing overhead using direct labor hours as the activity base.

a. What was the predetermined overhead rate used by Trackers?
b. What was the total cost of Job 66?
c. What are the costs incurred to date for Job 67?

E3-10
Objs. 2, 3

Small Company produces custom manufacturing equipment. The company uses job-order costing in conjunction with normal costing. Information pertaining to a recently completed job is as follows:

Job 423	
Direct labor	$2,500
Direct materials	$750
Machine hours	60
Units produced	100

(Continued)

Small Company applies manufacturing overhead using machine hours as the activity base. The predetermined overhead rate is $5 per machine hour.

    a. What was the total cost of job 423?
    b. What was the cost of one unit for job 423?

E3-11

Obj. 3

Basic Closet Company manufactures stand-alone cedar-lined wardrobe closets. Basic received an order for ten specially designed wardrobes to be delivered in eight weeks. The order was assigned job number 293. During production of the wardrobes, the following activities took place:

1. Requisitioned $2,500 of wood and $500 of hardware.
2. Time sheets revealed direct labor costs of $1,450 and indirect labor costs of $345.
3. Overhead was assigned using a predetermined overhead rate of 130% of direct labor costs.
4. Completed units were shipped to the customer. The selling price was 140% of cost.

    a. Calculate the manufacturing cost of one wardrobe.
    b. Calculate the selling price of each wardrobe.
    c. Describe how Basic traces material, manufacturing overhead, and labor costs to job 293.

PROBLEMS

If your instructor is using Personal Trainer® in this course, you may complete your assignments online.

P3-1

Objs. 1, 2

Unit Cost Using Actual and Normal Costing

Rocky Mountain Outfitters manufactures cowboy boots. Information related to a recent production period is as follows:

Estimated manufacturing overhead, 2004	$240,000
Estimated machine hours, 2004	12,000
Direct labor cost, September	$8,000
Direct materials cost, September	$5,000
Supervisor's salary, September	$3,000
Factory rent, September	$1,800
Factory utilities, September	$800
Indirect materials cost, September	$2,000
Machine hours worked, September	400

During September, 500 pairs of boots were produced.

Required

A. Using actual costing, what is the unit cost of one pair of boots produced during September?
B. Using normal costing, with machine hours as the activity base, what is the unit cost of one pair of boots produced during September?
C. If normal costing is used, was manufacturing overhead over- or underapplied during September? By how much?
D. What might have caused the amount of overhead applied to be different from the actual amount?
E. Why would managers at Rocky Mountain choose to use normal costing rather than actual costing?

P3-2

Objs. 1, 2

Unit Cost Using Actual and Normal Costing

Triple Play Sports manufactures baseball gloves. Information related to a recent production period is as follows:

Estimated manufacturing overhead, 2004	$100,000
Estimated machine hours, 2004	4,000
Direct labor cost, October	$5,000
Direct materials cost, October	$5,000
Supervisor's salary, October	$4,000
Factory rent, October	$1,000
Factory utilities, October	$1,000
Indirect materials cost, October	$1,400
Machine hours worked, October	300

During October, 2,000 gloves were produced.

Required

A. Using actual costing, what is the unit cost of one glove produced during October?

B. Using normal costing, with machine hours as the activity base, what is the unit cost of one glove produced during October?

C. If normal costing is used, was manufacturing overhead over- or underapplied during September? By how much?

D. What might have caused the amount of overhead applied to be different from the actual amount?

E. Why would managers at Triple Play Sports choose to use normal costing rather than actual costing?

P3-3   ## Applying Overhead Using a Job-Order Costing System

Objs. 2, 3   TCC Inc. has prepared the following estimates for the current year:

Direct labor hours	80,000
Direct labor cost	$1,000,000
Machine hours	60,000
Manufacturing overhead	$600,000

Required

A. Compute the predetermined overhead rate based on (1) direct labor hours, (2) direct labor cost, and (3) machine hours.

B. Assume the following jobs were worked during the year:

Job	Labor Hours	Labor Dollars	Machine Hours
123	18,000	$204,000	9,500
124	8,500	132,000	4,800
125	5,100	86,000	5,200
	31,600	422,000	19,500

Compute the amount of overhead that would have been applied to each of these jobs using the various overhead rates you computed in part (A).

C. Explain why the amount of overhead applied to each job varies with the activity base.

P3-4   ## Job-Order Costing Using Multiple Predetermined Overhead Rates

Objs. 2, 3   Granger Shirt Assembly Company runs a printing operation that produces customized T-shirts. These shirts usually are manufactured with either hand-created embroidery, individual holograms, or customized beaded accessories. Most often the shirts are produced in a small run to satisfy the needs of an individual rock performer, who uses the shirts as a promotional item when his or her band is on tour. Granger currently uses job-order costing in conjunction with normal costing to measure and assign unit costs.

The following information is provided regarding the company's two production departments:

	Layout Department	Printing Department
Estimated MOH cost for the year	$180,000	$450,000
Activity base for department	Direct labor hours	Machine hours
Budgeted activity for the year	10,000 DL hours	9,000 machine hours

Three jobs were started during a recent period and two were completed, job 101 and job 102:

	Job 101	Job 102
Materials cost	$10,200	$24,000
Direct labor cost	$24,500	$22,000
Labor hours, layout department	1,130	220
Machine hours, printing department	30	190

The selling price for each job includes a markup on cost of 50%.

(Continued)

Required

A. Calculate the predetermined overhead rate for the layout and printing departments.
B. Why would Granger use two different predetermined overhead rates?
C. What is the total cost of job 101?
D. What is the total selling price of job 102?
E. Granger also started, but did not complete, job 103 during this period. At the end of the period, the balance in the work-in-process account was $17,600, all of which related to job 103. Four hundred labor hours costing $8,000 were worked in the layout department. No work was performed in the printing department. How much in materials costs had been incurred to date for job 103 at the end of this period?

P3-5 Job-Order Costing Using Multiple Predetermined Overhead Rates

Objs. 2, 3   Pike Skateboard Company makes specialized skateboards. Pike seeks to be the leader in designs for skateboards and produces designs in lot sizes of 1,000 units. Pike sells the full batch of skateboards to its marketing subsidiary. Pike uses job-order costing in conjunction with normal costing to measure and assign unit costs.

The following information is provided regarding the company's two production departments:

	Design Department	Assembly Department
Estimated overhead cost for the year	$100,000	$300,000
Activity base for department	Direct labor hours	Machine hours
Budgeted activity for the year	10,000 DL hours	5,000 machine hours

Three jobs were started during a recent period and two were completed, job 201 and job 202:

	Job 201	Job 202
Materials cost	$16,000	$24,000
Direct labor cost	$5,000	$12,000
Labor hours, design department	120	240
Machine hours, assembly department	100	120

Pike sells the skateboards to its marketing subsidiary at a markup on cost of 30%.

Required

A. What is the predetermined overhead rate for the design department? For the assembly department?
B. Why would Pike use two different predetermined overhead rates?
C. What is the total cost of job 201?
D. What is the total selling price of job 202?
E. Pike also started, but did not complete, job 203 during this period. At the end of the period, the balance in the work-in-process account was $6,000, which all related to job 203. One hundred labor hours costing $4,000 were worked in the design department. No work was performed in the assembly department. How much in materials costs had been incurred to date for job 203 at the end of this period?

P3-6 Allocating Overhead Costs

Objs. 2, 3   Art's Custom Cabinetry manufactures and installs custom cabinetry built to customer specifications. The prices of cabinets depend on the quality of the lumber selected by the customers and the complexity of designs.

The company is owned and operated by Art Bruce. Five years ago, he started the company in his garage. Over the five years, Art invested heavily in special equipment. Art assigns job numbers by customer name. The only job still in process at the end of 2004 was for Clara Cummins. That job had been charged with direct materials of $750, direct labor of $1,000, and overhead of $250.

Art is the sole employee of his company. He works an average of 2,800 hours a year and pays himself $20 an hour. Art bids on all jobs in his spare time and feels his overhead rate has kept him from obtaining some of the jobs he has bid on.

A summary of activity for January is as follows:

Job	Direct Materials	Direct Labor Cost	Direct Labor Hours
Clara Cummins	$ 600	$ 800	40
John Ryan	1,200	1,000	50
Kyle Smith	750	700	35
Ken Woods	950	600	30

The Kyle Smith job was completed during January and billed at cost plus 10%. All other jobs are still in process at the end of the month.

Required

A. Assume the overhead allocation rate for 2005 is $5 per labor hour. Calculate the total costs for each of the jobs Art worked on during January.
B. Calculate the balance of the company's work-in-process inventory account as of January 31, 2005. Which jobs are reflected in that balance?
C. Calculate the cost of goods sold in January 2005.
D. Calculate the unit profit margin that the company earned from jobs completed in January.
E. If the primary overhead cost was an electric bill from running Art's machines, is an overhead allocation based on direct labor a good allocation method or should another allocation method be used? Explain.

P3-7 Allocating Overhead Costs

Objs. 2, 3

Handywoman Holly builds log cabins based on customer specifications. The only job still in process on January 1, 2005, was job 100. That job had been charged with direct materials of $40,000, direct labor of $30,000, and overhead of $5,000.

A summary of activity for 2005 is as follows:

Job	Direct Materials	Direct Labor Cost	Direct Labor Hours
100	$20,000	$22,500	450
200	50,000	40,000	800
300	10,000	10,000	200

Job 100 was completed during 2005. The other jobs are still in process at the end of the year. Overhead costs were $10,000 for 2005.

Required

A. Calculate the overhead rate based on direct labor hours.
B. Calculate the total costs for each of the jobs Holly worked on during 2005.
C. Calculate the balance of the company's work-in-process inventory account as of December 31, 2005.
D. Assume the only overhead cost is speculation work that Holly does to try to land new customers. The cost of speculation work is the same regardless of the size of the cabin to be built. Based on this information, do you feel overhead should be based on direct labor hours or is there be a better allocation method? Explain.

P3-8

Objs. 2, 3

The law firm of Dewey, Louie, and Howe has six lawyers and ten support people. The firm uses a job-order costing system to accumulate costs by client. There are two departments, research and litigation. The firm uses a different predetermined overhead rate for each department. At the beginning of the year, the partners made the following estimates:

	Department	
	Research	Litigation
Planned attorney hours	2,500	11,600
Number of clients	1,000	230
Legal supplies	$12,000	$4,600
Direct attorney cost	$132,000	$696,000
Department overhead	$70,000	$406,000

(Continued)

The costs to clients are separated into three components: supplies, attorney costs, and overhead. Both departments base overhead on the number of attorney hours charged. Supplies are charged on a per-client basis. Clients are billed all costs plus 20%.

Case DR9312 was opened on January 3 and closed June 17. During that period, the following costs and time were recorded:

Attorney hours, research	55
Attorney hours, litigation	175
Attorney cost	$13,800

Required

A. Compute the rate each department should use to assign overhead costs.
B. Compute the amount per client that each department should use to allocate supply costs.
C. Using the rates computed in requirements (A) and (B), compute the total cost of case DR9312, including overhead, supply charges, and attorney fees.
D. Calculate the billing for case DR9312.

P3-9 **Applying Overhead in a Service Organization**

Objs. 2, 3

PPGV provides auditing services. PPGV developed the following estimates for the current year:

Direct labor hours	70,000
Direct labor cost	$2,800,000
Overhead	$1,500,000

Required

A. Compute the predetermined overhead rate based on (1) direct labor hours and (2) direct labor cost.
B. Assume the following jobs were worked during the year:

Job	Labor Hours	Labor Dollars
100	40,000	$1,520,000
200	20,000	$820,000
300	10,000	$460,000

Compute the amount of overhead that would have been applied to each of these jobs using the various overhead rates you computed in part (A).
C. Explain why the amount of overhead applied to each job varies with the activity base.
D. The reason some jobs have a higher billing rate is because more senior people are working on the job. Assume the primary overhead cost is secretarial assistance. If the senior-level people require more secretarial work than their subordinates, which of these two overhead rates better reflects this situation? Explain.

P3-10 **Ethics and Overhead Allocation**

Objs. 2, 3

Cape Horn Yacht Company produces custom sailboats. A potential client has selected a design that is estimated to cost the company $300,000 to manufacture. To establish the selling price, the company typically adds a 40% markup to its manufacturing cost. Therefore, the selling price for the boat will be $420,000. Cape Horn pays a sales commission of 10% of the selling price. Hal, one of the sales representatives, is eager to close a deal with a potential customer. Unfortunately, the client is not willing to spend more than $385,000.

The cost estimate of the yacht is as follows:

Materials	$105,000
Labor	75,000
Manufacturing overhead ($75,000 × $1.60)	120,000
	$300,000

Cape Horn uses a predetermined overhead rate of $1.60 per dollar of direct labor cost.

Assume you are the company's accountant. Hal is looking for ways to reduce costs in order to make the deal. He argues the predetermined overhead rate is just an estimate; actual costs may be less. If you would simply reduce the predetermined overhead rate, the company could get the order. Otherwise, the sale (and commission) will be lost. He also reminds you of the generous bonus that awaits everyone in the company if certain sales targets are met. At year-end, you could simply close the underapplied overhead to cost of goods sold. Your report to management would state that overhead costs were higher than expected.

Required

A. Is this situation considered an ethical issue? Why or why not?

B. How would you respond to Hal's argument for reducing the predetermined overhead rate?

P3-11

Excel in Action

SPREADSHEET

Music Makers uses a job-order system for its production process. Orders are received for specific CDs, and costs are tracked for each order. Job A310 was completed in April. Costs associated with the job included 2,500 blank CDs at a cost of $0.75 per CD, 2,500 plastic containers at $0.10 per container, 2,500 printed inserts at $0.08 per insert, and 2,500 feet of cellophane at $0.02 per foot. Labor costs included copying (20 hours at $12 per hour) and packaging (45 hours at $8 per hour). Manufacturing overhead is applied at the rate of $30.092 per direct labor hour.

Required Use a spreadsheet to prepare a job cost sheet for job A310. The format should be as follows:

	A	B	C
1	Job Cost Sheet		
2	Order Number	A310	
3		Unit	Total
4	Number of CDs		
5	Material Costs:		
6	Blank CDs		
7	Containers		
8	Inserts		
9	Cellophane		
10	Total Materials		
11	Labor Hours:		
12	Copying		
13	Packaging		
14	Labor Costs:		
15	Copying		
16	Packaging		
17	Total Labor		
18	Overhead:		
19	Rate		
20	Total Cost		
21	Average Unit Cost		

Column B should identify unit amounts (number of CDs, unit costs, and labor hours). Column C should provide job costs for each material, labor, and overhead category. Subtotals should be provided for materials, labor, and overhead. These amounts should be computed by using cell references to compute the amounts and the SUM function to compute subtotals and total cost. Shaded cells will contain no data. Use the Format, Cells command, or the Fill Color button to shade cells. Use underlines, alignment, and bold type as indicated in the format provided.

Format cells to properly indicate the type of data entered in the cells. Quantities should be whole numbers, with commas as needed. Dollar amounts should provide for cents and

(Continued)

commas as needed. Average unit cost should provide three decimal places. Use the Comma Style and Increase or Decrease Decimal buttons to format cells.

Once completed, the spreadsheet should be useful for computing other job cost amounts. For example, suppose job A310 had included 5,000 units rather than 2,500. By changing the number of CDs in cell B4, the costs for the job should be recomputed automatically. Use absolute cell referencing for the number of CDs (B4) so that copying formulas from one cell (C6 for example) to another (C7 for example) does not alter the reference to the number of CDs. A major advantage of spreadsheets is that, once designed, they permit reuse and recomputation with minimal data entry.

P3-12 Multiple-Choice Overview of the Chapter

1. Overapplied overhead would result if:
   a. the plant was operated at less than full capacity.
   b. factory overhead costs incurred were less than estimated overhead costs.
   c. factory overhead costs incurred were less than the overhead costs charged to production.
   d. factory overhead costs incurred were greater than the overhead costs charged to production.

2. Scott Corporation uses labor hours as the basis for allocating manufacturing overhead costs to production. At the beginning of last year, Scott estimated total manufacturing costs at $300,000 and total labor hours at 75,000 hours. Actual results for the period were total manufacturing overhead costs of $290,000 and total labor hours of 75,000 hours. As a result of this outcome, Scott would have:
   a. applied more overhead to work-in-process inventory than the actual amount of overhead costs for the year.
   b. applied less overhead to work-in-process inventory than the actual amount of overhead cost for the year.
   c. applied an amount of overhead to work-in-process inventory that was equal to the actual amount of overhead.
   d. found it necessary to recalculate the predetermined rate.

3. Melrose Company uses a job-order costing system. The company recorded the following data for July:

Job Number	July 1 Work-in-Process Inventory	Added During July Direct Materials	Direct Labor
475	$1,500	$ 500	$ 300
476	1,000	700	900
477	900	1,000	1,500
478	700	1,200	2,000

Melrose charges overhead to production on the basis of 80% of direct materials cost. Jobs 475, 477, and 478 were completed during July. The balance of Melrose's work-in-process inventory account on July 31 was:
   a. $7,280.
   b. $2,600.
   c. $3,160.
   d. $3,320.

4. Last year, Rembrandt Company incurred $250,000 in actual manufacturing overhead costs. The manufacturing overhead account showed that overhead was overapplied in the amount of $12,000 for the year. If the predetermined overhead rate was $8 per direct labor hour, how many direct labor hours were worked during the year?
   a. 31,250
   b. 30,250
   c. 32,750
   d. 29,750

5. Birk Inc. uses a job-order costing system. The following information appeared in Birk's work-in-process inventory for April:

Balance, April 1	$ 4,000
Direct materials added	24,000
Direct labor added	16,800
Factory overhead applied	13,440
Transferred to finished goods	(48,000)

Birk applies overhead to production at a predetermined rate of 80% of direct labor costs. Work-in-process on April 30 includes direct labor costs of $2,000. The amount of direct materials in the ending work-in-process inventory for April was:
   a. $3,000.
   b. $5,200.
   c. $9,600.
   d. $6,640.

6. During May, Roy Company produced 6,000 units of product X in job 344. The costs charged to job 344 were as follows:

Direct materials	$10,000
Direct labor	20,000

At the beginning of the year, management estimated the following costs would be incurred to produce 120,000 units for the year:

Factory overhead	$168,000
Selling expenses	84,000

Roy applies overhead to work-in-process on a per-unit basis. The cost to produce one unit of product X in job 344 was:
   a. $6.40.
   b. $5.10.
   c. $3.80.
   d. $3.50.

7. A job cost sheet contains which of the following information?
   a. Materials requisition number
   b. Employee labor rate
   c. Job number
   d. All of the above are correct.

8. The product life cycle consists of each of the following phases except the:
   a. growth phase.
   b. harvest and divest phase.
   c. first-quarter phase.
   d. hold phase.

9. In the growth phase, after a product has been introduced, the producer normally is interested in building:
   a. market share.
   b. greater levels of profit.
   c. a cash balance at the bank.
   d. a better cost accounting system.

10. Traditional overhead allocation bases include all of the following except:
   a. machine hours.
   b. direct labor hours.
   c. direct labor dollars.
   d. electricity costs.

CASES

C3-1   Unit Costing Policy

Objs. 1, 2, 3

Knight Manufacturing produces three different products: A, B, and C. Knight applies overhead to the products on the basis of direct labor dollars. The company has collected the following information about its overhead and labor costs:

Manufacturing overhead:	
Machine setup	$ 53,000
Depreciation	400,000
Receiving and handling	200,000
Factory operations	650,000
Packing and shipping	400,000
Total	$1,703,000
Total direct labor	$ 225,000

Predetermined overhead rate 757% of direct labor dollars ($1,703,000 ÷ $225,000)

Knight can produce:

Product A—2 units per hour
Product B—3 units per hour
Product C—4 units per hour

The costs of direct materials and direct labor are charged to each product under a job-order costing system. The average cost per unit based on the first of several production runs is as follows:

	Product		
	A	**B**	**C**
Direct materials	$ 25.00	$ 35.00	$ 15.00
Direct labor*	10.00	6.67	5.00
Overhead applied	75.70	50.49	37.85
Total per-unit cost	$110.70	$ 92.16	$ 57.85
Current selling price	$163.00	$125.00	$102.00

The average labor rate is $20 per labor hour.

The company manufactures each product in different batch sizes. Product A is manufactured in lot sizes of 10,000 units per run, product B in lots of 5,000 units per run, and product C in lots of 1,000 units per run. The average shipment size is 2,000 units of product A, 500 units of product B, and 100 units of product C. Over the past year, the company has sold 22,000 units of product A, 15,000 units of product B, and 32,000 units of product C.

In recent months, management at Knight has been puzzled by the company's sales and profit figures. The sales of product A have declined significantly since a competitor of that product reduced its selling price below Knight's current cost of manufacturing that product. In addition, Knight has increased its selling price of product C three times over the past year without losing any sales. Even though more product C is being sold, and it has the largest gross margin of the three products, overall profits have been falling.

Required

A. What problems do you see with the current unit costing methods Knight is using?
B. What reasons can you suggest for the market reactions to the pricing of products A and C?
C. What changes would you suggest to management about its current costing policies?

C3-2 Allocation of Overhead Costs

Objs. 1, 2, 3

(This case is a variation of P3-6.) Art's Custom Cabinetry manufactures and installs custom cabinetry built to customer specifications. The prices of cabinets depend on the quality of the lumber selected by the customers and the complexity of designs.

The company is owned and operated by Art Bruce. Five years ago, he started the company in his garage. Over the five years, Art invested heavily in special equipment. The annual depreciation on that equipment is $1,200. He also has moved operations to a building he rents for $4,800 per year. During 2004, Art incurred the following costs: utilities, $1,500; repairs and maintenance, $600; shop supplies, $2,100; paint and varnish, $800; insurance and taxes, $3,000. All of these costs are considered to be production costs and are assigned to jobs as overhead expense. These costs are expected to stay the same in 2005.

Art assigns job numbers by customer name. The only job still in process at the end of 2004 was Clara Cummins. That job had been charged with direct materials of $600, direct labor of $1,000, and overhead of $400, using an overhead allocation rate of 25% of direct costs (direct materials plus direct labor).

Art is the sole employee of his company. He works an average of 2,800 hours a year and pays himself $20 an hour. Art bids on all jobs in his spare time and feels his overhead rate has kept him from obtaining some of the jobs he has bid on.

A summary of activity for January is as follows:

Job	Direct Materials	Direct Labor Cost	Direct Labor Hours
Clara Cummins	$ 600	$ 800	40
John Ryan	1,200	1,000	50
Kyle Smith	750	700	35
Ken Woods	950	600	30

The Kyle Smith job was completed during January and billed at cost plus 10%. All other jobs are still in process at the end of the month.

Required

A. Comment on the overhead base used by Art's Custom Cabinetry. What changes would you recommend, if any, for the company?
B. Select a base for 2005, and calculate the predetermined overhead rate that should be used in the coming year.
C. Using your predetermined overhead rate [part (B)], calculate the total costs for each of the jobs Art worked on during January.
D. Calculate the balance of the company's work-in-process inventory as of January 31, 2005. Which jobs are reflected in that balance?
E. Calculate the cost of goods sold in January 2005.
F. Calculate the unit profit margin that the company earned from jobs completed in January.

PRODUCING GOODS AND SERVICES: CONTINUOUS PROCESSING

How do we account for products manufactured in a continuous process?

Erin and Seth now understand the importance of unit costs and realize they need monthly reports to show the costs of manufacturing each type of product. Erin and Seth use two different manufacturing processes in their furniture company. Because they believe their futon will be very popular with several customers, they are making it on a continuous basis. Other products are manufactured when they are ordered. Frequently a job requires specific modifications to meet customer needs. Seth is particularly concerned about matching the costing procedure to the type of manufacturing process.

FOOD FOR THOUGHT

If you were advising Seth and Erin, what would be your recommendation for associating costs with the furniture they are producing? Does manufacturing a product continuously versus building it to order make a difference in how product costs are collected and reported? Let's join Erin, Seth, and Roberta again as they discuss the situation.

Erin: *We've been trying to decide how to assign manufacturing costs to our products. We're not sure if we can use the same approach for all of our products. Seth and I have been discussing this question and think we need two different costing methods. We should use job-order costing to assign manufacturing costs to our made-to-order products. If we divide the month's total overhead costs by the month's total for direct labor hours, we'll have an average we can apply for each labor hour. Then, we can assign overhead to each order by multiplying the overhead average by the number of labor hours worked on a particular job. Next, we will use job cost cards to record materials and labor costs for our batches of unique products. However, we need a different system to account for our futons that are produced continuously.*

Seth: *I agree. We are producing futons all the time and shipping them when orders are received. A futon may sit in the warehouse for three or four months before it is sold and shipped. How would we know how much cost to assign to a futon under these circumstances?*

Roberta: *An accounting system for a continuous process should track the costs of materials, labor, and overhead over a period. For example, each month the system should produce an average unit cost by dividing the manufacturing cost by the number of units produced during the period. Using two different product costing procedures should provide greater accuracy in product costs. You have to decide if the benefits of greater cost accuracy derived from using two procedures are worth the effort required to get the information.*

Erin: *I think I'm beginning to understand the differences between the two costing methods. Using job-order costing, we track costs to a specific job. In the continuous process situation, since there is no job, we have to assign some sort of average cost to the units produced. An average cost should work fine for the futons, because they are identical. How do we set up this type of costing system?*

OBJECTIVES

Once you have completed this chapter, you should be able to:

1 Distinguish between job-order and process costing and describe when each method should be used.

2 Explain the concept of equivalent units.

3 Prepare and evaluate a departmental production report.

ASSIGNING UNIT COSTS

OBJECTIVE 1

Distinguish between job-order and process costing and describe when each method should be used.

Cost accounting systems are designed to provide product cost information to decision makers. These systems capture important characteristics of a company's underlying manufacturing process. To develop unit costs, a company must determine how to measure costs and assign them to individual units. Two methods, job-order costing and process costing, traditionally have been used to assign unit costs. Each method is suited to a specific type of manufacturing or service environment. Companies that build ships; provide legal, medical, or accounting services; manufacture airplanes; and repair automobiles would likely use job-order costing to assign unit costs to their products or services. Those products or services share certain characteristics:

- The units of a particular job are easy to identify because they are unique.
- Much of the cost of producing the product or service can be traced directly to a particular job.

Suppose **Boeing**, an aircraft manufacturer, builds a jumbo jet and a small commuter plane in the same plant. Obviously, the physical characteristics and costs of producing a jumbo jet are very different from the characteristics and costs of producing a small plane. If the company assigns manufacturing costs by simply dividing its total costs for the period by the number of planes it has produced, it will assign too little cost to the jumbo jet and too much to the commuter plane. The company has to know the cost of producing each type of plane. Thus, a company such as Boeing would use job cost sheets, as illustrated in the previous chapter, to accumulate costs for each type of airplane.

In contrast, process costing is best suited for production situations with the following characteristics:

- The products are alike.
- The processes used to manufacture those products flow from one into another.
- The costs of producing the products cannot be traced easily to individual units.

Process costing **totals the costs of all units produced in a given accounting period and divides by the units produced.** Thus, unit costs are calculated as follows:

Unit cost for the period = Cost of production for the period ÷ Units produced in the period

Consider a petroleum processing company, such as **Shell Oil**, where gasoline is produced in a continuous flow. The oil flows through a series of processes that transform it into gasoline. Once produced and stored, it is impossible to distinguish one gallon of gasoline from another, much less to identify when that particular gallon was produced. A refinery cannot trace the cost of manufacturing gasoline to individual gallons. In this case, an average cost is sufficiently accurate because the physical characteristics and costs of producing each unit of product are very much the same.

Batch processing **combines elements of individual-job and continuous-flow processing.** When Shell Oil produces a batch of Shell Regular gasoline followed by a batch of Shell Plus gasoline on the same production line, it is using batch processing. When products are produced in batches, the decision to use job-order costing or process costing often depends on the answers to the following questions:

- How much accuracy in the unit cost calculation does management require?
- How accurate is process costing compared to job-order costing?
- How difficult and costly is tracing costs to individual batches using a job-order system?

When products are processed in batches, the choice of a cost-assignment method involves weighing the need for accurate information against the cost of developing that information. The need for accuracy depends on the type of business and how the information is going to be used. The cost of developing accurate information is a function of the production process. Job-order costing generally is more accurate than process costing. However, a job-order system can be more costly and more difficult to implement in many manufacturing situations.

Exhibit 1 compares the two traditional methods for assigning costs to units of products. Job-order costing is more effective when jobs are manufactured separately rather than in continuous processes. In addition, job-order costing performs well when the units of each product vary in characteristics and costs. Process costing works best when production is continuous and when the units of each product are similar in characteristics and cost.

Exhibit 1

Job-Order and Process Costing: Choosing a Cost-Assignment Method

	Job-Order Costing	Process Costing
Manufacturing Context	Products are manufactured in separate and distinct jobs.	Products are manufactured in a continuous process.
Computation of Unit Costs	Costs are traced to each job. The total cost of a job is divided by the number of units produced in the job to determine the unit cost.	Costs are accumulated for all units produced during a period. To determine the unit cost, total cost is divided by the number of units produced during the period.
Accuracy	Job-order costing tends to be more accurate because costs are traced directly to a particular job.	Process costing usually is less accurate because the unit cost is the average of all units produced during the period.

---

1 SELF-STUDY PROBLEM

Which method, job-order costing or process costing, would be most appropriate for each of the following organizations? Briefly justify your answer.

WebTUTOR Advantage

a. A paint manufacturer
b. A glue manufacturer
c. An aircraft manufacturer
d. A home building company
e. An accounting firm
f. A hospital
g. A tire manufacturer
h. A manufacturer of specialty factory equipment
i. An interior decorator
j. A film studio
k. A brewery

The solution to Self-Study Problem 1 appears at the end of the chapter.

PROCESS COSTING

OBJECTIVE 2

Explain the concept of equivalent units.

The objective of process costing, like that of job-order costing, is to determine a unit cost for each finished product. Products manufactured in a process environment usually pass through a series of steps. In each step materials, labor, and overhead costs are added to the product. Processes usually are carried out in specific departments or process centers. When units of a product are completed, they are transferred as finished goods to a warehouse until they are shipped to customers. This section uses Syntex Fabrics to illustrate cost accumulation in a continuous manufacturing environment.

Syntex Fabrics: The Manufacturing Process and Cost Flows

Syntex Fabrics is an example of a manufacturing company that uses a process costing system. As shown in Exhibit 2, the manufacturing processes at Syntex Fabrics require three departments, A, B, and C. In the first process, fiber production (known as spinning), liquid synthetic resin is placed into a machine. At the top of the machine, fibers emerge from spinnerets (discs resembling a showerhead). Each hole in the spinneret produces a continuous strand of fiber. These fibers are wound onto spools for use in the weaving process. Exhibit 2 illustrates that direct materials, direct labor, and manufacturing overhead costs are added by Department A during the fiber production process.

Exhibit 2 Tracing Costs Through Syntex Fabric's Process Costing System

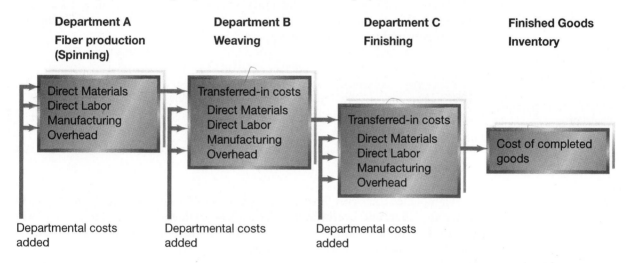

The second process, known as weaving, uses fiber transferred in from Department A to manufacture cloth on large high-tech looms. Various materials and supplies are used in preparing the loom (the machine used to weave fibers into cloth). First, fibers are wound side-by-side onto the loom in a process called warping. After the warping process, the loom contains fibers that are parallel and run the length of the loom. These fibers are called the warp. Fabric is created when weft fibers are woven over and under the warp fibers across the width of the loom. As shown in Exhibit 2, the weaving department adds direct materials, direct labor, and manufacturing overhead costs to convert the fiber into fabric.

When the weaving process is complete, the fabric is transferred to the third process, known as finishing, where various waterproofing and flame retarding coatings are applied. As shown in Exhibit 2, fabric costs are transferred in from the weaving department. The finishing department also adds direct materials, direct labor, and manufacturing overhead costs to the product during the conversion process. After the finishing process, the completed roll of fabric is transferred to finished goods inventory.

When the completed goods are sold, their accumulated costs are transferred from finished goods inventory to cost of goods sold.

Equivalent Units

In process costing systems, manufacturing costs are accumulated by department and are applied to equivalent units of production. *Equivalent units* **are the number of units that would have been produced during a period if all of the department's efforts had resulted in completed units.** For example, two units that are each one-half complete would be treated as one complete unit for purposes of assigning costs (2 units $\times \frac{1}{2}$ complete = 1 equivalent unit). Equivalent units are computed separately for each process center. The need to compute equivalent units arises because all of a department's efforts do not result in fully completed units during a period. Thus, process costing is complicated by work-in-process (WIP) inventory at the end of an accounting period. WIP for a particular department is made up of those units that are partially completed in that department.

Exhibit 3 illustrates how to calculate equivalent units for a department that transferred 65,000 units to another department. Though the units transferred out are not 100 percent complete, they are complete to the extent possible by the transferring department. Thus, units transferred out always are multiplied by 100 percent to calculate equivalent units. Remaining in the ending WIP inventory are 20,000 units that are 40 percent complete. As Exhibit 3 illustrates, these units are multiplied by the percentage of completion to determine the equivalent units remaining in ending WIP inventory. The total equivalent units produced by a department within an accounting period is calculated by adding the equivalent units transferred out to the equivalent units remaining in WIP inventory. Exhibit 3 reports 73,000 total equivalent units produced by the department during an accounting period.

Exhibit 3
Equivalent Unit
Calculation

Equivalent units transferred out	65,000	(65,000 × 100%)
Equivalent units remaining in ending WIP inventory	8,000	(20,000 × 40%)
Total equivalent units	73,000	

Companies track cost flows using *departmental production reports* **that describe materials, labor, and overhead used by each department during a given accounting period. The** *initial department* **is the department that begins producing a product. A** *subsequent department* **is a department that continues production activities on a product.** Using our Syntex example in Exhibit 2, fiber production is the initial department and the weaving and finishing processes are subsequent departments. The production cost follows the physical flow of the product as it moves from the initial department to subsequent departments. *Transferred-in costs* **are costs that have been transferred from a prior department in the production process to a subsequent department.**

To use process costing, a company must have a system keeping track of units produced, accumulating costs incurred during the period, and applying those costs to the units produced. The departmental production report summarizes all activities that affect the department's WIP inventory during a given period. Exhibit 4 presents an overview of a departmental production report that would be prepared for a continuous processor, such as Syntex. We later provide a numerical example to illustrate the details of a departmental production report. For now, let's look at the big picture.

The box at the left of Exhibit 4, the quantity schedule, provides a structure to guide you through the entire process of preparing a departmental production report. The quantity schedule reports the physical flow of units through the department. Thus, some companies refer to it as a physical flow schedule. The unit cost calculation associates dollar amounts (in the costs box) with the units to account for in the quantity schedule. The equivalent units calculation also is based on the quantity schedule. After the costs and equivalent units have been calculated, we simply divide costs by equivalent units to determine the cost per equivalent unit. Finally, in the cost reconciliation portion of the production report, we associate the cost per equivalent unit with the number of equivalent units produced during a period. As a result, the total costs in the cost reconciliation section equal the total costs to account for (in the costs box of the unit cost calculation).

Exhibit 4 Departmental Production Report—An Overview

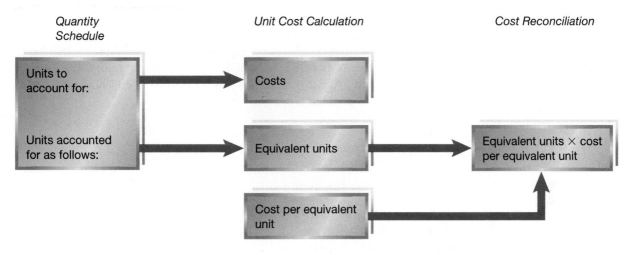

---

2 SELF-STUDY PROBLEM

WebTUTOR Advantage

Halyard Company uses two departments, braiding and finishing, to produce its primary product, $\frac{1}{2}$ inch diameter rope. During June, the braiding department transferred 30,000 yards of braided rope to the finishing department. The ending WIP inventory in the braiding department consisted of 800 yards of rope that were 30% complete.

Required Calculate the equivalent units that would be used to determine a cost per equivalent unit in the braiding department.

The solution to Self-Study Problem 2 appears at the end of the chapter.

PREPARING A DEPARTMENTAL PRODUCTION REPORT

OBJECTIVE 3

Prepare and evaluate a departmental production report.

Recall that Syntex Fabrics requires three departments, fiber production (or spinning), weaving, and finishing, to produce a completed roll of fabric. Accountants prepare departmental production reports for each department at the end of every month. We use the spinning department to illustrate the steps involved in producing a departmental production report for a continuous process manufacturer. The output from the department is measured in yards. The fiber is a high-tech material used in manufacturing fabric intended for rigorous outdoor applications. The high manufacturing cost per yard reflects the technical nature of the product. The objective is to determine the cost per yard and to assign material and conversion costs transferred to the weaving department and to the yards of unfinished product remaining in the department.

Assume the spinning department had 20,000 yards of partially completed fiber as WIP inventory on October 1, 2004. Material and conversion costs associated with the beginning inventory were $320 and $420, respectively. *Conversion costs* **are the direct** labor and manufacturing overhead costs required to convert raw materials into finished goods. During the month the department began working on an additional 120,000 yards of fiber. Costs of materials and conversion added during the month were $3,050 and $4,500, respectively. The spinning department transferred 110,000 yards of fiber to the weaving department during October. The remaining 30,000 yards of WIP inventory at October 31, 2004, were 50 percent complete as for materials and 40 percent complete for conversion.

Step 1: Account for the Physical Flow of Units. The first step in developing a production report is to account for the physical flow of units worked on during the month. As shown in Exhibit 4, this portion of the production report is known as the quantity schedule. The spinning department at Syntex Fabrics had 20,000 yards of WIP inventory on October 1. They began working on an additional 120,000 yards during the month. Thus, the spinning department had 140,000 yards of fiber to account for (20,000 + 120,000 = 140,000). The department completed and transferred to the weaving department 110,000 yards of fiber. Thus, 30,000 yards of partially spun fiber remain in the department's ending WIP inventory (140,000 − 110,000 = 30,000). Using this information, we complete the quantity schedule as follows:

Units to account for:	Units
Work-in-process, October 1	20,000
Units started in production in October	+120,000
Total	140,000

Units accounted for as follows:	
Units completed and transferred out in October	110,000
Work-in-process, October 31	+ 30,000
Total	140,000

Step 2: Account for the Department's Production Costs. In this step, the company adds the costs of beginning WIP inventory and the costs added during the month. Often, labor and overhead are added together and are accounted for as a single conversion cost in process-costing systems. Notice the "Units to account for" section of the quantity schedule is included to illustrate where to assign the materials and conversion costs. For example, the beginning inventory consisted of 20,000 partially complete units. These units contained materials and conversion costs of $320 and $420, respectively. In addition, 120,000 yards were started during the month. The materials and conversion costs associated with these yards are $3,050 and $4,500, respectively. Thus, the total cost associated with the spinning department during the month of October is $8,290 ($320 + $420 + $3,050 + $4,500).

			Costs	
	Units	Materials	Conversion	Total
Work-in-process, October 1	20,000	$ 320	$ 420	$ 740
Costs added during October in the spinning department	120,000	3,050	4,500	7,550
Total for October	140,000	$3,370	$4,920	$8,290

Step 3: Calculate the Equivalent Units of Production. In this step, the company converts the physical units of production into equivalent units. Using the quantity schedule as a guide, we calculate the equivalent units associated with the units completed and transferred to the weaving department. In addition we calculate the equivalent units associated with the fiber remaining in ending WIP inventory. The percentage of completion associated with products transferred out is always 100 percent. These units are complete to the extent possible by the spinning department. For further processing, these units are transferred to the weaving department. Thus, if 110,000 yards

are transferred out, 110,000 equivalent units of materials and 110,000 equivalent units of conversion are transferred to the weaving department.

Unlike the number of units transferred out, we must adjust the ending inventory for the percentage of completion. For example, the ending WIP inventory consists of 30,000 yards that are 50 percent complete for materials and 40 percent complete for conversion costs. In other words, the department has added only one-half of the materials necessary to complete the 30,000 yards of fiber. They have added only 40 percent of the conversion costs (labor and overhead) necessary to complete the 30,000 yards of fiber. Therefore, the department has 15,000 equivalent units of materials (30,000 whole units × .50) and 12,000 equivalent units with respect to conversion (30,000 whole units × .40). During the month, the division produced a total of 125,000 equivalent units of materials (110,000 + 15,000 = 125,000) and 122,000 equivalent units of conversion (110,000 + 12,000 = 122,000). The equivalent unit calculation is shown as follows:

	Units	Materials	Conversion
Units completed and transferred out in October (100% complete)	110,000	110,000	110,000
Work-in-process, October 31:			
30,000 units × 50% complete for materials	30,000	15,000	
30,000 units × 40% complete for conversion			12,000
Equivalent units of production for October	140,000	125,000	122,000

Step 4: Calculate the Cost of Equivalent Units. The fourth step in developing the production report is to divide total costs (from step 2) by equivalent units (from step 3) to obtain the cost per equivalent unit. Total material costs of $3,370 are divided by 125,000 equivalent units of materials. The result is a material cost of $0.026960 per equivalent unit. Likewise, total conversion costs of $4,920 are divided by 122,000 equivalent units of conversion. The result is a conversion cost of $0.040328 per equivalent unit of conversion. The total unit product cost of $0.0673 is obtained by adding the equivalent unit cost for materials and conversion.

		Costs		
	Units	Materials	Conversion	Total
Work-in-process, October 1	20,000	$ 320	$ 420	$ 740
Costs added during October in the spinning department	120,000	3,050	4,500	7,550
Total costs for October	140,000	$3,370	$4,920	$8,290

	Units	Materials	Conversion
(100% complete)	110,000	110,000	110,000
Work-in-process, October 31:			
30,000 units × 50% complete for materials	30,000	15,000	
30,000 units × 40% complete for conversion			12,000
Equivalent units of production for October	140,000	125,000	122,000
		$3,370	$4,920
		125,000	122,000
		$0.026960 +	$0.040328 = $0.067288

Step 4 indicates the spinning department incurred $0.027 in material cost and $0.040 in conversion cost for each yard of completed fiber. The cost of a yard of spun fiber transferred to the weaving department is $0.067 ($0.027 + $0.040).

Step 5: Assign Costs to Inventory. In the final step of the departmental production report, the company assigns production costs for the period to the units that are transferred out. These costs move into the WIP inventory of the weaving department. The costs transferred out equal the number of units transferred out multiplied by the total cost per equivalent unit. The costs assigned to WIP inventory equal the number of equivalent units in WIP multiplied by the cost per unit. Costs are assigned to units transferred out to the weaving department and to ending WIP inventory as follows:

	Units		
Costs transferred to the weaving department:			WIP
(110,000 units × $0.067288)	110,000		$7,402
Costs assigned to work-in-process inventory:			Ending WIP
Materials (30,000 units × 50% × $0.026960)	30,000	404	
Conversion (30,000 units × 40% × $0.040328)		484	
Costs assigned to work-in-process inventory			888
Total costs assigned to units in October	140,000		$8,290

Notice that the total costs assigned to units in October ($8,290) equal the total costs to be accounted for in step 2.

Exhibit 5 combines steps 1–5 into a completed production report using the layout shown in Exhibit 4.

Exhibit 5 Completed Departmental Production Report for the Spinning Department at Syntex Fabrics

Units to account for:	Units	Materials	Conversion	Total
Work-in-process, October 1	20,000	$ 320	$ 420	$ 740
Units started during October	120,000	3,050	4,500	7,550
Total	140,000	$3,370	$4,920	$8,290

Units accounted for as follows:				
Units transferred out in October	110,000	110,000	110,000	Transferred out 110,000 × $0.067288 = $7,402
Work-in-process, October 31	30,000	15,000	12,000	Ending WIP 15,000 × $0.026960 = 404
Total	140,000	125,000	122,000	12,000 × $0.040328 = 484
				$8,290
Cost per unit		$3,370	$4,920	
		125,000	122,000	

$$\$0.026960 + \$0.040328 = \$0.067288$$

Managers use cost information provided by the departmental production report in a variety of ways. For example, they can evaluate whether material, labor, and manufacturing overhead costs are consistent with expectations, based on prior periods. Most companies that use process costing systems are continuous manufacturers. Thus, managers should expect production levels and unit costs to remain stable unless the company experiences a manufacturing problem or a price increase for resources required in production. Companies also use output from a process costing system to help them value work-in-process and finished goods inventory. As we have seen, these values are reported in a company's published financial statements.

Case In Point

http://albright.
swlearning.com

Learn more about the
Dow Chemical Company.

Cost Information and Decision-Making in a Continuous Process Industry

Understanding production costs, such as materials and conversion, are important to continuous processors. **Dow Chemical** recently was able to raise prices without losing volume. The company beat analysts' earnings forecasts by aggressively controlling operating costs and increasing prices. Management believes price increases were possible because of increased demand, and lower supply of their products.

Source: Chemical Week. New York, July 2–9, 2003. Vol. 165, Issue 24, page 49.

3 SELF-STUDY PROBLEM

webTUTOR Advantage

Fizz Pop produces one product (a soft drink) that flows through two departments, mixing and bottling. Costs in WIP inventory on March 1 included $4,000 of materials and $2,500 of conversion costs. Costs added during March included $50,000 of materials and $35,000 of conversion costs.

A production report for the mixing department for March showed the following information:

	Units	Percentage Complete	
		Materials	Conversion
Units to account for:			
Work-in-process, March 1	50,000		
Units started in production in March	600,000		
Total units in production in March	650,000		
Units accounted for as follows:			
Units completed and transferred out in March	570,000		
Work-in-process, March 31	80,000	100%	50%
Total units accounted for	650,000		

Required Compute the total and unit costs for March. Also compute the amount of cost transferred to the bottling department during March and the amount of WIP on March 31 for the mixing department.

The solution to Self-Study Problem 3 appears at the end of the chapter.

REVIEW

SUMMARY of IMPORTANT CONCEPTS

1. Most companies use either process costing or job-order costing to assign costs to units of products.
   a. Each method is more effective in certain processing environments.

2. Equivalent units are used to determine unit costs for materials and conversion.

3. Process costing yields an average cost for each unit produced during a particular period.
   a. The departmental production report summarizes costs and units that flow through a department each period.
   b. A production report consists of three sections as follows:
      1. Quantity schedule
      2. Unit cost calculation
      3. Cost reconciliation
   c. As units of product move from one department to the next, the production costs of those products are transferred from department to department.

DEFINE

TERMS and CONCEPTS DEFINED in this CHAPTER

batch processing   (M79)
conversion costs   (M83)
departmental production report   (M82)
equivalent units   (M82)

initial department   (M82)
process costing   (M79)
subsequent department   (M82)
transferred-in costs   (M82)

SELF-STUDY PROBLEM SOLUTIONS

SSP4-1 Job-order costing is used in situations where many different products, jobs, or batches are produced each period. Process costing is used in situations where a homogeneous product is produced on a continuous basis.

	Process Costing	Job-Order Costing
a. A paint manufacturer	X	
b. A glue manufacturer	X	
c. An aircraft manufacturer		X
d. A home building company		X
e. An accounting firm		X
f. A hospital		X
g. A tire manufacturer	X	
h. A manufacturer of specialty factory equipment		X
i. An interior decorator		X
j. A film studio		X
k. A brewery	X	

SSP4-2

Yards transferred out	30,000	(30,000 × 100%)
Ending WIP	240	(800 × 30%)
Equivalent units	30,240	

SSP4-3

	Materials	Conversion	Total
Cost to account for:			
Work-in-process, March 1	$ 4,000	$ 2,500	$ 6,500
Costs added during March in mixing department	50,000	35,000	85,000
Total costs for March	$54,000	$37,500	$91,500

Equivalent units:

	Materials	Conversion
Units completed and transferred out in March	570,000	570,000
Work-in-process, March 31:		
80,000 units × 100% complete	80,000	
80,000 units × 50% complete		40,000
Equivalent units of production in March	650,000	610,000

Cost per equivalent unit:
Materials $54,000 ÷ 650,000 equivalent units = $0.083077 per equivalent unit
Conversion $37,500 ÷ 610,000 equivalent units = $0.061475 per equivalent unit

Total $0.144552 per equivalent unit

Costs assigned to inventory:		
Costs assigned to units transferred out 570,000 units × $0.144552		$82,395
Costs assigned to work-in-process inventory:		
Materials	80,000 units × 100% × $0.083077 =	6,646
Conversion	80,000 units × 50% × $0.061475 =	2,459
Costs assigned to work-in-process inventory		9,105
Total costs assigned to units in March ($82,395 + $9,105)		$91,500

Thinking Beyond the Question

How do we account for products manufactured in a continuous process?

Reflect back on Erin and Seth's discussion of batch versus continuous process costing. Earlier in the chapter, you learned to account for partially completed units using the equivalent units concept because some units manufactured during a given period may not be completed during that same period. You learned how to develop equivalent units for materials and conversion and to compute costs per equivalent unit for each category of cost. What happens, however, when more than one type of labor or material is used in a given department? How would you suggest accounting for such situations?

QUESTIONS

Q4-1
Obj. 1
During a family gathering you announce that you are studying managerial accounting and fully understand product costing. Your brother says that he works for a company that assigns product costs using job-order costing. Your sister says that her company uses something called process costing to assign product costs. Uncle Nick asks you to explain the difference between job-order costing and process costing. What do you tell him?

Q4-2
Obj. 1
Clark Lights produces lightbulbs. The plant is new, and the process is highly automated. All production is completed in a single two-step department. First, a bulb casing is made and is passed to a second machine process where a filament is inserted. The company manufactures several different wattage bulbs, including 40, 75, and 100. Once the machinery is set up, the company will produce the same wattage bulb for up to four days before changing to another wattage bulb. The only difference in processing the different wattage bulbs is the size of the filament that is inserted in the second step. The cost difference of the different size filaments is insignificant. Clark produces approximately 5,000 bulbs of each wattage per month. Identify the costing procedure that would be most appropriate given the different style bulbs that are produced. Explain the reason for your answer. Would your answer change if the cost of the materials was considered significantly different? Explain why or why not.

Q4-3
Obj. 1
Which method, job order or process costing, would be the most appropriate for each of the following organizations? Under what circumstances would managers choose job order costing? Under what circumstances would managers choose process costing?

a. A bakery that produces a variety of goods
b. A bank
c. A gasoline refinery
d. A printing shop
e. A cement manufacturer
f. A law firm
g. A pharmaceutical firm
h. A soft drink bottler
i. A jewelry repair shop
j. A custom boat builder
k. A fertilizer producer

Q4-4
Obj. 1
You work in consulting and have been hired to redesign Hoyt Industries' costing systems. Hoyt produces soft drinks. You have already decided to use normal costing to measure costs, but must decide what method to use to assign costs to units of products, job-order or process costing. What are the differences between the two approaches?

Q4-5
Obj. 1
Carter Lumber Company processes timber into finished lumber. For 20 years, Carter has calculated the cost of lumber using job-order costing. Each production run was treated as a separate job. Carter recently changed accounting procedures and now calculates product costs using process costing. Do you think making the change was a good idea? Why or why not?

Q4-6
Obj. 2
The equivalent unit calculation adjusts ending WIP for partially completed units. The purpose is to make the cost per equivalent unit more accurate. Can you think of a situation in which adjusting for equivalent units would be unnecessary? Explain.

Q4-7
Obj. 2
Pegasus Wire Harness Company produces an electrical-wire harness used in the automotive industry. Pegasus accounts for product costs using process costing. Managers of Pegasus focus on two elements of product costs for planning and control purposes. What are the two elements that are assigned costs in process costing? Why are the two elements treated separately?

Q4-8
Obj. 2
The equivalent unit calculation attaches material, labor, and overhead costs equally to each unit produced during an accounting period. Under what circumstances does this system produce reasonably accurate product costs? Explain.

Q4-9
Obj. 3
How might a manager use a departmental production report to understand and manage costs?

Q4-10
Obj. 3
Assume you are the manager of the third department in a three-department process. Your company uses process costing to determine its product costs. When a product passes through your department, it is taken to the finished goods inventory warehouse. At the same time, an accounting entry is prepared to reduce WIP inventory in your department and to increase finished goods inventory. How would you know the total value of goods to transfer? Where did these costs come from?

Q4-11
Obj. 3
Paula Locum is a department manager for Dempsey Lumber Mill. She supervises the kiln drying operations and is directly responsible for ten employees and three large kiln dryers. Each month, Paula prepares a production report for the drying operation and submits her report to accounting. What are the key elements of a departmental production report?

EXERCISES

If your instructor is using Personal Trainer® in this course, you may complete your assignments online.

E4-1
Write a short definition for each of the terms listed in the *Terms and Concepts Defined in this Chapter* section.

E4-2
Obj. 1
For each characteristic listed below, indicate whether the characteristic is more descriptive of a (a) job-order costing system or a (b) process costing system.

1. More detailed information is required for costing purposes.
2. Products are similar in cost and in required manufacturing activities.
3. Cost estimates are less accurate because of averaging.
4. Costs are accumulated for a given period of time.
5. Products usually vary in and required manufacturing activities.
6. Identical units pass through a series of different processes.
7. The total cost for the period is divided by the total units produced during the period.
8. Costs are accumulated by batch or job number.
9. Each unit of product receives a similar amount of manufacturing costs.
10. Units of different products may receive a different amount of manufacturing costs.

E4-3
Obj. 1
If you were the manager of each of the following firms or companies, which costing system would you recommend: (a) job-order costing or (b) process costing?

1. An oil refinery
2. A ship builder
3. A management consulting firm
4. A paper mill
5. A dairy
6. A construction firm
7. A manufacturer of fertilizer
8. An advertising company

E4-4
Obj. 2
Wise Foods Company produces a high-protein food product. The following information relates to the baking department's activities during the month of April:

Beginning work-in-process	600 units	
Units started into production	380 units	
Ending work-in-process	400 units	(100% complete as to material costs 75% complete as to conversion costs)

Prepare a physical flow schedule and a schedule of equivalent units.

E4-5
Obj. 2

Medi-Syrup is a large cough syrup producer. The cough syrup passes through several stages during production. In department B, the following activity was recorded for October:

- Beginning work-in-process on October 1 was 40,000 gallons.
- 20,000 gallons were started into production in department B during October.
- 55,000 gallons were completed and transferred out to department C during the month.
- The gallons remaining in work-in-process in department B at the end of the month were 80% complete as to material costs and 60% complete as to conversion costs.

Prepare a physical flow schedule and a schedule of equivalent units for the department.

E4-6
Obj. 2

Aladdin Company manufactures a product that passes through two processes. The following information was available for the first department for January:

1. Beginning WIP consisted of 6,000 units.
2. Ending WIP consisted of 4,400 units, 100% complete with respect to material costs and 25% complete with respect to conversion costs.
3. 10,000 units started into production in January.

a. Prepare a physical flow schedule for the department.
b. Calculate equivalent units for materials and conversion costs.

E4-7
Obj. 2

Blue Line Company makes two kinds of ink and uses a process costing system. The company's WIP inventory for blue ink on November 1 consisted of 10,000 units. An additional 8,000 units were entered into production in November, and 3,000 units were completed and transferred to finished goods inventory. The 15,000 units in ending WIP inventory were 100% complete as to materials and 80% complete as to conversion costs. Cost information for November for blue ink production is as follows:

Costs in beginning WIP:	
Direct labor	$20,000
Direct materials	10,000
Manufacturing overhead	30,000

The following costs were added during the month:

Direct labor	$ 5,000
Direct materials	14,840
Manufacturing overhead	20,000

a. Prepare a schedule of equivalent units.
b. Compute the cost per equivalent unit for materials.
c. Compute the cost per equivalent unit for conversion.

E4-8
Obj. 3

SPREADSHEET

Holbert Company produces a product that passes through two departments, mixing and heating. The following information relates to activities in the mixing department for June:

Beginning WIP, June 1, 100,000 pounds. Costs in beginning WIP inventory were as follows:

Materials	$20,000
Labor	10,000
Overhead	30,000

Ending WIP, June 30, 50,000 pounds, 100% complete with respect to material costs and 40% complete with respect to conversion costs.

Units completed and transferred out totaled 370,000 pounds. The following costs were added during the month:

Materials	$211,000
Labor	100,000
Overhead	269,500

a. Prepare a physical flow schedule.
b. Prepare a schedule of equivalent units.
c. Compute the cost per equivalent unit.
d. Compute the cost of goods transferred out and the value of the ending WIP inventory.

E4-9 A varnish manufacturer uses process costing. Information concerning a recent production pe-
Obj. 3 riod is as follows:

Units in beginning work-in-process	12,000
Units started into production	16,000
Units completed and transferred out	4,000
Units in ending work-in-process	24,000

The units in ending WIP were 100% complete as to direct materials and 80% complete as to conversion costs.

The following costs were incurred:

Direct materials, beginning work-in-process	$10,000
Direct materials, added during the period	14,920
Conversion costs, beginning work-in-process	2,032
Conversion costs, added during the period	4,000

a. Compute the cost of the units completed and transferred out.
b. Compute the cost of the units in ending WIP.

E4-10 Company X produces organic fertilizer and uses process costing. At the end of 2004, 20,000
Obj. 3 bags of fertilizer were completed. The total value of these completed units was $12,000, of which $8,000 constituted conversion costs.

a. What was the cost per equivalent unit for materials?
b. If 10,000 units remained in WIP at the end of the year (30% complete as to direct materials, 40% complete as to conversion costs), what was the total value of ending WIP?

E4-11 Smith Inc. produces plastic pellets. The following information refers to production activity
Obj. 3 during March:

Beginning work-in-process	5,000 units
Started into production	4,000 units
Completed	3,000 units
Ending work-in-process	6,000 units (60% complete as to direct materials, 75% complete as to conversion costs)

The value of the completed units was $6,000, of which $4,500 was direct materials costs and $1,500 was conversion costs. What was the value of direct materials and the value of conversion costs in ending WIP?

PROBLEMS

If your instructor is using Personal Trainer® in this course, you may complete your assignments online.

P4-1 ### Unit Costs under Process Costing
Obj. 2

Perfect Bread Company makes bread in its midwestern plant. The production process is described as follows:

Flour, milk, yeast, and salt are combined and mixed in a large vat. The resulting dough is transferred by conveyor to a machine that shapes the dough into loaves and places the loaves into pans. The dough is allowed to rise for several hours. Then the pans move slowly through a long oven, where they bake for 45 minutes. When the baked bread emerges from the oven, another machine removes the loaves from the pans. The bread cools for 10 minutes and then is fed through a slicing machine and wrapped.

Last week, Perfect produced 5,000 loaves of bread. The total cost of materials for the week, including ingredients and packaging, was $750. The costs of labor and overhead totaled $1,600. There were no beginning or ending inventories.

Required

A. Compute the unit cost of the 5,000 loaves produced during the week.
B. Perfect does not maintain WIP inventory. What implications does that fact have on the calculations the company must perform?

C. Suppose that Perfect uses the same machinery to produce rolls and buns but that processing those other products is significantly different in terms of cost. What implications would that have on the company's accounting procedures?

P4-2 Cost Calculation Using Process Costing

Obj. 3

SPREADSHEET

Chester Smith manufactures cheddar cheese. The manufacture of cheese requires one period of production and storage in huge vats and two periods of aging in a cellar. The company uses process costing and prepares departmental production reports in each of its two departments, production and aging. All units in beginning WIP are transferred out by the end of that period.

		% Complete at Beginning of Period	
	Units	**Ingredients**	**Conversion**
Beginning work-in-process for production	2,400	90%	60%
Cheese started into production	2,600	0%	0%

Costs in the beginning work in process totaled $230,000 for ingredients and $406,000 for conversion costs. Costs incurred during the period included $258,000 for ingredients and $492,000 for conversion costs. During the period, all the cheese in beginning WIP was completed and transferred to the first aging process. The ending WIP for the cheese will have the same percent completions as the beginning WIP.

Required

A. Compute the cost per equivalent unit for ingredients (round to two decimal places).
B. Compute the cost per equivalent unit for conversion costs (round to two decimal places).
C. Compute the value of the cheese completed and transferred to aging (round to nearest whole dollar).
D. Compute the value of the cheese in ending work in process (round to nearest whole dollar).
E. What is the importance of having these unit costs? How would Chester use this information?

P4-3 Process Costing

Obj. 3

Metallic Company produces steel. At the end of 2005, 10,000 tons of steel I-beams were completed. The total value of these completed I-beams was $20,000,000, of which $17,000,000 constituted conversion costs.

Required

A. What was the cost per equivalent unit for materials?
B. If 200 tons of steel remained in WIP at the end of the year (90% complete as to direct materials, 30% complete as to conversion costs), what was the total value of ending WIP?
C. Metallic determines that if it uses higher-quality inputs, it can reduce the conversion costs. The extra inputs would cost $20 per ton and the conversion costs would decrease by $150,000 per year. Assuming Metallic produces 10,000 tons of steel each year, should it switch to these higher-quality inputs?

P4-4 Job-Order and Process Costing

Objs. 1, 3

SPREADSHEET

Forever Green Co. manufactures artificial Christmas trees. In 2004, Forever Green only produced one type of tree, the Merry Green Tree. However, in 2005 Forever Green introduced a new, top-of-the-line product, the Green As Can Be Tree. The two products require different materials and are manufactured in separate batches. Overhead is allocated on the basis of machine hours. The information from 2005 is as follows:

	Total	**Merry Green**	**Green As Can Be**
Units produced	110,000	100,000	10,000
Materials cost	$4,800,000	$4,000,000	$800,000
Direct labor cost	$9,900,000	$9,000,000	$900,000
Machine hours	130,000	100,000	30,000
Overhead	$1,000,000		*(Continued)*

Required

A. For each product, what is the cost per unit using process costing?
B. For each product, what is the cost per unit using job-order costing?
C. Which costing method is more accurate for this example? Explain.
D. Assume Forever Green decides to use process costing to calculate unit cost. If Forever Green prices its trees at a 30% markup on cost, what would be the unit price for the trees? Is this a good pricing strategy or is one product being overcharged and the other being undercharged?

P4-5   Job-Order and Process Costing

Objs. 1, 3

SPREADSHEET

Call Me manufactures telephones. In 2004, Call Me introduced a stylish telephone with a clear plastic casing, allowing you to see the parts of the phone. The two products are manufactured in separate batches. Overhead is allocated on the basis of machine hours. The information from 2004 is as follows:

	Total	Easy Touch	Clear Phone
Units produced	110,000	80,000	30,000
Materials cost	$640,000	$400,000	$240,000
Direct labor cost	$110,000	$80,000	$30,000
Machine hours	140,000	80,000	60,000
Overhead	$500,000		

Required

A. For each product, what is the cost per unit using process costing?
B. For each product, what is the cost per unit using job-order costing?
C. Which costing method is more accurate for this example? Explain.
D. Assume Call Me decides to use process costing to calculate unit cost. If Call Me prices its phones at a 30% markup on cost, what would be the unit price for the phones? Is this a good pricing strategy or is one product being overcharged and the other being undercharged?

P4-6   Elements of the Departmental Production Report

Obj. 3

Bella Cucina processes olive oil. Information regarding production during October is as follows:

Beginning work-in-process	200 litres
Oil started into production	300 litres
Oil completed	400 litres

The oil in ending WIP was 100% complete as to direct materials and 50% complete as to conversion costs. Costs in beginning WIP totaled $500 for direct materials and $630 for conversion costs. Costs incurred during the month included $750 for direct materials and $900 for conversion costs.

Required

A. Compute the cost per equivalent unit for direct materials.
B. Compute the cost per equivalent unit for conversion costs.
C. Compute the value of the oil completed.
D. Compute the value of the oil in ending WIP.

P4-7   Elements of the Departmental Production Report

Obj. 3

Pet Products manufactures dry dog food. The following information pertains to the month of February:

Beginning work-in-process	5,000 pounds
Started into production	6,000 pounds
Completed	4,000 pounds
Ending work-in-process	7,000 pounds (60% complete as to materials, 40% complete as to conversion costs)

Costs in beginning work-in-process:

| Direct materials | $10,000 |
| Conversion costs | 2,460 |

Costs incurred during February:

| Direct materials | $5,990 |
| Conversion costs | 4,000 |

Pet Products uses a process costing system to value its inventories.

Required

A. Compute the cost per equivalent unit for materials.
B. Compute the cost per equivalent unit for conversion.
C. Compute the value of ending WIP.
D. Compute the value of the units completed.

P4-8

Excel in Action

SPREADSHEET

Assume Music Makers has begun to produce blank CDs for its use and for sale to outside customers. Because the CDs are produced in a continuous process and are identical, management at Music Makers uses process costing. The unit of measure for Music Makers is a box of CDs. Management has gathered the following information from the molding department for January:

Units (boxes) in beginning inventory	10,000
Units (boxes) started into production	40,000
Units (boxes) transferred out	35,000
Units (boxes) remaining in work-in-process inventory	15,000

Cost of beginning inventory:
Materials	$60,000
Conversion	80,000

Costs added during the period:
Materials	$240,000
Conversion	320,000

Ending inventory—percentage of completion:
Materials	50%
Conversion	30%

Required Use a spreadsheet to prepare a production report for the molding department for the month of January. The format should be as follows:

	A	B	C	D	E	F	G	H
1	Departmental Production Report							
2								
3	Ending WIP percentage of completion - materials	0.5						
4	Ending WIP percentage of completion - conversion	0.3						
5								
6		Quantity		Materials	Conversion	Total		Cost
7		Schedule		cost	cost			Reconciliation
8	Beginning inventory	10,000		$60,000	$80,000			
9	Units started	40,000		240,000	320,000			
10	Total units to account for							
11								
12	Transferred out	35,000						
13	Ending work-in-process inventory	15,000						
14	Total units accounted for							
15								
16								
17	Cost per unit							
18								
19								
20								

Sheet1 / Sheet2 / Sheet3 /

(Continued)

The data provided have been entered into the spreadsheet. You should prepare formulas for the shaded cells. Remember to format cells containing dollar values using the **format, cell, currency** commands. Once completed, the spreadsheet can be used to compute costs for later accounting periods. For example, suppose Music Makers reported the following during February:

Units in beginning inventory	15,000
Units started into production	29,000
Units transferred out	39,000
Units remaining in work-in-process inventory	5,000

Assume all production costs remain unchanged from January.

Calculate the unit cost for February. Compare your January and February spreadsheets. What do you observe?

P4-9 Multiple-Choice Overview of the Chapter

1. In a process costing system, costs flow from finished goods to:
   a. work-in-process.
   b. raw materials inventory.
   c. cost of goods sold.
   d. None of the above is correct.

2. In a process costing system, costs flow to finished goods from:
   a. work-in-process.
   b. raw materials inventory.
   c. cost of goods sold.
   d. None of the above is correct.

3. In a process costing system, costs are accumulated by:
   a. department.
   b. individual job.
   c. both job and department.
   d. neither job nor department.

4. Which of the following characteristics applies to process costing but does not apply to job-order costing?
   a. The need for averaging
   b. The use of equivalent units of production
   c. Separate, identifiable jobs
   d. The use of predetermined overhead rates

5. Equivalent units are calculated as follows:
   a. Equivalent units transferred out − Equivalent units in beginning inventory
   b. Equivalent units transferred out + Equivalent units in beginning inventory
   c. Equivalent units transferred out − Equivalent units in ending inventory
   d. Equivalent units transferred out + Equivalent units in ending inventory

6. An artist creates original works on commission. She is likely to use:
   a. job-order costing.
   b. process costing.
   c. actual costing.
   d. normal costing.

7. If a company that uses process costing did not adjust for partially completed units in the equivalent unit calculation, the effect on the cost per equivalent unit:
   a. would be zero.
   b. would be overstatement.
   c. would be understatement.
   d. cannot be determined from the information provided.

8. In process costing, a transferred-in cost is:
   a. a cost transferred from an earlier department.
   b. a cost that has been transferred in from the vendor who has supplied the raw materials.
   c. the cost of the labor that has been added to the process during the month.
   d. the conversion costs that were included in the beginning work-in-process inventory.

9. Listed below are the steps to calculate costs per equivalent unit using a process costing system. The steps are not presented in their proper order. Select the answer that places the steps in the correct order.
   i. divide the total costs for the department by the equivalent units
   ii. account for the flow of physical units
   iii. multiply the cost per equivalent unit by the goods transferred out and the equivalent units in ending inventory
   iv. account for the department's production costs recorded in the work in process
   v. convert the physical units into equivalent units

   The correct order is:
   a. v, iv, i, iii, ii.
   b. i, ii, iii, iv, v.
   c. ii, iv, v, i, iii.
   d. v, ii, i, iv, iii.

10. Companies in the service sector can use:
    a. job-order costing only.
    b. process costing only.
    c. either job-order or process costing.
    d. neither job-order nor process costing.

CASE

C4-1 Deciding on a Costing System

Obj. 1

Lux Electronics is completing a new plant that will begin manufacturing circuit boards within six months. Joan Keyes has just been appointed plant controller and must decide what type of cost accounting system the plant will use. The plant will manufacture many different models of two basic types of circuit boards: made-for-inventory boards and made-to-order boards.

In discussions with marketing and production managers, Joan learns that all models of the made-for-inventory circuit boards are commodity products, similar in design and requiring nearly identical materials, labor, and time in production. The commodity boards are made in very large batches that require long production periods. It is expected that a typical batch of commodity boards will take over a week to manufacture and result in tens of thousands of boards. Batches of commodity boards will be produced on a continuous basis.

The various models of made-to-order boards, on the other hand, are differentiated products. Each model is custom designed, and different models require modifications to the production process and times to manufacture. Differentiated models also require very different materials and varying amounts of labor. Differentiated boards will be manufactured sporadically in small batches of only a few hundred boards.

The two basic types of boards will be made using separate production lines within the same plant facility. Manufacturing overhead will comprise about 60% of the total manufacturing cost. Direct labor, direct materials, most indirect materials, line supervision, equipment costs, and some electrical costs can be traced directly to one of the two lines. Other manufacturing costs, such as those associated with plant supervision, personnel department, cafeteria, and plant office, are common to both lines. Some indirect labor will be shared by both types of boards. Further, some plant overhead costs, such as the cost of heating and air conditioning the plant, are difficult to assign except on some basis such as the amount of square footage occupied by each line.

Lux management expects that the commodity products will compete mainly on cost with low profit margins and will be priced based upon established market prices. Company management is therefore very concerned that the costing system accurately reflect the cost of manufacturing for these products. If commodity product costs are not reasonably accurate, Lux may experience poor cost control and lose money on these products.

Conversely, the differentiated models generally will be priced at cost plus a percentage markup over cost. Company management is therefore concerned that inaccurate product costing will lead to low profit margins if the boards are priced too low or lost sales if the boards are priced too high.

While gathering information before deciding on a costing system, Joan recently sent an e-mail message to Lux's assistant vice president in charge of marketing the new circuit boards, Joe Bally, asking how accurate the unit costs of the boards need to be. Joan is troubled by Joe's response to her question: "I have always assumed that unit costs are accurate to the nearest penny. Why would that not be the case? That's the way you accountants report them."

Joan is eager to get off on the right foot with the other managers involved with the new plant's operations and those engaged in marketing the products it will make. She knows that an inaccurate costing system can lead to poor operating performance. She is concerned that the wrong decisions now will lead to serious problems later.

Required

A. What type of costing system, job-order or process, is most appropriate for the commodity products and why?

B. What type of costing system, job-order or process, is most appropriate for the differentiated products and why?

C. If you recommended different costing systems for the different types of products, what problems do you foresee in using two costing systems?

D. Should Joan use actual or normal costing to assign overhead costs to commodity products? To differentiated products? Is this decision affected by the decisions about job-order and process costing? Explain your answers.

E. What problem do you see with Joe's response to Joan's question about the need for accuracy in unit costs? How should Joan respond to Joe?

Cost Allocation & Activity-Based Management

Cost Allocation: Why is it a problem?

As we discussed in Chapter M4, Erin and Seth have been concerned about selling enough products to cover their manufacturing, administrative, and selling expenses. Moreover, they are beginning to wonder whether their cost accounting system is giving them correct information about the profitability of each product in their line. Seth has observed that some of the most profitable products, according to the cost accounting system, are complex and difficult to make. These products require lengthy machine setup activities and time-consuming special handling during manufacturing. However, selling prices for these products are not significantly more than the less complex products in the line. Seth is puzzled because his intuition tells him greater complexity must mean higher costs. Also, he has noticed products manufactured in large quantities are reported to be more costly to produce than those made in small quantities. Once again, his observation is counter-intuitive. He believes high-volume products must cost less on a per-unit basis than products manufactured in small batches.

Both Erin and Seth agree that material and labor costs are being properly traced to their products. They have established effective accounting procedures that accurately identify the quantity and cost of each material used in the production of a piece of furniture. Also, they have added electronic card readers on each production machine to record the name of the operator, wage rate, number of hours worked, and product produced. Thus, Erin and Seth believe labor is recorded and accurately traced to each product. However, they are not convinced manufacturing overhead is accurately traced to their products. Currently, overhead is attached to products using labor hours as an activity base. As a result, products requiring greater amounts of labor time receive more overhead costs than those requiring lesser amounts of labor time.

FOOD FOR THOUGHT

If you are an advisor to Erin and Seth, how might you help them understand overhead costs? Are there activity drivers that may more accurately connect overhead costs to products? What kinds of activities would you look for in their manufacturing process to help identify better activity drivers? After Seth and Erin discussed his observations, the following conversation took place between Seth, Erin, and their financial advisor, Roberta.

Roberta: *I think you are right about the cost system misallocating overhead costs to products. The overhead allocation base that you currently use, labor hours, is a volume-based activity driver. Volume-based activity drivers typically assign more overhead costs to high-volume products and fewer overhead costs to low-volume products.*

Seth: *Maybe that's our problem. I can't imagine why high-volume products would be more costly to produce. That's like expecting to pay more at Kmart or Wal-Mart because they buy products in high volume.*

Erin: *I agree. We should see some per-unit savings as a result of producing in large batches. For example, if we spend $150 to make a machine changeover, shouldn't we spread that cost over the number of units produced following the machine changeover?*

Roberta: *Yes, of course. Using your example, if you make one product following a $150 machine changeover, the changeover overhead cost per unit is $150. However, if you make ten products, the changeover overhead cost is only $15 per unit. That is called "economies of scale." Your existing cost system doesn't allocate costs in this way.*

Seth: *Ok, that partially explains why some of our product costs don't make sense. At least we can understand why the high- and low-volume product costs may be wrong. But what about the complexity issue?*

Roberta: *We will have to examine your production processes to look for better allocation bases for certain types of overhead. I'm confident that we can design a better cost-allocation system.*

Erin: *Let's do it soon. I believe our cost system may be responsible for our losing a bid to produce furniture for a new children's hospital. If the cost system overstates the cost of high-volume products, we probably overbid the contract. Our main competitor bid lower and won the contract.*

Seth: *That's true. Incorrect product costs can cause problems for us in many ways. What if we set our prices too low for our low-volume, complex products? We may make lots of sales, but these sales may be unprofitable.*

Erin: *We could actually lose money on each sale because our cost system incorrectly allocates overhead costs!*

OBJECTIVES

Once you have completed this chapter, you should be able to:

1 Explain the importance of overhead and how overhead traditionally has been applied to products and services.

2 Identify problems with traditional methods of allocating overhead costs.

3 Describe an activity hierarchy for classifying overhead costs.

4 Explain how activity-based costing works.

5 Explain how service organizations use cost information for decision making.

THE REASONS FOR COST ALLOCATION

OBJECTIVE 1

Explain the importance of overhead and how overhead traditionally has been applied to products and services.

Cost allocation is the process of assigning indirect costs to a product or service. Allocations are necessary because different products or services often share common resources. Companies cannot trace the work of a plant supervisor to a specific product, but the supervisor's work adds to the value of each product the plant manufactures. Hospitals cannot trace the work of a nursing supervisor to a specific patient, but the supervisor's efforts add to the value of the service each patient receives. Thus, companies must allocate the cost of this work. The accuracy of the allocation, and ultimately the usefulness of cost information in decision making, is a function of the allocation method an organization uses.

Recall that costs can be classified according to a number of criteria such as fixed or variable, product or period, and direct or indirect. Direct costs—the costs of direct materials and direct labor—are easy to trace to a specific product. Materials requisition forms, as discussed in Chapter M3, document the type and amount of materials used in production. Direct labor costs are traced to products using time sheets to record the hours workers spend on each job. On the other hand, indirect costs—the costs of materials handling, supervisors' salaries, and depreciation of factory equipment—usually cannot be traced to a particular product or product line. Instead, indirect costs are allocated to products. Allocating overhead costs accurately is especially important in a company that produces multiple products. Without accurate cost information, managers cannot make good decisions about their product mix. For example, managers cannot determine whether to promote or eliminate product A if they cannot distinguish the costs of product A from those of products B and C. When overhead costs increase as a percentage of a company's total manufacturing costs, accurate cost allocation becomes even more important. In this chapter we illustrate overhead allocation using Adventure Trails' sleeping bag manufacturing process.

Adventure Trails: Product Mix and Manufacturing Process

Adventure Trails produces a variety of outdoor products at numerous manufacturing sites. The company makes all of its sleeping bags at one manufacturing location. Because the plant produces only sleeping bags, all materials, labor, and overhead costs incurred in the plant are associated with the sleeping bag product line. The company's products are sold to a variety of retail stores. These stores add a markup and sell the sleeping bags to three different customer groups. A high-volume consumer product, targeted to a broad consumer market, is sold through large discount stores. These bags are the least expensive of Adventure Trails' product line and are designed for light-duty use, such as weekend camping trips or summer camps. The selling price of the high-volume consumer bag is $70. The second product is a medium-volume, three-season bag that sells for $100. This bag can be used in the spring, summer, and fall in moderate climates. The medium-volume bag is constructed from heavier materials than the high-volume consumer bag. This bag typically is sold through specialty outdoor shops to consumers who are more demanding of their outdoor gear. This bag is rugged enough to be used for prolonged outings.

The third bag produced by Adventure Trails is manufactured in very low volume. The selling price of $200 is twice the price of the medium-volume bag and over three times the price of the high-volume bag. This low-volume specialty bag is popular with serious climbers and backpackers who are likely to encounter severe weather conditions. Exhibit 1 summarizes the annual production volume of each type of sleeping bag.

Exhibit 1

Adventure Trails: Annual Production Volume

Product	Annual Production Volume
High-volume consumer bag	12,000
Medium-volume bag	6,000
Low-volume specialty bag	500
Total	18,500

The company uses automated cutting and sewing equipment. As a result, the machine time to cut and sew the material is equal across the three products. Material costs differ because the high- and medium-volume products consume less insulation and demand lower-cost, less technical fabrics. The high-volume and medium-volume bags require the same amount of labor; however, the complexity of the low-volume bag requires more inspection and attention to detail. The low-volume bag represents less than 3 percent of the units produced, but consumes 15 percent of the inspection activities.

Volume-Based Allocation: The Traditional Method

Management accounting techniques for calculating the cost of goods and services have been around a long time. In this section we briefly explore traditional techniques for allocating overhead costs and describe the changes that have taken place in manufacturing since those techniques first were introduced. In a later section, we examine today's business environment, an environment that has forced managers to find new ways to attach overhead costs to products and services.

Background

Many changes have taken place in manufacturing processes and in the information needs of managers since the early days of the industrial revolution in the United States.[1]

---

[1] See H. Thomas Johnson and Robert S. Kaplan, *Relevance Lost* (Boston: Harvard Business School Press), 1991.

Yet methods for allocating costs remain surprisingly similar to those used by early industrialists.

Before the industrial revolution, manufacturing was dominated by cottage industries. Skilled artisans worked in their homes on specialized tasks. Farmers produced wool or cotton. Spinners produced yarn from the wool or cotton provided by farmers and usually were paid according to the pounds of yarn they delivered. Weavers produced cloth from yarn; they usually were paid by the yards of cloth they produced. Finally, tailors were paid a certain amount for each garment they sewed from the cloth the weavers supplied. To obtain a woolen shirt, for example, a merchant would buy wool from a farmer, yarn from a spinner, cloth from a weaver, and the finished product from a tailor. The cost of each shirt was easy to calculate because each transaction was driven by market prices. The unit product cost was simply the sum of the various components purchased at market prices. Exhibit 2 shows how a merchant might have accumulated costs in pre-industrial times.

Exhibit 2

A Pre-Industrial Cost Summary: 150 Woolen Shirts

Paid to Tom Farmer for wool	$ 200
Paid to Harriet Spinner to spin wool into yarn	800
Paid to Cynthia Weaver to weave yarn into fabric	600
Paid to Chris Taylor to sew shirts from fabric	500
Total costs	$2,100
Total shirts produced	150
Cost per shirt ($2,100 ÷ 150)	$14

The industrial revolution brought raw materials, equipment, spinners, weavers, and tailors together in one facility. When factory owners hired craftspeople to work for them, they could not use external market prices to determine the cost of delivering a product. They needed a new source of information. Radical changes in manufacturing practices created new challenges for those who managed textile, steel, and transportation companies.

In the past, engineers (rather than accountants) developed management control techniques in response to changing production methods and competition. They needed to know how much material and labor should be consumed during the production process. As a result, engineers developed standards for material and labor consumption. This information enabled managers to determine whether manufacturing processes were working at peak efficiency. Through bar coding technology and electronic scanning devices, direct material costs (and other information) can be traced from a supplier to a final product. In many factories production workers electronically log on to equipment and identify the product on which they are working. The system records the time spent by an operator on a particular job. Accounting databases also store information, such as hourly wage rates, that are used to determine direct labor costs for products manufactured by a machine operator. However, allocating indirect costs—overhead costs that are not directly related to products or processes—can be troublesome. The problem has been made larger with the growing importance of overhead costs.

At one time, manufacturing overhead was a relatively small part of total manufacturing costs. Direct materials and direct labor costs dominated the costs of production. As a result, a simple process for attaching overhead costs to inventory was developed. That process used activity bases, such as direct labor hours, direct labor costs, or machine hours, to apply overhead costs to products. We considered these allocation bases in our discussion of predetermined overhead rates in Chapter M3.

Today, cost structures have changed. Overhead has become the dominant cost in many manufacturing and service industries. Advances in technology have led to the dramatic growth of support functions, while the number of employees directly involved in production has decreased. Consider what happens when automated equipment replaces skilled machinists. The machinists' wages, a direct labor cost, are replaced with wages of technical support engineers, an overhead cost. As a result of automation, companies incur higher indirect costs for support activities as well as more depreciation on expensive production equipment. Unfortunately, traditional allocation bases often do not yield accurate product costs for individual products in a product line. Traditional cost allocation systems can misallocate costs by attaching too much overhead to some products and not enough overhead to others. Misallocation can create problems for managers who make pricing and product mix decisions. Later in this chapter we consider how inaccurate cost information may mislead decision makers.

Volume-Based Allocation

Suppose Adventure Trails' marketing manager needs cost information to make a pricing decision for a large order of sleeping bags. The accounting department has been asked to prepare a product cost report that identifies overhead, materials, and labor costs for each of the three sleeping bags. Overhead is calculated using a predetermined overhead rate, or burden rate, as discussed in Chapter M3 of this text. The company uses machine hours as its activity base; the estimated machine hours for the year is 9,250. Total manufacturing overhead is estimated at $231,250 for the coming year. The predetermined overhead rate is calculated at $25 per machine hour as follows:

$$\text{Predetermined overhead rate} = \text{Estimated overhead costs} \div \text{Estimated machine hours}$$
$$= \$231,250 \div 9,250$$
$$= \$25 \text{ per machine hour} \qquad 9,250 \div 18,500$$

The company uses automated cutting and sewing equipment. As a result, the machine time required to cut and sew the materials for a sleeping bag is equal across the three products. Each bag requires 0.50 hour of machine time. Using the overhead rate of $25.00 per machine hour, Exhibit 3 illustrates the overhead cost applied to each product. Observe the overhead is $12.50 per product, regardless of sales volume or product characteristics.

Exhibit 3
Overhead Cost per Unit

Product	Machine Hours	×	Predetermined Overhead Rate	=	Unit Overhead Cost
High-volume bag	0.50		$25.00		$12.50
Medium-volume bag	0.50		25.00		12.50
Low-volume bag	0.50		25.00		12.50

Exhibit 4 identifies the materials, labor, overhead, and total cost per sleeping bag. The high-volume, medium-volume, and low-volume bags require materials costing $30.00, $55.00, and $130.00, respectively. Material costs for the three bags are not equal because of differences in the amount of insulation, as well as differences in the quality of the materials. The high-volume and medium-volume bags require the same amount of labor, $20.00 per bag. The complexity of the low-volume specialty bag requires more labor. As shown in Exhibit 4, the labor cost of the high-volume specialty bag is $30.00. The overhead costs calculated in Exhibit 3 are added to the materials and labor costs in Exhibit 4. The resulting costs for the high-volume, medium-volume, and low-volume bags are $62.50, $87.50, and $172.50, respectively. The volume-based cost allocation system allocated equal amounts of overhead to the products because all three products required the same amount of machine time. If some types of overhead costs are not caused by machine hours, the accounting system may inaccurately allocate overhead to products. Inaccurate product costs can result in poor management decisions.

Exhibit 4
Unit Manufacturing
Costs

Product	Unit Materials Cost	+	Unit Labor Cost	+	Unit Overhead Cost	=	Total Unit Cost
High-volume bag	$ 30.00		$20.00		$12.50		$ 62.50
Medium-volume bag	55.00		20.00		12.50		87.50
Low-volume bag	130.00		30.00		12.50		172.50

Strategic Implications

Managers use product cost information to help them make strategic decisions. For example, a strategic decision at Adventure Trails may involve deciding to shift the product mix away from the high-volume consumer sleeping bag to the low-volume specialty bag. Exhibit 5 lists the selling price, manufacturing cost, and profit margin for each sleeping bag in Adventure Trails' product line. Using cost information, managers observe the profit margins vary widely across the product mix. The high-volume consumer bag has a profit margin of $7.50 per unit, while the low-volume specialty bag has a profit margin of $27.50 per bag. Each specialty bag produces roughly four times the profit margin of a consumer-grade bag ($7.50 versus $27.50). The accounting system is indicating the most profitable product (per unit) is the specialty bag.

Exhibit 5
Adventure Trails—
Profitability by Product
Line Using Volume-
Based Costing

Product	Selling Price	−	Manufacturing Cost	=	Profit Margin
High-volume bag	$ 70.00		$ 62.50		$ 7.50
Medium-volume bag	100.00		87.50		12.50
Low-volume bag	200.00		172.50		27.50

How might cost and profitability information influence decision makers? Based on the profit margins reported in Exhibit 5, managers may plan to add more low-volume, specialty products to the product line, while de-emphasizing the high-volume consumer market. The decision would be based in large part on the method Adventure Trails uses to allocate its manufacturing overhead costs. Does the traditional method of cost allocation give Adventure Trails' managers the information they need to make good decisions about the company's marketing strategy? Are they using accurate information to determine the company's product mix and to set sales policies? We answer these questions in the next section.

1 SELF-STUDY PROBLEM

WebTUTOR Advantage

Troy Company is a small manufacturer of high-quality home gardening tools. Each tool in Troy's line is the product of years of ergonomic research and development.

Troy's marketing manager is thinking about changing the selling price of certain products and has asked the company's accountant for a summary of production costs. Information that was gathered from accounting and production records during the past six months is as follows:

Depreciation on plant assets	$50,000
Energy for plant operations	$20,000
Indirect labor costs	$60,000
Manufacturing supplies	$12,000
Direct labor hours worked	10,000

Product A consumes $7 in direct materials and requires one-half hour of direct labor. Direct labor is paid at a rate of $10 per hour.

Required

A. Using the number of direct labor hours as an allocation base, calculate Troy's predetermined overhead rate.
B. Prepare a summary of the manufacturing costs for one unit of product A.

The solution to Self-Study Problem 1 appears at the end of the chapter.

THE PROBLEMS WITH VOLUME-BASED ALLOCATION

OBJECTIVE 2

Identify problems with traditional methods of allocating overhead costs.

The previous section addressed the traditional, volume-based method for allocating overhead costs to products and services. As shown in Exhibit 4, the volume-based system produces questionable results by allocating overhead costs equally to all three products. The bags are different in many ways; therefore, we may conclude they consume manufacturing resources differently. Overhead costs may be inaccurately allocated to the products because the accounting system does not recognize economies of scale or use accurate allocation bases.

Economies of Scale   *less costly / product compared to 24*

Most manufacturing companies could produce hundreds if not thousands of different products by offering many variations of a basic product. For example, an automobile maker that produces an SUV and a sports sedan offers two basic products. What if each vehicle could be manufactured with a V-6 or V-8 engine? What if the company also offered each customer a choice of leather or cloth interior, and left-hand or right-hand steering (for U.S. and British markets)? Suddenly, our two-product company offers 24 unique products. Some of these products will be sold in large quantities, while others will be sold in very small quantities. Most manufacturers limit the number of different products they produce because they want to benefit from economies of scale. *Economies of scale* **are the savings a company realizes in unit costs by spreading fixed overhead costs over a larger number of units.** Making 100 units of the same product is less costly than making 100 different products. A company that is able to produce a product at a lower cost than its competitors has a distinct advantage in the market.

Look again at Exhibit 1. Adventure Trails manufactures 12,000 high-volume consumer sleeping bags per year and just 500 low-volume specialty bags. The company clearly can achieve economies of scale when producing consumer bags that it cannot achieve when producing specialty bags. Cost associated with machine setup activity is a good example. Let's assume setup costs are $800 to prepare the cutting and sewing machines for each new production run. Assume the company produces 4,000 consumer-grade sleeping bags at a time. The company incurs a unit setup cost of $0.20 per bag ($800 ÷ 4,000 bags per batch). Even if Adventure Trails produced all 500 specialty bags in a single batch, the unit cost of the machine setup would be $1.60 ($800 ÷ 500 bags per batch), a cost of eight times that of the consumer bags.

One of the problems with the traditional method of allocating overhead costs is that it does not take into account economies of scale. Recall that all overhead costs (including machine setup costs) are divided by an activity base, such as machine hours.

The predetermined overhead rate spreads all overhead to products without regard for economies of scale. The savings Adventure Trails realizes from its high-volume products are not reflected in the unit cost of overhead. Instead, all of the company's products, high-volume, medium-volume, and low-volume, are allocated the same overhead cost per unit.

Accurate Allocation Bases

A second problem with traditional cost allocation is the allocation base, the activity used to determine the predetermined overhead rate. Think about activities that cause manufacturing overhead in Adventure Trails' sleeping bag plant. When raw materials are received, workers unload, inspect, move, and store them. During the manufacturing process, workers move work-in-process to various production areas and prepare machines to make different products. Quality control inspectors draw samples and test the products to ensure products meet specifications. Supervisors assist production workers with any problems that arise during a production run. The supervisors, quality engineers, materials handlers, and machine setup operators are paid wages, consume supplies, and use assets that depreciate. Each of these costs is classified as manufacturing overhead.

Now think about the way Adventure Trails allocates its overhead costs. The company uses machine hours as its activity base. How do machine hours relate to the costs of receiving materials, moving work-in-process, and performing quality inspections? Does the number of machine hours explain those costs? Does the use of machine hours produce those costs? No, they do not.

Critics of the volume-based allocation method argue that it distorts unit overhead costs. Remember, volume-based cost allocation systems assume manufacturing overhead costs vary in proportion to an allocation base. Examples of traditional allocation bases include direct labor hours, machine hours, or direct labor dollars. If product A uses 10 machine hours and product B uses five machine hours, product A is allocated twice as much overhead as product B. Managers who want to cut overhead costs in their departments are given little guidance by a cost accounting system that assumes all overhead costs result from machine hours, direct labor hours, or direct labor dollars. Adventure Trails' managers cannot reduce the number of machine hours and expect overhead costs in the receiving department to go down. Those costs simply are not affected by machine hours.

To understand the shortcomings of volume-based allocation, consider the manufacturing environment that was in place when the accounting system was designed. Overhead costs were a much smaller percentage of total costs in years past. Thus, managers were not as concerned with precise allocations. In addition, accounting systems were developed to help companies put a value on inventory in their published financial statements. External auditors were concerned that the value of total inventory on the balance sheet was correct. They did not care if the cost per unit of one product was overstated while the cost of another was understated. Today's information needs are dramatically different, however. Accountants are developing better ways of allocating overhead to products.

A HIERARCHY OF OVERHEAD ACTIVITIES

OBJECTIVE 3

Describe an activity hierarchy for classifying overhead costs.

Recognizing that overhead costs are not always related to volume, Robin Cooper, a management accounting professor, developed a hierarchy of overhead costs. **The** *overhead hierarchy* **is a framework that explains how overhead costs change with various activities.** Exhibit 6 illustrates the hierarchy consisting of four categories: unit level, batch level, product level, and facility level.

Exhibit 6

Cooper's Hierarchy: Allocating Costs by Activity

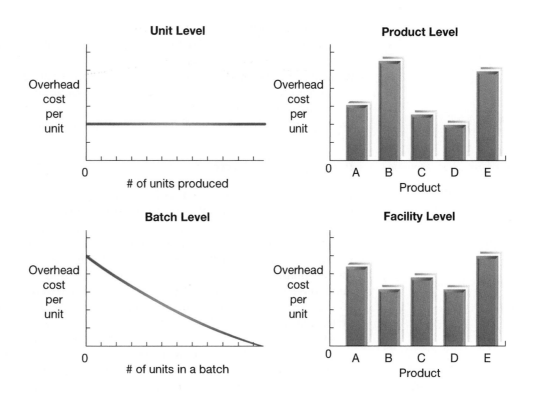

Unit-Level Costs

Unit-level costs behave like variable costs. Remember that variable costs change in total with the number of units produced but do not vary per unit with changes in volume. For example, the costs of manufacturing supplies and utilities are a function of production volume. Traditional allocation bases, such as machine hours, direct labor hours, and direct labor dollars, are appropriate for allocating unit-level costs. Suppose the cost of electricity to run a machine is $20 per hour. If the machine produces 100 units in one hour, the cost per unit is $0.20 ($20 ÷ 100 units). If the machine runs for 10 hours, the total cost of electricity is $200 ($20 × 10 hours), but the cost per unit is still $0.20 [$200 ÷ (100 units per hour × 10 hours)]. Traditional volume-based allocation systems attach overhead to products as if all costs were unit level. Some costs are allocated appropriately using machine hours or direct labor hours, but other costs are not. The overhead hierarchy offers managers three additional kinds of allocation bases.

Batch-Level Costs

Batch-level activities address one of the volume-related problems of traditional cost-allocation systems. By using a single activity base to allocate overhead costs, volume-based systems ignore economies of scale. They assume the cost of setting up a machine is the same per unit whether 10 units or 10,000 units are manufactured following the setup. Certain activities, such as raw materials handling and machine setups, are associated with each batch of production without regard to the number of units in a batch. To measure the overhead costs of a product accurately, batch-level costs must be allocated to specific production runs as follows:

Batch-level cost per unit = Total activity cost ÷ Units in the batch

If a machine setup costs $500 and the company produces 10 units in the batch, the setup cost per unit is $50 ($500 ÷ 10 units). If the company produces 1,000 units in the batch, the setup cost per unit is just $0.50 ($500 ÷ 1,000 units).

The batch-level cost per unit decreases as the number of units in the batch increases. Conversely, the batch-level cost per unit increases as the number of units in the batch decreases. Think of batch-level activities as a fixed cost. A batch-level cost is not influenced by the number of units produced following the batch-level activity. Batch-level overhead allocations capture economies of scale. Products manufactured in large batches typically benefit from an activity-based costing system, because the cost per unit will be lower. Products manufactured in small batches typically are allocated more overhead per unit.

Product-Level Costs

Product-level costs relate to a specific family of products. For example, suppose a company that manufactures brake systems for automobiles and trucks sells their products through automotive parts stores. The company also has a contract to provide brake systems for government vehicles. The governmental contract requires quality control tests on one unit out of each 50 produced to ensure the system complies with engineering specifications. The quality control test destroys the product. Assume the company has numerous quality control procedures in place to ensure the safety of its products. However, tests conducted on government products are significantly more rigorous than those performed on products sold through automotive stores. The cost of more rigorous quality testing should be allocated only to the governmental product family.

Another example is a design change for a product that currently is in production. Usually a design change affects newer product lines. Newer products often are redesigned to make them easier to assemble. Mature products typically have been in production for a long period of time. As a result, the manufacturing process is stable and does not require many engineering change orders. The cost system should not attach the cost of an engineering design change to well-established products that do not need modification. To do so may lead a marketing manager to over-price a mature product and under-price a new one because overhead costs were erroneously assigned.

Facility-Level Costs

Facility-level overhead costs include all overhead activities that are not unit level, batch level, or product level. Accurately allocating facility-level costs is difficult. Unfortunately, not all costs can be associated directly with a product. For example, the salary of a security guard does not relate directly to a specific unit, batch, or family of products. Therefore, facility-level costs tend to be allocated arbitrarily. Cost drivers of facility-level costs include the percentage of value-added, or the percentage of time a product remains in the manufacturing plant. The logic behind both of these measures is that products remaining in process longer, or requiring more value-added activities, probably consume greater levels of indirect manufacturing overhead costs.

---

2 SELF-STUDY PROBLEM

WebTUTOR Advantage

Highlands Machining Company produces bicycle gears from high-quality stainless steel. Assume you are an assistant department manager helping to develop a new cost-allocation system. Because you understand the weaknesses of the traditional volume-based method, you have been asked to classify some of the company's costs using Cooper's hierarchy. You have been given a list of four types of costs:

- Lighting costs for the production areas
- Raw materials movement costs: the wages and supplies consumed in moving raw materials from inventory storage to a production area (Materials are moved each time a different production order begins.)
- The costs of cooling the metal-cutting equipment (Metal-cutting equipment requires constant cooling during the production process. The cooling costs include

the costs of liquid coolant, pumps and hoses, and the energy to power the cooling system.)
- Research and development expenses incurred to develop a new product

Required Classify each cost as a unit-level, batch-level, product-level, or facility-level cost, and explain your classifications.

The solution to Self-Study Problem 2 appears at the end of the chapter.

Case In Point

http://albright.
swlearning.com

Learn more about ABC

Many larger firms use enterprise-wide accounting software, such as SAP. These software packages integrate and account for all key activities throughout a company. For example, when goods are received, workers at the loading dock enter various information such as product identification, cost, and quantity received. The accounting system automatically updates the inventory and accounts payable accounts. Since 1997, activity-based costing has been an important component of SAP. Costs and driver information are recorded in the software package and are used to calculate the cost of activities, products, and services. In addition, SAP helps managers predict future costs using activity-based budgeting.

Source: Osheroff, M. "The 123s of ABC in SAP," *Strategic Finance*, November 2002.

ACTIVITY-BASED COSTING

OBJECTIVE 4

Explain how activity-based costing works.

Activity-based costing (ABC) **allocates overhead costs to a product using activities required to produce the product.** The allocation bases are known as cost drivers. These cost drivers should relate to activities performed while manufacturing a good or providing a service. For example, machine hours do not drive the costs of moving materials from a loading dock into storage or from storage to a production area. The number of movements does. So a company might choose the number of material movements as a basis for attaching the costs of moving materials to products. The number of direct labor hours does not drive the costs of admitting patients to a hospital, but the number of admissions does. Thus, admitting costs could be allocated to patients by an allocation base such as the number of admissions.

Exhibit 7 illustrates the conceptual design of an ABC system. In an ABC system, cost allocation involves two stages. In the first stage, overhead costs such as depreciation, indirect salaries, and utilities are allocated to activity pools according to the type of activity carried out in each pool. *Activity pools* **are collections of costs that relate to an activity.** Exhibit 7 illustrates four kinds of activity pools, volume-based, setup, handling and inspection, and general overhead. Let's use the machine setup pool as an example to understand how costs flow through an ABC system. A pool for machine setups would include the cost of supplies, indirect labor, energy, and depreciation of equipment used in setup activities. A common method of allocating costs to a pool is in proportion to time or effort. Suppose 60 percent of an engineer's time is spent supervising machine setups and 40 percent is spent supervising material movements. The engineer's salary and benefits would be allocated in those proportions to a setup pool and a materials movement pool. Supplies, energy, and depreciation costs would be assigned to pools in a similar manner. They are pro-rated to cost pools based on an activity's proportionate consumption of a cost.

In the second stage, costs are allocated from activity pools to a cost object, such as a good or service. For example, all costs in the setup pool would be divided by the number of setups to determine the cost per setup. Alternatively, if setups vary in complexity, the allocation base could be the number of setup hours. In that case, output from the setup pool would be expressed in terms of a setup cost per hour. In Exhibit 7, setup costs are allocated to Adventure Trails' three products using the number of setups as an activity base. Notice the direct materials and direct labor costs are traced directly to products that consume the resources.

Exhibit 7 Conceptual Design of an ABC System

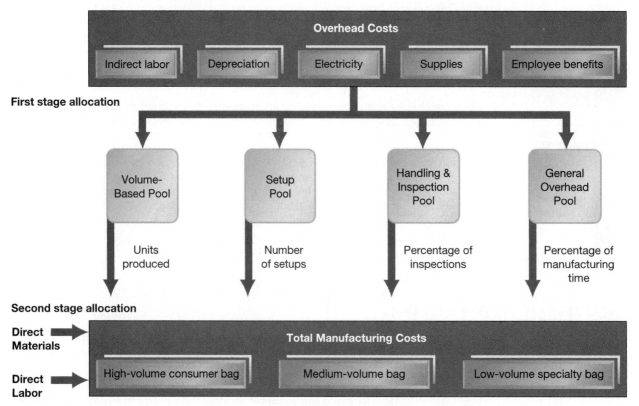

Using Exhibit 7 as a guide, we calculate activity-based costs for Adventure Trails' three products. Exhibit 8 classifies Adventure Trails' total overhead costs into pools using Cooper's hierarchy and identifies activity bases used to attach the costs to products. Assume the company used a variety of surveys and interviews to determine the proportion of costs that should be allocated in the first stage to each activity pool. Exhibit 8 presents the results of the first-stage allocation process. Total overhead costs of $231,250 have not changed from the amount used to calculate the predetermined overhead rate in our earlier example of $25 per machine hour. Exhibit 8 simply classifies the $231,250 of overhead into pools to gain a better understanding of the activities that cause overhead. Instead of using one predetermined overhead rate based on machine hours, Adventure Trails is using four allocation bases: units produced, number of setups, percentage of inspections by product line, and percentage of manufacturing time. Each base is the denominator in an overhead rate calculation. We also add direct materials and direct labor as before, to complete the product cost calculation.

Exhibit 8 Adventure Trails' Overhead Classified by Cooper's Hierarchy

	Overhead Costs	Activity Bases
Unit level	$ 90,000	Units produced
Batch level (setups)	8,800	Number of setups
Product level (handling and inspection)	60,000	Percentage of inspections by product line
Facility level	72,450	Percentage of manufacturing time
Total overhead costs	$231,250	

Before we can assign overhead to products, we need additional process information. Exhibit 9 reports Adventure Trails' batch sizes, number of setups, cost per setup, percentage of handling and inspections, handling and inspection costs, and percentage of manufacturing time. These values are used to calculate the activity-based cost of producing the three sleeping bags. For example, the high-volume bag is produced in batches of 4,000 units. During the year, the high-volume bag is produced three times (number of setups = 3). Observe that Adventure Trails makes three batches of the high-volume and medium-volume bag and five batches of the low-volume bag per year. This production schedule helps match production with demand to minimize inventory carrying costs. The cost to prepare the machines for each batch or production run is $800. Notice the setup cost does not vary in total with the batch size. Management estimates the high-volume bag consumes 60 percent of the handling and inspection activities. Thus, the cost of handling and inspection for this product line is $36,000 ($60,000 × .60). Finally, the high-volume bag consumes 50 percent of the manufacturing time.

Exhibit 9 Adventure Trails: Machine Hours, Batches, and Handling and Inspection by Product

Product	Batch Size	Number of Setups	Cost per Setup	Percentage of Handling & Inspections	Handling and Inspection Costs	Percentage of Manufacturing Time
High-volume bag	4,000	3	$800	60%	$36,000	50%
Medium-volume bag	2,000	3	800	25%	15,000	40%
Low-volume bag	100	5	800	15%	9,000	10%
Total						

Exhibit 10 illustrates how to calculate the unit cost of each product using activity-based costing. The first two columns report the materials and labor costs that were given in Exhibit 4. Traditional and ABC unit costs for materials and labor costs are the same. However, the ABC calculation uses four overhead allocation bases, rather than one. Exhibit 10 illustrates the amount of unit-level, batch-level, product-level, and facility-level costs allocated to each product.

Notice the unit-level cost is equal across the three product lines. Unit-level costs are calculated by dividing the total unit-level costs of $90,000 (shown in Exhibit 8) by the total units produced (shown in Exhibit 1). Unit-level costs shown in Exhibit 10 are calculated as follows:

Unit-level costs = Unit level costs ÷ Total units produced
= $90,000 (Exhibit 8) ÷ 18,500 units (Exhibit 1)
= $4.86

Next, batch-level costs are calculated by dividing the setup cost of $800 by the number of units manufactured in a batch. Notice the batch size varies across the three products. The high-volume, medium-volume, and low-volume products are manufactured in batches of 4,000, 2,000, and 100 units, respectively (see Exhibit 9). Batch-level costs shown in Exhibit 10 are calculated as follows:

Batch-level costs
High-volume bag = Setup costs ÷ Batch size
= $800 ÷ 4,000
= $0.20

Medium-volume bag = Setup costs ÷ Batch size
= $800 ÷ 2,000
= $0.40

Exhibit 10 Adventure Trails: Activity-Based Cost by Product*

Product	Unit Materials Cost	Unit Labor Costs	Overhead				Total
			Unit Level	Batch Level	Product Level	Facility Level	
High-volume bag	$ 30.00	$20.00	$4.86	$0.20	$ 3.00	$ 3.02	$ 61.08
Medium-volume bag	55.00	20.00	4.86	0.40	2.50	4.83	87.59
Low-volume bag	130.00	30.00	4.86	8.00	18.00	14.49	205.35

*A slight rounding error would occur if unit-, batch-, product-, and facility-level overhead was added for each product and multiplied by the units produced.

Total overhead from Exhibit 8	$231,250	
Total overhead assigned using ABC (see calculation below)	231,175	
Difference due to rounding	$ 75	

Product	Units Produced Annually (Exhibit 1)		Overhead Costs per Unit					Total Overhead Assigned Using ABC
			Unit	Batch	Product	Facility		
High-volume bag	12,000	×	($4.86	+ $0.20	+ $3.00	+ $3.02)	=	$132,960
Medium-volume bag	6,000	×	($4.86	+ $0.40	+ $2.50	+ $4.83)	=	75,540
Low-volume bag	500	×	($4.86	+ $8.00	+ $18.00	+ $14.49)	=	22,675
								$231,175

$$\text{Low-volume bag} = \text{Setup costs} \div \text{Batch size}$$
$$= \$800 \div 100$$
$$= \$8.00$$

Product-level costs are allocated according to the amount of resources each type of product consumes. For example in Exhibit 9, production engineers estimate the high-volume bag demands 60 percent of the handling and inspecting activities. The medium-volume and low-volume bags demand 25 percent and 15 percent, respectively. The ABC system allocates resources to products according to the activities demanded by them. Product-level costs shown in Exhibit 10 are calculated as follows:

Product-level costs

$$\text{High-volume bag} = (\text{Inspection \& handling costs} \times \text{Percentage of inspections by product line}) \div \text{Units produced}$$
$$= (\$60,000 \times .60) \div 12,000$$
$$= \$36,000 \div 12,000$$
$$= \$3.00$$

$$\text{Medium-volume bag} = (\text{Inspection \& handling costs} \times \text{Percentage of inspections by product line}) \div \text{Units produced}$$
$$= (\$60,000 \times .25) \div 6,000$$
$$= \$2.50$$

$$\text{Low-volume bag} = (\text{Inspection \& handling costs} \times \text{Percentage of inspections by product line}) \div \text{Units produced}$$
$$= (\$60,000 \times .15) \div 500$$
$$= \$18.00$$

Facility-level costs are allocated to products according to the percentage of manufacturing time consumed by each type of product. Managers recognize that facility-level cost allocation is less precise than the other levels of overhead activity. However, they believe products consume resources according to the length of time they remain in the manufacturing process. Thus, the accounting system allocates facility-level overhead to products as a percentage of manufacturing time. Exhibit 9 reports management's estimates of the percentage of manufacturing time by product. Facility-level costs shown in Exhibit 10 are calculated as follows:

Facility-level costs

High-volume bag = (Facility-level costs × Percentage of manufacturing time) ÷
 Units produced
 = ($72,450 × .50) ÷ 12,000
 = $36,225 ÷ 12,000
 = $3.02

Medium-volume bag = (Facility-level costs × Percentage of manufacturing time) ÷
 Units produced
 = ($72,450 × .40) ÷ 6,000
 = $28,980 ÷ 6,000
 = $4.83

Low-volume bag = (Facility-level costs × Percentage of manufacturing time) ÷ Units
 produced
 = ($72,450 × .10) ÷ 500
 = $7,245 ÷ 500
 = $14.49

Exhibit 10 reports the total cost of producing the high-volume, medium-volume, and low-volume bag is $61.08, $87.59, and $205.35, respectively. How do the ABC values compare with those calculated using the traditional volume-based system? Exhibit 11 compares Adventure Trails' unit product costs using traditional volume-based allocation with those of activity-based costing. The exhibit suggests the volume-based method overstated the unit costs of the high-volume consumer sleeping bags and understated the unit costs of the low-volume specialty sleeping bags. The ABC system produced unit costs that were 2.3 percent less than traditional costs for the high-volume products. The low-volume product costs using the ABC system were 19 percent greater than those reported by the traditional system. The cost of medium-volume sleeping bags remains unchanged.

Exhibit 11 Volume-Based Costs per Unit versus Activity-Based Costs per Unit

Allocation Method	High-Volume Bag	Medium-Volume Bag	Low-Volume Bag
Volume-based (Exhibit 5)	$62.50	$87.50	$172.50
ABC (Exhibit 10)	61.08	87.59	205.35
Percentage change (ABC − volume-based) ÷ volume-based	−2.3%	0%	+19%

Why do the two allocation methods yield different unit costs? More specifically, why does the ABC method yield different unit costs for the high- and low-volume products? The unit-level overhead costs listed in Exhibit 10 do not explain the differences in unit product costs among the three products. The unit-level costs ($90,000) are divided by the total number of units produced (18,500). The resulting unit cost is $4.86 per bag, regardless of the type.

The batch-level costs explain much of the difference in unit costs across Adventure Trails' product line. Remember that batch-level costs address economies of scale. Here production volume makes a difference. Each batch of products requires a machine setup costing $800. The batch-level costs of consumer sleeping bags is $0.20 per product (setup cost ÷ batch size = $800 ÷ 4,000 = $0.20), while the batch-level costs of the specialty bags are $8.00 per unit (setup cost ÷ batch size = $800 ÷ 100 = $8.00). By not recognizing economies of scale, traditional allocation penalizes high-volume products and subsidizes low-volume products.

The product-level costs also help explain some of the variation in unit costs across the three types of sleeping bags. The exhibit also reports the profit margin using a traditional volume-based allocation method (from Exhibit 5). The ABC system tells managers that the specialty bags use far more handling and inspection resources than the other bags. Handling and inspections add to the unit costs of the specialty bags. Customers who purchase these bags depend on an extremely high level of quality. Thus, we are not surprised that the low-volume bags consume so many handling and inspection activities. What about the facility-level costs? Adventure Trails assigned them as a percentage of total manufacturing time. Thus, products that remain in process longer are allocated more overhead costs.

Exhibit 12 reports the selling price, activity-based manufacturing cost, and profit margin for each sleeping bag. What are the implications of our findings for Adventure Trails' management? First, specialty bags are not as profitable as the company's managers had thought. In fact, the company is losing money on them. The traditional volume-based system produced costs resulting in cross-subsidy. **Accountants use the term** *product cross-subsidy* **to describe a situation in which one product subsidizes (supports) the reported costs of another.** The high-volume consumer bags are subsidizing the low-volume specialty bags. Although Adventure Trails can sell the specialty bags for a higher price, the cost of producing those bags in low volume is extremely high. A long-run strategy of adding other specialty bags to the company's product line could be disastrous.

Of course, a company's long-run strategies for marketing and production are based on more than manufacturing costs. A company may choose to offer a full line of products because retailers would rather order from one manufacturer than from six. Also, a company may wish to establish its reputation as an expert, full-line producer. A well-designed system for allocating costs to activities and products cannot answer all of management's questions. It can give the basic information managers need to chart the future course of their company.

Exhibit 12 Adventure Trails—Profitability by Product Line Using Activity-Based Costing and Traditional Volume-Based Allocations

Product	Selling Price	−	ABC Manufacturing Cost	=	ABC Profit Margin	Traditional Profit Margin
High-volume bag	$ 70.00		$ 61.08		$ 8.92	$ 7.50
Medium-volume bag	100.00		87.59		12.41	12.50
Low-volume bag	200.00		205.35		(5.35)	27.50

COST ALLOCATION AND DECISION MAKING IN THE SERVICE SECTOR

OBJECTIVE 5

Explain how service organizations use cost information for decision making.

This chapter used the term *cost object* to refer to the product of a manufacturing process. ABC allows us to define cost objects very broadly. Services offered by organizations also may be classified as cost objects. ABC is used by service organizations to understand the cost of its core and noncore activities. **The primary activities a service organization carries out are its** *core activities*; **its supporting activities are called noncore activities.**

The core activity of a public school is education, teaching students subjects such as math, chemistry, biology, history, a foreign language, and English. To carry out that primary activity, schools rely on a host of noncore activities. For example, most school districts offer bus transportation to students. What are the costs of providing that supporting service? How do the people who manage school districts use that cost information?

Some school districts outsource their transportation services. In other words, they contract with a company that provides bus services for the district. For those districts the direct costs of transportation are defined in their contract with the bus company. For districts that provide their own transportation services, the direct costs of those services include the costs of buses, tires, fuel, drivers' wages and benefits, repairs, maintenance, and insurance. In both cases, there are the indirect costs of the administrators who set busing policy and develop the bus routes. A school district could have several different activity pools that capture the costs of delivering transportation services.

How do school districts use activity-based costing in their decision making? For some, that information is a basis for the decision to outsource transportation services. By focusing on their core activity (education) and reducing noncore activities (such as busing), some districts have reduced the costs of supporting activities and applied the savings to core areas.

Case In Point

http://albright.
swlearning.com
....
Learn more about the
electric utility industry.

Customers who demand specialized services, greater supply choice, and lower costs are transforming the once-regulated electric utility industry into a competitive industry. The regulated electric utility industry provides consumers with a package of services, including the generation, transmission, and distribution of energy and a host of energy management services (metering, billing, dunning, and energy services). However, with the advent of competition, individual consumers will decide whether they want to purchase a package of services from a single vendor or whether they want to purchase different services from a variety of vendors. Compounding the situation, new organizations will enter markets where monopolies once dominated. When the transition to competition is complete, consumers will be able to shop around for energy services.

The electric utility industry's transition to competition has managerial accounting implications because questions persist about what parts of the energy services processes actually generate value. After the transition is complete, old cost accounting models for the electric utility industry may not be relevant. Under the old system, profitability is only measured on the corporate level. Public service commissions limit public utilities' revenues to prevent these organizations from taking advantage of their customers. However, in the competitive environment, managers must consider what is happening within individual departments because companies will provide services beyond the traditional package. This is where the value-added problem comes into play. One tool that has been proposed to combat the problem is activity-based costing. Under the new system, revenue will be generated four ways—electricity sales to individual customers, buying from and selling to other utility networks, selling and delivering other synergistic products and services to customers through the network distribution channel, and leasing capacity to other companies that can use this distribution channel (leasing space on electric poles to telephone companies so the telephone companies may hang their wires). Electric utilities may use activity-based costing to control overhead, to determine the cost of utility services, to compare revenues and costs for probability analysis, and to prepare strategic plans for the future in each profit center.

Source: Johnson, Scott. "The ABCs of the Electric Utility Industry," *Management Accounting* (November 1998): 25–28.

3 SELF-STUDY PROBLEM

WebTUTOR Advantage

Athena Company produces high-quality hand tools for wood-working. The company is conducting an ABC study. You are a manager at Athena, and you have been given the following information:

Costs and Activity Rates by Overhead Category

	Unit Level	Batch Level	Product Level	Facility Level
Estimated cost	$50,000	$20,000	$10,000	$20,000
Estimated activity	500 machine hours	80 materials movements	25 engineering drawings	(applied as a percentage of unit-, batch-, and product-level costs)

You have been asked to calculate the overhead costs associated with products A and B. The units produced of and the resources consumed by products A and B are as follows:

	Units Produced	Machine Hours	Materials Movements	Engineering Drawings
Product A	40	40	1	0
Product B	10	10	2	2

Required

✳ A. Calculate the:
   1. cost per machine hour.
   2. cost per materials movement.
   3. cost per engineering drawing.
   4. predetermined overhead rate for facility-level costs.
B. Determine the total overhead costs and the unit overhead cost of products A and B.
C. Explain why the overhead costs of the two products are different.

The solution to Self-Study Problem 3 appears at the end of the chapter.

REVIEW

SUMMARY of IMPORTANT CONCEPTS

1. The volume-based method of allocating costs to products was developed at a time when overhead costs were a relatively small portion of product costs.
   a. The method uses a single activity base and a single predetermined overhead rate to allocate overhead costs to products.
   b. Throughout a period, overhead is allocated to products by multiplying the actual amount of the activity base used (machine hours, for example) by the predetermined overhead rate.
   c. Today, overhead costs make up the largest portion of a company's product costs.

2. With the growing importance of overhead costs has come a need for greater accuracy in the allocation of those costs.
   a. The traditional method ignores volume diversity; it makes no allowance for economies of scale.
   b. By limiting a company to a single activity base, the traditional method of cost allocation distorts costs.

3. Cooper's hierarchy of costs is based on allocation by activity rather than volume.
   a. Unit-level costs are like variable costs; they are constant per unit but change in total with the number of units produced.
   b. Batch-level costs are like fixed costs; they vary per unit but are constant in total. These costs recognize economies of scale.
   c. Product-level costs are incurred in manufacturing a product or product family.

    d. Facility-level costs are not related to a particular unit or batch or family of products; they are necessary to sustain a company's overall operations.

4. Activity-based costing allocates overhead costs on the basis of the activities that are necessary to produce a product.
    a. In the first stage of the allocation process, a company assigns overhead costs to activity pools and chooses an activity base (a cost driver) for each pool.
    b. In the second stage, costs are assigned to a cost object, such as a good or service.

5. Activity-based costing gives managers of manufacturing and service companies the accurate cost information they need to make planning decisions.

DEFINE

TERMS and CONCEPTS DEFINED in this CHAPTER

activity pool   (M109)
activity-based costing   (M109)
core activities   (M114)

economies of scale   (M105)
overhead hierarchy   (M106)
product cross-subsidy   (M114)

SELF-STUDY PROBLEM SOLUTIONS

SSP5-1   A. Troy's predetermined overhead rate is $14.20 per direct labor hour:

Predetermined overhead rate = Estimated overhead costs × Estimated direct labor hours
= ($50,000 + $20,000 + $60,000 + $12,000) ÷ 10,000
= $142,000 ÷ 10,000
= $14.20 per direct labor hour

   B. The unit cost of product A is $19.10:

Direct material costs per unit	$ 7.00
Direct labor costs per unit	5.00
Manufacturing overhead costs per unit ($14.20 × 1/2 hour)	7.10
Total cost per unit	$19.10

SSP5-2 Lighting costs for the production areas are a facility-level cost. The lighting costs are not associated with any specific unit, batch, or family of products; they are related indirectly to all of the company's products.

    Raw materials movement costs are a batch-level cost because raw materials are moved each time a new batch of product is placed into production.

    The costs of cooling metal-cutting equipment are a unit-level cost. Those costs are a function of the number of hours the equipment is operating. When the equipment is idle, the cooling system also is idle.

    The research and development expenses incurred to develop a product are a product-level cost. Those expenses can be associated with one product or product family. Although GAAP require that research and development costs be expensed in the period in which they are incurred, internal decision makers often treat those costs as overhead.

SSP5-3 A.
    1. The cost per machine hour is $100 ($50,000 ÷ 500 hours).
    2. The cost per materials movement is $250 ($20,000 ÷ 80 moves).
    3. The cost per engineering drawing is $400 ($10,000 ÷ 25 drawings).
    4. The facility-level predetermined overhead rate is .25 [$20,000 ÷ (50,000 + $20,000 + $10,000)].

B.

	Product A		Product B
Machine hours:			
40 hours × $100 per hour	$4,000		
10 hours × $100 per hour			$1,000
Movements:			
1 movement × $250	250		
2 movements × $250			500
Engineering drawings:			
0 drawings × $400	-0-		
2 drawings × $400			800
Subtotal (cost to date)	$4,250		$2,300
Facility-level cost subtotal × .25	1,063		575
Total overhead costs	$5,313		$2,875
Units produced	40		10
Overhead cost per unit	$133		$288

Economies of scale are evident in the lower cost per unit for product A, which is produced in a quantity four times that of product B. Also, product A was produced in one large batch versus two small batches of product B (one movement versus two). In addition, product A does not consume engineering services. Product A might be a mature product whose manufacturing process is stable and requires little attention.

Thinking Beyond the Question

Cost Allocation: Why is it a problem?

In the chapter opening scenario, you learned that Erin and Seth's cost accounting system allocates costs using direct labor hours as an activity driver, or allocation base. The owners believe costs allocated to some products are too high, while costs allocated to other products are too low. Why might the activity hierarchy developed by Robin Cooper help Erin and Seth more accurately allocate costs to their products? How does the activity hierarchy differ from traditional cost system design?

QUESTIONS

Q5-1
Obj. 2
Last month when his father, Nathan, retired, Norm Gregory became president of his family's manufacturing business. The company produces camping and mountain-climbing equipment that is sold in specialty shops throughout the country. At a retirement party, Nathan told his son, "I started this business 40 years ago producing a single model of tent. Now we make five models of tents and hundreds of other items! Our plant has been updated with the most modern equipment and manufacturing technologies." How do you think the company's expanded product line and technological advances have affected its allocation of manufacturing overhead?

Q5-2
Obj. 2
Quantro Enterprises has invested heavily in automated equipment over the past 10 years. In that time Quantro has installed materials handling systems and automated flexible manufacturing systems. All of these changes have allowed Quantro to reduce its labor costs by more than 35% while increasing production by 150%. Quantro has been applying overhead to products based on direct labor hours. What impact do the changes in Quantro's manufacturing

process have on its application of its overhead? What impact on overhead assignment is created by economies of scale? Explain your answers.

Q5-3
Objs. 2, 3

Denver Materials Company operates a recycling center that separates metals and then sells them to steel mills. The company uses large machinery to sort, move, and crush the metals. Denver's business throughout the year is uneven, in large part because the collection of recyclable materials varies greatly from month to month. In some months, the plant is slow. In others, supervisors have to authorize overtime to work the mountains of materials that the company receives. Management charges overhead costs to each job based on total machine hours for each batch processed. Explain how changes in volume and activity can distort the cost of each batch.

Q5-4
Objs. 2, 3

T-Bar Industries, Inc., manufactures radios and compact disc players. For years T-Bar's production process has been labor-intensive; its primary production cost has been the wages of many direct laborers who assemble components along its production lines. Management at T-Bar is considering an investment in new technology that will automate 80% of the production process. The new machinery and the computer systems to operate it cost hundreds of thousands of dollars. T-Bar historically has allocated manufacturing overhead on the basis of direct labor hours. What change in cost structure should T-Bar expect if the company decides to invest in the new technology? What problems will that change in cost structure create? Explain your answer.

Q5-5
Obj. 3

Leslie Dunn is the controller of Demarco Company. Demarco produces six separate product lines in a single plant. Each line has a product manager who is accountable for the production costs of that line. Leslie is preparing for a meeting with the product managers to discuss the facility-level costs that will be allocated to each product line over the next year. She knows that the product managers are going to argue over these costs and the method of allocation to their product lines. Why would facility-level charges be a source of disagreement among the managers?

Q5-6
Obj. 4

Minor Medical Company is a manufacturer of blood pressure monitors, catheters, surgical instruments, and other medical products. In each of the past five years, Minor has added approximately 10 new products. Although its product line has become more diversified and its manufacturing processes more complex, Minor continues to apply overhead costs using a single activity base—direct labor hours. Explain why activity-based costing would benefit this company.

Q5-7
Obj. 4

Alice Glidden is the chief financial officer of Brown Ribbon Industries, Inc., a manufacturer of gift wraps, ribbons, and party supplies. A local certified management accountant has suggested that Alice implement an ABC system. The accountant told Alice that activity-based costing would not "overload" high-volume products with overhead costs. What did the accountant mean?

Q5-8
Objs. 1, 5

Jose Glass had a car accident last month and spent a night in the hospital. The bill came yesterday, and when he looked it over he noted that he had been charged $7 for a single aspirin. Believing it was a clerical error, Jose called the hospital and was told that the charge was correct. The person he spoke to in the billing department said that part of the charge was "overhead allocation" that included purchasing, handling, and other support-related costs. How does overhead allocation affect the cost of aspirin?

Q5-9
Objs. 2, 5

The law firm of Menard and Baker specializes in civil litigation. The overhead costs of operating the office are charged to clients as an administrative surcharge. The surcharge is based on attorneys' hours. The managing partner of the firm, Cynthia Menard, has noticed that clients who require extensive legal service often complain about the administrative surcharge. After reviewing costs and time sheets, Cynthia has determined that administrative costs usually are not a function of attorneys' hours, but of the time incurred by administrative personnel. How does volume affect the allocation of administrative costs? What changes should the firm consider? Why?

Q5-10
Objs. 4, 5

Apply the concepts of activity-based costing to an airline flight in which each passenger is a "unit of product." Give examples of unit-, batch-, product-, and facility-level costs.

EXERCISES

If your instructor is using Personal Trainer® in this course, you may complete your assignments online.

E5-1   Write a short definition of the terms listed in the *Terms and Concepts Defined in this Chapter* section.

E5-2   Average production costs representing three industries are as follows:

Obj. 1

	Paper	**Chemicals**	**Computer Manufacturing**
Raw materials	$ 5,000,000	$ 9,240,000	$1,440,000
Labor	5,000,000	1,760,000	560,000
Overhead	10,000,000	11,000,000	6,000,000
Total	$20,000,000	$22,000,000	$8,000,000

    a. Calculate the material, labor, and overhead costs as a percentage of total production costs.
    b. Explain how overhead costs differ from material and labor costs.
    c. Explain why overhead costs might be significantly higher than labor and material costs in these industries.

E5-3   Traditional cost systems allocated overhead costs using a single allocation base, such as direct labor hours, direct labor costs, or machine hours. These simple allocation systems were appropriate because overhead costs typically did not represent a significant proportion of total manufacturing costs. Overhead costs were traced to a product as shown:

Obj. 1

Assume the traditional method of overhead allocation is no longer relevant because of changes in manufacturing technology and support-related overhead costs. Significant activities and allocation bases are as follows:

Activity	**Allocation Base**
Quality control testing	Number of quality tests
Machine setup	Number of setups
Machine run time	Machine hours

Prepare a sketch to illustrate the application of overhead using relevant allocation bases. Then, explain why cost systems evolved in response to changes in manufacturing systems.

E5-4   Round Tire Company (RTC) uses a predetermined overhead rate to apply assembly overhead to products. Tire assembly is a labor-intensive process that requires one person to build a tire from a variety of components including inner liner, tread, and sidewall. Thus, the allocation base used by RTC is direct labor hours. During the month of June, RTC incurred overhead costs in the amount of $750,000 and worked 12,000 hours. Estimated assembly overhead for the year is $9,000,000 based on 120,000 labor hours. (*Hint:* Refer to Chapter M3 to review over- and underapplied overhead concepts.)

Obj. 1

    a. Calculate the predetermined overhead rate used by RTC.
    b. Determine the amount of assembly overhead to be applied to production during June.
    c. Is the overhead overapplied or underapplied? By how much?
    d. What is the effect of the overapplied or underapplied overhead on the financial statements before they are adjusted?
    e. Does the traditional allocation base, direct labor hours, make sense for RTC? Why or why not?

E5-5

Objs. 1, 2, 4

Auto Detail Company manufactures two basic types of products: vinyl and metallic adhesive-backed striping used by automobile manufacturers. The company traditionally has allocated manufacturing overhead to its product line using direct labor hours as a cost driver. More recently, the company has explored the use of two additional cost drivers as it evolves into an activity-based costing system. The following data summarize overhead application drivers and rates for the traditional and activity-based cost system.

Traditional: $175 per direct labor hour
Activity-based cost:
$120 per direct labor hour
$345 per machine changeover
$100 per inspection

	Per Production Run	
	Vinyl Striping	**Metallic Striping**
Direct labor hours	10 hours	8 hours
Batch size	180 rolls	65 rolls
Number of inspections	0	3

a. Calculate the overhead cost per roll to manufacture the vinyl striping and the metallic striping using the traditional method.
b. Calculate the overhead cost per roll to manufacture the vinyl striping and the metallic striping using the activity-based cost method.
c. Explain the cause or causes of the differences in cost for each product when using traditional and ABC methods.

E5-6

Objs. 1, 3, 4

Birmingham Cycle Manufacturing Company uses three activity pools to assign costs to products. Each activity pool has a unique cost driver, or activity base, used to apply overhead costs to products.

Activity	**Cost Driver**	**Estimated Overhead Costs**	**Estimated Activity Level**
Materials handling	Number of batches	$ 60,000	500 batches
Machine setup	Number of setups	150,000	300 setups
Machine operations	Machine hours	500,000	4,000 machine hours

Calculate the predetermined rate for each activity. Then, classify each activity as unit level, batch level, product level, or facility level.

E5-7

Objs. 1, 4

Second-stage activity drivers in an activity-based costing system allocate costs from activity pools to products. Cost system designers often make choices among a variety of potential drivers. Listed below are three cost pools and two potential allocation bases for each pool.

Activity Pool	**Driver #1**	**Driver #2**
Machine setup activities	Number of setups	Number of setup hours
Materials handling	Number of batches handled	Number of hours handling materials
Quality inspection	Number of inspections	Hours of quality inspection

Choosing the appropriate cost driver can make the difference between accurate and inaccurate product cost calculations.

a. For each activity, specify the circumstances that would favor the use of cost driver #1. Explain your rationale.
b. For each activity, specify the circumstances that would favor the use of cost driver #2. Explain your rationale.

E5-8

Objs. 1, 4

Taylor Sweets, Inc., produces a popular brand of chocolate candies. The company's manufacturing process is labor-intensive: Chocolate, sugar, and other ingredients are measured by hand, blended in a large mixer, and then heated. Next, the mixture is spread by hand into molds. When the mixture is cool, the candies are removed from the molds, placed in paper cups, and then boxed. All of these steps are done by hand.

(Continued)

Tim Gabet, Taylor's president, is considering a modernization project that would significantly increase the amount of candy the company can produce. Under his plan, the measuring and mold-filling procedures would be automated, and a single machine would remove the candies from the molds, wrap them individually, and box them.

Tim is excited about the possibility of increasing production volume but realizes that automation can be very expensive. If automation would increase Taylor's overhead cost more than $0.04 per unit, Tim knows he will have to reject the project. Taylor allocates overhead costs to production based on direct labor hours. Estimates of production volume and overhead costs under the current process and the automated process are as follows:

	Current Process	Automated Process
Production volume in units	50,000	450,000
Total overhead costs	$15,000	$162,000

a. Calculate the overhead cost per unit for the current process and the automated process.
b. Given Tim's target increase, should he go ahead with the automation project?
c. What is the minimum number of units (rounded to the nearest unit) that Taylor would have to produce at the expected level of overhead cost per unit to accept the project?
d. Suppose that Taylor allocates overhead on the basis of machine hours instead of direct labor hours. Would the project be accepted or rejected? Explain your answer.

E5-9

Objs. 2, 4

Complete the following sentences with the appropriate term(s) from the chapter.

1. To calculate a single plant-wide _____, a company does not have to separate indirect manufacturing costs into individual cost pools.
2. To calculate a burden rate, a company must estimate its indirect costs and a(n) _____.
3. _____ are the costs that sustain a company's general manufacturing facilities.
4. Activity-based costing more accurately traces the costs of production by shifting overhead costs from _____ goods or services to _____ goods or services.
5. _____ costs are incurred each time a batch of goods is processed.
6. Cost _____ is a problem when a company uses a single basis for allocating the costs of _____.
7. Using activity-based costing, overhead costs that vary in direct proportion to the number of units produced would be _____ costs.
8. Using activity-based costing, the costs of engineering a particular product line would be _____ costs.
9. The objective of activity-based costing is to associate as many costs as possible with specific _____.
10. The savings a company realizes by spreading fixed manufacturing overhead costs over a large number of products is called _____.

E5-10

Obj. 3

Classify the following activities as unit level, batch level, product level, or facility level according to the activity-based costing hierarchy developed by Cooper.

- Machine setups between batches of two different products
- Quality control inspections for specialty items
- Hours of machine run-time
- Plant security
- Refrigeration and special handling of certain inventory items in a pharmaceutical warehouse
- Hospital admissions (Assume admission costs do not vary according to length of stay.)
- Engineering costs for product redesign

E5-11

Obj. 4

Managers often make decisions about keeping or dropping a product after evaluating the profitability of each product in the product line. Bimini Products, Inc., recently completed an activity-based costing study. Management wishes to compare the results with the cost data produced by their traditional cost system. Product data are as follows:

SPREADSHEET

Product	Selling Price	Cost Traditional	Cost ABC
A	$100	$ 80	$ 65
B	150	120	140
C	130	80	90

Product A is produced in high volume using a stable process that does not require excessive support activities. Product B demands high levels of support activities and is produced in low volume. Product C is produced in moderate volume.

a. For each product compute:
   1. Profit margin, traditional
   2. Profit margin, ABC
   3. Percentage change in profit margin as follows: (profit margin ABC − profit margin ÷ profit margin traditional)
b. What kinds of product line decisions might your calculations support?

E5-12
Obj. 4

U-Build-It produces carpentry tools for homeowners. The company recently completed an activity-based costing study and is attempting to understand the results. The following table summarizes sales volume and overhead cost information for a sample of five products. In some cases, the activity-based costing study produced costs below the traditional product cost. In other instances, the activity-based cost study produced costs above the traditional product cost.

Product	Volume	Overhead Cost Traditional	Overhead Cost Activity-Based
A	Moderate	$100	$112
B	Moderate	75	75
C	High	87	73
D	Low	160	232
E	High	95	70

a. Compute the percentage change for each product using the formula (activity-based cost − traditional cost) ÷ traditional cost.
b. Sort the percentages calculated in requirement (a) from largest to smallest and prepare a bar graph summarizing the results.
c. What relationship do you observe between volume and cost?
d. How might you explain this relationship?

E5-13
Obj. 4

Good Earth Bakery traditionally has allocated manufacturing overhead to its product line using raw material weight as a cost driver. Assume the dough and other ingredients for one loaf weigh one pound. While evolving into an activity-based costing system, Good Earth explored the use of different cost drivers. The following data summarize overhead application drivers and rates for the traditional and activity-based cost systems.

Traditional: $0.95 per pound
Activity-based cost:
   $75 per oven hour
   $50 per blender setup (The blender is cleaned before each batch of product.)

	Whole Wheat Bread	Raisin Bread
Oven time	1/2 hour	3/4 hour
Batch size	100 loaves	50 loaves

a. Calculate the overhead cost per loaf to manufacture whole wheat bread and raisin bread using the activity-based cost method.
b. Identify the types of overhead cost pools (unit, batch, product, or facility) added by the Good Earth Bakery.
c. Explain why the traditional and ABC methods produce different results.

E5-14   Data from the accounting and production records of Hasgrow Company are as follows:

Obj. 4

	Product 1	Product 2	Product 3
Units per batch	150	200	60
Direct materials per unit	$50	$75	$90
Direct labor per unit	$20	$15	$21
Number of setups	2	5	3
Machine hours per unit	0.10	0.15	0.20
Number of engineering change orders associated with each product	0	1	2

Activity Costs	
Cost per setup	$300
Cost per machine hour	600
Cost per engineering change order	250

Managers wish to understand material, labor, and activity costs of each product to help guide their pricing decisions.

Compute the cost per unit of product 1, product 2, and product 3. Why do the costs differ across the three products?

E5-15   Refer to the facts as shown in E5-14. The cost system designers at Hasgrow selected the num-
Obj. 4   ber of setups as a cost driver to allocate setup costs to products. As an alternative, they could allocate setup costs to batches based on the number of setup hours for each changeover.

    a. What assumption did the cost system designers make when they chose number of setups rather than number of setup hours to allocate machine setup costs?

    b. Which alternative might result in easier (and perhaps less costly) data collection?

E5-16   Gonzalez Manufacturing traced the following levels of activity to the products it manufac-
Obj. 4   tured during the first quarter of this year:

Activity Pool	Cost per Activity	Product A	Actual Level of Activity Product B	Product C	Product D
Machine setups	$50/setup	500 setups	600	800	650
Inspection	$15/inspection	3,165 inspections	2,155	780	3,000
Receiving	$100/receipt	420 receipts	175	655	500
Factory	$20/machine hour	19,250 hours	14,300	21,500	15,950
Number of units		20,000	17,500	25,000	22,500

Determine the total overhead cost charged to each product for the quarter. In addition, calculate the overhead cost per unit.

E5-17   America Outback is a rapidly growing service company that offers wilderness backpacking,
Obj. 5   canoeing, and rock-climbing expeditions at numerous locations across the United States. Management wants to gain a better understanding of overhead costs associated with various expeditions. The following is a brief overview of the company's activities and costs:

- The company provides all equipment, except personal items, for the expeditions. Overhead cost, which consists mainly of depreciation, varies according to the difficulty level of the expedition. More sophisticated and expensive gear is required for expeditions of greater difficulty.
- Each expedition requires one guide. However, enrollments vary by expedition to ensure a proper guide-to-participant ratio.
- Most of the expeditions are offered on National Park Service property. Thus, America Outback pays a park entrance fee for each participant.
- America Outback hires experienced naturalists as route planners who also schedule treks and order necessary provisions.

    a. Identify the cost objects (products or services) associated with the operations of America Outback. Explain why you selected these services as cost objects.

    b. Does a service company, such as America Outback, require materials, labor, and overhead to deliver its product? Explain.

E5-18

Obj. 3

Refer to the facts presented in E5-17.

a. Identify each cost as a unit-level, batch-level, product-level, or facility-level overhead cost.
b. Justify your answer.
c. How might America Outback use more accurate cost information in planning future expeditions?

PROBLEMS

If your instructor is using Personal Trainer® in this course, you may complete your assignments online.

P5-1   **The Ethics of Overhead Allocation**

Obj. 1

Justin owns a small factory that produces buttons for the garment industry. He wants to buy a new machine and has applied to a bank for financing. The loan officer has asked for operating statements for the past year. The company's net income has not been very good over that time, and inventory has grown substantially. Justin is concerned that the bank is not going to be as optimistic as he is about future sales and the company's ability to reduce its inventory.

Yesterday, Justin had the following conversation with Beth, the company's controller.

Justin: You know that I've applied for a bank loan and that the bank wants copies of our operating statements for the last twelve months.
Beth: I can have those ready for you in an hour.
Justin: I'd like you to make some changes before you prepare those statements, Beth.
Beth: What sort of changes?
Justin: I want you to increase our predetermined overhead rate by 30% and then recalculate the inventory figures and last year's income statement using the new rate. Also, move my salary and our office rent into the manufacturing overhead pool. I'll need those statements first thing in the morning.

Required

A. What effect would the change in predetermined overhead rate have on the company's inventory values?
B. What effect would the reclassification of Justin's salary and the office rent have on the company's product costs?
C. Do you agree with the changes Justin is asking for? What parts of the financial statements would reveal Justin's changes to the loan officer?

P5-2   **Predetermined Overhead Rates Using Volume-Related Drivers**

Objs. 1, 2

Mallory Chemical Corporation produces two products: A and B. The company's expected factory overhead costs for the coming year are as follows:

Overhead Category	Estimated Costs
Utilities	$ 300,000
Indirect materials	150,000
Indirect labor	50,000
Depreciation	100,000
Materials handling and storage	200,000
Repairs and maintenance	200,000
Supplies	180,000
Insurance	120,000
Other	50,000
Total	$1,350,000

Its expected levels of production activity are as follows:

	Product A	Product B	
Machine hours	35,000	15,000	= 50,000
Direct labor hours	20,000	25,000	= 45,000
Number of units produced	10,000	5,000	
Direct materials used, in pounds	75,000	125,000	*(Continued)*

All labor costs $10 per hour; materials cost $1.80 per pound for product A and $2.40 per pound for product B.

Required

A. Calculate the predetermined overhead rate based on direct labor hours and based on machine hours.
B. Calculate the unit cost of each product if overhead is applied on the basis of direct labor hours.
C. Calculate the unit cost of each product if overhead is applied on the basis of machine hours.
D. Compare the unit costs you have just calculated. Why does the choice of an activity base affect unit cost? What implications would the selection of an activity base for allocating overhead have on managerial decisions? What factors should management consider in choosing an activity base for assigning costs?

P5-3   **Overhead Allocation: Traditional Method**

Obj. 2

Cast-Rite Company produces a variety of cast iron pipe products used by municipalities for water and sewer systems. Though many different product configurations are possible, products primarily differ on the basis of pipe diameter, length, and bell type (the type of fitting applied to the end of a pipe to enable it to be attached to other pipes).

The process begins when molten iron is poured into molds on the casting line. Casting machine setups are required between batches of different product types because casting molds must be changed between runs of pipes with different diameters. Following the casting process, all pipes are annealed (heated) in an oven to strengthen the pipe. Finally, some pipe products are lined on the inside with a thin concrete mixture.

Management is concerned that the traditional cost system, which assigns overhead using a predetermined rate based on a cost per ton, may not produce accurate results. Use the following information to prepare your responses to P5-3 and P5-4.

Product	Length	Diameter	Weight	Batch Size	Lined
A	10 ft.	12"	1,000 lbs.	50 units	yes
B	10 ft.	15"	1,200 lbs.	100 units	no
C	15 ft.	12"	1,500 lbs.	100 units	yes
D	15 ft.	15"	2,000 lbs.	150 units	yes
E	10 ft.	20"	2,300 lbs.	5 units	yes

The old cost system applied overhead at a rate of $407.68 per ton. Cast-Rite pays $200 per ton for scrap iron used in the melting process. Labor cost is insignificant and is included in the overhead rate.

Required

A. Using the traditional method of applying overhead, determine the cost for each product manufactured by Cast-Rite.
B. What can you learn about overhead consumption across the product classes?
C. What are the weaknesses of the traditional approach from a decision maker's perspective?

P5-4   **Overhead Allocation: Traditional versus ABC**

Obj. 4

Refer to the facts presented in P5-3. The activity-based costing study revealed the following revised cost estimates:

Predetermined overhead rate based on cost per ton	$300
Cost to change molds between batches of product	700
Cost to apply cement lining (per pipe)	100

Note: Total costs for traditional and ABC are the same ($191,875).

Required

A. For each product, calculate the activity-based cost of production.
B. Prepare a table with four headings as follows: Product, Traditional Cost, Activity-Based Cost, Percentage Change (defined as follows: [ABC cost − traditional cost] ÷ traditional cost). Complete the table using your calculations from P5-3 and part (A) of this problem.

C. What can you learn about overhead consumption across the product classes? Explain.

D. What types of decision alternatives might management consider in light of the new cost information?

P5-5
Obj. 3

The Conceptual Design of an ABC System

Auto-Plex produces windshields for a major international automobile manufacturer. The company is under increasing pressure to reduce costs. Thus, management authorized an activity-based costing study to help understand how various activities contribute to overhead costs. The following is an excerpt from the ABC study:

Cost Pool	Explanation
Glass melting oven	Silica (sand) is melted in a continuous flow, resulting in glass sheets used by all windshield types. The major cost is the natural gas consumed on an hourly basis.
Machine setup	Windshield molding machines must be reconfigured between runs of different products.
Special inspection	Radio antennas are molded into certain types of windshields. These specialty windshields require extra handling and inspection activities.
Supervision	Each shift employs three supervisors who support all manufacturing processes and products within the plant.

Required

A. Using Exhibit 7 as a model, construct a diagram of a two-stage cost allocation system for Auto-Plex.

B. Identify each activity pool in your model as unit level, batch level, product level, or facility level.

P5-6
Obj. 4

The Two-Stage Allocation Process

Refer to the information provided in P5-5. Assume the company employs six individuals who set up the equipment between runs of different products. Setup crew members devote approximately 90% of their time to physically changing machine specifications and molds to accommodate a different product. In addition, they spend approximately 10% of their time on special inspection activities. Crew salaries and related setup costs total $200,000 per year. Engineering studies indicate natural gas and other melting oven costs approximate $700,000 per year. The company employs two full-time quality control engineers, who each earn $65,000 annually. These engineers are responsible for special inspections (75% of their time) but also work with setup crews (25% of their time) to help minimize scrap rates. The company's three supervisors each earn $70,000 per year.

Required

A. Using your diagram from P5-5 as a guide, allocate the costs to each activity pool.

B. For each activity pool in your diagram, identify a reasonable cost allocation base (second-stage cost driver). Justify your answer.

P5-7
Objs. 1, 4

Multiple Cost Drivers: Calculating Predetermined Overhead Rates

Randall Foundry uses four activity pools to assign costs to its products. Each pool has its own cost driver, the activity base used to calculate and apply overhead costs. Last year Randall prepared the following estimates of overhead costs and activity levels for the first quarter of this year:

Activity Pool	Cost Driver	Estimated Overhead Costs	Estimated Activity Levels
Machine setups	Number of setups	$560,000	2,500 setups
Inspection	Number of inspections	$245,000	10,000 inspections
Receiving	Number of receiving reports	$21,300	1,200 receiving reports
Machine operations	Machine hours	$590,000	73,750 machine hours

(Continued)

Assume product A was produced in three 50-unit batches over the course of the first quarter. Additional information relevant to product A is as follows:

3 setups

150 units

Number of inspections	9
Number of receiving reports	3
Number of machine hours	150

Required

A. Calculate the predetermined overhead rate for each activity pool.
B. Calculate the overhead cost per unit to produce product A.
C. Randall is planning to run smaller batch sizes in an effort to reduce its inventories. The flow of raw materials will not be affected by that decision. What concerns should management address before it actually implements the plan?

P5-8 Using the Activity Hierarchy to Classify Activities

Obj. 3

Dynamic Products, Inc., manufactures a wide variety of products in its plant in Macon, Georgia. Management has identified the following manufacturing and administrative activities:

1. Special equipment is used to add a protective finish to various products.
2. Purchase orders are issued to acquire raw materials.
3. Factory managers run training programs in quality control for new employees.
4. Machine setups are necessary for each batch of goods produced.
5. Janitors clean the offices and the plant floor each evening.
6. Warehouse personnel pull the stock needed for production and move the materials to the plant floor.
7. Receiving clerks inspect incoming materials and prepare receiving reports.
8. Quality control inspectors test each batch of goods before it is stored or shipped.
9. Payroll clerks process the factory workers' time cards and prepare weekly paychecks for distribution.
10. Engineers develop new-product specifications and redesign existing products as needed.

Required

A. Classify each of the activities listed as a unit-level, batch-level, product-level, or facility-level activity.
B. Identify a cost driver for each of the activities that could be used to apply costs to Dynamic's products.
C. For each activity, identify one or more traceable costs.
D. Explain how the hierarchy provides insights that affect decision making.

P5-9 The Conceptual Design of an ABC System—An Internet Company

Objs. 3, 5

Web-books.com is an Internet company that sells books on the World Wide Web. The president of the company authorized an activity-based costing study to understand the cost of various activities that are driving overhead at Web-books.com. Selected activities include:

- Web site maintenance—costs do not vary as a function of sales volume.
- Retrieving the order from the Web site and locating the product—costs vary as a function of order size (the number of books per order) because more time is required to fill larger orders.
- Specialty handling—unique packaging is required for oversized (large) products.
- Standard packaging—costs do not appear to vary by the number of books in the order, but are constant across all orders.

Required Using Exhibit 7 as a model, construct a diagram of a two-stage cost allocation system for Web-books.com. Identify each activity pool in your model as unit level, batch level, product level, or facility level.

P5-10 The Two-Stage Allocation Process

Objs. 4, 5

Refer to the information in P5-9. Assume the company employs three systems engineers at an annual salary of $75,000 each. The engineers devote 85% of their time to Web site maintenance and 15% to improving technical aspects of order retrieval. Eight people who pick orders consume supplies and equipment-related overhead costs of $20,000 each. Interviews during the activity-based costing design process indicated these employees devote 90% of their time to picking, but occasionally help with specialty handling requirements of large orders (10% of their time). Depreciation on equipment and tools for special handling activities total $70,000 per year. The packaging department employs four people who devote approximately 70% of their time to standard packaging activities and 30% to specialty handling. Each person consumes $15,000 annually in support-related overhead costs.

Information is presented in tabular form as follows:

Resource	Number	Resource Consumption	Activity Allocation
Systems engineers	3	$75,000 each	85% Web site maintenance
			15% order retrieval
Order pickers	8	$20,000 each	90% order retrieval
			10% specialty handling
Depreciation		$70,000	100% special handling
Packaging	4	$15,000	70% standard packaging
			30% specialty handling

Required

A. Using your diagram from P5-9 as a guide, determine the costs to be allocated in the first stage to each activity pool.
B. For each activity pool in your diagram, identify a reasonable cost allocation base (second-stage cost driver).
C. What factors might cost system designers consider when choosing among numerous potential cost drivers for cost-allocation purposes?

P5-11 Cost Allocation: Service Industry

Objs. 1, 4, 5

Franklin County Bank has a commercial loan department that makes loans to businesses that meet the bank's strict criteria. The department is staffed by eight loan officers. Each loan officer can grant loans up to a certain amount without the approval of the bank's lending committee. Loans that exceed that limit must be approved by the lending committee, which meets weekly.

The commercial loan department incurs significant costs administering and monitoring commercial loans. Among those costs are the wages of the credit analysts who review borrowers' financial statements; the wages of the administrative personnel who prepare loan packets; filing fees for security agreements; office rent; depreciation expense on office equipment, computers, and furniture; and fees for credit reports.

Anita Andrews, vice president of commercial loans, wants to allocate and collect administrative costs from borrowers in the form of a processing fee.

Required

A. What cost drivers could the bank use to allocate its overhead costs of processing commercial loans? What factors affect the choice of an activity base?
B. What estimates would be necessary to establish a processing fee if all costs are included?
C. How could activity-based costing be used to allocate overhead costs in the commercial loan department?

P5-12 Overhead Allocation: A Service Environment

Objs. 1, 4, 5

The East State Veterinary Clinic provides veterinary services for small domestic animals. Three certified veterinarians and four technical assistants work at the clinic. The clinic has three separate areas of operations: examinations, surgeries, and laboratory tests. The technical assistants help with exams and surgery and perform the majority of laboratory tests.

The clinic allocates administrative and operating overhead to the three service areas using a single rate based on the veterinarians' direct labor hours. Information about services and costs for the past fiscal quarter are as follows:

(Continued)

	Veterinarians' Direct	
Area of Operations	Labor Hours	Number of Patients
Examinations	1,200	800
Surgeries	200	60
Laboratory tests	100	600
Total	1,500	

Overhead Item	Cost
Maintenance and supplies, exam rooms	$ 8,500
Depreciation, surgical equipment	6,000
Surgical supplies	2,000
Depreciation, laboratory equipment	2,000
Laboratory supplies	4,000
Total	$22,500

Required

A. Calculate the clinic's predetermined overhead rate based on the activity in the most recent quarter, and use that rate to allocate costs to each service area.

B. How does the use of a single activity base and rate disproportionately allocate costs among the three service areas? Explain your answer.

C. Calculate separate overhead rates for each of the three service areas using the veterinarians' direct labor hours incurred in each area as the activity base. Why do the rates differ for each service area? Calculate the overhead cost (rounded to the nearest dollar) that would have been allocated to each area using the three separate rates.

P5-13   ABC—A Conceptual Design

Objs. 3, 4, 5

The Clearwater SCUBA Shop, owned and operated by Floyd Ridges, offers three types of services: retail sales, SCUBA instruction, and dive boat charters. As with many service organizations, the three elements of Floyd's business are not independent. Floyd earns revenue from SCUBA instruction and sales of gear to students. He uses the boat for open-water dives that are part of a student's SCUBA training. In addition, Floyd transports experienced divers to dive sites for a fee. After a student is certified, Floyd believes the dive boat generates additional equipment sales and dive charter revenue as newly certified divers acquire advanced skills and equipment.

Floyd wants to understand the costs associated with each business segment, retail sales, SCUBA instruction, and dive charters. Other than cost of goods sold for retail sales, he believes the dive boat is the single most expensive service he provides. Major costs include fuel, insurance, depreciation, dockage fees, interest costs, and wages for the mate who assists divers while on board. Floyd also carries extra liability insurance for higher risk certifications such as cave diving and wreck exploration.

Required

A. Identify the cost objects in Floyd Ridges' company.

B. What problems will Floyd experience as he undertakes the cost allocation?

C. The overhead costs associated with the dive charter operation may be classified according to a cost hierarchy. Using Clearwater's business description, identify an example of the following:

- Unit-level cost
- Batch-level cost
- Product-level cost
- Facility-level cost

P5-14   Excel in Action

Music Makers manufactures CDs for software and music companies. It classifies its products into two types: data CDs and music CDs. Because of the greater quality demands of music CDs, the manufacturing process requires greater quality control and longer manufacturing time for this product type. Music Makers produces 500,000 CDs per month. Eighty percent of the production is data CDs.

SPREADSHEET

Management of Music Makers has become concerned about the price it is charging for its products and the profitability of each product line. It sells its products for $2.40 per unit, regardless of product type. This price is higher than some of the company's competitors are charging for data disks, and Music Makers has begun to lose orders to these competitors. Because profits have been slipping a bit, management is worried. It has decided to analyze its production costs using activity-based costing.

For purposes of the analysis, the company has collected the following manufacturing overhead information. Unit-level costs include depreciation, $70,000; utilities, $51,000; and supplies and repairs, $8,500. Unit-level costs will be allocated on the basis of machine hours. The manufacturing process requires 100,000 machine hours per month. Data CDs require 60,000 hours, and music CDs require 40,000 hours. Batch-level costs include materials handling, $63,000; quality inspections, $41,000; and machine setups, $35,000. The company runs 50 batches per month. Half of the batches are for data CDs and half are for music CDs. Product-level costs include special quality inspections for music CDs of $25,000 per month. Facility-level costs include plant management costs of $30,000 per month and are attached to products using the number of units produced as an allocation base.

Required

A. Use Exhibit 10 in this chapter as an example and prepare a calculation of activity costs for Music Makers using a spreadsheet. Costs should be separated into unit, batch, product, and facility levels. Use cell references and formulas as appropriate to prepare the spreadsheet. The analysis should use the following format.

	A	B	C	D	E	F	G	H
1	Activity - Based Cost by Product							
2								
3		Units	Machine					
4	Product	Produced	Hours	Batches				
5								
6	Data							
7	Music			(129,500 × .6)/400,000				
8								
9				Per	Overhead Costs			
10	Product	Materials	Labor	Unit	Batch	Product	Facility	Total
11	Data	.92	.20	.19				
12	Music	.92	.20	.52				
13								
14		Selling	Unit	Unit				
15		Price	Cost	Profit				
16	Data	2.4						
17	Music	2.4						

Direct materials cost is $0.92 per unit. Direct labor cost is $0.20 per unit.

B. Compare the unit production costs of each product with the unit selling price. What actions should Music Makers' management take as a result of this analysis? How would your analysis differ if total machine hours used in production had been 80,000 per month and 70,000 of these hours had been for data CDs?

P5-15 Multiple-Choice Overview of the Chapter

1. Overhead allocation based on volume alone:
   a. is a key element of activity-based costing.
   b. systematically overcosts high-volume products and undercosts low-volume products.
   c. systematically overcosts low-volume products and undercosts high-volume products.
   d. must be used to prepare external financial reports.

(Continued)

2. Using activity-based costing, overhead costs are accumulated in:
    a. a single, company-wide pool.
    b. departmental pools.
    c. pools created according to the number of cost drivers that can be identified.
    d. batches and allocated to products based on the costs of materials or labor.

3. First-stage allocations in an activity-based cost system:
    a. typically use percentages to allocate costs to activities.
    b. allocate fixed costs only.
    c. allocate variable costs only.
    d. are unnecessary because ABC requires a one-stage allocation process.

4. Activity-based costing would be least effective when:
    a. products differ substantially in volume and lot size.
    b. there is a close link between direct labor hours and overhead costs.
    c. managers use cost information to make pricing or other product decisions.
    d. the processes used to manufacture products differ substantially in terms of complexity.

5. All of the following are characteristic of activity-based costing except the:
    a. use of cost drivers as a basis for allocating costs.
    b. accumulation of costs by activities.
    c. failure to recognize economies of scale.
    d. use of volume as a possible cost driver.

6. The allocation of overhead costs:
    a. is used by service and manufacturing organizations to assign costs to products.
    b. is used only by manufacturing organizations.
    c. is used to assign the costs of direct materials and labor.
    d. must be based on sales or production volume.

7. The denominator used in calculating a predetermined overhead rate:
    a. should have a causal relationship to the costs being assigned.
    b. is not affected by varying levels of volume.
    c. should change monthly to allow for fluctuations in volume.
    d. is determined once volume and actual costs are known.

8. The level of activity that is most likely to use volume for the allocation of overhead is the:
    a. unit level.
    b. product level.
    c. batch level.
    d. facility level.

9. An example of a product-level cost is the cost:
    a. of setting up machines for different products.
    b. incurred to operate a break room.
    c. of a factory's payroll.
    d. incurred to operate a product-testing center.

10. An example of a batch-level cost is the cost:
    a. of setting up machines for different products.
    b. incurred to operate a break room.
    c. of a factory's payroll.
    d. incurred to operate a product-testing center.

CASES

C5-1   **Activity-Based Costing versus Traditional Cost Allocation**

Objs. 2, 4   C. Berry Manufacturing Company produces two guitar models. One is a standard acoustic guitar that sells for $600 and is constructed from medium-grade materials. The other model is a custom-made amplified guitar with pearl inlays and a body constructed from special woods. The custom guitar sells for $900. Both guitars require 10 hours of direct labor to produce, but the custom guitar is manufactured by more experienced workers who are paid at a higher rate.

Most of C. Berry's sales come from the standard guitar, but sales of the custom model have been growing. Following is the company's sales, production, and cost information for last year:

	Standard Guitar	Custom Guitar
Sales and production volume in units	900	100
Unit costs:		
Direct materials	$ 150	$375
Direct labor	180	240
Manufacturing overhead	135	135
Total unit costs	$ 465	$750
Manufacturing overhead costs:		
Building depreciation	$ 40,000	
Maintenance	15,000	
Purchasing	20,000	
Inspection	12,000	
Indirect materials	15,000	
Supervision	30,000	
Supplies	3,000	
Total manufacturing overhead costs	$135,000	

The company allocates overhead costs using the traditional method. Its activity base is direct labor hours. The predetermined overhead rate, based on 10,000 direct labor hours, is $13.50 ($135,000 ÷ 10,000 direct labor hours).

Nick Fessler, president of C. Berry, is concerned that the traditional cost-allocation system the company is using may not be generating accurate information and that the selling price of the custom guitar may not be covering its true cost.

Required

A. The cost-allocation system C. Berry has been using allocates 90% of overhead costs to the standard guitar because 90% of direct labor hours were spent on the standard model. How much overhead was allocated to each of the two models last year? Discuss why this might not be an accurate way to assign overhead costs to products.
B. How would the use of more than one cost pool improve C. Berry's cost allocation?
C. C. Berry's controller developed the following data:

Manufacturing Overhead Cost	Amount	Cost Driver	Standard Guitar	Custom Guitar
Building depreciation	$40,000	Square footage	3,000	1,000
Maintenance	15,000	Direct labor hours	9,000	1,000
Purchasing	20,000	Number of purchase orders	1,500	500
Inspection	12,000	Number of inspections	400	600
Indirect materials	15,000	Number of units	900	100
Supervision	30,000	Number of inspections	400	600
Supplies	3,000	Number of units	900	100

Use activity-based costing to allocate the costs of overhead per unit and in total to each model of guitar.
D. Calculate the cost of a custom guitar using activity-based costing. Why is the cost different from the cost calculated using the traditional allocation method? At the current selling price, is the company covering its true cost of production? Explain your answer.

C5-2 Forest Industries Paper Company: An ABC Costing Analysis*

Objs. 2, 4

Forest Industries Paper Company (FIPC) was a small, closely held paperboard manufacturer that produced a broad line of paperboard in large reels, termed parent rolls. These parent rolls were sold to converters who further processed them into containers used for a variety

*Case prepared by Dr. Thomas Albright for use in the Institute of Management Accountant's Regional Education Assistance Program (REAP) course in Strategic Cost Management. Used with permission.

of consumer products. The owners of FIPC had long pursued the strategy of producing a full range of products. While product diversity within a paperboard plant would not readily be apparent to the casual observer, subtle differences existed. For example, paperboard differs by basis weight (or thickness determined by caliper measurements) for a specified length of product.

FIPC produced 20 different grades of paperboard. Some were produced in large quantities requiring production runs of several days, while others were produced in smaller quantities requiring runs of only a few hours.

Pulp manufacturing begins with hardwood or softwood timber in the form of wood chips. The second step in the process is termed "digesting." Wood chips are cooked at 325 degrees Fahrenheit to break down the glue-like material bonding the wood fibers. Following the digesting process, brown fibers are washed and screened. A bleaching process is used to convert brown pulp into white pulp.

The paperboard manufacturing process begins by mixing pulp with water and chemicals in the first stage of a paper machine. The mixture is applied to a porous wire mesh; formation of paper actually occurs within this step. The wire mesh travels through a press that forces the pulp mixture against the wire to eliminate water within the mixture and to form the desired paper thickness. The material then proceeds to a drying section where it travels across numerous cylindrical dryers that are heated with steam. In the final section of the paper machine, long sections of paperboard are rolled up into parent rolls and are removed from the machine. The parent roll is further processed by FIPC's customers to make various types of paperboard containers.

Sometimes customers require additional processes to be performed on parent rolls. For example, food processors often require widths of 18 inches, rather than the standard width of a reel (approximately 12 feet). Thus, reels are loaded onto a rewinder slitter to produce eight reels 18 inches wide from one reel 12 feet wide. For convenience, Forest Industries had always combined labor and machine costs of the rewinder slitter with those of the paper machine for allocation purposes. Thus, all grades of paperboard shared in the costs of slitting even though most grades were not slit. Additionally, only a minor setup fee was charged to customers requesting slit parent rolls, as this was viewed as incidental customer service. Engineering studies suggest the slitting may be more expensive than previously thought.

Forest Industries traditionally applied overhead to production as a function of materials costs: thicker materials required more machine time to process as they demanded slower machine speeds and more energy to dry. Thus, unit-level drivers made sense for applying certain types of overhead to products. However, other important costs were incurred without respect to volume. For example, grade changes induce instabilities into the process that result in scrap until the process resumes stability. On average, production engineers estimate that approximately one-half reel is lost to scrap each time a grade change is made. Just as discrete-part manufacturers incur machine setup costs between production runs of two different products, scrap produced following grade changes is a predictable cost of production.

A sample representing significant categories of grades is presented in Exhibit A. The sample contains thin paperboard grades (caliper 0.013) as well as heavier grades (caliper 0.02). In addition, Exhibit A identifies whether a grade typically is slit. The sample is representative of the variation in batch quantities. As shown below, some grades are produced in small quantities, while the market demands significantly more production in other grades. Materials cost per reel includes pulp and chemical costs, while the selling price reflects recent market prices.

Exhibit A
Selected Product Grades with Production and Financial Data

Product	Caliper	Slit	Average Reels per Batch	Materials Cost per Reel	Selling Price per Reel
A	0.013	yes	50	$4,800	$12,600
B	0.014	no	2	5,200	13,500
C	0.015	yes	35	5,600	14,200
D	0.020	no	175	7,400	19,500

Total reels slit: 85 (50 + 35)
Total grade changes: 4 (grade A, grade B, grade C, grade D)

In the past, Forest Industries' accountants estimated that manufacturing overhead, including labor, energy, and depreciation on capital equipment, approximated 105% of material costs. Historically, product costs at Forest Industries were calculated by multiplying the overhead rate by direct material costs. However, brand managers had begun to suspect that some grades were subsidizing others with respect to costs. Two significant activities, grade changes and slitting, were identified to help reduce cross-subsidy and provide more accurate cost estimates. Exhibit B summarizes information obtained from the activity-based costing study.

Exhibit B

Activity Cost Pools and Activity Volumes

Total grade change costs	$47,000	Number of grade changes	4
Total slitting costs	$195,000	Number of reels	85
General overhead	0.911 × material costs per reel		

The capital-intensive structure of a paper company coupled with the cyclical nature of the industry makes accurate cost information an important strategic tool. Though current demand exceeds existing capacity, managers at Forest Industries know that a downturn is inevitable. They understood different pricing and production mix strategies are necessary when the economic environment changes. Gaining an understanding of the costs associated with grade changes and slitting is a first step that will enable managers to more effectively manage their business in good times and in bad.

Required

A. Compute the volume-based, traditional cost per reel for grades A–D identified in Exhibit A.
B. What is the total cost for Forest Industries to conduct a grade change?
C. What is the grade change cost for each reel? (*Hint:* The reel cost will differ because batch sizes are not equal.)
D. What is the cost to slit a reel of paperboard? (*Hint:* How many reels are slit? Do all reels require slitting services?)
E. Using the information in Exhibit B, calculate the amount of general overhead to be applied to each reel of paper.
F. Determine the activity-based cost for grades A–D.
G. Prepare a chart that illustrates the percentage change in costs between the volume-based system and the strategic activity-based cost system (ABC cost − volume-based system cost) ÷ volume-based system cost.
H. As a consultant to Forest Industries, what action would you recommend?

COMPUTERIZED MANUFACTURING SYSTEMS

How do we implement a computerized manufacturing system?

In previous chapters, we examined accounting systems for accumulating production costs. Job-order, process costing, and activity-based systems provide means for a company to track the flow of materials, labor, and overhead costs through the manufacturing process and to attach these costs to particular units of production. Managers use these systems to determine production costs and to monitor and evaluate the manufacturing process. The systems also are used to determine inventory costs and cost of goods sold for a particular fiscal period.

Like other components of a company's accounting system, the manufacturing systems used by most companies are computerized. Costs and physical data (number of units, production time, product identification) are maintained in databases. Data about purchases and use of materials, labor used in particular processes, and overhead are entered into the computer system by employees. The computer system accumulates these costs and attaches them to particular products or jobs.

This chapter describes the components and functions of computerized manufacturing systems. It provides an example of a simple computerized job-order system that could be used by a small business to accumulate job costs.

FOOD FOR THOUGHT

How does a computerized manufacturing system differ from a manual system? What issues must a company consider in using a computerized system? Erin and Seth discuss these questions with Roberta, their accountant.

Erin: *Recording transactions and preparing financial reports with our current accounting system is labor-intensive and a bit slow. It takes us several hours a week to record transactions and prepare reports. Sometimes we are several days or even weeks behind in updating our accounts.*

Seth: *At times, these delays are a major problem because we do not have accurate cost data for pricing our products. In some cases, we have sold products at prices below their costs, because our data are not timely. Should we be looking at a computerized accounting system?*

Roberta: *Yes, there are a number of good systems on the market that are not expensive and that will meet your needs.*

Seth: *How different are these systems from what we have been using? Will a computerized system be difficult for us to learn?*

OBJECTIVES

Once you have completed this chapter, you should be able to:

1 Identify the primary modules of a computerized manufacturing system.

2 Describe the components of a computerized information system used to process data in a manufacturing company.

3 Explain the use of relational databases to perform product cost functions.

COMPONENTS OF A COMPUTERIZED MANUFACTURING SYSTEM

OBJECTIVE 1

Identify the primary modules of a computerized manufacturing system.

Many of the mechanical functions of an accounting system, keeping track of cost data and updating account balances, and preparing schedules and reports from account data can be automated. Computers are capable of processing data through a series of steps to produce standard outputs such as reports. Consequently, certain accounting functions are automated in most companies.

Computerized accounting systems, even those for small companies like Young Designs, Inc., are composed of modules. Each module provides a mechanism for recording and reporting specific types of business activities. Common modules are those associated with the most common business activities: sales and customer relations, purchasing and inventory management, production, human resources, asset management, and financial management. A separate module is usually responsible for the general ledger and external financial reporting (GAAP-based financial statements) functions. Exhibit 1 illustrates an accounting system as a set of component modules.

Exhibit 1 Components of an Accounting Information System

Each component in the information system has a particular role:

- The **sales module** receives sales order data from customers and maintains accounts receivable information.
- The **purchasing and materials management module** provides purchase order data to vendors. Vendors are those who supply specific products to a company. This module maintains accounts payable and inventory information. In a manufacturing company, this module is especially important for keeping track of the costs and use of raw materials.
- The **human resources module** maintains data about employees, hours worked, and wage rates. It is used for preparing payroll and payroll tax information.
- The **production module** tracks the flow of costs through the manufacturing process.
- The **asset management module** identifies long-term asset costs, their expected useful lives, and where these assets are located in a company.
- The **financial management module** keeps track of debt, when repayment is due, interest rates, and shareholder information. Also, it is used for managing a company's cash flows.
- The **general ledger/financial reporting module** provides information for use by external stakeholders, including shareholders and government regulators.

All of the modules are linked together in the system so they can interact with each other to share data. Some businesses use one software application that integrates all of these functions. **Systems that integrate most of the business information functions as a basis for management decisions are referred to as** *enterprise resource planning (ERP) systems.* Many large companies have implemented these systems from ERP developers such as **SAP**, **PeopleSoft**, and **Oracle**. Other companies may rely on software from different vendors for different components of their systems. Many smaller companies rely on software that handles most of the company's accounting functions. These systems lack the capabilities of larger systems but provide for most of the common accounting and financial reporting functions small businesses need. Thus, computerized accounting systems can be small basic systems such as QuickBooks, MAS, Peachtree, or Simply Accounting; middle-market systems such as Microsoft Business Solutions or ACCPAC; or large-scale systems such as SAP and Oracle Financials. Regardless of size, each of these systems is made up of component modules.

The modules available in SAP are described in the following sections. These modules are typical of those in other ERP systems. Most large manufacturing companies have implemented ERP systems, SAP being the most common for these companies. The primary modules, nearly all of which are linked to the manufacturing process, include:

- Financial accounting
- Controlling
- Asset management
- Project management
- Human resources
- Quality management
- Production planning
- Materials management
- Sales and distribution

These functions are integrated so that the work of one module overlaps with others in some cases.

The **financial accounting** module is designed for automated management and external reporting of general ledger, accounts receivable, accounts payable, and other accounts based on a user-defined chart of accounts. Key elements of the financial accounting module include:

Financial Accounting
Financial system for recording of transactions
General ledger for maintaining account balances and preparing financial statements

http://albright.
swlearning.com
....
Learn more about these
ERP developers and
other computerized ac-
counting systems.

Accounts payable for tracking amounts owed to vendors
Accounts receivable for tracking amounts owed by customers
Treasury for cash flow management
Consolidation for consolidation of a parent company's subsidiaries

The **controlling** module maintains and reports information about costs and revenues associated with specific functions or divisions of a company. Controlling is a tool for management decisions. Key elements of the controlling application module include:

Controlling
Cost center accounting for determining the costs of specific functions or divisions of a company
Internal order accounting for tracking the flow of costs among functions or departments within a company
Product costing analysis for determining and evaluating product costs
Profitability analysis for evaluating divisional and product profit performance
Activity-based costing for determining activity-based costs and allocation of overhead in the manufacturing process

The **asset management** module is designed for keeping track of property and equipment and similar long-term fixed assets. The asset management module includes:

Asset Management
Maintenance and repair for tracking costs and timing of these activities
Sale of assets for monitoring disposal decisions
Asset replacement for evaluating replacement decisions
Depreciation for determining and tracking asset depreciation for financial reporting, cost, and tax purposes
Investment management for making decisions about new acquisitions or replacements of property and equipment

The **project management** module supports the planning, control, and monitoring of long-term, highly complex projects with defined goals. It accelerates work and data flows and reduces routine tasks. The module includes:

Project Management
Funds and resource management to help project managers keep track of resources used in a project
Quality control to help with including quality issues in a project
Time management to assist in scheduling activities associated with a project

The **human resources** module is used for managing human resources and for maintaining employee and related financial data. The module includes a range of capabilities such as:

Human Resources
Recruitment for keeping track of job requirements and postings
Benefits for tracking employee benefits
Time management for determining and scheduling employee labor hours
Incentive wages for determining bonuses
Business trip management for maintaining reimbursement information and determining travel costs
Payroll for processing employee wages
Training and events management for coordination of training activities
Personnel development for tracking development activities for individual employees
Workforce planning for determining labor and labor cost requirements for various functions or divisions

The **quality management** application module is a quality control and information system supporting quality planning, inspection, and control for manufacturing, costing, and procurement. Primary elements of the module are:

Quality Management
Quality inspection for monitoring quality control
Quality planning for determining quality control requirements

The **production planning** module is used to plan and control the manufacturing activities of a company. The module includes:

Production Planning
Bills of material for identifying the materials that are used in each product
Master production scheduling for determining production schedules and the use of equipment and labor in the production process
Material requirements planning for coordinating the amount and availability of materials for scheduled production runs
Shop floor control for coordinating the flow of materials through production processes
Production orders for tracking order status and completion dates
Product costing and activity-based costing for determining the costs of units of production

The **materials management** module supports the procurement and inventory functions occurring in day-to-day business operations. This module includes:

Materials Management
Material procurement for purchasing materials and maintaining vendor data
Inventory management for determining inventory availability and costs
Reorder point processing facilitates determining when to reorder and placing orders
Invoice verification tracks orders and ensures company policies are followed in the ordering process
Material valuation provides for identifying quality or quantity problems with materials received
Vendor evaluation for monitoring vendor quality
External services procurement for facilitating the outsourcing of services
Warehouse management for maintaining data about the location of materials and for transferring materials into and out of the warehouse

The **sales and distribution** module helps to optimize all the tasks and activities carried out in sales, delivery, and billing. Key elements of the module include:

Sales and Distribution
Inquiry processing for responding to customer inquiries
Quotation processing for providing pricing information to customers
Sales order processing for recording and tracking sales orders
Delivery processing for recording and tracking delivery of goods to customers
Billing for submitting sales invoices to customers

For a large manufacturing company, these modules facilitate the financial, marketing, and production processes necessary for managing the company. A large-scale system of this type is complex but provides a mechanism for recording, maintaining, and reporting information for decisions throughout a company. The computer processes and infrastructure necessary to support the system are described in the next section.

A goal of modern information systems is to automate the supply chain (also referred to as the supply chain) to reduce delays in the production and delivery process and to reduce costs associated with data entry. The supply chain includes the entities and functions associated with procuring materials and labor, employing these materials and labor in the manufacturing process, and selling and distributing completed goods to customers. Exhibit 2 illustrates the supply chain and specific ERP modules that are important in the automation process.

The supply chain is automated when most of the functions occur without direct human intervention. The system identifies resource requirements and automatically

Exhibit 2 Automating the Value Chain

places orders with suppliers. Once goods are received, they are requisitioned and placed into production and tracked by the information system. Orders are received from customers and are processed by the system, which then schedules the production of goods to meet these orders. The goal is not the elimination of human interaction, which may still be needed for the physical movement and production of goods, but to reduce human involvement in support services associated with purchasing and order processing.

Case In Point

The Values of Manufacturing Systems

Profitable construction companies understand the cost of each job and use proper software for accounting and job costing. A purchasing component is a significant aspect of job costing software. For example, contractors who use such a system report improved control over purchasing activities and cost flow.

Source: Contractor's Business Management Report. New York, October 2002. Issue 10, page 3.

1 SELF-STUDY PROBLEM

Marco Co. constructs commercial buildings. Marco must keep accurate and timely information about its construction activities and costs.

Required Describe the modules of a computerized information system that Marco would need to keep track of its cost information and why they are important.

The solution to Self-Study Problem 1 appears at the end of the chapter.

DATA PROCESSING IN A COMPUTERIZED SYSTEM

OBJECTIVE 2

Describe the components of a computerized information system used to process data in a manufacturing company.

Each module of an information system receives data, stores the data, processes the data to create useful information, and reports that information to decision makers, as indicated in Exhibit 3.

Input into the system originates in business activities and can come from a variety of sources. It may originate as paper documents, such as **sales orders** prepared by or for customers or **sales receipts** indicating the sale of goods to customers. In computerized systems, data must be entered into the computer system. Data entry may be in the form of keystrokes entered by clerical personnel who transfer data from paper documents to computer files. Increasingly, data are entered directly into computer systems. For example, many retail stores use scanners to read bar code data from products. The bar codes are linked to the company's inventory data so that sales prices, costs, and inventory amounts can be recorded without keying data into the system.

Data associated with production processes can be entered by factory workers using computer terminals or scanning devices. Employees can enter identification codes

Exhibit 3 Data Processing in a Computerized Information System

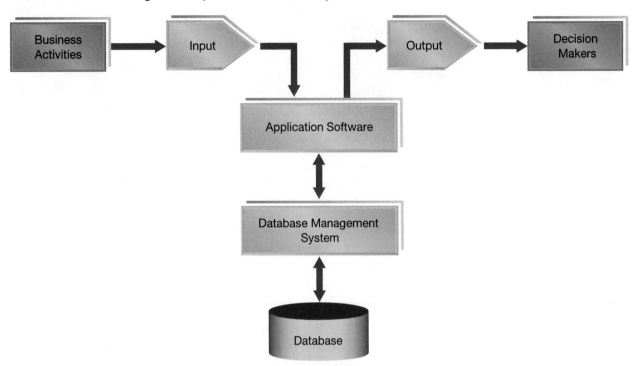

at the beginning and end of a process that can be used to track the labor associated with that process. Tags attached to materials can be scanned to track their use in the production process.

Many companies provide web-based input systems that permit customers to place orders directly using the Internet. Companies such as **Amazon**, **Southwest Airlines**, and **Banana Republic** provide for online shopping, reservations, and sales. Data entered by customers updates company order and inventory files. Customers also can retrieve information about their orders from these systems.

The use of computer networks, like the Internet, to provide for customer sales is referred to as *E-business.* Some E-business systems provide a means for a company to receive sales orders from customers. These systems are referred to as business-to-customer (b2c) systems. Other systems permit companies to order goods from vendors and to track order information. These systems are referred to as business-to-business (b2b) systems. In either system, most of the customer data entry is prepared by the customer. These data become a basis for recording sales, accounts receivable, materials purchased, accounts payable, cost of goods sold, and related transactions. Thus, many routine transactions can be recorded and processed automatically without the seller or buyer having to take special steps to record these transactions.

Application software **includes the computer programs that permit data to be recorded and processed.** If a customer enters an order using a web browser, application software is needed to collect that data, to record it in the company's files, and to process the data to ensure that the appropriate actions occur. For example, a customer order must be recorded, shipping must be notified of the order so the goods can be shipped, a bill may need to be prepared and sent to the customer, and sales and accounts receivable accounts need to be updated. Application software automates these functions.

Databases often are used to store data that can be accessed by various components of a system. Data are transferred by application software to databases. **A** *database* **is a set of computerized files where company data are stored in a form that facilitates retrieval and updating of the data. A** *database management system* **controls database functions to ensure data are recorded properly and can be accessed only by those authorized to record, update, or retrieve the data.**

http://albright.
swlearning.com
....
Visit the online shopping
sites of Amazon.com,
Southwest Airlines, and
Banana Republic.

Many internal controls are built into computerized information systems. These controls are important for protecting data and for helping to prevent errors. Controls, such as passwords, are needed to make sure data are not accessed or modified by unauthorized personnel. Controls built into database management systems prevent more than one user from updating a particular record at the same time and make sure that all appropriate parts of a database are updated when a transaction is recorded.

Other controls require management action. For example, databases must be backed up on a regular basis so data will not be lost if a computer system fails or is destroyed. A company also must have a plan in case its computer system is destroyed because of natural disaster, sabotage, or terrorism. Failure to provide backup systems can result in a company being unable to do business if its primary system is unusable.

Output from information systems often is in the form of reports. These reports may contain prescribed information and may be prepared automatically by a system. They may be paper reports or electronic documents that are sent to users. Many output reports can be modified and retrieved as needed by the user. For example, production managers need information about outstanding orders and the status of existing orders.

Regardless of which of the modules in a company's accounting system is involved, data flow through the system from inputs to outputs. The processes that take place in association with these data flows depend on the module. Data flows are initiated by business activities but also stimulate these activities. For example, a request for materials results from a need for materials to be used in a production process. However, data about the request also result in a company ordering materials from vendors.

Computerized systems rely on networks for processing data. *Computer networks* **include the cables that connect the clients and servers and the hardware and software needed to make the networks function properly.** Exhibit 4 illustrates a computer network. Input devices, such as scanners, and client workstations provide a basis for data input and for users to access information from the computer system. A **client** is a computer or other network device that uses software that requests services from other software. The services are provided by server software that resides on other computers, referred to as **servers**.

Exhibit 4
An Illustration of a
Computer Network

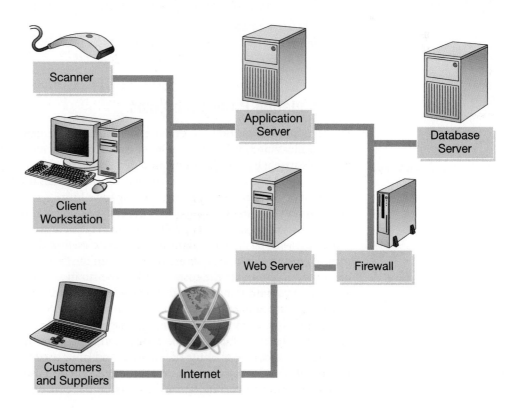

Application software usually resides on one or more **application servers** on the network. Application servers are connected to **database servers** where data are stored and managed. Companies engaged in E-business or which permit their employees to connect to their network from locations outside of the business, such as customer businesses, often use web servers to provide the software needed to interact across the Internet. The Internet provides a network so that almost any computer can connect to a company to do business.

Automating a company's supply chain and production process involves network connections among a company, its suppliers, and customers. Application software at the manufacturer identifies when materials are needed and places orders with suppliers with which the company partners. Arrangements with the suppliers provide for access by the manufacturer's computer system with the suppliers' systems so that purchase orders can be processed on a real-time basis. Orders placed by the manufacturer are filled by suppliers who ship goods to the manufacturer and submit bills to the manufacturer through its computer system. Bills can be processed by the manufacturer and funds can be transferred to suppliers.

Once materials are received by the manufacturer they can be transferred to production automatically as called for in production schedules or as requested by factory employees. Many companies now use just-in-time systems that move materials directly from receiving into production with a need for storing the materials in a warehouse. The fewer movements and less handling associated with the materials reduces production costs. Materials are tagged with computer-readable tags so that they can be tracked through the production process. Thus, at any time, the manufacturing company can determine the physical location, quantity, and cost of materials in production.

Customers can place orders with a manufacturer using the manufacturer's computer system. The orders can be placed directly through a web interface, for example, that provides access to the manufacturer's product price list. Because of the efficiencies of automated systems, a manufacturer may not produce goods until orders are received, thereby eliminating costs of maintaining finished goods inventories. Orders from customers pull the production process. The order is recorded by the manufacturer's production scheduling system, which notifies the materials management system to order materials. As soon as they are completed, goods are delivered to the customer. Streamlining the production process and eliminating unnecessary operations and costs is a major objective of ERP systems.

The next section examines various processes in a company's production system associated with the accumulation of production costs.

Accumulating Production Costs

Production costs include direct materials, direct labor, and manufacturing overhead costs as illustrated in Exhibit 5. Direct materials costs are derived from a company's materials management system or module. That module records the costs of materials and provides a basis for determining the costs of materials used in a production process. Direct labor costs are derived from a company's human resources module. That module identifies the amounts paid to various types of employees. Some manufacturing overhead costs are derived from the asset management module, which tracks the costs associated with facilities, equipment, and tools used in the production process. Other manufacturing overhead costs are derived from the financial accounting or other modules, which accumulate the costs of utilities, insurance, supplies, and similar items that are associated with the manufacturing process. Indirect labor costs included in manufacturing overhead are derived from the human resources module.

The cost data from the materials management, human resources, and other modules in Exhibit 5 are inputs to the production system. In the production system, these costs are linked to the quantity of materials and labor used in a particular job or period.

The difference between a job-order and a process costing system is largely in the cost object used for accumulating the costs. In the case of a job-order system, the cost

Exhibit 5 Accumulating Production Costs in Job-Order or Process Systems

object is a job. Materials, labor, and overhead costs are accumulated for each job. In a process costing system, the costs are accumulated for a fiscal period for each product that is produced during that period. These costs are then assigned to each unit of product that results from the job or the period to determine unit costs. In a traditional system, manufacturing overhead costs are assigned to the production process using a predetermined allocation rate and basis, such as labor hours or labor costs.

In an activity-based costing system, manufacturing overhead costs are first grouped based on the types of costs, such as batch-, product-, or facility-level costs, as illustrated in Exhibit 6. These costs are allocated to each job or production process based on the drivers that are associated with each level of cost. Otherwise, the accumulation of costs is similar between traditional and activity-based costing systems.

The key to understanding any production system is to understand that the objective is to determine the cost of each unit produced. That cost is determined from the cost of materials that were used in producing those units (cost per item times the number of each item used), the cost of labor used in producing those items (labor rate for each type of employee times the amount of time each employee worked), and the amount of overhead allocated to those units. The total cost associated with the units produced is then divided by the number of units produced to determine the unit cost.

Automating a production cost system involves linking the modules that identify and track materials labor and overhead costs so that these costs can be accumulated throughout the production process. The next section of this chapter examines database management systems that are used to identify and track production costs and provides a simple example of a job-order cost system.

2 SELF-STUDY PROBLEM

Suppose you want to automate a production system so that materials and labor costs can be determined and tracked based on inputs within the production system.

Required Describe a computerized system for this purpose.

The solution to Self-Study Problem 2 appears at the end of the chapter.

Exhibit 6 Accumulating Production Costs in an Activity-Based Costing System

DATABASE SYSTEMS AND PRODUCT COSTS

OBJECTIVE 3

Explain the use of relational databases to perform product cost functions.

This chapter uses the example of Kwiki Oil Company to describe a computerized job-order system. Kwiki Oil is a small company that provides motor oil changes for passenger cars and light trucks. Most of the company's business is drive-in. The driver pulls into a bay where the oil and oil filter are replaced. The company's goal is to complete the process in 15 minutes or less. Three employees work on each vehicle, though two of the three often are working on more than one vehicle at the same time. Kwiki Oil's production system tracks the materials and labor that are used in each vehicle, as a basis for determining the cost of each job. After examining the components of a database, we will describe a simple job-order system for Kwiki Oil.

Most computerized accounting, including ERP, systems are constructed as relational databases. A *relational database* **is a set of related files that are linked together so that the files can be updated and information can be retrieved from the files efficiently.**

A relational database stores data in tables. A *table* **is a file that contains data represented as rows and columns.** Each column identifies a particular attribute of the entity or process described in the table. Each attribute is referred to as a **field** in the table. A vendor table would include vendor name and address attributes, for example. Each row in the table contains a record of data for a particular entity. Rows in a vendor table would contain data for each vendor. Separate tables are used for specific types of entities (vendors and products) and processes (purchase orders and production). Each table contains one or more **primary keys** that uniquely identify the entities or processes recorded in the rows of the table. These primary keys are used to connect the tables into relationships. The primary key in one table connects to the primary key or a **foreign key** in another table. A foreign key is a field that is a primary key in a different table. For example, Part_Number might be a primary key in a materials table. The same field might be a foreign key in a vendor table that identifies which parts are ordered from that vendor.

Exhibit 7 illustrates the tables and relationships in a database. The boxes represent tables, identified by their captions at the top. Fields stored in each table are listed in the boxes. Fields in bold are primary keys. Lines connect the keys that form the relationships in the database.

Exhibit 7
Tables in a Relational
Database

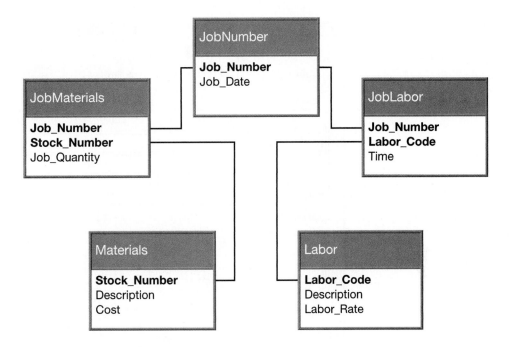

The relationships permit a change to a field that is in more than one table to affect each table containing that field. For example, when a job number is entered into the system, the Job_Number field is updated in the JobNumber, JobMaterials, and JobLabor tables. The relationships also permit a user to obtain data from more than one table. For instance, a particular job number can be used to obtain data from the JobMaterials and JobLabor tables because these tables are linked to the job number.

Thus, a relational database is a network of information objects that permits data to be stored and retrieved efficiently. Knowing the relationships in the database, a user can retrieve any combination of fields to serve a particular decision need.

Individual tables in the database store data about a particular entity or activity. Exhibit 8 provides an example of a simple table. The top row identifies the attributes stored in the table. The remaining rows are records. The first column of each record identifies the stock number that uniquely identifies that record. Records are listed sequentially by the stock number, which is the primary key for the table. Other fields identify other attributes associated with each stock number, such as the description and unit cost of each stock item.

Exhibit 8
An Example of a Table
in a Database

Stock_Number	Description	Cost
F150	oil filter	$6.43
F160	oil filter	$7.20
F170	oil filter	$8.35
L235	5-30 weight	$0.92
L236	10-30 weight	$0.98
L245	5-30 weight premium	$1.15
L246	10-30 weight premium	$1.21

Data are entered into a database using **forms**. Forms are computer templates for entering data. Exhibit 9 provides an illustration of a simple form. The form provides input areas where data are keyed into the system. Form fields are linked to attributes in tables in the database. Thus, when a new job number is entered in the form in Exhibit 9, data are added to the JobNumber table and related tables in the company's database.

Exhibit 9

An Example of a Form for Data Entry

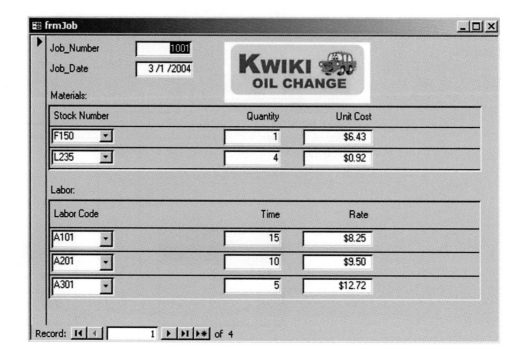

As noted earlier, much of the data needed by a computerized system may be entered automatically through scanning devices. Customers enter data in forms when they place orders using web-based systems. Much of the data needed in database systems are entered by a company's employees who are responsible for various data entry functions.

Each module of a computerized accounting system consists of tables and forms that collect and store data needed for the activities associated with that module. Individual tables often are part of more than one module. For example, an inventory table may be accessed by the sales module to determine product availability and price. It may be accessed by the production module to update it for finished goods.

The following section illustrates a database accounting system that is typical of a computerized production system, though it uses simple examples with limited transactions and examines only a small part of a total manufacturing system. The illustration is designed to help you see how accounting data are processed in actual systems from data entry to storage and reporting.

http://albright.
swlearning.com

Download database file (also available on the student CD).

An Illustration of an Accounting System

This section illustrates various components of a computerized manufacturing system. The illustration examines the job cost module of Kwiki Oil Co.'s system. Example transactions are provided for March 2004 to illustrate production activities: creating a job number, accumulating direct materials and direct labor costs, allocating manufacturing overhead costs, and creating a job cost report.

The software used in this module is a Microsoft® Access database, which can be found on the CD that accompanies this text or downloaded from http://albright.swlearning.com. Directions for use of the software are provided as part of the description that follows.

To use the database, you must have a computer with a Microsoft® Windows® operating system and Access 2000 or a more recent version.

Access is application software built around a database system. It is inadequate for large-scale accounting applications but is useful for illustrating database systems. Unlike most business systems, all of the software runs on a workstation. Though it can be configured to run on a network with separate client and server components, it is easier to use and to understand when it is operated from a single computer.

Copying and Opening the Database

We highly recommend copying the database to another disk or your hard drive before using it. To copy the database, first insert the CD into your CD-ROM drive, open Windows® Explorer and select your CD-ROM drive where the database is located. Click on KwikiOil.mdb and drag it to a folder on your other disk or hard drive. Release the mouse button, and the database will be copied. It is a good idea to make several copies of the database under different names (KwikiOil1.mdb, KwikiOil2.mdb, and so on). If the database is modified or accidentally corrupted, you still have an unmodified version for use.

Use one of the following options to open the database.

Option 1. Open Access by clicking Start, Programs, Microsoft Access. Once Access has opened, click File, Open. Double-click KwikiOil.mdb in the folder to which it was copied.

Option 2. Open Windows Explorer. Select the folder in which the database was copied. Double-click on KwikiOil.mdb.

Database files can become large when they are modified through use. It is a good idea to compact the database periodically. To compact the database, open it in Access, click Tools, Database Utilities, Compact and Repair Database. The database will be compacted automatically. Compacting removes unused space in the database. Running a database from a 3.5″ disk requires frequent compacting.

Database Contents

A database consists of objects. Once the KwikiOil.mdb database has been opened, these objects appear in various categories: tables, queries, forms, reports, pages, macros, and modules. **Tables** contain the data stored in the system. **Queries** are short programs that permit a user to obtain data from one or more tables. **Forms** provide a means for entering or reading data stored in the database. **Reports** provide summary information intended primarily to be printed. Macros are sequences of steps a user performs to complete a particular task. A macro runs a task without the user having to enter each keystroke separately. **Pages** provide a means of creating web documents for accessing a database. **Modules** are computer programs (written in Visual Basic) to provide higher level functions in the database. The Kwiki Oil Co. database contains no macros or modules.

Tables. Tables are the key to understanding a database. Tables contain the data in the database. Other objects manipulate these data by adding new data, modifying existing data, deleting data, or retrieving data.

Begin by examining the tblJobNumber table. Click on the Tables tab in the Database window. Double-click on tblJobNumber or click on tblJobNumber and then click the Open button. Columns in the table identify categories (also known as fields or attributes) of data. The Job_Number is a code that uniquely identifies each job. Numbers are listed consecutively so that any missing jobs are easy to identify. Job_Date identifies the date that the job was completed and provides a basis for determining when revenues and costs associated with the job should be recognized. Close the table by clicking the X box in the upper right corner of the table window. Do not click the X box in the Access window (top right of screen) or you will close the Access program. If you close Access by mistake, reopen it and the KwikiOil.mdb database.

Next examine the tblMaterials table. This table identifies materials that Kwiki Oil uses in its jobs. The Stock_Number uniquely identifies each item. Description provides a narrative explanation for each item, and Cost identifies the unit cost for each item. The example assumes that each item has a specific cost.

The tblMaterials table is an example of a master file. Master files contain data that are relatively stable and that may be updated periodically. The tblJobNumber table is an example of a transaction file. Transaction files are updated each time a new transaction, such as a job, is recorded.

Other tables in the database include the tblLabor table that identifies the types of employees who work on jobs and the hourly rate earned by each type of employee. The tblJobMaterials table links data about materials with each job. It describes the materials that were used in a job and the quantity of those materials for each job. The tblJobLabor table links data about labor with each job. It identifies the employees who worked on each job and the time each employee spent on each job. Time is measured in minutes in this table.

You can examine the relationships among all the tables in the database by clicking on the Relationships button ▭▭ in the top row of buttons in the database window. The relationship diagram that appears contains the tables and identifies the fields in each table. Lines in the diagram link the primary and foreign keys. Close the Relationship window by clicking on the bottom X in the upper right corner of the screen.

Entering Transactions. Job cost data would be entered by the supervisor in charge of each job. To enter a transaction, click on the Forms tab of the Database window. Then open the frmJob form. Notice that the form identifies the Job Number and Date. It also identifies materials and labor that were used in each job. You can click on the Record selector arrow ▶| at the bottom of the form window to view completed jobs.

To enter a new job, click on the New Record selector arrow |▶*| at the bottom of the form window. Two sets of arrows appear near the bottom of the form. Use the bottom set of arrows to move among the jobs. Enter a new Job Number, 1006. You may wish to press the Caps Lock key when entering transaction data. Press the Tab key to go to the Job_Date box. Type 03/06/2004 in the box. Click on the Stock Number selector arrow ▼ to see a list of materials. Click on F150. The unit cost of the material appears in the Cost box. Enter 1 for the Quantity. In the next row, click on the selector arrow and select L245. Enter 5 for the Quantity.

Repeat the process to enter the labor used in the job. In the first row under labor code, select A101 from the drop-down box and enter 13 for Time. On the next row select A201 and enter 7; then select A301 on the third row and enter 4. To save the order, you can click the New Record selector arrow |▶*| at the bottom of the form or close the form window.

To view the data entered for the order, open the tblJobNumber, tblJobMaterials, and tblJobLabor tables, scroll to the last row, and observe the new data.

Job Cost Reports. You can view a job cost report, including the one just entered, by selecting the Reports tab on the Database window and double-clicking on rptJob. A report appears listing the orders that have been entered in the database. To see the entire report you may need to enlarge the window and the zoom control on the menu bar. Jobs are listed in the report by Job Number. Each job appears on a separate page. The job you just entered is listed on the last page of the report. Use the page selection arrow at the bottom of the report to view page 6. A copy of the report can be printed if a printer is available. Close the report when you have finished examining it.

Determining production costs for Kwiki Oil is straightforward. Each job represents a unit of product. Costs are accumulated for each unit based on the quantity of each type of material used in the job times the cost of each type of material, the quantity of each type of employee that worked on the job times the wage rate paid that type of employee, and an allocation of manufacturing overhead based on a rate per hour times the total number of labor hours associated with the job.

The job cost report identifies the materials, labor, and manufacturing overhead costs applied to each job. Manufacturing overhead is applied on the basis of total labor hours at a rate of $9.00 per labor hour.

Some of the data in the Kwiki Oil Co. Job Cost reports are derived from queries. Queries obtain data from tables, manipulate these data to produce new data items, and store them temporarily. Click on the Queries tab to view the queries. Double-click on qryMaterials and view the data that appear in the query. The query is used to compute the total cost for each item of materials used on a job. The qryLabor query is used to compute the labor cost for each job.

3 SELF-STUDY PROBLEM

The description of Kwiki Oil Company's job-order system refers to tables, forms, queries, and reports that are used in the system.

Required Describe the purpose of tables, forms, queries, and reports and how each of these is related to the others.

The solution to Self-Study Problem 3 appears at the end of the chapter.

REVIEW

SUMMARY of IMPORTANT CONCEPTS

1. Most manufacturing companies use computerized accounting systems. Typically, these systems are part of larger information systems that integrate various management functions throughout an organization.

2. Computerized information systems are separated into modules. Common modules include sales, purchasing and materials management, human resources, production, asset management, financial management, and general ledger/financial reporting.

3. Enterprise resource planning (ERP) systems integrate the various management functions into a comprehensive information system.

4. ERP systems, like SAP, include many functions such as financial accounting, controlling, asset management, project management, human resources, quality management, production planning, materials management, and sales and distribution.

5. A goal of many companies is to automate their supply chain so that interaction with customers and vendors can be handled by the computer system with little human intervention.

6. Computer systems receive, store, and process data to create useful information that can be reported to decision makers.

7. E-business uses computer networks to provide customer sales.

8. Application software is part of a computer system that includes computer programs that permit data to be recorded and processed.

9. Data are stored in databases, and database management systems control the database functions to ensure accuracy and security of data.

10. Client-server networks provide for interaction by users through client workstations to application and database servers that process and store data.

11. The production module obtains input from the materials, human resources, asset management, and other modules. The production module accumulates production costs

and allocates these to individual units based on the number of units produced during a period or job.

12. Computerized information systems use relational databases, which store data in related tables. Forms are used to enter data in tables, and queries are used to retrieve and manipulate data for preparing reports.

DEFINE

TERMS and CONCEPTS DEFINED in this CHAPTER

application software (M142)

computer network (M143)

database (M142)

database management system (M142)

E-business (M142)

enterprise resource planning (ERP) systems (M138)

relational database (M146)

table (M146)

SELF-STUDY PROBLEM SOLUTIONS

SSP6-1 Materials, labor, and overhead costs are important for a construction company. The company must determine the materials required for each construction project and track the use of those materials at each project. It must determine the amount of time employees spend on each project. Asset costs associated with the use of construction equipment also are important. The company must determine which types of equipment are used on each project and how much time the equipment is used. Consequently, materials management, human resources, asset management, and production are all essential. If the company borrows money to finance its projects during the construction process, the financial management module also may be important.

SSP6-2 Input data for the system would require computer-readable identifiers for materials and employees. Tags that could be scanned would be attached to materials. The tags would identify the item; the system could then link the item code back to a database that recorded the cost of the item and when and where the item was used. Electronic cards or badges could be issued to employees. These would be scanned at the beginning and end of a production process. The cards would identify the employee and permit the system to determine the amount of time an employee spent on a particular process or job. These data could be used by a database to determine labor costs for a period or job. The scanning devices would provide the clients for the network, which would connect to application servers that processed the data and database servers that maintained the data.

SSP6-3 Tables are used to store data in a relational database. Some of the data may be relatively fixed and provide information for other tables or processes. Some of the data changes in response to events or transactions associated with operations of the business, such as a production process or sale. Forms are used primarily to provide a means of entering data into a system. The data entered are stored in and used to update tables. Thus, the items in a form must be linked directly to fields in tables. Queries provide a means for obtaining data from various tables and summarizing these data (by summing, computing new variables, etc.) to provide a basis for preparing reports. Reports summarize data from the system in a format useful for decision makers.

Thinking Beyond the Question

How do we implement a computerized manufacturing system?

Computerized manufacturing systems are used by most manufacturing companies to facilitate the collection, reporting, and analysis of manufacturing cost information. What are some of the risks associated with using these systems?

QUESTIONS

Q6-1
Obj. 1
Why are integrated business systems more efficient than using individual systems for different functions in a business?

Q6-2
Obj. 1
How would the human resources module for a manufacturing company differ from that for a retail or service company?

Q6-3
Obj. 1
Irmo Co.'s asset management module lists each piece of equipment the company has purchased, when it was purchased, its cost, its expected life, and its location in the company. Why would the company want this information?

Q6-4
Obj. 1
Kreel Co.'s financial management module lists each loan the company has outstanding, when the money was borrowed, the amount borrowed, the interest rate, the dates payments were made, and the amounts of these payments. Why is this information important to the company?

Q6-5
Obj. 1
What purposes does a manufacturing company's purchasing module serve? What accounts and types of transactions will be associated with this module?

Q6-6
Obj. 1
What purposes does a manufacturing company's human resources module serve? What accounts and types of transactions will be associated with this module?

Q6-7
Obj. 1
Street Inc.'s purchasing module lists each vendor's name, address, the materials purchased from the vendor, and when purchases were made. What uses might the company make of this information?

Q6-8
Obj. 1
Why would the sales module of **Dell Computer Corporation** differ from the sales module of **Wal-Mart**? What transactions would Dell record as part of its sales process that would differ from those of Wal-Mart?

Q6-9
Obj. 1
Why is it important for the accounting department of a manufacturing company to receive data from human resources? What internal control function is served by this process?

Q6-10
Obj. 1
Why is it important for the accounting department of a manufacturing company to receive data from purchasing and receiving? What internal control function is served by this process?

Q6-11
Obj. 2
What is a computer network? Why are they used by businesses to maintain accounting systems?

Q6-12
Obj. 2
What is the purpose of a database management system?

Q6-13
Obj. 3
Suppose a company sells to customers through the web. Customers are required to pay for their orders with credit cards at the time of the order. What primary activities would be required of the sales module to process and account for these orders?

EXERCISES

If your instructor is using Personal Trainer® in this course, you may complete your assignments online.

E6-1
Write a short definition for each of the terms listed in the *Terms and Concepts Defined in this Chapter* section.

E6-2
Objs. 1, 2
Complete each sentence with the appropriate term.

1. Systems that integrate most of the business information functions are referred to as _____.

2. The use of computer networks, like the Internet, to provide for customer sales is referred to as _____.

3. _____ includes the computer programs that permit data to be recorded and processed.

4. A _____ is a set of computerized files where company data are stored in a form that facilitates retrieval and updating of the data.

5. A _____ controls database functions to ensure data are recorded properly and can be accessed only by those authorized to record, update, or retrieve the data.

6. The interaction of a company and its suppliers and customers is known as the company's _____.

7. A _____ is a set of related files that are linked together so that the files can be updated and information can be retrieved from the files efficiently.

E6-3

Objs. 1, 2

Match each term with the appropriate definition.

a. application software
b. database management system
c. database
d. E-business

e. enterprise resource planning (ERP) systems
f. relational database
g. supply chain

1. a set of computerized files where company data are stored in a form that facilitates retrieval and updating of the data
2. a set of related files that are linked together so that the files can be updated and information can be retrieved from the files efficiently
3. controls database functions to ensure data are recorded properly and can be accessed only by those authorized to record, update, or retrieve the data
4. includes the computer programs that permit data to be recorded and processed
5. systems that integrate most of the business information functions
6. the interaction of a company and its suppliers and customers
7. the use of computer networks, like the Internet, to provide for customer sales

E6-4

Obj. 1

Complete each sentence with the appropriate term for a component in the information system.

1. The _____ receives sales order data from customers and maintains accounts receivable information.
2. The _____ provides purchase order data to vendors. Vendors are those who supply specific products to a company. This module maintains accounts payable and inventory information.
3. The _____ maintains data about employees, hours worked, and wage rates. It is used for preparing payroll and payroll tax information.
4. The _____ tracks the flow of costs through the manufacturing process.
5. The _____ identifies long-term asset costs, their expected useful lives, and where these assets are located in a company.
6. The _____ keeps track of debt, when repayment is due, interest rates, and shareholder information. It is also used for managing a company's cash flows.
7. The _____ provides information for use by external stakeholders, including shareholders and government regulators.

E6-5

Obj. 1

Dell Computer Corporation is a large, well-known manufacturer of computers for home and business. Assume you logged onto its web site, ordered a computer system, and paid for it by credit card. Describe the business activities that would occur at Dell, including linkages from the sales order system to other modules of the company's information system, in handling your order.

E6-6

Obj. 1

Great Plains Manufacturing Co.'s receiving department received an order of raw materials. How will information about the order affect the various modules of the company's information system?

E6-7

Obj. 1

For each of the functions listed below, identify the module of an ERP system that would provide that function from the following list.

a. financial accounting
b. controlling
c. asset management
d. project systems
e. human resources

f. quality management
g. production planning
h. materials management
i. sales and distribution

1. cash flow management
2. coordination of employee training
3. coordination of the flow of materials through the production process

4. determining and evaluating product costs
5. determining and tracking asset depreciation
6. determining costs of specific functions or divisions of a company
7. determining employee hours
8. determining production schedules
9. determining quality control requirements
10. evaluating asset replacement decisions
11. identifying materials used in each product
12. maintaining account balances and preparing financial reports
13. monitoring vendor quality
14. planning for long-term projects
15. processing employee wages
16. purchasing materials
17. recording sales orders
18. responding to customer inquiries
19. tracking amounts owed to vendors
20. warehouse management

E6-8
Obj. 1

What does it mean to automate a company's supply chain? What are the advantages of automating the supply chain for a manufacturing company?

E6-9
Obj. 2

What is a computer network? Why are they used by businesses to maintain accounting systems?

E6-10
Obj. 2

What is the purpose of a database management system?

E6-11
Obj. 2

Computer networks in many organizations include client applications, business management programs and databases on servers, and connections among the computers running these programs. For each of the following activities, identify the portions of the computer system that would be affected. Explain how the portions are affected.

1. Access to company data is requested
2. Records are updated
3. Data are transferred between a client and a server
4. New data for processing are entered
5. Data that are being used by another user are required
6. Data to print a report are obtained

E6-12
Obj. 3

Modern accounting information systems often are maintained as relational databases. What is a relational database, and what are the advantages of these database systems? Identify the parts of a relational database and explain the purpose of each part.

E6-13
Obj. 3

Howard Co. manufactures household goods and maintains its accounting system using a relational database. In order to prepare information about purchase transactions, the company uses the following tables in its database. The fields that appear in each table are in brackets following the table.

- vendors [vendor ID, name, address, phone number]
- purchase orders [purchase order number, vendor ID, order date, product ID, order quantity]
- materials [product ID, product name, quantity on hand, unit cost]
- purchase invoice [purchase invoice number, purchase order number, invoice date]
- cash payments [purchase invoice number, cash payments amount, payment date]

A purchase order is prepared when materials are ordered from a vendor. A purchase invoice is recorded from billing information supplied by the vendor.

For each of the following events, identify the tables that would be needed to record the event.

1. Placed an order with Jones Co. for materials on November 3.
2. Received the materials from Jones Co. on November 16.
3. Received a bill from Jones Co. for the purchase order on November 28.
4. Sent a check to Jones Co. for the purchase on December 5.

E6-14
Obj. 3

Refer to the information provided in E6-13.

1. If a manager for Howard Co. wanted to query the company's database to obtain information about orders during November, which tables would be used to obtain the information? Explain why.
2. If a manager wanted to query the database to obtain information about amounts owed to vendors at the end of November, which tables would be used to obtain the information? Explain why.

PROBLEMS

If your instructor is using Personal Trainer® in this course, you may complete your assignments online.

P6-1   Modules in an ERP System

Obj. 1

The chapter describes the primary modules available in SAP, a producer of ERP systems.

Required Explain the functions provided by each of the following modules and why they are important for a manufacturing company: (a) financial accounting, (b) controlling, (c) materials management, and (d) production planning.

P6-2   Interaction with System Modules

Obj. 1

ERP systems provide for a variety of functions associated with planning, operating, and evaluating production activities.

Required In what ways would you be likely to interact with an ERP system in a manufacturing system if you were (a) a shop employee, (b) a manufacturing division supervisor, (c) a sales representative, (d) a cost accountant?

P6-3   Cost Systems

Obj. 1

Job-order, process, and activity-based costing systems are similar with respect to the accumulation of production costs.

Required Describe the similarities and differences in these cost systems. Why are different cost accumulation systems needed by different companies? What are the primary inputs and outputs of each of these cost accumulation systems?

P6-4   Computer Networks

Obj. 2

You have just been hired as a human resources manager for a large manufacturing company. Your supervisor shows you to your desk, which contains a workstation. She explains that the workstation is part of a network connecting all of the company's manufacturing operations through a client-server system. All of the company's data are maintained in databases on servers and are accessed through a database management system. To obtain employee information, you must log on to the network and use the company's human resources program on your workstation to retrieve data from the database.

Required What is the supervisor talking about? Explain the function of each part of the company's computer network. Why do most companies use computer networks for their accounting systems?

P6-5   Controlling Networks

Obj. 2

Dora Company uses a client-server network for its accounting system. The company's database servers are kept at a central computer center. Users of the system access the company's database through workstations on their desks. Data are updated continuously throughout the day based on sales, production, billing, and other transactions that are recorded by users. Dora is a large company and its network connects offices in several states.

Required Identify four threats to the accounting system and accounting data that exist in Dora's network system that should be managed through internal controls. Identify an internal control that would be useful for dealing with each threat.

P6-6 Database Management Systems

Obj. 2

Open an Access database like the Kwiki Oil Co. database described in this chapter. Examine the Tools menu in the database window.

Required What database management functions are provided by the Tools menu options? Based on your examination, what are some of the primary purposes of a database management system?

P6-7 Network Components

Obj. 2

DVC Co. has decided to automate its supply chain. It has developed a web site so that customers can identify products and order them online. It has signed agreements with vendors that permit it to place orders through the Internet for materials.

Required Describe a network configuration that DVC could use to support its E-business activities. What is the purpose of each network component?

P6-8 Purpose of Relational Databases

Obj. 3

Newbury Company produces industrial machinery. Materials are purchased from vendors throughout North America, primarily using Internet connections. Purchases are made on credit and materials are placed into production when received. Newbury uses a relational database for its information system.

Required Explain the purpose of a relational database and why it is useful to a company. Describe the parts of a relational database and identify specific examples of how these parts would be used by Newbury to place vendor orders.

P6-9 Tables and Forms in Relational Databases

Obj. 3

Exhibit 8 in this chapter provides an example of a table that might appear in a company's relational database. Exhibit 9 provides an example of a form.

Required Using these exhibits as examples, explain the purpose of tables and forms in a relational database. Be specific about what the rows and columns in a table represent and how individual entities are identified in tables. Explain how forms are related to tables.

P6-10 Web Interfaces to Relational Databases

Obj. 3

Connect to http://www.dell.com on a web browser.

Required Identify the data items that are collected and processed by Dell's web interface as part of selecting and placing an order for a computer. Which components of Dell's database system are likely to be directly affected by a customer's interaction with the system if (a) the customer is browsing for information about Dell computers, (b) the customer places an order for a computer?

P6-11 Tables in Relational Databases

Obj. 3

You have been assigned the responsibility of developing a purchasing module for a manufacturing company.

Required Identify the tables that you think would be necessary as part of a relational database that will store data for the module. Identify the fields that will be important in each table and the primary and foreign keys that will link the tables together.

P6-12 Fields in a Relational Database

Obj. 3

Linden Co. uses over 100 different types of nuts, bolts, and screws in its manufacturing process. Each type has an identification number and is described by its type, size, and material composition.

Required Linden Co. is developing a database system for its materials inventory. What fields would be important to include in the database for the inventory items? Why would these fields be important?

P6-13   Relational Database Design

Obj. 3

Niven Co. manufactures ornamental flamingoes. The flamingoes are sold to wholesalers who then sell the goods to retailers. The flamingoes come in a variety of colors, sizes, and materials. Niven produces its products once an order is received. Each order is treated as a job and the company tracks costs using a job-order system.

Required Design a relational database system that Niven might use for tracking the costs of its orders. Identify the tables, fields, primary, and foreign keys that would be part of the database.

P6-14   Diagramming a Relational Database

Obj. 3

Plaxa Co. developed a design for its material ordering system that consisted of three tables. Tables and associated fields are listed below. The primary keys for each table are underlined.

> Materials Table [Product ID, Description, Quantity Available]
> Vendor Table [Vendor ID, Name, Address, City, State, Zip, Email]
> Purchase Order Table [Vendor ID, Materials ID, Order Date, Quantity Ordered, Cost]

Required Provide a relational diagram for the order system like that illustrated in Exhibit 7.

P6-15   Multiple-Choice Overview of the Chapter

1. All of the following are advantages of a computerized accounting system EXCEPT:
   a. many accounting cycle steps are performed by the computer.
   b. it is easier to control than a manual system.
   c. it is faster than a manual system.
   d. fewer opportunities for error exist than in a manual system.
2. The following are parts of a computer network EXCEPT:
   a. transmitters.
   b. clients.
   c. servers.
   d. databases.
3. A field that is a primary key in a different table is called a:
   a. query key.
   b. foreign key.
   c. domestic key.
   d. validation key.
4. An information system that integrates most of the business information functions of a company is known as an:
   a. enterprise resource planning system.
   b. enterprise manufacturing relations system.
   c. enterprise resource module system.
   d. enterprise business planning system.
5. The part of a computer system that controls access to data and ensures reliability of processing in the system is the:
   a. relational database.
   b. application software.
   c. database management system.
   d. control module.
6. The part of a client-server system that requests services from the system is the:
   a. database server.
   b. application server.
   c. web server.
   d. client.

7. The Internet is an example of a:
   a. client.
   b. network.
   c. server.
   d. database.
8. The module in an accounting system that is most concerned with vendors is the:
   a. sales module.
   b. purchases module.
   c. human resources module.
   d. financial management module.
9. The field in a table that uniquely identifies records in the table is the:
   a. primary key.
   b. foreign key.
   c. relation key.
   d. access key.
10. The part of a relational database system that permits users to define the information needed as output from the system is a:
    a. form.
    b. table.
    c. query.
    d. report.

CASE

C6-1
Obj. 3

http://albright.
swlearning.com

Download database file (also available on the student CD).

Working with a Relational Database System

Kwiki Oil Co. completed job number 1007 on March 8, 2004. The job required an F150 oil filter and six quarts of L245 oil. Labor time for the job was as follows: staff 1–10 minutes, staff 2–5 minutes, supervisor–2 minutes.

This case is based on the information provided in the Kwiki Oil Co. example in the chapter.

Required Use Kwiki Oil Co.'s database to record the job. Begin with the job form. Follow the example in the chapter for processing the job order. Once the job has been recorded, print the job cost report for this job.

ANALYZING COST BEHAVIOR

How much do we need to sell to make a profit?

Erin and Seth are staring rather dejectedly at the first quarter's financial report. The company is not yet close to making a profit, and they are concerned about how long the company can continue to operate at a loss. During the last month of the quarter, however, sales began to increase.

FOOD FOR THOUGHT

Seth and Erin are most concerned about not losing any more money. If you were running Young Designs, Inc., what would be the first step you would take to make the business profitable? Erin and Seth are meeting right now to discuss this question.

Erin: I think the business is improving overall. Sales are growing. I think we'll eventually be ok if we can hang on long enough and keep paying the bills until we make a profit.

Seth: How much cash do we need?

Erin: That depends on how long it takes before we stop losing money—that is, how long before we break even. We need to know the minimum amount of sales needed so we are no longer operating at a loss. Then, we can determine what level of sales is required to reach the profit we want.

Seth: I agree. I think we can use our present sales growth rate to calculate when we will reach the breakeven level.

Erin: Yesterday, I talked with Roberta about our struggle to stop losing money. She told me cost-volume-profit, or CVP, analysis would help us calculate our sales breakeven point. Basically, she said that CVP analysis involves understanding how costs behave.

Seth: Huh, seems like our costs have been misbehaving. What's this cost behavior stuff?

Erin: Remember when we talked about some costs being variable and some being fixed?

Seth: Yes, we found out certain costs, like raw materials and direct labor, vary with the amount of products we produce. But, certain other costs, like the lease on our building, don't.

Erin: Evidently, part of our problem is our sales aren't high enough to cover our fixed costs.

Seth: We could just raise our prices, but that might make us more expensive than our competition. Then, we'll have fewer sales.

Erin: I agree. Roberta said our breakeven is the point where total sales equal total costs. What we have to do is figure out what our total variable and total fixed costs are, and then we will know the minimum amount of sales revenue we must have.

Seth: Ok, that's easy enough. It also sounds like we can use CVP analysis to determine how many units we need to sell to reach a certain level of profitability.

Erin: CVP can certainly be used to determine the amount of sales necessary to reach a certain target profit. In a breakeven calculation, the target profit is zero because the company's revenues equal its costs. In a target profit calculation, we would simply use the breakeven equation of total revenues = variable costs + fixed costs and add profits to the equation so that it becomes total revenues = variable costs + fixed costs + profits.

Seth: *I understand. Since we know revenues, which are calculated as price times the number of units sold, the variable costs, which are calculated as unit variable cost times units sold, the fixed costs, and the target profit, we can solve for the number of units required.*

OBJECTIVES

Once you have completed this chapter, you should be able to:

1 Describe how costs respond to changes in activity.

2 Explain what contribution margins and breakeven points are and how the contribution margin is reflected in a variable-costing income statement.

3 Use CVP analysis to determine the breakeven point in sales and the sales volume necessary to earn a target profit.

4 Calculate unit product costs using variable and absorption costing.

5 Explain why costs are important for decision making in service companies.

COST BEHAVIOR

OBJECTIVE 1

Describe how costs respond to changes in activity.

This section considers the details of how managers explain changes in costs in regard to changes in activity. Direct materials, direct labor, and manufacturing overhead are categories of product costs. In this section we look at the behavior of those costs. First, consider how costs respond to changes in activity levels.

Black & Blue Manufacturing: The Product and Manufacturing Process

Black & Blue Manufacturing Company is a small company that manufactures skateboards. The boards are produced from composite fiberglass. Synthetic materials are prepared and poured into molds. The boards are finished and wheel assemblies are added. After inspection, the boards are shipped to retail sporting goods and specialty shops. Though the company produces several models based on the grade of materials used, the manufacturing process is the same for each model.

Cost Behavior in Relation to Changes in Activity Levels

Managers often make decisions about pricing, production levels, product mix, and external purchases after considering cost information. Later in this chapter, we examine the types of decisions managers commonly face. First, it is important to understand which costs are relevant to certain types of decisions. Often, whether a cost is relevant depends on how costs change (or do not change) when volume changes. The following paragraphs explore the impact of volume on manufacturing costs and identify examples of costs that typically are classified as variable, fixed, semivariable, and step-pattern.

Variable Costs. *Variable costs* **are costs that change in total with volume but remain fixed on a per-unit basis.** For example, the cost of materials Black & Blue uses in its manufacturing process is a variable cost because the total cost of materials varies in relation to the number of products manufactured. The cost of materials for each XR100 board produced is $20. If a single board is produced, the total cost of materials is $20. However, if 100 boards are manufactured, the total cost of materials would be $2,000.

Variable costs go up as the level of activity (volume) rises. Exhibit 1 illustrates that behavior pattern. Managers can predict the total cost of a direct material at any level of production by multiplying the cost per unit times the number of units produced:

Exhibit 1
Behavior Pattern:
Variable Costs

Stays same

Cost per unit	× Number of units produced	= Total variable cost
$20	× 1 unit produced	= $20
$20	× 3 units produced	= $60
$20	× 100 units produced	= $2,000

Fixed Costs. *Fixed costs* **are costs that do not change in total with volume but vary on a per-unit basis.** Generally, depreciation is a fixed cost. A company's *total* depreciation cost does not change whether it produces 2,500 units or 5,000 units in a year, as illustrated in Exhibit 2. However, the cost *per unit* does vary with output because fixed depreciation costs are spread over a greater or lesser number of units.

Exhibit 2
Behavior Pattern:
Fixed Costs

Suppose, for example, that a company has $50,000 in depreciation expense this year. The total cost is fixed, but the cost per unit depends on the number of units produced:

Total fixed cost	÷ Number of units produced	= Cost per unit
$50,000	÷ 2,500 units produced	= $20
$50,000	÷ 5,000 units produced	= $10

Notice that fixed costs per unit fall as the number of units produced rises.

Semivariable or Mixed Costs. *Semivariable* or *mixed costs* **are a combination of variable and fixed costs.** For example, total electricity consumption at Black & Blue changes with production levels as the number of machine hours varies. Machinery consumes most of the electrical energy used in the plant. However, even if production falls to zero, electricity would be used for lighting and heating or cooling of plant facilities. Exhibit 3 shows how mixed costs react to changes in the amount of output. The key point: Total cost is a function of both variable and fixed costs; costs vary with output but cannot drop to zero as long as a company is in business.

Exhibit 3
Behavior Pattern:
Semivariable Costs

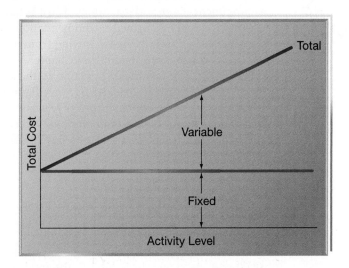

Step-Pattern Costs. *Step-pattern costs* **are costs that increase or decrease in total over a wide range of activity levels. However, these costs remain fixed over a narrow range of activity levels.** The relationship between variable costs and volume is linear as shown in Exhibit 1. Every unit produced increases total costs by the same amount. Step-pattern costs also vary with respect to volume but not in a linear pattern, as illustrated in Exhibit 4.

Exhibit 4
Behavior Pattern:
Step-Pattern Costs

For example, assume that one quality control engineer can inspect up to 1,000 units a month. If Black & Blue increases its production to 1,500 units, it must hire another quality control engineer. The company cannot hire a portion of a quality control engineer;

it has to hire the entire person. If production levels increase to more than 2,000 units a month, the company is going to have to hire a third quality control engineer. Quality inspection costs move in a step pattern with respect to volume.

Cost Behavior and Decisions: A Make-or-Buy Example

A manager who must decide between manufacturing a component or buying that component from an outside source (outsourcing) is facing a make-or-buy decision. Typically managers evaluate many factors, including costs, before choosing to make or buy a component. Your understanding of cost behavior will enable you to analyze these situations and make informed recommendations to management.

Currently, Black & Blue is buying from an outside supplier the wheels it uses on its XR100 skateboards. Recall from Chapter M2, suppliers are part of a value chain that extends from raw material production to the sales and service of a product. The company's management is considering reconfiguring the value chain by outsourcing and would like to know which costs are relevant to its decision. *Relevant costs* **are costs that change under two or more decision alternatives.** For example, plant depreciation costs are not relevant to a make-or-buy decision because depreciation costs are fixed and will not change regardless of the decision. However, wheels and other materials used to produce the boards are relevant because these costs differ between the two decision alternatives of make or buy.

Let's evaluate the costs of outsourcing and manufacturing the wheels. Assume the wheels cost $8.00 per board. The $8.00 unit cost is relevant to the make-or-buy decision because if Black & Blue manufactures the wheels internally, it does not incur the $8.00 outsourcing cost. If the company purchases the product externally, it incurs the $8.00 cost. As shown in Exhibit 5, the total cost of making one unit is $8.70. At first glance, we may conclude outsourcing is the better option because $8.00 is less than $8.70. However, applying our understanding of cost behavior, we may reach a different conclusion. Included in the total cost calculation are both variable and fixed costs. However, the relevant cost calculation includes only variable costs totaling $7.75. The fixed costs of depreciation and supervision are not relevant to the make-or-buy decision because these costs do not change between the two decision alternatives. If the product is purchased externally, the materials, direct labor, electricity, and supplies costs disappear. However, the depreciation and supervision costs remain whether the company manufactures the product internally or purchases it externally. Thus, depreciation and supervision costs are not relevant to the outsourcing decision.

Exhibit 5
Make-or-Buy
Cost Analysis

	Total Cost to Make	Total Relevant Cost to Make	Outsourced Cost
Outsource cost			$8.00
Cost to make			
Direct materials (variable)	$5.45	$5.45	
Direct labor (variable)	2.00	2.00	
Manufacturing overhead:			
Electricity (variable)	0.25	0.25	
Supplies (variable)	0.05	0.05	
Depreciation costs (fixed)	0.70	0.00	
Supervision costs (fixed)	0.25	0.00	
Total cost per unit	$8.70	$7.75	$8.00

Our cost analysis suggests Black & Blue should make the wheels internally and save $0.25 ($8.00 − $7.75) per unit. However, cost is not the only factor managers consider when analyzing a make-or-buy decision. By manufacturing the wheels internally, the company controls both quality and product availability. Availability is especially important if a labor dispute or other event interrupts production at a supplier's facility. When a company outsources a product, it depends upon suppliers to meet delivery schedules. Outsourcing can bring other complications, as well. Sometimes external firms make low bids in an attempt to attract customers. Management must be careful when deciding to discontinue production of a component in favor of outsourcing, especially if they eliminate their ability to produce it later. Cost savings that initially appear attractive may disappear just as quickly if suppliers later increase prices.

Other Behavior Considerations: Management Policies and Time

Not all costs are inherently variable or fixed. Workers in an assembly department, for example, could be paid by the piece: the higher the level of production, the larger their paychecks. Here the terms of the contract tie the workers' wages to output; wages are a variable cost. On the other hand, if the company contracts with the same workers to pay them a fixed amount every week, whatever their output, their wages are fixed. You should be careful when you classify costs by behavior because costs that appear variable may in fact be fixed. For example, assume a factory worker is being paid on an hourly basis. Are these wages variable or fixed? Most people would say that the wages are variable because the total wage costs vary according to the number of hours worked. Suppose you have one more bit of information: workers in this factory are never told to go home, even during times when the factory is producing below expected volume. In other words, each employee works 40 hours a week. In this case, management's policy has changed what is traditionally a variable cost—the wages of hourly employees—into a fixed cost. Here the total hours worked do not vary with the level of production.

Another important factor in understanding the effect of volume on costs is time. For example, the cost of raw materials generally is thought to be variable; however, if raw materials have been purchased and are available in the warehouse, one could argue that their costs are fixed. In the short run, raw material costs do not vary because the materials have been paid for and are available. There are times when fixed costs respond more like variable costs. Depreciation on plant assets generally is considered a fixed cost. However, in the long run, as assets are acquired or sold in response to changes in demand, plant depreciation behaves like a variable cost. Thus, general patterns of cost behavior exist; however, most costs can be affected by management actions.

1 SELF-STUDY PROBLEM

WebTUTOR Advantage

Atta Baby Company produces infant seats for use in automobiles. During a recent fiscal period, the company incurred the following costs:

Metal for frames	$40,000
Foam filler	25,000
Plastic seat covering	15,000
Manufacturing wages	23,000
Inspector salaries	7,000
Administrative salaries	12,000
Depreciation	4,000
Utilities	1,600

The company produced and sold 3,190 seats at $50 per seat. Each inspector can inspect up to 2,000 seats during a period. Half of the utilities costs are associated with manufacturing and vary with production. Manufacturing employees are paid for hours worked.

Required

A. Classify each cost as variable, fixed, semivariable, or step.
B. For variable costs, including the variable portion of semivariable costs, calculate the unit cost of each seat produced and sold. Round unit costs to the nearest cent.
C. If the company had produced and sold 3,500 seats, what would you expect the total costs to have been? How much profit would the company have earned?

The solution to Self-Study Problem 1 appears at the end of the chapter.

CONTRIBUTION MARGIN AND THE VARIABLE-COSTING INCOME STATEMENT

OBJECTIVE 2

Explain what contribution margins and breakeven points are and how the contribution margin is reflected in a variable-costing income statement.

An organization has to assign costs to price its products and evaluate its performance. Managers have a choice. They can assign costs using either absorption or variable costing. *Absorption costing* **assigns costs by function, separating the costs of manufacturing products from the costs of selling, administration, and other nonmanufacturing activities.** Absorption costing is also called the *full-cost method.* That's because absorption costing assigns the full costs of manufacturing to product costs. It makes no distinction between variable and fixed manufacturing costs.

Variable costing **assigns costs by their behavior, separating them into variable and fixed components.** Key to this costing method is the *contribution margin,* **the difference between sales revenue and variable costs over an accounting period.** (In fact, variable costing is sometimes called the *contribution-margin method.*) It is the contribution margin that covers a company's fixed costs and defines its profits.

A traditional income statement lists expenses by function: the cost of goods sold, selling, and administration. The format does not distinguish between variable and fixed costs. In the administrative expenses category, for example, both variable and fixed administrative costs are reported as one amount. The traditional income statement provides information about revenues and expenses for investors and other external decision makers. It does not always give a company's management the information it needs to make planning and control decisions, however.

LEARNING NOTE

The term *costs* in cost behavior decisions refers to the costs of resources that have been consumed in producing goods sold during a period. Therefore, the terms costs and expenses are used interchangeably.

Managers need information in a format that can help them make decisions. **The** *variable-costing income statement* **is a managerial decision-making tool that measures net income by subtracting variable expenses from sales and then subtracting fixed expenses from the difference.** The difference between sales revenue and variable expenses for a period is the contribution margin. The contribution margin "contributes" to covering fixed expenses. What remains after fixed expenses have been covered is net income for the period. If the contribution margin is too small to cover all fixed expenses, the company reports a net loss. The order in which the contribution margin is applied is very important: first to cover fixed expenses, and then to provide profits.

Exhibit 6 shows a variable-costing income statement for Black & Blue Company. Notice that the amounts are listed both in total and per unit. In their analysis of profitability, managers can look at both overall performance and the per-unit effect of variable expenses.

Black & Blue generates a contribution margin of $10.40 per skateboard: Each skateboard the company sells contributes $10.40 toward covering fixed expenses. If the company sells enough skateboards to generate a $6,000 contribution margin, it can then cover all of its fixed expenses and break even for the month. **The** *breakeven point* **is that level of sales at which all variable and fixed expenses are covered, but no profit is generated.** Once sales reach the breakeven point, each additional unit sold contributes a profit equal to the contribution margin of that unit. As more units are sold, net income continues to go up by the contribution margin of each additional unit sold.

Exhibit 6

Black & Blue Company:
A Variable-Costing
Income Statement

Black & Blue Company
Variable-Costing Income Statement
For the Month Ended August 31, 2005

	Total	Per Unit
Sales revenue (1,000 skateboards)	$26,000	$26.00
Less variable expenses	15,600	15.60
Contribution margin	$10,400	$10.40
Less fixed expenses	6,000	
Net income	$ 4,400	

why isn't fixed expense put in

In addition to being expressed in total or on a per-unit basis, the contribution margin can be expressed as a percentage of sales as shown in Exhibit 7.

Exhibit 7

Black & Blue Company:
Contribution Margin as a
Percentage of Sales

	Total	Per Unit	Percentage
Sales (1,000 skateboards)	$26,000	$26.00	100%
Less variable expenses	15,600	15.60	60%
Contribution margin	$10,400	$10.40	40%
Less fixed expenses	6,000		
Net income	$ 4,400		

The ratio (expressed as a percentage) of contribution margin to total sales is called the *contribution margin ratio* **or the profit volume ratio:**

Contribution margin ratio = Contribution margin ÷ Sales
40% = $10,400   ÷ $26,000

When fixed costs stay the same, a company can use the contribution margin ratio to determine the effect on net income of a change in total sales. For example, suppose that Black & Blue plans to increase its sales next month by $10,000. That means it plans to increase the total contribution margin by $4,000 ($10,000 increase in sales × 40% contribution margin ratio). If the company's fixed costs do not change, Black & Blue can expect its net income to go up by $4,000.

The contribution margin ratio can also help managers allocate limited resources. Products that have a higher contribution margin ratio are more profitable to a company, and so a company is more likely to focus its advertising and production resources on those products.

COST-VOLUME-PROFIT ANALYSIS

OBJECTIVE 3

Use CVP analysis to
determine the breakeven
point in sales and the
sales volume necessary to
earn a target profit.

The variable-costing concept can be extended to help managers plan and make decisions about sales and profits. *Cost-volume-profit (CVP) analysis* **is the use of the relationships among costs, volume, and profits to make managerial decisions.** A change in any one of those components affects the others. As Exhibit 8 shows, an understanding of the relationships among product prices, activity levels, variable costs, and fixed costs can help managers develop marketing strategies, set pricing policies, and make resource decisions. Once costs have been separated into variable and fixed components, CVP analysis can be used to determine a company's breakeven point, to determine the sales volume necessary to earn a target profit, to measure the effect on net income of a

Exhibit 8

Cost-Volume-Profit
Analysis and
Managerial Decision
Making

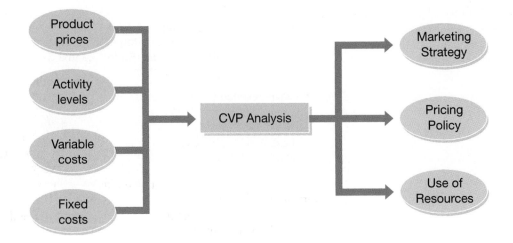

change in expenses, and to determine the most profitable mix of products in a multiple-product environment. CVP analysis also helps managers evaluate sales options and a company's level of operating risk.

CVP analysis makes certain assumptions about costs and activities. If those assumptions are violated, the analysis can be flawed. One assumption, for example, is that fixed costs remain constant over the range of production. If fixed costs change, the analysis is not valid. A company can provide only a certain volume of production and sales without adding workers or plant assets, which translates into higher fixed costs. If the existing machinery at Black & Blue is capable of producing just 60 skateboards a day, the company cannot produce 70 boards a day without additional equipment. That additional equipment would increase maintenance and depreciation expenses, which are part of the fixed cost of production.

CVP analysis is complicated by mixed (semivariable) costs. Remember that mixed costs have both fixed and variable components. A salesperson's compensation, for example, is a mixed cost if it is made up of a base salary plus a bonus that increases with sales.

Whenever possible, mixed costs should be separated into their variable and fixed components. For example, some equipment is depreciated on the basis of units of production. That is a variable expense. Other equipment is depreciated on a straight-line basis. That is a fixed expense. By keeping records of depreciation for individual pieces of equipment, a company can separate its depreciation expense into variable and fixed components.

Of course it is difficult to separate mixed costs because the costs are intermingled in the accounting records. For instance, a company may use a single account to record the costs of generating reports on a computer. The cost of reports that are produced weekly and sent to all departments in the company would be fixed. The cost of reports that are produced only at the request of a department would be variable. Although the company could separate the costs, it may choose not to if the additional accuracy does not justify the cost of keeping two accounts.

CVP analysis also is complicated by the fact that the cost of materials for a unit of product may not remain constant. For example, as a company produces more units, it buys more materials. As it buys more materials, volume discounts can lower the cost per unit of those materials. Another example is a shortage of materials in the market, which would push the price of those materials up. CVP analysis assumes that the cost of materials remains constant for each unit of a partic-

LEARNING NOTE

Remember our discussion in an earlier chapter about costs and the need for accurate information. Generally the more accurate the accounting information, the more costly it is to produce.

ular product. It is important, then, for managers using CVP analysis to talk with purchasing managers to be sure that variable costs per unit and fixed costs will not change over the period being considered.

Breakeven-Point Analysis

Breakeven-point analysis is one of the most common uses of CVP analysis. **Breakeven-point analysis** is a technique used to find the volume of sales—in units or dollars—at which a company just covers its total costs. Erin and Seth's situation at the beginning of the chapter underscores the importance of breakeven-point analysis. They need to know what sales level Young Designs, Inc., must reach for the company to cease being unprofitable. Breakeven-point analysis is a simple calculation that often has profound implications. Two ways to calculate the breakeven point are the equation method and the unit-contribution method.

The Equation Method. The equation method builds on the relationship among sales, total costs, and profits. In its simplest form,

Sales − Total costs = Profits

The next step is to separate the variable and fixed components of total costs:

Sales − (Variable costs + Fixed costs) = Profits

At the breakeven point, profits are zero. That means the equation can be rewritten as:

Sales = Variable costs + Fixed costs

Remember that we're looking for the volume of sales at which a company covers its total costs. Fixed costs are a given: we assume that however many units a company sells, its fixed costs remain constant. Our focus is on two terms: sales and variable costs. For the sales term we can substitute the selling price per unit multiplied by the number of units sold; for the variable-costs term, we can substitute the variable cost per unit multiplied by the number of units sold:

Sales = Variable costs + Fixed costs
Selling price per unit × Units sold = (Variable cost per unit × Units sold) + Fixed costs

How does it work? Black & Blue sells its skateboards for $26.00 apiece, each skateboard has variable costs of $15.60, and the company has fixed costs each month of $6,000 (see Exhibit 6). How many skateboards does the company have to sell each month to break even?

Breakeven sales = Variable costs + Fixed costs
Selling price per unit × Units sold = (Variable cost per unit × Units sold) + Fixed costs
$26.00 × Units sold = ($15.60 × Units sold) + $6,000
($26.00 − $15.60) × Units sold = $6,000
$10.40 × Units sold = $6,000
Units sold = 577

Black & Blue's breakeven point is 577 units a month. If it sells 577 skateboards a month, the company can cover its fixed costs.

The Unit-Contribution Method. The unit-contribution method also can be used to determine the number of units a company must sell to break even. The method is based on the idea that each unit sold contributes toward covering fixed expenses. To determine the number of units that must be sold to break even, then, we divide fixed costs by the contribution margin per unit:

Breakeven units = Fixed costs ÷ Unit contribution margin

According to Exhibit 6, Black & Blue generates a $10.40 contribution margin on each skateboard it sells. On that basis, the company has to sell 577 skateboards a month to break even:

Breakeven units = Fixed costs ÷ Unit contribution margin
              = $6,000 ÷ $10.40
              = 577 skateboards

The unit-contribution method also can be used to determine the breakeven point in sales dollars—the amount of sales in dollars at which a company covers its fixed costs:

Breakeven sales dollars = Fixed costs ÷ Contribution margin ratio

Black & Blue's contribution margin ratio is 40% (Exhibit 7). So the company must sell $15,000 in skateboards each month to break even:

Breakeven sales dollars = Fixed costs ÷ Contribution margin ratio
                     = $6,000 ÷ 40%
                     = $15,000

Target-Profit Analysis

CVP analysis also can be used to determine the sales (in units or dollars) necessary to earn a target profit. A *target profit* is the profit that a company wants to make over a given period. The Food for Thought section in the beginning chapter scenario provides an intuitive feel for how this type of situation can arise in the business world. As Erin explained to Seth, the basic breakeven-point equation can be modified to permit a target profit calculation. As Erin indicated, breakeven-point analysis is the same thing as target-profit analysis with the target profit set at zero.

Suppose that Black & Blue wants to earn a profit of $2,000 a month. How many skateboards would it have to sell? One way to answer that question is to rework the breakeven-point equation, inserting target profit:

Target profit = (Selling price per unit × Units sold) −
             (Variable cost per unit × Units sold) − Fixed costs
$2,000   = ($26.00 × Units sold) − ($15.60 × Units sold) − $6,000
$8,000   = $10.40 × Units sold
Units sold = 770 skateboards

Black & Blue can earn its target profit by selling 770 skateboards a month.
We can get the same answer using a variation of the unit-contribution method:

Units sold = (Target profit + Fixed costs) ÷ Contribution margin
          = ($2,000 + $6,000) ÷ $10.40
          = $8,000 ÷ $10.40
          = 770 skateboards

Profit-Sensitivity Analysis

CVP analysis also answers questions about how profits would change if the selling price, the units sold, or costs change. Black & Blue is selling 1,000 skateboards for $26.00

apiece at a variable cost per skateboard of $15.60. Suppose that the company's management is thinking about lowering the selling price to $24.00, a change that should increase sales by 20 percent, and cutting the variable cost per unit to $15.00. Do the changes make sense in terms of the company's profits?

To gauge the impact of the changes on profits, we can use the equation we used to determine the number of units the company would have to sell to earn its target profit. Here, though, we substitute profit for target profit:

Profit = (Selling price per unit × Units sold − (Variable cost per unit × Units sold) − Fixed costs
  = ($24.00 × 1,200)* − ($15.00 × 1,200) − $6,000
  = $28,800 − $18,000 − $6,000
  = $4,800

*1,200 units = 1,000 units × 1.20

At the new selling price, the new sales volume, and the new variable cost per unit, Black & Blue's profit would go up $400 ($4,800 − $4,400) (see Exhibit 6).

Cost Behavior and Operating Risk

Cost behavior affects operating risk. *Operating risk* **is the risk that a drop in sales volume will cause a company to earn an unsatisfactory profit.** Operating risk increases as the percentage of a company's fixed costs to total costs increases. As the percentage of fixed costs to total costs increases, reductions in sales result in smaller and smaller reductions in total costs. For example, major commercial airlines have enormous fixed costs associated with owning or leasing aircraft. If an airline's fixed costs to total costs percentage is 80 percent, then a drop in sales of $1.00 will result in a reduction in total cost of only $0.20 [(100% − 80% = 20%) × $1.00]. This is because only 20 percent of the total costs vary with sales volume.

When a company's operating risk becomes too high, managers frequently take steps to reduce this risk. This often means reducing discretionary fixed costs. *Discretionary fixed costs* **are fixed costs that can be eliminated in the relatively short term.** An example of a discretionary fixed cost is an advertising contract that is renewable each month. If a company does not wish to incur this cost next month it can simply choose not to renew the contract. In contrast, *committed fixed costs* **are costs that cannot be eliminated in the relatively short term.** An example of a committed fixed cost is a long-term lease on a warehouse. Even if the company does not need the warehouse space, it is still obligated to make lease payments.

Once committed fixed costs are incurred, it may be years before these costs can be eliminated. Well-managed companies often take great care before committing to large, nondiscretionary fixed costs. One way in which companies do this is by requiring that large expenditures for property, plant, and equipment be thoroughly evaluated through a formal approval process before a purchase is approved. Such evaluations are intended to identify the expected benefits, costs, and risks associated with the expenditures.

2 SELF-STUDY PROBLEM

WebTUTOR Advantage

Calhoun Carpets is considering a new line of carpeting for boats. The carpet would cost $3.00 a yard to make and would sell for $10.00 a yard. Calhoun would have to build a new plant and buy new equipment—at an annual cost of $4.2 million—to produce the new line.

Required

A. How many yards of carpet would Calhoun have to sell annually to break even? What would the company's breakeven point in sales dollars be?

B. How many yards would the company have to sell to make a target profit of $700,000 on the line? What is the sales dollars equivalent of that number of yards?

The solution to Self-Study Problem 2 appears at the end of the chapter.

VARIABLE AND ABSORPTION COSTING: A COMPARISON

OBJECTIVE 4

Calculate unit product costs using variable and absorption costing.

GAAP require companies to use absorption costing to develop their financial statements for external reporting. Under absorption costing, both variable and fixed production costs are recognized as the cost of goods sold. The Internal Revenue Service (IRS) also requires the use of that method to determine federal tax liability. However, a company can choose the costing method it uses for internal purposes—to set the selling price of products and to evaluate performance. Some companies use absorption costing for both external reporting and internal decision making. Other companies set up two accounting systems, using absorption costing for external reports and variable costing for internal reports.

The choice of costing method affects both the unit product cost—a measure sometimes used to determine a product's selling price—and a company's net income—a performance measure.

Unit Product Cost

A key measure in the pricing decision is the unit cost of the finished product—the unit product cost. That cost determines the value of finished goods inventory and, eventually, the cost of goods sold.

Remember that variable costing classifies costs by their behavior: variable or fixed. In calculating the unit product cost, variable costing uses only those costs that vary directly with production: the costs of direct materials, direct labor, and variable manufacturing overhead. Fixed manufacturing overhead costs are treated like period expenses. Like selling and administrative costs, those costs are expensed in the period in which they are incurred. The variable unit product cost never includes fixed costs.

Absorption costing, on the other hand, classifies costs by their function: manufacturing or nonmanufacturing. The unit product cost calculation using the absorption-costing method includes all the costs of manufacturing—variable and fixed. By definition, then, the variable unit product cost is always smaller than the absorption unit product cost because it does not include fixed production costs.

The Variable-Costing Calculation. The variable unit product cost is a measurement that helps managers make decisions about cost-volume-profit relationships. For example, as you have just seen in the discussion of CVP analysis, the variable unit cost of a product is key to breakeven-point analysis, target-profit analysis, and profit-sensitivity analysis.

Exhibit 9 shows how variable costing is used to calculate unit costs. Observe that unit cost includes only variable costs. Fixed costs are never part of the calculation. The unit variable cost is a *product cost.* Only the costs of direct materials, direct labor, and manufacturing overhead are part of its calculation. Selling and administrative expenses—whether they are variable or fixed—are treated as period expenses. Like fixed manufacturing overhead, they are recorded as expenses in the period in which they are incurred. The variable unit product cost times the number of units produced is recorded in finished goods inventory and then charged to cost of goods sold when the units are sold.

The Absorption-Costing Calculation. Absorption costing includes *all* production costs in the unit-cost calculations, whether those costs are variable or fixed. So the unit-

Exhibit 9
Calculating the Variable
Product Cost per Unit

Number of units produced in the period	10,000
Variable costs per unit:	
Direct materials	$5
Direct labor	3
Variable manufacturing overhead	2
Variable selling and administrative expenses	2
Fixed costs per period:	
Fixed manufacturing overhead	$50,000
Fixed selling and administrative expenses	35,000
The variable unit product cost calculation:	
Direct materials cost per unit	$ 5
Direct labor cost per unit	3
Variable manufacturing overhead cost per unit	2
Total variable cost per unit	$10

[handwritten: Point included selling Admin]

cost calculation allocates fixed manufacturing overhead to each unit of product in addition to variable production costs. The cost of each unit in finished goods inventory and cost of goods sold include both variable and fixed components.

Exhibit 10 shows how costs are classified under variable and absorption costing. Notice that the only difference between the two methods is in the way each treats the costs of fixed manufacturing overhead.

Exhibit 10
Variable and Absorption
Costing: Classifying
Costs

Costs	Variable Costing	Absorption Costing
Direct materials	Product cost	Product cost
Direct labor	Product cost	Product cost
Variable manufacturing overhead	Product cost	Product cost
Fixed manufacturing overhead	**Period expense**	**Product cost**
Variable selling & administrative expenses	Period expense	Period expense
Fixed selling & administrative expenses	Period expense	Period expense

Let's calculate a unit product cost using absorption costing from the information in Exhibit 9. The unit product cost for the period would be $15:

Direct materials cost per unit	$ 5
Direct labor cost per unit	3
Variable manufacturing overhead cost per unit	2
Fixed manufacturing overhead cost per unit*	5
Total cost per unit	$15

[handwritten: 50,000 ÷ 10,000]

*$50,000 ÷ 10,000 units. See Exhibit 9.

Performance Evaluation: Net Income

Income calculated using variable costing differs from income calculated using absorption costing. Absorption-costing income is affected by changes in the ending inventory of finished goods. Variable-costing income is not affected by these changes.

Exhibit 11 compares income statements for Black & Blue Company for January using the variable- and absorption-costing methods.

Exhibit 11

Black & Blue Company:
Income Statements for
January

Absorption Costing	
Sales (8,000 units × $25)	$200,000
Cost of goods sold (8,000 units × $10) + $40,000	120,000
Gross margin	$ 80,000
Less administrative expenses ($35,000 fixed + $20,000 variable)	55,000
Net income	$ 25,000
Variable Costing	
Sales (8,000 units × $25)	$200,000
Cost of goods sold (8,000 units × $10)	80,000
Gross margin	$120,000
Less administrative expenses ($35,000 fixed + $20,000 variable)	55,000
Less fixed manufacturing overhead costs	50,000
Net income	$ 15,000

The following data were used to prepare the statements:

Direct materials cost per unit	$5
Direct labor cost per unit	$3
Variable manufacturing overhead cost per unit	$2
Total variable unit cost	$10
Fixed manufacturing overhead cost	$40,000
Unit selling price	$25
Units sold	8,000
Beginning finished goods inventory in units	0
Ending finished goods inventory in units	2,000
Fixed administrative expenses	$35,000
Variable administrative expenses	$20,000

Exhibit 11 reveals a $10,000 ($25,000 − $15,000) difference in income between the two costing methods. This $10,000 difference is a function of the way the costs of fixed manufacturing overhead are treated. Using the absorption-costing method, fixed overhead costs are carried as an asset in finished goods inventory until the units are sold. Black & Blue produced 10,000 units (2,000 units in inventory + 8,000 units sold) in January; it sold just 8,000 units. The company assigned each of the 2,000 units in ending inventory $5 of fixed manufacturing overhead costs. That means $10,000 (2,000 × $5) of fixed manufacturing overhead costs remained in inventory until the units were sold.

Under the variable-costing method, fixed manufacturing overhead is a period expense. The entire cost of fixed manufacturing overhead, $40,000, was deducted as an expense in the January period in which the costs were incurred. Again, using variable costing, all fixed overhead costs are recognized as expenses each period; no fixed overhead costs are recorded in inventory.

The differences in net income between the absorption- and variable-costing methods had to do with the level of finished goods. When the number of units in ending inventory *increases* from that of the *previous period*, net income reported under the absorption-costing method is *higher* than net income reported under the variable-costing method. When inventory *decreases*, however, net income reported under the absorption-costing method is *lower* than net income reported under the variable-costing method.

If manufacturing costs are constant (i.e., inventory levels do not change from the beginning to the end of a period) and production equals sales, variable costing and absorption costing produce the same net income. But production costs, inventory levels, and sales in a manufacturing company usually vary over time. That means that the methods should produce different income numbers from period to period. That difference can lead to important differences in managers' decisions, a subject considered in the next section.

Arguments For and Against Variable Costing

Many accountants argue that variable costing is more accurate than absorption costing because it treats fixed overhead as a period expense. They insist that it is theoretically wrong to inventory fixed costs because most fixed costs are incurred whether or not any products are produced during a period. Another argument for variable costing is the usefulness of variable-cost information in certain types of analyses, like breakeven-point analysis and target-profit analysis. Variable costing clarifies the cost-volume-profit relationship.

If decision makers think of each sale independently from all other sales, any sale that covers its variable costs is good because it increases the company's contribution margin. But there are two difficulties with that logic. First, in the long run a company must cover its fixed costs and make a profit or it cannot survive. If an airline's average ticket price doesn't cover the fixed costs of buying airplanes, the company is not going to be able to pay for its assets. Second, often one sale is not independent of other sales. Airline customers who have flown on discount tickets that just cover variable costs are more likely to shop for low-priced tickets in the future. This makes it important for the airline to sell full-priced tickets. This also makes it difficult for the airline to cover its fixed expenses and make the profit it needs to stay in business.

Despite the contribution fallacy, variable costing and the contribution method can be helpful when managers understand how they should be used. For instance, it may be fine to price above variable cost but below absorption cost in selling a one-time order in a market in which a company normally does not do business. It can be very dangerous, however, to set prices this way in markets in which the company routinely does business. Variable costing also is useful in profit-sensitivity analysis (to determine the effect on profits as sales go up or down) and breakeven-point analysis (to measure operating risk). The key to its usefulness is remembering that variable costing can lead to decisions that seem good in the short run but create serious problems in the long run.

MEASURING COSTS FOR DECISION MAKING IN SERVICE COMPANIES

OBJECTIVE 5

Explain why costs are important for decision making in service companies.

Cost information is as important for service companies as it is for manufacturers. A bank, for example, has to know how much it costs to execute a particular transaction or provide a particular service in order to price that transaction or service. The cost of a car loan is more than the amount being borrowed. The loan application has to be printed and processed, the amount has to be updated each month, and a bad-debt assessment and the bank's target profit have to be included in the pricing.

The process of measuring costs in service organizations is often more complex than in manufacturing organizations. Two factors are at work here. First, services do not have the tangible, physical nature of products. It is much easier to trace the costs of materials and labor to a physical object than it is to trace costs to a particular service and the transactions that make up that service. Second, services often require many transactions that are carried out by a number of departments. The same employees may work on many different services. Again, this makes it difficult to determine the cost associated with a particular transaction and to trace the cost of that transaction to a particular service.

The following Case in Point demonstrates two important aspects of using costs to make decisions in service organizations: (1) the difficulty of tracing costs to services and (2) the way in which costing decisions can influence pricing, marketing, and operations.

Case in Point

http://albright.
swlearning.com

Find out about online
services offered by
some banks and sav-
ings and loans.

First National Bank, a bank, and **Home Federal Savings**, a savings and loan (S&L) association, were considering how to price a new service, a checking account that pays interest. In the past, the bank had offered checking accounts, but they did not pay interest. Based on cost estimates, the bank set a minimum balance of $2,200 for interest-paying accounts. The S&L set its minimum balance at $800. Why were the amounts so different?

In its estimates, the bank included all indirect costs of doing business. For example, it developed a charge for heating the building used by the customer service representatives who, in addition to their other duties, would handle customers' inquiries about their accounts. Citing the difficulty of accurately estimating certain indirect costs, the S&L's management chose to ignore any indirect costs that it could not estimate easily. The result was that the bank's estimate of the account costs was much higher than the S&L's.

The bank subsequently lost a great deal of its checking account business, but it continued to be very profitable. The S&L got many new accounts but was less profitable.

Which institution made the best pricing decision? It is difficult to say. The bank may have included costs that it should not have included. The S&L may have excluded too many costs. The process of measuring costs to make decisions in service companies is not an easy one.

---

3 SELF-STUDY PROBLEM

WebTUTOR Advantage

Kokomo Manufacturing Company produces a single product, model airplanes. A list of selected cost and operating data for last year follows:

Beginning finished goods inventory in units	0
Units produced during the year	15,000
Units sold during the year	13,500
Ending finished goods inventory in units	1,500
Selling price per unit	$60
Manufacturing costs:	
Variable costs per unit:	
Direct materials	$20
Direct labor	12
Variable manufacturing overhead	8
Fixed manufacturing overhead	$60,000
Selling and administrative expenses:	
Variable costs per unit sold	$5
Fixed expenses	$50,000

Required

A. Assuming that Kokomo uses absorption costing, compute the inventory cost per unit, and prepare an income statement for the year using a *traditional format*.

B. Assuming that the company uses variable costing, compute the product cost per unit, and prepare an income statement for the year showing the *contribution margin*.

C. Explain the difference between the variable-costing and absorption-costing net income figures.

D. Assuming that Kokomo had finished goods in inventory at the beginning of the year, what would have happened to the company's net income if the number of units sold during the period had been greater than the number of units produced? Explain your answer.

The solution to Self-Study Problem 3 appears at the end of the chapter.

REVIEW

SUMMARY of IMPORTANT CONCEPTS

1. Manufacturing costs may be classified according to their behavior with respect to changes in production volume as follows:
   a. Variable costs change in total with volume but are fixed per unit.
   b. Fixed costs do not change in total with volume but vary per unit.
   c. Semivariable or mixed costs combine variable and fixed costs.
   d. Step-pattern costs are fixed over a small range but vary over a wide range of activities.

2. Companies can use two different methods to assign product cost.
   a. The variable-costing method classifies costs by behavior, breaking costs down into variable and fixed components.
   b. The absorption-costing method classifies costs by function, manufacturing and non-manufacturing.

3. Key to variable costing is contribution margin, the difference between sales and variable expenses over a period. Profit is the contribution margin less fixed expenses.

4. The variable-costing method helps managers understand the relationship among costs, volume, and profits, an understanding that is basic to breakeven-point analysis, target-profit analysis, and profit-sensitivity analysis.

5. Operating risk increases as the percentage of fixed costs to total costs rises.

6. Both variable and absorption costing can be used to calculate unit product cost, an important element in a company's pricing decisions.
   a. Using variable costing, only those production costs that vary with volume are included in the unit product cost calculation.
   b. Using absorption costing, all product costs—fixed and variable—are part of the unit product cost calculation.
   c. The difference in the value of finished goods inventory between variable and absorption costing is a function of the way the methods treat fixed overhead costs.
      (1) Variable-costing expenses all fixed costs in the period in which they are incurred.
      (2) Absorption costing holds fixed overhead costs in inventory until the products are sold.

7. The way in which the methods treat inventory also has an impact on the net income figure each produces—a factor in the evaluation of managerial performance.

8. Variable costing is a managerial tool.
   a. Its proponents insist that it is more accurate than absorption costing and that it is critical to managerial decisions about costs, volume, and profits.
   b. Its critics argue that it is a tactical decision-making tool, useful only for making short-run decisions.

9. Absorption costing must be used for financial reporting. Some companies also use absorption costing for internal decision making.
   a. Absorption costing can be more effective than variable costing for strategic decision making.
   b. One limitation of the method is that it can create an incentive for overproduction.

10. Service organizations, like manufacturing companies, rely on variable or absorption costing to make managerial decisions, particularly decisions about pricing.

DEFINE

TERMS and CONCEPTS DEFINED in this CHAPTER

absorption costing (M166)   committed fixed costs (M171)
breakeven point (M166)   contribution margin (M166)

SELF-STUDY PROBLEM SOLUTIONS

SSP7-1   A. Materials and manufacturing wages are variable; administrative salaries and depreciation are fixed; utilities are semivariable; inspector salaries are step.

B.

	Total	Unit	
Metal for frames	$ 40,000	$12.54	
Foam filler	25,000	7.84	
Plastic seat covering	15,000	4.70	
Manufacturing wages	23,000	7.21	
Inspector salaries	7,000		
Administrative salaries	12,000		
Depreciation	4,000		
Utilities	1,600	0.25	($800 ÷ 3,190)
Total	$127,600	$32.54	

C.

Variable costs: 3,500 units × $32.54 =	$113,890
Inspector salaries	7,000
Administrative salaries	12,000
Depreciation	4,000
Fixed utilities	800
Total costs	$137,690
Revenues (3,500 × $50)	$175,000
Total costs	137,690
Net income	$ 37,310

SSP7-2   A. Calhoun would have to sell 600,000 yards to break even:

$$\text{Unit contribution margin} = \$10 - \$3$$
$$= \$7 \text{ per yard}$$
$$\text{Breakeven units} = \$4,200,000 \div \$7$$
$$= 600,000 \text{ yards}$$

The company's breakeven point in sales dollars would be $6 million (600,000 units sold × $10).

B. Calhoun would have to sell 700,000 yards of the carpet to earn a target profit of $700,000:

$$(\$700,000 + \$4,200,000) \div \$7 = 700,000 \text{ yards}$$

In sales dollars, sales of 700,000 yards equal $7 million (700,000 yards × $10).

SSP7-3   A. Using absorption costing, both fixed and variable manufacturing costs are included in the unit product cost. The unit product cost is $44:

Direct materials costs per unit	$20
Direct labor costs per unit	12
Variable manufacturing overhead costs per unit	8
Fixed manufacturing overhead costs per unit	
($60,000 ÷ 15,000 units)	4
Total cost per unit	$44

The absorption-costing income statement looks like this:

Sales revenue (13,500 × $60)	$810,000
Less cost of goods sold (13,500 × $44)	594,000
Gross margin	$216,000
Less selling and administrative expenses*	117,500
Net income	$ 98,500

*Variable selling and administrative	
expenses (13,500 units sold × $5)	$ 67,500
Fixed selling and administrative expenses	50,000
Total selling and administrative expenses	$117,500

B. Using variable costing, only variable product costs are included in the unit cost. The unit product cost is $40:

Direct materials	$20
Direct labor	12
Variable manufacturing overhead	8
Total cost per unit	$40

The income statement looks like this:

Sales revenue (13,500 × $60)		$810,000
Less variable expenses:		
Variable cost of goods sold (13,500 × $40)	$540,000	
Variable selling and administrative		
expenses (13,500 × $5)	67,500	
Total variable expenses		607,500
Contribution margin		$202,500
Less fixed expenses:		
Fixed manufacturing overhead	$ 60,000	
Fixed selling and administrative expenses	50,000	
Total fixed expenses		110,000
Net income		$ 92,500

C. Kokomo's absorption-costing net income ($98,500) is $6,000 more than the variable-costing net income ($92,500). That difference equals the fixed overhead costs of the units that remained in finished goods inventory at the end of the year under the absorption-costing method:

1,500 units in finished goods inventory × $4 fixed manufacturing overhead costs per unit = $6,000

D. If Kokomo had sold more units than it produced during the year, the absorption-costing net income would have been less than the variable-costing net income. Using absorption costing, a company's selling more units than it has produced has the effect of releasing fixed overhead costs that were deferred in previous periods.

Thinking Beyond the Question

How much do we need to sell to make a profit?

In Chapter M2, you learned how fixed costs remain fixed only within a relevant range. If sales and production are not in that relevant range, fixed costs do not stay constant. In the real world, the variable cost of making one unit may also change if sales and production vary a great deal. For example, if production exceeds the amount that can be produced within the normal work week, a higher-cost overtime wage is likely to be required. A certain amount of "normal" overtime may be assumed in the unit variable cost, but unusual amounts of overtime for extended periods will alter temporarily the unit variable cost and the company's breakeven point.

Think about Erin and Seth's dilemma at the beginning of the chapter. They want to determine the level of sales required to break even or to make a target profit. Suppose Young Designs, Inc.'s, sales and production temporarily exceed certain levels, and the unit variable cost changes substantially because of increased overtime costs. How can Erin and Seth deal with such changes within the context of breakeven analysis? Does this issue have any similarities to step fixed costs? Does the existence of multiple breakeven points invalidate breakeven analysis?

QUESTIONS

Q7-1
Obj. 1
You decide to study for an upcoming accounting exam with a friend. Your friend says that fixed costs are considered fixed because they remain constant, or "fixed," for each unit produced. Do you agree? Explain your answer.

Q7-2
Obj. 1
Pagoda Company manufactures metal picture-framing materials. Part of the manufacturing process is the coating and painting of the metal with finishes. Management of Pagoda believes the painting process is a variable cost that is incurred evenly for each unit that passes through the painting operation. An analysis of several recent production runs revealed, however, that costs differ on a per-unit basis when the run sizes differ. Is the cost of painting a variable cost? What explanation could you provide for the cost behavior of the painting operation?

Q7-3
Obj. 1
Explain the importance of cost behavior as it relates to various levels of production activity. Why is information about cost behavior important to managers? Identify some decisions that managers make that require information about cost behavior.

Q7-4
Obj. 2
Jane Pratt is the president of Capital Products, Inc. Capital manufactures adjustable baseball caps embroidered with the logos of college teams. The company is planning to produce a special hat with the logo of a university that recently won the national football championship. The hats will be sold throughout the country over the next three months. After meeting with the managers of sales, production, and purchasing, Jane has determined that the special hat will have a positive contribution margin of $1.50. Capital currently is earning a profit for the year. What does the contribution margin represent? Why is it important to Jane?

Q7-5
Obj. 2
Ampco Industries, Inc., produces audio and video circuit boards. Ampco sold 12,500 circuit boards last month, which was its breakeven point in sales units. Explain what the breakeven point is.

Q7-6
Obj. 2
Enterprises produces and sells a specialty soft drink called PowerPunch. The contribution margin ratio for PowerPunch is 40%. What percentage of total sales is used to cover variable costs? Will these percentages change with a rise or fall in sales volume? What does PowerPunch's contribution margin in dollars equal at the breakeven point?

Q7-7
Obj. 3
Snow Manufacturing Company produces a snowshoe that is sold in many parts of the upper Midwest. The company's production manager has decided to change the materials used in the production process, a change that should produce a savings in direct materials costs of $12

per pair of snowshoes. The sales manager has decided to pass the savings on to the customer by reducing the selling price of the snowshoes $12 a pair. What effect will these changes have on Snow's breakeven point in units?

Q7-8
Obj. 3
An automobile manufacturer is considering buying new robotic welders for its frame assembly operations that will replace existing manual welding. This change is expected to result in lower overall costs and higher quality. Explain the impact of this decision in terms of operating risk.

Q7-9
Obj. 4
Hendee Productions Company does personal and commercial videotaping. Hendee accumulates the cost of each video production on a per-job basis using the variable-costing method. Pete Conrad, the owner of the company, recently noticed that selling and administrative expenses are not included in the costs of production. Pete is considering a switch to absorption costing. Would selling and administrative expenses be treated differently under absorption costing? Explain your answer.

Q7-10
Obj. 4
Sam Merchant was recently hired as a cost accountant by Dolls and Such Manufacturing. The company's management desires more useful information. The controller asked Sam to review the company's inventory records and to convert the carrying value of each item in inventory from an absorption-costing value to a variable-costing value. What differences does Sam have to consider in making his calculations? Why might the controller have chosen to convert to variable costing?

Q7-11
Obj. 4
Over the past year, Darren, Inc., has seen its finished goods inventory go up significantly. Darren prepares financial statements for its stockholders using absorption costing. The company prepares another set of financial statements for its managers using variable costing. Which of the two statements is going to show a greater net income for the year? Why?

Q7-12
Obj. 4
Juanita Perez is the president of Allgood Manufacturing, Inc. Allgood manufactures electric power tools. The company uses the absorption-costing method. Over the past year, sales increased significantly at Allgood, reducing the company's inventories 60% from the beginning of the year. When she looked at the year's sales figures, Juanita was surprised that net income was lower than anticipated. What factors might have been at work here?

Q7-13
Obj. 4
Suppose that the number of units in a company's ending inventory equals the number of units in its beginning inventory and that its fixed costs have not changed from the previous year. Which costing method—variable or absorption costing—would yield a higher net income?

Q7-14
Obj. 4
Coyote Battery Company manufactures rechargeable nickel cadmium batteries. The company uses the variable-costing method to accumulate inventory costs. At the end of its fiscal year, Coyote has to prepare its financial statements and tax returns. Can Coyote use its inventory values for financial-reporting and tax purposes? Explain your answer.

Q7-15
Obj. 4
Jan and Fran Hook are hairdressers with over 40 years of experience between them. Recently they decided to combine their savings and buy a factory to produce men's hairpieces. Jan has assumed responsibility for administration, including the development of accounting procedures. Fran does not understand why the inventory value of a hairpiece should include plant and supervisory costs. How should Jan explain the process of placing a value on inventory to Fran?

Q7-16
Obj. 4
Absorption costing defers certain costs. Which costs are deferred? Where? When are these costs expensed? How does variable costing treat these costs?

Q7-17
Obj. 4
Randy Lightfoot is vice president of operations for MultiCo, Inc. He is responsible for the operations of the company's two manufacturing plants, one in Atlanta and one in St. Louis. Each plant has a manager who oversees the daily operations. During a recent review of operations for the year, prepared using absorption costing, Randy noted that the Atlanta plant reported net income and that the balance in finished goods inventory had grown significantly over the year. The St. Louis plant showed no net income, but its inventory fell over the year. According to MultiCo's policy, the Atlanta plant manager will receive a bonus this year based on the income generated at the plant; the St. Louis manager will not receive a bonus. Comment on Randy's observation. What conflicts are created when a company determines its managers' bonuses based on net income alone?

Q7-18
Obj. 4
Ruth Peevey is president of Tuffee Tools Company. Tuffee manufactures a wide variety of hand tools and sells them throughout the South. Ruth just completed a review of next year's budget and plans, which project an operating loss. Knowing that Tuffee's stockholders and

the bank that is financing the company will not be happy with an operating loss, Ruth has asked the company's controller to recalculate next year's predetermined overhead rate to include 50% of all budgeted administrative costs. What problems does this create for the controller? Should the controller make the changes?

EXERCISES

If your instructor is using Personal Trainer® in this course, you may complete your assignments online.

E7-1 Write a short definition of each of the terms listed in the *Terms and Concepts Defined in this Chapter* section.

E7-2 Use (a) variable costs, (b) fixed costs, (c) semivariable costs, and (d) step-pattern costs to classify
Obj. 1 each of the following costs based on its cost behavior. Provide a brief explanation of your answer.

a. Direct materials
b. Direct labor
c. Depreciation
d. Salary of production supervisor
e. Telephone expense

f. Machine repairs
g. Factory janitor wages
h. Property taxes
i. Sales commissions
j. Material handling

E7-3 The data for costs A, B, and C are as follows. Determine the cost behavior (variable, fixed, or semi-
Obj. 1 variable) of Cost A, Cost B, and Cost C. Prepare a graph depicting the cost behavior of each of the three costs, using total cost as the vertical axis and production volume as the horizontal axis.

[handwritten margin note: — Salary + commission is a step pattern]

	Number of Units Produced	Unit Cost	Total Cost
Cost A	1	?	$ 15
	10	?	150
	100	?	1,500
	1,000	?	15,000
Cost B	1	$6,000	?
	10	600	?
	100	60	?
	1,000	6	?
Cost C	1	?	$ 4,025
	10	?	4,250
	100	?	6,500
	1,000	?	29,000

E7-4 Sheldon Nast, an entry-level cost accountant, was asked by his supervisor to analyze mainte-
Obj. 1 nance costs. Sheldon produced the following plot of maintenance costs by production level:

He immediately recognized how costs vary with production levels and remembered how to plot a line through data points to describe its slope. Convinced he had discovered a linear relationship that describes cost at any level of production, Sheldon produced the following graph to demonstrate his point at the next managers' meeting:

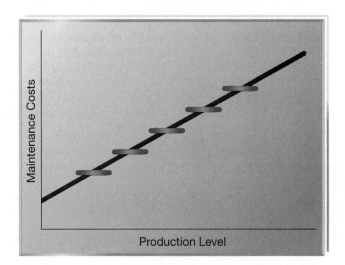

a. Do maintenance costs increase in a linear fashion as production levels increase? Why or why not?
b. What effect, if any, would cutting production by 10% have on maintenance department costs? Explain your answer.

E7-5
Obj. 2
Taylor, Inc., produces a child's wall clock that chimes the tune "Three Blind Mice" every hour. The contribution margin for this clock is $8, and the breakeven point is 8,000 units. How much profit will Taylor make if it sells 11,000 clocks? What are the company's total fixed costs?

E7-6
Obj. 2
The following partial information is from Brown Bag, Inc.'s income statement for 2006, prepared using variable costing:

Sales revenue	—
Less variable costs	—
Contribution margin	—
Less fixed costs	$30,000
Net income	$10,000

Brown Bag's contribution margin ratio is 40%. What percentage of Brown Bag's revenue is used to cover variable costs? What were variable costs at this sales volume? What was sales revenue in 2006?

E7-7
Obj. 2

SPREADSHEET

Double R Company's most recent income statement, prepared on a contribution-margin basis, is as follows:

	Total	Per Unit
Sales	$500,000	$25
Less variable costs	360,000	18
Contribution margin	$140,000	$ 7
Less fixed costs	110,000	
Net income	$ 30,000	

Prepare a new income statement under each of the following independent conditions:

a. Sales volume increases 20%.
b. The selling price drops $4 per unit, and sales volume increases 30%.
c. The selling price increases $2, fixed costs increase $10,000, and sales volume decreases 5%.

(Continued)

    d. The selling price increases 20%, variable costs increase $2 per unit, and fixed costs increase 20%.

    e. Variable costs increase $2 per unit, and fixed costs decrease by $40,000.

E7-8
Objs. 2, 3

Joey Company manufactures a product that sells for $27 per unit. Its variable costs are $15 per unit, and its fixed costs are $132,000 per year.

    a. What is the product's contribution margin ratio?

    b. What is the breakeven point in sales dollars?

    c. Assume that sales go up $60,000 next year. If fixed costs do not change, how does the increase affect net income (or net loss)?

    d. If Joey spends $30,000 on advertising, sales should go up $60,000. If the increased sales do not change the company's contribution margin ratio, should Joey buy the advertising?

E7-9
Objs. 2, 3

Penquin Industries, Inc., manufactures a variety of plastic food containers and serving dishes. The company's income statement for this year in a variable-costing format is as follows:

SPREADSHEET

Sales revenue	$960,000
Less variable production costs	192,000
Less variable selling expenses	96,000
Contribution margin	$672,000
Less fixed manufacturing overhead	300,000
Less fixed selling expenses	139,000
Net income	$233,000

    Penquin's management believes that it can increase prices by an average of 6% next year without affecting the number of products sold. Advertising costs are expected to go up next year by $9,000; administrative expenses by $30,000. Production costs are not expected to change.

    a. Calculate Penquin's breakeven point in sales dollars for this year.

    b. Use the estimates for next year to prepare a variable-costing income statement for that year.

    c. Using the forecasted changes, calculate Penquin's breakeven point in sales dollars for next year.

E7-10
Objs. 2, 3

JLC Enterprises is a rapidly growing gardening supply company. Information for the year just ended is as follows:

SPREADSHEET

Sales revenue	$300,000
Units sold	20,000
Unit contribution margin	$10
Total fixed costs	$120,000

What is JLC's breakeven point in dollars?

E7-11
Objs. 2, 3, 5

Green Acres is a lawn care service. Rachel Webb, the owner of the service, is trying to increase her number of regular customers. She has developed several proposals and is trying to decide which one to choose. Following is an income statement for the current year prepared using variable costing:

Green Acres Income Statement		
	Total	**Per Job**
Revenue	$80,000	$40.00
Less variable costs:		
Variable product costs	$15,000	7.50
Variable selling and administrative expenses	20,000	35,000 10.00
Contribution margin		$45,000 $22.50
Less fixed costs:		
Fixed product costs	$10,000	
Fixed selling and administrative expenses	6,000	16,000
Net income		$29,000

Prepare a new income statement under each of the following independent conditions:

a. Rachel increases her fixed advertising budget by $2,000 and sales increase by 10%.
b. Rachel reduces the selling price by $5 per job, and volume increases 50%.
c. Rachel reduces the selling price $3 per job, reduces fixed costs 8%, and volume increases to 2,500 jobs.

E7-12

Obj. 3

Carbon Industries, Inc., is considering buying new equipment to use in the manufacture of its product. The new machines, which would increase production capacity, would also require annual fixed costs of $480,000. Carbon expects variable costs to go down with more efficient use of materials and fewer direct labor hours. Those savings would be offset in part by higher variable manufacturing overhead costs related to machine maintenance. The net effect of the changes would be a 20% reduction overall in Carbon's variable manufacturing costs. Total sales are not expected to change in 2005. If the company does not buy the new machines, it expects the following next year:

Sales revenue	$8,000,000
Variable costs	70% of sales
Fixed costs	$1,600,000

If Carbon does buy the new equipment, what will be the net income next year?

E7-13

Obj. 3

Home Company never advertises. The Ad group, an advertising agency that has been trying to win Home over, claims that an aggressive advertising campaign would increase Home's sales by 22%. A summary of Home's sales and costs for the year just ended is as follows:

Units sold	150,000
Selling price per unit	$50
Variable manufacturing costs per unit	$10
Fixed costs:	
Manufacturing overhead	$800,000
Selling and administrative expenses	$700,000

Using this information, determine how much Home could pay for advertising and earn a target profit of $300,000.

E7-14

Obj. 3

Stillman, Inc., manufactures light bulb filaments and other miscellaneous parts for electronic equipment. Stillman has the opportunity to fill a large special order for a new customer. The special order would require Stillman to incur extra production costs. Selected cost information regarding the part is as follows:

Number of parts ordered	3,000
Revenue from special order	$25,000
Additional production costs for special order	$5,000
Contribution margin ratio	30%

Calculate the difference in profit or loss that would result if Stillman accepts the special order versus rejecting it.

E7-15

Obj. 3

SPREADSHEET

Matt Ledesma has recently been hired as vice president for marketing by Glencoe, Inc. Matt is convinced that Glencoe should launch a major new promotion that includes a tie-in with a movie. For every one of Glencoe's products sold, the customer would be given two free tickets to the movie. Glencoe's most recent income statement, based on sales of 100,000 units, is as follows:

Sales revenue	$300,000
Less variable costs	120,000
Contribution margin	$180,000
Less fixed costs	70,000
Net income	$110,000

(Continued)

Matt has conducted some market research and concluded that the promotion would increase sales by 15,000 units. The movie tickets would cost Glencoe $0.50 each. What would net income be if Glencoe does the promotion? What would net income be if one ticket instead of two is given away with each purchase?

E7-16
Obj. 3

Carol's Creations produces and markets a unique product. The president of the company has set a target profit of $50,025 for the coming year. Cost information for the company is as follows:

SPREADSHEET

Selling price per unit	$ 125
Variable product cost per unit	36
Variable selling and administrative expense per unit	14
Fixed manufacturing overhead per year	43,975
Fixed selling and administrative expense per year	56,000

a. Calculate the breakeven point in units.
b. Calculate the number of units Carol's Creations will need to sell to achieve the target profit of $50,025.

E7-17
Obj. 3

Atwater Enterprises sold 5,000 units of product A during July. It reported the following sales and cost information for the month:

Sales revenue	$400,000
Less variable costs	240,000
Less fixed costs	120,000
Net income	$ 40,000

Suppose Atwater increases the selling price of product A by 10%. How many units would it have to sell to continue generating a monthly income of $40,000?

E7-18
Obj. 3

In planning its operations for next year, Petrie, Inc. estimated sales of $6,000,000 and the following costs:

	Costs and Expenses	
	Variable	**Fixed**
Direct materials	$1,600,000	
Direct labor	1,400,000	
Factory overhead	600,000	$ 900,000
Selling expenses	240,000	360,000
Administrative expenses	60,000	140,000
Total	$3,900,000	$1,400,000

Calculate Petrie's breakeven point in sales dollars.

E7-19
Obj. 3

The following CVP graph shows the relationships in one company among costs, volume, and profits:

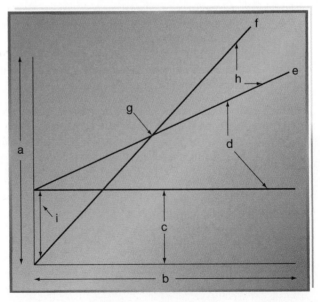

    a. Label each of the lettered elements on the graph.

    b. List the lettered elements in the graph that would be affected by each of the following actions and the nature of the effect. Treat each case independently. Ignore the effect on element h.

      (1) The selling price per unit goes down from $50 to $45.

      (2) Variable costs per unit go up from $18 to $23.

      (3) Fixed costs fall $3,000.

      (4) Sales volume goes up 1,500 units.

      (5) The company sells a piece of production equipment, increasing labor hours and reducing fixed costs.

      (6) Both variable costs and the selling price go up 10%.

      (7) The company incurs advertising costs in the amount of $25,000 a year. Sales increase as a result.

E7-20
Obj. 4

Yellow Jacket Company manufactures one product, an organic bath soap. Information concerning production during the past year is as follows:

Units produced and sold	25,000
Direct labor cost	$40,000
Direct materials cost	$10,000
Factory supervisor's salary	$15,000
Other fixed manufacturing overhead	$5,000
Indirect materials (varies with production)	$1,300
Other variable manufacturing overhead	$1,200
Variable selling expenses	$1,000
Fixed selling and administrative expenses	$40,000

    a. What is unit product cost using absorption costing?

    b. What is unit product cost using variable costing?

    c. What is the total unit variable cost?

E7-21
Obj. 4

Azure Company went into business two years ago. Information concerning production, costs, sales, and inventory levels for the last two years is as follows:

	2005	2004
Sales revenue	$1,200,000	$1,000,000
Sales in units	22,000	15,000
Production in units	20,000	20,000
Variable product cost per unit	$30	$30
Fixed manufacturing overhead	$10,000	$10,000
Fixed selling and administrative expenses	$30,000	$30,000
Variable selling and administrative expenses (per unit sold)	$5	$5

    a. Calculate unit product cost using absorption costing.

    b. Calculate unit product cost using variable costing.

    c. Which costing method, variable or absorption, will report a higher net income for 2004?

    d. Which costing method, variable or absorption, will report a higher net income for 2005?

E7-22
Obj. 4

Proto, Inc., manufactures a single product. The company's production results, sales, costs, and inventory levels last year is as follows:

Total production in units	96,600
Total sales in units	82,200
Fixed selling and administrative costs	$113,880
Selling price per unit	$12
Variable-costing net income	$11,880
Absorption-costing net income	$17,640

Calculate the total fixed manufacturing overhead costs and the fixed manufacturing overhead cost per unit. Prepare an income statement using the absorption-costing method.

E7-23 During 2005, C & R Industries, Inc., produced 10,000 units and sold 8,000 units of its prod-
Obj. 4 uct. It began 2005 with no units in its finished goods inventory. The ending balance in finished goods inventory was $18,000 using absorption costing and $6,000 using variable costing.
What was the total fixed manufacturing overhead cost for 2005? What was the difference in
net income for the year if variable costing is used rather than absorption costing?

E7-24 Hill County Bank, a small, locally owned institution, is reexamining the way it prices its ser-
Objs. 4, 5 vices. The bank's managers are concerned that some of their customers are less profitable than
was believed, and are trying to decide what to include in the cost of various services. Cost estimates related to these services are as follows:

	Transaction	
	Withdrawal, Teller	**Withdrawal, ATM**
Direct labor per transaction	$0.75	—
Other variable costs per transaction	$0.25	$0.80
Average # transactions per month	10,000	15,000

Building utilities, depreciation expense on equipment (including the ATM machine), and other
fixed costs total $5,000 per month.

a. What is the cost of a withdrawal using a teller if both fixed and variable costs are included? (Allocate the fixed costs to all transactions.)
b. What is the cost of an ATM withdrawal if both fixed and variable costs are included?
(Allocate the fixed costs to all transactions.)
c. Monthly depreciation expense on the ATM machine totals $750. What is the cost of an
ATM withdrawal if that is the only fixed cost included in your calculations?

....

PROBLEMS

*If your instructor is using Personal Trainer® in this course, you may complete your assignments
online.*

P7-1   Cost Behavior

Obj. 1
Tim Ricker lives in Atlanta. He is a toolmaker for Georgia Industries, a manufacturer of heavy
equipment such as backhoes, graders, and earthmoving equipment. Tim makes specialty tools
and jigs that are used on different machines in the plant. His annual salary is $35,000. Ann
Thompson also works for Georgia Industries. She is an independent sales representative who
lives in El Paso, Texas. She is paid a straight salary of $25,000 but also earns a 5% commis-
sion on sales. Ann is responsible for accounts in the west Texas area, works out of an office
in her home, and is reimbursed by Georgia Industries for her travel expenses. The company
provides Ann with a leased vehicle and a gasoline credit card.

Required
A. Classify Tim and Ann's income as fixed, variable, or semivariable expenses.
B. Classify Ann's travel expenses as fixed, variable, or semivariable. What considerations
are important in arriving at your answer?

P7-2   Cost Behavior and Employee Motivation

Objs. 1–4 Refer to the facts presented in P7-1.

Required
A. For financial reporting purposes, are Tim and Ann's salaries and expenses considered a
product cost or a period expense?
B. As illustrated in the problem, top management at Georgia Industries has established
different compensation systems for manufacturing and sales employees. These managers made their decisions, based on an understanding of cost behavior, to help reduce
risks and to motivate certain types of behavior. Would you classify Ann's salary as
fixed, variable, or mixed? Why?
C. What type of behavior are managers at Georgia Industries attempting to motivate?
D. Does this type of compensation package reduce risk for Georgia Industries? Explain.
E. Describe various types of analyses the partners might conduct using monthly financial
information.

P7-3   Cost Behavior

Obj. 1

A company's cost structure may contain numerous different cost behavior patterns. Below are descriptions of several different costs; match these to the appropriate graphs. On each graph, the vertical axis represents cost and the horizontal axis represents level of activity or volume.

Required Identify, by letter, the graph that illustrates each of the following cost behavior patterns. Graphs may be used more than once.

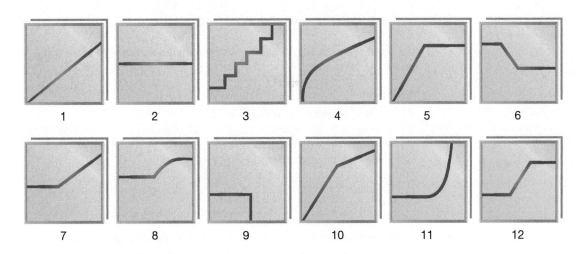

A. Cost of raw materials, where the cost decreases by 6 cents per unit for each of the first 150 units purchased, after which it remains constant at $2.75 per unit.

B. City water bill, which is computed as follows:

First 750,000 gallons or less	$1,000 flat fee
Next 15,000 gallons	$0.002 per gallon used
Next 15,000 gallons	$0.005 per gallon used
Next 15,000 gallons	$0.008 per gallon used
Etc. Etc.	

C. Rent on a factory building donated by the city, where the agreement provides for a fixed-fee payment, unless 250,000 labor hours are worked, in which case no rent needs to be paid.

D. Cost of raw materials used.

E. Electricity bill—a flat fixed charge of $250 plus a variable cost after 150,000 kilowatt-hours are used.

F. Salaries of maintenance workers if one maintenance worker is needed for every 1,000 hours or less of machine time.

G. Depreciation of equipment using the straight-line method.

H. Rent on a factory building donated by the county, where the agreement provides for a monthly rental of $100,000 less $1 for each labor hour worked in excess of 200,000 hours. However, a minimum rental payment of $20,000 must be made each month.

I. Rent on a machine that is billed at $1,000 for up to 500 hours of machine time. After 500 hours of machine time, an additional charge of $1 per hour is paid up to a maximum charge of $2,500 per period.

(Material from the Uniform CPA Examination Questions and Unofficial Answers, Copyright © by the American Institute of Certified Public Accountants, Inc., is reprinted [or adapted] with permission.)

P7-4   Cost Behavior and the Income Statement

Objs. 1–4

Lauren Stephens owns William's Restaurant, which sells hamburgers for carry out or drive through only. Each hamburger sells for $2. Lauren employs several part-time employees and a full-time manager. She leases the building and hires a cleaning company to provide services on a weekly basis. The manager, who is paid a monthly salary, carries out all administrative functions such as hiring, scheduling, and counting cash.

(Continued)

The following expenses were incurred in November.

Ground meat	$1,500	Manager's salary	$2,100
Lettuce	350	Utilities	600
Tomatoes	400	Depreciation, grill	350
Buns	400	Depreciation, signs	100
Condiments	70	Advertising	75
Part-time labor, cooks	2,500	Rent	800
Part-time labor, servers	2,250	Cleaning service	300
Wrapping paper and bags	30		

The restaurant sold 10,000 hamburgers during the month, and there is no WIP inventory at the end of the month.

Required

A. Identify each expense as fixed or variable.
B. Classify each cost as one of the following: direct materials cost, direct labor cost, overhead cost, or period expense.
C. Prepare an income statement for November.
D. Compute gross margin as a percentage of sales.
E. Compute net income as a percentage of sales. What are the implications of your findings in terms of risk? Elaborate.

P7-5   **Cost Behavior and Management Decisions**

Objs. 1, 3

Shiny Company produces a line of cleaning products for both industrial and household use. While most of the company's products are processed independently, a few are related, such as Glow and Satin Silver Polish.

Glow is an abrasive cleaner used in industrial applications. It costs $1.60 per pound to produce and sells for $2.40 per pound. A small portion of Glow each year is combined with other ingredients to form Satin Silver Polish. Satin sells for $5.00 per jar.

Each jar of Satin uses $1/4$ pound of Glow. The other costs of ingredients and labor required for further processing are as follows:

Additional ingredients	$1.00
Additional direct labor	1.48
Total added cost	$2.48

The additional overhead costs required each month for further processing are:

Variable overhead	50% of additional labor costs
Fixed overhead	$3,000, related mainly to depreciation (none of the fixed costs are avoidable)

Advertising costs for Satin total $5,000 per month; the variable selling costs related to Satin are 10% of sales.

Because of a recent drop in demand for silver polish, the management of Shiny is thinking about stopping production of Satin. The sales manager believes it would be more profitable to just sell Glow.

Required

A. What is the additional revenue less the additional processing costs, per jar (contribution margin), from further processing Glow into Satin?
B. Assume that marketing projections indicate the company can sell 5,000 jars of Satin each month. What advice would you give to Shiny management? Support your advice with a calculation.

P7-6   **Contribution Margin Ratio**

Objs. 2, 3

Skyler Industries, Inc., produces and sells swimwear. The following information is for a recent period:

Production	10,000 units
Sales	7,000 units
Unit selling price	$50
Variable product costs	$80,000
Variable selling and administrative	$2 per unit sold
Fixed manufacturing overhead	$51,000
Fixed selling and administrative	$70,000

Required

A. What is the unit contribution margin? What are some actions Skyler could take to increase the unit contribution margin?

B. What is the contribution margin ratio? What does this mean?

C. Use the contribution margin ratio to calculate sales dollars at the breakeven point.

P7-7

Objs. 2, 3

SPREADSHEET

Contribution Margin and Breakeven Point

Elizabeth McClary recently began a small snowboard company called Pure Powder. She and her staff have assembled cost information regarding the snowboards.

Variable unit costs (per snowboard):		
Direct materials	$ 25	
Direct labor	20	} 55
Variable manufacturing overhead	7	
Variable selling and administrative	3	
Fixed costs (for the period):		
Fixed manufacturing overhead	24,300	
Fixed selling and administrative	40,075	

The snowboards sell for $180.

Required

A. What is the unit contribution margin per snowboard?

B. What is the breakeven point in units?

C. Explain what the contribution margin is, and why it is useful information for Elizabeth.

P7-8

Objs. 2, 3

SPREADSHEET

Breakeven Point

Small Fries is a company that processes gourmet potatoes into little french fries. Each package has a contribution margin of $2.50. Small Fries has total fixed costs of $40,000 each period. The selling price of one package is $5. Sales for the most recent period totaled $90,000.

Required What is the company's breakeven point in units? In dollars?

P7-9

Objs. 2, 3

SPREADSHEET

Breakeven Point, Cost Structure, and Target Sales

Plainfield Bakers, Inc., manufactures and sells a popular line of fat-free cookies under the name Aunt May's Cookies. The process Plainfield uses to manufacture the cookies is labor-intensive; it relies heavily on direct labor. Last year Plainfield sold 300,000 dozen cookies at $2.50 per dozen. Variable costs at this level of production totaled $1.50 per dozen, and fixed costs for the year totaled $150,000.

300,000   .90

Required

A. Prepare a contribution-margin income statement for last year.

B. Calculate the company's contribution-margin ratio and breakeven point in sales units for last year.

C. Plainfield's direct labor rate is going to go up $0.40 a dozen next year. Assuming that the selling price stays at $2.50 a dozen, calculate next year's contribution margin and breakeven point in sales units.

D. Plainfield's management is thinking about automating the production process, a change that would reduce variable costs by $0.60 a dozen but would raise fixed costs by

(Continued)

$150,000 a year. If the company undertakes the automation project, how would its contribution margin and breakeven point in sales units be affected?

E. Assuming that Plainfield does go ahead with the automation project [see requirement (D)], how many dozen cookies would the company have to sell at $2.50 a dozen to earn the same income it earned last year?

F. What are some of the nonfinancial aspects of the automation decision that Plainfield's management should consider when deciding whether to embark on the automation project or not?

P7-10   Graphing the Cost-Volume-Profit Relationship

Objs. 2, 3   Two CVP graphs and cost information for two unrelated companies, each of which manufactures a single product, follow:

 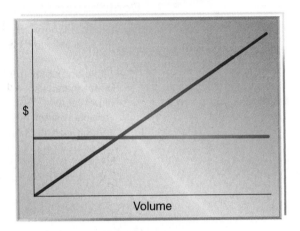

Company A
Fixed costs = $400,000
Sales = $150 per unit
Contribution margin = $20 per unit

Company B
Fixed costs = $400,000
Sales = $150 per unit
Contribution margin = $40 per unit

Required

A. Complete each graph by adding a total-cost line and the breakeven point, and by labeling each of the CVP graph lines.
B. Calculate the variable unit product cost for each company.
C. Calculate the breakeven point in sales units for each company.
D. Why are the companies' breakeven points different when both sell their products for the same price? How is that difference reflected in the CVP graphs in requirement (A)?

P7-11   Ethics and CVP Analysis

Obj. 3   Nathan Dechter is the controller of Specialty Candies, Inc., a manufacturer of candies and confections. The company's executive planning committee has asked Nathan to prepare an analysis of two alternatives the committee is considering. The first alternative is labor-intensive. Nathan's analysis revealed the following:

Sales revenue (projected at 6,000,000 units)	$1,800,000
Less variable costs	1,000,000
Contribution margin	$ 800,000
Less fixed costs	600,000
Net income	$ 200,000

The second alternative would automate the factory, increasing fixed costs and reducing variable costs:

Sales revenue (projected at 6,000,000 units)	$1,800,000
Less variable costs	800,000
Contribution margin	$1,000,000
Less fixed costs	800,000
Net income	$ 200,000

Before sharing his analysis with the executive planning committee, Nathan thought about the probable outcome of the committee's decision making. He knows that if the committee decides to automate the plant, many of his friends in the production department will lose their jobs. Although both alternatives yield net income of $200,000 at the projected level of sales, Nathan is afraid that management will opt for automation. Nathan could recalculate depreciation using a method that would increase fixed costs in the short run, which would encourage management to reject the automation alternative.

Required

A. Is there an argument that Nathan could make to support the labor-intensive alternative without manipulating the financial data? (*Hint:* Calculate the breakeven point for each alternative.)
B. Do you think Nathan should alter the fixed costs of the automation alternative? Would this be ethical? Would the manipulation be justified if it helps a number of employees keep their jobs? Why or why not?

P7-12

Obj. 3

Contribution Margin and Purchase Decisions

Douglas Cabinet Company manufactures a single model of bathroom cabinet. The company's contribution margin ratio is 45%. Douglas is considering an advertising campaign that would cost $8,000 but is expected to increase sales by $22,000.

Required

A. What dollar amount of the additional revenue will go to cover variable costs?
B. Should Douglas buy the advertising? Explain your answer.
C. If Douglas's contribution margin ratio is 30% instead of 45%, should it still buy the advertising? Explain your answer.

P7-13

Objs. 2, 4

Variable Costing and Production Variations

Jerry Sanchez is president of Heatco, Inc., a manufacturer of a single product. He is comparing this year's income statement with last year's and is wondering why net income is different for the same level of sales. "Our costs have not changed at all, yet look at our income. What did we do right this year?" The statements, both prepared using absorption costing, look like this:

	This Year	Last Year
Sales revenue (40,000 units each year)	$800,000	$800,000
Less cost of goods sold	400,000	460,000
Gross margin	$400,000	$340,000
Less selling and administrative expenses	300,000	300,000
Net income	$100,000	$ 40,000

Last year, the first year of operations, the company produced 40,000 units and sold them all. This year, the company increased production to maintain a margin of safety in its finished goods inventory. Fixed costs are applied to products on the basis of the number of units produced each year. Here is a summary of Heatco's production results, variable production costs, and fixed manufacturing overhead cost for both years:

	This Year	Last Year
Production in units	50,000	40,000
Production costs:		
Variable cost per unit	$4	$4
Fixed manufacturing overhead	$300,000	$300,000

(Continued)

Required

A. Calculate the unit product cost under variable costing and absorption costing.
B. Prepare an income statement for each year using variable costing.
C. Compare the net income figures in the variable-costing income statement [requirement (B)] and the absorption-costing income statement for each of the years. Explain any differences.
D. Why did Heatco earn more this year than last year using absorption costing, even though the company sold the same number of units?

P7-14   Absorption and Variable Costing

Obj. 4

SPREADSHEET

Joan Tyler started a small manufacturing company, JT Enterprises, at the beginning of 2005. Joan has prepared the following income statement for the first quarter of operations.

JT Enterprises
Income Statement
For the Quarter Ended March 31, 2005

Sales revenue (25,000 units)		$1,200,000
Less variable costs:		
Variable cost of goods sold	$540,000	
Variable selling and administrative expenses	260,000	800,000
Contribution margin		$ 400,000
Less fixed costs:		
Fixed manufacturing overhead	$300,000	
Fixed selling and administrative expenses	150,000	450,000
Net loss		$ (50,000)

The variable <u>cost of goods sold</u> includes the costs of direct materials, direct labor, and variable manufacturing overhead. The company began the quarter with no inventory; it manufactured 30,000 units over the period. Variable selling and administrative expenses are based on units sold.

Required

A. Calculate the unit product cost using absorption costing.
B. Rework the income statement using absorption costing.
C. Does the net loss figure change using absorption costing? If yes, explain why.
D. During the second quarter of operations, JT again manufactured 30,000 units but sold 35,000 units. Prepare income statements for the second quarter using both the variable- and absorption-costing methods.
E. Explain the difference in net income (or loss) in the second quarter between the two statements prepared in requirement (D).

P7-15   Absorption- versus Variable-Costing Income

Obj. 4

A company that makes cameras uses both variable and absorption costing. The following information pertains to the year just ended:

Units produced	1,000
Units sold	750
Selling price per unit	$375
Variable product costs per unit	$100
Variable selling expense per unit	$20
Fixed manufacturing overhead for the year	$70,000
Fixed administrative expense for the year	$70,000

Required

A. Prepare an income statement using absorption costing.
B. Prepare an income statement using variable costing.
C. Assume that at the beginning of the year, the balance in the finished goods inventory was $0. What is the value of the finished goods inventory at the end of the year using absorption costing? What is the value using variable costing?
D. What causes the difference in net income between the two costing methods?

P7-16 Using Variable Costing and Full Costing in Pricing Decisions

Obj. 4

Beat You to the Punch is a young company specializing in computer game software. The company is facing stiff competition from larger, well-established companies. These companies are lowering their prices considerably in an effort to force Beat You out of the market. Managers at Beat You are trying to decide how much they can lower their price in order to remain competitive. Cost information for Beat You from a recent period is as follows:

Production	300 units
Variable product costs	$7 per unit
Variable selling expenses	$3 per unit sold
Fixed manufacturing overhead	$600
Fixed selling and administrative expenses	$20,000

Required

A. If Beat You's managers make their pricing decision based on variable cost and would like a minimum markup of 20%, what should the selling price be?
B. What are some arguments for and against using variable cost alone as the basis for making a pricing decision?
C. If Beat You bases its pricing decision on full cost, and still would like a 20% markup, what would be the selling price?
D. What are some arguments for and against using full cost as the basis for making a pricing decision?

P7-17 Choosing a Costing Method

Obj. 4

SPREADSHEET

Cedar Products is a company that produces wooden novelties. The controller has been asked by the president to review the company's costing methods. Currently, the company uses absorption costing for internal as well as external purposes, but they are considering using variable costing for internal reporting and decision making. Information related to a recent production period is as follows:

Units produced	6,000
Units sold	4,000
Direct labor	$6 per unit
Direct materials	$5 per unit
Variable manufacturing overhead	$4 per unit
Fixed manufacturing overhead	$36,000
Variable selling and administrative	$1.50 per unit sold
Fixed selling and administrative	$40,000

Required

A. Calculate the unit product cost using absorption costing.
B. Calculate the unit product cost using variable costing.
C. Cedar's president does not see any need to spend the extra time and money to develop a second costing system. The controller is in favor of doing so. What might the controller tell the president when trying to convince him to agree to use variable costing?

P7-18 Absorption- and Variable-Costing Income Statements

Obj. 4

MT Designs, Inc., manufactures a motorcycle accessory. The company was very successful in 2006 and demand for their product was much higher than anticipated. Use the following production and sales information to answer the questions.

(Continued)

Production	5,000 units
Sales	9,000 units
Selling price	$220
Direct materials used, 2004	$125,000
Direct labor cost, 2004	$200,000
Variable manufacturing overhead, 2004	$25,000
Fixed manufacturing overhead, 2004	$60,000
Variable selling expenses	$90,000
Fixed administrative and selling expenses	$130,000

Note: Assume all fixed costs and all variable unit costs remained the same from the previous year.

Required

A. Prepare an income statement using variable costing.
B. Prepare an income statement using absorption costing.
C. Explain why net income is higher using variable costing than absorption costing.
D. Suppose that MT Designs was facing an extended slump in demand for its product, and that the production manager is evaluated based on net income. What would be a possible drawback to using absorption costing in this instance?

P7-19 **Using Variable Costing to Make Business Decisions**

Objs. 3, 5

John Chang is president of Clean Machines, a new car washing service that makes house calls. John has decided that his goal for the coming year is to earn a profit of $40,000. Clean Machines reported the following sales and cost information for the year just ended:

Sales revenue	$60,000	120
Less all variable costs	20,000	40
Less all fixed costs	40,000	80
Net income	$ 0	

Clean Machines performed 500 car washes during the year.

Required

A. How many car washes will Clean Machines need to do in order to earn John's target profit of $40,000?
B. If John thinks that that number of car washes is an unrealistically high goal, what else could he do to achieve his target profit?
C. John is considering raising the price of a car wash to $130. However, he anticipates that if he raises the price, demand will fall and he will perform 450 car washes. What will his net income be if this occurs? What do you think John should do?

P7-20 **Using Variable Costing to Make Pricing Decisions**

Objs. 3, 5

Letitia Green owns a small, independent off-Broadway theater. Her theater is about to begin performing a new play titled "Franklin County Blues." Letitia has invested her own funds to get the play off the ground, and wants to know how many tickets need to be sold before the theater breaks even. Information about the play follows: *40 plays*

Variable costs	$1,000 per performance
Fixed costs	$50,000 for the entire run of the play *5000*
Letitia's investment in the play	$60,000
Ticket price	$40
Theater capacity	300 seats

Required

A. How many performances must be put on before the theater breaks even? (Assume that each performance will be sold out.)
B. Letitia believes that the arts should be accessible to everyone, so she has decided to change the price structure for the play. If she offers 50 tickets at a reduced rate of $10

per ticket, and the other 250 tickets at $42 per ticket, how many performances would be necessary to break even?

C. Suppose instead that, based on past experience, Letitia anticipates there will only be enough demand for eight performances of the play. Although the play would not break even, what other factors might cause Letitia to go ahead with the production?

P7-21 Variable and Absorption Costing in the Service Sector

Obj. 5

PS Consultants specializes in computer systems design and programming. Most of the company's employees have a background in both computers and management. PS's average job takes three to four months to complete. The price PS quotes for consulting services is based on the expected number of consultant hours and an estimate of out-of-pocket expenses. When a job is finished, PS bases its charges on the actual number of hours and costs incurred on the job. The firm usually does not collect its fee until a consulting job is completed.

Currently PS records all of the firm's expenses in the periods in which they are incurred. Those expenses include the hourly wages of consultants and programmers as well as indirect costs—employee benefit packages, travel expenses, and other out-of-pocket expenses. Fixed overhead costs for administering the office, rent, advertising, depreciation on computer equipment, and software license fees also are expensed each period.

Leslie Rinauro is the firm's managing partner. She is concerned because the company's income fluctuates significantly from month to month. In the months when several jobs are billed, the firm shows respectable profits. In other months, the firm shows large losses, even though all of the consultants and programmers are busy. Leslie wants to use a costing method that will better reflect PS's income and smooth out the month-to-month profit fluctuations.

Required

A. How could PS better match the costs of its services with the income it generates?

B. How does the deferral of costs relate to PS's client services?

C. How do the concepts of variable and absorption costing affect PS?

P7-22 Excel in Action

SPREADSHEET

Music Makers expects to produce and sell 500,000 CDs each month. The sales price per unit is $2.45. Variable costs per unit are $1.20. Total fixed costs per month are $540,000. The company's target profit is $75,000 per month.

Required Use a spreadsheet to prepare a profit analysis for Music Makers. Use the following format.

	A	B	C
1		Unit	Total
2	**Profit Analysis**		
3	Units		
4	Sales price		
5	Variable costs		
6	Fixed costs		
7	Total costs		
8	Profit		
9	**Breakeven Analysis**		
10	Unit contribution margin		
11	Contribution margin ratio		
12	Breakeven		
13	**Target Profit Analysis**		
14	Target profit		
15	Units required		

(Continued)

Volume, unit cost, and ratio amounts should appear in column B. Total dollar amounts should appear in column C. Data will not appear in the shaded cells. Amounts in cells C4, C5, C7, C8, B10, B11, B12, C12, and B15 should be calculated using formulas and references to other cells. Cell B12 should report the breakeven point in units. Cell C12 should report the breakeven point in dollars. Appropriate formatting should be used throughout.

The spreadsheet should be designed so that a change in any of Music Makers' price or cost data can be entered and numbers in the spreadsheet will be recalculated automatically. What is the breakeven point if variable costs increase to $1.22 per unit? How many units must be sold to generate a target profit of $75,000 if the variable unit cost is $1.22? What is the breakeven point if fixed costs increase to $560,000?

P7-23   Multiple-Choice Overview of the Chapter

1. The breakeven point is that point where:
   a. total sales revenue equals total variable and fixed expenses.
   b. total contribution margin equals total fixed expenses.
   c. Both a and b are correct.
   d. Neither a nor b is correct.

2. Garth Company sells a single product that generates a positive contribution margin. If the selling price per unit and the variable cost per unit both increase 10% and fixed costs do not change, the:

	Unit Contribution Margin	Contribution Margin Ratio	Breakeven in Units
a.	increases	increases	decreases
b.	no change	no change	no change
c.	no change	increases	no change
d.	increases	no change	decreases

3. Honeybee Company's contribution margin ratio is 60%; the company's breakeven point in sales is $150,000. If the company wants to earn net income of $60,000 over the period, its sales would have to be:
   a. $200,000.   c. $250,000.
   b. $350,000.   d. $210,000.

4. Carlton Company sells its product for $40 per unit. The company's variable costs are $22 per unit; its fixed costs are $82,800 a year. Carlton's breakeven point is:
   a. $184,000.   c. $150,545.
   b. 3,764 units.   d. 2,070 units.

5. Fixed manufacturing overhead costs are allocated to each unit of product using:
   a. the absorption-costing method only.
   b. the variable-costing method only.
   c. both the absorption- and variable-costing methods.
   d. neither the absorption- nor the variable-costing method.

6. Last year Clarence Company sold 3,600 units at a price of $50 per unit. The company's variable cost per unit was $15; its fixed costs for the year were $40,530. If the company wants a profit of $40,000 next year, all other factors remaining constant, it will have to sell:
   a. 1,158 units.   c. 2,300 units.
   b. 1,958 units.   d. 800 units.

7. When production exceeds sales, absorption-costing net income generally:
   a. is less than variable-costing net income.
   b. is more than variable-costing net income.
   c. equals variable-costing net income.
   d. is higher or lower than variable-costing net income because no generalization can be made.

8. Last year, Bone Company produced 10,000 units of product X and incurred the following costs:

Direct materials costs	$10,000
Direct labor costs	14,000
Variable manufacturing overhead costs	5,000
Variable selling and general expenses	3,000
Fixed manufacturing overhead costs	9,000
Fixed selling and general expenses	4,000
Total	$45,000

Under absorption costing, any unsold units of product X would be carried in Finished Goods Inventory at a unit cost of:

a. $4.50.

b. $4.20.

c. $3.80.

d. $2.90.

9. Selling and administrative expenses are:
   a. a product cost under variable costing.
   b. a product cost under absorption costing.
   c. part of fixed manufacturing overhead under variable costing.
   d. a period expense under both variable and absorption costing.

10. Last year Smith Company had net income of $125,000 using variable costing and $105,000 using absorption costing. The company's variable production costs were $20 per unit; its total fixed overhead was $176,000. The company produced 11,000 units. Production levels and fixed costs have not changed in three years. During the year, Smith's finished goods inventory:
    a. increased by 1,000 units.
    b. increased by 1,250 units.
    c. decreased by 1,000 units.
    d. decreased by 1,250 units.

CASES

C7-1 Relevant Costs for Decision Making: Keep or Drop a Product Line

Objs. 1, 2

John Randazzo is the owner of a successful machine shop that produces automotive brake components for national auto parts chains. These auto stores sell "after-market" parts to replace those made by original equipment manufacturers such as **General Motors**, **Ford**, and **Toyota**. A great deal of volume diversity exists across the products manufactured by Randazzo's shop. For example, Randazzo may produce 80,000 brake components per year for vehicles such as the Chevrolet Lumina, Ford Taurus, or Toyota Corolla; however, he may produce only 5,000 for the Corvette market. Selling prices vary greatly across the product line as a result of market supply and demand.

The machine shop is highly automated and uses the most current computer-numerically controlled (CNC) equipment. By changing cutting tools and entering different measurements into the system, a variety of products can be manufactured. Thus, machine costs are not traceable to a single product line, but are common to all products. Alternatively, many production costs are variable and can be traced to individual products. For example, energy, material, and supply costs differ among the products.

Randazzo's cost accountant recently completed a study that associated cost and revenue data with each product listed in the company's catalog. Exhibit A identifies sales volume, selling prices per unit, and variable costs for a sample of ten products representing the mix manufactured by Randazzo. In addition to the variable costs identified in Exhibit A, the accountant estimated $600,000 of fixed costs would be associated with the production of these ten products.

Exhibit A

Product	A	B	C	D	E	F	G	H	I	J
Sales volume in units (× 1,000)	50	80	10	20	70	25	5	12	11	15
Selling price per unit	$12	$15	$2	$10	$15	$10	$2	$5	$5	$8
Variable cost	$10	$11	$3	$8	$10	$8	$4	$4	$5	$6

(Continued)

The study produced startling results; two of the ten products in the sample had variable costs exceeding their selling prices. Upon analyzing the cost report, Randazzo's marketing vice president immediately defended the current strategy of manufacturing a full product line. She argued that even though some products had costs in excess of their selling prices, Randazzo should consider the big picture. Many of their customers were controlling costs by reducing the number of vendors from which they purchased merchandise. She argued that if Randazzo no longer produced product G (Corvette brake components), retail chains would likely turn to Randazzo's competitors for other products as well.

Randazzo knew that dropping products from the line would necessitate lay-offs of some salaried and hourly employees. In the short run, lost production volume could not be made up by increases in production of other products. Over the years, he had worked hard to achieve a culture of trust and cooperation within the company and the community. He wondered about the options available to him.

Required

A. What financial and nonfinancial considerations are relevant to the management team's decision to keep or drop a product line?

B. Assume $70,000 of the $600,000 in fixed costs can be saved if products C and G are dropped. What is the total benefit to the company of dropping the two products?

C. Do you agree with the marketing vice president's concern about carrying a full product line?

D. As a consultant to Randazzo, what would you recommend to:
   1. ensure each product in the line is profitable, or
   2. ensure the entire line is profitable?

C7-2 Absorption versus Variable Costing—Effects on Income

Obj. 4

Rachel Yablonka assumed the responsibilities as executive manager of the Chair Division, Office Furniture and Fixtures, Inc. (OFF), on January 1, 2005, taking the place of her recently promoted predecessor. Rachel's own performance evaluation is directly tied to the division's annual net operating profit determined under absorption costing, and her quarterly bonus is determined as a percentage of net operating income.

Rachel immediately began taking measures designed to reduce costs during future periods. Part of her cost-reduction efforts involved examining better ways to deal with inventory. After a careful review of the division's sales and production over the past quarter, Rachel concluded that inventory had been accumulating faster than sales. The division makes to order and does not normally carry any excess inventory. She decided that the buildup of excess inventory might be contributing to low profits. Rachel knows that excess inventory can lead to higher costs of material-handling, warehousing, insurance, and auditing as well as keeping capital tied up when it could be more useful elsewhere. Further investigation disclosed that the excess inventory was being stored off site in newly rented warehouse facilities because of inadequate storage space in the division's own warehouses.

Rachel immediately set out to eliminate the excess inventory by slowing down the rate of production during the first quarter of 2005. However, she was very disappointed when she saw the first quarter 2005 results. Instead of profits improving, the division experienced a net operating loss even though sales were flat and there was some reduction in warehousing and material handling costs. Quarterly performance data for the two quarters are as follows:

	Fourth Quarter 2004	First Quarter 2005
Units of beginning inventory	0	50,000
Units sold	200,000	200,000
Units produced	250,000	150,000
Average selling price per unit	$500	$500
Unit cost of production:		
Direct labor cost per unit produced	$ 50	$ 50
Direct material cost per unit produced	200	200
Variable overhead cost per unit produced	30	25
Fixed overhead assigned to each unit produced	70	115
Total unit cost	$350	$390

	2004	2005
Revenue	$100,000,000	$100,000,000
Cost of goods sold	70,000,000	76,000,000
Gross margin	$ 30,000,000	$ 24,000,000
Selling and administrative expenses	25,000,000	25,000,000
Operating income	$ 5,000,000	$ (1,000,000)

Required

A. Why was the division's income significantly lower in first quarter 2005 than in fourth quarter 2004?

B. Why do you think the inventory buildup occurred at the end of the previous manager's term?

C. If you were Rachel, how would you handle this situation? Should you keep inventory levels low or high?

D. If you were the CEO of OFF, Inc., would you change Rachel's performance measurements? Explain why or why not?

C7-3 Effects of Cost-Plus Pricing—Beyond Absorption and Variable
Obj. 4   Costing

The Dobson Specialty Valve Division of American Industrial Group, Inc. (AIG) develops and manufactures complex valves and fittings for commercial uses. AIG has long operated other divisions engaged in making products such as furniture, metal doors, and windows. Dobson has just been acquired by AIG from another company, and AIG's management is considering what management accounting system to use for Dobson's cost-plus product pricing. A group of senior AIG officials recently held a meeting to discuss the issue.

Karen Sanchez (vice president and chief financial officer): AIG has always used variable costing when it was necessary to price our products on a cost-plus basis, but I have been reading that variable costing does not always work well for this purpose. Some consultants claim that using variable costing to cost products leads managers to overlook fixed costs and price products too low. These consultants say that absorption costing results in better recovery of fixed costs in product because it includes fixed costs in the cost of manufacturing.

John Warren (vice president, marketing): Although the consultants may be correct in some situations, I disagree in the case of Dobson. Dobson manufactures many small lots of specialty valves that require individual design and special handling. This means that direct labor and raw materials represent almost 70% of Dobson's manufacturing costs. After deducting variable overhead, fixed costs represent less than 20% of total manufacturing costs. There is little fixed manufacturing cost to recover. Further, only a small amount of our selling costs are fixed. We sell mostly through independent sales representatives who are paid on a 5% commission basis.

Susan Sabbagh (vice president, production): Given that Dobson's after-tax profit margins are in the 5%–6% range and our goal is to raise that to 8%, I would think that a 20% fixed manufacturing cost percentage is still very significant. If we do not recover our fixed costs on each job and make a profit, it will be difficult to increase our profit margins to the desired levels.

Sanchez: I am looking at a product cost and margin sheet for valve #2032 that was specially developed for one particular customer only. We do not know if this valve will ever be manufactured again. The job cost sheet only includes manufacturing costs. It does not include the costs of research and development (R&D) for the valve. The price is based upon a 30% markup over manufacturing costs. As you may remember from your financial accounting classes, generally accepted accounting principles require that R&D costs be expensed in the period in which they are incurred. R&D costs may not be inventoried. Therefore, R&D costs are not normally included in product costs, and neither our variable manufacturing-cost system nor the proposed absorption-cost system captures R&D costs. It seems to me that the cost of manufacturing the valve under either system is inadequate for product pricing because neither manufacturing cost captures the cost of R&D.

Product Unit Cost and Gross Margin—Job 99-1-2032

Direct labor	240 hours at $16.00 per hour	$ 3,840.00
Direct materials	50 units at $125.00 per unit	6,250.00
Manufacturing overhead	240 DL hours at $9.00 per hour	2,160.00
Total product manufacturing cost		$12,250.00
Unit cost	$12,250.00 ÷ 50 units	245.00
Cost-plus price per unit	$245.00 + (30% × $245.00)	318.50
Total sales value of order	$318.50 × 50 units	15,925.00
Gross margin	$15,925.00 − $12,250.00	3,675.00

Warren: We have not discussed that concern before, but you are correct. We have assumed that R&D costs are a small percentage of the total cost of a product because we expect to sell a large quantity of the product through many orders. In a situation where we incur significant R&D to develop a particular valve that we are unsure will sell in large quantities, we likely will lose money on the valve if we do not make provision for recovering R&D costs in our pricing.

Sabbagh: I believe that I understand everything that has been said, and yet I am more confused than ever. This discussion began with a debate about whether to use variable or absorption manufacturing costs to price products, and now we seem to have concluded that neither is adequate. Is there another type of costing that I have not heard about that would solve this problem? And why have we not discussed this problem before with respect to our other divisions? It seems to me that Karen is saying that every product should cover its fair share of all costs, but is it possible to accurately determine that fair share?

Required

A. Assess the arguments made by the various participants in the meeting. Are these arguments correct? Explain.

B. Why do you think that the problem of including R&D costs in product pricing has not been discussed before by AIG's senior management?

C. Suppose AIG estimates that it took approximately 50 hours of engineering design time to develop valve #2032 at $50.00 per hour and general administrative costs are allocated at $1,000 per job. How should AIG have priced the job to make the desired profit percentage on a full absorption-cost basis? Based upon this price, how well does the practice of using a 30% markup above gross margin appear to work in the case of job #99-1-2032?

D. What potential benefits and problems do you see for AIG if it attempts to assign a fair share of all costs to each product?

Cost Evaluation and Performance Measurement

THE BUDGETING PROCESS—PLANNING BUSINESS ACTIVITIES

Why should budgets be carefully constructed?

Erin and Seth are comparing their actual financial performance of Young Designs, Inc., to the budgeted performance. The two sets of numbers are very different. It looks like the costs for last month are much greater than expected. They are meeting with Roberta later today, and they plan to ask her to explain why Young Designs' actual financial performance varied from budgeted performance and what they can do with the budget to better understand how well costs are being controlled.

FOOD FOR THOUGHT

What would you do to design a budget that considers differences between expected and actual sales? How would this budget help Erin and Seth better understand how well different types of costs are being controlled? How could this concept be extended to help managers anticipate different financial outcomes for different levels of sales? Now, let's join Erin and Seth in their meeting with Roberta.

Erin: *Last month we produced and sold more futons than we projected. Our raw material costs per unit were higher than expected because we got hit with unexpected price increases from our suppliers. Apparently there is a lumber shortage right now.*

Seth: *Selling more than we expected is a good thing, but unexpected raw material price increases are not. Overall, we ended up missing our profit goal by a fairly large margin. I guess that means the higher raw material prices more than offset the gains we got from selling more units.*

Erin: *That may not be the only reason. We also had higher than expected labor costs because we had to pay overtime for higher than expected production. In addition, our overhead costs exceeded projections.*

Seth: *So, Roberta, how do we go about sorting out all these revenues and costs to get a better understanding of what actually happened? We need to know how well we are controlling each type of manufacturing and selling cost. It seems to me that we need to produce a budget that shows what our costs should have been for the amount we actually sold.*

Roberta: *In budgeting, predicting the levels of sales is often the most important but most difficult task. This is because the level of sales drives much of the company's costs. For example, raw material, direct labor, variable overhead, and variable selling costs all vary with the level of sales.*

Seth: *If sales are that important yet that hard to predict accurately, won't we frequently have budgets that do not reflect reality?*

Roberta: *What you need is a flexible budget, which shows what you would have budgeted for costs and profits if you had known the actual amounts you would sell.*

Seth: *In other words, a flexible budget is a budget created after the fact to show what our costs should have been given actual levels of sales activity. I would suppose that this flexible budget concept uses the notion that some costs vary with production while other costs are fixed.*

Roberta: *Correct. This will allow you to better understand how well different costs were controlled. By comparing the flexible budget to the actual costs and profits, you will be able to see which costs are higher or lower than they should have been given the actual sales.*

Erin: *Will this work if we have more than one product with different costs?*

Roberta: *Certainly. In situations where there is more than one product, you simply develop the flexible budget to calculate the costs for each different product and then sum the results to get total revenues and expenses.*

Seth: *What about manufacturing overhead? Will this help us to better understand how much overhead was expensed and why?*

Roberta: *Yes, flexible budgets typically break down manufacturing overhead into its fixed and variable components. You will be able to compare how much variable overhead is expensed because of the actual level of sales versus the original budgeted sales.*

Erin: *I don't see why we couldn't use this same concept of flexible budgeting to assist us in another way. When we are preparing the budget, we could forecast what our company's financial performance would be for different levels of sales. This would help us establish a range of possible financial outcomes.*

Roberta: *That's called sensitivity analysis. Companies often use sensitivity analysis in flexible budgeting to develop best-case, worst-case, and most-likely-case scenarios. Since variations in sales can sometimes be difficult to predict, developing these scenarios helps management see how good or bad the financial results for a given period are likely to be.*

OBJECTIVES

Once you have completed this chapter, you should be able to:

1 Explain how budgets provide information to help managers prepare a pro forma (predicted) income statement and balance sheet.

2 Prepare the budgets and schedules that make up the master budget.

3 Prepare reports that describe the timing of cash receipts and payments during a fiscal period.

4 Describe the elements of a successful budgeting culture.

5 Explain the role of budgets in service organizations.

SIERRA CANOE: BUDGETING AND THE MANUFACTURING PROCESS

In this chapter, we consider elements of the master budget using Sierra Canoe Co. Before accounting for a product, managers should understand the processes and components that are necessary to manufacture it. Exhibit 1 illustrates the key parts of Sierra Canoe Co.'s product. The company produces canoes from plastic polymers and various accessories purchased from suppliers. The company also incurs direct labor costs during the manufacturing process. Workers operate machines that mold polymers to form the hull of the canoe. In addition, they attach various components, such as the seats, decks, and gunwales. Other manufacturing costs include overhead in the form of electricity, small tools, and supplies consumed during the manufacturing process. Sierra Canoe Co. also employs workers who perform sales and administrative duties.

Exhibit 1
Canoe Diagram

Demand for canoes varies throughout the year. Because Sierra Canoe Co. sells most of its products through retail stores in North America, the most active sales period occurs from April through August. The least active sales period occurs during the winter months of the first quarter of the year. Because sales vary in a predictable manner, management believes a budget can help them understand the timing of cash receipts and cash payments. If cash receipts are not sufficient to cover cash payments during the winter months, the company will need a short-term loan. During the summer months when cash receipts are expected to exceed cash payments, the company will repay the loan. Thus, managers at Sierra Canoe Co. are interested in determining the timing and amount of future cash inflows and outflows. In addition, they wish to understand the expected future financial position of the company.

TRANSACTION AND BUDGET SYSTEMS COMPARED

OBJECTIVE 1

Explain how budgets provide information to help managers prepare a pro forma (predicted) income statement and balance sheet.

As explained when you studied financial accounting, businesses enter the results of actual transactions into the accounting system to measure income for a fiscal period, such as a month, quarter, or year. Actual transactions, such as inventory purchases, wage payments, and sales, are recorded in the accounting system. These transactions are summarized, and account balances are calculated. Then, financial statements are prepared from the account balances. Using financial statement information, managers, lenders, and owners evaluate actual performance for an accounting period.

A *budget* **is a detailed plan describing the use of financial and operating resources over a specific period.** A company's budget system differs from its transaction system. Rather than collecting data from actual events, the budget system is based on *forecasts* from various departments within an organization. Preparing company-wide budgets requires coordination among the sales, production, and purchasing functions. For example, sales managers provide sales forecasts to production managers, who estimate the number of units necessary to ensure an adequate supply of products for sale. Using estimates provided by production managers, purchasing managers forecast the type, amount, and cost of resources to satisfy production requirements. Also, sales forecasts help managers estimate selling and administrative expenses. The budget process helps managers understand whether short-term loans will be needed during the forecast period, as materials and other manufacturing resources are purchased to meet production demands. Exhibit 2 illustrates differences between a transaction system and a budget system.

Exhibit 2

The Transaction System and Budget System Compared

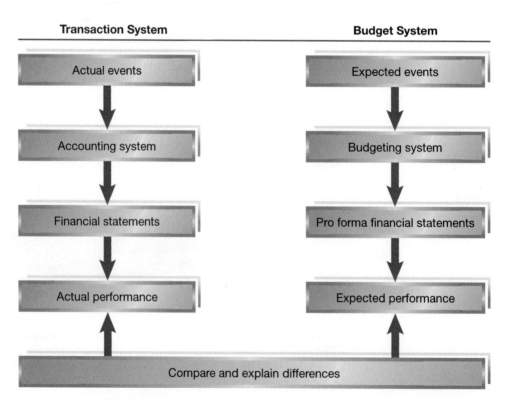

Pro forma, or predicted, financial statements are prepared by combining information from various budgets. The purpose of a pro forma balance sheet is to predict the financial position of the company. The purpose of the pro forma income statement is to predict revenues, expenses, and earnings. As shown in Exhibit 2, the transaction system produces financial statements based on *actual performance*; the budget system produces financial statements based on *expected performance*. Management can compare actual performance with expected performance to explain why differences may have occurred and to correct problems that create these differences.

Pro forma financial statements are produced at the end of the budgeting process. However, our discussion of the various budgets begins with a familiar set of financial statements, the pro forma income statement and balance sheet. The remainder of the chapter illustrates how account balances in these financial statements were determined using the budgeting process. The format of pro forma financial statements is the same as that of financial statements. The only difference is that pro forma financial statements report estimated, rather than actual, account balances. Exhibit 3, panel A, illustrates a pro forma income statement for Sierra Canoe Co. for the first quarter of 2005, ending on March 31. Panel B illustrates a balance sheet at December 31, 2004, and a pro forma balance sheet at March 31, 2005.

Exhibit 3
Panel A—The Pro Forma
Income Statement

Sierra Canoe Co.
Pro Forma Income Statement
For the Quarter Ended March 31, 2005

Panel A

Sales	$336,000
Cost of goods sold	247,800
Gross margin	$ 88,200
Selling and administrative expenses	68,400
Net income	$ 19,800

Exhibit 3
Panel B—The Balance
Sheet and Pro Forma
Balance Sheet

Sierra Canoe Co.
Balance Sheet and Pro Forma Balance Sheet
At December 31, 2004 and March 31, 2005

Panel B

	Balance Sheet 12/31/2004	Pro Forma Balance Sheet 3/31/2005
Assets		
Cash	$ 50,000	$ 71,428
Accounts receivable	21,600	52,800
Inventory		
Raw materials	1,296	5,508
Finished goods	2,950	14,750
Property, plant, and equipment	350,000	350,000
Total assets	$425,846	$494,486
Liabilities and Equity		
Accounts payable	$ 33,491	$ 82,331
Contributed capital	300,000	300,000
Retained earnings	92,355	112,155*
Total liabilities and equity	$425,846	$494,486

*Beginning retained earnings	$ 92,355
Net income	19,800
Ending retained earnings	$112,155

THE MASTER BUDGET

Prepare the budgets and schedules that make up the master budget.

Chapter M2 contrasted product expenses, such as materials, labor, and manufacturing overhead, with period expenses, such as selling and administrative expenses. Recall that materials, labor, and manufacturing overhead become part of inventory for a manufacturing company and are not expensed until the products are sold. Period expenses have an effect on the income statement in the period in which they are incurred. **A *master budget* is a collection of related budgets that includes the sales, production, purchasing, labor, overhead, selling and administrative, and cash budgets.** The master budget of a manufacturing company, such as Sierra Canoe Co., includes both product and period expenses. Managers want to understand the amount of resources to be consumed (both product and period) and when the resources are expected to be consumed. Exhibit 4 illustrates an overview of the budgeting process that results in a master budget. Exhibit 5 identifies the people at various levels of an organization who are responsible for information needed in the budgeting process. We consider the individual budgets that make up the master budget in this chapter.

The budgeting process for Sierra Canoe Co. begins with an estimate of expected unit sales for the coming year. As Exhibit 5 illustrates, the chief executive officer (CEO) works

Exhibit 4 Master Budget

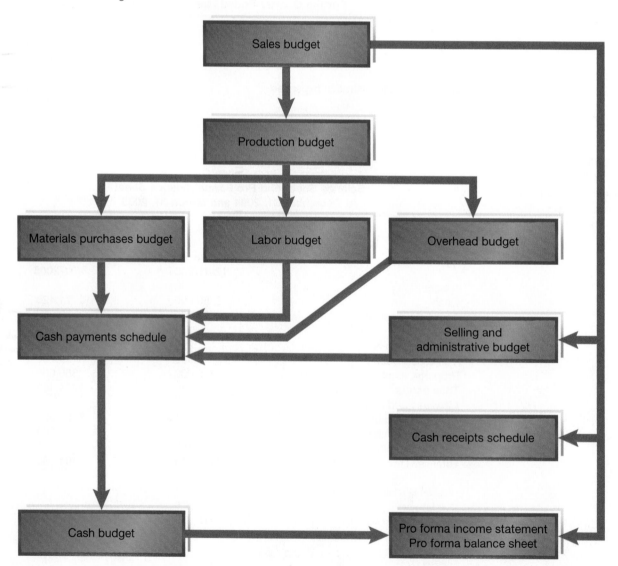

with the vice presidents (VP) of finance, marketing, manufacturing, and human resources (HR) to devise a sales forecast that results in a sales budget. The team agrees on a sales target after considering a variety of resource issues. As shown in Exhibit 4, production will be scheduled to meet expected sales demand. If sufficient units are not produced to meet sales demand, the company will lose sales. If production exceeds sales demand, the company will incur additional inventory expenses associated with damage, insurance, handling, and storage. Therefore, the sales budget drives the production budget.

After sales and production estimates are complete, the purchasing department prepares a materials purchases budget. As Exhibit 5 illustrates, the production manager

Exhibit 5 The Organizational Chart and the Budgeting Process

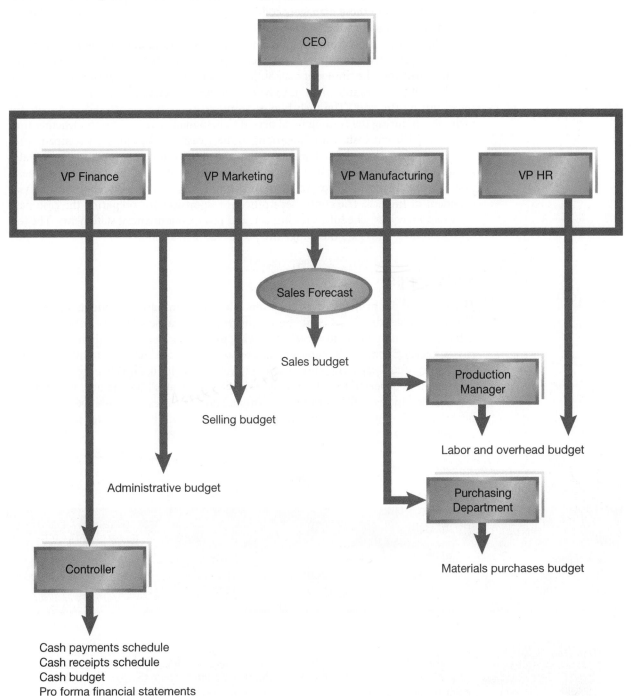

works with the VP of human resources to develop a labor and overhead budget. Purchase budgets permit managers to estimate the amount of raw materials, labor, and overhead necessary to meet production requirements. The costs that result from production activities appear as finished goods inventory on a company's balance sheet until the product is sold. When the product is sold, these costs appear as cost of goods sold on the income statement.

In addition to forecasting product expenses, managers at Sierra Canoe Co. must forecast period expenses associated with selling and administrative activities. As shown in Exhibit 4, the sales budget (or forecast) affects selling and administrative expenses. Selling and administrative expenses are an example of a semivariable expense, as discussed in Chapter M2. Therefore, they have a fixed component that is unaffected by sales volume and a variable component that changes with the number of products sold. As Exhibit 5 illustrates, the administrative expense budget is prepared at the vice president level, because these managers collectively understand the amount of administrative activity throughout the company.

Using information from the materials, labor, overhead, and selling and administrative budgets, accountants prepare a cash payments schedule. The cash payments schedule identifies the timing of cash outlays for various purchases during the year. The sales budget provides information to help managers understand the timing of cash receipts during the year. The cash budget summarizes cash receipts and payments for each month during the coming fiscal period to help managers understand whether they will have sufficient cash from operations to meet cash needs. Finally, a company prepares pro forma financial statements at the end of the budgeting process. These statements help managers understand what the financial position of the company will be, if forecasts are correct. The controller is an accountant that typically reports to the vice president of finance. The controller's office is responsible for preparing the cash payments and receipts schedule, cash budget, and pro forma financial statements. The following sections illustrate the budgeting process at Sierra Canoe Co.

Sales Budget

The *sales budget* **projects revenues from sales of a company's products or services.** The sales budget drives the entire budgeting process because sales expectations directly determine future production levels. Likewise, production levels directly influence purchases. Sierra Canoe Co.'s management prepared a forecast for each month of the first quarter. Expected sales are 50, 150, and 220 canoes for January, February, and March. Each canoe is expected to sell for $800. Exhibit 6 illustrates how the unit sales forecast is multiplied by the selling price to determine budgeted sales revenues. December sales information is not included in the quarter total, but will be used later in the budget process.

Exhibit 6 Sales Budget

	Actual	Expected			
	December	January	February	March	Quarter
Unit sales	90	50	150	220	420
Selling price per unit	$ 800	$ 800	$ 800	$ 800	$ 800
Sales revenue	$72,000	$40,000	$120,000	$176,000	$336,000

Exhibit 6 indicates expected revenues of $336,000 for the first quarter. Refer to the pro forma income statement in Exhibit 3, panel A. Note the pro forma sales account balance equals the quarterly sales amount calculated in Exhibit 6.

Case in Point

Forecasting "Sales" for a Bank

To a bank, loans to customers are like sales to manufacturers or retailers. Banks often use sophisticated forecasting models to project demand for loans. Some of the factors banks may consider in forecasting loans are economic growth, changes in interest rates, trends in consumer spending, and competition from other banks. A bank may develop a sales forecasting model that contains these and other variables. The expected value of each of these variables is inserted into the model to arrive at an estimate of future loan demand.

Production Budget

The *production budget* **identifies the amount of a product that must be produced to meet a company's needs for sales and inventory.** Using the unit sales forecast from Exhibit 6, management prepares the production budget shown in Exhibit 7. The number of units to be produced is based on expected sales, desired ending finished goods inventory, and beginning finished goods inventory. Sierra Canoe's management keeps a finished goods inventory of 10 percent of the following month's expected sales to ensure they do not run out of inventory for sale. The unit sales forecast is added to desired ending finished goods inventory to determine total inventory requirements. Next, beginning finished goods inventory is subtracted from total inventory requirements to determine the number of units to be produced.

Exhibit 7 Production Budget

	Actual December	Expected				
		January	February	March	Quarter	April
Unit sales	90	50	150	220	420	250
Desired ending finished goods	5	15	22	25	25	30
Total units required	95	65	172	245	445	280
Beginning finished goods	9	5	15	22	5	25
Units to produce	86	60	157	223	440	255

For example, the sales forecast for January is 50 units. The desired ending inventory of 15 units is calculated by multiplying 10 percent times February sales of 150 units. Thus, Sierra Canoe Co.'s total inventory needs at the end of January are 65 (50 + 15) units. The company began the month with 5 units in inventory. Therefore, only 60 (65 − 5) units must be produced in January. Having calculated the number of canoes to be manufactured, the production manager will send the information to the purchasing manager. December information is included in Exhibit 7 because December's finished goods inventory balance, 5 units, becomes the beginning finished goods inventory balance for January. Likewise, April inventory information is included to permit us to determine desired ending finished goods inventory of 25 units for March (10% × 250). However, only January, February, and March are included in the quarterly total.

Materials Purchases Budget

The materials purchases budget links directly to the production budget. After production demands are known, the purchasing manager can determine how much material to acquire. In a similar fashion, the production manager can estimate labor and overhead requirements.

The canoe produced by Sierra Canoe Co. requires two types of raw materials:

- polymer (for use in molding the canoe), and
- an accessory package consisting of seats, gunwale, thwart, and decking.

Because of an imbalance in supply and demand, the company's polymer orders frequently are delayed. Therefore, management maintains an ending polymer inventory of 20 percent of the following month's production requirements to help prevent stockouts. However, no inventory of accessory packages is kept at the factory because Sierra Canoe Co. has agreements with reliable suppliers to deliver these materials daily as they are needed.

The *materials purchases budget* **identifies the amount of materials that will be required to support a company's total production needs.** Exhibit 8 illustrates the materials purchases budget for polymer. Each canoe requires 12 gallons. Thus, total polymer requirements are computed by multiplying total production (from Exhibit 7) times 12. Desired ending polymer inventory is added to production requirements to calculate total needs. Finally, beginning polymer inventory is subtracted from total requirements to calculate gallons to be purchased. The number of gallons to be purchased is converted into a dollar value by multiplying the purchase quantity by the cost per gallon.

Exhibit 8   Materials Purchases Budget for Polymer*

	Actual	**Expected**				
	December	**January**	**February**	**March**	**Quarter**	**April**
Production units	86	60	157	223	440	255
Gallons of polymer per unit	× 12	× 12	× 12	× 12	× 12	× 12
Total gallons required for production	1,032	720	1,884	2,676	5,280	3,060
Plus: Desired polymer ending inventory	+ 144	377	535	612	612	1,215
Total requirements in gallons	1,176	1,097	2,419	3,288	5,892	4,275
Less: Beginning polymer inventory	− 206	144	377	535	144	612
Total gallons to be purchased	970	953	2,042	2,753	5,748	3,663
Cost per gallon	× $9	× $9	× $9	× $9	× $9	× $9
Total polymer purchases	$8,730	$8,577	$18,378	$24,777	$51,732	$32,967

*Amounts in this exhibit are rounded to whole units and whole dollar values.

For example, from the production budget we know Sierra Canoe Co. plans to manufacture 60 canoes during January. Each canoe consumes 12 gallons of polymer. Thus, to meet production demand, 720 (12 × 60) gallons are required. In addition, the company desires to maintain an ending inventory of polymer equal to 20 percent of the next month's production needs. For January, the desired ending inventory of polymer is 377 gallons (1,884 × .20 = 377). The purchasing manager needs 1,097 (720 + 377) gallons to meet production and inventory requirements; however, 144 gallons already are in beginning inventory. As a result, the purchasing manager must purchase 953 gallons (1,097 − 144) at $9 per gallon. Exhibit 8 indicates total polymer purchases of $8,577 (953 × $9) for January. Purchases for each month may be calculated in an identical manner.

The materials purchases budget provides information to help estimate the value of the ending raw materials inventory account shown on the pro forma balance sheet. For example, Sierra Canoe Co. wants to have 612 gallons of polymer on hand at the end of the quarter. Each gallon costs $9. Thus, the value of the ending raw materials inventory as shown in the pro forma balance sheet in Exhibit 3, panel B, is $5,508 (612 × $9 = $5,508).

In addition to polymer, Sierra Canoe Co. purchases an accessory package for $50. The budget for purchases of the accessory package is greatly simplified because Sierra Canoe Co. does not maintain an inventory of this item. By partnering with reliable suppliers who make daily deliveries, Sierra Canoe Company minimizes handling and storage costs. Using production values from Exhibit 7, purchase quantities for the accessory package are calculated in Exhibit 9. Purchase quantities are converted to dollar values by multiplying by the cost per package. For example, the production manager plans to manufacture 60 canoes in January. Therefore, 60 accessory packages at $50 each must be purchased to meet production requirements. The cost of polymer and accessory kits is placed on the balance sheet as inventory until the canoe that contains the materials is sold. Thus, accountants refer to materials, labor, and overhead as costs until a product is sold, and as an expense after the product is sold.

Exhibit 9 Materials Purchases Budget for Accessory Packages

	Actual	Expected			
	December	January	February	March	Quarter
Total production (units)	86	60	157	223	440
Component packages per unit	× 1	× 1	× 1	× 1	× 1
Total packages required	86	60	157	223	440
Cost per component package	× $50	× $50	× $50	× $50	× $50
Total component packages	$4,300	$3,000	$7,850	$11,150	$22,000

1 SELF-STUDY PROBLEM

WebTUTOR Advantage

A retail organization may prepare a merchandise purchases budget similar to the production budget illustrated in Exhibit 7. Assume a retail company that sells outdoor equipment expects to sell backpacks as shown in the following table. The company wants to keep a backpack inventory equal to 50 percent of the following month's expected sales volume. The backpacks cost the company $45 each.

	Actual	Expected				
	December	January	February	March	Quarter	April
Unit sales	16	10	6	20	36	30
Plus: Desired ending finished goods inventory	5	3	10	15	15	30
Total units required	21	13	16	35	51	60
Less: Beginning finished goods inventory	8	5	3	10	5	15
Total units purchased	13	8	13	25	46	45
Cost per unit	$45	$45	$45	$45	$45	$45
Cost of purchases	$585	360	585	1125	2070	2025

Required Complete the inventory purchases table.

The solution to Self-Study Problem 1 appears at the end of the chapter.

Labor Budget

The *labor budget* **identifies labor resources required to meet production needs.** Labor costs, as shown in Exhibit 10, are based on production quantities from Exhibit 7. Industrial engineers have determined each canoe requires 6 hours of direct labor at an average rate of $22 per hour. Thus, the number of canoes to be produced is multiplied by the required number of labor hours per unit to determine total labor hours. Total labor expense is calculated by multiplying the labor rate per hour times the total hours required. For example, the production budget indicates 60 canoes will be manufactured in January. Each canoe requires 6 hours of labor; therefore, 360 hours (60 × 6) of labor are required for the month. Since each hour of labor costs $22, the total labor budget for January is $7,920 (360 hours × $22).

Exhibit 10 Labor Budget

	Actual	Expected			
	December	January	February	March	Quarter
Total production (units)	86	60	157	223	440
Hours per unit	× 6	× 6	× 6	× 6	× 6
Total hours required	516	360	942	1,338	2,640
Labor rate per hour	× $22	× $22	× $22	× $22	× $22
Total labor cost	$11,352	$7,920	$20,724	$29,436	$58,080

Overhead Budget

The *overhead budget* **provides a schedule of all costs of production other than materials and labor.** Manufacturing overhead costs are not as easily associated with specific products as are direct materials and direct labor. Manufacturing overhead costs usually are associated with activities that support a production process but often are not directly related to any specific product. Thus, overhead costs are classified as indirect manufacturing costs. Overhead costs typically are estimated using production forecasts, as shown in Exhibit 7. Sierra Canoe Co. associates overhead with products using a rate of $50 per direct labor hour. Recall that industrial engineers have determined each canoe requires 6 hours of direct labor. The number of units produced is multiplied by labor hours per unit to calculate total labor hours required. Total budgeted overhead costs are calculated by multiplying the overhead rate times the total hours required. For example, overhead cost for January is calculated in Exhibit 11 by multiplying total production of 60 canoes by 6 hours, the time required to assemble each canoe. Based on January production levels, 360 (60 × 6) hours of labor are required. Overhead is added to the product at a rate of $50 per labor hour; therefore, total budgeted overhead costs for January are $18,000 (360 × $50).

Exhibit 11 Overhead Budget

	Actual	Expected			
	December	January	February	March	Quarter
Total production (units)	86	60	157	223	440
Hours per unit	× 6	× 6	× 6	× 6	× 6
Total hours required	516	360	942	1,338	2,640
Overhead rate per hour	× $50	× $50	× $50	× $50	× $50
Total overhead costs	$25,800	$18,000	$47,100	$66,900	$132,000

Predetermined overhead rate (handwritten annotation)

Having completed the materials, labor, and overhead budgets, management may calculate an expected product cost. For example, by adding polymer, accessory package, labor, and overhead expenses we may determine a product cost of $590 as shown in Exhibit 12. Notice that overhead is a large portion of Sierra Canoe Co.'s total manufacturing cost. This is not uncommon for manufacturing companies. As we have seen in earlier chapters, companies design cost systems to help them understand, and reduce, overhead costs.

Exhibit 12

Canoe Cost Calculation

Materials:			
Polymer	($9 × 12 gallons)	$108	(Exhibit 8)
Accessory kit		50	(Exhibit 9)
Labor	(6 hours × $22 per hour)	132	(Exhibit 10)
Overhead	(6 hours × $50 per hour)	300	(Exhibit 11)
Total unit cost		$590	

(handwritten: Total)
(handwritten: × 25 = 14,750)

Total product cost is used to determine cost of goods sold on the pro forma income statement. We may calculate cost of goods sold of $247,800, as shown in the income statement in Exhibit 3, panel A, by multiplying $590 times the number of units expected to be sold, as reported in the sales budget ($590 × 420 = $247,800). Likewise, we determine ending inventory by multiplying $590 times the desired number of finished canoes shown in the production budget (25). Thus, the desired finished goods inventory on the pro forma balance sheet in Exhibit 3, panel B, is $14,750 (25 units × $590).

Our pro forma income statement and balance sheet in Exhibit 3 are prepared using accrual concepts. As illustrated, pro forma cost of goods sold is calculated using the expected number of units sold, while the desired ending inventory of finished canoes is appropriately included on the balance sheet as a current asset. Unlike product costs that are expensed when goods are sold, selling and administrative expenses are reported on the income statement of the period in which they are incurred. The next section illustrates the budgeting process for selling and administrative expenses.

Selling and Administrative Budget

The *selling and administrative budget* contains expenses related to selling a company's products and administering the business. Exhibit 13 illustrates the selling and administrative budget. As Chapter M4 discussed, management can predict net income at various sales levels by understanding how expenses respond to changes in sales volume. The selling and administrative budget shown in Exhibit 13 uses a similar approach to forecast expenses.

Exhibit 13 Selling and Administrative Budget

	Actual	Expected			
	December	January	February	March	Quarter
Total sales	$72,000	$40,000	$120,000	$176,000	$336,000
Variable expense per sales dollar	× 0.15	× 0.15	× 0.15	× 0.15	× 0.15
Total variable expense	$10,800	$ 6,000	$ 18,000	$ 26,400	$ 50,400
Fixed expense per month	6,000	6,000	6,000	6,000	18,000
Total selling and administrative expense	$16,800	$12,000	$ 24,000	$ 32,400	$ 68,400

Management at Sierra Canoe Co. estimates variable selling expenses are 15 percent of sales, while fixed selling expenses are $6,000 per month. Sales commissions are an example of a variable selling expense, while advertising and administrative salaries are examples of fixed selling expenses. Advertising expenses will not change if sales volume increases or decreases; however, sales commissions vary according to sales levels. Total selling and administrative expenses for January are calculated in two steps. Using sales volume from the sales budget shown in Exhibit 6, the variable expense is calculated at 15 percent of total sales ($40,000 × .15 = $6,000). Next, fixed selling expenses are added to variable selling expenses to determine the budgeted selling and administrative expense for January ($6,000 + $6,000 = $12,000).

The pro forma income statement shown in Exhibit 3, panel A, reports selling and administrative expense of $68,400 based on total quarterly selling and administrative expenses calculated in the selling and administrative budget.

2 SELF-STUDY PROBLEM

webTUTOR Advantage

Assume the managers for the retail company introduced in Self-Study Problem 1 want to predict administrative expenses for the company during the months of January, February, and March. They believe fixed administrative expenses will be $20,000 per month. In addition, variable selling expenses are expected to be 20 percent of sales.

Required Prepare a selling and administrative budget for January, February, and March, assuming forecast sales are $30,000, $45,000, and $50,000, respectively.

The solution to Self-Study Problem 2 appears at the end of the chapter.

CASH BUDGET

OBJECTIVE 3

Prepare reports that describe the timing of cash receipts and payments during a fiscal period.

The *cash budget* summarizes expected cash collections and payments during an accounting period. For example, Exhibit 14 illustrates the cash budget for Sierra Canoe Co. during the first quarter of an accounting period. Expected cash collections are added to the beginning cash balance. Next, expected cash payments are subtracted to determine whether a cash excess or deficit exists. The amounts shown in Exhibit 14 are based on cash collection and payment schedules that are explained in later sections. Because the cash budget often is prepared for a twelve-month period, management can understand how cash balances vary throughout the year. If a cash shortage is expected in certain months, management can make arrangements to borrow necessary cash. The cash budget also provides information to lenders who want to know when short-term loans will be repaid. For example, assume Sierra Canoe's management wants to maintain at least $50,000 in cash at the end of each month. The cash budget indicates borrowing will be necessary in January. Also, the budget indicates sufficient cash will be available to repay the loan in March.

Exhibit 14 Cash Budget

	December	January	February	March	Quarter
Beginning cash balance		$50,000	$50,360	$ 62,586	$ 50,000
Plus: Cash collections		49,600	96,000	159,200	304,800
Less: Cash disbursements		58,240	83,774	141,358	283,372
Cash excess or deficit		41,360	62,586	80,428	71,428
Plus: Bank loans		9,000	0	0	9,000
Less: Bank repayments		0	0	9,000	(9,000)
Ending balance	$50,000	$50,360	$62,586	$ 71,428	$ 71,428

A cash budget can help managers make short-term and long-term cash management decisions. For example, managers may choose to invest excess cash in securities that earn a higher rate of return than typically is paid on business checking accounts. Also, if the cash budget permits, management may invest excess cash in long-term investments to enable them to pay off debt or to purchase equipment in the future.

The cash budget is used to determine the ending cash balance reported in the pro forma balance sheet. For example, the cash budget indicates an ending balance of $71,428. The same value is reported on the balance sheet shown in Exhibit 3, panel B. Thus, the cash budget is necessary to estimate the ending cash balance on the pro forma balance sheet. So far, we have assumed the cash collections and disbursements are given. The information about expected cash flows comes from two different schedules, the schedule of cash collections and the schedule of cash payments. Next, we consider these schedules.

Schedule of Cash Collections

The accrual basis can be used for determining value created during an accounting period. When you studied financial accounting, you considered how revenue is recorded when earned, not necessarily when cash is collected. As the budgeting process illustrates, cash collections often differ from revenues in the short run. **A** *schedule of cash collections* **identifies the timing of cash inflows from sales.** For example, assume Sierra Canoe Co. typically collects cash from sales in the following pattern:

- 70 percent in the month of sale
- 30 percent in the month following the sale

The schedule of cash collections is based on the sales budget and the company's historical experience with collecting cash from credit sales. Monthly cash receipts for Sierra Canoe Co. are affected by sales from the current month and from the previous month. Exhibit 15 describes the two-month collection pattern based on Sierra Canoe's collection experience. January cash collections are expected to be $49,600 (December sales of $72,000 × .30 = $21,600 plus January sales of $40,000 × .70 = 28,000). Cash collections for each month in the quarter may be calculated in an identical manner. As shown in Exhibit 15, Sierra Canoe Co. expects to collect $49,600, $96,000, and $159,200 in January, February, and March. Refer to the cash budget shown in Exhibit 14. Notice the monthly cash collections from Exhibit 15 also appear in the second row of Exhibit 14.

Exhibit 15 Schedule of Cash Collections for January, February, March, and Quarter* Ex 6

	December	January	February	March	Quarter
December collections for December sales	$50,400				
January collections for December sales		$21,600			$ 21,600
January collections for January sales		28,000			28,000
February collections for January sales			$12,000		12,000
February collections for February sales			84,000		84,000
March collections for February sales				$ 36,000	36,000
March collections for March sales				123,200	123,200
		$49,600	$96,000	$159,200	$304,800

*See Exhibit 6 (Sales Budget). Each month's total collection is the sum of (prior month sales × 30%) + (current month sales × 70%).

The schedule of cash collections also is used to estimate ending accounts receivable. Notice Exhibit 3, panel B, reports an ending accounts receivable balance of $52,800 on the pro forma balance sheet. Consequently, Sierra Canoe Co. must have $52,800 of accounts receivable on March 31, the end of the quarter. From the sales budget we know March sales were estimated to be $176,000. March collections from March sales are expected to be $123,200 ($176,000 × .70). The remaining accounts receivable balance of $52,800 ($176,000 − $123,200) should be collected in April.

Schedule of Cash Payments

The *schedule of cash payments* **identifies the timing and amount of cash outflows related to production and administrative activities.** A schedule of cash payments is useful to help managers understand the timing of cash outlays resulting from purchases. For example, assume Sierra Canoe Co.'s cash payments typically occur in the following pattern:

- 50 percent in the month of purchase
- 50 percent in the month following a purchase

Before determining the timing of cash outflows for purchases, we must determine total purchases for materials, labor, overhead, and selling and administrative expenses by month by summing information from the purchases budgets as follows:

	December	January	February	March	Source
Materials:					
Polymer	$ 8,730	$ 8,577	$ 18,378	$ 24,777	Exhibit 8
Accessory					
packages	4,300	3,000	7,850	11,150	Exhibit 9
Labor	11,352	7,920	20,724	29,436	Exhibit 10
Overhead	25,800	18,000	47,100	66,900	Exhibit 11
Selling and					
administrative	16,800	12,000	24,000	32,400	Exhibit 13
	$66,982	$49,497	$118,052	$164,663	

Exhibit 16 identifies cash payments during January, February, and March. For example, January cash payments include the remaining 50 percent from December pur-

Exhibit 16 Schedule of Cash Payments*

	December	January	February	March	Quarter
December disbursements for December purchases	$33,491				
January disbursements for December purchases		$33,491			$ 33,491
January disbursements for January purchases		24,749			24,749
February disbursements for January purchases			$24,748		24,748
February disbursements for February purchases			59,026		59,026
March disbursements for February purchases				$ 59,026	59,026
March disbursements for March purchases				82,332	82,332
		$58,240	$83,774	$141,358	$283,372

*Each month's total payment is the sum of (prior month total purchases × 50%) + (current month total purchases × 50%).
Note: Amounts are rounded up to the nearest whole dollar.

chases ($66,982 × .50 = $33,491) plus 50 percent of the January purchases ($49,497 × .50 = $24,749). Therefore, January cash payments equal $58,240 ($33,491 + $24,749). Cash payments for each month are calculated in the same manner. The monthly disbursement totals are transferred to the cash budget.

The cash payment schedule provides accounts payable information to help prepare the pro forma balance sheet. For example, the amount remaining unpaid from March purchases totals $82,331 ($164,663 − $82,332 = $82,331). Recall that Sierra Canoe Co. pays 50 percent in the month of purchase and 50 percent in the first month following the purchase. Thus, the accounts payable balance at the end of March is $82,331 and appears in Exhibit 3, panel B, as the accounts payable balance in the pro forma balance sheet.

DEVELOPING A SOUND BUDGETING CULTURE

OBJECTIVE 4

Describe the elements of a successful budgeting culture.

The budgeting methods adopted by a company will greatly influence how successful the budgeting process will be. The culture of a business is the way people in the business think and behave. A sound budget culture relies on establishing a process that encourages participation by key employees in the development of budgets. Key employees are those charged with making critical decisions about sales, production, and expenditures. Key employees include top managers and others who are held accountable for critical decisions. Companies can undertake a variety of activities to develop a sound budget culture. These activities include directing attention to the budget, educating participants in the budget process, ensuring availability of information necessary to develop the budget, evaluating actual versus budgeted results, and motivating management to be active in the budget process.

Preparation of the master budget requires the involvement of managers throughout an organization. Each department or manager who participates in the planning process should understand the goals of the budget and the methods used to develop it. Therefore, a company should educate managers about the goals and procedures of the budgeting process.

To create an accurate budget, a thorough understanding of an organization's cost structure is required. Managers must understand expenses that affect their particular department or function. In addition, managers must understand the accounting methods a company uses in measuring expenses and accumulating data in their areas of responsibility. Responsibility accounting assigns responsibility for the performance of a company's departments to department managers. It requires that each manager's performance be evaluated on the basis of expenses or revenues that are directly under the manager's control. Responsibility accounting reports are produced periodically for the purpose of evaluating a department manager's effectiveness in generating revenues or controlling expenses.

Coordination is needed to bring together the various components of the master budget. In many organizations, a standing budget committee is responsible for the coordination of the master budget. This committee generally consists of the president and vice presidents in charge of various departments, such as sales, production, and finance. One role of the budget committee is to resolve disputes or misunderstandings among those involved in budget preparation.

Generally, the most successful budget processes are those that permit managers to participate in developing the budgets. Participative budgeting (or bottom-up budgeting) is a process that allows individuals at various levels of a company to participate in determining the company's goals and the plans for achieving those goals. It signals that senior managers value employee judgment and also results in a greater degree of employee acceptance of the budget. Senior managers often are not in a position to know the details of day-to-day operations as well as employees involved in these operations. Therefore, participation by employees can result in more accurate and achievable budgets. Further, employees who are involved in the development of a budget are more likely to work toward achieving budget goals.

Budget Revisions

As we illustrated earlier in this chapter, budgets forecast future costs of materials, labor, overhead, and selling and administrative activities. However, these forecasts are not always accurate. Substantial differences between a company's actual costs and those assumed in developing the budget can make the budget less useful. For example, a large increase in materials costs can cause the materials budget to be grossly understated. Evaluating managers responsible for materials purchases against such a budget would be unrealistic. Consequently, companies may find it necessary to revise the original budget if there are unforeseen changes.

Inaccurate forecasts raise two concerns. First, when is a forecast sufficiently inaccurate to justify a change in the budget? If budgets are changed frequently because of minor differences in expenses, they will lose meaning. Second, is the difference between the forecast and the actual amounts due to a bad forecast or to the failure of managers to control costs? If managers are allowed to escape responsibility too easily, the budget will lose its value. In deciding whether to permit a budget revision, senior management must weigh these concerns against the concern that the budget is inaccurate.

Behavioral Concerns in Budgeting

http://albright.
swlearning.com
....
**Find out more about
the Hawthorne
Research.**

During the 1920s, a series of studies were conducted at the Hawthorne plant of the **Western Electric Company** to determine whether various elements of the physical environment in the plant affected employee efficiency and output. The experimenters varied employee work environments and measured resulting employee performance. At first, the researchers believed that increasing the levels of light had a positive effect on productivity. They later discovered that productivity increased whenever the researchers measured employees' work, regardless of the change in environment. The Hawthorne studies provide evidence that observing and measuring human behavior can alter behavior. Budgets provide benchmarks for measuring performance. By observing and measuring performance, companies hope to improve efficiency and effectiveness.

Participation in the Budget Process

Different leadership styles can lead to different types of budgeting processes. Budgets can be described as either top-down or bottom-up. Top-down budgets are established by management and then provided to lower levels of management. Bottom-up budgets involve all levels of an organization working to achieve the organization's goals.

For a bottom-up budget, the department managers usually submit proposed budgets and then negotiate with senior managers to create a master budget. This budget is used to evaluate the department's performance. There is two-way communication in bottom-up budgeting. In a bottom-up, participative budget setting, the chief executive officer might direct the vice president of sales to solicit information on sales goals for the coming year from the regional sales offices or departments. After reviewing the goals submitted by the regional sales offices and negotiating any desired changes, the vice president of sales would present a consolidated sales budget for the company to the chief executive. If the chief executive accepts the proposed budget, no further action is required. If the chief executive does not accept the budget, the vice president of sales renegotiates the regional sales budgets with the regional sales offices until an acceptable budget is reached.

Resources are necessary to meet objectives, but resources usually are limited. In many companies, departments compete with each other for a greater share of available resources. Sound planning requires decisions about the allocation of limited resources. Middle and lower-level managers tend to accept these decisions more readily if they have an active role in planning and setting budget goals. Participative budgeting encourages the acceptance of resource allocation decisions by creating a budget culture in which employees have a voice in decisions.

Case in Point

Bottom-Up Budgeting

The **National Bank of Georgia** conducted an annual budgeting process that included loan and deposit goals for each of its branches. Top management established budget targets for the entire bank and for the branch division as a whole. Branch managers participated in this process by developing budgets for their branches and submitting these budgets to Branch Administration. Branch administrators reviewed the budgets and compared them to the targets set for the division. If the branch budgets were not as aggressive as the targets set by top management, branch administrators negotiated with individual branch managers in an attempt to get them to increase their budget targets so that the sum of the individual branches' goals was equal to the division's goal.

Slack in Budgets

When budgets are prepared, departmental managers have incentives to build slack into budgets to make performance goals easier to achieve. *Budgetary slack* **is the difference between a less demanding budget value and a value managers believe they realistically can achieve.** The process of building slack into budgets is called padding. Budgets that have little or no slack are referred to as tight budgets. Managers perform best when faced with moderately difficult, but achievable, goals. Not all factors that affect department performance are under the control of departmental managers. While managers have little control over external variables, such as the general economy, they should understand the effect those variables will have on their department's performance. Examples of external factors that should be considered in the budgeting process include economic forecasts related to a particular product, market conditions that affect a particular industry, and interest rates.

Because external factors affect performance, department performance may not reflect managers' efforts. Budgetary slack reduces the risk that factors beyond the control of managers will cause them to fail to meet their budget goals. On the other hand, if budgets contain too much slack, department managers can perform at a less than optimal level. Senior managers and department managers must work together to create budgets that lead to satisfactory performance.

Budgets and Undesirable Behavior

Senior managers also should be aware that budget goals sometimes can cause lower-level managers to make decisions that are not in the best interest of the company as a whole. For example, suppose a plant's maintenance expenses are high relative to the budget. Further assume the plant manager expects to be promoted if plant performance targets are met. The plant manager may be tempted to defer needed maintenance in the hope of meeting budget targets and winning the promotion. The downside of such a decision, however, will be higher maintenance expenses in the future. Delaying maintenance leads to abnormal wear of a plant's equipment.

Managers need to be aware of the behavioral effects of the budgeting process. With proper planning, managers can reduce those problems. For example, some slack can be included in the budget to reduce incentives for undesirable behavior. Companies also can attempt to detect behavior problems. As an example, a company can monitor unusual decreases in maintenance expenses prior to the end of a budget period to make sure a department is not foregoing necessary maintenance activities.

BUDGETING IN SERVICE COMPANIES

OBJECTIVE 5

Explain the role of budgets in service organizations.

Service companies use budgets similarly to manufacturing companies. The preparation of budgets in service companies, however, can differ from budget preparation in manufacturing companies because service companies do not manufacture goods. Although service companies do not have to develop production and raw materials budgets, some aspects of budgeting can be more difficult in service organizations because it is often harder to trace costs to a particular service than to manufactured goods. In service companies, workers may be involved in the delivery of several different types of services during the same time period. In manufacturing companies, workers usually manufacture only one type of product at a time. When workers are involved with several different types of services at the same time, it is much more difficult to determine how much time (and therefore labor cost) is associated with providing one particular service. This makes it more difficult to develop budgets based on the expected amounts of services to be provided.

Consider checking account services, one of many services provided by banks. One of the costs bank management must budget for is the cost of the labor directly involved in providing checking accounts. This includes the work of tellers, new account personnel, and customer service personnel. These same personnel, however, help to provide many other types of services in addition to checking accounts, often at the same time they are dealing with checking accounts. For example, a teller may process a checking transaction, a loan payment, and a savings deposit for a given customer. How much of the cost of the teller's idle time should be assigned to each type of transaction? Although these cost allocation difficulties may be present in a manufacturing company to some extent, they are present to a greater extent in banks. The result is that banks are less able to accurately budget for the costs of providing for particular services than are manufacturing companies.

Although some aspects of service companies make budgeting more difficult than in manufacturing companies, other aspects potentially make budgeting easier and more useful. For example, some service companies, such as banks and automobile rental companies, operate many offices in different locations. The similarity of these separate offices provides a basis for analyzing budgets and evaluating performance that is not present in many manufacturing companies. The information for each unit can be compared with company-wide averages. This makes determination of good and bad performers easier than with manufacturing companies.

3 SELF-STUDY PROBLEM

WebTUTOR Advantage

Assume a company's management has forecast sales of $30,000, $37,000, $40,000, and $62,000, for June, July, August, and September, respectively. They estimate that 80 percent of their sales are collected the month of sale and 20 percent are collected in the month following the sale.

The company typically pays for 60 percent of its inventory purchases in the month of purchase. The remaining 40 percent is paid in the month following purchase. Assume purchases for June, July, August, and September are $15,000, $20,000, $22,000, and $30,000, respectively.

Required

A. Prepare a schedule of cash receipts for July, August, and September.
B. Prepare a schedule of cash payments for July, August, and September.

The solution to Self-Study Problem 3 appears at the end of the chapter.

REVIEW

SUMMARY of IMPORTANT CONCEPTS

1. The transaction system records actual events. The budget system records expected events.
   a. Pro forma, or predicted, financial statements are prepared by combining information from various budgets.
   b. The transaction system produces financial statements based on actual performance, while the budget system produces financial statements based on predicted performance.

2. A master budget has the following components:
   a. The sales budget shows the quantity and price of goods expected to be sold during the coming period.
   b. The production budget shows the type and quantity of products expected to be produced.
   c. The direct materials budget reflects the amount of raw materials expected to be purchased and used in production.
   d. The direct labor budget indicates the expected labor requirements for production.
   e. The manufacturing overhead budget reflects anticipated overhead costs.
   f. The selling and administrative expense budget shows anticipated costs.
   g. The cash budget shows expected cash receipts and disbursements.
   h. The pro forma income statement indicates the expected net income for the period.
   i. The pro forma balance sheet indicates anticipated levels of assets, liabilities, and owners' equity.

3. The cash budget summarizes expected cash collections and payments during an accounting period.
   a. A schedule of cash collections identifies the timing and amount of expected cash receipts.
   b. A schedule of cash payments identifies the timing and amount of cash outflows.

4. The budgeting culture influences the success of a company's budgeting efforts.
   a. Budget revisions may become necessary if assumptions made during the budgeting process later are found to be incorrect.
   b. Studies have shown that the process of observing and measuring behavior can influence behavior.
   c. Participation in the budgeting process often leads to budget acceptance.
   d. Budgetary slack is padding built into a budget in case cost and revenue targets are not met.
   e. Strict use of budgets can cause undesirable behavior as managers make short-term decisions that may have negative long-term effects.

5. Budgeting in service companies differs in some respects from budgeting in manufacturing companies.
   a. Workers in service companies often perform more than one type of service at the same time, making budgeting the cost of individual services more difficult.
   b. Service companies often operate many branches, providing a basis for analyzing budgets and evaluating performance that is not present in many manufacturing companies.

DEFINE

TERMS and CONCEPTS DEFINED in this CHAPTER

budget (M206)	overhead budget (M214)
budgetary slack (M221)	production budget (M211)
cash budget (M216)	sales budget (M210)
labor budget (M214)	schedule of cash collections (M217)
master budget (M208)	schedule of cash payments (M218)
materials purchases budget (M212)	selling and administrative budget (M215)

SELF-STUDY PROBLEM SOLUTIONS

SSP8-1

total (handwritten)

	Actual	Expected				
	December	January	February	March	Quarter	April
Unit sales	16	10	6	20	36	30
Plus: Desired ending finished goods inventory	5	3	10	15	15	30
Total units required	21	13	16	35	51	60
Less: Beginning finished goods inventory	8	5	3	10	5	15
Total units purchased	13	8	13	25	46	45
Cost per unit	$ 45	$ 45	$ 45	$ 45	$ 45	$ 45
Cost of purchases	$585	$360	$585	$1,125	$2,070	$2,025

SSP8-2

	January	February	March
Sales	$30,000	$45,000	$50,000
Variable expenses*	$ 6,000	$ 9,000	$10,000
Fixed expenses	20,000	20,000	20,000
Total expenses	$26,000	$29,000	$30,000

Variable expenses are .20 × sales.

SSP8-3   A.

	July	August	September
From June sales (.2 × 30,000)	$ 6,000		
From July sales (.8 × 37,000)	29,600		
From July sales (.2 × 37,000)		$ 7,400	
From August sales (.8 × 40,000)		32,000	
From August sales (.2 × 40,000)			$ 8,000
From September sales (.8 × 62,000)			49,600
Total	$35,600	$39,400	$57,600

B.

	July	August	September
From June purchases (.4 × 15,000)	$ 6,000		
From July purchases (.6 × 20,000)	12,000		
From July purchases (.4 × 20,000)		$ 8,000	
From August purchases (.6 × 22,000)		13,200	
From August purchases (.4 × 22,000)			$ 8,800
From September purchases (.6 × 30,000)			18,000
Total	$18,000	$21,200	$26,800

Thinking Beyond the Question

Why should budgets be carefully constructed?

Think about the chapter opening scenario. Suppose Erin and Seth want to develop a sound budgeting culture with Young Designs, Inc. Based upon what you learned in this chapter about the ways in which budgets can affect human behavior, would you suggest that Erin and Seth share their best-case/worst-case/most-likely-case sensitivity analysis with their sales and production managers and also with their lower-level employees? What advantages and disadvantages do you foresee in sharing this information?

QUESTIONS

Q8-1
Obj. 1
Why do managers compare expected results and actual results at the end of a fiscal period, after their actions can no longer influence results for that period?

Q8-2
Obj. 2
Why is communication among marketing and production managers necessary when developing a master budget?

Q8-3
Obj. 2
Why is the production budget necessary for estimating labor costs?

Q8-4
Obj. 2
Why is it important to the budgeting process to have an accurate sales forecast?

Q8-5
Obj. 2
Paul Reynolds recently was hired as a salesman for The Rocky Company, which sells gardening tools and potting soil through retail outlets. Paul has been asked to attend a meeting next week to discuss the preparation of the master budget for the coming year. Paul has asked you to explain what is meant by a master budget so that he can prepare for the meeting. What will you tell Paul?

Q8-6
Obj. 2
Markle Company is a merchandising firm that operates 26 stores. Marvle Industries is a manufacturer that operates a single plant. Both firms prepare detailed master budgets each year. How will the master budgets of the two firms differ?

Q8-7
Obj. 2
Vantage Incorporated is preparing a master budget for the coming quarter of operations. As part of the budget process, inventory policies are being reviewed at a senior management planning meeting. Which budgets will policies concerning the level of inventories affect? Why?

Q8-8
Objs. 2, 3
Susan Broyer is a marketing manager for Glow Industries, which produces lamps and lighting fixtures. Susan's department is preparing a sales budget for the company's lighting fixtures. She has issued a memo to her staff that says in part: "I expect an annual increase in sales next year of 12% across the board. Every line and product should reflect this sales increase." What budget(s) will be affected by the estimated increase in sales?

Q8-9
Objs. 2, 3
Frank Sheffield is the vice president of finance for Hercules Company. Recently, Hercules completed preparation of its master budget for the coming year. Frank has scheduled a meeting with the company's banker. What portions of the master budget, if any, do you believe Frank should review with the bank?

Q8-10
Obj. 3
If management prepares a pro forma income statement that suggests the company will be profitable, why is a cash budget necessary?

Q8-11
Obj. 4
Why is an understanding of an organization's cost structure necessary for successfully preparing a master budget?

Q8-12 Why is employee participation important when developing a budget?
Obj. 4

Q8-13 Leroy Smith is the production manager of Alum Company. In addition to his salary, Leroy
Obj. 4 receives bonus compensation based solely on his ability to meet the budgeted production of
units. Comment on Leroy's bonus arrangement. What weaknesses might exist in this arrangement?

Q8-14 Discuss the implications associated with a budgetary approach in which budgetary data are
Obj. 4 imposed on managers from above. Contrast such an approach with one in which budgetary
data are self-imposed in a participative manner.

Q8-15 Rona Abraham is the purchasing manager for Flextech Incorporated, a manufacturer of fur-
Obj. 4 niture and bedding. Rona knows that as part of her bonus compensation, she must meet the
material purchasing budget that was established at the beginning of the year. In an effort to
meet this budget, Rona has been purchasing lower-grade materials at reduced costs and is
proud of her ability to spend less than the budgeted amounts on materials. What implications
do Rona's actions have for Flextech as a whole?

Q8-16 Lester Arbuckle is owner of Sheetco, a manufacturer of snow shovels. Lester and his managers
Obj. 4 do no budgeting or planning for Sheetco. Sheetco management does not anticipate problems
that arise, and as a result the company has slow production, missed shipment deadlines, and
lost sales. Discuss the reasons why Lester should wish to engage in budgeting and planning.

Q8-17 Service firms do not manufacture products; therefore, budgeting is not important to service
Obj. 5 firms. Do you agree? Explain your answer.

EXERCISES

*If your instructor is using Personal Trainer® in this course, you may complete your assignments
online.*

E8-1 Write a short definition of each of the terms listed in the *Terms and Concepts Defined in this
Chapter* section.

E8-2 Match the following budgets with their definitions.
Obj. 2
  a. sales budget
  b. production budget
  c. direct materials budget
  d. direct labor budget
  e. manufacturing overhead budget
  f. selling and administrative budget
  g. cash budget
  h. pro forma budgeted income statement
  i. pro forma budgeted balance sheet

  1. identifies the labor resources required to meet production needs
  2. identifies the amount of materials that will be required to support a company's total
     production needs
  3. a schedule of revenues and expenses prepared from information developed in the bud-
     get process
  4. identifies the expected amount of assets, liabilities, and owners' equity at the end of the
     budget process
  5. contains a list of anticipated expenses for the period for activities other than manufac-
     turing
  6. identifies the amount of a product that must be manufactured to meet a company's
     needs for sales and inventory
  7. provides a schedule of all costs of production other than direct materials and direct labor
  8. describes cash requirements for the budget period
  9. projects revenues from sales of a company's products or services

E8-3 Hoop Action manufactures basketballs, which it sells for $50 each. Cash collections from sales
Obj. 2 are expected to be 80% in the quarter of the sale and 20% in the following quarter. The un-
collected portion of sales at January 1 was $40,000. The sales forecast for the next year is:

Expected Sales in Units

Quarter 1	2,000
Quarter 2	3,000
Quarter 3	5,000
Quarter 4	5,000

Create a sales budget and a schedule of cash collections.

E8-4
Obj. 2

Spooks Company makes a popular Halloween mask. Peak sales are in October of each year. The company's partial sales budget, in units, for 2004 is as follows:

August	**September**	**October**	**November**
15,000	35,000	50,000	10,000

The company has an inventory policy in which the end-of-month inventory must equal 10% of the following month's sales. The inventory as of July 31 was 1,500 units.

Prepare a production budget for the three months ended October 31, 2004. In your budget, show the number of units to be produced each month and for the quarter in total.

E8-5
Obj. 2

Razor Sharp produces a hedge trimmer used for lawn care. The company's sales budget for April through July is as follows:

April	**May**	**June**	**July**
300,000	350,000	250,000	150,000

The company has an inventory policy in which the end-of-month inventory must equal 5% of the following month's sales. The inventory as of March 31 was 15,000 units.

Prepare a production budget for April, May, and June. In your budget, show the number of units to be produced each month and for the quarter in total.

E8-6
Obj. 2

Young Company produces a dietary product called Veggy Bars. Each six-ounce Veggy Bar contains five ounces of mixed vegetables, which Young purchases for $.05 an ounce. Budgeted sales of vegetable bars for the first four months of 2004 is as follows:

	Units
January	100,000
February	120,000
March	110,000
April	100,000

Young has an inventory policy that requires the ending inventory of Veggy Bars to be 10% of the following month's sales.

Prepare a production budget for the first quarter of 2004 by month and for the quarter in total. Calculate the amount of materials, in ounces and in dollar amounts, required to meet production.

E8-7
Obj. 2

Refer to the data in E8-6. Each Veggy Bar requires .02 direct labor hour. The average labor rate is $10 per hour.

Prepare a direct labor budget for the first quarter of 2004, showing the number of hours needed and the total labor cost required by month and for the quarter in total.

E8-8
Obj. 2

Chugalot Company produces soda mugs. Each 32-ounce mug contains 1.1 pounds of glass, which Chugalot purchases for $1.05 a pound. Budgeted production of mugs for the first four months of 2004 is as follows:

	Units
January	10,000
February	12,000
March	8,000
April	10,000

(Continued)

Chugalot has an inventory policy that ending inventory of mugs should be 10% of the following month's sales.

Prepare a purchasing budget for the first quarter of 2004 by month and for the quarter in total. Show the amount of materials required in unit and in dollar amounts.

E8-9
Obj. 2

Refer to the data in E8-8. Each mug requires .05 direct labor hour. The average labor rate is $20 per hour.

Prepare a direct labor budget for the first quarter of 2004, showing the number of hours needed and the total labor cost required by month and for the quarter in total.

E8-10
Obj. 2

Office Supply 4U manufactures staplers. The activity base used to allocate overhead is direct labor hours. The variable overhead rate is estimated at $1.50 per direct labor hour for 2004. The fixed overhead is budgeted at $20,000 per quarter, of which $5,000 represents depreciation. The budgeted direct labor hours are as follows:

Quarter	Direct Labor Hours
1	9,500
2	10,500
3	11,500
4	11,000

Prepare a manufacturing overhead budget for 2004, showing the total budgeted manufacturing overhead and the cash disbursements for manufacturing overhead by quarter and for the year in total. (*Hint:* Is there a periodic cash flow associated with depreciation?)

E8-11
Obj. 2

A+ Company manufactures study guides for students. A+ sells its study guides through door-to-door sales. Its salespeople receive a $20 commission per book sold. Fixed annual selling and administrative expenses for 2004 are estimated as follows:

Insurance	$ 200,000
Executive salaries	1,000,000
Property taxes	30,000
Depreciation	30,000

The sales for 2004 are estimated as follows:

Quarter	Unit Sales
1	5,000
2	10,000
3	20,000
4	7,000

Prepare a selling and administrative budget for 2004, showing the total budgeted selling and administrative expenses by quarter and for the year in total.

E8-12
Obj. 2

Tough Terrain Company manufactures professional quality lawn mowers. Tough Terrain incurs variable selling expenses of $15 per lawn mower. Other annual selling and administrative expenses for 2004 are estimated as follows:

Advertising	$200,000
Insurance	100,000
Executive salaries	500,000
Property taxes	20,000
Depreciation	10,000

The sales for 2004 are estimated as follows:

Quarter	Unit Sales
1	5,000
2	30,000
3	20,000
4	2,000

Prepare a selling and administrative budget for 2004, showing the total budgeted selling and administrative expenses and the cash disbursements for selling and administrative expenses by quarter and for the year in total. (*Hint:* Is there a periodic cash flow associated with depreciation?)

E8-13
Objs. 2, 3

On April 30, Sterling Enterprises had an inventory of 38,000 units of finished goods, and it had accounts receivable totaling $85,000. Sales, in units, have been budgeted as follows for the next four months:

May	60,000
June	75,000
July	90,000
August	81,000

Sterling has a policy that 40% of the following month's sales should be maintained in ending inventory. Each unit sells for $2. All sales are on account. The budgeted cash collections anticipate that one-third of sales will be collected in the month of sale and the remainder in the following month.

a. Prepare a production budget for the months of May, June, and July.
b. Prepare a schedule of cash collections for the months of May, June, and July.

E8-14
Obj. 3

Elm Company makes a product that has peak sales in September of each year. Excerpts from the annual sales budget are as follows:

	May	June	July	August	September
Budgeted sales	$450,000	$500,000	$500,000	$600,000	$750,000

The company is in the process of preparing a cash budget for the third quarter (July, August, and September) and must determine the cash collections by month. Collections on sales are expected to be as follows:

70% in the month of sale
20% in the month following the month of sale
8% in the second month following the month of sale
2% uncollectible

What are the expected cash collections for each month of the third quarter? (*Hint:* When calculating cash inflows, ignore the amount that is uncollectible.)

E8-15
Obj. 3

Beany-Toys Company makes small toys that it sells to retailers. Following are excerpts from the annual sales budget:

	August	September	October	November	December
Budgeted sales	$1,000,000	$800,000	$1,000,000	$2,500,000	$3,000,000

The company is in the process of preparing a cash budget for the third quarter (October, November, and December) and must determine the cash collections by month. Collections on sales are expected to be as follows:

50% in the month of the sale
40% in the month following the sale
7% in the second month following the sale
3% uncollectible

What are the expected cash collections for each month of the fourth quarter? (*Hint:* When calculating cash inflows, ignore the amount that is uncollectible.)

E8-16
Obj. 3

Cross Blade manufactures pocket knifes. The activity base used to allocate overhead is machine hours. The variable overhead rate is estimated at $4 per machine hour for 2004. The fixed overhead is budgeted at $80,000 per quarter. The budgeted machine hours are as follows:

(Continued)

Quarter	Machine Hours
1	5,000
2	4,000
3	4,500
4	5,000

Prepare a manufacturing overhead budget for 2004, showing the total budgeted manufacturing overhead by quarter and for the year in total.

PROBLEMS

If your instructor is using Personal Trainer® in this course, you may complete your assignments online.

P8-1   Pro Forma Income Statement

Obj. 1

Say Cheese Company manufactures picture frames that sell for $25 per frame. Say Cheese does not maintain an inventory; all items produced are sold during the period. Thus, all production costs appear on the income statement. The company has fixed manufacturing overhead of $30,000 per year. The company's fixed selling and administrative expense is $40,000 per year. Other expenses are as follows:

	Cost per Unit
Direct materials	$5.00
Direct labor	2.00
Variable manufacturing overhead	3.00
Variable selling and administrative expense	2.00

Say Cheese would like to estimate its net income if sales for 2004 are expected to be 8,000 units.

Required

A. Create a pro forma income statement using Exhibit 3 as a guide.
B. Discuss the uses for a pro forma income statement.

P8-2   Pro Forma Income Statement

Obj. 1

Technology Team manufactures laptops that sell for $2,200 each. Assume Technology Team does not maintain an inventory; all items produced are sold during the period. Thus, all production costs appear on the income statement. The company has fixed manufacturing overhead of $4,000,000 per year. The company's fixed selling and administrative expense is $3,000,000 per year. Other expenses are as follows:

	Cost per Unit
Direct materials	$1,200
Direct labor	150
Variable manufacturing overhead	50
Variable selling and administrative expense	30

Management at Technology Team believe sales for 2005 will be 10,000 units.

Required

A. Create a pro forma income statement using Exhibit 3 as a guide.
B. Discuss how a pro forma income statement helps managers make better decisions.

P8-3   Cash Budget

Objs. 1, 3

Kim Incorporated is preparing its master budget for 2004. Shown at the top of the next page are expected cash inflows and outflows resulting from the sales, purchases, and administrative budgets. In addition to these cash flows, assume the company expects to pay $10,000 in income taxes each quarter. Also, assume Kim expects to pay a $20,000 dividend in the fourth quarter. The beginning cash balance is $160,000.

SPREADSHEET

	Quarter				
	1	**2**	**3**	**4**	**Year**
Cash Collections from Sales Budget					
Total cash collections	$120,000	$140,000	$230,000	$250,000	$740,000
Cash Disbursements from Direct Materials Budget					
Total cash disbursements	$ 60,000	$ 70,000	$115,000	$125,000	$350,000
Direct Labor Disbursements					
Total direct labor disbursements	$ 16,000	$ 24,000	$ 40,000	$ 40,000	$120,000
Manufacturing Overhead Disbursements					
Cash disbursements for manufacturing overhead	$ 31,000	$ 39,000	$ 55,000	$ 55,000	$180,000
Selling and Administrative Disbursements					
Cash expenditures for selling and administrative expenses	$ 29,000	$ 31,000	$ 35,000	$ 35,000	$130,000

Required

A. Create a cash budget for 2004.

B. Assume that Kim has $1,000,000 of debt outstanding as of January 1, 2004. Given the cash budget should Kim borrow additional funds or repay any of the debt during 2004? Why or why not?

C. Why is it important to create a cash budget?

P8-4   ## Purchasing Budget, Strategic Considerations

Obj. 2

Noise Hollow launched a new stereo in January. The budget for the stereo is as follows:

	January	February
Unit sales	1,000	1,500
Add: Desired ending inventory	300	400
Subtotal	1,300	1,900
Less: Beginning inventory	0	300
Total production	1,300	1,600
Units of materials per finished good	10	10
Required units of materials	13,000	16,000
Cost of materials per unit	× $5	× $5
Total purchasing costs	$65,000	$80,000

Actual units of materials required per finished good were 12 units in January and 11 units in February. Actual cost of materials was $6 per unit in January and $5.50 per unit in February.

Required

A. Show what the budget would have looked like with the actual material requirements and costs.

B. What strategic considerations should be taken into account when reviewing this product?

P8-5   ## Budgeting Culture and Behavior

Objs. 2, 4

Bob Haskins is the purchasing manager for Regal Products. Each year Regal Products develops a master budget. Bob is responsible for preparing a purchasing budget, which he bases on budgeted levels of production. Bob carefully plans purchasing costs and raw material inventory levels to meet production needs.

Each year, Yvonne Lang, president of Regal Products, conducts performance evaluations, and bonuses are paid to key employees, including Bob, based on meeting budgeted results. For the past two years, Bob has received a very small bonus and has been chided by Yvonne for poor planning. Specifically, Yvonne has pointed out that the purchasing department has not maintained adequate levels of raw material inventory and is always in a rush to obtain materials, resulting in increased shipping and handling charges. Further, Regal must often pay

(Continued)

premium amounts for immediate shipment of materials. In her most recent evaluation, Yvonne stated to Bob, "The sales department and production department are doing an excellent job. They consistently exceed their budgets by 10% or more. I just don't understand why you can't meet your numbers. Perhaps it is time for some changes around here."

After getting chided by Yvonne, Bob went back and looked at his budget. He knew he had ordered the amount required by the budget. The budget for January and February is as follows:

	January	February
Unit sales	300,000	350,000
Add: Desired ending inventory	35,000	25,000
Subtotal	335,000	375,000
Less: Beginning inventory	30,000	35,000
Budgeted production	305,000	340,000
Pounds of raw materials per unit	1.1	1.1
Required pounds of raw materials	335,500	374,000
Add: Desired ending inventory of raw materials	37,400	27,500
Less: Beginning inventory of raw materials	33,550	37,400
Total raw material needs (pounds)	339,350	364,100

Required

A. If sales levels were 10% higher than budgeted, how many pounds of raw materials would Bob need to rush order each month so he can meet demand and the required ending inventory as shown in the budget?
B. Why does it appear that the purchasing department is having trouble meeting its budget?
C. Is it appropriate to blame Bob for all of the purchasing problems?
D. If Yvonne does "make some changes," what changes would you suggest she consider?

P8-6 Budgeting Culture and Behavior

Objs. 2, 4

Sue is the purchasing manager for Paper Goods Incorporated. Sue's budget for January and February was as follows:

	January	February
Finished goods to produce (units)	10,000	11,000
Add: Desired ending inventory	1,100	1,100
Subtotal	11,100	12,100
Less: Beginning inventory	1,000	1,100
Total	10,100	11,000
Pounds of raw materials per unit	2.0	2.0
Required pounds of raw materials	20,200	22,000
Add: Desired ending inventory of raw materials	2,200	2,200
Less: Beginning inventory of raw materials	2,020	2,200
Total raw material needs (pounds)	20,380	22,000

At the end of February, Sue's boss asked her, "Why are you ordering so many materials? The inventory stockroom is overflowing with materials." Puzzled, Sue checked her order amounts and saw that she had ordered the exact amount as stated by the budget. Sue then spoke to the production manager who explained that the plant had been running at only 90% capacity for the past two months due to lower demand.

Required

A. If sales and production levels were 10% lower than budgeted, how many pounds of raw materials are on hand at the end of February?
B. What is the problem with this system, and how would you suggest it be improved?

P8-7 Labor Requirement Planning, Service Provider

Objs. 2, 5

Ceco Grass Care is a small lawn maintenance service that provides a variety of landscape services. A large part of Ceco's sales are generated through lawn maintenance. Jeff Roberts manages Ceco. Jeff has reviewed the job order log for the next 12 weeks (three months ending July 26, 2005), and the log is full. Ceco recently acquired several commercial property accounts and has plenty of work planned. A summary of accounts shows that Ceco now has 11 commercial properties and 45 residential properties to maintain on a routine basis.

Each property is scheduled for maintenance every two weeks. The commercial accounts require 16 worker-hours to service, and the residential accounts require four worker-hours.

Ceco currently has a cutting crew of three, each of whom is paid $8.50 an hour.

Required

A. Prepare a direct labor budget for Ceco covering the next three months.
B. Does the budget raise any concerns for Ceco? Explain your answer.

P8-8
Obj. 3

SPREADSHEET

Sales Budget, Strategic Considerations

A new high-tech product was launched in July. This is the first product of its type in the marketplace. The budget for this product is as follows:

	July	August
Expected sales in units	2,000	3,000
Selling price per unit	$ 50	$ 50
Total sales	$100,000	$150,000

However, the actual sales were not quite as high as was anticipated. The actual sales were:

	July	August
Actual sales in units	1,000	2,500
Selling price per unit	$ 50	$ 50
Total sales	$50,000	$125,000

Mary, the vice president of finance, spoke harshly to John, the product manager, for not meeting the budgeted amounts. She threatened to discontinue the product if John did not meet budgeted sales for September. Mary also wants to know how much cash would have been collected if the budgeted sales had been achieved.

Required

A. Create a schedule of cash collections for the budgeted sales for July and August. Assume that 80% of sales are collected in the month of sale and the remaining 20% of sales are collected the following month.
B. What strategic considerations should Mary take into account? Explain.

P8-9
Obj. 3

Budgeted Production and Cash Collections

On August 31, Blake & Sons had an inventory of 50 units of finished goods, and it had accounts receivable totaling $75,000. Sales, in units, have been budgeted as follows for the next four months:

September	300
October	400
November	450
December	500

Blake has a policy that 20% of the following month's sales should be maintained in ending inventory. Each unit sells for $500. All sales are on account. The budgeted cash collections anticipate that one half of sales will be collected in the month of sale and the other half in the following month.

Required

A. Prepare a production budget for the months of September, October, and November.
B. Prepare a schedule of budgeted cash collections from sales for the months of September, October, and November.

(Continued)

C. Actual sales values (which drive the entire budgeting process) are not known with certainty. Are the various budgets and schedules meaningful since they are based on management's estimate of sales in the coming year? Can you identify other examples of accounting estimates?

P8-10   Budgeting and Behavioral Implications

Obj. 4

An effective budget converts the goals and objectives of management into specific performance targets. The master budget serves as a blueprint that reflects management's plans for the budgeted period. Moreover, the master budget serves as a basis for control in that performance can be evaluated by comparing actual results to budgeted or planned results.

Given the importance of budgeting within a company, the creation of an effective budget is essential for the successful operation of the company. There are several methods of generating budget information that can be employed, all of which require extensive contact with people at various operating levels within the company. The way in which people see their involvement with the budget process is important to the successful use of the budget as a management tool.

In the budget-setting process, budget A was put together by lower management, including sales representatives, purchasing managers, and factory supervisors. Budget B was put together by senior management.

	A	B
Unit sales	10,000	15,000
Dollar sales	$2,000,000	$3,000,000
Less variable expenses:		
Direct materials	$1,100,000	$1,500,000
Direct labor	220,000	300,000
Variable overhead	110,000	150,000
Variable selling and administrative expense	88,000	120,000
Total variable expenses	$1,518,000	$2,070,000
Contribution margin	$ 482,000	$ 930,000
Less fixed expenses:		
Manufacturing overhead	$ 350,000	$ 300,000
Selling and administrative	200,000	200,000
Taxes and interest	10,000	10,000
Total fixed expenses	$ 560,000	$ 510,000
Net income (loss)	$ (78,000)	$ 420,000

Required

A. Calculate the cost per unit for the variable costs.
B. Why do you think budget A has high costs and low sales forecasts?
C. Why do you think budget B has low costs and high sales forecasts? What are the behavioral implications of this top-down approach?
D. How should the two groups participate to come to a consensus on the budget? What are the advantages of this approach?

P8-11   Budgeting and Behavioral Implications

Obj. 4

Crunch Numbers is a manufacturer of calculators. In the budget-setting process, budget A was put together by lower and middle management. Budget B was put together by senior management.

	A	B
Unit sales	20,000	30,000
Dollar sales	$600,000	$900,000
Less variable expenses:		
Direct materials	$260,000	$360,000
Direct labor	40,000	60,000
Variable overhead	60,000	75,000
Variable selling and administrative expense	60,000	60,000
Total variable expenses	$420,000	$555,000
Contribution margin	$180,000	$345,000

Less fixed expenses:		
Manufacturing overhead	$ 60,000	$ 50,000
Selling and administrative	100,000	80,000
Taxes and interest	10,000	10,000
Total fixed expenses	$170,000	$140,000
Net income (loss)	$ 10,000	$205,000

Required

A. Calculate the cost per unit for the variable costs.
B. Why do you think budget A has high costs and low sales forecasts?
C. Why do you think budget B has low costs and high sales forecasts? What are the behavioral implications of this top-down approach?
D. How should the two groups participate to come to a consensus on the budget? What are the advantages of this approach?

P8-12 ## Excel in Action

SPREADSHEET

Music Makers expects to sell 500,000 CDs per month, including 350,000 data CDs and 150,000 music CDs. The selling price per unit is $2.30 for data CDs and $3.10 for music CDs. The desired level of ending inventory of raw materials is 5,000 units for blank CDs, containers, and cellophane wrap. Wrap is measured in feet, and each unit requires one foot of wrap. Paper inserts are obtained as needed, and the desired ending inventory is zero for these materials. At the beginning of May, Music Makers has 9,500 blank CDs, 2,500 containers, and 20,000 feet of cellophane in stock. The cost per unit of raw materials is $0.72 for CDs, $0.12 for containers, $0.07 for inserts, and $0.01 per foot of cellophane. Direct labor hours to produce each CD is 0.023 for copying and 0.015 for packaging. Direct labor cost is $12 per hour for copying and $8 per hour for packaging.

Required Use the data provided to prepare a (A) sales budget, (B) direct materials budget, and (C) direct labor budget for Music Makers for May. Use the following format. Use cell references and formulas where possible.

5,000 enc

	A	B	C	D	E	F
1	Monthly Sales Budget					
2		Data	Music	Total		
3	Expected sales in units	350,000	150,000	500,000		
4	Selling price per unit	×2.30	3.10			
5	Total sales					
6						
7	Direct Materials Budget					
8		CDs	Containers	Inserts	Cellophane	Total
9	Expected sales					
10	Desired ending inventory					
11	Total needs					
12	Beginning inventory	9,500	2,500		20,000	
13	Units to purchase					
14	Cost per unit	.72	.12	.07	.01	
15	Cost of materials					
16						
17	Direct Labor Budget					
18		Copying	Packaging	Total		
19	Units to produce					
20	Direct labor hour per unit	.023	.015			
21	Total hours					
22	Direct labor cost per hour					
23	Total direct labor cost	12	8			

(Continued)

Use appropriate formatting for numbers.

If expected sales were 400,000 data CDs and 100,000 music CDs, what would be the effect on the budgets?

P8-13   Multiple-Choice Overview of the Chapter

1. Which of the following represents the correct order in which the budget documents for a manufacturing company would be prepared?
   a. Sales budget, cash budget, direct materials budget, direct labor budget
   b. Production budget, sales budget, direct materials budget, direct labor budget
   c. Sales budget, cash budget, production budget, direct materials budget
   d. Sales budget, production budget, direct labor budget, cash budget, pro forma financial statements

2. Which of the following is *not* included as one of the four major sections of the cash budget?
   a. The receipts section
   b. The financing section
   c. The selling and administrative expense section
   d. The cash excess or deficiency section

3. A major advantage of budgeting is that it:
   a. eliminates major uncertainties associated with the business environment.
   b. ensures that management's objectives will be met.
   c. requires managers to give priority to the planning process.
   d. eliminates the need for stringent controls.

4. Which of the following is *not* correct with respect to the manufacturing overhead budget?
   a. The manufacturing overhead budget includes selling and administrative expenses.
   b. Manufacturing overhead can be broken down by cost behavior.
   c. The manufacturing overhead budget should include all costs of production other than direct materials and direct labor.
   d. The budgeted variable cost of manufacturing overhead is dependent on the number of units to be produced, as shown in the production budget.

5. Budgeted production needs are computed by:
   a. adding budgeted sales to the desired ending inventory and deducting the beginning inventory.
   b. adding budgeted sales to beginning inventory and deducting the desired ending inventory.
   c. adding budgeted sales to the desired ending inventory.
   d. deducting beginning inventory from budgeted sales.

6. Which of the following is *not* true with respect to a participative budgeting process?
   a. Participative budgeting requires less managerial involvement.
   b. Participative budgeting motivates managers by involving them in the budget process.
   c. Participative budgeting requires greater coordination between departments and disciplines.
   d. Participative budgeting relies on a bottom-up approach.

7. The materials purchases budget is prepared using which format?
   a. Beginning inventory + units to be produced − ending inventory
   b. Raw material required for production + desired ending raw materials inventory − beginning raw materials inventory
   c. Ending inventory + beginning inventory − units to be produced
   d. None of the above is correct.

8. The cash budget is comprised of all the following except:
   a. cash receipts.
   b. cash disbursements.
   c. accrued sales revenue.
   d. proceeds from loans and loan repayments.

9. A collection of related operating budgets is known as a:
   a. pro forma financial statement.
   b. flexible budget.
   c. static budget.
   d. master budget.

10. Budgeting in service companies:
   a. can be more difficult than in manufacturing companies because of complexities involved in tracing costs to a particular service.
   b. typically does not involve materials purchases.
   c. can help managers understand the cost of providing services.
   d. All of the above are correct.

CASES

C8-1

Objs. 2, 3

The Master Budget

Columbo Company manufactures a single model trench coat sold throughout the United States. Projected sales in units for the first five months of 2005 are as follows:

January	35,000
February	20,000
March	15,000
April	8,000
May	6,000

The following information relates to Columbo's production and inventory policies and balances:

1. Finished goods inventory is maintained at 80% of the following month's sales. Finished goods inventory at January 1, 2005, was 28,000 units.
2. Two materials are required for each trench coat manufactured, as follows:

Direct Materials	Yards per Unit	Cost per Yard
Polyester	5	$8
Lining material	3	2

   Raw materials inventory is maintained at 10% of the following month's production needs. Inventory at January 1, 2005, was 51,000 yards of polyester and 30,600 yards of lining.

3. Direct labor used per unit is two hours. The average rate for labor is $9.50 per hour.
4. Overhead each month is estimated by adding the fixed cost component to the variable cost component. Direct labor hours is used as the basis for variable costs. A summary of expected overhead costs is as follows:

	Fixed Cost Component	Variable Cost Component
Factory supplies		$1.00
Utilities		0.75
Shop maintenance	$ 3,000	0.50
Supervision	4,000	
Depreciation	60,000	
Taxes	5,000	
Other	10,000	2.00
Total	$82,000	$4.25

(Continued)

5. Selling, general, and administrative expenses are also calculated by summing the fixed cost component and the variable cost component. The variable cost component is based on the number of units sold. Cost estimates are as follows:

	Fixed Cost Component	Variable Cost Component
Salaries	$18,000	
Commissions		$3.00
Depreciation	22,000	
Shipping		0.75
Other	10,000	1.50
Total	$50,000	$5.25

6. Each trench coat sells for $85.
7. All purchases are made in cash. All sales are on account. Collection of accounts receivable is planned as follows: 90% in the month of sale; 10% in the month following the month of sale. The accounts receivable balance at January 1, 2005, is $145,000, all of which is collectible. The cash balance at January 1, 2005, is $202,000.

Required

A. Prepare the following portions of the operating master budget, by month, for the first quarter of 2005:
   1. Sales budget
   2. Production budget
   3. Materials purchases budget
   4. Labor budget
   5. Overhead budget
   6. Selling and administrative budget
   7. Cash budget
B. Suppose Columbo's management believes that unseasonably warm weather in March and April could cause its sales in units to differ from the original projections as follows:

January	35,000
February	20,000
March	10,000
April	6,000
May	6,000

Explain how these fluctuations in sales will affect the other portions of the master budget developed in the previous requirements. What are the implications for the importance of forecasting sales accurately?

C8-2 Budgeting in a Service Company

Obj. 5

Juanita Testor owns and operates a hair salon under the name Clips n' Curls. There are currently seven hair stylists, including Juanita. In addition to hair styling, Clips n' Curls sells nail care, facials, skin and hair care products, fashion jewelry, and tanning bed time.

A full-time receptionist is employed to arrange appointments and perform other clerical duties, such as counter sales and record keeping. The receptionist is paid $1,500 a month.

Juanita has eight styling bays, each equipped with a sink, cabinet, and vacuum system. Each stylist provides his or her own instruments. Each stylist, including Juanita, "rents" a bay at a cost of $400 per month. Charges for all client services are billed and collected by the receptionist, who accumulates totals for each stylist. Collections for services are paid to the stylists on a weekly basis after deducting bay rent and cost of supplies. Any supplies used by the stylists must be purchased through the shop at Juanita's cost.

Nail care and facials are offered on a limited basis three days a week by a single individual, who receives 50% of collected billings as compensation. The tanning bed is owned by the shop. All income received from the bed goes to the shop. Variable shop costs are incurred based on the number of stylists. Based on a two-year study, Juanita has assembled the following information on monthly activity and costs to operate Clips n' Curls:

Average monthly billings per stylist	$4,000
Average product sales	600
Average gross margin on product sales	55%
Average gross nail and facial billings	$1,000
Average gross tanning bed billings	450
Fixed operating costs:	
Shop rent	500
Depreciation	400
Advertising	150
Other	100
Variable operating costs:	
Maintenance, utilities, and other	1,400*

Note: Variable operating costs are incurred as follows: 50% by stylists, 30% by tanning, nail care, and facials, 15% by product display, and 5% administrative.

Required

A. Assume that Juanita can hire an additional stylist who can generate the same average amount of business as the other stylists. Assume also that the additional stylist would have no impact on administrative expenses. What would be the change in average monthly shop income if Juanita hires the stylist to fill the remaining open bay? (*Hint:* Compare the change in revenues with the change in costs related to the incremental increase of one stylist.)

B. What is the average total monthly income of the shop given the number of stylists currently employed?

C. Juanita is considering a change in the bay rent agreement. Instead of charging a fixed amount per month, she is thinking of charging a stylist 12% of the stylist's billings. Would Juanita be better off with this new fee arrangement? Explain your answer.

COST VARIANCES AND QUALITY MANAGEMENT

How are budgets used to evaluate performance?

Chapter M8 illustrated how Seth and Erin might use the budget process to plan future costs and expenses. Budgets also are useful to help managers understand performance at the end of an accounting period. For example, the accounting software that Erin and Seth use automatically compares expected, or budgeted, performance with actual performance. The difference is termed a variance. Seth and Erin must understand how to interpret variance reports and make process improvements based on their interpretations. One year has elapsed since they started their furniture business in a garage. They have been successful in producing and selling their line of juvenile furniture. However, actual financial results differ from expectations.

FOOD FOR THOUGHT

Put yourself in the role of Erin and Seth. You just received a report indicating the actual costs of materials, labor, and overhead are greater than the predicted, or budgeted, amount. As a result, actual income as reported by the income statement is less than budgeted net income. How could this difference have occurred? What would you do to correct the problem? Let's join Erin and Seth as they consider the use of variance information.

Seth: Wow, look at these figures! In some cases we really missed the mark when we budgeted our manufacturing costs. Our materials, labor, and overhead variances are all unfavorable.

Erin: So what does that mean?

Seth: An unfavorable cost variance means that all our actual costs for materials, labor, and overhead were larger than the budgeted amount. On the other hand, when an actual cost is less than the budgeted amount, the variance is favorable.

Erin: Okay, so now we know our actual cost of materials was greater than the budgeted cost of materials. What caused the difference, and how do we fix it? Did we spend more for materials than we planned?

Seth: That's certainly a possibility. However, the report shows a favorable materials price variance. That means our actual materials cost was less than the budget called for.

Erin: Have lumber prices changed since we prepared the budget?

Seth: Actually, I was able to get a better price on lumber by purchasing it in larger quantities. So our lumber prices were lower than we budgeted.

Erin: But this makes no sense. Paying less for materials should cause a favorable variance, yet you said our materials variance was unfavorable.

Seth: The price variance is only part of the total materials variance.

Erin: The other part must be the quantity of materials used. I'd be willing to bet we used more lumber than we should have.

Seth: I think that's the answer. The report says our materials quantity variance is unfavorable. In fact, we have a huge unfavorable quantity variance as compared to the small favorable price variance. Thus, our overall materials variance is unfavorable.

Erin: *How do we explain the unfavorable quantity variance, and how do we keep it from happening again?*

Seth: *You are asking the right questions, Erin. I need to go back and look at the production records to see if I can find a reason for using so much material. We could have had a machine problem that resulted in too much scrap or waste material. Sometimes the machine cutting tools become dull or damaged and ruin a piece of lumber.*

Erin: *Is it possible that we had an inexperienced craftsman making some of the furniture?*

Seth: *There could be lots of possibilities. Variance analysis can help us understand where problems may have occurred so we can make changes to prevent the same problems in the future. We also need to look at the labor and overhead variances in a similar manner to see why our budgeted costs differed from actual costs in these accounts.*

Erin: *I agree. If we can find where we are creating waste and inefficiency, we can improve our profitability.*

OBJECTIVES

Once you have completed this chapter, you should be able to:

1 Calculate and evaluate cost variances for direct materials and direct labor.

2 Explain how variance analysis can enhance managerial decision making.

3 Identify four types of quality costs and explain how managers use these costs to improve performance.

4 Describe how variability can affect production costs.

5 Explain how statistical process control provides useful information to managers of both production and administrative functions.

6 Explain the application of performance evaluation methods in service organizations.

MetalArt: Performance Evaluation and the Manufacturing Process

Successful companies provide a return to investors by producing sales revenues in excess of costs. Thus, managers always are mindful of their customers' needs for quality, innovation, and reasonable prices. Control systems are used to ensure key processes are functioning as intended. Furthermore, compensation often is linked to outcomes as indicated by these control systems. As this chapter illustrates, a variety of techniques may be used to manage costs and to improve profitability. Thus, managers may use outcomes from these techniques as a *scorecard* to evaluate their success in achieving targets from internal operations.

The examples in this chapter are based on the experience of MetalArt, a company that prints graphic designs on flat metal sheets. The sheets are processed by other companies to make containers for ground coffee sold in grocery stores. Exhibit 1 illustrates the manufacturing process at MetalArt. Four interrelated processes (coil shearing, coating, printing, and wrapping and shipping) are required to produce MetalArt's product line. The following section briefly explains the activities taking place within each process.

Coil Shearing

The manufacturing process begins with coils of steel and ends with printed metal sheets that will be cut and welded into coffee cans by MetalArt's customers. Large rolls of steel (weighing approximately 20,000 pounds and called *coils*) are loaded onto a spindle that permits the coil to rotate as it is unwound for processing. Next, the steel passes through a pinhole detector, an optical scanning device that identifies light passing through the steel sheet. This step ensures that the finished can will be airtight and provide a perfect seal.

Exhibit 1 The Manufacturing Process at MetalArt

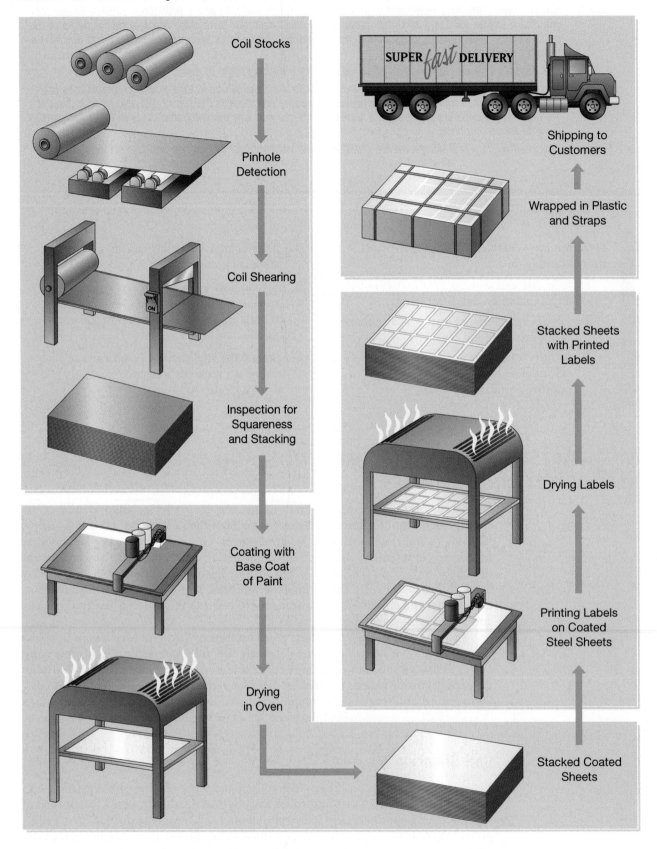

As a coil unwinds, the steel is sheared (cut) into sheets approximately three feet square. The steel sheets are randomly tested for squareness and must fall within specification limits to be passed on to the next stage of production. Those sheets that meet the quality standards are stacked in preparation for coating.

Coating

Coating is the first step in the printing process. A coat of white paint is applied to the metal sheet to provide a base to which colored ink will adhere. Following the base coat application, the sheet advances into an oven for drying. Since 18 or more cans are cut from one sheet of steel, the base coat is applied in rectangular patterns with strips of bare steel separating the rectangles. This frame of bare metal, called the *weld margin* (Exhibit 2), is very important. When the individual rectangles are cut from the sheet and welded to form the cylindrical can body, paint in the weld margin would cause major damage to the welding machine and disrupt the assembly process. Thus, a computer equipped with optical scanning devices monitors the coating of each sheet. A red flashing signal from the computer's control system lets the machine operator know when the coating process is beginning to produce weld margins that are too narrow. At the end of the coating step, the sheets are stacked and placed in a work-in-process area on the plant floor.

Exhibit 2 Sheet of Can Bodies

Printing

Printing is the next step in the process. The printing machines are capable of applying up to three colors to the sheets before they pass through a dryer that promotes rapid drying of the paint. The image that appears on the final product is printed using a process similar to silk screening. Three colors (such as red, blue, and yellow) are applied one after the other. Exhibit 2 illustrates a typical sheet of can bodies after coating and printing. At the end of the printing step, the sheets are stacked on platforms called *pallets* to await wrapping.

Wrapping and Shipping

Pallets of finished printed sheets are covered with plastic and bound with metal straps for shipping. Wrapping is a manual operation that requires two workers. After wrapping, pallets are loaded directly into trucks and delivered to customers. Finished goods inventory is not allowed to accumulate for more than a few hours.

METALART: COST AND QUALITY MANAGEMENT

This section documents the events occurring at MetalArt over a two-year period. The company found that its product quality was lower than that of its competitors. In addition, production costs were soaring out of control. MetalArt's managers discovered various cost management techniques to improve quality and reduce production costs.

We begin our discussion with the following events.

MetalArt—March 2005

Pat Allan, manager of the MetalArt plant, looked around the conference table in hopes that someone at the managers' meeting could explain why production costs had gone through the roof during the past few weeks. "I just don't understand. After all of our efforts to control costs, things have gotten worse. Corporate isn't going to be happy with our profitability figures."

Mary Smith, the production manager, replied, "Pat, remember the problems we had last week with bad raw materials? Everyone knows that rusty steel causes all kinds of headaches when we run it through the printing line. I suspect our profitability problems somehow are related to that. Also, I'm sure that some defective prints left the plant and that we'll hear about it from our customers. But we can't inspect everything; we don't have the resources."

"Mary, I don't think 'off-grade' material could have had *that* much impact on our bottom line," replied Lee Jones, the purchasing manager. "Anyway, by my estimates, I saved thousands of dollars by finding good steel prices."

Mary said, "Lee, we appreciate your efforts to control raw materials costs, but I scheduled a lot of overtime because our production line had to slow down to deal with off-grade raw material."

"I'm hearing two important issues," said Pat. "We have to find a way to *measure* the impact of material and labor cost overruns, and also to *prevent* production problems and their related costs before they get out of hand. It's clear to me that our disappointing financial results are linked to our operating problems. Let's get busy and put some controls in place that will help us improve operations and reduce costs. First, let's calculate cost variances for materials and labor. I'll evaluate those reports on a weekly basis to make sure we are staying on track."

"That's okay for you, Pat, but I need on-line, real-time tools to let me know when our process is out of control," said Mary. "I can't wait a week to find out that I need to look for a solution to a manufacturing problem. I think statistical process control methods would help us determine quickly when something has gone wrong."

"I agree," said Pat. "In addition, I think we should install a system for accounting for the costs of quality. I don't think we should rely on inspections to ensure that few defective units leave the plant. We can improve our processes so that they are reliable. In addition, we can illustrate to everyone from the shop floor worker to plant management how their actions affect our bottom line. We have good people, and I'm sure we can turn this plant around. Let's go to work!"

MetalArt—2007

Like other companies, MetalArt is constantly reviewing its operations, looking for ways to cut costs and improve quality. The employees have risen to the challenge and have managed to cut costs by 40 percent over the last two years while maintaining product quality. These improvements are due largely to employee suggestions and implementation efforts.

At each stage of production, the machine operator is assisted by software that signals when production quality slips out of control. With newer machines, data go directly from the machine to the computer. However, for older machines, the operator must enter the machine readings manually into the computer. The data are analyzed by a computerized statistical model that checks relevant variables to determine if production is within quality control limits. In addition, workers at all stages select samples from work in process, visually inspect printing quality, and reject products that do not meet very tight guidelines.

VARIANCE ANALYSIS FOR DIRECT MATERIALS AND DIRECT LABOR

OBJECTIVE 1

Calculate and evaluate cost variances for direct materials and direct labor.

As you learned from the discussion in the opening scenario to this chapter, Seth and Erin are interested in learning the cause of their unfavorable variances. Unlike the managers at MetalArt, Seth and Erin had established a standard cost system. Their job is to interpret the output. Let's learn how to set up a standard cost system from the managers at MetalArt.

The managers' meeting at MetalArt revealed an absence of controls. Pat Allen suggested the team must find a way to measure the cost of material and labor overruns and to implement systems that help prevent excessive costs. This section considers variance analysis as a tool for determining whether managers are using resources efficiently. We consider the environment in which the technique developed and its relevance to modern manufacturing companies. MetalArt is used to illustrate variance calculation and analysis.

MetalArt—April 2005

The first task undertaken by Pat Allan and the management team was to establish a standard cost reporting system that would allow *actual* material and labor costs to be compared with *standard* material and labor costs. *Standard costs* **represent the cost of the material and labor that should have been used to achieve actual production levels.** Accountants have used variance analysis for many years to evaluate how actual costs and quantities compare with predetermined standards.

In the later part of the nineteenth century and early part of the twentieth century, engineer-managers embraced a manufacturing philosophy known as scientific management. Frederick Taylor, who generally is regarded as the father of scientific management, believed that for every process there was one best way of doing it. He identified standards for labor efficiency and material usage. Then he compared these standards with actual operating performance. Typically, *standards* are based on engineering studies to determine the amount of a resource (such as labor hours or pounds of material) necessary to manufacture a product. Thus, standards tell us how much of a resource we should use or how much we should pay for materials and labor, given the number of units actually produced. Today, managers use variance analysis, which evolved from scientific management, to evaluate performance and to help them identify solutions to production problems. In addition, managers of service organizations use variance analysis. For example, hospitals use it to monitor the amount of nursing labor and hospital supplies used in treating patients. Retail organizations often analyze sales performance by comparing actual costs at a certain sales level with standard (or expected) costs. Examples may include travel and entertainment expenses, sales commissions, and other administrative support costs.

Direct Materials and Direct Labor Variances

We will calculate and interpret cost variances for the direct materials and direct labor used by MetalArt. At the most basic level, a variance is simply the difference between an actual cost and a standard cost. Using the diagram in Exhibit 3, total *actual* costs are compared with total *standard* costs to determine a total variance. Whether direct labor or direct materials is analyzed, the format is the same.

Exhibit 3
Total Variance Diagram

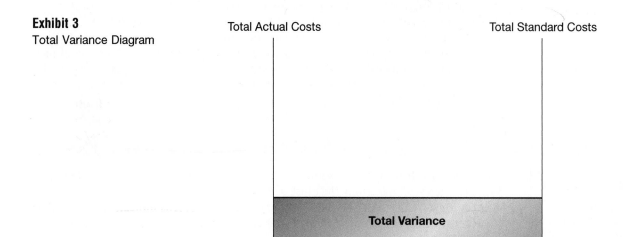

As shown in Exhibit 4, the total variance may be divided into two parts, a *price* component and a *quantity* component, by adding a middle prong to the total variance diagram. The reason for dividing a variance into its component parts is to determine whether a variance resulted from:

- *costs* of resources consumed that differed from standards,
- *physical amounts* of resources consumed that differed from standards, or
- a combination of *both costs and physical amounts* that differed from standards.

Exhibit 4
Variances Divided into
Price and Quantity
Components

Accountants typically use the terms material *price* and *quantity* and labor *rate* and *efficiency* to describe the price and quantity components of each variance.

MetalArt's experience illustrates how to calculate and interpret variances. Under the direction of Pat Allan, a team consisting of an engineer, an accountant, a personnel manager, and a purchasing manager prepared the information in Exhibit 5. They wanted to understand why manufacturing costs went through the roof during the second week of March 2005, as discussed in the weekly managers' meeting.

Exhibit 5

Production Information and Cost Information—Second Week of March 2005

Materials (Steel)		
Actual usage	× Actual price per pound	= Actual cost
500,000 pounds	× $0.25	= $125,000
Standard usage	× Standard price per pound	= Expected cost
460,000 pounds	× $0.30	= $138,000
Labor		
Actual usage	× Actual rate per hour	= Actual cost
5,300 hours	× $29	= $153,700
Standard usage	× Standard rate per hour	= Expected cost
4,600 hours	× $24	= $110,400

Materials (Steel). As shown in Exhibit 5, production records indicate that the actual quantity of steel purchased and used in the second week of March 2005 was 500,000 pounds. However, according to engineering standards, only 460,000 pounds should have been used during this period to make 6,000,000 finished coffee cans. Engineers designed coffee containers to precise specifications for length, width, thickness, and weight. Therefore, by multiplying the actual number of coffee cans manufactured times the standard weight per can, MetalArt's accountants determined the amount of steel that *should* have been used in production. In addition to physical standards for steel consumption, MetalArt established raw materials cost standards to evaluate the effectiveness of the purchasing department. Recall that MetalArt's purchasing manager, Lee Jones, had found a "good deal" on steel coils and had paid only $0.25 per pound, although the standard price was $0.30 per pound.

Labor. MetalArt employs many factory workers, each of whom is scheduled to work 40 hours per week; however, some are willing to work overtime when necessary to achieve production targets. In our opening discussion, Mary Smith indicated that extra labor time was needed because the manufacturing process had to operate at slower speeds as a result of inferior raw materials. As shown in Exhibit 5, the total number of hours worked during the second week of March was 5,300, at an actual cost of $29 per hour. By contrast, only 4,600 hours should have been worked during the period, at a rate of $24 per hour, to achieve the actual production level. Engineers developed time standards for producing a printed image for a coffee container. By multiplying the number of containers actually produced by the standard time per container, MetalArt's accountants determined the number of labor hours that *should* have been worked. Standard labor rates also were provided by MetalArt's personnel department. Recall that overtime wages, which are higher, were paid, causing the actual average hourly wage ($29) to exceed the standard hourly wage ($24).

The differences between actual and standard costs and usage for both materials and labor have been identified. In addition to calculating the amount of a variance, accountants also classify variances as favorable or unfavorable. A *favorable variance* results when the actual price (or quantity) is less than the standard price (or quantity) for materials or labor. On the other hand, an *unfavorable variance* results when the actual price (or quantity) exceeds the standard. Because variances may be interrelated, you must be careful when interpreting favorable and unfavorable variances. The term *favorable* does not always imply that something good has happened.

Calculation and Interpretation of Materials and Labor Variances

Recall that Erin and Seth are attempting to make sense of their standard cost report. This section outlines how to calculate materials and labor variances and provides more insight into how the standard cost reports are used for decision making. The managers at MetalArt face similar challenges. Pat Allan called another managers' meeting in May 2005 to review the work of the standard cost team.

Total Materials Variance. The plant controller began the discussion after passing copies of the variance report to each member of the team. "Refer to Exhibit 4, where the left-hand side is defined as *actual* cost. We multiplied the actual quantity of steel purchased by the actual price per pound to determine the total actual cost of our steel purchases. The right-hand side identifies the total *standard* cost allowed for actual production. We multiplied the standard quantity of steel allowed for actual production by the standard price to determine the standard cost. Thus, the total materials variance represents the difference between actual cost and standard cost, calculated as shown here."

Total materials variance = (Actual quantity × Actual price) − (Standard quantity × Standard price)

500,000 × $0.25 = $125,000	**Total Materials Variance**	460,000 × $0.30 = $138,000
	$13,000 Favorable	

Pat examined the total materials variance and commented, "The plant's cost problems do not seem to be related to materials after all. A $13,000 favorable materials variance actually means that total material costs were *less* than the standards allowed."

However, Mary was quick to point out that a total variance does not tell the entire story. "Let's look beyond the total materials variance to the price and quantity elements and see what we find."

Materials Price Variance. "We divided the total variance for materials into price and quantity elements by adding a middle prong to the total variance diagram," explained the controller.

The middle prong shown in Exhibit 4 is defined as an actual quantity multiplied by a standard price. Thus, the price variance equation compares an *actual price* with a *standard price* to determine the *price variance per unit*.

MetalArt's controller continued, "We multiplied the number of pounds of purchased steel by the cost per pound (on the left side) and multiplied the actual number of pounds of purchased steel by the standard price (on the middle prong). The materials price variance is determined by subtracting the value found on the middle prong from that on the left side."

Materials price variance = (Actual quantity × Actual price) − (Actual quantity × Standard price)

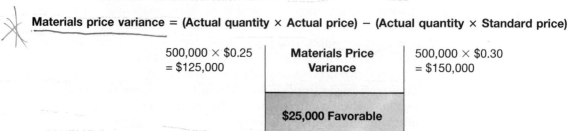

500,000 × $0.25 = $125,000	**Materials Price Variance**	500,000 × $0.30 = $150,000
	$25,000 Favorable	

The purchasing manager, Lee Jones, smiled when the discussion turned to the materials price variance; he actually paid $0.05 ($0.30 − $0.25) per pound less than standard rates for steel purchases. Since 500,000 pounds were purchased, the result was a favorable price variance of $25,000 (500,000 × $0.05). Next, the discussion focused on the materials quantity variance.

Materials Quantity Variance. The plant controller continued, "As you know, we produced approximately 6,000,000 cans. Standards suggest that we should have used 460,000 pounds of steel. Thus, we multiplied the standard quantity of steel allowed for actual production by the standard cost per pound to arrive at the value found on the right side of the diagram. The materials quantity variance calculation compares the value on the middle prong with that on the right side."

Materials quantity variance = (Actual quantity × Standard price) − (Standard quantity × Standard price)

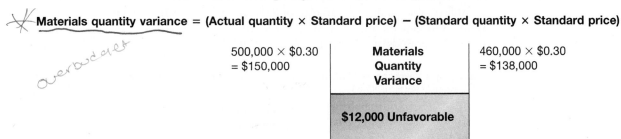

overbudget

500,000 × $0.30 = $150,000	Materials Quantity Variance	460,000 × $0.30 = $138,000
	$12,000 Unfavorable	

"Unfortunately, the materials quantity variance of $12,000 is unfavorable. The difference between the actual quantity of materials used (500,000 pounds) and the standard quantity allowed for actual production (460,000 pounds) represents excess consumption of 40,000 pounds of material at a standard cost of $0.30 per pound," the controller explained. "Our calculations indicate that the total materials variance of $13,000 (favorable) can be divided into a $25,000 favorable price variance and a $12,000 unfavorable quantity variance ($25,000 favorable − $12,000 unfavorable = $13,000 favorable). As Mary suggested, off-grade materials affect the amount of steel required for production. The steel coils were blemished by small rust spots that did not affect the strength of the steel. Unfortunately, the blemishes were visible through the printed image, resulting in 40,000 pounds of scrap (500,000 actual pounds of steel − 460,000 standard pounds of steel)."

LEARNING NOTE

When the quantity of material purchased differs from the quantity actually used in production, the materials price variance is calculated using the actual quantity purchased, and the materials quantity variance is calculated using the actual quantity used in production. Thus, the purchasing agent is evaluated based on the amount purchased, whereas the production manager is evaluated based on the amount used. If more materials are purchased than are used, the difference is not a variance; it simply increases the value of the raw materials inventory.

Jones leaned back in his chair. "So what's the problem? Even though we used $12,000 more materials than our standards allow, I saved $25,000 by finding good steel prices. The net effect is still positive."

Mary turned the page to the labor variance report. "Lee, look at the next report. Poor-quality materials affect our process in other ways. I think a clearer picture will emerge after we consider labor variances."

Total Labor Variance. The controller continued, "The total labor variance is calculated in the same way as the total materials variance. Referring to Exhibit 4, the difference between actual labor costs and standard labor costs allowed for actual production (6,000,000 cans) is calculated as shown here."

Total labor variance = (Actual hours × Actual rate) − (Standard hours × Standard rate)

5,300 × $29 = $153,700	Total Labor Variance	4,600 × $24 = $110,400
	$43,300 Unfavorable	

"Look at how our labor costs were affected," said Mary.

"Wow, the $43,300 unfavorable labor variance wiped out my favorable materials variance. What caused the variance to be so large?" asked Lee.

Labor Rate Variance. The controller explained, "Lee, the labor variance is made up of two elements, the labor rate variance and the labor efficiency variance. Exhibit 5 identifies the actual and standard hourly labor rates as $29 and $24, respectively. We actually paid $5 per hour ($29 − $24) more than the standards allowed because we had to pay overtime. Since 5,300 hours actually were worked during the second week of March, an unfavorable labor rate variance of $26,500 (5,300 × $5) resulted. Many employees were asked to work overtime (at higher hourly wage rates) to achieve a production level of 460,000 pounds of printed steel. We computed the labor rate variance as shown here."

Labor rate variance = (Actual hours × Actual rate) − (Actual hours × Standard rate)

5,300 × $29 = $153,700	**Labor Rate Variance**	5,300 × $24 = $127,200
	$26,500 Unfavorable	

Labor Efficiency Variance. Mary said, "I not only paid higher hourly wages because of overtime, but also scheduled more hours trying to get materials to run properly. Our efficiency is really poor. Look at the labor efficiency report."

The controller explained, "We calculated the labor efficiency variance by subtracting the value found on the right side from the value on the middle prong."

Labor efficiency variance = (Actual hours × Standard rate) − (Standard hours × Standard rate)

5,300 × $24 = $127,200	**Labor Efficiency Variance**	4,600 × $24 = $110,400
	$16,800 Unfavorable	

"Only 4,600 hours were allowed by engineering standards to produce 6,000,000 cans. Our actual labor time was 5,300 hours. Thus, an excess of 700 hours (5,300 − 4,600) at a standard rate of $24 per hour caused an unfavorable labor efficiency variance of $16,800 (700 × $24). Our calculations indicate that the unfavorable labor variance of $43,300 is made up of an unfavorable rate variance of $26,500 and an unfavorable efficiency variance of $16,800 ($26,500 + $16,800 = $43,300)."

The team began to understand the financial impact of materials and labor variances. In addition, the relationship between purchasing and production decisions became apparent. Pat commented that perhaps management was to blame for the problem. In closing the meeting, Pat stated, "It appears that we are motivating managers to achieve local performance objectives without considering how their actions affect the organization as a whole."

"So, I'm not such a bad guy after all," quipped Lee.

"No, just a bit misdirected," teased Pat.

LEARNING NOTE

In a standard cost system, costs flow through the inventory accounts (Raw Materials Inventory, Work-in-Process Inventory, and Finished Goods Inventory) at standard values. Thus, the balance sheet reflects these standard costs. However, since actual costs of materials, labor, and overhead seldom equal standard costs, variances are created. At the end of an accounting cycle, these variances typically are closed out to cost of goods sold on the income statement. Thus, the cost of goods sold calculation on the income statement reflects actual (rather than standard) costs.

LIMITATIONS OF TRADITIONAL VARIANCE ANALYSIS

OBJECTIVE 2

Explain how variance analysis can enhance managerial decision making.

The MetalArt example illustrates a potential problem associated with using price variances to motivate behavior. Because he was focusing only on meeting price standards, Lee Jones cut corners on quality. In addition, purchasing managers may be encouraged to purchase inventory in quantities far greater than reasonable needs in order to receive volume purchase discounts. Unfortunately, costs saved on an initial purchase may be offset by inventory carrying charges, damage, and obsolescence.

In saving the company $25,000 in material costs, Lee Jones contributed to unfavorable variances totaling $55,300. Managers may add up the variances to determine whether a change (such as buying less expensive materials or using a different mix of labor) results in a favorable or an unfavorable net variance. In MetalArt's case, the unfavorable net variance may be calculated as follows:

Materials price variance		$25,000 favorable
Materials quantity variance	$12,000 unfavorable	
Labor rate variance	26,500 unfavorable	
Labor efficiency variance	16,800 unfavorable	55,300 unfavorable
Net variance		$30,300 unfavorable

While the MetalArt example suggests that poor raw material quality significantly contributes to the unfavorable labor efficiency variance, other factors also can hurt labor efficiency. For example, workers may simply make mistakes. In addition, poor training or problems with scheduling may affect workers' abilities to perform as desired.

The tendency in many organizations is to point the finger at plant managers when production-related variances occur. However, managers in marketing divisions can contribute to variances as well. For example, when a manufacturing facility gears up for a certain level of production in response to a sales forecast made by the marketing manager, it often takes on additional labor and equipment. If actual sales do not meet expectations, the factory cannot immediately eliminate the unnecessary resources. The lag in the response time will result in some workers being temporarily idle, creating an unfavorable labor efficiency variance. Alternatively, if sales exceed the forecast, unexpected overtime costs will be incurred, thereby affecting the labor rate variance. Thus, proper planning is an important element of cost control.

LEARNING NOTE

While variance analysis helps managers identify sources of inefficiency, some managers believe that the use of standards does not promote continuous improvement. For example, workers may focus merely on meeting the standards rather than finding better ways to manage existing processes.

In addition to materials and labor variances, some companies calculate variable and fixed overhead variances. Variable overhead variances are calculated in the same way as variances for labor and materials. In other words, variable overhead rate and efficiency variances may be calculated using the diagrams discussed earlier in this chapter. Many accountants, including the authors of this text, do not believe that overhead variances are especially useful; however, alternative methods for evaluating overhead are described in an earlier chapter. Also, recall that we have considered cost behavior with respect to volume; some costs change with activity levels, whereas others remain fixed. Fixed overhead can be analyzed in terms of two variances, budget and volume.

The fixed overhead budget variance is simply the difference between actual spending for fixed overhead and planned spending for fixed overhead. Alternatively, the fixed overhead volume variance is a measure of plant use. Managers who produce at higher levels have more units over which to spread fixed costs, making the fixed cost per unit smaller and creating more favorable variances. Thus, managers are encouraged to manufacture products in large quantities even if there is no market for them.

Many accountants argue that managers should focus instead on process improvements and product quality. The remainder of this chapter considers methods for evaluating processes and improving product quality. Both statistical process control charts and Taguchi's quality loss function were developed by statisticians and engineers for use in understanding factory operations. We also consider how accountants and managers can use engineering methods to improve administrative, as well as production, processes.

SELF-STUDY PROBLEM

Greasy Grimes is a chain of automotive repair shops owned by entrepreneur Terrel Grimes. Grimes established the company during the 1960s to compete with local garages and the service departments of new car dealerships. In addition to performing basic oil change and lubrication services, Greasy Grimes' mechanics do major and minor repairs on engine, transmission, and brake systems.

The company is unionized and has three labor classes, with the following wage rates:

	Hourly Rate
Apprentice mechanic	$25
Journeyman mechanic	30
Master mechanic	40

Each shop has a manager who prepares cost estimates for customers and assigns jobs to mechanics. Labor estimates are prepared using a book that identifies the number of standard labor hours required to perform various repairs.

Grimes is reviewing a monthly report that summarizes the transmission service activities of shop 222. The shop recently had a change in management, and Grimes is anxious to evaluate the new manager's ability to use labor effectively. Relevant data are as follows:

Shop 222 July Transmission Services Standard Labor Class: Apprentice			
Actual Hours	**Actual Rate**	**Standard Hours**	**Standard Rate**
500	$30	800	$25

Required Calculate the labor rate and labor efficiency variances for shop 222 during July and interpret your results.

The solution to Self-Study Problem 1 appears at the end of the chapter.

QUALITY COST CONCEPTS[1]

OBJECTIVE 3

Identify four types of quality costs and explain how managers use these costs to improve performance.

Quality costs **are costs incurred because poor quality can or does exist in a particular product, function, or business.**[2] Quality refers to conformance to design specifications. Thus, quality costs are costs incurred to ensure that quality standards are met or because quality standards are not met. These costs of conformance often are divided into three categories: prevention, appraisal, and failure.

Prevention costs are costs incurred to prevent the production of poor-quality units (in manufacturing organizations) or poor-quality services (in service organizations). MetalArt uses statistical process control to monitor production and to make necessary

---

[1]   This section draws heavily from the following article: Albright, T. L., and H. P. Roth. 1992. The Measurement of Quality Costs: An Alternative Paradigm, *Accounting Horizons* (June): 15–27.

[2]   The definitions in this section are based on Morse, Wayne J., Harold P. Roth, and Kay M. Poston. *Measuring, Planning, and Controlling Quality Costs* (Montvale, N.J.: National Association of Accountants, 1987).

changes if a process slips out of control. Thus, the cost of implementing statistical process control techniques to prevent paint from being applied in the wrong place is an example of prevention costs.

Appraisal costs are costs incurred to identify poor-quality products (or services) before a customer receives the goods or services. The cost of inspections within the MetalArt plant is classified as an appraisal cost. A goal of world-class organizations is to design a production process that is in a state of control and exhibits little random variation. A good process that is in control produces high-quality products, making less inspection necessary. Therefore, a company usually benefits by investing in prevention, rather than appraisal, activities.

Failure costs are costs incurred because poor quality exists. Failure costs may be divided into two categories: internal failure costs and external failure costs. If a defective product or service is discovered before it is delivered to the customer, the cost is considered an internal failure cost. However, if a customer discovers a defective product or service, the cost is considered an external failure cost. For example, if paint is applied outside of the proper location during printing and subsequently damages welding equipment when a customer manufactures a can, MetalArt has incurred an external failure cost. Some failure costs are easy to quantify; however, customer ill will associated with discovering a defective product or service is difficult to measure. When W. Edwards Deming, a famous industrial statistician, said that the costs of poor quality are unknown and unknowable, he referred to the inability to determine the cost of unhappy customers.

Firms that measure quality costs wish to track the level of internal failure, external failure, appraisal, and prevention costs over time. Typically, a firm that embraces a quality program invests additional resources in prevention and appraisal activities to reduce failure costs. Over time, as processes become more reliable, failure costs decline. Of course, the objective is not merely to substitute one type of quality cost for another. Managers wish to see a decline in total quality costs as investments in improved processes produce results.

Exhibit 6 illustrates MetalArt's experience in managing quality costs. At first, failure costs were high. Then management implemented appraisal and prevention measures. Over time, the quality of production at MetalArt improved, and total quality costs began to decline. Finally, total quality costs reached a level far below their initial amounts.

Exhibit 6
Quality Cost Mix

In attempting to use a quality cost system that classifies a product as defective or nondefective, several problems may be encountered. One of these problems is determining the amount of failure costs. Many failure costs, such as the costs of rework and warranty repairs, are available from accounting records, but others must be estimated. Costs such as lost customer goodwill, which occur because an organization produces poor-quality products, are not recorded by an accounting system. Thus, they often are referred to as hidden quality costs.

The traditional view of quality (defective versus nondefective) usually defines defective products as products with some characteristic that does not fall within the specification limits. By this definition, all units that fall within the specification limits are good, and all units outside the specification limits are defective. The problem with this view is all units within the specification limits are considered to be equally good, regardless of whether they fall near the target value or near the upper or lower specification limit.

Case in Point

http://albright.
swlearning.com

Learn more about the
Malcolm Baldrige
Award.

Malcolm Baldrige Award for Quality

Recent recipients of the Malcolm Baldrige National Quality Award include **Motorola, Inc.** in the manufacturing category, **Branch-Smith Printing Division** in the small business category, and **SMM Health Care** in the health care division. Applicants for the Baldrige award are evaluated in seven categories: leadership, strategic planning, customer and market focus, information and analysis, human resources focus, process management, and business results.

Branch-Smith Printing's management team has developed a strong culture that emphasizes quality. For example, management frequently evaluates the company's action plans and quality improvement teams. Management also reviews all suggestions for improvement including customer complaints and supplier and internal reports concerning substandard products and processes. The review ensures timely communication, involvement, and accountability across all levels within the organization.

Quality and excellence are the foundations of the Baldrige award. At the awards ceremony, Commerce Secretary Don Evans stated, "For America to have a strong economy, we need sound businesses with ethical, responsible leaders. Great authority is vested in the men and women who run our public corporations, and with such power comes responsibility. Corporate leaders aren't simply stewards of their individual companies. They are stewards of American capitalism itself."

Source: Quality Troy: February 2003. Vol 42, Iss. 2, p. 12.

Many quality experts believe that units that fall within specification limits are not all equally desirable. Even if a unit is within limits, higher costs may result as a unit's deviation from expected value increases. The Taguchi loss function, considered in the next section, attempts to measure these costs of variability.

TAGUCHI'S QUALITY LOSS FUNCTION

OBJECTIVE 4

Describe how variability can affect production costs.

http://albright.
swlearning.com

Learn more about
Taguchi's quality loss
function.

Genichi Taguchi is a Japanese engineer who recognized the relationship between variation and cost. He developed a model, termed the quality loss function (QLF), to explain in financial terms the engineering concept of variability. In theory, **the *quality loss function* measures the loss to society from a product that does not perform satisfactorily.** In the quality loss function model, costs increase dramatically as actual product characteristics deviate from a target (expected) value. The loss function is quadratic, which means that when the deviation from a target value doubles, the loss increases by four times.

Taguchi justifies the quality loss function on the basis of experience:

> This is a simple approximation, to be sure, not a law of nature.... But the tremendous value of QLF, apart from its bow to common sense, is that it translates the engineer's notion of deviation from targets into a *simple cost estimate* managers can use.[3] (Emphasis added.)

[3] Taguchi, Genichi, and Don Clausing. 1990. Robust Quality, *Harvard Business Review* (January–February): 68.

The quality loss function estimates the loss that results from producing products that vary from a target value, regardless of whether they fall inside or outside the specification limits. This differs from the traditional view of losses from poor quality, which is illustrated in Exhibit 7. The traditional view suggests that no failure costs or losses are incurred if actual product measurements fall within the specification limits. However, total loss in the form of scrap, rework, or warranty replacement occurs if the product's actual dimensions are outside the specification limits.

Exhibit 7
Traditional Cost
Function

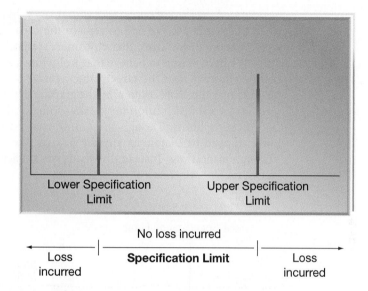

As an alternative to the traditional view, the quality loss function shown in Exhibit 8 shows a loss due to variability whenever a product deviates from a target value, even if the actual value falls within the specification limits. The loss is shown by the U-shaped curve that touches the horizontal axis at the target value. Thus, the quality loss function suggests that hidden quality costs exist any time a product varies from a target value. Once again, we use MetalArt to illustrate how a company may use the information from the quality loss function to make better decisions.

Exhibit 8
Taguchi Cost Function

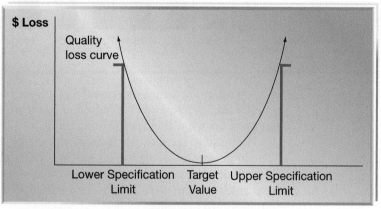

METALART—DECEMBER 2006

Pat Allan, plant manager of MetalArt, called another managers' meeting to address the cost of variability and the intense competition from KolorKan. The team has made a great deal of progress since its original meeting to discuss production problems and related costs. MetalArt has installed a quality cost system and added extra inspectors to the process. However, the team knows that prevention costs in the form of statistical process control soon will allow them to shift resources away from inspections as processes improve.

Pat said, "As you know, KolorKan has made production changes to reduce variability in color density during the printing process.[4] Our market studies suggest that as color densities vary from target values, customers become dissatisfied."

"I could have told you that," interjected Mary. "Remember what happened when we shipped the load of containers with images that varied from dark pink to dark red?"

"I certainly do. We had to replace the cans, and I don't think we've been able to get any more orders from that customer," responded Pat.

"We have reason to believe that KolorKan's products follow a normal distribution with an average near the target value," said Pat, while wrestling to assemble an easel. Producing a flip chart containing the graphic shown in Exhibit 9, Pat continued, "However, a normal distribution means that some of their products actually fall outside the specification limits. Though these products did not conform to specifications, they were shipped to customers anyway because the plant did not strive for zero defects through inspections. Instead, the focus was on achieving output consistent with a target value."

Exhibit 9

Normal Distribution of KolorKan

After flipping the page to reveal a graph identical to that shown in Exhibit 10, Pat pointed out, "Alternatively, as indicated by the uniform distribution shown here, all of our products fell within specification limits."

"I'm glad to see that our investment in inspection costs is paying off," said Mary. "The inspectors are doing a great job. We didn't ship a single out-of-spec order."

"While it's true that inspections prevented some embarrassing deliveries, we still have much work to do to reduce our variability," responded Pat. "The uniform distribution shown here suggests that our process is equally likely to produce a product at the target value, the upper specification limit, or the lower specification limit."

[4] The MetalArt example is based on Taguchi and Clausing's article describing the experience of Sony Corporation. Taguchi, Genichi, and Don Clausing. 1990. Robust Quality, *Harvard Business Review* (January–February): 65–75.

Exhibit 10

Rectangular Distribution
of MetalArt

"Pat, what are you driving at?" Mary asked. "Who cares about normal and uniform distributions? Our quality is good; we didn't ship any defective units."

Pat replied, "Assume that we want to assign letter grades to MetalArt and KolorKan; an A represents achieving target specifications, while an F represents exceeding specification limits. We may say that KolorKan produced many more As than we did, even if they did get an F now and then. Most of KolorKan's production was in the A and B range. We earned an equal number of As, Bs, Cs, and Ds. We also made some out-of-specification prints, but we didn't ship our Fs; they were inspected out of the process. KolorKan shipped everything it printed without bothering to inspect anything."

Pat continued to flip pages on the chart. "I think we may have discovered a hidden source of costs. If the Taguchi model is right, our quality costs are approximately *double* KolorKan's. I have made some estimates based on the cost of production and the way in which our customers respond to product variation. Let me summarize the Taguchi model in terms of how it affects us.

"First of all, let's review the elements of the model," said Pat, pointing to the easel containing the following equation and definitions:

Quality loss $= K(y - T)^2$

y = actual value of a quality measurement

T = target value of a quality measurement

K = dollar value of loss associated with deviation from target. The value is based on estimates of the cost of rework, scrap, and customer ill will.

"In other words, the loss function simply takes the difference between a target specification and an actual measurement $(y - T)$ and squares the difference. Therefore, the larger the distance from the target value to the actual measurement, the greater the loss. Squaring the difference makes the cost increase dramatically!"

Lee responded, "So that means that as our products deviate more from a target value, our costs increase dramatically. The farther away they are, the greater the cost."

"Exactly. I've made some estimates of the cost of deviation; let's assume it's $5 and our target value for color density is 100. Assuming that our actual measure for color density is 95, our loss is $125." Pat turned the flip chart to reveal the following calculations:

Loss of color density = 95	Loss of color density = 135
Quality loss = $K(y-T)^2$	Quality loss = $K(y-T)^2$
$5(95-100)^2$	$5(135-100)^2$
$5(25)	$5(1,225)
$125	$6,125

"By contrast," continued Pat, "if our actual measure for color density is 135, our loss is $6,125! The losses become large very quickly if we have many deliveries that are too far from the target specification."

Pat continued, "I have made some assumptions about KolorKan's process. If most of their production is close to the target value, as I have illustrated in Exhibit 11, their total quality costs approximate $359,000. On the other hand, our quality costs are approximately $651,000, because of variability in our process. We are equally likely to produce a unit at the upper specification limit, the lower specification limit, or the target."

Lee interjected, "Let me get this straight. Although we produced 248 units, the same number as KolorKan, our quality costs are approximately double theirs because our units are spread evenly between color densities of 65 and 135. On the other hand, KolorKan had most of their products clustered around the target value of 100."

After a few moments, Mary spoke. "I think I see the big picture. The manner in which we conduct our operations affects the income statement because costs and expenses reduce net income. Customer ill will also can affect net income through reduced sales. First, we used variance analysis, a tool that helps Pat and other upper-level managers compare actual performance with a standard. Statistical process control charts provide too much detail for the needs of upper management."

"That's right," responded Pat. "However, statistical process control tools help shop floor workers maintain control over their processes, thereby reducing operating costs."

"After we improve our processes and can maintain them in statistical control, we can work to reduce the common causes of variability. You have shown us that variability has a cost," Lee added. "All of our efforts are interrelated and ultimately affect profitability."

2 SELF-STUDY PROBLEM   Terrel Grimes wishes to implement a quality cost program at each Greasy Grimes service center. His goal is to reduce total quality costs by 30% over the next five years, but he does not fully understand how quality costs are classified.

Required Provide examples of each type of quality cost (internal failure, external failure, appraisal, and prevention) that Grimes may expect to incur at his service centers.

The solution to Self-Study Problem 2 appears at the end of the chapter.

Exhibit 11

Unit and Total Costs: The Taguchi Quality Loss Function

(From Exhibit 9) KolorKan			
Observed Value	Number of Units	Total Cost	Cost per Unit
55	1	$ 10,125	10,125
65	9	55,125	6,125
75	20	62,500	3,125
85	40	45,000	1,125
95	54	6,750	125
105	54	6,750	125
115	40	45,000	1,125
125	20	62,500	3,125
135	9	55,125	6,125
145	1	10,125	10,125
Total	248	$359,000	

(From Exhibit 10) MetalArt			
Observed Value	Number of Units	Total Cost	Cost per Unit
55	0	0	0
65	31	189,875	6,125
75	31	96,875	3,125
85	31	34,875	1,125
95	31	3,875	125
105	31	3,875	125
115	31	34,875	1,125
125	31	96,875	3,125
135	31	189,875	6,125
145	0	0	0
Total	248	$651,000	

STATISTICAL PROCESS CONTROL[5]

OBJECTIVE 5

Explain how statistical process control provides useful information to managers of both production and administrative functions.

As businesses seek to improve the quality of products and processes, methods for monitoring and evaluating performance have become increasingly important. One such tool that has become popular is the statistical process control (SPC) chart. Statistical process control charts can be applied to many different types of situations. When maintained continuously, they provide an early warning signal that a quality problem may exist. For example, control charts may be used to (a) identify errors or unpredictable processes and determine basic causes, (b) provide a warning of an unexpected change within a

[5] The authors relied on the following articles in preparing the section on statistical process control: Albright, T. L., and H. P. Roth. 1993. Controlling Quality on a Multidimensional Level, *Journal of Cost Management* (Spring): 29–37.

Walter, R., M. Higgins, and H. Roth. 1990. Applications of Control Charts, *The CPA Journal* (April): 90–93, 95.

Duarte, J. 1991. Statistical Process Control in Marketing and Finance, *CMA Magazine* (May): 20–23.

process, (c) evaluate service or product consistency over time, and (d) decrease process variability and associated inspection costs.

Control charts measure two types of variation, special cause and common cause. A *special cause variation* **has an identifiable source, such as faulty equipment or processes. Alternatively, a** *common cause variation* **is the result of randomness inherent in a process.** Statistical control results when special causes of variation have been eliminated. Once a process is in a state of statistical control, the process is considered stable and predictable. A process in a state of statistical control is not necessarily a good process; rather, it is a *predictable* process. Once a process is in control, managers can focus their attention on making improvements that reduce common cause variation.

Though companies use many different types of statistical process control charts, the charts have common elements. In general, a control chart is a graph that shows measurements for a characteristic of interest. The characteristic may be a quantitative variable such as weight, length, or thickness of material, or it may be a qualitative attribute such as whether or not a product is defective.

Statistical process control charts typically include (a) a center line, representing the expected value of a characteristic, (b) a line above and another below the expected value, indicating the limits within which a characteristic is considered to be in control, (c) a horizontal axis, indicating the time order of observations of the characteristic, and (d) a vertical axis, measuring the values of the observations. A control chart used to monitor the printing line at MetalArt serves as an example to illustrate the elements and uses of control charts.

As described at the beginning of this chapter, the printing line sprays paint onto steel sheets to produce a finished image. Paint is applied to the surface of metal sheets through sprayer nozzles. If the sprayer nozzles become clogged, printing quality is affected because the images do not receive the correct amount of paint. Thus, MetalArt maintains on-line control charts to monitor paint flow coming from the nozzles. Exhibit 12 is an example of a control chart used by MetalArt.

Exhibit 12

Example of a Statistical
Process Control Chart

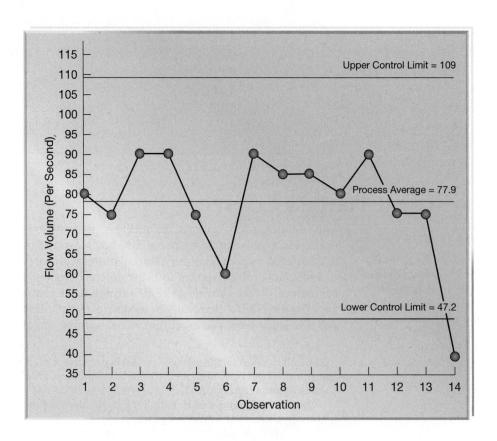

The vertical axis measures the flow volume per second through the sprayer nozzle. Values can range from zero, indicating no paint flow, to 120, indicating the maximum possible flow. The horizontal axis represents individual flow measurements taken throughout the day. Points on the chart represent flow values (y axis) for individual observations (x axis). A horizontal center line, or process average (expected value), is drawn through the center of the points. The process average (77.9) is the sum of the individual measurements divided by the total number of measurements [(80 + 75 + 90 + 90 + 75 + 60 + 90 + 85 + 85 + 80 + 90 + 75 + 75 + 40) ÷ 14 = 77.9].

In addition to the center line, the MetalArt control chart has an upper and a lower control limit, placed at 109 and 47.2, respectively. The area between the upper and lower control limits represents the band of normal variability for the printing process. **Control charts are designed to signal when a process is out of control.** At observation number 14, which exceeds the lower control limit, the sprayer process is no longer in statistical control. The chart informs the machine operator that an unusual situation has occurred so that the operator can take corrective action.

Thus, statistical process control charts are used to identify measurements of a characteristic that deviate from the process average and to discover changes in the measurement. If points on a control chart are randomly scattered around the center line and fall within the upper and lower control limits, the process is considered to be in statistical control. An out-of-control condition is indicated if points fall above or below the control limits. By analyzing conditions existing at the time an out-of-control signal occurs, a manager may discover the cause of the problem.

Control charts are appropriate for measuring and evaluating many different types of processes. Generally, they can be used in any repetitive situation in which a quantitative variable or qualitative attribute is measurable. However, statistical process control charts also can be used in other areas, including accounting, finance, and marketing. For example, MetalArt's accounting department prepares payroll checks and payments for inventory purchases. Internal auditors typically verify that proper internal control procedures, such as authorization of bills and approval to make payments, are used in preparing payroll checks and payments to suppliers. To do this, they can collect samples of paid invoices or canceled payroll checks and record the percentage of cases with proper authorization and approval on a control chart. An out-of-control signal would suggest that an unusually large percentage of cases did not conform to proper procedures. By investigating samples in which control limits are exceeded, auditors may trace the cause of errors. For example, a new employee may not be familiar with company policies. Employee training should keep this problem from occurring in the future. Thus, control charts may be used to identify and correct administrative problems, as well as problems within the manufacturing process.

Other examples of using control charts in an administrative capacity include monitoring (a) the number of invoices processed during each month, (b) the average age of accounts receivable, (c) the time required to prepare monthly financial statements, and (d) sales returns per salesperson. Thus, managers in many different areas can use statistical process control analysis to help them evaluate the quality of their activities.

When first implementing statistical process control methods, managers should use charts where they expect to find trouble. In addition, they should use charts in those areas where financial benefits from improving a process and reducing special causes of variability are most likely. Managers are more likely to support continued use of statistical process control methods if they are able to see positive, tangible financial results. Unfortunately, SPC does not measure variation in financial terms. Recently, Six Sigma techniques have evolved to fill this need.

Six Sigma is a management philosophy that is becoming popular with manufacturing and service organizations. The approach is based on statistical methods that help identify and reduce process variation. Proponents argue Six Sigma begins where statistical process control methods end. Like SPC, one goal of Six Sigma is to reduce process variation. However, Six Sigma is a management philosophy that attempts to link reduced variation to improved customer satisfaction and, ultimately, improved financial performance.

The term *Six Sigma* means that organizations should aspire to processes that virtually are error free. For example, six standard deviations (six sigma) from a process average represents only one misspelled word in all the books found in a small library. Put another way, if one product were produced each second for a century, only six products would be defective.[6] Clearly, these examples represent very low error rates. The Six Sigma approach enables management to financially justify process changes that help the company meet these high standards.

Case in Point

http://albright.
swlearning.com

Find out more about
Six Sigma.

Six Sigma

Six Sigma requires rigorous analysis of business processes in order to achieve a low error, or defect, rate of 3.4 per million. A defect is defined as anything that does not meet customer expectations. In the banking industry a defect could be a loan application review that exceeds the promised 48 hours, a telephone inquiry that is not answered, or the bank's failure to pay property taxes held in escrow for a customer.

Industry experts estimate that 80 of the top 100 banks have implemented (or plan to implement) Six Sigma programs. **Bank of America Corporation** used Six Sigma techniques to develop a loan application process that requires 80 percent less paperwork than other banks require. Some have predicted that in a few years every bank will have an Internet-based, fully automated loan application process. Engineering-based Six Sigma techniques will be useful to make the transition from human-based to Internet-based lending.

Source: 2003. Six Sigma: Some Home Lenders See a Natural Fit, *American Banker* (February 12).

PERFORMANCE EVALUATION FOR SERVICE ORGANIZATIONS

OBJECTIVE 6

Explain the application of performance evaluation methods in service organizations.

Service organizations such as CPA firms, law firms, hospitals, cable TV companies, and telecommunications companies face performance issues similar to those encountered by manufacturing organizations. Though these organizations do not manufacture a tangible product, managers can nonetheless evaluate the effectiveness of service delivery processes. For example, both CPA firms and hospitals often develop labor standards, or estimates of the time required to perform certain activities. A new staff accountant in a CPA firm is expected to prepare a client's payroll tax return in a certain (standard) amount of time. Additionally, hospitals often use critical paths to estimate the amount of services required for each type of medical procedure. Physicians whose use of services deviates significantly from a critical path may be asked to justify such deviations. Thus, as in manufacturing organizations, the efficiency of labor may be monitored. Service organizations often seek to improve customer satisfaction by making the experience pleasurable. For example, minimizing the time it takes to receive the service may result in satisfied customers. Therefore, managers often monitor customer satisfaction in order to improve the company's service quality.

Statistical process control charts originally were developed for use in manufacturing organizations. However, these charts commonly are used within service organizations to determine if a service process is "in control." For example, some hospitals maintain control charts to determine if the time from admission to the beginning of hydration (adding fluid) for a leukemia patient meets expectations. Another example would be plotting the variable cost of each appendectomy surgery to determine if certain physicians significantly exceed the average cost.

[6] Breyfogle, F. W., J. Cupello, and B. Meadows. 2001. *Managing Six Sigma* (New York, NY: John Wiley and Sons, Inc.).

Many service organizations use quality cost systems that attempt to measure the cost of external failure. For example, many companies measure the amount of time a customer spends "on hold" before receiving assistance from a company representative. Additionally, many firms measure the number of customers who hang up while waiting to receive assistance. Costs or lost revenues associated with customers who "drop off" the line are seen as external failure costs. Thus, many processes in service organizations can be monitored in the same way as manufacturing processes.

3 SELF-STUDY PROBLEM

WebTUTOR Advantage

Corporate managers at Greasy Grimes began collecting data from each service center to analyze material price and quantity variances. Some managers are concerned that too much is being paid for materials and too many materials are being used in conducting repairs.

Managers collected quantity data from the past 12 months to use as a comparison with the variance figures for July of the current year:

12-Month Material Quantity Variance Data

Jul.	$1,000 F	Jan.	$350 F
Aug.	1,000 U	Feb.	400 F
Sep.	500 F	Mar.	250 F
Oct.	750 F	Apr.	300 U
Nov.	800 U	May	250 U
Dec.	750 U	Jun.	150 F

July Material Price and Quantity Data

Actual price	$200
Actual quantity	25
Standard price	$190
Standard quantity	23

Required

A. Construct a statistical process control chart for material quantity variances. In calculating the process average, treat favorable variances as positive values and unfavorable variances as negative values.
   1. Calculate the process average for the 12 months listed.
   2. Place the upper control limit at +$1,875.
   3. Place the lower control limit at −$1,825.
   4. Plot the material quantity variances for the past 12 months.

B. Calculate the material price and quantity variances for July of this year and add the quantity variance to your statistical process control chart.

C. Is the process in statistical control? Should managers investigate this July's material quantity variance for special causes? Explain.

The solution to Self-Study Problem 3 appears at the end of the chapter.

REVIEW

SUMMARY of IMPORTANT CONCEPTS

1. Companies may perform variance analysis of direct materials, direct labor, and overhead.
   a. A variance is defined as the difference between total actual costs and total standard costs allowed for actual production.
   b. Variances may be divided into a price (rate) component and a quantity (efficiency) component.
   c. Variances are defined as favorable if actual prices or quantities used are less than standard prices or quantities. However, because variances often are interrelated, *favorable* variances are not always good.

2. Quality costs:
   a. Quality costs are classified as internal failure, external failure, appraisal, and prevention.

b. External failure costs are the most expensive type of quality costs, though their amount can never be known with certainty. External failure costs include customer ill will as well as replacement and warranty costs.

3. Taguchi quality loss function:
   a. The Taguchi quality loss function is important because it associates costs with the engineering concept of variability.
   b. Customer dissatisfaction (and costs) occurs when product characteristics deviate from a target value, even if the characteristics are within specification limits.

4. Statistical process control:
   a. Statistical process control charts separate special cause variation from random variation in manufacturing or administrative processes.
   b. Statistical process control charts have a center line (representing a process average) and upper and lower control limits.

5. Service organizations:
   a. Service organizations generally can establish standards for measuring the efficiency and effectiveness of their delivery process.
   b. Many processes in service organizations can be evaluated with statistical process control charts.
   c. Quality costs are not limited to companies that manufacture tangible products. Service organizations also incur quality costs in delivering services to customers.

DEFINE

TERMS and CONCEPTS DEFINED in this CHAPTER

common cause variation (M260)   special cause variation (M260)
favorable variance (M247)   standard costs (M245)
quality costs (M252)   standards (M245)
quality loss function (M254)   unfavorable variance (M247)

SELF-STUDY PROBLEM SOLUTIONS

SSP9-1   Labor rate variance

$$= (\text{Actual hours} \times \text{Actual rate}) - (\text{Actual hours} \times \text{Standard rate})$$
$$= (500 \times \$30) - (500 \times \$25)$$
$$= 500 \times (\$30 - \$25)$$
$$= \$2,500 \text{ unfavorable}$$

Labor efficiency variance $= (\text{Standard rate} \times \text{Actual hours}) -$
$$(\text{Standard rate} \times \text{Standard hours})$$
$$= (\$25 \times 500) - (\$25 \times 800)$$
$$= \$25 \times (500 - 800)$$
$$= \$7,500 \text{ favorable}$$

Total variance $= \$5,000 \text{ favorable} (\$7,500 \text{ favorable} - \$2,500 \text{ unfavorable})$

The new manager appears to have changed the mix of labor for services. Typically, an apprentice mechanic, receiving the lowest wage rate, performs the transmission services. The new manager assigned higher-paid journeyman mechanics to these jobs and created an unfavorable labor rate variance. However, the experienced journeyman mechanics were more efficient in performing the service, as indicated by the favorable labor efficiency variance. In fact, the higher labor rate was more than offset by greater efficiencies. The shift in mix resulted in a net $5,000 favorable labor variance. The new manager has found a way to improve the efficiency of transmission service at Greasy Grimes.

SSP9-2   *Internal Failure.* Costs resulting from repairs that have been performed incorrectly but are found before an automobile is returned to the customer are classified as internal failure. The costs of dealing with loose bolts or oil pan drain plugs that later could cause mechanical failure are examples.

External Failure. Costs resulting from repairs that were performed incorrectly and are discovered by the customer are classified as external failure costs. Examples include the cost of replacement parts, labor, customer ill will, and lost revenue (time spent reworking a repair is not available for other revenue-generating repairs). External failure costs also include the costs of lawsuits resulting from damages suffered by customers whose vehicles were damaged because of poor workmanship.

Appraisal. Appraisal costs generally relate to inspection costs. For example, the time spent by a mechanic on a test drive to ensure that repairs were made properly is an appraisal cost.

Prevention. Prevention costs can include training or technical workshops for mechanics. In addition, resources invested to identify reliable suppliers of high-quality parts are classified as prevention costs.

SSP9-3 A. In summing the favorable and unfavorable variances for the 12 months, the average is calculated as follows:

$$(1,000 - 1,000 + 500 + 750 - 800 - 750 + 350 + 400 + 250 - 300 - 250 + 150) \div 12 = 25$$

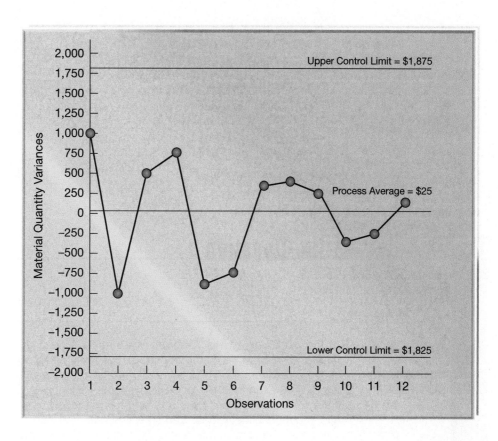

B.

Price variance = (Actual quantity × Actual price) − (Actual quantity × Standard price)

$\quad$ = (25 × \$200) − (25 × \$190)

$\quad$ = 25 × (\$200 − \$190)

$\quad$ = \$250 U

Quantity variance = (Standard price × Actual quantity) − (Standard price × Standard quantity)

$\quad$ = (\$190 × 25) − (\$190 × 23)

$\quad$ = \$190 × (25 − 23)

$\quad$ = \$380 U

The revised statistical process control chart appears in part (C).

C. The material quantity variances are in a state of statistical control. Though the July variance deviates from the process average, it is within the control limits. The variation seems to be random and normal. Managers should not attempt to find a special cause for the variation during the month of July.

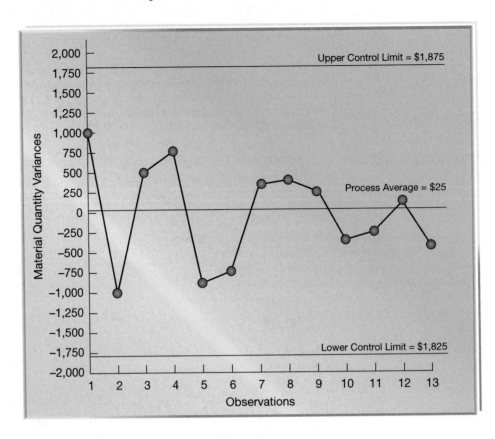

Thinking Beyond the Question

How are budgets used to evaluate performance?

At the beginning of this chapter, Erin and Seth were discussing their variance report. They were concerned because materials, labor, and overhead variances all were unfavorable. To determine why the budgeted and actual numbers differed, they examined the price and quantity variances. Seth and Erin will continue to grow their business and employ managers who will make purchasing and production decisions. Variance analysis also can be used to assess performance of individual managers. Typically, who is responsible for materials price and quantity variances? Explain your reasoning.

QUESTIONS

Q9-1
Obj. 1
Managers are held accountable for variances that occur in the areas under their control. Variances may arise in a manufacturing environment and in administrative functions as well. In general, what is meant by the term *variance*?

Q9-2
Obj. 1
Doall Company is establishing production standards for the coming year. Matt Mellon, the production manager, argues that the standards need to be relaxed. "Last year's standards were

based on ideal performance and did not reflect the practical realities of what could be achieved," he said. In establishing standards, what is the difference between practical and ideal standards?

Q9-3
Obj. 1
Keene, Inc., separates material variances into price and quantity components for purposes of management control and analysis. Why are variances generally separated into price and quantity components? What effect, if any, can the price variance have on the quantity variance?

Q9-4
Obj. 1
The cost records of Prichter Company reveal that as the unfavorable material price variance increased, the unfavorable material usage variance decreased. What might this suggest?

Q9-5
Obj. 1
Cadet Industries utilizes a standard cost system. When Cadet purchases raw materials, the materials are recorded at standard cost. Is this treatment by Cadet proper in a standard cost accounting system? Why or why not? What is the appropriate time to recognize material price and usage variances? Why?

Q9-6
Obj. 2
In a manufacturing environment, who would most likely be responsible for the materials price variance? The labor efficiency variance?

Q9-7
Obj. 2
In addition to material and labor variances, a company that utilizes standard cost accounting can compute fixed overhead variances. What are the two components of fixed overhead variance? What do the fixed overhead variances measure?

Q9-8
Obj. 2
Tim Winker Manufactured Housing, Inc., produces prefabricated modular housing. The company manufactures four styles of homes and uses a standard cost accounting system. The company uses a single account for capturing material variances and another account for recording labor variances. During a review of the general ledger for the past operating period, Tim Winker, the president, noted that the material variances were favorable and the labor variances were unfavorable. In general, what do these variances indicate regarding production costs for the period? What further information would management find useful in analyzing production costs and variances for the period?

Q9-9
Obj. 3
Electro Industries wants to analyze the costs associated with quality conformance in its manufacture of electronic capacitors and transistors, which are sold primarily to manufacturers of cellular telephones. What four broad categories of conformance costs should Electro use? What are the differences between these cost groups?

Q9-10
Obj. 3
Rayco Products manufactures audio speakers that are used in many applications. At the beginning of the current year, Rayco developed detailed operating budgets for all aspects of the company. Rayco now is considering purchasing new test equipment for the inspection department to use in checking the acoustical quality of speakers. This purchase was not considered during the preparation of operating budgets for the current year. If the equipment is acquired, depreciation will begin to be recognized immediately, using straight-line depreciation over an estimated useful life of five years; the result will be a monthly charge of $2,200. What effect would the equipment purchase have on quality costs and on meeting the company's current year budget?

Q9-11
Obj. 5
A machine operator cuts metal rods into six-inch lengths, measures output periodically, and records the measurements on a statistical process control chart. Over an eight-hour shift, the operator notes that the measurements vary greatly but are always within the acceptable limits of plus or minus 0.005 inch. Are these variations most likely examples of common cause or special cause variations? Explain your answer.

Q9-12
Obj. 5
Nathan Stuart is employed in the accounting department of a local manufacturer. During a recent management staff meeting, Nathan suggested that statistical control charts be established at key production steps to help increase quality and minimize defects. What is a statistical control chart? How is it used?

Using Minitab and Excel

For Statistical Process Control Charts

SPREADSHEET

What is Minitab?

Minitab for Windows is a package that permits a variety of analyses including basic statistics, regression, analysis of variance, and statistical control charts. Many college and university computer centers have a site license that permits students to use the package. Data are entered into a spreadsheet format similar to Microsoft Excel. Drop-down menus permit the user to specify the type of analysis. Certain problems and exercises in this chapter may be solved using the control chart menu.

Using Microsoft Excel to draw the statistical process control charts.

- Open Microsoft Excel and enter the data points in column A.
- Highlight column A and click on the Chart Wizard.
- A drop-down menu titled Step 1 of 4—Chart Type will appear. Click on Line. Click on Next>.
- A drop-down menu titled Step 2 of 4—Chart Source Data will appear. Click on Next>.
- A drop-down menu titled Step 3 of 4—Chart Options will appear. Select the Gridlines tab. Remove any check marks in boxes under Value (Y) axis.
- Click on Legend tab. Remove check mark in box before Show Legend.
- Click on Next>.
- A drop-down menu titled Step 4 of 4—Chart Location will appear. Click "as a new sheet." Click on Finish.

At this point you have a line graph. The last step is to draw the horizontal lines representing upper and lower control limits and the process average.
Using the drawing toolbar, select this button.

- Click on the left side of your line graph and drag the cursor to the right to create a horizontal line. Next press Copy one time and press Paste two times to make two more horizontal lines.

You now have a line graph containing your data points and three horizontal lines. Move the cursor to one of your horizontal lines. To create the upper control limit line, click on the horizontal line and drag it to the appropriate position. In the same manner, click and drag a second horizontal line to the appropriate position to represent the process average. Finally, click and drag the remaining horizontal line to the appropriate position for the lower control limit.

EXERCISES

If your instructor is using Personal Trainer® in this course, you may complete your assignments online.

E9-1   Write a short definition of each of the terms listed in the *Terms and Concepts Defined in this Chapter* section.

E9-2   Multiflow Products manufactures a single product, for which the following standards have
Obj. 1   been developed:

	Standard Quantity or Hours	Standard Price or Rate	Standard Cost
Direct materials	5 feet	$3 per foot	$15
Direct labor	? hours	? per hour	?

During October, the company purchased 15,200 feet of direct materials at a cost of $47,880, all of which was used in the production of 3,000 units.

A total of 5,400 hours was spent on production during the month. The actual cost of direct labor was $61,560. The following labor variances have been computed:

Total labor variance	$1,185 Unfavorable
Labor rate variance	$540 Favorable

a. For direct materials, compute (1) the actual cost paid for materials per foot, (2) the materials price variance, and (3) the materials usage variance.
b. For direct labor, compute (1) the standard labor rate per hour, (2) the standard hours allowed for the output of 3,000 units, and (3) the standard hours allowed per unit of product.
c. What is the value of direct materials and direct labor that has been applied to the work-in-process inventory account during the month, in total and on a per-unit basis?

E9-3
Obj. 1

World Wide Products has developed the following standards for one of its products:

Direct materials	25 pounds at $4 per pound
Direct labor	8 hours at $10 per hour

The following activity was recorded for the production of 12,000 units during the month of August: _ use

Materials purchased	355,000 pounds at $4.15 a pound
Materials used	305,000 pounds
Direct labor	95,400 hours at $10.75 an hour

a. Compute the materials price variance.
b. Compute the materials usage variance.
c. Compute the labor rate variance.
d. Compute the labor efficiency variance.

E9-4
Objs. 1, 2

A nationally known blue jeans manufacturer purchases denim material and cuts it into a variety of components and sizes. Following the machine-intensive cutting operation, the parts are flown to another location for assembly. The following data summarize the assembly operations:

Standard hours allowed per pair	0.30	Actual hours worked	4,500
Standard wage rate per hour	$7.00	Actual labor rate per hour	$6.50
Actual pairs assembled	16,000		

Calculate the labor rate variance and the labor efficiency variance. Determine whether each variance is favorable or unfavorable. How might managers use variance information such as this to support decisions about changing a manufacturing process?

E9-5
Objs. 1, 2

Tawanda's Bakery uses variances to help control production-related costs. The following data summarize the production activity for June:

Standard resource consumption per 50-loaf batch

Materials	60 lbs. at $2.00 per pound
Labor	3 hours at $16.00 per hour

Actual resource consumption during June

Materials	1,100 lbs. at $2.10 per pound
Labor	80 hours at $15.00 per hour

During the month, Tawanda produced 20 batches.
Calculate each of the following and determine whether the variance is favorable or unfavorable:

a. materials price variance
b. materials quantity variance
c. labor rate variance
d. labor efficiency variance

At what level within an organization is variance analysis useful to support decision making? Explain.

E9-6   Metalworks, Inc., produces castings for various applications in the plumbing industry. Be-
Objs. 1, 2   cause the industry is mature, standardized products with known materials and labor requirements are the primary revenue generators for the company. The following information has
been assembled for the month of January:

	Standard resource consumption per batch of Faucet Value No. 337
Materials	500 lbs. at $2.50 per pound
Labor	40 hours at $11.00 per hour

	Actual resource consumption
Materials	530 lbs. at $2.10 per pound
Labor	45 hours at $14.00 per hour

Calculate each of the following for Faucet Value No. 337 and determine whether the variance
is favorable or unfavorable:

a. materials price variance
b. materials quantity variance

c. labor rate variance
d. labor efficiency variance

How might management determine whether a variance is significant and worthy of investigation? Explain.

E9-7   Sunclear Glass Company is a producer of architectural glass products sold through national
Objs. 1, 2   retail outlets. Glass production begins with sand and other chemicals that are placed into a
gas-fired melting chamber. The river of molten glass flows from the melting chamber through
equipment that cools the glass sheet and defines its width and thickness. As the solid ribbon
of glass emerges from the machine, it is cut into a variety of dimensions, packaged, and sold.
The following data summarize the production activities for Sunclear Glass Company. (*Hint:*
Remember to be consistent in your use of tons and pounds.)

Actual raw materials consumed:
200 tons at $0.07 per pound

Standard raw materials allowed for actual production:
198 tons at $0.05 per pound

Calculate the materials price variance and the materials quantity variance. Determine whether
each variance is favorable or unfavorable. Is variance analysis a meaningful exercise in an industry such as this? Explain. What are typical causes of price and quantity variances?

E9-8   Refer to the process description in E9-7. The following information was pulled from the com-
Obj. 3   pany's records:

- A container of glass was broken as the result of a forklift accident at the end of the production line.
- Customers returned 25% of a shipment to the company because the glass contained im-
purities.
- The melting oven crew members attended a national glass manufacturers' conference to
learn about new manufacturing technologies and methods.
- The company implemented a three-step raw materials inspection program to verify raw
material quality and purity.
- Managers at all levels were trained in statistical process control methods.

Classify each event as internal failure, external failure, prevention, or appraisal. Support your
answers.

E9-9   Companies that implement quality cost systems typically use four cost categories.
Obj. 3   Classify the following costs as internal failure, external failure, prevention, or appraisal:

- Scrap
- Warranty claims
- First-part inspection of a new production run
- Quality control education

- Unexpected machine downtime for repairs
- Litigation defense costs associated with product recalls
- Vendor certification
- Manufacturing process redesign

E9-10
Obj. 3

Cable-Op, Inc., is a manufacturer of fiber-optic cable used in the communications industry. Management is considering implementing a cost of quality program to monitor progress in achieving targets. The following information has been accumulated for a four-year period:

Category	2004	2005	2006	2007
Internal failure	300,000	300,000	350,000	400,000
External failure	500,000	450,000	525,000	545,000
Prevention	60,000	72,000	70,000	65,000
Appraisal	80,000	105,000	110,000	110,000

Prepare a bar graph for each year that includes the four categories of quality costs. What trends do you observe? What types of managerial decisions may result from reviewing your cost of quality graph?

E9-11
Obj. 3

Edwards Deming, a pioneer in the area of statistical quality control, stated, "The cost of poor quality is unknown and unknowable." The quality categories—internal failure, external failure, prevention, and appraisal—are used to categorize costs from the general ledger for use by management.

a. Identify the category of quality cost to which Deming most likely refers. Justify your answer.
b. Which of the four quality cost categories is most controllable by management in the short run? Explain.

E9-12
Obj. 3

The following quality cost graph identifies the levels of four quality cost categories over a three-year period. External and internal failure costs have increased each year, while investments in prevention and appraisal activities have remained constant. Assume management wishes to reduce total quality costs in the long run.

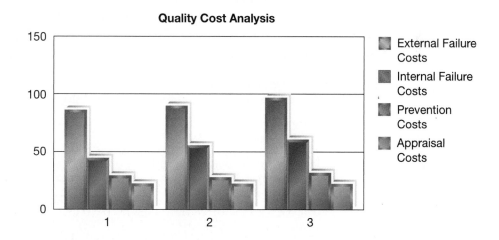

Discuss various management decisions that could be made to better manage quality costs in the organization. What kinds of quality costs are controllable by management in the short run? Are other kinds of quality costs controllable by management in the long run? Explain your answers.

E9-13
Obj. 4

Sony Corporation conducted a survey to determine customer satisfaction levels with their television sets. Interestingly, after matching the survey satisfaction data with production records, Sony discovered the customers who purchased televisions manufactured in Plant 1

(Continued)

were more satisfied than customers whose sets were produced in Plant 2. Upon further investigation, Sony discovered the following distributions for a critical component in the television picture tube:

a. Which plant has more process variation?
b. Plant 2 did not ship any "defective" products because each television set was inspected. Plant 1 shipped a small number of "defective" products because products were not inspected. Why were customers whose sets were manufactured in Plant 1 generally happier with their purchases?

E9-14   In Exhibits 9 and 10 in this chapter, Pat Allan related the concept of variation to letter grades
Obj. 4   that could be assigned for plant performance.

a. Explain how the lessons Sony learned in E9-13 relate to the Taguchi loss function.
b. If you were assigning letter grades (A, B, C, D, and F) to the Sony factories illustrated in E9-13, how might you distribute the grades? (Assume each factory made 1,000 television sets.) You may make reasonable assumptions about how to divide the television sets so your distributions resemble those shown in Exhibit 9 in the text.

E9-15   The Taguchi loss function is represented as a U-shaped function. At the target specification,
Obj. 4   the quality loss is zero. As actual measurements move up or down from the target, quality losses occur at an increasing rate.

Taguchi also describes two variations of the U-shaped function as follows:

a. More is better.
b. Less is better.

The "more is better" function describes quality losses as a critical quality characteristic declines from a target. For example, weld strength is an example of a "more is better" function. This function is illustrated as follows:

Using your understanding of the Taguchi loss function, prepare a sketch of the "less is better" loss function. Identify three examples of quality costs that might be described by the "less is better" loss function.

E9-16
Obj. 4

Traditionally, a product was considered acceptable if actual product characteristics fell within the upper and lower specification limits as determined by design engineers. This method of evaluating product conformance to specifications is known as the "goalpost" approach to quality. In the game of football, whether the ball is centered between the uprights or marginally passes inside either upright, a point after touchdown or field goal is considered good. Taguchi believed this concept is not applicable to product quality and developed the Taguchi loss function to explain the cost of variation from a target specification.

    a. Prepare a sketch of the traditional loss function and label each component.
    b. Prepare a sketch of the Taguchi loss function and label each component.
    c. Explain the reasoning that Taguchi used to support the loss function.
    d. List three examples of how the Taguchi loss function may apply to an industrial or service industry setting.

E9-17
Obj. 5

Travel-Tow, Inc., is a producer of small utility trailers. The company partners with suppliers to help reduce inventory carrying costs. Raw material deliveries are made every two hours. Materials are brought directly to the production line for immediate use. The following statistical process control chart captures variation in raw material delivery times.

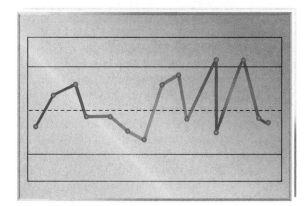

    a. Label the following elements on the control chart:
       1. Upper control limit
       2. Lower control limit
       3. Process average
    b. Is the process subject to common cause variation? Explain.
    c. Is the process subject to special cause variation? Explain.
    d. What might be an example of special cause variation in this manufacturing setting?

E9-18
Obj. 5

SPREADSHEET

Felicidad, Inc., uses statistical process control charts to determine whether material quantity variances are the result of special or common cause variation. The following variances represent the results of analyses over the previous 16 weeks. The week number is in parentheses. U and F indicate unfavorable and favorable.

(1) 520 F	(4) 325 F	(7) 200 U	(10) 115 F	(13) 1,500 U	(15) 125 F
(2) 550 F	(5) 127 U	(8) 200 U	(11) 150 U	(14) 225 U	(16) 130 F
(3) 250 U	(6) 525 U	(9) 150 F	(12) 530 F		

    a. Prepare a statistical process control chart to determine whether any of the material quantity variances might represent unusual circumstances worthy of investigation. (Treat favorable variances as positive numbers and unfavorable variances as negative numbers.) To solve the problem using Minitab, use the following instructions: Open Minitab. Enter variances for weeks 1–6 in column C1. Click on Stat. Click on Control Charts. Click on Individuals. Enter C1 into Variable field. Click OK.

(Continued)

Note: If you choose to manually solve the problem (or to use Excel), upper and lower control limits should be placed on your graph at Y-axis values 1,296 and −1,388, respectively. Refer to Exhibit 12 in the chapter for an illustration of control limit and process average placement. You may manually calculate the process average or use the average function within Excel.

b. Refer to the control chart that you prepared in part (a). In general, what may be potential causes of unfavorable material quantity variances?

c. How does statistical process control assist managers in making decisions about cost accounting information?

E9-19
Objs. 5, 6

SPREADSHEET

As part of a continuous quality improvement initiative, an accounting department quality team at Dexmar Pharmaceuticals was evaluating the quality of payroll services provided to employees. The team decided to use the percentage of payroll checks containing errors as a measure of payroll quality. Errors could be in the form of incorrect withholding for FICA, health insurance, or charitable contributions. Errors also may include the incorrect calculation of overtime pay, or use of an incorrect hourly wage rate. The following table illustrates the percentage of weekly payroll checks without errors for a six-month period:

1	0.98	8	0.99	15	0.95	22	0.98
2	0.99	9	0.80	16	0.97	23	0.98
3	0.95	10	0.85	17	1.00	24	0.96
4	0.96	11	0.90	18	0.99	25	0.96
5	0.99	12	0.97	19	0.96	26	0.94
6	0.98	13	0.97	20	0.98		
7	0.97	14	0.98	21	0.95		

a. Prepare a control chart using the data presented. To solve the problem using Minitab, use the following instructions: Open Minitab. Enter observations 1–26 in column C1. Click on Stat. Click on Control Charts. Click on Individuals. Enter C1 into Variable field. Click OK.

Note: If you choose to manually solve the problem (or to use Excel), upper and lower control limits should be placed on your graph at Y-axis values 1.036 and 0.879, respectively. Refer to Exhibit 12 in the chapter for an illustration of control limit and process average placement. You may manually calculate the process average or use the average function within Excel.

b. Is the process in control?

c. Which types of variation are present? Explain.

E9-20
Objs. 5, 6

Refer to the information provided in E9-19. Control charts are designed to signal when an out-of-control event has occurred. However, the chart does not indicate the reason for the out-of-control event. Individuals must serve as detectives to investigate possible reasons for special cause variation.

a. Identify the *types* of questions you would ask in attempting to understand the cause of the lower percentages in periods 9 and 10. (For example, was there turnover in payroll staff during these periods?)

b. Though control charting techniques originally were developed to monitor manufacturing processes, their use has expanded beyond the manufacturing floor. Identify other examples of how control charts could be used to monitor the quality of administrative (or service-related) processes.

PROBLEMS

If your instructor is using Personal Trainer® in this course, you may complete your assignments online.

P9-1
Obj. 1

Establishing Material and Labor Standards, Multiple Departments

TCC Industries produces specialty tires in a variety of sizes and tread designs for use on trailers and farm equipment. TCC is planning to implement a standard cost accounting system. Valerie Siewert, the controller, has accumulated the following information on the standard cost of a particular bias tractor tire.

Each tire requires 15 pounds of carbon black, the basic tire component, which is added in the mixing department. Other materials, such as zinc and sulfur, which are added in the molding department, are required in such small quantities that they are treated as indirect materials and included as part of overhead. Each tire requires 15 minutes of processing time to mold and cure. An additional 45 minutes of time is required to mix the ingredients in the mixing department.

The standard cost for carbon black is $3.50 a pound. The standard cost of direct labor in the mixing department is $10.00 per labor hour, while the standard cost of direct labor in the molding department is $11.00 per hour.

Required

A. Develop the standard cost of materials and labor for the tractor tire. The standard cost should identify the standard quantity, the standard rate, and the total standard cost per unit.

B. Identify the advantages of implementing a standard cost system.

C. Explain the role each of the following people would have in developing the standard costs:
   1. Purchasing manager
   2. Mixing department supervisor
   3. Molding department supervisor
   4. Cost accountant
   5. Product engineer

D. Assume that a batch of tires has been completed and the following actual amounts were used to produce the batch:
   1. Actual output: 4,500 tires
   2. Actual carbon black utilized: 68,000 pounds
   3. Carbon black purchased: 75,000 pounds at a cost of $258,000
   4. Direct labor in mixing department: 3,220 hours at a cost of $31,073
   5. Direct labor in molding department: 1,075 hours at a cost of $12,384

Compute the materials price variance and the material usage variance. Also, compute the labor rate variance and labor efficiency variance for each department.

P9-2 Performance Evaluation and Variance Analysis

Obj. 2

Timber Industries manufactures unfinished furniture, which it sells through retail outlets. Timber produces many different styles of bookcases, tables, chairs, desks, and dressers that customers finish themselves with stain or paint. Timber utilizes a standard cost system and performs variance analysis. The company recently increased production to meet anticipated demand from several new retail outlets that opened in new sales territories. To accommodate the expected increase in sales demand, the production department hired five new employees from a local community college program. These new employees were immediately assigned to various production processes, such as milling, lathe, and assembly.

To meet the anticipated production needs, the purchasing department had to seek additional sources of lumber. The company ordered large quantities of high-grade oak, maple, and pine. The purchasing department insisted on obtaining high-quality materials, since poor-quality materials result in excess scrap, rework, and defects during the manufacturing process. Some of the new suppliers delivered materials that were warped or had too many knots or blemishes. Instead of returning the materials, the purchasing department negotiated "quality" credits from the suppliers. The poorer-quality wood then was sorted, remilled by Timber, and used in places where lower-quality material was acceptable, such as drawer bottoms and sides.

Several of the new retail outlets did not reach the sales volume that was originally expected. The sales department insists that with time, the new stores will gain recognition and their sales will increase. To deal with the increase in finished goods inventory, the sales department negotiated with a discount department chain to sell a limited line of Timber products in markets that did not compete directly with company-owned retail outlets.

Material and labor variances for Timber Industries were as follows:

Material price variance	Favorable
Material usage variance	Unfavorable
Direct labor rate variance	Favorable
Direct labor efficiency variance	Unfavorable

(Continued)

Required

A. Based on the facts stated, identify contributing factors for the variances noted.
B. Discuss how Timber Industries could use variance analysis to analyze the performance measures of the purchasing, production, and sales departments.

P9-3   Changes in Costs, Effects on Variances

Objs. 1, 2

Tempro, Inc., uses a standard cost accounting system. Variances for the year ended December 31, 2005, were as follows:

Material price variance	Unfavorable
Material usage variance	Favorable
Labor rate variance	Favorable
Labor efficiency variance	Unfavorable

Managers at Tempro are considering the following changes in operations for the year ending December 31, 2006.

1. An across-the-board pay increase of 5% will be given to all personnel.
2. The purchasing department will be allowed to purchase lower grades of materials.
3. Several key production workers will be transferred into managerial positions. These workers will be replaced either by new hires or by production personnel who will be transferred from another department.
4. Additional inspectors will be hired to ensure quality production. The cost of these inspectors will be considered administrative and general expense.

Required Assuming that product standards are not changed from the previous year, what impact, if any, would you expect each of the changes to have on the company's variances? Consider each decision separately, and identify the variance that would be affected by the decision and whether the change would increase or decrease the prior-year variance. Explain your answers.

P9-4   Establishing Labor Standards

Objs. 1, 2

Greenbriar Company is considering the addition of a new machine in its mold injection plant. Greenbriar already has five such machines that are operating three shifts a day. The company uses a standard cost accounting system. The number of pieces that currently are being produced on the existing machines is 300 per worker-hour. The vendor of the new equipment has stated that its studies indicate that the new machinery should be able to produce 400 pieces per worker-hour. Greenbriar engineers agree that under ideal conditions, the equipment should be able to generate 400 pieces an hour, and they support that rate as a labor standard. Production managers point out that the new machine is identical to the machines currently in use, and that the current production rate is only 300 pieces per worker-hour. Accordingly, production managers advocate the use of 300 pieces as the labor rate standard. The accounting staff believes that the most appropriate standard labor rate would be 350 pieces per labor hour.

Required

A. What arguments are most likely to be offered by engineering, production, and accounting to support their respective proposed standards?
B. Which alternative do you support? Consider the motivational aspects of establishing a standard and explain the reasons for your choice.

P9-5   Establishing a Standard Cost Accounting System

Objs. 1, 2

Tasha Smith is the president of Modern Machinery, Inc., which manufactures flexible manufacturing systems used in a wide variety of production processes. To remain competitive, Modern is continually improving product performance by increasing the sophistication of electronic controls, diversifying product offerings, and enhancing the quality of existing products. Many of Modern's customers dictate specific performance expectations and system designs. Modern employs a large engineering staff that coordinates system requirements with the designed components. Each manufactured system requires extensive design work and often results in over a hundred individual component drawings. Each drawing is developed in the engineering department and contains detailed manufacturing specifications. The use of computer-assisted design (CAD) allows Modern to provide system designs in an efficient manner, and has reduced design time. Since each system is manufactured to meet specific requirements, very few parts are interchangeable between systems.

Tasha is considering implementation of a standard cost accounting system. Her objective is to identify both rate and usage variances related to material and labor that are in excess of allowable standards. Tasha will require the engineering department to develop a standard cost sheet with each CAD design. The standard cost sheet will identify the amount of materials that should be used. For components already in use, the standard will assume the cost rates for materials that existed at the beginning of the year. For standards for new components, material costs will be taken from supplier catalogs. Standards for labor will be developed jointly by product and process engineers.

Tasha has determined that material price variances will be the responsibility of the purchasing department. Material usage and labor efficiency variances will be the responsibility of shop supervisors in each of four manufacturing areas (Mill Shop, CNC Manufacturing, Electrical Shop, and Assembly). The labor rate variance will be the responsibility of the human resource department.

Required Prepare a memo to Tasha Smith giving your advice concerning her plans. Specifically comment on the purpose of a standard cost system, the cost-benefit element of implementing such a system, and the inherent weaknesses in Tasha's proposed implementation plans.

P9-6 **Quality Cost Analysis**

Obj. 3

Management at Precise Manufacturing would like to analyze quality costs associated with the manufacturing process. In Year 1, Precise implemented a statistical process control system. In Year 2, further steps were taken in an effort to improve quality and focus on customer satisfaction. These included the addition of inspectors, expansion of statistical process control to additional processing steps, and further development of products through quality engineering. The benefits of the quality focus at Precise are apparent, as warranty costs and customer returns have declined since quality programs were implemented. However, total quality costs continue to be significant, and management is concerned that the quality focus has not reduced total costs, but has simply shifted costs from one area to another. Accordingly, management would like to analyze quality costs for the past two years. Precise had sales of $18,000,000 in both Year 2 and Year 1, and incurred the following costs related to quality control during those years:

	Year 2	Year 1
Inspection	$ 61,000	$ 30,000
Quality engineering	57,000	12,000
Quality training programs	26,000	39,000
Customer allowances	22,000	104,000
Scrap, net	25,000	8,000
Product testing	92,000	42,000
Rework	130,000	68,000
Statistical process control	50,000	34,000
Downtime due to defects	25,000	18,000
Warranty repairs	75,000	189,000
Field service	45,000	143,000
Testing supplies	15,000	16,000

Required

A. Categorize the costs and compute the total costs of conformance for each year by category.
B. Evaluate the distribution of quality costs at Precise. Discuss the distribution of quality costs and any trends in cost distribution. What effect does the distribution of quality costs have on total quality at Precise? Explain your answer.
C. What future trends should Precise expect if the current focus of quality programs continues? Explain your answer.

P9-7   Quality Loss Function Analysis

Obj. 4

Journal Paper Manufacturing produces newsprint paper for use in newspaper publishing. The thickness of the paper can vary slightly during the manufacturing process. If the paper is too thin, it will not hold up under the printing process and will tear, while paper that is too thick can result in printing press malfunction. As the paper is manufactured, it is rolled onto spools for shipping to newspaper publishers. Each spool is weighed after the manufacturing process is complete. The target value for a spool is exactly one ton (2,000 pounds). Management at Journal has determined that each pound deviation from the target value will increase quality costs by $0.50. The following production figures reflect production for the most recent month:

Spool Number	Total Gross Product Weight (in pounds)
1	2,119.20
2	1,924.62
3	1,907.32
4	2,141.91
5	1,974.43
6	2,030.21
7	2,053.92
8	2,142.12
9	1,936.90
10	1,899.97
11	1,997.87
12	2,112.25
13	1,943.40
14	2,071.75

Required

A. Calculate the total quality loss cost for Journal Paper Manufacturing, using the quality loss function.

B. What do your calculations suggest about the manufacturing process? What do your calculations suggest must be done by Journal? Explain your answer.

P9-8   The Taguchi Loss Function: Plot Preparation and Interpretation

Obj. 4

SPREADSHEET

Taguchi explained the basis for his loss function by providing an example from the nursery industry in Japan. Greenhouses typically are covered with plastic sheeting that permits the correct amount of sunlight to penetrate. If manufacturers of plastic sheeting deviate from target specifications, quality losses occur. For example, if the material is too thick, insufficient light will penetrate. If the material is too thin, it lacks sufficient strength to withstand inclement weather and will tear.

Assume the target specification is 50 microns (a micron is 1/1000 of a millimeter) and the dollar value of loss associated with variation is $200 [(k) = $200].

Required

A. Calculate the quality losses at the following points:
   1. 30 microns
   2. 40 microns
   3. 50 microns
   4. 60 microns
   5. 70 microns

B. Prepare a plot of the quality losses calculated in requirement (A).

C. Explain the results of your calculations and plot.

D. How might management use information from your plot to support decisions about quality improvement?

P9-9   Statistical Process Control Charting

Obj. 5

Power Source, Inc., produces electrical control harnesses used in the production of battery-powered carts and cars for children. These harnesses are sold to a toy manufacturer who re-

SPREADSHEET

quires close tolerances related to cable length. Power Source has implemented a statistical process control system to monitor harness production and performs statistical control charting related to cable length.

During a recent four-hour morning shift, the operator on the cable assembly line performed a cable measurement every 20 minutes and recorded the observation on a SPC control chart. The observed measurements were as follows:

Measurement		Measurement	
1	30.75 inches	7	33.50 inches
2	32.25 inches	8	31.95 inches
3	31.67 inches	9	32.00 inches
4	33.25 inches	10	31.08 inches
5	30.45 inches	11	30.99 inches
6	32.80 inches	12	32.15 inches

Required

A. Prepare a statistical process control chart to evaluate whether the process is in control. To solve the problem using Minitab, use the following instructions: Open Minitab. Enter observations 1–12 in column C1. Click on Stat. Click on Control Charts. Click on Individuals. Enter C1 into Variable field. Click OK.

   Note: If you choose to solve the problem manually (or to use Excel), upper and lower control limits should be placed on your graph at Y-axis values 35.11 and 29.69, respectively. Refer to Exhibit 12 in this chapter for an illustration of control limit and process average placement. You may manually calculate the process average or use the average function within Excel.

B. Do any of the observed measurements indicate that an out-of-control condition exists? Which measurement(s)? What steps should be taken to remedy this situation?

P9-10

Obj. 5

SPREADSHEET

Control Chart Preparation

Tuscaloosa Brickworks uses variance analysis to track materials price and quantity variances. Managers recognize that normal fluctuations occur, but want to investigate the cause of significant favorable or unfavorable variances. To help them assess whether a variance is significant, managers use statistical process control charts. Materials price variance data are presented for 25 periods as follows:

(1) 420 F	(6) 555 F	(10) 135 F	(14) 325 U	(18) 235 F	(22) 155 F
(2) 570 F	(7) 1,050 U	(11) 170 U	(15) 325 F	(19) 550 F	(23) 200 F
(3) 350 U	(8) 250 U	(12) 550 F	(16) 230 F	(20) 350 F	(24) 140 F
(4) 355 F	(9) 155 U	(13) 1,600 U	(17) 525 U	(21) 375 U	(25) 200 U
(5) 125 F					

Required

A. Prepare a statistical process control chart to evaluate whether materials price variances are in a state of statistical control. Use positive values for favorable variances and negative values for unfavorable variances. To solve the problem using Minitab, use the following instructions: Open Minitab. Enter observations 1–25 in column C1. Click on Stat. Click on Control Charts. Click on Individuals. Enter C1 into Variable field. Click OK.

   Note: If you choose to solve the problem manually (or to use Excel), upper and lower control limits should be placed on your graph at Y-axis values 1,564 and −1,572, respectively. Refer to Exhibit 12 in this chapter for an illustration of control limit and process average placement. You may manually calculate the process average or use the average function within Excel.

B. Which, if any, observations should management investigate?

C. Is the process subject to common and special cause variation? Explain.

D. Typically, who is responsible for a significant materials price variance? Explain.

P9-11, P9-12, & P9-13   These three problems are based on one business situation. The three-problem series links quality costs, the Taguchi loss function, and statistical process control.

P9-11   Quality Costs and Management Decisions

Obj. 3

AutoSafe, Inc., produces windshields for major international automobile manufacturers. To produce a shatter-proof windshield, a sheet of plastic-like material is sandwiched between two sheets of glass. The completed product must conform to a number of engineering specifications. For example, a completed windshield must not vary significantly from an established target thickness. Products that are too thick or too thin will not fit properly in the vehicle for which they are intended. Quality costs include extra installation time to make a poorly manufactured windshield fit properly; in a worst case scenario, the windshield may leak.

Management is interested in tracking internal failure, external failure, prevention, and appraisal costs.

Required

A. Machine operators indicate that a critical part in the assembly machine is subject to random failure. New tooling costing $250,000 is required to prevent future problems from occurring. How would the company classify capital expense associated with the process improvement initiative?

B. Assume management decided to invest in new tooling and quality training. As a result, total quality costs increased when compared to the prior year. How would you defend these decisions against critics who complained that total quality costs are increasing?

P9-12   The Taguchi Loss Function and Quality Costs

Obj. 4

SPREADSHEET

Refer to P9-11 for a description of AutoSafe's manufacturing process. Managers at AutoSafe collected twenty data points representing a batch of windshield XXR531. These data follow. The target thickness specification for product XXR531 is 2.5 millimeters. Management has estimated the cost of variability, or (k), in the Taguchi loss function at $12,000.

1	2.60	6	2.60	11	2.65	16	2.50
2	2.55	7	2.55	12	2.65	17	2.55
3	2.40	8	2.55	13	2.50	18	3.10
4	2.40	9	2.60	14	2.55	19	2.45
5	2.50	10	2.55	15	2.45	20	2.60

Required

A. Calculate the quality losses associated with process variability.

B. Will these losses appear in the accounting general ledger? Explain.

C. What types of costs are included in the Taguchi loss function?

D. Does the Taguchi function describe failure, prevention, or appraisal cost? Explain.

P9-13   Control Chart Preparation and Interpretation

Obj. 5

As part of AutoSafe's quality program, control charts are prepared on a regular basis to evaluate whether the process is in a state of statistical control. Using process data shown in P9-12, complete the following requirements.

SPREADSHEET

Required

A. Prepare a control chart for the AutoSafe glass windshield production process. To solve the problem using Minitab, use the following instructions: Open Minitab. Enter observations 1–20 in column C1. Click on Stat. Click on Control Charts. Click on Individuals. Enter C1 into Variable field. Click OK.

Note: If you choose to solve the problem manually (or to use Excel), upper and lower control limits should be placed on your graph at Y-axis values 2.90 and 2.23, respectively. Refer to Exhibit 12 in this chapter for an illustration of control limit and process average placement. You may manually calculate the process average or use the average function within Excel.

B. Determine whether the process is in a state of statistical control. Explain your answer.

P9-14   Variance Analysis, Service Environment

Objs. 1, 6

Todd Judd separated from his wife, Stella, and filed for divorce. As part of the divorce, Todd realized that he would have to engage in a legal battle with Stella since the couple owned several parcels of property and had considerable investments, including a business Todd had acquired from his father. Todd spoke with several attorneys, explained his case, and asked each for an estimate of the cost to represent him in the proceedings. Perry Schmidt, a practicing attorney, provided Todd with the following estimate of costs if he were to represent Todd:

Item	Hours	Billing Rate	Total Cost
Attorney hours, planning and court time	150	$185 per hour	$27,750
Admin. and clerical support	60	75 per hour	4,500
Witness fees	n/a	n/a	1,500
Court costs	n/a	n/a	500
Total			$34,250

Todd hired Perry based on the estimate. In the course of the trial several unforeseen issues arose, continuances were granted, and the proceedings dragged on for 18 months. At the end of the trial, Perry provided Todd with a bill totaling $42,840. The following billing details were also provided:

Item	Hours	Total Cost
Attorney hours, planning and court time	187	$34,595
Admin. and clerical support	52	3,640
Witness fees	n/a	2,750
Deposition fees		1,255
Court costs	n/a	600
Total		$42,840

Perry offered the following explanations for the difference between the estimated and final billings.

1. Continuances and unforeseen issues resulted in the extra attorney hours.
2. Deposition fees were not anticipated in the original quote.
3. Although the number of filings was exactly as anticipated, Perry was not aware that the court had increased its filing fees, resulting in an extra $100.

Required

A. Calculate the average rate per hour that Todd was billed for attorney time and clerical assistance.
B. Based on the original budget estimate, was the labor efficiency variance for attorney time favorable or unfavorable?
C. Is the court filing fee variance related to volume? Explain your answer.
D. Calculate the labor rate, efficiency, and total variances associated with clerical support.

P9-15 Excel in Action

SPREADSHEET

Music Makers normally produces 500,000 CDs each month. Standard quantities and prices per unit of direct materials are as follows:

	Quantity	Price
Blank CDs	1	$0.75
Containers	1	0.11
Printed inserts	1	0.05
Cellophane	1	0.02

Standard labor hours per unit and rates per hour are:

	Hours	Rate
Copying	0.00667	$13.00
Packaging	0.01500	7.50

(Continued)

Production during June was higher than normal at 560,000 units. To meet the higher demand, Music Makers purchased a higher than normal amount of materials. Luckily the company's purchasing department found a manufacturer willing to provide some surplus CDs and containers at a discount. Actual quantities of direct materials used and prices per unit for June were as follows:

	Quantity	Price
Blank CDs	565,430	$0.71
Containers	562,109	0.09
Printed inserts	560,139	0.05
Cellophane	561,240	0.02

Because of the higher than normal production, Music Makers' labor hours and rates were higher than normal. The company paid extra overtime to complete the additional units. Actual labor hours and rates per hour were as follows:

	Hours	Rate
Copying	3,820	$12.25
Packaging	8,300	8.15

Required

A. Use the data provided to prepare an analysis of direct materials and direct labor variances for Music Makers for June. Column headings for material variances should include: Units Produced, Standard Quantity per Unit, Standard Price per Unit, Actual Quantity, Actual Price per Unit, Actual Quantity × Actual Price, Actual Quantity × Standard Price, and Standard Quantity × Standard Price. Rows should provide data for each type of direct material. Quantity × Price columns should be totaled and the differences should be calculated to determine the total price and quantity variances. A positive number should be a favorable variance, and a negative number should be an unfavorable variance.

Below the direct material variance calculations, repeat the same process for direct labor variances. Column headings should be: Units Produced, Standard Hours per Unit, Standard Rate per Hour, Actual Hours, Actual Rate per Hour, Actual Hours × Actual Rate, Actual Hours × Standard Rate, and Standard Hours × Standard Rate. Separate rows should be provided for copying and packaging labor. Hours × Rate columns should be totaled and used to determine rate and efficiency variances.

B. Use cell references and formulas where possible. Use appropriate formatting throughout. Evaluate Music Makers' direct materials and direct labor variances. What were the likely causes of the variances? Were the decisions to produce the extra CDs and purchase the blank CDs and containers at a discount good decisions?

C. Suppose Music Makers had paid $0.73 for CDs and $0.13 for containers used in June. What would the price and quantity variances have been? Suppose the company's actual labor hours had been 3,700 for copying and 8,300 for packaging. What would the rate and efficiency variances have been?

P9-16   Multiple-Choice Overview of the Chapter

1. A favorable material price variance coupled with an unfavorable material usage variance would most likely be the result of:
   a. labor efficiency problems.
   b. machine efficiency problems.
   c. the purchase and use of higher than standard quality materials.
   d. the purchase and use of lower than standard quality materials.

2. Standards preferably should be set so that:
   a. no allowance is made for machine breakdowns or other work interruptions.
   b. they are based on practical levels that can be achieved rather than on ideal levels.
   c. they reflect a level that can be achieved only by the most skilled and efficient employee working at peak effort 100% of the time.
   d. they can be used for motivational purposes rather than in forecasting cash flows and in planning inventory.

3. Inspection of products would be a(n):
   a. prevention cost.
   b. appraisal cost.
   c. internal failure cost.
   d. external failure cost.

4. Which of the following is NOT true with respect to statistical process control?
   a. It places the monitoring of quality at a workstation.
   b. It eliminates the need for a final inspection of goods.
   c. It is considered a prevention cost.
   d. It requires the charting of observed measurements.

Questions 5 through 8 are based on the following information.

Jackson Industries employs a standard cost system in which direct materials inventory is carried at standard cost. Jackson has established the following standards for the costs of one unit of product:

	Standard Quantity	Standard Price or Rate
Direct materials	5 pounds	$3.60 per pound
Direct labor	1.25 hours	$12.00 per hour

During May, Jackson purchased 125,000 pounds of direct material at a total cost of $475,000. The total factory direct labor wages for May were $327,600. Jackson manufactured 22,000 units of product during May, using 108,000 pounds of direct material and 28,000 direct labor hours.

5. The price variance for the direct material acquired by Jackson Industries during May is:
   a. $21,600 favorable.
   b. $25,000 unfavorable.
   c. $28,000 favorable.
   d. $21,600 unfavorable.

6. The direct material quantity (usage) variance for May is:
   a. $7,200 unfavorable.
   b. $7,600 favorable.
   c. $5,850 unfavorable.
   d. $7,200 favorable.

7. The direct labor rate variance for May is:
   a. $8,400 favorable.
   b. $7,200 unfavorable.
   c. $8,400 unfavorable.
   d. $6,000 favorable.

8. The direct labor efficiency variance for May is:
   a. $5,850 favorable.
   b. $7,200 favorable.
   c. $6,000 unfavorable.
   d. $5,850 unfavorable.

9. For the month of January 2006, Crabapple's records disclosed the following data related to direct labor:

Actual direct labor costs	$10,000
Labor rate variance	$1,000 Favorable
Labor efficiency variance	($1,500) Unfavorable

For the month of January, actual direct labor hours totaled 2,000. What was Crabapple's standard direct labor rate per hour?
   a. $5.50
   b. $5.00
   c. $4.75
   d. $4.50

(Continued)

10. Quality costs:
    a. relate only to the manufacturing process.
    b. should focus on appraisal activities.
    c. are minimized by having well-trained inspectors.
    d. cut across departmental lines and are often not reported to management.

CASES

C9-1

Objs. 1, 2

Establishing Standards, Variance Analysis

Stellhorn Snacks produces high-quality potato chips. The manufacturing process is highly automated, yet requires labor to handle, inspect, and sort potatoes and chips. Stellhorn has accumulated product costs using process costing in the past and is considering adopting a standard cost accounting system.

At the beginning of the manufacturing process, potatoes are scrubbed and cleaned in an automatic washer. The potatoes then are placed automatically on a conveyor that feeds them into an automatic peeling machine. After the potatoes are peeled, they are inspected manually to remove blemishes and to cut out eyes. After inspection, they are placed on another conveyor that feeds them into an automatic slicing machine. The slicer feeds the chips into vats, which are loaded manually into deep fryers and monitored closely by production personnel. After cooking, the chips are drained and placed on another conveyor for final inspection and seasoning. At this point, unacceptable chips are sorted from good production, and the good chips are fed into an automatic bagger. The bagging process is highly automated, requiring one operator to load the empty bags for filling, and another person to remove the bags once they have been sealed and place them in cartons for final shipment.

Stellhorn expects to purchase potatoes of acceptable grade and quality for $0.08 a pound. Based on historical records, Stellhorn has determined that it can produce 152 ounces of chips for every 10 pounds of potatoes placed into production. Each bag of chips produced contains 19 ounces of chips. Other direct materials include bags and boxes, which amount to $0.14 per bag of chips. All other materials, such as oil and seasoning, are treated as indirect costs.

Stellhorn operates under a union contract and has three distinct classes, or categories, of employees. The established classes and the agreed-upon hourly rates for direct laborers are as follows:

Handlers	$ 8.00 an hour
Machine operators	10.50 an hour
Inspectors	12.00 an hour

For the coming year, Stellhorn expects to produce six million bags of chips. For this level of production, the company has determined that it will require 10,800 hours of handler time, 12,000 hours of machine operator time, and 14,800 hours of inspection.

Variable overhead is applied on the basis of direct labor hours and historically has averaged 110% of labor dollars. The budgeted fixed overhead for the coming year is $1,350,000, and also is applied based on direct labor hours.

Required

A. Discuss the benefits Stellhorn would realize by adopting a standard cost accounting system.
B. Using the following format, develop a standard cost sheet for material, labor, and overhead for each bag of potato chips.

Cost Category	Standard Quantity	Standard Cost or Rate	Total Standard Cost

For requirements (C) and (D), assume that Stellhorn produced 6,200,000 bags of chips and incurred the following costs and levels of activity:

Materials: 7,800,000 pounds of potatoes purchased and used, at a cost of $608,400.

Labor:

Handlers	12,480 hours, at an actual cost of $89,280
Machine operators	13,650 hours, at an actual cost of $130,200
Inspectors	15,475 hours, at an actual cost of $185,700

C. Calculate the material price and usage variances for potatoes.

D. Calculate the labor rate variance and labor efficiency variance for each labor category.

C9-2 Performance Measurement

Obj. 3

Petro-Flo Corporation designs and manufactures fluid transfer components found in engine and transmission systems of expensive, heavy equipment. These systems often are contained in earth-moving equipment used under harsh conditions ranging from Middle Eastern oil fields to Canadian real estate development projects. Because of protection granted by patented designs and the company's uncompromising dedication to service, Petro-Flo has enjoyed a dominant position within the industry. If a Petro-Flo fuel system malfunctions, regardless of where the equipment is in use, an engineer will be assigned to assist the customer. Sometimes the engineer can ship a replacement part by express air. However, occasionally he or she must travel to the job site to personally assess the cause of the problem and to make recommendations for repairing the system.

The business environment is changing as a result of innovations introduced by Petro-Flo's competitors. Therefore, cost management and quality control have received greater attention in recent years. In 2005, top management believed some managers had grown complacent as a result of previous successes in a very different business climate. As within many companies, the production, marketing, and service departments traditionally had functioned independently. In order to call attention to quality costs, management established a program to identify and manage quality expenditures as well as to serve as a basis for performance evaluation. Excerpts from the company's general ledger appear in Exhibit A.

Exhibit A Quality Cost Data (in thousands)

General Ledger Account	2004	2005	2006	2007
Sales	$2,000,000	$2,300,000	$2,500,000	$2,700,000
First-part inspection costs	30,000	35,000	40,000	50,000
Scrap/rework	70,000	60,000	50,000	45,000
Warranty claims	20,000	20,000	19,000	17,000
Product liability litigation	30,000	30,000	20,000	10,000
Vendor certification programs	0	20,000	30,000	20,000
Travel associated with field repairs	40,000	40,000	35,000	15,000
Quality training/education programs	5,000	20,000	15,000	10,000
R & D for better processes	20,000	40,000	40,000	20,000

After three years of using quality cost as a performance measurement criterion, some managers disagreed with the emphasis placed on identifying quality spending. These managers argued their main focus should be on nonfinancial variables such as scrap rates, machine downtime, on-time delivery, and the number of field breakdowns. They believed statistical process control charts provided immediately useful detailed process information for making quality improvements. These managers argued that after four years of tracking quality costs, total quality spending is not significantly lower than in 2004, one year prior to the introduction of the quality program.

Consider the following guidelines when preparing your analysis of the case.

Required

A. Discuss the purposes of a quality cost system as envisioned by management (such as cultural change and attention-getting).

(Continued)

B. Classify the costs in Exhibit A according to the following categories: internal failure, external failure, prevention, and appraisal.

C. Analyze the trends in quality spending. Prepare a stacked bar graph to analyze total quality costs. Prepare another graph to identify trends in spending by each type of cost category. (*Hint:* You may wish to prepare graphs in absolute dollars and percentage of sales.)

D. Consider the appropriate use of quality measures such as SPC charts and other nonfinancial measures of performance. Do these measures complement financial measures of quality?

E. How frequently should a company capture financial and nonfinancial measures?

MANAGING MULTI-DIVISIONAL ORGANIZATIONS

How do we set up meaningful performance measures?

Erin and Seth are continuing to grow their manufacturing business. They have learned about product costing and cost behavior. They also have become very adept at accurately budgeting their revenues and costs. As discussed in Chapter M9, they are beginning to understand how to use variance analysis as a type of performance measure for process improvement. They now have numerous employees with marketing, accounting, or production responsibilities. Seth and Erin share financial information throughout their organization hoping everyone will use the information to make the company more efficient, effective, and profitable. However, Erin and Seth realize their employees do not understand much of the information they are sharing. Also, the employees don't seem to understand how to use the information to make decisions that are consistent with the mission of the company. Erin and Seth would like to develop financial and nonfinancial performance measures that will help guide the actions of everyone.

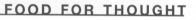

FOOD FOR THOUGHT

Put yourself in the position of Erin and Seth. How would you design your performance measurement system so that it is understandable by everyone throughout the company? The system should promote decisions and behavior that are consistent with the company's strategy. Let's see what Erin and Seth are considering as they plan their system design.

Erin: *I have been considering launching a project to develop a better method of evaluating and rewarding performance.*

Seth: *What's wrong with our bonus plan based on earnings? After all, the purpose of our company is to make money. If everyone does his or her job well, we should be profitable. Our bonus system shares some of the profits with our employees.*

Erin: *I agree that financial performance is the bottom line, but basing rewards on financial performance alone seems very short-sighted. We could do an excellent job on things that really matter, but because of events beyond our control, our earnings could be disappointing. Also, I believe nonfinancial measures may provide more guidance for decision making.*

Seth: *I'm not sure that I follow you.*

Erin: *Ok. What if I ask one of our marketing managers to improve net income? Or, what if I ask the production manager to improve earnings this month? What actions should he or she take?*

Seth: *So, how would other measures help?*

Erin: *If we partially based the marketing manager's performance evaluation on the number of new customers signed up during the month, she would develop a plan to increase our customer base. Likewise, if the production manager's bonus is affected by the percentage of on-time deliveries, he would be more interested in making sure delivery dates are not missed.*

Seth: *I see your point. By establishing a variety of financial and nonfinancial performance measures, everyone would be made aware of important factors that ultimately affect net income. Also, these measures can be used to communicate competitive strategy throughout the company.*

Erin: *Right. For example, we have built our business around the principle of developing innovative, high-quality products, delivered on time, at a reasonable price. We could build performance measures into our system that encourage actions consistent with our strategy.*

Seth: *I can think of a few measures, such as defect rate, number of new product innovations, and percentage of on-time deliveries, that are consistent with our strategy.*

Erin: *We will need to involve everyone in the process of developing appropriate measures. Buy-in is important in order for people to support what we are trying to accomplish.*

Seth: *I agree. We also need to tailor the performance measures to specific areas of responsibility. It makes no sense to evaluate a production manager on the number of new customers or to evaluate a marketing manager on the number of defective products produced.*

Erin: *The key will be to develop a small number of measures that capture various aspects of our competitive strategy. If we can identify a few processes that we must do well and focus on these, I believe profits will follow.*

OBJECTIVES

Once you have completed this chapter, you should be able to:

1 Explain problems associated with managers acting on behalf of owners.

2 Identify various organizational levels within a company and explain how performance at each level may be evaluated.

3 Explain the historical context in which return on investment (ROI) was developed.

4 Calculate ROI and economic value added. Explain how they can motivate behavior that is consistent or inconsistent with the strategic objectives of an organization.

5 Discuss the four elements of the balanced scorecard approach to evaluating performance.

6 Explain how a manager who acts in the best interests of a division may harm the company as a whole.

7 Discuss various transfer pricing methods that have been developed to influence managerial behavior.

8 Explain how the performance of managers can be evaluated in decentralized service organizations.

AMERICAN PAPER COMPANY: THE MANUFACTURING PROCESS

This chapter uses American Paper Company to illustrate the concepts of responsibility centers, performance evaluation, and transfer pricing. American Paper is organized into two divisions, Pulp and Paper. Each division is responsible for producing and selling its products. Though most of the output from the Pulp Division is sold to external customers worldwide, some of it is sold to the Paper Division to be used as raw material.

As shown in Exhibit 1, pulp manufacturing begins with timber in the form of logs or wood chips. If raw materials are received in the form of logs, the first step in the process is debarking. A rotating debarking drum tumbles the logs to remove the bark. After the debarking, chippers cut the logs into one-inch cubes.

The second step in the process is "digesting." Wood chips are cooked to break down the glue-like material bonding the wood fibers. Chemicals used in the digestor are reclaimed and used in future pulp production. Following the digesting process, brown fibers, which are used in manufacturing so-called natural-colored coffee filters and paper towels, are washed and screened. A bleaching process may be used to convert natural-colored brown pulp into white pulp, which is used to manufacture products such as writing and printing paper. As a final step, the pulp mixture is dried, cut into sheets, and packaged for shipment.

The Paper Division of American Paper manufactures large rolls of paper. These rolls are sold to companies that convert the paper into writing, printing, and computer

Exhibit 1 The Pulp Manufacturing Process

paper. As shown in Exhibit 2, the paper manufacturing process begins with the mixing of pulp with water and chemicals in the first stage of a paper machine. The mixture is spread out on a porous wire mesh; the actual formation of paper begins in this step. The wire mesh travels through a press that forces the pulp mixture against the wire to remove water from the mixture and make the paper the desired thickness. The material then proceeds to a drying section, where it travels across numerous cylindrical dryers that are heated with steam. In the final section of the paper machine, long sections of paper are rolled up into "parent rolls" and removed from the machine. The parent rolls are processed further by American Paper's customers to make various types of printing paper.

Exhibit 2   The Paper Manufacturing Process

A paper plant requires a large amount of expensive production equipment—a new pulp mill can cost $750 million. In addition to the initial investment in equipment, these mills consume resources in the form of pulp, water, and chemicals. Some mills purchase electricity to power their operations, while others use heat produced by the chemical recovery process to generate electric power. The capital and organizational structures of a company, as well as its operating costs, are directly related to decisions managers face in a decentralized environment. The remainder of this chapter considers the related topics of responsibility accounting, performance measurement, and transfer pricing.

THEORETICAL FRAMEWORK FOR BEHAVIOR WITHIN ORGANIZATIONS

OBJECTIVE 1

Explain problems associated with managers acting on behalf of owners.

Seth and Erin are beginning to share decision-making authority with others in their company. This chapter illustrates some of the issues involving the sharing, or transferring, of authority to professional managers. Throughout this text you are learning how managers use accounting information to make marketing and operations decisions. In most large companies, professional managers make these decisions, thereby acting as agents for the owners (shareholders). *Agents* **are hired by owners and are expected to manage the company in a way consistent with the owners' interests.** Thus, a major consideration when designing a performance evaluation system is to build incentives for managers to act according to the owners' wishes.

Economic theory assumes the objective of a company is to maximize stockholder wealth. However, the theory does not assume managers will always behave in a way consistent with this objective. Thus, compensation packages often are constructed to give the managers incentives to maximize company value. For example, compensation arrangements often include bonuses when certain income targets are met. In a decentralized organization, divisional managers have authority to make many types of decisions, but are held accountable for the results of their decisions. Next, this chapter addresses various types of responsibility areas within decentralized organizations, and how managers of these areas may be evaluated.

MANAGEMENT OF DECENTRALIZED ORGANIZATIONS

OBJECTIVE 2

Identify various organizational levels within a company and explain how performance at each level may be evaluated.

Exhibit 3 presents the organizational chart of American Paper. Each division manager reports to a corporate-level vice president. Operations managers, who report to the division managers, are responsible for supervising the activities of the manufacturing and marketing functions.

Managers typically are evaluated on the basis of variables over which they have control. Thus, managers at different levels within an organization are evaluated by different criteria. For example, some managers can control costs but not revenues. Other managers may be responsible for controlling costs, earning revenues, and making decisions about acquiring additional plant assets. Thus, divisions within an organization often are categorized according to the types of responsibilities placed on managers. For example, the organizational structure of American Paper consists of four levels or types of responsibility centers:

- Cost centers *paper*
- Revenue centers *sales*
- Profit centers *sales and controlling costs/exp.*
- Investment centers *profits and managing assets*

A *cost center* **is a division of an organization that consumes resources while performing its responsibilities, yet has no direct involvement in generating sales or acquiring property.** Thus, managers of cost centers are evaluated on their ability to control costs. For example, manufacturing plant managers can influence materials, labor, and overhead costs, but they cannot set selling prices for products, manage marketing campaigns, or acquire equipment without approval from divisional or corporate-level management. Thus, to evaluate the performance of a manufacturing plant manager on profitability would not be consistent with the objective of evaluating managers on activities over which they have control. Additionally, cost center managers often are evaluated on their ability to meet quality standards and delivery schedules. The two manufacturing plants identified in Exhibit 3 are examples of cost centers.

A *revenue center* **is a division of an organization that has responsibility for generating sales.** Thus, managers of revenue centers often are responsible for meeting sales quotas and managing distribution channels. However, these managers do not control most of the costs that affect net income. Therefore, revenue center managers should be

Exhibit 3 American Paper Company—Organizational Chart

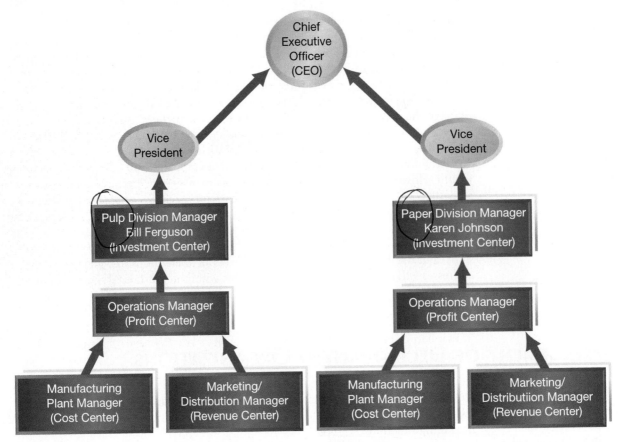

evaluated using sales, rather than income, as a performance criterion. In addition, revenue center managers may be responsible for managing inventory and may be evaluated using inventory measures. The Marketing and Distribution functions shown in Exhibit 3 are examples of revenue centers.

A *profit center* **is a division of an organization that is responsible for both generating sales and controlling costs and expenses.** Profit center managers typically have the responsibility for setting prices for products, determining product mix, and monitoring production activities. Thus, profit center managers are responsible for costs, sales volume, and profitability. As shown in Exhibit 3, American Paper has two operations managers whose departments function as profit centers. Since profitability is determined by the difference between sales revenue and costs, operations managers who are evaluated on profitability must have control over both variables.

An *investment center* **is a level within an organization that has the strategic responsibility for generating profits and managing assets.** In the American Paper example, division managers are considered investment center managers. Typically, performance measures such as return on assets (ROA) or a similar measure, return on investment (ROI), are used to evaluate investment center managers because they have control over costs, revenues, and assets. Investment center managers are evaluated using these measures because profit, or operating income, tells only part of the story about their effectiveness as managers. Typically, measures such as ROI or ROA are appropriate only if managers can determine the level of assets used by their area of responsibility. In this example, division managers can acquire and dispose of equipment. Thus, it is appropriate to evaluate division managers using ROA or ROI as a performance criterion. In addition, investment center managers are responsible for the strategic direction of the company. Thus, they are responsible for improving market share and successfully introducing new products.

Exhibit 4 summarizes responsibility centers often found within decentralized organizations and gives examples of relevant performance measures.

Exhibit 4

Performance Measures by Type of Responsibility Center

	Performance Measures
Cost centers	Manufacturing cost (materials, labor, overhead)
	Quality (defect rate)
	Percentage of on-time deliveries
Revenue centers	Sales volume in units
	Inventory turnover
	Sales revenue
Profit centers	Manufacturing costs
	Distribution costs
	Sales volume
	Profitability
Investment centers	ROI Return on Investment
	Market share
	Successful new product introductions

Benefits of Decentralization

A decentralized organization permits local managers, such as bank branch managers who are located far from corporate offices, to make certain decisions without approval from a central administrator. Localized decision making has many benefits for an organization. For example, local managers should be in touch with the economy and business conditions in their geographical areas; therefore, they often are in a better position to make informed judgments than their supervisors, who may be located hundreds of miles away.

The decentralized structure offers other benefits as well. Lower and middle managers are given the opportunity to develop and exercise their skills in preparation for greater responsibilities. Thus, a decentralized structure provides a training ground for future top-level managers. In addition, lower and middle managers' job satisfaction should be enhanced because they are allowed to have control over their areas of responsibility and should experience pride of ownership.

---

1 SELF-STUDY PROBLEM Assume you are the plant manager for a medium-sized company that manufactures a variety of types of telephones. The phones are produced by assembling an array of components, including electronic circuit boards that are purchased from another division within the company. Every Friday morning your corporate headquarters faxes you a production schedule indicating the type and amount of products to be produced during the following week. Thus, a major aspect of your job is meeting production schedules as efficiently as possible. Selling prices are set by senior-level management.

The following income statement and supporting schedule reflect sales, product costs, and expenses for your plant during the last twelve months. As you prepare for your annual performance evaluation, you recall a conversation from last year in which upper management set a net income target for products manufactured in your plant. However, you believe that certain costs on the income statement are beyond your control. Also, you wonder why net income is used to evaluate your performance at the plant level.

Required

A. In preparation for your meeting, identify the costs over which you have control.
B. Should your plant be evaluated as a cost center, revenue center, profit center, or investment center? Explain.

Income Statement

Sales	$100,000,000	
Cost of goods sold	75,000,000	
Gross margin		$25,000,000
Selling and administrative expenses:		
Depreciation on corporate aircraft	$ 1,000,000	
Sales commissions and other sales expenses	10,000,000	
Other direct plant-related expenses	13,000,000	
Total expenses		24,000,000
Net income		$ 1,000,000

Cost of Goods Sold Schedule

Beginning finished goods inventory	$ 5,000,000
Cost of goods manufactured	77,000,000*
Total	$82,000,000
Ending finished goods inventory	(7,000,000)
Cost of goods sold	$75,000,000

*Cost of goods manufactured includes materials, labor, and overhead costs. Overhead includes allocated corporate-level costs, such as quality assurance and computer time used for production scheduling.

The solution to Self-Study Problem 1 appears at the end of the chapter.

PERFORMANCE EVALUATION USING ROI

OBJECTIVE 3

Explain the historical context in which return on investment (ROI) was developed.

http://albright.
swlearning.com
....
Find out about the DuPont Company today.

Recall that return on assets (ROA) is a ratio used to understand financial performance. This chapter considers a similar measure, return on investment (ROI), commonly used by internal managers to evaluate performance. The measures are used for different purposes. In this section, ROI is calculated and divided into its two components. In addition, the strengths of using ROI as a performance indicator to motivate managers are evaluated, and some criticisms of using ROI as the sole measurement of performance are considered.

Johnson and Kaplan[1] trace the roots of return on investment (ROI) to the **Du Pont Powder Company**. Three cousins purchased the assets of **E.I. du Pont de Nemours and Company** in exchange for corporate bonds and created the Du Pont Powder Company in 1903. The bond interest rate was based on the earnings of the old company. The new owners had to use the company's resources wisely in order to generate sufficient earnings to pay the bond interest and produce a profit. The cousins developed ROI for the purpose of assessing the performance of various departments and for making resource allocation decisions. They could not afford to invest assets in projects that earned less than the interest rate they were paying on the bonds issued to acquire their assets.

Of what benefit is ROI? Why don't managers simply compare the net incomes from their various operations to determine which is the most and least profitable? Net income tells only part of the story; other factors also must be considered. For example, assume that you are a senior manager in a corporation that has two divisions. Both division managers report directly to you. During the past year, both managers reported $500,000 in net income. Do you evaluate them equally? How would your answer change if you assume that one division employed assets of $2,500,000 while the other division

[1] Johnson, H. Thomas, and Robert S. Kaplan. 1991. *Relevance Lost* (Boston: Harvard Business School Press).

employed assets of $5,000,000? A different picture now emerges; the smaller division (in terms of assets employed) produced the same net income as the larger division. This suggests that the smaller division is managed more efficiently than the larger division.

Recall that ROA can be divided into two components, profit margin and asset turnover. Profit margin is determined by dividing net income (adjusted for interest expense) by operating revenues (sales). Asset turnover is computed by dividing operating revenues (sales) by average total assets. From an external perspective, such analysis provides useful information about a company as a whole. For example, we can determine whether a company uses a high margin, low turnover strategy, in which the profit on each sale is high and the amount of sales compared to assets is low (as is the case with a phone company like **Southwestern Bell**), or a low margin, high turnover strategy, in which the profit on each sale is low and the amount of sales compared to assets is high (as is the case with a discount store like **Wal-Mart**). *Return on investment (ROI)* **is calculated by dividing operating income by operating assets.** Like ROA, ROI can be divided into two components, *margin* and *turnover*. As illustrated in Exhibit 5, *margin* **for ROI is operating income expressed as a percentage of sales.** For example, a 6 percent margin suggests that 6 cents of operating income are earned for every dollar of sales. *Turnover* **for ROI is sales divided by average operating assets employed.** A turnover value of 1.07 indicates that $1.07 of sales were generated for each dollar of operating assets used. Thus, as shown in Exhibit 5, ROI for the Pulp Division is margin times turnover ($0.064 = 0.06 \times 1.07$).

OBJECTIVE 4

Calculate ROI and economic value added. Explain how they can motivate behavior that is consistent or inconsistent with the strategic objectives of an organization.

Exhibit 5
ROI Data and Calculations for the Pulp and Paper Divisions

Handwritten note: Cost of Goods Sold = DM, DL, MOH

	Pulp	Paper
Average operating assets	$750,000,000	$200,000,000
Sales	800,000,000	275,000,000
Cost of goods sold	640,000,000	206,000,000
Operating expenses *(Period cost)*	112,000,000	58,000,000
Operating income	48,000,000	11,000,000

Pulp Division

Margin	×	Turnover	=	ROI
$\dfrac{\text{Operating income}}{\text{Sales}}$	×	$\dfrac{\text{Sales}}{\text{Average operating assets}}$	=	ROI
$\dfrac{\$48,000,000}{\$800,000,000}$	×	$\dfrac{\$800,000,000}{\$750,000,000}$	=	ROI
0.06	×	1.07	=	0.064

Paper Division

Margin	×	Turnover	=	ROI
$\dfrac{\text{Operating income}}{\text{Sales}}$	×	$\dfrac{\text{Sales}}{\text{Average operating assets}}$	=	ROI
$\dfrac{\$11,000,000}{\$275,000,000}$	×	$\dfrac{\$275,000,000}{\$200,000,000}$	=	ROI
0.04	×	1.38	=	0.055

Managers typically use *operating income* as the numerator of the margin calculation and *average operating assets* as the denominator of the turnover calculation. Operating income, rather than net income, is used because operating income is not affected by nonoperating revenues and expenses (such as interest and taxes). **Recall that** *operating income* is sales − (**cost of goods sold** + **other operating expenses**). *Operating assets* **are those assets controlled by the division; they include investments in cash, accounts receivable, inventory, and plant assets used in production.** Excluded from operating assets are assets such as land held for investment or long-term investments in marketable equity securities. While ROI and ROA are similar in their approach to measuring margin and turnover, ROI uses assets, revenues, and expenses that are more directly related to the daily operations of an investment center.

In the following paragraphs, information about American Paper Company is used to illustrate the calculation of margin, turnover, and ROI. In addition, the types of decisions managers make to improve ROI for their areas of responsibility are considered. From the organizational chart, note that the managers of the Pulp and Paper Divisions are Bill Ferguson and Karen Johnson, respectively. These division managers compete with each other; their salary levels, bonuses, and opportunities for promotion are related to their performance. Exhibit 5 presents information that permits us to evaluate the performance of each division using ROI.

Discussion of Results

The Pulp Division has a higher ROI than the Paper Division. An ROI of 0.064 means that for every dollar of assets, the Pulp Division earns almost six and a half cents. In contrast, the Paper Division earns only five and a half cents from every dollar of assets. How could Karen Johnson, manager of the Paper Division (who is embarrassed by her performance relative to the Pulp Division), improve her division's margin, turnover, and ROI?

Margin. To improve an investment center's margin, a manager must increase the size of operating income relative to sales. In other words, Johnson needs to earn more operating income from each dollar of sales. Since operating income is determined by subtracting cost of goods sold and operating expenses from sales, managers usually focus on cost control to improve the *margin* element of ROI. Of course, another alternative is to raise selling prices. However, managers typically are reluctant to raise prices because of competitive pressures. Margin may be expressed as follows:

$$\text{Margin} = \frac{\text{Operating income}}{\text{Sales}} = \frac{\text{Sales} - (\text{Cost of goods sold} + \text{Operating expenses})}{\text{Sales}}$$

Let's assume that Johnson decides to reduce costs in the next period to improve the division's margin. She predicts that she can achieve a cost savings of $2,750,000 by reducing production overhead costs (which become part of cost of goods sold) by $2,000,000 and reducing operating expenses by $750,000. Specifically, Johnson plans to change administrative procedures to eliminate costs associated with activities such as purchasing and payroll. She understands that if non-value-added work can be eliminated, the associated costs also will disappear. Most of the savings will be realized by reducing the size of support departments and eliminating unnecessary job classifications.

In addition, Johnson plans to realize savings from redesigning the product mix and manufacturing process. For example, analysts within the plant currently are examining the product mix to eliminate product types (termed "grades") that are manufactured in small batches, or that require special handling or expensive finishing operations. Exhibit 6 provides examples of the product and volume diversity within Johnson's plant. The process of changing the paper machine from the production of one grade to another results in scrap, and so Johnson expects to reduce the plant's scrap rate by making fewer grade changes. The number of grade changes can be reduced by eliminating products that are manufactured in small quantities. This should result in significant scrap reductions and cost savings. Eliminating some of the product line will not affect the plant's overall output. The remaining grades will simply be produced in larger quantities. Currently, demand for paper exceeds supply. Thus, Johnson is confident sales revenues will not decline. Additionally, she plans to redirect the quality control engineers' efforts to pulp inspection. If only top-quality raw materials are allowed into production, scrap rates and related costs should further decline.

Exhibit 6 Product and Volume Diversity within the Paper Plant

As illustrated in Exhibit 5, the Paper Division's cost of goods sold and operating expenses are $206,000,000 and $58,000,000, respectively. Let's evaluate the Paper Division's margin under the proposed cost-cutting program as follows:

$$\text{Margin} = \frac{\text{Operating income}}{\text{Sales}} = \frac{\text{Sales} - (\text{Cost of goods sold} + \text{Operating expenses})}{\text{Sales}}$$

$$0.05 = \frac{\$13,750,000}{\$275,000,000} = \frac{\$275,000,000 - (\$206,000,000 - \$2,000,000 + \$58,000,000 - \$750,000)}{\$275,000,000}$$

$$= 0.05$$

This calculation indicates that the Paper Division's margin should improve from 0.04 to 0.05 after establishing the cost-cutting program. Therefore, if Johnson's predictions are correct, the cost-cutting program will improve the division's ROI from 0.055 to 0.069, as follows:

	Margin	×	Turnover	=	ROI
Paper Division ROI before cost-cutting program	0.04	×	1.38	=	0.055
Paper Division ROI after cost-cutting program	0.05	×	1.38	=	0.069

Savings resulted in 6.9%

In addition to cost-cutting strategies, managers also can improve ROI by effectively managing assets under their control. The next section addresses turnover decisions.

Turnover. Sales are divided by operating assets to calculate turnover. Because larger turnover values are preferred to smaller values, managers are motivated to keep asset levels low while maintaining or increasing sales levels. Let's use the information from Exhibit 5 to illustrate the concept of turnover and to consider the types of decisions managers may make in an attempt to improve turnover within their area of responsibility.

Assume that Johnson has identified assets in the form of inventory, accounts receivable, and equipment totaling $25,000,000 that can be eliminated. For example, she plans to aggressively pursue collections of accounts receivable. She plans to permanently reduce the level of accounts receivable and submit excess cash to the corporate offices. In addition, by reducing the level of raw materials, finished goods, and supplies inventory, Johnson can reduce the asset base of her plant. She may do this by employing just-in-time inventory techniques. Modifying the product line and manufacturing process may make certain types of equipment unnecessary. Thus, further decreases in the asset base will be possible. How would these reductions affect the Paper Division's turnover ratio? After removing $25,000,000 from the asset base, turnover is calculated as follows:

$$\text{Turnover} = \frac{\text{Sales}}{\text{Operating assets}} = \frac{\$275,000,000}{\$200,000,000 - \$25,000,000} = 1.57$$

This calculation indicates that eliminating $25,000,000 from the asset base improves turnover from 1.38 (before reducing the asset level) to 1.57 (after reducing the asset level).

How does improving the turnover ratio affect the Paper Division's ROI? First, let's look at the improvement in ROI attributable only to improved turnover. Then we calculate the predicted ROI if both margin and turnover ratio are improved.

	Margin	×	Turnover	= ROI
Paper Division ROI—improved turnover only	0.04	×	1.57	= 0.063

If Johnson improved only turnover, without undertaking a cost-cutting campaign, her division's ROI would improve from 0.055 to 0.063.

However, by improving both margin and turnover, Johnson can report an ROI of 0.079, as follows:

	Margin	×	Turnover	= ROI
Paper Division ROI—improved margin and turnover	0.05	×	1.57	= 0.079

This analysis shows that Johnson can improve ROI *in the short run* by increasing margin, turnover, or both margin and turnover simultaneously. In a competitive environment, managers make decisions to improve the measures that are used to evaluate their performance. Unfortunately, a focus on short-term performance may have disastrous long-term consequences.

Criticisms of Using ROI to Evaluate Performance

Earlier, this chapter discussed managers' roles as agents and the objective of selecting performance measures that align the interests of agents with those of owners. How can using ROI as a performance indicator achieve this objective? What does it communicate to managers? Using ROI instructs managers to earn the greatest net income possible, while minimizing assets employed. Thus, managers are motivated to increase the numerator and to reduce the denominator of the ROI calculation. The discussion of margin identified strategies to increase the income component (numerator) of the ROI calculation, while the discussion of turnover considered methods to reduce the average operating asset level (denominator) of the ROI calculation.

Some accountants argue that focusing on ROI promotes short-sighted decision making that can harm a company in the long run. The following discussion gives examples of decisions that improve ROI in the short run but may have negative long-term effects. The first set of examples involves decisions affecting the margin component of ROI. Since managers are encouraged to reduce operating costs and administrative expenses, they may be encouraged to sacrifice "investments" necessary for future growth. Such investments include research and development (R&D) expenses.

Generally accepted accounting principles (GAAP) require companies to expense R&D in the period incurred, even though most companies view R&D as an investment to benefit future periods. By cutting R&D expenses, managers may realize an immediate improvement in operating income. However, the long-term consequences of a reduced R&D budget may include less competitive products, which are likely to lead to lost market share and lower profitability.

Managers also may capture short-term savings by reducing maintenance expenditures for manufacturing equipment. Typically, maintenance costs, such as lubricants, spare parts, and salaries of maintenance crews, are treated as overhead cost items. Therefore, trimming maintenance costs may improve a division's operating income in the short run. However, a reduced maintenance program may result in very large equipment repair or replacement costs in the future.

Finally, since using ROI encourages reduced asset levels, some managers may be reluctant to make the investments in plant assets necessary to ensure superior quality and reliable product delivery. Therefore, while ROI has many positive attributes as a performance measure, if used improperly it may encourage managers to make short-term decisions that negatively affect long-term performance.

Exhibit 7 summarizes some of the criticisms of using ROI as the only measure of performance.

Economic Value Added Compared to ROI

Chapter M1 briefly introduced the concept of economic value added,[2] a new term for a traditional concept, residual income. Companies must provide an adequate return to

Exhibit 7
Criticisms of Using ROI as the Only Measure of Performance

ROI Downside

Short-Term Decisions

Research & Development

Managers reduce operating costs by cutting research & development expenses

Maintenance

Managers reduce operating costs by reducing maintenance expenditures

Long-Term Effects

Production

Cutting R&D expenses may cause less competitive products to be produced

Equipment

Reducing maintenance costs may result in large equipment repairs or replacement

---

[2] EVA is a trademarked measure of Stern Stuart & Co., New York.

encourage investors to help finance the company's activities. This return represents a cost to the company. The first step in calculating economic value added involves producing an income statement. After calculating operating income, the cost of investors' capital is deducted. The result is economic value added. Examples of organizations that have adopted economic value added concepts include **Best Buy**, **California Public Employees Retirement System**, **Coca-Cola**, **Quaker Oats**, and **Bank of America**.[3]

To illustrate residual value concepts, we use the Western Division of Crimson Company. Crimson Company is a multi-divisional company with offices located across the North American continent. Assume Crimson Company's investors require a 20 percent return on their invested capital. The division manager of the Western Division employs invested capital of $1,000,000. As shown in Exhibit 8, Western Division management produced an economic value added of $50,000. Thus, they produced revenues in excess of all operating and capital costs.

Exhibit 8
Residual Income
Calculation for the
Western Division

Sales	$2,000,000
Cost of goods sold	1,300,000
Gross profit	$ 700,000
General selling and administrative costs	450,000
Operating income	$ 250,000
Cost of capital (0.20 × $1,000,000)	200,000
Economic value added	$ 50,000

residual income

Using financial information presented in Exhibit 8 we can calculate ROI for the Western Division. Earlier in this chapter we used average operating assets as the denominator for the ROI calculation. For purposes of comparison, we assume invested capital was used to acquire operating assets. Thus, in our example, operating assets and invested capital are the same. ROI for the Western Division is calculated as follows: Operating income ÷ average operating assets ($250,000 ÷ $1,000,000 = 0.25). The Western Division produced an ROI of 0.25 and an economic value added of $50,000. Which measure should corporate managers use to assess a division manager's performance?

Both ROI and economic value added have strengths and weaknesses. ROI permits managers to compare performance across large and small divisions. Using ROI as a performance measure, operating income is divided by asset size to capture a manager's efficiency in using assets to produce operating income. Alternatively, economic value added is not as useful in comparing divisions of different sizes because economic value added is not divided by assets employed. However, using ROI as a performance measure also may discourage managers from making investments that are good for the company.

Using the Western Division as an example, assume the manager could make an investment in a new product line. Also, assume the investment is expected to produce the financial results shown in Exhibit 9.

Exhibit 9
The Western Division
Forecast for a New
Product Line

Sales	$600,000
Cost of goods sold	450,000
Gross profit	$150,000
General selling and administrative costs	95,000
Operating income	$ 55,000
Cost of capital (0.20 × $250,000)	50,000
Economic value added	$ 5,000

[3] Lucey, Brian, and Louise Turner. 1999. Out with the Old, In with the New? *Accountancy Ireland* (December): 14–15.

Management believes an investment of $250,000 will produce an operating income of $55,000. If forecasts are correct, the new investment will generate an ROI of 22 percent ($55,000 ÷ $250,000). If management is rewarded based on ROI, they will not invest in the new line. Why? Currently the Western Division is earning an ROI of 25 percent. The new investment will earn only 22 percent. Thus, the new investment will reduce the division's ROI.

If division management were evaluated using economic value added, rather than ROI, would they invest in the new product line? Yes, because the investment produces a *positive* economic value added. The new investment is expected to generate revenues sufficient to satisfy all operating and capital costs. The company would be better off with the investment than without it. Thus, in this case, economic value added would motivate management to make the correct investment decision, while ROI would not.

How do managers design performance measurement systems that encourage behavior consistent with the long-term objectives of an organization? The next section considers an evaluation method that permits performance criteria to be linked to a company's strategy. Both financial and nonfinancial performance criteria are used in the approach termed the balanced scorecard.

THE BALANCED SCORECARD APPROACH

OBJECTIVE 5

Discuss the four elements of the balanced scorecard approach to evaluating performance.

http://albright.
swlearning.com

Learn more about the balanced scorecard.

Recall that Seth and Erin were discussing the use of both financial and nonfinancial measures in their new performance measurement system. They want a few carefully selected measures to help guide managers in their decision making. This section considers the balanced scorecard as a method for providing structure to the design of a performance measurement system.

People use information continuously to evaluate their environment and to help them make appropriate decisions. For example, if you drove a car to class today, you probably monitored your speed, checked the rear-view and side-view mirrors to evaluate the position of other vehicles relative to yours, glanced at the gasoline gauge, and so forth. However, while the rear-view mirror is certainly an important piece of safety equipment, driving your car using only the rear-view mirror would produce disastrous results. People must view and react to many different types of performance measures at the same time.

Some accountants have argued that ignoring important nonfinancial performance measures while focusing exclusively on financial measures can spell disaster for organizations. Therefore, managers need a short list of key indicators that signal current as well as future performance. A "balanced scorecard" approach has been used by some companies to bring together many different aspects of their corporate *strategy* in one report. **The** *balanced scorecard* **has key performance criteria in four categories: financial, customer satisfaction, internal business processes, and learning and growth.** Thus, operating performance measures are developed that are consistent with an organization's strategic goals. In addition, the balanced scorecard prevents managers from improving only one aspect of performance while simultaneously allowing other important aspects of performance to decline.

The balanced scorecard approach to performance evaluation is based on linking a company's strategic goals with specific, concrete measures designed to motivate behavior consistent with factors that will help the organization achieve success in the long run. The approach views a financial measure, such as ROI, as an important indicator, but not the only measure at which managers must excel. Thus, the approach represents a broader, more balanced view of an organization's success in achieving its long-term strategic goals.

Financial performance measures motivate managers to consider how the company looks in the eyes of the shareholders. Typically, managers are evaluated using criteria such as profitability, ROI, market share, and cash flow. Thus, managers are encouraged to make decisions that increase revenues, contain costs, or both.

In line with the objectives of total quality management (TQM), the balanced score-card contains a category of indicators that encourage managers to consider how their company looks in the eyes of customers. Customer satisfaction performance measures may include the percentage of on-time deliveries and customer response time for service or other assistance. When customer satisfaction is included as a key performance indicator, managers are encouraged to make decisions consistent with customers' needs.

Managers who are evaluated by internal business criteria ask themselves, "At what must we excel?" Thus, the link to customer satisfaction is made explicit. Managers are encouraged to improve processes internally to ensure customer satisfaction. Internal business indicators include measures that promote manufacturing excellence, such as cycle time, scrap rate, and lead time from placing an order until delivery. Managers are encouraged to improve internal processes that add value for customers. Once again, the balanced scorecard emphasizes long-term investments and continuous improvement, rather than short-term savings from cost reductions.

The learning and growth category requires management to consider the question, "What is necessary to meet the ambitious goals of the financial, customer, and internal-business perspectives?" Common objectives for the learning and growth category include improving employee skills through training, providing adequate resources to employees who strive to meet difficult targets, empowering employees to make decisions, and motivating employees with meaningful rewards when goals are met. Companies that have found a strategic payoff from implementing balanced scorecard concepts include **Whirlpool Europe**, **Lands' End Direct Merchants**, and **Bass Brewers**.[4]

Exhibit 10 illustrates the relationships among the various components of the balanced scorecard, using the Paper Division of American Paper Company as an example.

Exhibit 10

Performance Measures Using the Balanced Scorecard Approach for the Paper Division of American Paper Company

Perspective	Actual	Desired
Financial		
ROI	0.055	0.08
Customer		
On-time deliveries	80%	85%
Response time to inquiries	2 days	3 hours
Internal Business Processes		
Cycle time	6 weeks	5 weeks
Scrap rate	5%	2%
Manufacturing lead time	10 hours	8 hours
Learning and Growth		
Percentage of employees with specialized training or skills	8%	25%

Using American Paper Company as an example, how would Johnson's decision to restructure the division and reduce costs affect other important factors identified by a balanced scorecard approach? Certainly reducing the scrap rate (and presumably improving the quality of products delivered to customers) would be viewed favorably from the customer perspective. Additionally, reducing the number of different products would result in faster cycle and delivery times. However, her strategy to pursue collections of accounts receivable aggressively may have an adverse effect on customer relations (though in the short run cash flow would be improved).[5] Finally, using ROI as a

---

[4] Anonymous. 1999. Building and Implementing a Balanced Scorecard. Management Services; Enfield (February): Vol. 43.

[5] Customers who wish to purchase all of their paper from one supplier may be disappointed to learn that Johnson no longer produces a full line of products. These customers may take all of their business elsewhere.

measure does not encourage Johnson to invest resources in seeking opportunities to develop new products. In a mature industry such as pulp and paper, innovation may result in long-term financial rewards.

This section has considered how to evaluate performance in decentralized organizations and how to motivate behavior to achieve long-term success. The next section examines how transfer pricing policies can affect decisions made by divisional managers. Often, financially based performance measures encourage managers to optimize divisional earnings, yet harm the overall organization. Thus, transfer pricing and performance measurement issues are of key importance to managers in decentralized organizations.

Case in Point

http://albright. swlearning.com

Learn more about Southwest Airlines.

Balanced Scorecard

Southwest Airlines Co. has developed a variety of balanced scorecards for use throughout the organization. Historically, accountants have understood terms such as "profit and loss," while operations personnel understood terms such as "fast ground turnaround." The company hopes the balanced scorecard will associate rapidly preparing an airplane for its next flight with profitability. Southwest plans to continue collecting hundreds of detailed operational measures; however, the balanced scorecard will be used to display a few of the most important ones. The company wants management to focus on key measurements that impact financial performance.

Source: 2003. Balanced Scorecard. *Computerworld* (February 17).

2 SELF-STUDY PROBLEM

WebTUTOR Advantage

Refer to the financial information presented in Self-Study Problem 1. In addition to the financial statement data, your records indicate that the division employed operating assets valued at $20,000,000.

Required

A. Calculate the division's operating profit margin and describe various ways a manager may improve his or her performance with respect to operating profit margin.
B. Calculate the division's turnover and describe various ways a manager may improve his or her performance with respect to turnover.
C. Calculate the division's ROI.
D. What are some of the criticisms of using ROI as the sole performance measure?
E. Identify other measures that may promote organizational success in the long run.

The solution to Self-Study Problem 2 appears at the end of the chapter.

TRANSFER PRICING

OBJECTIVE 6

Explain how a manager who acts in the best interests of a division may harm the company as a whole.

Transfer pricing **involves setting appropriate selling prices for goods or services when both buyer and seller are within the same company.** Thus, transfer pricing decisions typically arise within multi-divisional organizations. In a decentralized business, managers are free to make many decisions locally. Some of the decisions managers make relate to the acquisition of materials, labor, and overhead to be used in production. When a corporation has many divisions, situations often occur in which one division buys products from another division. Because internal transfer prices affect revenues (for the selling division) and costs (for the buying division), transfer pricing policies affect a division's ROI. Thus, divisional managers are very interested in the price at which goods are transferred internally.

The classical transfer pricing problem involves setting a transfer pricing policy that encourages managers to act in the best interests of the overall organization. Naturally, when *divisional* managers are evaluated by a measure such as ROI, they take actions that produce the highest possible *divisional* ROI. To maximize ROI, what options are available to a manager? Since ROI boils down to operating income ÷ operating assets, the manager has an incentive to increase income or reduce assets (or some combination of the two). For purposes of our discussion, let's focus on the management of operating income. If you are Bill Ferguson, manager of the Pulp Division, you wish to receive the highest possible price for pulp sold to the Paper Division. On the other hand, if you are Karen Johnson, manager of the Paper Division, you maximize ROI by paying the lowest possible price for raw materials (assuming quality is not affected adversely). As a result of divisional competition and performance evaluations exclusively based on ROI, the following scenario is unfolding within American Paper Company.

The Scenario

Karen Johnson, manager of the Paper Division, was unhappy with her division's performance in comparison to that of the Pulp Division (refer to Exhibit 5). Her division purchased all of its raw materials from the Pulp Division at a transfer price of $400 per ton. However, Karen wondered if she could outsource (buy pulp from an outside supplier) at a cost below that quoted by her sister division. Since the divisions were decentralized and had a *market-based* transfer pricing policy, she was free to purchase raw materials from any source. **A *market-based transfer pricing policy* requires buyers and sellers to transfer goods based on externally verifiable market prices.** Thus, bids from outside vendors often are used to establish a market price to serve as a basis for transferring goods.

Karen knew that market prices for pulp had been falling because of worldwide oversupply. Thus, she requested a bid from Southland Pulp Company to determine if the transfer price charged by her sister division was competitive. This morning, a bid of $350 per ton arrived by fax from Southland. The bid specified that to qualify for the reduced price of $350 per ton, the Paper Division must purchase one-half of its annual demand from Southland. Karen quickly made a few computations to determine the potential impact on her division's ROI.

She understood that her division's cost of goods sold ($206,000,000, as shown in Exhibit 5) represented pulp costs as well as other manufacturing costs incurred by her division to convert pulp into paper. She estimated that one-half of the cost of goods sold value, $103,000,000 ($206,000,000 ÷ 2 = $103,000,000), represented pulp costs. The remaining portion of the cost of goods sold value represented labor, electricity, water, chemicals, and overhead costs for depreciation and supervision. Thus, "If our annual pulp cost is $103,000,000 at an average of $400 per ton, we must have used 257,500 ($103,000,000 ÷ $400) tons last year," Karen reasoned. "Southland wants one-half of our volume, or 128,750 tons."

"Wow," Karen said under her breath. "Bill isn't going to like losing the sale of almost 130,000 tons, especially in this slow market."

Karen continued to work with the bid. "Let's see, what's the bottom-line savings if I agree to this deal? Okay, at a savings of $50 per ton ($400 from Bill versus $350 from Southland), that works out to be a total savings of $6,437,500 ($50 per ton × 128,750 tons to be purchased). What does that do for my ROI?" Karen said to herself as she continued to enter values into her calculator.

"Our operating income was $11,000,000, to which we can add an expected savings of $6,437,500. That results in an estimated operating income of $17,437,500. Now, if I divide by operating assets of $200,000,000, I have a predicted ROI of 0.087."

Karen reclined at her desk. The prospects for outsourcing one-half of her pulp requirements looked promising. Assuming that her sales and other expenses remained at a constant level, she could improve the division's ROI from 0.055 to 0.087, a whopping

60 percent improvement [0.58 = (0.087 − 0.055) ÷ 0.055]! Karen did not look forward to announcing her intentions to Bill Ferguson, manager of the Pulp Division.

Bill had been in a bad mood recently because of soft market conditions and a union contract that required a 40-hour work week for each of his three shifts. Because of sluggish demand, each shift required only 30 hours per week in production time. The remaining 10 hours were spent maintaining equipment and making general repairs. Therefore, Bill was watching sales volume fall while most of the division's manufacturing costs continued unchanged. Karen was certain that her decision to outsource one-half of the Paper Division's pulp requirements would send shock waves throughout the corporation.

Karen was correct. Her company subscribed to a "hands-off" policy with regard to letting divisional managers make their own decisions. However, Karen contacted Deborah Truth, a vice president at the corporate office, and revealed her intention of acquiring one-half of her pulp requirements from an external supplier. Karen's phone rang, and Deborah was on the other end of the line requesting a meeting with both divisional managers as soon as possible to discuss their transfer pricing problem.

A few days later, Karen made her way from the airport to the corporate offices. Because her flight had arrived before Bill's, she had a few minutes to review her notes before the meeting. Deborah was the next to enter the conference room, and finally Bill arrived. Following greetings and casual chatter, Deborah began the meeting by referring to the analysis Karen had faxed after receiving the bid from Southland.

"You must admit," Karen began, "a $50 savings per ton can have a dramatic effect on my division's profitability. That represents a 13 percent price reduction. Do you realize how difficult it would be to reduce operating costs by that amount and still maintain the same level of quality?"

Bill could hardly contain himself any longer. "Karen, let's talk about quality. The first time you ship a load of unbleached paper that contains strands of chlorinated fibers, there will be trouble." Bill was referring to "twilight pulp" that is temporarily produced between production runs of bleached and unbleached pulp. This "twilight" mixture is produced until the system cleans out all the chlorine from the pulp mill. Bill's mill has stringent quality control measures to prevent the shipment of mixed, or twilight, pulp.

Karen understood Bill's point. Customers who are environmentally sensitive will not tolerate bleached fibers mixed with environmentally friendly "unbleached" fibers. She certainly had no complaints about the quality she was receiving from Bill.

"And what about reliable delivery?" Bill continued. "In a continuous-process manufacturing environment, such as pulp and paper, you know very well what happens if production interruptions occur. You can't just turn your paper machines on and off like a saw. Remember the studies that show how scrap costs are associated with paper machine downtime? If you start messing around with your process and making late shipments yourself, you'll soon see that 13 percent cost savings evaporate into thin air."

Karen knew that Bill was right. A paper process is complex. Any production interruption introduces instabilities into the process, with undesirable consequences. However, Karen also knew that Bill was suggesting that Southland's quality was poor and their delivery times were unreliable. Admittedly, Karen had never had a problem with quality or on-time delivery from Bill's division.

Bill was on a roll, and he continued his assault against Southland. "Furthermore, I'll bet Southland will give you one contract at that price and later will raise their bid. I think they are bidding below market price so that they can get their foot in the door."

Deborah considered all that had taken place. She knew why Bill was fighting to keep Karen's business. Since Bill had idle capacity (the division could produce more pulp than the market currently required), his production costs per unit were increasing. "Let's try to remember we are all on the same team here," Deborah began. "Bill has made some good points regarding quality, delivery reliability, and cost. We need to work together to make sure that American Paper Company doesn't suffer as a result of decisions that improve divisional performance." Deborah walked to the board at the head of the conference table and wrote the following outline:

OBJECTIVE 7

Discuss various transfer pricing methods that have been developed to influence managerial behavior.

"What do you two remember from your college accounting course about different ways to set up transfer pricing policies?" Deborah asked.

"Not much," admitted Bill. "I memorized some formulas, but beyond that . . ."

"Then, let's reason through these methods and consider the pros and cons of each. Maybe we can find a mutually agreeable solution to our transfer pricing problems," continued Deborah.

"Market-based. That's our existing policy," volunteered Karen. "The market determines the value at which transfers take place. As a buyer, I'm in favor of a market-based approach because it keeps guys like Bill honest."

Karen continued, "I operate a division that sells paper to the outside market at competitive prices. If my costs are too high, I can't compete. Therefore, using a market-based policy throughout the company seems to be a control that forces our internal divisions to be competitive with those outside our company. I'll buy from Bill if he meets the external price. I'd like to keep the business within the company."

Bill walked to the board and scribbled the following numbers:

Variable cost per ton	$110	
Fixed cost per ton	250	
Total cost per ton	$360	Fully absorbed

"Karen," he said, "I recently completed a major capital expansion at my plant. As a result, I estimate that next year my cost structure will look like this. As you can see, if I sell at $350 a ton, I won't even cover my costs. My variable costs include items such as timber, chemicals, water, and electricity; however, the majority of my costs are fixed. These fixed costs include depreciation on my plant equipment and most labor costs. Unfortunately, those costs will be incurred whether the machines are making pulp or not."

Karen looked at the figures. She now understood why Bill was fighting so hard to convince her to reject the Southland bid. If Bill's production volume declined further, the cost of each ton would become larger because his fixed costs would be spread over fewer tons. To cover his higher unit costs, he would have to raise prices. However, raising prices would cause further declines in volume, which in turn would raise his unit costs—definitely not a happy scenario.

Deborah interjected, "Bill, you have moved the discussion to the topic of cost-based transfer pricing policies. Leave your numbers on the board. Some accountants advocate using a cost-based approach," she added. "However, two distinct versions of cost definition emerge, variable and fully absorbed. Variable-cost transfer prices include only variable manufacturing costs, while fully absorbed transfer prices include both variable and fixed manufacturing costs."

Karen spoke quickly, "As a buyer, I'd be in favor of a cost-based approach if cost is defined as variable cost."

Bill retorted, "Sure you would. Your profits would look great because you would leave me holding the bag for all the fixed costs of your raw materials production. I could not pass those along to you. How could you expect me to show a profit under those circumstances?"

Deborah intervened. "Most companies do not use a variable-cost transfer policy for that reason. The buyer's profitability is overstated, and the seller's profitability is understated."

Bill added, "What about using a full-cost approach, one that includes both variable and fixed costs? Admittedly, I would not earn a profit, but at least I could recover my costs. Since sales to Karen represent only a portion of my total sales volume, a breakeven situation would not hurt my division's profitability too badly."

Karen squirmed in her seat. "Bill, remember our discussion about market-based policies. I really don't want to have my profitability affected by your decisions. If your costs increase, a full-cost transfer price permits you simply to pass them along to me. I find that unacceptable."

Deborah interjected, "Perhaps there is room for compromise. The third method for determining transfer prices is through negotiation. Perhaps we can put aside our divisional interests momentarily and look at the problem from the corporate point of view." Deborah returned to the board and wrote the following equation:

> Transfer price = Variable cost + Opportunity cost

"Bill, is this the equation you memorized for your accounting class?" asked Deborah.

"I think so. Somehow it looks familiar," responded Bill.

"Karen, what is the most you would be willing to pay per ton?" Deborah asked.

"I can't see why I should pay more than Southland's bid of $350, all other things being equal," responded Karen.

Deborah wrote $350 on the board with the word "Ceiling" beside it. Next, she turned to Bill. "What is the lowest price you would be willing to accept?"

"Deborah, I've already told you. I need $400 per ton to cover my costs and make a decent profit," responded Bill.

"Let's step back a moment. What is American Paper Company's cost to make a ton of pulp?" asked Deborah.

"Look at the board. It's $360 per ton," responded Bill.

"But, what is our direct out-of-pocket cost?" continued Deborah.

"Are you talking about my variable cost of $110 per ton?" asked Bill.

"Exactly," said Deborah. "You have already told us that your fixed costs are incurred whether you make pulp or not. Thus, let's use your variable cost as a floor, below which you would never consider selling the product." Deborah completed the board, which now looked like this:

> Transfer price = Variable cost + Opportunity cost
> Ceiling $350 Karen's max
> Floor $110 VC

Deborah began the discussion. "Bill, if you could sell every ton you could produce at $400, would you be willing to negotiate with Karen for a lower price?"

"Of course not. Why should I? If I can sell everything I can make at $400 per ton, why should I take less?"

"Let's put your answer into our formula," responded Deborah. "In other words, your 'opportunity cost' of taking a ton off the market and selling it to Karen is the difference between the selling price of $400 and your variable costs of $110, as follows:"

> Selling price $400
> Variable cost   110 — Minimum
> Contribution margin (opportunity cost) $290 OCost

"If we add your variable cost to the opportunity cost, our transfer price formula gives us a value of $400, or the original selling price."

$$\text{Transfer price} = \text{Variable cost} + \text{Opportunity cost}$$
$$\$400 = 110 + 290$$

"That makes sense," replied Bill. " Since I can sell all I can make at $400 per ton, the formula says that if Karen wants some of my tons, she will have to pay $400 for them. Otherwise, I'll sell them to other customers."

"Exactly," responded Deborah.

"But, Bill, aren't you forgetting something?" interjected Karen. "You have excess capacity—you can't sell everything you make. Thus, you are not forgoing profits by selling me a ton of product because you cannot sell that product to someone else. Your opportunity cost is zero when you have excess capacity. According to Deborah's model, if your opportunity cost is zero, the transfer price should be $110, your variable cost. When you have idle capacity, the opportunity cost becomes zero because external sales are not forgone."

Karen walked to the board and plugged new numbers into the equation as follows:

$$\text{Transfer price} = \text{Variable cost} + \text{Opportunity cost}$$
$$\$110 = 110 + 0$$

"Karen, you seem to be suggesting that I sell to you at variable cost. We already dismissed that plan when we discussed cost-based transfer policies."

Deborah once again broke into the conversation. "What do these calculations suggest? From a company-wide viewpoint, what can we learn from our model?"

Bill spoke first. "Since I have excess capacity, the model says that the company is better off if I sell to Karen at a price that at least covers my variable costs. Since my fixed costs are incurred whether I produce or not, they are not relevant to the decision. From the company's perspective, the variable cost to produce pulp is $110; if we purchase it from Southland, the variable cost to the company is $350. Thus, the company would lose $240 per ton."

Karen responded, "So that's what the floor and ceiling represent. The floor represents the minimum acceptable transfer price to the seller, and the ceiling represents the maximum acceptable transfer price to the buyer."

"Exactly," said Deborah.

Bill spoke after a few moments of thought. "Deborah, you've certainly given us a lot to think about. But somehow, I can't help but believe that the problem is not with the transfer pricing policy, but rather with our performance evaluation policies. Everything is tied to divisional profitability and ROI. Who knows how many times decisions are made that may affect corporate profitability in the long run, but in the short run make managers look good on paper."

Deborah agreed. "That sounds like a problem for another day. Think about what we discussed and let me know what you decide. I appreciate the time you took from your busy schedules to meet with me today. Have a safe flight home."

As Karen and Bill left the room, they both knew that corporate management would not permit them to optimize divisional performance at the expense of the overall organization. American Paper was decentralized; however, corporate management had sent a strong signal regarding the outsourcing decision. Both Karen and Bill knew that the transfers would take place internally; however, they had a great deal of work still to do to negotiate a transfer price acceptable to both of them.

Transfer Pricing Summary

Given the preceding exchanges, how can we summarize the key issues with regard to transfer pricing? The exclusive use of financially based performance measures such as ROI and profitability may encourage managers to make decisions that benefit their divisions, but at the same time harm the overall organization. The use of market-based transfer prices helps managers assess their efficiency with respect to external companies producing similar products. Market-based transfer pricing policies rely on external market prices for identical (or comparable) goods or services to establish transfer prices. Cost-based transfer prices are easy to calculate and apply; however, their use can cause problems because inefficiencies may be passed along to subsequent departments. *Cost-based transfer pricing policies* **use either full cost or variable cost as a basis for determining a transfer price.** *Negotiated transfer pricing policies* **permit managers to consider factors such as cost and external market prices when negotiating a mutually acceptable transfer price between two business units.**

LEARNING NOTE

When divisions sell goods exclusively to other divisions within a company, market-based and negotiated transfer pricing policies generally are not used. If a division does not sell to external customers, the division should be evaluated as a cost center, rather than as a profit center, and transfers should take place at standard costs. The division managers' performance would be based on their ability to control costs when compared to standards.

Capacity issues should affect decisions concerning appropriate transfer prices. If a division has excess capacity, a transfer price between the variable cost of the selling division and the outside market price may be negotiated. Theoretically, if a company has excess capacity (thus, zero opportunity cost), it would be worse off if it purchased goods from an external supplier at a purchase price that exceeded the internal variable cost. Exhibit 11 summarizes the key points of each of the major transfer pricing methods.

Case in Point

Transfer Pricing and the IRS

Transfer pricing problems can occur within multi-divisional corporations if divisions buy and sell among themselves. The problems become even more complex if divisions are located in different states or countries. Typically, managers prefer to transfer costs from divisions in states (or countries) having low tax rates into divisions in states (or countries) having higher tax rates. Such a strategy reduces a company's tax payments because subtracting higher costs from revenues results in lower taxable income. Because of adverse tax consequences, tax authorities work diligently to ensure corporations transfer costs appropriately.

Prior to the May 2002 merger of **Compaq Computer Corporation** with **Hewlett-Packard Corporation**, the IRS challenged Compaq's transfer pricing policies in tax court. The IRS believed Compaq was transferring printed circuit assemblies from its Singapore division at inflated prices. As a result, the IRS believed Compaq's cost of goods sold was too high and its taxable income was too low. Fortunately, Compaq also had purchased printed circuit assemblies from external suppliers at prices comparable to the company's internal transfer price. Thus, Compaq could show the transfer price was not overstated, based on market conditions. The IRS lost the case.

Source: Lowell, Cym H. 1999. Compaq: A Rare Taxpayer Victory in a Transfer Pricing Case. *Journal of International Taxation.* Warren Gorham Lamont (October): 10–43.

MANAGEMENT OF DECENTRALIZED SERVICE ORGANIZATIONS

OBJECTIVE 8

Explain how the performance of managers can be evaluated in decentralized service organizations.

In this chapter, a manufacturing company was used to demonstrate issues facing decentralized organizations. However, managers of service organizations face many of the same issues. For example, banks often have branch offices in various locations. Rather than referring all loan applications to a centralized loan committee, branch managers are given authority to make certain types of lending decisions. Thus, a decentralized structure often permits faster processing of loan applications. In addition, local managers

Exhibit 11

Transfer Pricing
Methods

Cost-based
  Strengths: Cost-based transfer pricing methods are easy to apply because standard (or actual) product costs generally are available from the accounting system.
  Weaknesses: Cost-based transfer pricing methods do not encourage and reward efficiency. Often, costs are transferred from one department to the next without concern for the price at which the final product will sell.

Market-based
  Strengths: Market-based transfer pricing methods force departmental managers to be as cost-efficient as the best competitor.
  Weaknesses: Market-based transfer pricing methods require time and effort because external bids must be acquired and evaluated.

Negotiated
  Strengths: Negotiated transfer pricing methods encourage dialogue among division managers. Such conversations may promote transfers internally when they are in the best interest of the overall company. For example, when excess capacity exists, the opportunity cost is zero. Thus, the company will be better off if an internal transfer is made.
  Weaknesses: Negotiated transfer pricing methods take management time and can result in stronger negotiators acquiring better deals. Thus, performance may be affected by negotiating skills rather than by a manager's ability to control costs.

may better understand the risks associated with granting loans if they are familiar with the local economy.

Decentralized service organizations can be made up of cost centers, profit centers, revenue centers, and investment centers. For example, branch banks often are evaluated as profit centers. The performance of bank branch managers is evaluated using a number of criteria. For instance, they are responsible for generating profits by charging more interest on money loaned to their customers than they pay to depositors. In addition, they are responsible for increasing the amounts of deposits and loans at their branch. Thus, two common performance measures within the banking industry are (1) yield (a measure of loan profitability) and (2) loan growth (the rate by which a manager increases the dollar value of loans outstanding). Analogies in manufacturing organizations include ROI and sales growth. While this example illustrates financial measures of performance, service organizations also may use a balanced scorecard approach to evaluate performance. In addition to performance evaluation issues, managers in service industries face other challenges often associated with manufacturing companies.

LEARNING NOTE

Both service and manufacturing companies make special pricing decisions to attract customers who would otherwise buy goods or services from competitors. When negotiating special pricing arrangements, a manager must understand which costs are relevant and which costs are not relevant. Costs that change between alternatives typically are considered relevant to special pricing decisions. For example, pricing that covers variable costs of materials, labor, overhead, and special handling expenses will benefit the company in the short run. However, many academics warn against the long-term consequences of continuously basing prices on variable rather than full (variable + fixed) costs. Though special sales may appear profitable in the short term, all costs of production must be recovered in the long term if the company is to survive.

In a manufacturing organization, transfers between divisions occur when one division buys goods from another division. Transfer pricing is a major issue in banking also. For example, to meet legal requirements aimed at protecting depositors and other interested parties, banks must maintain a certain ratio of loans to deposits. A loan-to-deposit ratio of 65 percent means that a bank has loaned 65 cents for every dollar it holds in deposits. Assume that an aggressive branch manager has exceeded the maximum loan-to-deposit ratio, while another branch manager (within the same banking corporation) has not. Corporate management would transfer funds from the branch with excess funds to the branch exceeding the limit. The funds transfer would involve "interest charges" to the borrowing bank and "interest revenues" to the lending bank. The interest rate selected for the transfer is similar to the transfer price in a manufacturing organization. Many options exist for determining the interest charge, or transfer price. For example, the interest charge could be based on the corporation's average cost of funds, or perhaps on the highest rate paid on deposits. Thus, like manufacturing organizations, banks transfer goods and services among divisions and must determine an acceptable price for the transaction.

This chapter has shown that manufacturing and service organizations may use a decentralized organizational structure. The banking example illustrates the way service organizations face many of the same challenges as manufacturing organizations face. Managers of service organizations must find ways to be responsive to a changing environment, evaluate performance using a variety of indicators, and determine the cost of resources transferred among divisions.

3 SELF-STUDY PROBLEM

WebTUTOR Advantage

Refer to the financial data presented in Self-Study Problem 1. The financial statements represent the operations of your division during the past 12 months. Assume that you are a divisional manager who purchases raw materials from other divisions within the company. Your company has a market-based transfer pricing policy. Thus, managers commonly seek transfer prices consistent with bids submitted by outside companies.

Before entering into price negotiations to purchase raw materials from the manager of Division B, you wish to understand Division B's cost structure and other factors that may affect the negotiations.

Required Respond to the following questions.

A. You estimate that 25% of the materials used by your division was purchased from Division B. Assuming that your division's total cost of materials was $40,000,000, what was the cost of materials purchased from Division B?

B. If the selling division (Division B) typically earns a 20% gross margin [(sales − cost of goods sold) ÷ sales], what was Division B's cost of goods sold?

C. You recall from past meetings that Division B is very capital intensive (they use expensive equipment, whose costs are fixed in the short run). Their variable costs are 30% of total manufacturing costs, while fixed costs make up the remaining 70%. Using the transfer pricing equation, transfer price = variable cost + opportunity cost, calculate the minimum acceptable transfer price (from the seller's perspective). Assume that Division B is operating at full capacity.

D. Should the manager of Division B consider negotiating a lower transfer price if the division is not operating at capacity? Explain.

The solution to Self-Study Problem 3 appears at the end of the chapter.

REVIEW

SUMMARY of IMPORTANT CONCEPTS

1. Managers use accounting information to make marketing and operation decisions.
    a. Managers (agents) are hired by owners to make decisions consistent with the owners' interests.
    b. Compensation packages are designed to encourage managers to maximize company value.

2. A responsibility center is defined as any business unit or segment over which managers have control and managerial authority.
    a. Cost center managers are evaluated on their ability to control costs.
    b. Revenue center managers are responsible for generating sales or revenues.
    c. Profit center managers are responsible for both costs and revenues.
    d. Investment center managers are held accountable for costs, revenues, profits, and efficient asset use.

3. Managerial performance is often evaluated using ROI and economic value added.
   a. Return on investment (ROI) is made up of two elements, margin and turnover.
   b. Margin is defined as operating income ÷ sales.
   c. Turnover is defined as sales ÷ operating assets.
   d. The use of ROI for performance evaluation encourages managers to maximize operating income while at the same time minimizing the level of assets employed.
   e. Economic value added is calculated by subtracting the cost of invested capital from operating income.
   f. Economic value added motivates managers to invest in projects that produce a return above the cost of invested capital.

4. Performance evaluation using the balanced scorecard includes four sets of measures:
   a. Financial: How do we look to shareholders?
   b. Customer satisfaction: How do customers see us?
   c. Learning and growth: How may we continue to improve and create value?
   d. Internal business: At what must we excel?

5. A number of transfer pricing issues can arise in organizations.
   a. Transfer pricing issues typically occur in decentralized organizations.
   b. Financially based evaluation programs often encourage managers to act in the best interests of their own division, rather than the best interests of the company as a whole.
   c. Typically, three methods are used for determining transfer prices among business units:
      (1) Cost-based transfer pricing policies use either full cost or variable cost as a basis for determining transfer prices.
      (2) Market-based transfer pricing policies rely on external market prices for identical (or comparable) goods or services to establish transfer prices.
      (3) Negotiated transfer pricing policies permit managers to consider factors such as cost and external market prices when negotiating a mutually acceptable transfer price between two business units.

6. Many of the same issues arise in service organizations.
   a. Service organizations often are decentralized and face many of the same challenges as manufacturing companies.
   b. Managers of decentralized service organizations must develop financial (and nonfinancial) measures with which to evaluate performance.
   c. Transfer pricing policies are important to decentralized service organizations because services are transferred among divisions.

DEFINE

TERMS and CONCEPTS DEFINED in this CHAPTER

agents (M291)
balanced scorecard (M301)
cost center (M291)
cost-based transfer pricing policy (M309)
investment center (M292)
margin (M295)
market-based transfer pricing policy (M304)
negotiated transfer pricing policy (M309)

operating assets (M296)
operating income (M296)
profit center (M292)
return on investment (ROI) (M295)
revenue center (M291)
transfer pricing (M303)
turnover (M295)

SELF-STUDY PROBLEM SOLUTIONS

SSP10-1   A. A plant manager typically is responsible for controlling materials, labor, and overhead costs within the plant. These costs are included in the cost of goods manufactured as shown on the cost of goods sold schedule. Some of the overhead costs appear to be allocated from the corporate level and are not directly controllable by you, such as the cost of corporate computer time used for production scheduling. The income statement also includes corporate cost allocations over which a plant manager has no control, such as depreciation on corporate aircraft (used by the senior-level executives). Finally, as plant manager, you have no control over sales commissions and expenses.

B. The scenario presented suggests that the plant manager determines neither product mix nor selling prices. Thus, to evaluate the plant manager on his or her ability to generate income is not consistent with the principles of performance evaluation. This manager should be evaluated on his or her ability to manage costs, meet production schedules, and achieve quality specifications. Thus, the plant in our example should be evaluated as a cost center rather than a profit center.

Senior-level managers may evaluate a plant's ability to contribute to corporate income. An analysis based on income is appropriate at higher levels because higher-level managers make product mix and pricing decisions. However, the plant manager in our example is not responsible for decisions such as these.

SSP10-2   A. Margin = Operating income ÷ Sales
= \$1,000,000   ÷ \$100,000,000
= 0.01

Managers may consider ways to reduce direct materials, direct labor, manufacturing overhead, and other general or administrative costs. Such actions would increase operating income, assuming no changes in sales volume.

Another approach involves raising prices to generate more operating income per sales dollar. Managers must be careful when raising prices because both sales volume and operating income could decline, resulting in a lower profit margin.

B. Turnover = Sales   ÷ Operating assets
= \$100,000,000 ÷ \$20,000,000
= 5

Turnover motivates managers to create lean organizations by producing greater sales volume while simultaneously employing fewer operating assets. Thus, turnover can be improved by

1. increasing sales while maintaining the same level of operating assets,
2. reducing operating assets while maintaining the same level of sales, or
3. increasing sales and reducing the level of operating assets.

Strategies to reduce assets may include (1) collecting on accounts receivable and submitting excess cash to corporate management, (2) reducing inventory levels, and (3) eliminating unnecessary equipment that creates excess capacity.

C. Margin × Turnover = ROI
0.01   ×   5   = 0.05

D. Focusing exclusively on financial measures of performance may encourage managers to sacrifice long-term success for short-term gains. For example, managers may cut back on research and development expenditures, quality programs, and preventive maintenance in order to improve short-term performance.

E. The balanced scorecard identifies four classes of performance measures: financial, customer, learning and growth, and internal business. Financial measures may include ROI or market share. Customer measures may include percentage of on-time deliveries or external failure rate (percentage of products delivered that are defective). Innovation and learning measures may include such things as the number of technological innovations. Internal business measures may include such things as scrap rates.

SSP10-3   A. \$40,000,000 cost of materials × 0.25 = \$10,000,000.

B. First, let's establish the relationship among sales, cost of goods sold, and gross margin as follows:

Sales − Cost of goods sold   = Gross margin
Gross margin = 0.20 × \$10,000,000 = \$2,000,000

Selling price	\$10,000,000	100%
(less) Gross margin	(2,000,000)	20%*
Cost of goods sold	\$ 8,000,000	80%

$$* \frac{\$10,000,000 - \$8,000,000}{\$10,000,000} = 20\%$$

Therefore, it cost Division B $8,000,000 to produce the goods it sold to your division.

C.

Variable cost 0.3 × $8,000,000 = $2,400,000
Fixed cost　　0.7 × $8,000,000 = ___5,600,000

　Total cost　　　　　　　　　　$8,000,000

Opportunity cost = Sales　　　 − Variable cost
$7,600,000　　 = $10,000,000　− $2,400,000

Transfer price　　 = Variable cost + Opportunity cost
$10,000,000　　= $2,400,000　 + $7,600,000

Thus, the manager of Division B would have no incentive to reduce the selling price from $10,000,000 because all units could be sold to external buyers at a price of $10,000,000. Therefore, negotiations could be difficult.

D. Theoretically, the manager of Division B should be willing to make price concessions if the division has idle capacity. The transfer pricing formula suggests that if excess capacity exists, managers may consider prices that are sufficient to cover the variable costs of production as follows:

Transfer price = Variable cost + Opportunity cost
$2,400,000　 = $2,400,000　 + 0

When a division has idle capacity, the opportunity cost becomes zero because external sales are not forgone.

Thinking Beyond the Question

How do we set up meaningful performance measures?

Seth and Erin understand the importance of communicating goals and objectives throughout their organization. Also, they believe relevant, verifiable performance measures should be used to motivate decisions consistent with these goals and objectives. Why should they consider using both financial and nonfinancial measures as part of a balanced scorecard?

QUESTIONS

Q10-1　Heather Stone is a production manager for Bohemia Company. Her father, Alex, is a share-
Obj. 1　holder of the company but does not work for Bohemia. Which of the Stones would be considered an agent for Bohemia? What role does an agent play in an organization?

Q10-2　Tenco Company manufactures high-quality playground equipment. There are several plants
Obj. 2　within Tenco. Plant A produces plastic slides and swings that are used in manufacturing at Plant B. What type of responsibility center is Plant A? Explain your answer.

Q10-3　Assume that the performance of the plant manager at Tenco's Plant A, discussed in Q10-2, is
Obj. 2　being evaluated by the vice president of operations at Tenco's headquarters. What performance objectives are most likely to be used to evaluate the manager's performance?

Q10-4
Obj. 2
Granite Industries is a multi-divisional corporation in which each division operates autonomously. Division A is considered an investment center of Granite. Given this, would you expect the divisional manager of Division A to be able to make decisions regarding the acquisition of new machinery and equipment necessary to conduct divisional business? Explain your answer.

Q10-5
Obj. 2
Logistics, Inc., is a decentralized company with branch operations in 15 of the largest metropolitan areas of the United States. Each division is operated as a separate profit center, and there is a corporate vice president in charge at each location. The company has a decentralized decision-making philosophy by which the vice president at each location is empowered to make the necessary decisions to operate the profit center. What benefits would be realized from the decentralized decision-making philosophy at Logistics? What sort of localized decisions would the profit center managers be expected to make?

Q10-6
Obj. 2
Leslie Greenwood is a plant manager for Ambrose Manufacturing. Leslie's plant is operated and evaluated as a profit center. Leslie has reviewed the plant's sales and costs for the last 12 months in preparation for her annual review. She has noticed that while margins and the cost of goods manufactured have improved over the last year, overall profitability has declined as a result of increased corporate cost allocations. The corporate controller has told Leslie that the cost allocations relate mainly to insurance, interest, and data processing costs, which have increased significantly over the prior-year levels. What arguments should Leslie be prepared to make when her performance is evaluated?

Q10-7
Obj. 3
Assume that two different companies, Company A and Company B, have earned net income of $10 million and $1 million, respectively, over the same fiscal period. Would it be fair to say that Company A earned a higher ROI than Company B?

Q10-8
Obj. 4
The manager of Zelta Corporation's southeast region, Art McCormick, must improve the investment center's margin in order to achieve the performance goals established for his segment of the company. A 5% increase in sales price would achieve the desired margin. After meeting with the sales and marketing staff, however, Art is sure that an increase in sales price would result in a loss of sales and that target income would not be achieved, even though margins would increase. If sales prices cannot be increased, how can Art attain the desired margins?

Q10-9
Obj. 4
Elmer Woods is a plant manager for Lima Corporation, a producer of paints and solvents. Elmer's performance evaluation, and his bonus compensation, is based in part on his plant's turnover ratio. Elmer wants to increase the turnover ratio in order to maximize his bonus. What are the two elements of turnover, and how would they need to change in order to increase Elmer's turnover ratio?

Q10-10
Objs. 4, 5
The board of directors at Mays Company calculates the company president's performance based strictly on the turnover ratio. The denominator for the calculation is cash, accounts receivables, inventory, and fixed assets. The company has been engaged in a plant revitalization project over the past two years and has added or upgraded many of the fixed assets. How will these changes in fixed assets affect the president's performance evaluation assuming sales do not increase? Do you agree with the method the board uses to evaluate the president? Why or why not?

Q10-11
Obj. 6
Lana Martinez is a divisional manager with Power Source, Inc. Over the last several years, Lana has trimmed equipment maintenance costs in an effort to improve her division's operating income and improve financial performance measures. What effect, if any, will such a move have on the long-term profitability of the division?

Q10-12
Obj. 7
For establishing transfer prices between divisions of a company, what alternative is there to using current market prices or a cost-based formula? What are the strengths and weaknesses of such an approach?

EXERCISES

If your instructor is using Personal Trainer® in this course, you may complete your assignments online.

E10-1
Write a short definition of each of the terms listed in the *Terms and Concepts Defined in this Chapter* section.

E10-2
Obj. 1
Listed below are a number of actions that could be taken by managers within the context of an owner/agent relationship. For each decision, determine whether an agent's actions are

(Continued)

consistent with the best interests of owners who hired them. For each situation in which managers appear to act in their own interests, identify the economic benefits received.

- Currently, the company cannot produce enough goods to meet demand. Managers acquire additional assets to expand production.
- The marketing vice president authorized funds to remodel marketing department office space. He justified the lavish furnishings as a necessary investment to ensure the company projects a successful image.
- Managers hired additional research scientists to ensure the company's products remain technologically competitive in the future.
- Soon after the new vice president of finance arrived, she implemented plans to improve the company's visibility in the financial community. As such, the new vice president often was seen at the country club shooting 18 holes with community bankers.
- The production manager will receive a bonus if the quality and quantity of products manufactured during the quarter exceed targets by a certain percentage. The production manager understands the production processes better than higher-level managers and sets the targets at easily attainable levels.

E10-3
Obj. 2

The organizational structure of a decentralized organization often contains four levels, as follows:

Organizational level
Cost center
Revenue center
Profit center
Investment center

Match the correct definition below with the appropriate organizational level.

Definition
- A level within an organization that has the strategic responsibility for generating profits and managing assets
- A level of an organization that has responsibility for generating sales
- A level of an organization that consumes resources while performing its responsibilities yet has no direct involvement in generating sales or acquiring property
- A level of an organization that is responsible for both generating sales and controlling costs and expenses

E10-4
Obj. 2

Following are a variety of performance measures used to evaluate responsibility centers in decentralized organizations. For each performance measure, identify the organizational level for which the measure would be appropriate. Explain your reasoning.

- Manufacturing costs
- ROI
- Quality
- Profitability
- Percentage of on-time deliveries
- Successful new product introductions
- Market share
- Inventory turnover

E10-5
Obj. 2

The following are independent situations.

1. LonnMark, Inc., operates a *satellite plant* that produces components for many of the company's products. The plant is operated by a plant manager, who coordinates scheduling and material acquisition with the company's home office. The plant manager also is directly responsible for a labor force consisting of 350 employees. This manager controls overhead but may not add any equipment without home office approval.
2. A nationally known soft drink company acquires a *coal mining company*. The decision to acquire the mining operation is strategic and is based on anticipated growth in the industry. The mining operation is run by a local management group independent of soft drink management.

3. Black and Runyan, Inc., of Chicago, owns a grain elevator and storage facility in rural Iowa. The *grain facility* is run by Dave Bailey. Dave and 22 other grain facility operators report to the senior vice president of operations, located in Chicago. Dave has day-to-day control in running the Iowa facility and routinely buys and sells grain.

4. Sandra Falls is the California senior account representative for a national copier manufacturer. Sandra has overall responsibility for the 12 *showrooms* located in the state. Each showroom employs approximately six sales representatives. Sandra's representatives sell copiers, but maintenance on the copiers is provided by certified subcontractors who are coordinated through the national headquarters.

Categorize each of the organizations listed in italics as either a cost center, profit center, revenue center, or investment center. Briefly justify your answers.

E10-6

Obj. 3

In 1903, the du Pont cousins acquired the assets of **E.I. Du Pont de Nemours and Company** in exchange for bonds. In the language of today, the cousins conducted a leveraged buyout of the company. Explain why a measurement such as ROI was needed to help ensure financial survival of the new company. If the bond interest rate was 4%, explain how ROI might be used by the du Ponts to evaluate financial performance on existing assets and to consider additional investment opportunities.

E10-7

Obj. 4

LaKeesha Roberts is a successful division manager for Textron Industries. Her division's ROI currently is 22%. Roberts is evaluating a plant expansion opportunity that is expected to produce an annual income of $500,000 and require an investment of $3,000,000. The corporation's cost of capital is 12%.

a. If Roberts' performance is based on ROI, will she be inclined to make the investment? Explain.

b. Calculate the residual income for the proposed investment.

c. If Roberts' performance is based on residual income, will she be inclined to make the investment? Explain.

d. Would corporate management encourage Roberts to make the investment? Explain

E10-8

Obj. 4

The following information for the past two years relates to a division of Wheel Company:

	2006	2007
Sales	$31,000,000	$39,000,000
Net operating income	2,700,000	2,900,000
Average operating assets	55,000,000	55,000,000

a. Compute the return on investment for both years.

b. Compute the margin and turnover ratio for each year.

c. Explain why the return on investment increased from 2006 to 2007 despite a lower margin in 2007.

E10-9

Obj. 4

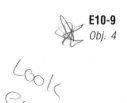

Look exam

	Company 1	Company 2	Company 3	Company 4
Sales revenue	$10,000	$20,000	$148,000	?
Expenses	7,000	?	126,000	?
Net income	3,000	7,000	?	?
Average assets	20,000	25,000	65,000	$120,000
Margin	?	40%	?	7%
Turnover	?	0̸.8 0.7	?	2
ROI	?	?	?	?

Calculate the missing information for each of the four companies. Treat each company independently.

E10-10

Obj. 5

One attribute of the balanced scorecard approach lies in performance measure diversity. For each scorecard category, identify appropriate performance measures from the following list:

(Continued)

Scorecard category	Performance measures
Financial	ROI
Internal business processes	Lead time
Learning and growth	On-time delivery
Customer satisfaction	Cash flow
	Manufacturing lead time
	Sales dollars per square feet of retail space
	Percentage of sales from new products

E10-11 ROI is computed by multiplying a margin times turnover as follows:

Objs. 4, 5

$$\frac{\text{Operating income}}{\text{Sales}} \times \frac{\text{Sales}}{\text{Operating assets}}$$

The ROI measure is intended to motivate managers to make their divisions lean, efficient, and profitable. However, the exclusive use of ROI may motivate short-sighted decision making.

a. Provide two examples of how the margin component of ROI may be managed for short-term benefit with long-run consequences.
b. Provide two examples of how the turnover component of ROI may be managed for short-term benefit with long-run consequences.
c. How does the balanced scorecard approach reduce the incentive for managers to focus on activities that result in short-term benefits and long-term consequences?

E10-12 Following are a variety of performance measures that could be used with the balanced score-
Obj. 5 card approach. Classify each measure as financial, internal business processes, customer satisfaction, or learning and growth. Justify your answer.

Customer loyalty	Defect rate
Net income	Material yield
Cycle time	Percentage of employees that participate in
Sales growth	annual training seminars
Employee retention and satisfaction	Market share

E10-13 Tide Company has two divisions, Division A and Division B. Division A currently sells com-
Obj. 6 ponents to Division B for $10 per unit. The cost of Division A to produce a component follows:

Variable cost per unit	$5
Fixed cost per unit	$2 (based on 100,000 units)

Division A typically sells 40,000 components to Division B and 40,000 components to external customers. The manager of Division B is considering buying components from an outside supplier that submitted a bid of $8.

a. Calculate the cost savings to Division B if the manager decides to purchase the component externally.
b. Assume Division A cannot replace lost sales in the short run if Division B purchases components externally. How does the fixed cost per unit change?
c. From the perspective of the corporation as a whole, should Division B purchase the components externally? Explain.
d. What other factors should Division B's management consider in its decision of whether to buy from an outside source?

E10-14 Java-Time Coffee Company is organized into two divisions. Division A roasts, blends, and
Obj. 6 packages gourmet coffees for sale to specialty shops and coffee bars. Division B designs and produces packaging materials for Division A as well as for external customers. The cost of producing a pound of Java-Time specialty coffee is $3.50, including the transfer price of $0.50 for the packaging materials. The cost to Division B to design and produce packaging materials is $0.35.

The manager of Division A has acquired a bid from an external producer that would reduce the cost of packaging materials by 20%. The reduced purchase price would significantly improve Division A's ROI.

What is motivating the manager of Division A to buy packaging materials from an outside supplier? Why might corporate-level managers at Java-Time Coffee Company encourage the manager of Division A to continue purchasing the packaging materials from Division B? Explain.

E10-15

Obj. 7

SportCo, Inc., is a multi-divisional company that produces and sells athletic equipment. Division 1 produces components for a variety of products, while Division 2 assembles the components and packages the finished product. Both divisions are free to buy and sell internally or externally. For a particular soccer ball, the cost structure within Division 1 and market price are as follows:

Variable cost	$ 4
Fixed cost	2
Market price	10

Depreciation, FMOH   VC

CM/OC = 6 + 4 = 10

a. Assuming Division 1 *is not* operating at capacity, calculate the minimum acceptable transfer price.
b. Assuming Division 1 *is* operating at capacity, calculate the transfer price.
c. Explain why capacity is a factor in the transfer pricing decision.

E10-16

Obj. 7

For each transfer pricing method identified, match the appropriate strength and weakness.

Transfer pricing method
a. Cost-based
b. Market-based
c. Negotiated

Strength or weakness
1. Easy to apply
2. Takes management time to help settle disputes
3. Requires time and effort because external bids must be obtained and evaluated
4. Performance may be affected by negotiating skills rather than by a manager's ability to control costs
5. Does not encourage and reward efficiency
6. Forces managers to be as cost-efficient as the best competitor
7. Encourages dialogue among division managers

E10-17

Obj. 7

Tandem Manufacturing transfers a product between two plants. The product has variable costs of $65 per unit and fixed overhead costs of $25 per unit. This product can be purchased from an outside source with acceptable levels of quality and quantity at $83 per unit. Assuming Tandem has excess production capacity for this product, what would be the acceptable ceiling and floor transfer pricing amounts for the product?

E10-18

Obj. 7

The Frame Division of Reliable Computers manufactures storage housings for personal and midsize computers, which it sells externally to computer manufacturers. The division is operating at full capacity. One of the most popular housings has variable costs of $34 and is sold to outside customers at $52 per unit. These housings also are needed by the Component Division of Reliable, which produces a line of small business computers. The Frame Division can sell all of its production to outside customers at $52 or can transfer a significant amount of its production to the Component Division. At what cost should the Frame Division transfer production? Why?

E10-19

Obj. 7

Transfer pricing terminology includes the concepts of floor and ceiling, representing the seller's minimum acceptable price and buyer's maximum acceptable price, respectively. The following data are presented from transfer pricing negotiations among managers at Douglas Company:

Ceiling	$550
Floor	315

(Continued)

a. What is the market price of the product?
b. What is the variable cost of the product?
c. Calculate the contribution margin.
d. Calculate the opportunity cost if the selling division is not at capacity.
e. Calculate the opportunity cost if the selling division is at capacity.

E10-20   Decentralized service organizations may be classified into a variety of responsibility centers

Obj. 8   including cost centers, profit centers, and investment centers. Following are a variety of responsibility centers from a national public accounting firm.

1. Managers and partners within the firm have the responsibility of managing the audit engagement and signing the audit opinion that is presented with a client's annual report. In addition, they are responsible for practice development activities, including bidding for audits and expanding professional services.
2. Lower-level accountants and their supervisors have the primary responsibility for conducting the work (audit tests) associated with the annual audit.
3. Managing partners at regional offices make decisions about expanding the firm by opening offices in new cities or by acquiring smaller firms.

Classify each responsibility center as a cost center, profit center, or investment center as appropriate. Justify your answer. How do you think the components of ROI would differ between a public accounting firm and a steel manufacturing company? Explain.

E10-21   Soldwell Bankers operates a national chain of realty offices. While some activities are con-

Obj. 8   ducted centrally, others are conducted on a decentralized basis. The following activities were conducted by Soldwell during December. Identify the activities that would be performed most efficiently on a centralized basis. Then, identify the activities that would be performed most efficiently on a decentralized basis. Explain your reasoning.

- A client, currently located in San Jose, California, is relocating to Atlanta, Georgia. Managers at Soldwell contacted the office manager in Atlanta and managed the client introduction.
- After discussions with a realtor, the client received neighborhood locator sheets with photographs and price listings.
- The client was taken on a real estate tour to view property.
- Realtors were present at the closing when all legal documents completing the real estate purchase were signed.
- A public accounting firm was hired to conduct the annual audit.
- Soldwell managers contracted with a national advertising agency to develop a television advertising campaign.
- The Atlanta office hired 20 new realtors.
- Soldwell modified its commission policy on a national basis.

PROBLEMS

If your instructor is using Personal Trainer® in this course, you may complete your assignments online.

P10-1   ### Compensation Strategies in the Owner/Agent Relationship

Obj. 1   As discussed in this chapter, managers are hired as agents to make decisions in the best interests of the owners. Often, employment contracts are put into place to help align the goals of managers and owners. For example, **Nike, Inc.** has implemented a variety of conditions within its executive compensation package. Below is an excerpt from DEF 14 A 1999 - 09 - 22 (the proxy statement) that Nike, Inc. filed with the Securities and Exchange Commission.

(1) The Compensation Plan Subcommittee established a series of performance targets based on fiscal 2000 and 2001 revenues and earnings per share corresponding to award payouts ranging from 10% to 150% of the target awards. Participants would have been entitled to a payout at the highest percentage level at which both performance targets are met, subject to the Committee's discretion to reduce or eliminate any award based on Company or individual performance. Under the terms of the awards, on August 15, 2000 and 2001 the Company would issue in the name of each participant a number of shares of Class B Stock with a value equal to the award payout based on the closing price of the Class B Stock on that date on the

New York Stock Exchange. The shares would be restricted for three years thereafter and subject to forfeiture to the Company if the participant ceases to be an employee of the Company for any reason during such three-year period.

Required Identify the types of incentive packages used by Nike stockholders to align the goals of management with theirs.

P10-2 Organizational Structure and Performance Evaluation

Objs. 2, 4

Timberline Corporation is a multi-divisional manufacturing company. Each of the two division managers has responsibility for sales, costs, and profitability. Division 1 has three manufacturing plants, while Division 2 has four plants that produce a variety of products as requested by the divisional marketing department. The divisional marketing department is responsible for setting prices, determining product mix, managing advertising, and meeting income projections. The division manager is responsible for coordinating production and marketing activities across the various levels within the division. Sales and operating data for each division are as follows:

	Division 1	Division 2
Sales	$10,000,000	$6,000,000
Cost of goods sold	6,000,000	4,200,000
Gross margin	$ 4,000,000	$1,800,000
Operating expenses	3,500,000	1,000,000
Operating income	$ 500,000	$ 800,000
Average assets	$ 8,000,000	$7,000,000

Required

A. Construct an organization chart that illustrates the various levels of responsibility within Timberline.
B. Classify each level according to the responsibility centers identified in this chapter.
C. Identify appropriate performance measures for each level of responsibility. Justify your answer.
D. Calculate ROI for the two divisions. Evaluate the results of your calculation.

P10-3 Responsibility Centers and Relevant Costs for Performance

Obj. 2 **Evaluation**

Darius Taylor, manager of the Industrial Products Division, was preparing for his annual performance evaluation. Though Darius has been successful in generating sales growth and controlling manufacturing costs, he has not achieved his income target for the year. Financial information for his division is as follows:

Industrial Products Division Statement of Income For the Year Ended 2006		
Sales	$18,500,000	
Cost of goods sold	10,000,000	
Gross margin		$8,500,000
General selling and administrative expenses:		
Advertising	$ 450,000	
Salaries	1,000,000	
Depreciation	2,000,000	
Insurance	600,000	
Other	900,000	
Total		4,950,000
Net income		$3,550,000

(Continued)

Industrial Products Division
Statement of Income
For the Year Ended 2007

Sales	$21,500,000	
Cost of goods sold	10,965,000	
Gross margin		$10,535,000
General selling and administrative expenses:		
Advertising	$ 760,000	
Salaries	1,900,000	
Allocation of corporate administrative overhead	1,500,000	
Depreciation	2,700,000	
Insurance	600,000	
Other	800,000	
Total		8,260,000
Net income		$ 2,275,000

Required

A. What type of responsibility center does Darius manage?
B. Identify the appropriate measures for the type of responsibility center identified in requirement (A). Explain your reasoning.
C. Prepare a revised income statement that more accurately reflects Darius' division performance. If you were Darius, what points would you make during your performance evaluation? Explain.

P10-4   The Use of ROI and Its Effect on Management Decision Making

Obj. 4

As discussed in this chapter, the use of ROI by managers can create incentives for managers to make short-term decisions that have negative effects on long-term performance. However, ROI, if used properly, can also encourage managers to utilize assets effectively to produce higher returns for investors.

Required

A. Write the ROI formula, breaking it down into its components as follows:

Margin: Operating income ÷ Sales
Turnover: Sales ÷ Average operating assets

For the numerator and denominator of each component, identify actions that may improve ROI in the short term but may harm the company in the long run.
B. Explain why managers often are under pressure to make short-term decisions that may have adverse long-term consequences.

P10-5   Enhancing Return on Investments: Ethical Considerations

Obj. 4

Carter Consumer Products has three operating divisions, which are appropriately treated as investment centers. Each of the investment centers is run by a divisional manager. The managers are evaluated on the basis of ROI performance. Those managers with the best ROI figures are most likely to be promoted to higher-level corporate positions. Edwin Jones is one of the divisional managers for Carter. He is an ambitious person who desperately wants a promotion to headquarters. The investment center for which Edwin is responsible manufactures a line of patio furniture. This investment center has two plants, which employ over 500 workers. Operating results for each of the plants and for the division in total for the most recent year are as follows:

	Total	Plant A	Plant B
Revenues	$180,000	$120,000	$60,000
Expenses	$150,000	$100,000	$50,000
Net income	$25,000	$15,000	$10,000
Average operating assets	$170,000	$110,000	$60,000

Carter's cost of capital is 11%. Sales, marketing, and production managers who work for Edwin have proposed adding production capabilities for the manufacture of picnic table umbrellas. They have compiled figures that show that the estimated cost of the assets needed to produce an umbrella line is $120,000. They further estimate that the umbrella line would increase net income by $15,000 a year. After careful consideration, Edwin rejected the idea and added, "This is no time to add to our production facilities. In fact, I've been thinking of closing Plant B and moving its production to Plant A."

Required

A. What is the most likely reason why Edwin turned down the proposal to produce umbrellas?

B. Would the company as a whole be better off by producing the umbrellas? Explain your answer. Using the economic value added (residual income) approach, provide computations to support your reasoning.

C. Why do you believe Edwin has suggested closing Plant B? How does ROI as a performance measure adversely affect the company in total?

P10-6 Segment Reporting and Analysis

Obj. 4

The following is Tennis Today's financial statement for the year ending December 31, 2006, in total and by division:

	Total	Division A	Division B
Assets:			
Cash	$ 46,000	$ 10,000	$ 36,000
Accounts receivable	89,000	37,000	52,000
Inventory	198,000	72,000	126,000
Fixed assets	1,850,000	900,000	950,000
Total	$2,183,000	$1,019,000	$1,164,000
Liabilities:			
Accounts payable	$ 65,000	$ 28,000	$ 37,000
Bank debt	1,620,000	800,000	820,000
Total	$1,685,000	$ 828,000	$ 857,000
Stockholders' equity	498,000		
Total liabilities and equity	$2,183,000		
Revenues	$1,500,000	$ 500,000	$1,000,000
Expenses	1,150,000	300,000	850,000
Net income	$ 350,000	$ 200,000	$ 150,000

Required

A. If the stockholders own shares of the company in total, and not in the individual divisions, how can the divisional managers' performance be evaluated in terms of building stockholder wealth?

B. From an ROI perspective, which of the two divisions has shown better performance? (Assume that ending assets reflect average operating assets for the year.)

P10-7 Scorecard Development: The Customer Perspective

Obj. 5

An internationally known electric guitar manufacturer produces its legendary instruments from a variety of purchased components. Suppliers are held accountable for strict quality standards. To ensure proper sound quality, meeting engineering tolerances is crucial. In addition, the guitar company does not carry a large parts inventory. Therefore, suppliers make small deliveries multiple times each week. A late or defective shipment would result in a major disruption of the production line.

Assume you are a manager for the company that supplies electrical pickups used in producing the instruments. Recently you have been assigned to design a balanced scorecard for your company. Currently, you and a group of team members are working on the customer aspect of the scorecard.

(Continued)

Required Using your knowledge of the balanced scorecard, develop performance indicators for the customer perspective. Consider the appropriate number of measures as well as the types of measures the company should include. Justify your answer.

P10-8 Balanced Scorecard Approach to Performance Evaluation

Obj. 5

Carol Rolfson is a divisional manager for Klinger Products. Carol operates a division that manufactures clocks and timepieces that are distributed through retail stores. Over the past year, Carol's division recorded the highest net income in the division's history. Internal records indicate that customer returns have declined significantly as a result of the division's improved quality. Many of the improvements were generated as a result of a vigorous program of enhanced technology in which most of the division's equipment was replaced or updated over the last 18 months.

Carol has noticed a change in morale as a result of the plant improvements. Employees have become more interested in their work and have suggested additional improvements to the production process. One of the suggestions led to a new product that has shown strong sales potential. The improved processes have also resulted in lower scrap rates and more timely shipments.

As a divisional manager, Carol is eligible for an annual bonus under Klinger's executive compensation plan. She has been notified, however, that her bonus for the year will be significantly less than in prior years. The executive compensation plan calculates a manager's effectiveness based solely on return on investment. The president of Klinger pointed out to Carol that while her division's income has improved, the addition of all the new equipment overshadowed the higher earnings.

Required

A. What weaknesses do you see in Klinger's executive bonus plan?
B. How does the company's current compensation plan differ from a balanced scorecard approach to bonus compensation?
C. If the company utilized a balanced scorecard approach, what do you believe would be the impact on Carol's bonus compensation? Explain your answer.

P10-9 Performance Evaluations

Objs. 2, 5

The Promotion and Advertising Department at Jefferson Corporation coordinates point of purchase promotions for its distributors. Employees of this department are graphic arts or marketing majors who develop campaign materials and conduct market research. The department does not collect any revenue for these services. The department manager is evaluated based on the department's ability to operate within its budget. For the last several years, the manager has had to curtail many promotional programs a month before year-end in order to stay within budget.

Sales personnel, marketing representatives, and customers frequently complain when these services are terminated. Dan Beck, the department manager, told a colleague, "I hate taking all this heat every year. But I just can't afford to blow the budget." He also noted that "soon the new budget will be out, and I can give everyone what they want!"

Required

A. What type of responsibility center is the Promotion and Advertising Department?
B. How is the department currently being evaluated? What are the important elements on which the department should be evaluated?
C. What appear to be the reasons for the department's budget problems? What implications does this have for the company?

P10-10 Outsourcing Decisions: Relevant Factors

Obj. 6

Salvo Corporation produces cast metal parts used in the plumbing industry. The company is organized into two divisions, mining and casting. Managers of the two divisions are evaluated based on divisional ROI.

The Mining Division sells ore to the Casting Division as well as to external customers. Currently, the Mining Division has excessive inventory and has reduced production because of weak demand for its product.

In an effort to reduce material costs, the manager of the Casting Division obtained bids from external suppliers to provide the ore. Some external bids were below the prices charged by the Mining Division at Salvo, making purchasing from external sources appear attractive.

Required

A. Identify the relevant facts for the outsourcing decision.
B. Explain why purchasing the ore from an outside company may not be the best decision for Salvo.
C. How would capacity and market conditions affect the outsourcing decision?

P10-11   ### Transfer Pricing, Idle Capacity
Objs. 6, 7

At its Video Division, Crew Enterprises manufactures computer monitors. These can be sold internally to the EDD Division of Crew or externally to independent customers. Sales and costs of the most popular monitor are as follows:

Per unit selling price	$134.00
Per unit variable cost	$103.00
Per unit fixed costs*	$28.00
Full production capacity	11,000 units per month
Current level of production	8,500 units per month

*Based on full production capacity

The Video Division of Crew plans to sell a maximum of 96,000 of these monitors to outside customers in the coming year. The EDD Division of Crew plans to buy 20,000 identical monitors from an outside supplier at a price of $134. The manager of the Video Division has offered to supply these 20,000 monitors to the EDD Division at a price of $130.

Required

A. What is the minimum transfer price for the monitor that the Video Division should be willing to accept on an internal transfer? What is the maximum price the EDD Division should be willing to pay for these monitors on an internal transfer?
B. Suppose the managers of the EDD Division learn of the idle capacity at the Video Division and make an offer of $122 for these monitors. Would you expect the Video Division to accept? What would be the effect on net income for the Video Division of accepting this offer?
C. What would be the effect on net income for Crew as a whole if the transfer price of $122 were accepted?

P10-12   ### Transfer Pricing, Full Capacity
Objs. 6, 7

The USA Company's Box Division produces cardboard boxes used for packaging microwavable fast foods. The Consumer Products Division produces a variety of fast-food entrees that are packaged in boxes. In the past the Consumer Products Division has purchased its boxes from the Box Division for $0.15 each. The Box Division currently is producing at capacity and sells 6,000,000 of these boxes each year at a price of $0.15. The Consumer Products Division has offered to buy 500,000 boxes per year from the Box Division at an internal transfer price of $0.13 per box. The Box Division's cost to produce each box consists of $0.09 of variable costs and $0.04 of fixed costs.

Required

A. What is the minimum transfer price that would be acceptable to the Box Division?
B. Assume that by selling the boxes internally, the Box Division would avoid $0.03 of variable costs. Should the internal transfer be accepted at $0.13 per box? Explain.

P10-13   ### Service Organizations versus Manufacturing Companies: The
Objs. 5, 8   ### Financial Perspective

Decentralized service organizations face many of the same problems as those faced by manufacturing companies. Service organization managers are responsible for profitable, efficient operations that result in sufficient returns for investors. The financial perspective of the balanced scorecard asks the question, "How do we look to shareholders?" Measures such as ROI, cash flow, and profitability may be used as financial performance measures.

(Continued)

http://albright.
swlearning.com

Required Go to the Internet site for this text; select the text and Student Resources. Select SEC under the hotlinks for this chapter. From this site you will be able to access the SEC's database. Search for the financial statements (Form 10k) for **H&R Block, Inc.** and for **General Mills.** Use your knowledge of financial performance measures to compare the results of H&R Block, Inc. (a service company) and General Mills (a manufacturing company). Include in your analysis a calculation of ROI for each company. Also compare the margin and turnover components. Are your results consistent with your expectations? Why or why not?

P10-14

Objs. 6, 8

Transfer Pricing in a Service Environment

Waldo and Company, LLP, is a partnership that provides public accounting services. Waldo has three offices located in New Orleans, Baton Rouge, and Lafayette. Each of the offices employs approximately 30 professional accountants who are hired by and work solely for the office to which they are assigned. The offices are run independently, and there is a managing partner in charge of each office. Bonuses are paid to each managing partner based on criteria that include the number of staff hours worked and total billings for the respective office.

The Lafayette office was recently hired by a large petroleum company to conduct an audit. This engagement will require more accounting personnel than are currently available in the Lafayette office. Nancy Bloom, managing partner of the Lafayette office, has asked the other offices to "lend" her some professional staff to assist on this engagement. The other offices want to help, but are concerned that "lending" their personnel will reduce the number of staff hours worked in their own offices, thereby reducing their billings and resulting bonuses.

Required Why does this situation reflect a transfer pricing problem for the firm? How should the firm handle the interoffice transfer of personnel from a pricing standpoint? If there are professional staff available in the New Orleans and Baton Rouge offices who are not servicing clients, would the interoffice transfer price be affected?

P10-15

Excel in Action

SPREADSHEET

As part of an effort to increase sales and profit margin, Music Makers' management is adopting a transfer pricing plan. The copying and packaging departments have been placed under divisional managers. As an incentive to cut costs, each division is expected to earn a gross margin of 10% on its divisional costs. The copying division will sell its output to the packaging division, and the packaging division will sell its output to the corporation. The company expects to produce and sell 535,000 units per month, and the maximum it is willing to pay to the packaging division for the units is $1,075,000.

Variable manufacturing costs per unit in the copying division include $0.70 for materials, $0.09 for labor, and $0.04689 for overhead. Fixed costs in the copying division are $268,000 per month. Variable manufacturing costs per unit in the packaging division include $0.20 for materials, $0.11 for labor, and $0.04 for overhead. Fixed costs in the packaging division are $76,000 per month.

Required Use a spreadsheet to determine the total costs for each division and the sales price each division will need to charge to earn a 10% gross margin. The sales price can be calculated as total cost ÷ (1 − profit margin).

Provide data for the copying division in column B and the packaging division in column C. Captions should appear in column A. Enter headings in row 1, the number of units to produce in row 2, and gross profit margin in row 3. In row 4, enter a heading "Variable Costs per Unit." Then, enter variable unit costs for materials, labor, and overhead in rows 5 through 7. Calculate total unit variable costs in row 8. Calculate total variable costs in row 9. Enter fixed costs in row 10. Calculate total manufacturing costs in row 11. Calculate the price including required margin in row 12. In the following rows, calculate the total price of the products transferred from the packaging division to the corporation and the amount under (over) the maximum transfer price of $1,075,000. Use cell references and formulas where possible. Use appropriate formatting throughout.

If you were manager of the copying division, what price would you want for the units sold to the packaging division? If you were manager of the packaging division, what price would you want to pay for the goods purchased from the copying division?

How would your answers change if the gross margin expected of each division were 8%?

P10-16   Multiple-Choice Overview of the Chapter

1. Which of the following responsibility centers would appropriately be evaluated in terms of the margin and turnover together?
   a. Cost center
   b. Profit center
   c. Investment center
   d. Revenue center

2. Which of the following is true regarding return on investment?
   a. An increase in sales would affect the margin but not the turnover.
   b. Return on investment is applied only to profit centers.
   c. An increase in assets will decrease the return on investment when sales remain constant.
   d. Plant and equipment are the only assets used to calculate the return on investment.

3. A company establishing transfer prices for products between divisions should:
   a. transfer products at prices that would be paid by outside customers.
   b. utilize transfer prices that will result in the highest income to the transferring division.
   c. allow negotiated prices that result in the greatest benefit to the corporation as a whole.
   d. require the transferee division to accept price quotes without negotiation.

4. A principal expectation for agents is that:
   a. agents will operate the company in a way consistent with the owners' interests.
   b. agents may not act on behalf of owners in important business matters.
   c. agents must always operate a company in order to maximize shareholder wealth.
   d. agents' compensation should not include incentives, as this can create conflicts of interest.

5. A decentralized organization:
   a. permits managers to make decisions based on local economic situations.
   b. allows middle managers to develop skills in preparation for greater responsibilities.
   c. is characterized by multiple divisions or operating segments.
   d. includes all of the above.

6. When used as an internal tool for evaluating managerial performance, ROI is:
   a. calculated by dividing operating assets by net income.
   b. calculated by dividing sales revenue by operating assets.
   c. calculated by dividing operating income by operating assets.
   d. not meaningful since it is subject to manipulation by division managers.

7. The turnover ratio:
   a. is considered to improve when the ratio decreases.
   b. demonstrates the effectiveness of asset management.
   c. encourages managers to increase the asset base.
   d. cannot increase unless the company's margin also increases.

8. The balanced scorecard approach to performance evaluation includes:
   a. financial performance measures.
   b. customer satisfaction measures.
   c. internal business criteria.
   d. All of the above are correct.

9. The transfer pricing policy that requires managers to transfer goods based on external price conditions is referred to as:
   a. negotiated transfer pricing.
   b. a market-based transfer policy.
   c. a cost-plus transfer policy.
   d. None of the above is correct.

10. When a division is operating at less than full capacity:
   a. the company as a whole would be better off utilizing a market-based transfer pricing policy.
   b. internal transfers generally should be made at a price that equals the variable cost of production.
   c. the turnover ratio will increase.
   d. fixed costs are being fully recovered.

CASES

C10-1   The Balanced Scorecard at Golden Grain Foods

Obj. 5

Golden Grain Foods produces consumer food products including cereals, dessert mixes, microwave popcorn, snack foods, and mixes that enhance and simplify meal preparation. During the previous year, reported sales grew at a rate of 8% to reach $6 billion. Earnings after taxes grew at a rate of 10% to $522 million. Every one of Golden Grain Foods' domestic operating divisions posted earnings gains of at least 10%, and combined international earnings grew at an even stronger rate.

The double-digit earnings growth was driven by unit volume gains. Worldwide unit volume increased 9%, with good performance from established businesses and strong contributions from the cereal and snack brands. In addition, productivity improvements helped lower the cost per case of manufactured products. In spite of double-digit earnings growth, the stock price grew just 6% while the S&P index grew 29%. The growth differential reflects concern among investors about the market for ready-to-eat cereal in the United States Investors also are concerned that recent sales growth of lower-priced bagged cereals and store brands will inhibit sales of premium quality brands such as those produced by Golden Grain Foods.

Management is optimistic about the future of cereal products because of favorable demographic trends and cereal's fit with today's emerging health and nutrition recommendations. Golden Grain Foods will use product improvement, health news and brand-building marketing, effective trade merchandising programs, and good new products to drive cereal growth.

The company's financial goals are to achieve 12% average annual growth in earnings per share, to generate a minimum 25% return on invested capital, to exhibit financial strength that merits an "A" bond rating, and to pay out between 50% and 60% of earnings as dividends. Three factors will be key to achieving 12% earnings per share growth as follows:

- Strong unit volume
- Improved productivity
- Profit contributions from international operations

Actions have been taken to stimulate more and better innovation throughout the company by sharpening the focus and increasing the level of resources committed to new products and business development. In addition, management has consolidated the supply chains for flour milling, foodservice, and packaged foods business. These changes will create productivity opportunities.

The company plans to keep leading brands vital with a steady diet of product improvements, innovation, and consumer-focused marketing. Plans include meaningful improvement on several key products, such as cake mixes and frosting. New products are critical to the company's long-term growth. In recent years, an average 27% of volume has come from products five years old or less.

Innovation will be focused on consumer needs. When it comes to snacks, consumers crave variety. New variations of microwave popcorn and new fruit snack products drove volume and share growth in the past. Consumers want mix products that make popular foods a snap to prepare. In addition, consumers are asking for nutritious foods to eat on the go. Strong levels of innovation have been key to increasing dollar market share for yogurt brands to nearly 27%. The company used a steady stream of indulgent new flavor varieties to drive growth in the core yogurt lines.

To meet its long-term goals, the company is after really big ideas—everything from new packaging concepts to new health benefits to new food technologies. Consistent with key strategic objectives, employee teams have been empowered to design and develop new and creative ways to use information and manufacturing technology. Additionally, procedures are in place to supply information to key users within the company. Management has recently taken actions to accelerate the flow of their innovation pipeline. Operating divisions now focus at least 25% of total resources on new products and new business ideas.

In addition to innovations in production, Golden Grain Foods is exploring new distribution channels. The company is targeting a broader penetration of products in vending machines and other foodservice outlets. New retail outlets include convenience stores, membership clubs, drug stores, and mass merchandisers.

Management has been finding ways to buy smarter, manufacture more efficiently, and distribute products at a lower cost. Strong productivity and improved operating leverage combined to lower average cost an additional 5%. Golden Grain Foods seeks to deliver ongoing productivity gains with innovative thinking and breakthrough performance. For example, the company borrowed techniques from racing pit crews to achieve a 30% reduction in the time it takes to change a cereal line from one product to another. The results are significant cost savings and an important increase in manufacturing capacity. In addition, managers are working to more closely integrate the flour milling, foodservice, and packaged foods supply chains. Across all functions, Golden Grain Foods is exploring outsourcing and other strategies to increase efficiency and reduce administrative expense.

Assume corporate managers at Golden Grain Foods want to develop a set of performance indicators to help align decision making with the company's strategic plans. These measures should encourage key activities within the four elements of the balanced scorecard, financial, internal, customer, and innovation and learning.

Required

A. In what businesses does Golden Grain Foods operate?
B. Discuss the financial performance of the company.
C. What are the primary concerns and opportunities identified by management?
D. Prepare a balanced scorecard for Golden Grain Foods. You may wish to classify key activities or initiatives cited in the case as financial, internal business processes, learning and growth, or customer satisfaction. Having identified key initiatives, develop a performance measure that could be used to evaluate progress in that particular activity or initiative.

C10-2 Transfer Pricing

Objs. 6, 7

Cameo Products has two divisions: Office Products and Furniture. Divisional managers are encouraged to maximize ROI at their respective divisions. Managers are free to decide whether goods will be transferred internally and to determine the prices at which transfers will occur.

The Furniture Division would like to purchase a particular chair manufactured in the Office Products Division and sell it with a computer desk the division recently has designed. The Furniture Division can purchase a similar chair from an outside supplier for $45. The Office Products Division currently is producing this chair at full capacity and sells it to outside customers at $45. The manager of the Furniture Division is hoping to receive a price concession if the chair is bought internally. The fully absorbed cost to produce the chair is $40 ($32 represents variable costs). If the chair is sold internally, $3 of variable selling expenses can be avoided.

The managers of the two divisions met to discuss the possible transaction. After some discussion and negotiation, it was decided that the Furniture Division would purchase the chair at the current outside selling price for the next six months. At the end of six months, negotiations can be reopened by either party if desired.

Required

A. Based on current information, what is the highest price that the Furniture Division should be willing to pay for the chair? What is the lowest price that the Office Products Division should be willing to accept?
B. Assume that the outside sales price of the chair increases to $47. How would this affect the internal transfer price of the chair?
C. Assume that because of soft market conditions, demand for the chair has decreased significantly, creating excess idle capacity within the Office Products Division. How would this change affect the internal transfer price of the chair?
D. Why is it in the best interest of the company as a whole to allow the division managers to negotiate internal transfer prices instead of using a fixed, nonnegotiable formula for establishing transfer prices?

IMPROVING OPERATIONAL PERFORMANCE

How can managerial accounting help beat emerging competition?

Young Designs, Inc., is confronted by competition from a foreign furniture producer that has a cost advantage because of lower labor rates. Because of this, Seth and Erin are considering ways to meet this competition by adding value to make their products more competitive. Their strategy is to provide innovative, high-quality products to their customers. Thus, they are focusing on product differentiation rather than on cost leadership. However, cost control is becoming increasingly important as competitors introduce products at significantly lower prices.

One of the challenges Seth and Erin face is that of converting their company into a lean enterprise. Lean enterprises are characterized by efficient operations that rely on minimal levels of raw materials, work-in-process, and finished goods inventory. Also, lean enterprises make efficient use of their assets.

FOOD FOR THOUGHT

Imagine yourself managing Young Designs, Inc. If your strategy is to sell differentiated products that command higher prices, how do you ensure your products provide value to customers? How do you offer significantly better quality and more features desired by customers to justify a higher price? In addition, how do you organize your production area to improve efficiency and reduce costs? Let's listen as Erin and Seth discuss ways of becoming a lean enterprise.

Erin: *I have been in touch with a number of our customers during the past few weeks. It seems we now have competition from an overseas furniture producer. Our customers tell me their products are quite a bit less expensive than ours.*

Seth: *How do their products compare with ours in terms of innovation and quality? Also, can the competition meet our reliable delivery record?*

Erin: *I'm sure our products are better; however, the cost differential is rather dramatic. I've been thinking that we should consider changing some of our processes in the production area. Maybe we can find a way to remove inefficiency and cost. While we currently do a good job with on-time delivery, I believe we have room for improvement.*

Seth: *There is no doubt that we have grown comfortable with our processes. We have far too much invested in inventory. Although the excess helps provide a margin of safety, we still need to become a lean producer.*

Erin: *I'm not sure that I follow you.*

Seth: *Right now, if we make a mistake in production, we simply go to the storage area and get more materials. We don't think about how to improve the process to prevent the mistake from occurring again. I order inventory in quantities large enough to last a month or so. That's a lot of material to count, move, store, and insure against loss. Thus, the excess inventory is very costly to maintain.*

Also, I sometimes believe we do not efficiently route products through the factory. I often walk through the production area and find batches of parts that should have been completed weeks ago. Some machines are churning away, while others seem to sit idle for days at a time. We need to figure out which machines are crucial to our production processes and make sure we don't lose valuable time on those machines.

Erin: *In other words, if we become a lean producer, we will reduce our costs and increase the number of products we are able to complete in a given time period. Our efficiencies should translate into lower prices for our customers. Also, we should be able to offer better service when a customer places an order.*

Seth: *That's right. If we can provide rapid, reliable delivery to our customers, they may reduce their investment in inventory. Again, we may be able to deliver cost savings to our customers. By working smarter, we can compete with companies that have lower labor costs or other cost advantages.*

OBJECTIVES

Once you have completed this chapter, you should be able to:

1 Explain the difference between strategic and operational decisions and how accounting information supports these decisions.

2 Explain the philosophy of total quality management (TQM) and how a modern cost management system can be used to support the philosophy.

3 Describe the just-in-time (JIT) manufacturing philosophy and evaluate its

strengths and weaknesses from financial and operating perspectives.

4 Explain how a traditional "process-oriented" plant layout differs from a "product-oriented" plant layout, and describe the financial consequences of each layout.

5 Identify the primary components of the theory of constraints.

6 Explain how new manufacturing environment concepts apply to service organizations.

THE NEW COMPETITIVE ENVIRONMENT

OBJECTIVE 1

Explain the difference between strategic and operational decisions and how accounting information supports these decisions.

In the opening scenario, Seth and Erin decided they must convert their company to a lean enterprise. The following pages address in more detail the concept of lean organizations and how they evolved.

The Japanese automobile industry generally is given credit for developing the concept of a lean enterprise.[1] The lean enterprise was born out of necessity. The Japanese automobile industry did not have a great deal of manufacturing equipment during the 1950s and 1960s. Thus, manufacturers were forced to produce automobiles in small quantities, using far less equipment than their competitors around the world. **Toyota** found ways to reduce setup time on metal presses from days to minutes. Small-batch production became economically possible as a result of efficient metal press setup times. Unfortunately, small-batch production created other problems that had to be resolved.

Because small-batch production results in lower inventory levels, extra components to replace a defective batch often were not available. Thus, lean production systems, while very efficient, demand strict attention to quality control. As a result, programs such as zero defects and total quality management (TQM) were developed to help minimize defects that could disrupt an entire production system. In summary, systems such as total quality management and just-in-time were developed in response to international competition. These concepts have been implemented by manufacturers around the world.

Modern management accounting systems should provide relevant information to support managers who make decisions in a rapidly changing competitive environment. For example, accounting systems should capture the economic results of small-batch production in highly automated processes, such as those found at Toyota. Management accounting systems also provide information to support customer-oriented TQM

---

[1] Cooper, Robin, 1995. *When Lean Enterprises Collide* (Boston: Harvard Business School Press).

programs. Because management accountants help design innovative performance measurement systems, they must have a solid understanding of manufacturing processes and the dynamics that drive these processes. This chapter considers many recent manufacturing innovations used by organizations throughout the world.

TUFF CUT: THE COMPETITIVE ENVIRONMENT AND MANUFACTURING PROCESS

Examples in this chapter are based on the experiences of Tuff Cut, a company that manufactures rotary mowers used for industrial and agricultural purposes. Its rotary mowers are towed behind tractors to clear brush from rough, wide terrain. Tuff Cut has produced mowers in the United States for the past 40 years and has enjoyed consistent growth and loyal customers because of its high-quality product line. Customers include agricultural companies; individual landowners; and city, county, and state governments.

In recent years, some of Tuff Cut's market share has been eroded by competing products manufactured in the United States and abroad. Thus, managers at Tuff Cut are looking for ways to become more competitive in terms of price, quality, and delivery. As part of their effort, corporate officers are considering strategic changes in the way they manage their organization. **Strategic decisions** include decisions about the types of products a company should manufacture (such as commercial, agricultural, or residential) and how these products should be distributed (through wholesale distributors or company-owned retail outlets). In addition, questions concerning whether to enter new markets, such as China, Europe, Japan, and South America, are strategic issues. **Operational decisions** focus on day-to-day activities of the organization, but are linked directly to strategic objectives. For example, if receiving a product very soon after placing an order is important to Japanese customers, improving machine setup times to reduce cycle time is an operational activity that can be carried out at the factory floor level in support of strategic objectives. **Cycle time** is the total minutes, hours, or days a product remains in a manufacturing system. Cycle time includes producing, moving, and waiting time.

Tuff Cut has embraced a "customer-focused" philosophy that places many operating decisions in the hands of teams of employees, rather than in the hands of management. To help reduce costs, improve competitiveness, and understand their position in the industry, Tuff Cut's managers evaluated the suppliers and manufacturing processes within the industry and used the information to assist in making strategic decisions. In addition, Tuff Cut made operational changes on the factory floor, such as maintaining very low inventory levels and strengthening relationships with suppliers. Finally, plant managers evaluated the flow of resources through their manufacturing facilities to identify bottlenecks and increase each plant's output. This chapter evaluates the changes implemented by Tuff Cut and explores the manufacturing philosophies supporting these changes. First, let's begin with a description of the manufacturing process.

As shown in Exhibit 1, Tuff Cut's manufacturing process involves fabricating (cutting metal to desired specifications), welding, painting, and assembling steel sheets and components to conform to engineering specifications. Sheets of steel are removed by an overhead crane from the steel stores area, located on the factory floor, and delivered to the fabrication area. In the fabrication area, steel is cut and pressed to the required shape. These cut shapes go to the welding area, where individual pieces of steel are welded together to make the mower body. Following the welding process, the mower body is painted and sent to the assembly area, where workers attach wheels, gear boxes, and various other components. Following assembly, finished units are transported to the loading dock for shipment to dealers.

Exhibit 1 The Manufacturing Process at Tuff Cut

Steel Stores

Steel Sheets   Steel Rods

Fabrication

Steel disks punched
from square steel
sheets

Stacked
steel
disks

Welding

Painting

PAINTING BOOTH

Assembly

Finished Goods

TUFF CUT: TOTAL QUALITY MANAGEMENT

Explain the philosophy of total quality management (TQM) and how a modern cost management system can be used to support the philosophy.

Total quality management (TQM) **is a management system that seeks continual improvement by asking everyone in an organization to understand, meet, and exceed the needs of customers.** A key question underlying all business activities should be, "Who are the customers, and what are their needs?" For example, total quality management as embraced by a university would include opening additional sections of classes to accommodate large student enrollments. Also, in response to long lines in university bookstores, managers may open additional cash registers to speed the checkout process at the beginning of each term.

Though total quality management is a continually evolving concept, the primary focus is on delivering value to a customer. As shown in Exhibit 2, every activity within an organization should contribute ultimately to the strategic objective of satisfying customers. Thus, the cascading set of TQM tasks shown in the exhibit links strategic objectives with operational activities. In the following paragraphs, Tuff Cut is used to illustrate examples of each task identified in Exhibit 2.

Exhibit 2 Elements of TQM

Who are our customers?

What are the needs of our customers?

How can our products/services satisfy their needs?

Which processes are crucial to meeting their needs?

How do we ensure our processes are satisfactory?

Which performance measures ensure high-quality processes?

http://albright.
swlearning.com
·····
Learn more about TQM.

- *Identify the customers.* At first glance, we may be tempted to say that dealers and retail buyers are Tuff Cut's only customers. However, closer examination reveals additional customers internal, as well as external, to the company. For example, welders are customers of the fabrication process, and painters are customers of the welding process. Each operation produces output that is used by later processes.
- *Identify customer needs.* Having identified its customers, Tuff Cut prepared a list of customer needs. For example, *internal customers* demand rugged, high-quality raw materials consistent with engineering specifications. *External customers* require dependable delivery times and sturdy products capable of withstanding the abuse associated with mowing rough terrain.
- *Identify product (or service) features.* For Tuff Cut customers, important *product* features include strong welds and sturdy gear boxes. Important *service* features include rapid delivery of spare parts and availability of repair services in the event of a mechanical breakdown.
- *Identify process (production or delivery) features.* Customers have identified rugged, high-quality products as essential. To meet this need, strong welds and sturdy components are required. Therefore, the next logical step is to design processes that result in strong welds and sturdy components. Tuff Cut evaluated various welding technologies, including robotic and manual, to ensure that these processes were consistent with the demands of the market.
- *Establish controls.* Having identified key quality processes, management put controls in place to ensure that processes are performed at the appropriate quality level. Often, entire processes are redesigned to meet process requirements for quality.
- *Assess performance against goals from the perspective of both internal and external customers.* Tuff Cut must continuously improve production processes and service functions critical to ensuring that customers are satisfied. Managers assess performance on a number of quality criteria by comparing actual performance with predetermined targets (or benchmarks).

Case in Point

http://albright.
swlearning.com
·····
**Learn more about
maquiladoras and man-
ufacturing in Mexico.**

Customer-Focused Quality Programs

Maquiladoras (pronounced ma kee' a dor as) are manufacturing plants established in Mexico by foreign companies. The goods produced by maquiladoras are for export only. A major factor in the success of these plants has been the fact that they meet the requirements for international quality certification. Thus, the maquiladoras are creating a quality culture based on the concepts shown in Exhibit 2 in this chapter. These concepts are being used successfully by Mexico's manufacturing companies to change the country's image from a relatively inexpensive source of labor to that of a global manufacturing power.

Source: Aly, Nael, and Danies Schloss. 2003. Assessing Quality Management Systems of Mexico's Maquiladoras, *The TQM Magazine.*

To support TQM activities managers also set benchmarks by comparing their products (or services) against the best on the market. Managers in world-class companies understand their competitors' products, manufacturing processes, and manufacturing costs. Often a competitor's product is purchased and disassembled to understand the types of materials and assembly processes used. Such information is useful during the design phase of a new product. However, when a product is in the production phase, managers look for opportunities to improve quality and to reduce costs. These activities often are termed "Kaizen," or continuous process improvement. Thus, competitive benchmarking and continuous process improvement are consistent with the TQM philosophy. These techniques help managers deliver higher quality products (or services) to their customers at a lower cost.

The remainder of this chapter explores two topics that are consistent with the objectives of total quality management. Just-in-time (JIT) inventory management and the theory of constraints have received much attention from business leaders in recent years. The operations of Tuff Cut are used to demonstrate these concepts. The purpose is to illustrate how real-world companies implement change in order to remain competitive in a dynamic environment.

1 SELF-STUDY PROBLEM

WebTUTOR Advantage

To illustrate the concepts in this chapter, all the self-study problems use the production process of Autobrake. Autobrake produces aftermarket (replacement) brake cylinders used by automobile repair companies. Autobrake purchases steel bar stock from wholesale distributors and manufactures and assembles components for brake cylinders at its plant. The purchasing manager seeks the lowest steel prices (consistent with strict quality standards) from a large number of vendors. Orders for raw materials must often be delivered very rapidly because of poor communication between the production floor and the purchasing department. The company has been growing at a rapid pace because of its reputation for high-quality products. Thus, Autobrake is in the position of having more orders than it currently can process. As a result, it maintains a production backlog of approximately 12 weeks.

The manufacturing process consists of five steps. First, steel bar stock is placed into automatic turning equipment (lathes) (step 1). Clamps secure each end of the bar stock, which spins rapidly while a cutting tool cuts the external dimensions to meet engineering specifications. The process requires two turning operations, first stage and second stage. The operations are similar; however, second-stage turning further refines the shape of the component. Studies conducted by the industrial engineering department suggest that average processing times for first-stage and second-stage turning are five and four minutes per component, respectively. Both turning operations require machine setups between runs of different brake systems. These setups are lengthy and require highly skilled machine operators.

Following second-stage turning, a milling operation takes place (step 2). The component is held in place while a cutting tool removes metal according to specifications. Engineering studies have determined that the milling operation requires approximately seven minutes for each component. The milling machines are old and subject to unexpected breakdowns. Because Autobrake does not maintain large amounts of work-in-process inventory, a machine failure often causes other machines to be idle from lack of input.

After milling, a component is ground to meet final specifications (step 3). The grinding operation requires approximately three minutes per component and is the last process before the cylinders are assembled.

Assembly of various components is a manual operation (step 4). The average assembly time per cylinder is six minutes. Following assembly, each cylinder is carefully packaged in an individual paperboard box that bears the name and logo of Autobrake (step 5). Autobrake gets its packaging materials from a company that buys rolls of paper stock from paper mills and produces custom-printed boxes. Management is considering automating the packaging line to reduce labor costs. Automated equipment would reduce the packaging time of 15 seconds to 8 seconds.

Autobrake contracts with trucking lines to transport its products to wholesalers, who then sell the brake cylinders to various retail stores. However, a major retailer of auto parts has contacted Autobrake to explore the possibilities of buying cylinders directly from the factory, without going through a wholesaler. In addition, the retailer wishes to buy cylinders in bulk containers rather than in individual packages.

Required

A. Draw a diagram that represents the five-step process Autobrake uses. Include processing times.
B. Discuss how Autobrake might apply TQM principles to improve its competitiveness.

The solution to Self-Study Problem 1 appears at the end of the chapter.

PRINCIPLES OF JUST-IN-TIME MANUFACTURING

OBJECTIVE 3

Describe the just-in-time (JIT) manufacturing philosophy and evaluate its strengths and weaknesses from financial and operating perspectives.

http://albright.swlearning.com

Learn more about JIT.

Erin and Seth discussed the costs of making infrequent, large raw material purchases. These costs included handling, storing, and insuring. They also discussed providing better service to their customers by improving delivery time, which in turn would minimize the finished goods inventory costs. Minimizing inventory levels is a condition of just-in-time (JIT) manufacturing systems, which have become popular in recent years. *Just-in-time manufacturing* **is a production system that pulls products through the manufacturing process on the basis of market demand.** Inventory levels are minimized (parts are delivered "just-in-time"), thereby improving asset turnover and reducing manufacturing costs. The concepts underlying just-in-time are not new; Japanese manufacturing companies have benefited from lean, integrated manufacturing systems for many years. A just-in-time manufacturing system typically has a number of related elements. For example, inventory is pulled through the system based on market demand. Companies using just-in-time have small inventories of raw materials and finished goods; therefore, high-quality raw materials are critical to success. Poor-quality raw materials can stop a production line. Because high-quality materials are extremely important, companies usually establish close business relationships with a small number of high-quality, certified suppliers. Engineers work to minimize machine changeover (setup) times to permit manufacturing products in small batches. Short manufacturing cycle times result from small-batch production. Thus, just-in-time manufacturing is an important element of time-based competition. High-quality materials, rapid setup times, small-batch production, and minimal inventory levels are all important elements of just-in-time systems.

Just-in-time principles require inventory to be pulled through the plant based on market demand. For example, the last operation in a process acts as a trigger, signaling earlier (upstream) work centers to begin production. The pull system is in contrast to traditional "push" systems, which determine production levels from forecasted demand.

The push system is illustrated in Exhibit 3, panel A. Production is started in Department 1 based on market forecasts of customer demand. The goods produced are placed in inventory until they are needed. The alternative, the pull (or just-in-time) system, is illustrated in panel B of the exhibit. When a customer places an order, a signal is sent to the assembly department to begin production. The assembly department removes components from work-in-process and assembles them, and the product is delivered to the customer. When components are removed from work-in-process, a signal to process additional components is sent to the painting department. Thus, the painting department takes cut components from work-in-process, paints them, and places the painted components into work-in-process. By removing cut components from work-in-process, the painting department sends a signal to the sawing department to cut more materials. Therefore, the sawing department places an order for materials from an outside vendor. The materials are cut and put into work-in-process. In summary, a just-in-time system pulls products through the factory at the rate of customer demand. Information flows from right to left, as indicated by the blue arrows in Exhibit 3 (B). Materials flow from left to right, as shown by the red arrows in the exhibit. A key component of the pull system is low work-in-process inventory and rapid product movement.

To move products through a plant quickly, a company looks for ways to reduce machine setup (or changeover) times. By making setup times short enough, a company can produce units in small batches. Small-batch production results in low inventory levels because products move through the process in small quantities, rather than in large blocks. The company enjoys fast cycle times. Cycle time is considered in the following section.

Just-in-time principles require small amounts of all types of inventory, even raw materials inventory. Therefore, a good relationship with vendors is extremely important. Vendors must make many deliveries of small amounts of high-quality raw materials, rather than making weekly or monthly deliveries of large quantities. Because only small amounts are delivered at a time, quality must be high, or the production line will stop because of lack of raw material. To achieve the objectives of just-in-time, **nonfinancial performance measures** are used to evaluate critical factors such as cycle time,

Exhibit 3 Push System (A) of Production Compared to Pull System (B)

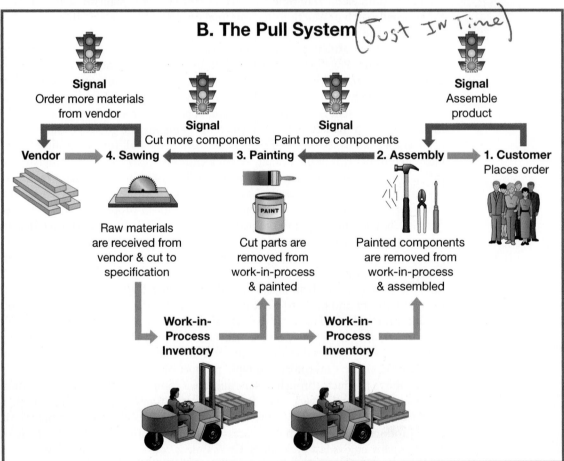

production rate, and throughput. The following section considers measures that are consistent with the philosophies of just-in-time and total quality management.

Nonfinancial Performance Measures

In today's manufacturing environment, employees often are asked to participate in cross-functional teams made up of individuals with various types of professional expertise. For example, teams may consist of accountants, industrial engineers, production managers, purchasing managers, and finance managers. Often, teams are responsible for improving processes, reducing manufacturing costs, and developing key nonfinancial performance indicators. Performance is no longer measured only in financial terms, such as net income or return on investment. While better financial performance is the ultimate goal, financial measures often do not provide guidance to managers who want to improve manufacturing performance. Thus, measurements such as *cycle time, throughput,* and *bottleneck management* have been added to the list of performance criteria.

To illustrate these concepts, Exhibit 4 contains processing times for various work centers within the Tuff Cut plant. For example, the fabrication area has the capacity to produce 20 units per hour, while the welding, painting, and assembly areas are capable of processing 10, 30, and 25 units per hour, respectively. From these data, we can determine several key performance indicators for the Tuff Cut plant. The following sections consider the concepts of cycle time, production rate, and throughput.

Cycle Time. *Cycle time* **is defined as the total time required to move a unit from raw materials inventory to finished goods inventory.** Cycle time is the sum of processing time, moving time, and waiting time. Exhibit 4 indicates that the **processing time** required to produce one rotary mower is:

	Processing Time (minutes)
Fabrication	3.0
Welding	6.0
Painting	2.0
Assembly	2.4
Total	13.4

Each rotary mower requires 13.4 minutes of total processing time from beginning (fabrication) to end (assembly). **Processing time is the number of minutes in which value is added to raw materials.** Does this mean that Tuff Cut can produce a unit from start to finish in 13.4 minutes? Probably not. Processing time is only one part of cycle time; the other part is **wait time, the time a unit spends waiting to be processed.** For example, assume that each work center has six hours of work-in-process inventory waiting to be processed. Six hours of work-in-process inventory represent the production of less than one shift. Most manufacturers have far more work-in-process inventory. Thus, 24 hours of wait time (6 hours before the fabrication area + 6 hours before the welding area + 6 hours before the painting area + 6 hours before the assembly area = 24 hours) are built into Tuff Cut's manufacturing process. Therefore, the cycle time for completing one mower is calculated as follows:

Wait time (24 hours × 60 minutes)	1,440.0 minutes
Processing time	13.4 minutes
Cycle time	1,453.4 minutes

Wait time makes up the major portion of the cycle time required to move a unit of product through the plant. Imagine a four-step class registration process at your university that requires a six-hour wait at each step to accomplish a task requiring only a

Exhibit 4   Workcenter Processing Times within the Tuff Cut Plant

Steel Stores

Steel Sheets   Steel Rods

Fabrication:
20 units per hour;
3 minutes per unit

Steel disks punched from square steel sheets   Stacked steel disks

Welding:
10 units per hour;
6 minutes per unit

Painting:
30 units per hour;
2 minutes per unit

PAINTING BOOTH

Assembly:
25 units per hour;
2.4 minutes per unit

Finished Goods

few minutes. You probably would say that the university registration process is inefficient. The same is true with a manufacturing process.

Why would Tuff Cut keep six hours of inventory at each work center? The answer involves process reliability. For example, without such inventory, if a work center becomes idle because of a mechanical breakdown, all later (downstream) work centers must stop processing because of lack of input. Therefore, inventory is viewed as insurance against unreliable equipment. Unfortunately, the insurance is not free. Just-in-time manufacturing practices require reducing the level of inventory to reduce carrying costs and to improve cycle time.

So, why are cycle time and work-in-process levels important? What is the downside of having high work-in-process levels and long cycle times? Maintaining high inventory levels is expensive because of the potential for damage or obsolescence as well as the cost of storage. Also, managers often are evaluated using return on assets[2] as a performance criterion. High inventory levels make the asset base larger and reduce a company's return. There are other considerations as well. A company that has low levels of work-in-process inventory can move an order through the process in much less time than a company whose inventory levels require many hours of waiting time. Thus, fast-cycle companies may enjoy a strategic advantage in the marketplace by being able to deliver goods faster than their competition.

In addition to cycle time, production rate often is used as a nonfinancial performance measure. The next section considers production rate in connection with the Tuff Cut plant.

Production Rate. *Production rate* **is the number of units a manufacturing system is capable of producing in a given time period.** For example, if a manufacturing system can produce 10 products every hour (or 10 units/60 minutes), a new product would be completed every six minutes (10 units/60 minutes = 1 unit/6 minutes). For Tuff Cut, which manufacturing center (fabrication, welding, painting, or assembly) drives the production rate? The slowest process in the chain, the welding area, drives the production rate for the entire system. Since welders need six minutes to process a unit, it does not matter that the fabrication department can process one unit every three minutes, or that the painting department can process one unit every two minutes. The welders take the longest time to process a unit, and the system as a whole cannot move faster than the slowest process will permit. **Processes that work at slow production rates and restrict the flow of goods or services are termed** *bottlenecks.* Just as the small-diameter opening in a bottle restricts the flow of liquid, a production bottleneck restricts the output of a process.

The fabrication area can process units twice as fast as the welding area; however, processing at a rate faster than ten units per hour merely results in excess work-in-process inventory accumulating in front of the welding area. The painting and assembly areas also process faster than the welding area. Unfortunately, their output is held down by the welding area's inability to provide parts fast enough for them to achieve their potential. Thus, the production rate of the entire plant is determined by the slowest manufacturing center, the welding process.

This section has evaluated cycle time and production rate as performance indicators. Another important measure of a manufacturing facility is throughput, which is discussed in the following section.

Throughput. *Throughput* **represents the number of units completed by a process.** Marketing managers are interested in both cycle time and throughput. Cycle time affects a salesperson's ability to deliver goods to customers quickly, and throughput affects the number of units available for sale. Of course, throughput is related to production rate. For example, to calculate the number of units Tuff Cut can produce in one eight-hour shift, multiply the available production time by the production rate.

---

[2] Recall that Return on assets = Asset turnover × Profit margin

$$= \frac{\text{Sales}}{\text{Average assets}} \times \frac{\text{Earnings}}{\text{Sales}}$$

Thus, by multiplying available production time by production rate, throughput can be determined as follows:

8 hours per shift × 60 minutes per hour =		480 available minutes per shift
Production rate	=	1/6 (or 1 unit every 6 minutes)
Throughput	= 480 × 1/6 =	80 units per eight-hour shift

Therefore, Tuff Cut has the ability to produce 80 units per eight-hour shift. During periods when demand for rotary mowers is high, managers must ensure that throughput is maximized to avoid lost sales.

PRODUCT-ORIENTED VERSUS PROCESS-ORIENTED PLANT LAYOUT

OBJECTIVE 4

Explain how a traditional "process-oriented" plant layout differs from a "product-oriented" plant layout, and describe the financial consequences of each layout.

Some organizations have explored various approaches to plant organization in an attempt to improve operations and reduce manufacturing costs. Innovative plant layouts have been developed that can support minimal inventory levels, fast setup times, high-quality products, and responsive cycle times. Traditionally, designs for manufacturing facilities were *process-oriented*. Each area of the plant was designed to carry out a certain type of process, and work-in-process inventory was transported between processes. For example, as illustrated in Exhibit 5, the steel storage area at Tuff Cut was located in the northwest corner of the plant. Materials were transported to the fabrication area in large batches by forklift. Following fabrication, the pieces were transported to the welding area to await processing. Following the welding operation, extensive handling and transportation was needed to move units to the painting process and back to final assembly. Clearly, Tuff Cut organized its factory by grouping similar processes together, an example of a process-oriented plant layout. *Process-oriented plant layouts* **typically are arranged according to machine function, with machines that perform similar functions placed together.**

Exhibit 5 Traditional "Process-Oriented" Plant Layout

What are some of the cost considerations in a traditional process-oriented plant? First of all, to make efficient use of assets and the people who move parts from one workstation to another, a process-oriented plant typically produces in large batches. Therefore, work-in-process levels are high and lead times are long.

As an alternative, many companies are reorganizing their plants. As illustrated in Exhibit 6, **a** *product-oriented plant layout* **is based on manufacturing cells that meet the production requirements of products or product families (products that have similar characteristics).**

Exhibit 6 Cellular "Product-Oriented" Plant Layout

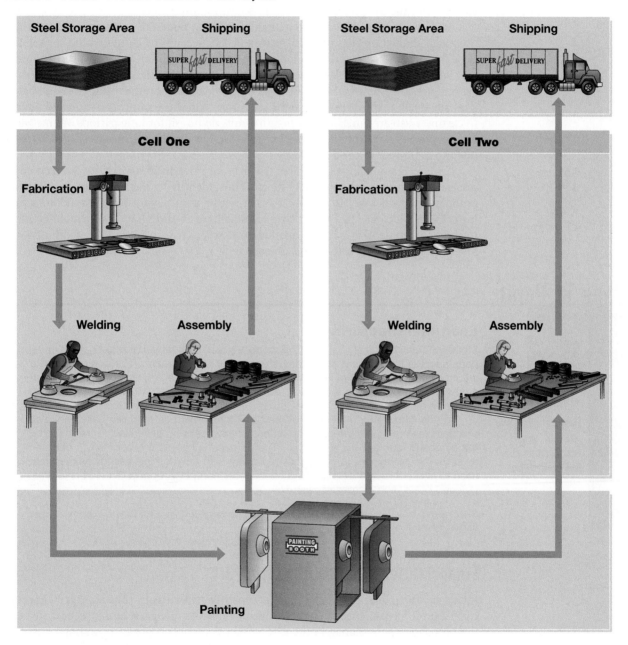

Because of rapid changes in product characteristics, manufacturing systems are developed to be flexible. Rather than buying a machine that serves only one function, such as drilling, cutting, or welding, companies are investing in flexible machinery that can perform a number of functions. Typically, flexible manufacturing systems are characterized by their ability to change rapidly from one type of process to another. For example, automatic tool changers may remove a drill bit that makes $\frac{1}{2}$-inch-diameter holes and replace it with a drill bit that makes $\frac{1}{4}$-inch-diameter holes. In addition, many flexible systems contain automatic error detection in the form of statistical process control software. Finally, most flexible systems have the ability to increase or decrease the rate of output.[3]

A *manufacturing cell* **is a group of related machines, typically arranged in the shape of a U.** Raw materials enter one prong of the U, and finished goods exit from the other prong. Exhibit 6 illustrates how Tuff Cut might reorganize its plant floor to achieve a product-oriented layout. The industrial engineers designed work cells by placing equipment in two cells based on the manufacturing requirements of their product line. The painting process presented a few problems because the paint line cannot be divided. Thus, the design linked both cells to the painting area.

As indicated by the arrows in Exhibit 6, raw materials enter the cell and are processed, and completed products leave the cell. Because machines within the cell are close to one another, extensive handling and transportation of work-in-process inventory is not required. Work cells are arranged according to the needs of product families and are consistent with the concepts of just-in-time manufacturing. Because batch sizes are small, work-in-process levels are lower than those of process-oriented plants. Cycle times also are much shorter because units do not sit for long periods of time waiting for processing. Plants that use a cellular design often have many cells, each dedicated to a product or product family.

Cellular manufacturing requires few arbitrary overhead allocations because costs associated with each cell tend to be direct. Thus, identifying the resources used by each product or product family usually is easier with a plant layout based on manufacturing cells. In addition, since batch sizes are small, waste and scrap costs should be minimal. For example, if a machine operator makes an error in setting the width of a cut for a small batch, only a few units are affected.

Case in Point

Lean Manufacturing

Medalist LaserFab is an Oshkosh, Wisconsin-based company that makes sheet metal parts such as fenders and steps for Oshkosh Truck Corporation. The company is doing more with less. Its goal is to reduce waste, inventory levels, and production stoppages. We "bring the raw material in, cut it, and get it out," according to John Mazur, president of Medalist LaserFab.

Ariens Company, a member of the same consortium as Medalist LaserFab, also practices lean manufacturing. Using manufacturing cells as described in this chapter, the company reported the following: "The process builds on the company's decision to assemble machinery in pods that did away with labyrinthine assembly lines that used to snake through the plant." As a result, the company reports reduced lead time, reduced costs, and increased cash flow.

Source: 2003. Manufacturers in Appleton, Wisconsin Area Learn to Think Like Service Suppliers, *Knight Ridder Tribune Business News* (April 30).

Financial Benefits Resulting from JIT

Managers who make operational changes consistent with just-in-time management principles expect these changes to improve profitability. As discussed in this section, just-in-time principles help managers increase revenues as well as reduce operating costs. For example, companies maintain minimal levels of raw materials, work-in-process, and finished goods inventories when products are pulled through the factory at the rate demanded by customers. Reduced inventory levels result in lower carrying costs, which

---

[3] For more information on flexible manufacturing systems, see Black, J. T. 1991. *The Design of the Factory with a Future* (New York: McGraw-Hill, Inc.).

include costs of financing, obsolescence, and damage. Fast setup times contribute to short manufacturing cycle times. Often, responsive factories gain a competitive advantage that translates into increased sales. This section considers the financial effects of reduced inventory levels, improved manufacturing cycle times, and increased throughput.

Selected financial information for Tuff Cut follows. The company currently has sales of $93 million annually while employing assets of $139.5 million. The controller estimates that variable manufacturing costs are 40 percent of sales. In addition, fixed manufacturing expenses and fixed administrative expenses are $28 million and $11 million, respectively. Thus, Tuff Cut's return on assets currently is 12 percent.

Annual sales		$93,000,000
Variable manufacturing expenses, 40% of sales		
(0.40 × $93,000,000)	$37,200,000	
Fixed manufacturing costs	28,000,000	
Fixed general and administrative costs	11,000,000	76,200,000
Operating income		$16,800,000

Return on assets before process changes:

$$\underbrace{\text{(Operating income}^4 \div \text{Sales)}}_{\textit{Profit Margin}} \times \underbrace{\text{(Sales} \div \text{Assets}^5)}_{\textit{Asset Turnover}} = \text{Return on assets}$$

$$(\$16,800,000 \div \$93,000,000) \times (\$93,000,000 \div \$139,500,000) = \text{Return on assets}$$

$$0.18 \times 0.67 = 0.12$$

Let's consider how implementing just-in-time can improve Tuff Cut's return on assets. First, assume that demand for Tuff Cut's products exceeds supply and that improvements in throughput will result in a 10 percent increase in sales. Further, assume that reductions in raw materials, work-in-process, and finished goods inventories will result in a 1 percent decrease in assets. In addition, variable manufacturing costs will be reduced from 40 percent of sales to 38.5 percent of sales because inventory carrying costs and scrap rates will decrease. Product and process reengineering efforts often reduce fixed manufacturing costs. In this case, Tuff Cut's fixed manufacturing costs will decrease from $28 million to $27 million because of reductions in materials handling activities and the elimination of unnecessary manufacturing equipment. Finally, fixed administrative costs will be reduced from $11 million to $10 million because of changes in administrative support functions. For example, fixed administrative costs can be reduced by restructuring processes and reducing the amount of indirect labor and equipment. The following calculations summarize our assumptions:

Annual sales ($93,000,000 × 1.1)		$102,300,000
Variable manufacturing expenses,		
38.5% of sales (0.385 × $102,300,000)	$39,385,500	
Fixed manufacturing costs	27,000,000	
Fixed general and administrative costs	10,000,000	76,385,500
Operating income		$ 25,914,500

Assets following a 1% decrease = $139,500,000 × 0.99 = $138,105,000

Return on assets after process changes:

$$\underbrace{\text{(Operating income} \div \text{Sales)}}_{\textit{Profit Margin}} \times \underbrace{\text{(Sales} \div \text{Assets)}}_{\textit{Asset Turnover}} = \text{Return on assets}$$

$$(\$25,914,500 \div \$102,300,000) \times (\$102,300,000 \div \$138,105,000) = \text{Return on assets}$$

$$0.25 \times 0.74 = 0.19$$

---

[4] Operating income is equivalent to earnings.

[5] The asset information given here is assumed to be equal to average costs.

These calculations suggest that Tuff Cut's return on assets will improve from 12 to 19 percent as a result of implementing just-in-time principles. Our example illustrates the potential financial effects of changes in manufacturing strategy. Companies that have successfully implemented just-in-time see it as a strategy for long-run continuous improvement. Thus, just-in-time is not a "magic pill" that suddenly will improve a company's profitability. However, as our example illustrates, just-in-time includes sound operating principles that affect a company's revenues and costs.

Drawbacks to the Just-in-Time Manufacturing Philosophy

Just-in-time manufacturing is a system with many positive attributes; however, it has its disadvantages. In the economic recovery of the early 1990s, many companies reduced inventories to record low levels. Unfortunately, some companies experienced difficulties because of these low levels. Assume that you are the general manager of two plants, a manufacturing plant and an assembly plant. The manufacturing plant provides components to the assembly plant. Unexpectedly, the union at the manufacturing plant goes on strike. In the past, negotiations were lengthy and difficult, but at that time, the assembly plant had six months of components in inventory. Now, consistent with the just-in-time philosophy, the assembly plant has three days of inventory. How do you think just-in-time will affect your ability to bargain effectively? The union at the manufacturing plant has successfully closed two plants instead of one.

In a just-in-time environment, cost savings from reducing inventories can be offset by increased delivery costs imposed by suppliers who are now making daily (or even hourly) deliveries. In addition, management must explain to workers why they are being asked to increase the number of batches and machine setups. Finally, in an economy experiencing rapid growth, managers may increase inventory to levels *inconsistent* with just-in-time because they fear that they will run out of inventory at a time when customers are ready to purchase goods.

On balance, just-in-time principles have helped many manufacturers improve operations and reduce waste. In addition, by reducing work-in-process inventory levels, bottlenecks become apparent. As we discussed earlier in this section, bottlenecks in a production process affect production rates, and thus the number of units processed through the system (throughput). Understanding how to manage bottleneck resources is important for improving operating performance. The following section addresses the issue of managing bottlenecks.

Case in Point

http://albright.
swlearning.com

**Learn more about
NUMMI.**

JIT

New United Motor Manufacturing, Inc. (NUMMI) is a joint venture between **General Motors Corporation** and **Toyota Motor Corporation**. Using a JIT system, NUMMI produces trucks and automobiles in its Fremont, California, plant. The company shut down its truck line for five days and its car line for two days as a result of a West Coast dock strike. The strike caused parts and supplies necessary for production to remain loaded on ships docked in the harbor. The port dispute is one of many examples of challenges that can disrupt production in a JIT manufacturing environment. Other events that could challenge JIT producers include terrorist attacks that would close borders, economic crises overseas, and weather disasters.

NUMMI responded to the port crisis by temporarily using very costly air transportation. The company has used trucks when flooding disrupted rail transportation. Will the company abandon its JIT program as a result of these "wildcard" events? According to Michael Damer of NUMMI, "Is it really reasonable to build up a couple of months inventory in the event this happens again? We don't have facilities for that inventory, and we don't want them."

Source: 2002. *Industry Week* (December).

2 SELF-STUDY PROBLEM

Refer to the information presented in Self-Study Problem 1.

Required

A. Calculate the following for the manufacturing process at Autobrake:
  1. Production rate
  2. Total processing time
  3. Throughput
B. Why would you expect cycle time to be different from the total processing time calculated in part (A2) above?
C. Assume that management at Autobrake is considering redesigning the plant layout from a process-oriented layout to a product-oriented layout by establishing work cells. Discuss the benefits of a product-oriented plant layout.

The solution to Self-Study Problem 2 appears at the end of the chapter.

THE THEORY OF CONSTRAINTS

OBJECTIVE 5

Identify the primary components of the theory of constraints.

Recall that Seth discussed the importance of efficiently routing products through the manufacturing process. As part of his discussion, he mentioned the importance of using resources wisely. This section considers the theory of constraints, a system that encourages managers to identify bottlenecks and manage them efficiently.

As indicated in the previous section, the welding area of the Tuff Cut factory was found to be a bottleneck. In this area, steel sheets are assembled to form the mower housing. As part of the strategic objective of reducing cycle time and increasing throughput, management began reducing the level of work-in-process inventory. In doing so, they observed some troubling outcomes. Certain machines were forced to become idle, which resulted in a *decrease*, rather than an increase, in throughput.

While touring the plant in search of answers to the decline in productivity, managers noticed several things that suggested the presence of a bottleneck. First, in the welding area, managers observed large stacks of work-in-process inventory sitting in front of the welding machines waiting to be processed. Though work-in-process inventories in most areas of the plant contained output from only a few hours of production, the work-in-process inventory in the welding area contained output from several days of production. Second, after observing the welding operation over a number of days, managers noticed that the welders never were idle, except during scheduled breaks. In contrast, they noticed that the downstream painting process often was forced to shut down temporarily because workers had no materials to paint. From observing the manufacturing process, management reasoned that the welding area must be a production bottleneck, or constraint.

Bottleneck processes exist in almost every manufacturing plant. They result when the processing speed of a machine or production area is less than that of other machines or production areas in the plant. Bottlenecks never can be eliminated entirely, because as the processing capability of one machine or production area is increased, a *different* machine or production area often becomes a bottleneck. Thus, in the spirit of continuous process improvement, managers continually adjust processes to improve throughput and reduce operating costs.

Steps to Improve Performance

This section explores various steps management can take to improve throughput consistent with the theory of constraints.[6] The *theory of constraints (TOC)* **states that by**

---

[6] The principles of the theory of constraints were developed and discussed in Goldratt, Eliyahn M., and Jeff Cox. 1992. *The Goal* (Great Barrington: North River Press).

identifying a constraint, such as a bottleneck, that exists in the processing of a good or service and taking corrective steps, the process will be improved. The five steps recommended for process improvement are as follows:

- Step 1: Attack a bottleneck by **identifying** the system's constraints.
- Step 2: Decide how to make the **best use** of the constraint.
- Step 3: **Subordinate** all other decisions to those made in step 2.
- Step 4: **Improve the performance** of the constraint.
- Step 5: If a constraint has been broken (the old bottleneck is gone) but a different bottleneck has been created, **go back to step 1 and start over.**

Implementation of the Theory of Constraints

Let's assume that managers at Tuff Cut have correctly identified the welding area as a bottleneck. Thus, the second step involves deciding how to make the best use of the welding area. For example, because a minute of lost time on a bottleneck results in a minute of lost production for the entire plant, the bottleneck resource must never be allowed to remain idle during lunchtime and breaks. If automated equipment is used, workers simply make certain the raw material supply bins are filled with parts before they leave the work area for a break. Alternatively, workers may be encouraged to have flexible break times and lunchtimes to ensure that the bottleneck is not idle.

Another way to reduce the effect of the bottleneck is to inspect materials before they are processed at the bottleneck. For example, if scrap rates are a problem in the manufacturing process, inspection centers can be located before the bottleneck. Thus, the bottleneck does not waste valuable processing time on parts that will be unusable.

Step 3 suggests that all other decisions should be subordinated to those made in step 2. In other words, the entire plant should be scheduled and managed by considering the bottleneck. For example, components that require processing on a bottleneck resource should receive highest priority at nonbottleneck work centers. Thus, all work centers should schedule production orders to ensure that the bottleneck resource is never idle.

The fourth step requires managers to improve the performance of the bottleneck. What are some strategies Tuff Cut can use to improve performance on the bottleneck in the welding area? They can minimize downtime on the bottleneck by making machine setups less time-consuming. One method of reducing setup time is to convert on-line setup time to off-line setup time. Production machinery often has removable parts, such as saw blades, grippers, and drill bits, called machine tools. Complex tool changes can be made more quickly if two or more sets of tools are used. While a machine is actively producing with one set of tools, a machinist prepares the settings of a second set of tools at a workbench. Changeovers become rapid because one set of tools is simply replaced by a second set that already has been prepared. Thus, productive time is gained by reducing downtime associated with setup activities.

Extra capacity can be created for the bottleneck resource in several ways. Purchasing additional machinery can reduce the effects of a bottleneck by providing more processing capability. If management decides that capital for additional equipment is not available, some components could be purchased from external sources, thereby increasing the output of the entire plant. Additionally, more workers can be hired. At Tuff Cut, management acquired a new machine to operate along with existing equipment. The new machine provided the capacity needed to increase throughput, while decreasing inventory. Let's assume that the new equipment was more efficient and increased the number of units processed from 10 per hour to 25 per hour. How will the investment affect throughput?

Exhibit 7 illustrates the relationships among Tuff Cut's processing centers after adding the new equipment. What is the production rate under the new arrangement? Just as before, the bottleneck controls the rate of product flow through the plant. Do we have the same bottleneck as before?

Exhibit 7 Revised Workcenter Processing Times within the Tuff Cut Plant

Steel Stores

Steel Sheets   Steel Rods

Fabrication:
20 units per hour;
3 minutes per unit

Steel disks punched
from square steel
sheets

Stacked
steel
disks

Welding:
25 units per hour;
2.4 minutes per unit

Painting:
30 units per hour;
2 minutes per unit

PAINTING BOOTH

Assembly:
25 units per hour;
2.4 minutes per unit

Finished Goods

Exhibit 8 indicates that with the capacity of the welding department increased to 25 units per hour, the fabrication department, with a productive capacity of 20 units per hour, now becomes the process bottleneck. Thus, the production rate has changed from one completed unit every six minutes (10 units per hour = 6 minutes per unit) to one completed unit every three minutes (20 units per hour = 3 minutes per unit). The theoretical throughput per eight-hour shift is calculated by multiplying the number of minutes in an eight-hour shift (60 minutes × 8 hours = 480 minutes) by the production rate. As the following calculations illustrate, improving the process capability of the bottleneck resource dramatically increases the throughput from 80 units per shift to 160 units per shift.

Exhibit 8

Throughput Comparison, Old System versus New System

	Before new CNC welder	After new CNC welder
Bottleneck	Welding area	Fabrication area
Production rate	6 minutes per unit	3 minutes per unit
Throughput per 8-hour shift	$480 \times 1/6 = 80$	$480 \times 1/3 = 160$

In Exhibit 9, panel A represents the four processes of Tuff Cut and work-in-process levels between each process. Under the old system, large amounts of inventory piled up in front of the welding area because it was the bottleneck, or slowest work center in the plant. The work-in-process areas before the painting and assembly processes were empty because these processes were faster than the welding process. Thus, painting and assembly workers had idle time between completing a unit and receiving another one from the welding area.

Exhibit 9 Bottleneck Identification

The new system is presented in Exhibit 9, panel B. Now, the fabrication department is the bottleneck, or slowest work center, in the plant. What is the difference in work-in-process levels between panel A and panel B? In panel B, since all processes are faster than the first one in the sequence, no work-in-process inventory accumulates between work centers. In other words, the welding, painting, and assembly work centers can complete a unit of product before the fabricating department places another unit into work-in-process.

In the spirit of continuous process improvement, the fifth step requires management to start over with step 1. As indicated by Exhibit 8, the improvements have shifted the bottleneck operation from the welding area to the fabrication area. Therefore, managers must look for ways to reduce the new constraint, the fabrication area.

If managers increase the processing capacity of nonbottleneck resources, will throughput increase? What if the managers of Tuff Cut learn of robots that can double the speed of the *assembly* process? Thinking every modern manufacturing plant needs advanced technology to survive, they redesign the assembly process and install robots. Press conferences are held in the community to advertise how the company has modernized the plant and how modernization will carry the company forward into the twenty-first century. The plant managers eagerly await the productivity reports in the month following the installation. What result do you predict? Assume the same information presented in Exhibit 7 except that the assembly department now produces at 50 units per hour. Where is the bottleneck? What is the production rate? What is the throughput? Of course, the fabrication area remains the bottleneck, the production rate continues to be the rate of the slowest production area, and throughput does not increase at all. What has happened? Managers invested in faster machines in an area that already had excess capacity. In other words, the bottleneck (the fabrication area) already restricted the rate at which the assembly area could produce. Adding speed to a nonbottleneck resource does nothing for throughput. However, it increases costs and investment, thus reducing operating income and return on assets.

Just-in-Time and Theory of Constraints Similarities and Differences

This chapter used the operations of Tuff Cut to illustrate the concepts of just-in-time inventory management and the theory of constraints. Just-in-time emphasizes external relationships in an attempt to improve operations and profitability. An example includes developing stronger relationships with fewer suppliers. Also, just-in-time emphasizes fast-cycle, low-inventory manufacturing practices. Performance measures consistent with just-in-time include cycle time, setup time, and work-in-process inventory levels.

The theory of constraints also emphasizes the external environment by considering market demand when determining production levels. Both just-in-time and the theory of constraints have the objective of reducing work-in-process inventory levels; however, the theory of constraints emphasizes placing small amounts of inventory in front of constraints to ensure that they are never idle. Both just-in-time and the theory of constraints emphasize the importance of reducing lead times. Thus, just-in-time and the theory of constraints embrace the concepts of total quality management with respect to satisfying customer needs.

Though the approaches discussed in this chapter have different characteristics, a pattern emerges. To compete in the global economy, companies are learning that identifying and serving customer needs is crucial. In addition, inventory management and cost control are major elements of most companies' competitive strategies.

SERVICE ORGANIZATIONS IN A GLOBAL BUSINESS ENVIRONMENT

OBJECTIVE 6

Explain how new manufacturing environment concepts apply to service organizations.

The concepts illustrated in this chapter also are directly applicable to companies that deliver services, rather than tangible products, to their customers. For example, an insurance company specializing in automobile coverage can apply TQM principles in its quest to meet the needs of policyholders. Assume that Fender Bender Insurance Company knows that customers want their insurance claims processed quickly in the event of an automobile accident. Fender Bender may analyze activities in its claims processing department to discover ways to reduce cycle time.

Assume that a study conducted by Fender Bender showed that the average policyholder waits three weeks (15 working days) after submitting a claim before receiving a check. Further studies showed that it takes four hours to process an average claim. Thus, value-added time represents a very small portion of total cycle time. Why does a claim remain in work-in-process so long? Perhaps a bottleneck exists.

For Fender Bender, the number of claims processed is equivalent to throughput for a manufacturing company. Thus, to improve throughput, bottleneck activities must be identified and improved. The check preparation function is an example of a bottleneck within Fender Bender. After cost estimates are received from three separate repair facilities and an insurance adjuster gives final approval, the final step is check preparation. Fender Bender's checks are computer-generated; however, an office employee must enter the amount and the payee into the computer. Fender Bender discovered that the employee responsible for entering check data sometimes waited three or four days between processing batches of checks. Rather than preparing checks several times per day, the employee allowed claim forms to accumulate for processing in one large batch. Thus, work-in-process levels and cycle time increased, resulting in slower claims service and dissatisfied policyholders.

The check-processing activity is only one potential bottleneck, but it illustrates the concepts of a customer-focused total quality management philosophy, bottlenecks, throughput, and cycle time within a *service* organization. Understanding administrative processes permits managers in various service industries to deliver value to their customers. Other examples of customer-oriented services include one-day mortgage loan approval offered by certain mortgage lenders, fast checkout procedures offered by major hotel chains, and rapid car rental and drop-off services provided by leading car rental agencies.

3 SELF-STUDY PROBLEM

Autobrake wishes to identify bottlenecks in the production process.

Required

A. How would you identify potential bottlenecks by observing a manufacturing process?
B. If the bottleneck in Autobrake's process is idle for one hour, what is the effect on plant throughput?
C. How would an hour of lost time on a nonbottleneck machine affect throughput?
D. Identify some ways to ensure that production time on the bottleneck process is not wasted.

The solution to Self-Study Problem 3 appears at the end of the chapter.

REVIEW

SUMMARY of IMPORTANT CONCEPTS

1. Managers use accounting information to help them make strategic and operational decisions.
   a. Strategic decisions are major, high-level decisions that affect the overall direction of an organization.
   b. Operational decisions focus on the day-to-day operations of the company.

2. Total quality management includes the following activities:
   a. Identify customers.
   b. Identify customer needs.
   c. Identify product (good or service) features.
   d. Identify process (production or delivery) features.
   e. Establish controls and conduct operations.
   f. Assess performance against goals from both internal and external customer perspectives.

3. Just-in-time (JIT) has the following key elements:
   a. High-quality input and output are required.
   b. Inventory levels are reduced.
   c. Production rates become faster.
   d. Suppliers become partners, rather than adversaries.
   e. Machine changeover (setup) times must be short.
   f. Production batch sizes are small.
   g. Inventory is pulled through a plant based on market demand.

4. Manufacturing plants typically are organized as process-oriented or product-oriented facilities.
   a. Process-oriented facilities typically group equipment by function; all welders, painters, or grinders are located together in one part of the facility.
   b. Product-oriented facilities arrange equipment according to the needs of products or product families; a production area may contain a welder, grinder, and painter to accommodate the needs of a particular product.

5. The theory of constraints has the following key steps:
   a. Identify the process constraint (the bottleneck).
   b. Decide how to make the most efficient use of the constraint.
   c. Subordinate all other decisions to those identified as making efficient use of the constraint.
   d. Improve the processing capability of the constraint.

6. The concepts of total quality management, just-in-time, and the theory of constraints can be applied to service organizations.
   a. All organizations use processes to deliver their goods or services to customers.
   b. TQM principles apply to service organizations as well as to manufacturing companies.
   c. Processes within service organizations can contain bottlenecks that affect lead time and throughput.

DEFINE

TERMS and CONCEPTS DEFINED in this CHAPTER

bottlenecks (M341)
cycle time (M339)
just-in-time manufacturing (M337)
manufacturing cell (M344)
process-oriented plant layout (M342)

production rate (M341)
product-oriented plant layout (M343)
theory of constraints (TOC) (M347)
throughput (M341)
total quality management (TQM) (M334)

SELF-STUDY PROBLEM SOLUTIONS

SSP11-1   A.

Step 1   First-stage turning (5 minutes)
Second-stage turning (4 minutes)

Step 2   Milling (7 minutes)

Step 3   Grinding (3 minutes)

Step 4   Assembly (6 minutes)

Step 5   Packaging (15 seconds)

Within the plant, raw material goes through five operations: turning (first and second stage), milling, grinding, assembly, and packaging. Following packaging, cylinders are shipped to wholesalers, who sell and ship to retailers.

B.   Using TQM principles, there are several clues for improvement in the process description. For example, Autobrake orders raw materials from many vendors, using the lowest cost as a criteria. In addition, communication between the plant floor and the purchasing department often is very poor. Perhaps Autobrake could reduce the costs of acquiring raw materials by working closely with a few selected vendors. Understanding suppliers' cost drivers may also help Autobrake reduce acquisition costs. For example, production needs could be forecast well in advance and provided to vendors, who then might pass along savings resulting from better communication between the two companies. Delivery costs often can be reduced by careful planning.

The process description also suggests that setup times between batches of different products are very lengthy. Since the process appears to be capacity-constrained (Autobrake has a backlog of orders), an hour used to set up equipment cannot be used to make brake cylinders. Therefore, if a faster method of performing machine setups can be developed, nonproductive setup time can be converted into productive manufacturing time.

The scenario at the close of the problem suggests that Autobrake has the opportunity to sell directly to a large retailer and to eliminate packaging costs. Packaging includes raw materials (in the form of paperboard boxes) and also labor and overhead costs associated with handling.

Thus, by identifying key process features and establishing controls to ensure that Autobrake meets or exceeds demands placed on these processes, Autobrake's quality may be improved and costs may be reduced. The end result is a satisfied customer who receives a quality product at a competitive price.

SSP11-2   A. 1.   Production rate is defined as the number of units a manufacturing system is capable of producing in a given time period. The production process consists of the following steps and associated manufacturing times:

First-stage turning	5 minutes	
Second-stage turning	4 minutes	
Milling	**7 minutes**	**(Milling is the bottleneck)**
Grinding	3 minutes	
Assembly	6 minutes	
Packaging	$\frac{1}{4}$ minute (15 seconds)	

To determine the production rate, identify the slowest process because it determines the rate of flow through the plant. In the Autobrake facility, the milling department requires seven minutes to process a component; thus, we would expect to see a component available for shipment every seven minutes.

2. Total processing time is determined by adding the time required to process a unit at each step in the process, as follows: $5 + 4 + 7 + 3 + 6 + \frac{1}{4} = 25\frac{1}{4}$ minutes.

3. Plant throughput (assuming no breakdowns) is calculated by multiplying 60 minutes by the production rate (60 minutes per hour $\times \frac{1}{7} = 8.6$) Thus, the plant would produce approximately nine cylinders per hour.

B. Total processing time should be shorter than cycle time. Cycle time is the sum of processing time, moving time, and waiting time. The cycle time required to move a unit of product from the raw materials inventory to the finished goods storage area is the sum of all processing and waiting times. Waiting and moving times are considered non-value-added activities. Alternatively, processing time is value-added time, in which materials are converted from their original form.

C. Traditionally, plants were organized according to the machine functions, and products were transported through the plant to carry out various manufacturing steps. These process-oriented plants consume many resources in moving and handling materials. Alternatively, work cells typically are U-shaped and consist of machines dedicated to a product or product family. Machines are arranged according to product requirements. Work-in-process inventory levels usually are small, and cycle times usually are short. In addition, materials moving and handling is reduced greatly as a result of locating machines close together. From a cost management perspective, production costs are associated more easily with products and product families because many costs can be traced directly to cells and then to products manufactured within the cells.

SSP11-3 A. Since bottlenecks produce at a slower rate than other machines in the plant, stacks of work-in-process inventory usually are piled up in front of the bottleneck to await processing. Other clues include a machine or work center that constantly is active. In other words, bottleneck resources do not have slack time because they are attempting to catch up with faster processes that continue to add work to their "to do" list.

B. An hour of lost time on a bottleneck resource translates into an hour of lost production for the entire plant. In Self-Study Problem 2, the production rate of the plant was found to be approximately nine units per hour. Therefore, an hour of lost time on the bottleneck resource results in a loss of nine units.

C. An hour of lost time on a nonbottleneck resource may have no impact on throughput. Since the rate of flow through the plant is determined by the processing speed of the bottleneck, other machines have faster processing speeds and can "make up for lost time."

D. Inspection points can be placed in front of the bottleneck, so that valuable time is not spent processing defective units. Also, workers can be asked to cooperate with respect to lunch and break periods, to permit constant operation of the bottleneck resource. Setup times can be reduced by either devising ways to perform setups faster or developing part or all of the setup "off-line" while the machine is engaged in production. This technique is referred to as converting on-line setup time to off-line setup time.

Thinking Beyond the Question

How can managerial accounting help beat emerging competition?

Erin and Seth have determined they must make better use of bottleneck resources within their production area. Seth has observed that some machines occasionally are idle during lunch breaks. He has attempted to explain the importance of minimizing downtime on these key resources. However, some of the production workers do not understand why bottleneck resources impact production levels differently from nonbottleneck resources. If Seth and Erin want to maximize the number of units produced, what are some strategies to ensure production time on a constraint is maximized?

QUESTIONS

Q11-1
Obj. 1
NCCB produces pool tables and billiard supplies. The company is considering changes in the billiard ball production process that would reduce operating costs but would not affect any physical aspects of the product. It also is considering an expansion of operations whereby it would begin manufacturing pinball machines, a product it has not produced in the past. Which of these plans represents an operating decision? Which represents a strategic decision? What is the difference between operating and strategic decision making?

Q11-2
Obj. 2
Madrid Manufacturing Company produces roller skates designed for use in indoor skating rinks. Over the past five years, Madrid has seen sales decline significantly. The company has not added any new products or changed manufacturing processes in the past 20 years. Some changes have been made in materials, but the basic product has not changed. The company produces standard roller skates with four polyurethane wheels and leather uppers. How could elements of TQM assist Madrid in improving performance and meeting customer needs?

Q11-3
Obj. 2
Quick Drain Plumbing has six full-time plumbers who perform residential and commercial plumbing services. Based on a review of service records over the last several months, it was noted that, on average, plumbers must return to the shop to obtain parts or equipment on one out of every three service calls. How could TQM philosophies improve the performance of the plumbers? Explain your answer.

Q11-4
Obj. 3
Many manufacturing companies experience inventory losses. These losses often result from excess inventory that must be handled, stored, and accounted for, during which time it risks being damaged, being lost, or becoming obsolete. Explain a key cause of excess inventory in an organization.

Q11-5
Obj. 3
Dexter Pharmaceuticals manufactures a variety of over-the-counter pain relievers. Each employee in the production area of Dexter has been trained on a single piece of equipment, which they operate during eight-hour shifts. How would implementation of a JIT philosophy at Dexter affect the workforce?

Q11-6
Obj. 3
Mitchell Gabriel is the plant manager for Carry-All Company. Carry-All produces a soft shell book bag/attaché that is popular with students and young business professionals. During production, the bag passes through a number of steps, such as cutting, sewing, assembly, and finishing. Mitchell wants to increase the number of products being packaged for shipment each day. What advice would you give Mitchell to help increase throughput?

Q11-7
Obj. 3
Leeza Vicaro is a divisional manager for Liddon Industries. Leeza is responsible for the production at three of Liddon's plants. Production at Plant 1 provides components to Plant 2, which in turn provides components to Plant 3. In the second and third plants, component parts from the previous plant are added to raw materials during the production process. Leeza is considering the implementation of JIT manufacturing at all three plants. What are some drawbacks of adopting the JIT system that Leeza should consider?

Q11-8
Objs. 2, 3
Tom Mast is a lathe operator for a company that manufactures precision metal products. The lathe is the first step in the manufacturing process. Jobs begin at the lathe based on customer orders that call for specific numbers of pieces to be shipped. When an order is started, Tom generates the number of pieces ordered, plus a 10% cushion. According to Tom, "This overrun is necessary to allow for errors and scrap in subsequent manufacturing steps." Since production begins based on customer demand, is the company using a JIT system? How could principles of TQM and JIT help the company?

Q11-9
Objs. 2, 3
Brayton Manufacturing has been utilizing JIT concepts in its single manufacturing plant for the past year. One of the key elements in Brayton's production process is the ability of any worker to completely stop the entire production line if he or she detects quality problems. Why is it essential for employees to have such control in a TQM production environment? Explain your answer.

Q11-10
Obj. 4
Alverez Manufacturing produces five different types of battery-operated hand tools. There are four production departments at Alverez, each of which performs similar functions on the various products. A great amount of time is spent in each department changing tools and setting

up machinery to work on the different products. How could a product-oriented plant layout assist Alverez in reducing cost and improving production? Explain your answer.

Q11-11
Obj. 4
Traditionally, companies have designed their plant floors so that similar machines are grouped together. Such a process-oriented layout results in all drill presses in one place, all lathes in one place, and so forth. How does the traditional plant layout add cost to the manufacturing environment? How would this layout change with the implementation of a product-oriented manufacturing system? Explain your answer.

Q11-12
Obj. 5
Step 4 in Goldratt's theory of constraints (TOC) involves improving performance on a constraint. Identify two examples of how managers may improve performance on a constrained resource. Explain.

Q11-13
Objs. 2, 6
Why is a commitment to continuous improvement necessary for the successful implementation of a total quality production process? Is the commitment to continuous improvement isolated to the manufacturing process? Explain your answer.

EXERCISES

If your instructor is using Personal Trainer® in this course, you may complete your assignments online.

E11-1
Write a short definition of each of the terms listed in the *Terms and Concepts Defined in this Chapter* section.

E11-2
Obj. 1
Five types of decisions follow. Classify each decision as strategic or operational. Justify your answer.

a. A steel company's managers implement a policy of charging extra handling fees for orders of less than a full truckload. The policy is intended to encourage customers to buy in larger quantities, which will improve the efficiency of the production process.
b. A South American producer of breakfast beverages decides to build a production and distribution facility in the People's Republic of China to service an expanding market.
c. A plant manager decides to use a third shift to increase production, rather than to ask employees to work overtime.
d. An automobile manufacturing company decides to build a new assembly plant. Rather than producing all of the components necessary to make a vehicle, the company decides to buy most of the components from suppliers. This plan permits the company to reduce investment costs for manufacturing equipment.
e. Management for Telxx Communication decides to accept a special order for one of its products at a reduced price because Telxx currently has excess capacity.

E11-3
Obj. 1
Five types of decisions follow. Classify each decision as strategic or operational. Justify your answer.

a. The head nurse for Riverview City Hospital revised the nursing schedule for July 5–11 because of changes in the hospital's patient load.
b. A company that previously sold its products using a door-to-door sales force began exclusively marketing its products through retail stores.
c. A major state university accepts applications for admission only through its Internet web site. Previously, all applications were received by mail.
d. An automobile company reduces the number of suppliers and forms new, long-term alliances with suppliers of key components.
e. A manufacturing company hires an additional quality control engineer to ensure only high-quality products are shipped to customers.

E11-4
Obj. 1
Managerial decisions may be classified as either operational or strategic. Five business decisions follow. Classify each decision as operational or strategic and justify your answer.

a. A manufacturing firm decides to pursue a low-cost strategy by reducing the number of products offered and increasing production volume of the remaining products.
b. A division manager of a retailing organization decides to increase spending for advertising in advance of the holiday season.

(Continued)

    c. A company decides to sell certain divisions that provide components used in the manufacture of a key product. In the future, the components will be acquired from high-quality suppliers.

    d. An engineering design team decides to change the specifications for purchased materials.

    e. A company attempts to differentiate its product line from competitors by introducing high-cost, high-quality features.

E11-5 The Northport YMCA operates an indoor pool that permits year-round swimming. The YMCA
Obj. 2 offers a variety of member services such as youth and adult swimming lessons, lap swimming, and unstructured open recreational swimming. The aquatics director wishes to implement TQM at the facility and has prepared a list of questions to help achieve her objective. Using your knowledge of recreational facilities, such as the Northport YMCA, provide examples of answers for each of the following TQM questions.

- Who are our customers?
- What are the needs of our customers?
- How can our services satisfy their needs?
- Which processes are crucial to meeting their needs?
- How do we ensure our processes are satisfactory?
- Which performance measures ensure high-quality processes?

E11-6 As discussed in Exhibit 2 of the chapter, six elements comprise the TQM philosophy. Match
Obj. 2 the correct description to each of the following TQM elements:

TQM Element	*TQM Description*
1. Who are our customers?	a. Visual inspection, statistical process control charts
2. What are the needs of our customers?	
3. How can our products or services satisfy their needs?	b. Wholesalers, retailers, patients, downstream processes
4. Which processes are crucial to meeting their needs?	c. Scrap rate percentage, on-time delivery percentage, number of new product introductions, cost per unit
5. How do we ensure our processes are satisfactory?	d. Welding, gold-plating, corrosion-proofing zinc bath
6. Which performance measures ensure high-quality processes?	e. Efficient, cost-effective products capable of operating in extreme climatic conditions
	f. Corrosion-resistant materials used in all products subject to adverse operating conditions

E11-7 The elements of TQM follow. Explain the logic supporting the ordering of the TQM elements.
Obj. 2
- Who are our customers?
- What are the needs of our customers?
- How can our products or services satisfy their needs?
- Which processes are crucial to meeting their needs?
- How do we ensure our processes are satisfactory?
- Which performance measures ensure high-quality processes?

E11-8 Three nonfinancial performance measures and definitions follow. Match the appropriate de-
Obj. 3 finition to each nonfinancial performance measure. Why is gaining an understanding of these measures important?

Nonfinancial performance measures
1. Cycle time
2. Production rate
3. Throughput

Definition
    a. The number of units completed by a process in a given period of time
    b. The number of units completed by a process
    c. Total time required to move a unit from raw materials inventory to finished goods inventory

E11-9
Obj. 3

The manufacturing process at SteelCo. Office Products consists of cutting, assembly, and finishing. Each product requires five minutes for cutting, seven minutes for assembly, and four minutes for finishing. Determine the production rate using the information provided. Explain how production rate affects throughput.

E11-10
Obj. 3

City Surgical Center specializes in outpatient surgery. Typically, each patient requires 12 minutes for admitting and completing insurance documentation, 19 minutes of surgical preparation, 25 minutes of surgery, and two hours of recovery time. During recovery, nurses continually monitor a patient's status by checking vital signs such as blood pressure and temperature. Typically, a 35-minute wait occurs between the admitting process and the surgical preparation process. Calculate the total cycle time for a typical patient at City Surgical Center. How much of the total cycle time would be considered processing time? Explain.

E11-11
Obj. 4

Following are characteristics of product-oriented plant designs. Explain why each characteristic is associated with product-oriented plant layouts.

    a. Minimal transportation (materials handling) cost
    b. Small batch sizes
    c. Short cycle times
    d. Few arbitrary allocations
    e. Minimal setup costs

E11-12
Obj. 4

Point Co. produces artificial stone materials used by landscapers. Investment in fixed assets totals $1,400,000. Sales and expense information is as follows:

Sales	$1,000,000
Variable manufacturing and administrative costs	600,000
Fixed manufacturing and administrative costs	300,000
Operating income	$ 100,000

Management at Point Co. believes variable costs could be reduced from 60% of sales to 53% of sales by using a product-oriented layout, rather than a process-oriented layout. To reconfigure the plant would require additional fixed costs of $25,000 annually, but total assets would remain constant. Assume the change also would help the company increase sales by 6%.

    a. Calculate the company's return on assets (NI/Assets) prior to converting to the product-oriented layout.
    b. Calculate the company's return on assets (NI/Assets) after converting to the product-oriented layout.
    c. Give examples of the types of costs the company might save as a result of reconfiguring the plant.

E11-13
Obj. 5

Arizona Jewelry Company makes individual pieces of sterling and turquoise jewelry in a multi-step process as follows:

    a. Identify the bottleneck process at Arizona Jewelry Company and explain your reasoning.
    b. If the silver preparation process breaks down for one hour and requires unscheduled maintenance, how much production would the company lose?
    c. If the soldering process breaks down for one hour and requires unscheduled maintenance, how much production would the company lose?
    d. Why is your answer to part (c) different from your answer for part (b)?

E11-14
Obj. 5

A manufacturing process consists of four steps as follows:

Materials Movement	12 minutes
Cutting	28 minutes
Assembly	120 minutes
Packaging	5 minutes

(Continued)

    a. Identify the bottleneck process. Explain your answer.

    b. Calculate the throughput that would result from an eight-hour manufacturing period.

E11-15
Obj. 5

Mary Wells sat in her office after a long walk through the manufacturing plant. She has been under a great deal of pressure from corporate to reduce the backlog of late orders. She knew the key to improving throughput was constraint management; however, the company has not managed the constraint very well. In fact, the bottleneck was idle as she toured the plant. The operators were taking their lunch break but failed to load the automated machine prior to leaving. Mary decided to call a meeting with production managers in the afternoon to discuss techniques for bottleneck management.

    a. Explain how managers may identify bottleneck processes.

    b. Why does an hour of lost production on a bottleneck affect throughput, but an hour of lost production on a nonbottleneck process does not?

    c. What kinds of decisions might managers make concerning the efficient use of a bottleneck?

E11-16
Obj. 5

The theory of constraints often is used to improve process performance by wisely managing bottlenecks or constraints. The proper ordering of the five steps recommended to improve process performance has been scrambled in the following list. Arrange the five steps of process improvement in the proper order. Provide an example of how performance on a constraint may be improved.

- Decide how to make the best use of the constraint.
- Attack a bottleneck by identifying the systems constraints.
- If a constraint has been broken but a different bottleneck has been created, start over at step 1.
- Subordinate all other decisions to those made in step 2.
- Improve performance on the constraint.

E11-17
Obj. 5

Deb Samson is the owner of a company that produces glass products, such as shower doors, table tops, and specialty windows for recreational vehicles. The process involves cutting glass into the proper shape, smoothing the edges, heat treating, and packaging. The cutting process is automated and very rapid; two minutes are required to cut a piece of glass to the proper dimensions. The smoothing, heat treating, and packaging processes require eight minutes, ten minutes, and three minutes, respectively. A simple diagram of the process is as follows:

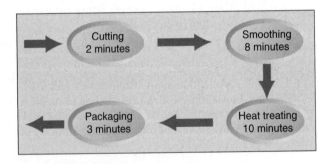

    a. Identify the bottleneck or process constraint.

    b. Explain how you identified the bottleneck.

    c. Calculate the throughput for an eight-hour shift.

E11-18
Obj. 5

Use the information presented in E11-17.

    Using the theory of constraints, Deb Samson invested in technology to improve the processing speed of the bottleneck from 10 minutes per unit to 7 minutes.

    a. Identify the bottleneck after the investment in technology.

    b. Calculate the throughput after investing in technology to improve the bottleneck.

    c. Explain why throughput changed.

E11-19
Obj. 6

A large regional financial consulting firm currently is making a number of important strategic and operational decisions as a result of rapid growth during the past three years. Examples of recent decisions follow. For each decision, determine whether it is considered operating or strategic. Explain your reasoning.

    a. Two years ago the company bought a smaller firm that specialized in estate tax planning. Prior to the acquisition, the parent company had limited experience in this area.

    b. Partners voted to upgrade the firm's telephone system.

    c. The firm implemented a "rapid response" policy to ensure high-profile clients are contacted by a partner within one hour of receiving a request for services.

    d. Partners have become concerned about the turnover rate among entry-level consultants. Many talented people leave the firm within two years, citing excessive travel and time away from family as reasons. The firm is exploring ways to make its work assignment policies less burdensome for their consultants.

E11-20
Obj. 6

A national automobile insurance company uses a multistep process to evaluate automobile damage and to settle damage claims for their policyholders. When a policyholder notifies the company that an accident has occurred, a claims adjuster is assigned to the case. He or she evaluates the damage and prepares a claims report. Multiple repair facility estimates are compared with the claims report prepared by the adjuster and repairs are authorized. This is the most time-consuming step in the claims process. When the repairs are complete, the repair facility is paid by check. The company typically completes 5,000 claims per week. Most claims are paid within 10 days from the time a claims adjuster initially evaluates the damage.

    a. Identify throughput for the insurance company.

    b. What is the cycle time associated with a typical claim?

    c. What is the bottleneck process?

    d. Are the concepts of throughput, cycle time, and bottlenecks relevant to both service and manufacturing firms? Explain.

E11-21
Obj. 6

Jiffy Lunch is a service organization that prepares and delivers meals to elderly people. As a service project, a university sorority provides most of the delivery services. Each of the 20 volunteer drivers typically delivers five meals. The kitchen facility is small but can potentially produce 120 meals per day. Currently, demand for services exceeds the number of meals Jiffy Lunch can provide.

    a. Which process appears to be the constraint or bottleneck?

    b. Using your understanding of constraint management, how might Jiffy Lunch increase the number of lunches served?

    c. Under what circumstances would the kitchen facility become the constraint or bottleneck?

    d. Assume the kitchen facility becomes the bottleneck. Identify examples of ways to improve the performance.

PROBLEMS

If your instructor is using Personal Trainer® in this course, you may complete your assignments online.

P11-1
Obj. 1

Operational versus Strategic Decisions

Gulf Coast Shipping Co. (GCSC) is interested in developing a new type of market for transportation services. They wish to develop a high-speed vessel to compete with slow-moving freight ships that offer low-cost transportation and with rapid-delivery cargo planes that offer high-cost transportation. Managers at GCSC believe a middle market exists that would enable the company to gain business from slower freight ships as well as from more expensive cargo planes. The proposed high-speed vessel would be faster than freight ships but slower than cargo planes.

The company has been experimenting with a number of hull forms and propulsion systems that would make the venture economically feasible. For example, multihull and single-hull designs have been considered. Additionally, engineers must determine whether the vessel should be constructed of steel, aluminum, or some kind of composite material. Possible propulsion systems include water-jet and propeller.

Required Using the information provided, respond to the following questions.

    A. Identify the major strategic issue facing managers at GCSC.

    B. What are some examples of operational decisions the managers must make? Explain.

    C. How do strategic decisions differ from operational decisions?

P11-2 TQM Principles Applied to a University Setting

Obj. 2

Professor Smith was discussing TQM with his accounting class. A student asked how TQM principles might be applied to a university setting. Smith replied, "There seems to be a great deal of confusion among many academics about the application of TQM principles to the classroom. Students are not customers; they are work in process. The customers of a university are the companies that hire our students upon graduation."

Required

A. Respond to Professor Smith's comment.
B. Identify three more customers of a university. Indicate if they are internal or external.
C. Using the concepts presented in Exhibit 2 in this chapter, explain the types of decisions university administrators may face when implementing TQM principles.

P11-3 JIT: Supplier Relationships

Obj. 3

Sung Yu Chen is a purchasing manager for Hilbert Construction, a builder of custom homes. Hilbert is implementing JIT philosophies and has informed Sung Yu that new purchasing procedures need to be developed. For the past 10 years, to obtain the lowest possible cost on building materials, Hilbert has requested quotes from many different suppliers.

Building materials usually are stored in the company's inventory area, where employees select the materials needed for the day, load the materials, and take them to the job site. Materials received in the inventory area are inspected by the shop supervisor. Sometimes the inspection occurs days after receipt. After inspection, poor-quality materials are separated and returned to the supplier.

Under the new plan, the inventory area would be eliminated and suppliers would deliver materials directly to job sites. The delivery of materials must be made as construction progresses, with no buildup or excess inventory held at any site.

Required

A. What changes in supplier relationships will result from the implementation of JIT philosophies?
B. How will the implementation of JIT affect internal and external communications?
C. Under the new plan, how would the inspection process change?

P11-4 Measuring Cycle Time and Throughput

Obj. 3

Clean Products, Inc., manufactures a dust-free computer enclosure that is designed to be used on plant floors and in other harsh environments. The steps required to manufacture the all-steel enclosure and the amount of time each step takes on a per-unit basis are as follows:

Department	Processing Time per Unit
Forming	8 minutes
Milling	11 minutes
Grinding	9 minutes
Assembly	32 minutes
Finishing	25 minutes

Required

A. Calculate the production rate for a completed enclosure.
B. Assume that the company has a total of 384 minutes per day available in each department. Calculate the total daily throughput of completed enclosures.
C. Assume that the company currently has a manufacturing cycle time of 123 minutes per enclosure. Calculate the total process time and total wait time for an enclosure. What does the wait time reveal about the manufacturing process?
D. Which of the departments represents a manufacturing bottleneck? If all departments are operating at maximum output, what effect does the bottleneck have on inventory levels and unit output? Explain your answer.

P11-5 Just-In-Time Objectives

Obj. 3

Apex Technologies produces automotive filters that are used by original equipment manufacturers of automobiles and light trucks. The company also markets a line of replacement filters that are sold through retail distributors.

Apex operates a single plant that manufactures over 100 different filters. The first manufacturing department is metal fabrication. This department stamps out casings and housings that are needed by other departments later in the production process. The metal fabrication department has implemented a JIT system with respect to raw material purchases. No other departments at Apex have yet implemented a JIT system.

Juan Spanoza is the production manager of the metal fabrication department. Although work-in-process inventories have declined significantly since the implementation of JIT, Juan is frustrated at the amount of time that he now spends coordinating with suppliers and with other departments in order to meet production demands. With no buildup of inventory in his department, Juan must now tend to problems immediately, since failure to do so could halt the department's production.

Other managers at Apex have observed Juan's problems and are reluctant to implement JIT in their areas. The plant manager, Chris O'Connor, has scheduled a meeting to discuss further JIT implementation plans for the plant with department supervisors.

Required

A. What are the objectives of a JIT system that Chris should communicate to the department supervisors?
B. What are some actions that Apex could take to ease the transition to a JIT system?
C. In order to successfully implement the JIT system, what arrangements must the company make with vendors? How will these arrangements be formalized?

P11-6 JIT, Ethical Considerations

Objs. 2, 3

McMahon Food Services is a provider of vending machine meals, snacks, and sandwiches. The company operates under a JIT philosophy. Each morning, food is received at the company's commissary, where meals are prepared and packaged. Company route drivers load trucks and deliver the food to vending machines throughout a large metropolitan area.

On a daily basis, the company relies on suppliers providing fresh food materials that are free of contamination, mold, and foreign objects. The only materials that McMahon stockpiles are cases of soda, which are purchased on a weekly basis and are stored in the company's warehouse.

Management at McMahon has received a notice from a food supplier indicating that a delivery of coffee may have been contaminated with a nontoxic cleaning solution used in the supplier's packaging machine. The notice indicated that the cleaning solution posed no risk to health, but would cause a significant foul taste in the coffee.

Managers at McMahon do not wish to recall the coffee from vending machines. They believe that the cost of retrieving the coffee is not warranted, since there is no foreseeable health risk involved. In support of this position, they also note that federal law allows food to contain small traces of foreign substances, provided there is no risk to consumers.

Required

A. What does the coffee contamination suggest about supplier responsibilities and a company's selection of supply sources under a TQM system?
B. In measuring the quality of the product, what ethical considerations should McMahon consider?
C. Comment on the measurement of quality in this situation. Who measures quality, and what implications do those measurements have for McMahon?

P11-7 Process-Oriented versus Product-Oriented Plant Layout

Obj. 4

Gearworks, Inc., manufactures parts for industrial machinery. The manufacturing process requires a variety of machines that grind, heat treat, and polish steel into various shapes. Three different product lines are produced using a traditional process-oriented plant layout as follows:

(Continued)

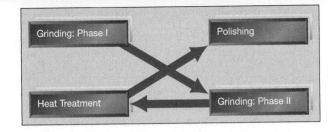

Required

A. Discuss the differences in traditional process-oriented plant layouts and cellular product-oriented plant layouts.

B. Draw a revised plant layout for Gearworks, assuming management wishes to redesign the plant layout to use three manufacturing cells.

C. Why are product-oriented plant layouts more efficient than process-oriented plant layouts? Explain.

D. What types of savings would managers expect to realize by redesigning the plant layout from process-oriented to product-oriented?

P11-8   A Product-Oriented versus Process-Oriented Plant Layout

Obj. 4   Millworks, Inc., is a manufacturer of defense systems used by the military. Typically, Millworks produces three types of components in four different work centers. Though the components are part of the same defense system, they differ in size and complexity. Presently, the company uses a process-oriented facility to manufacture the components. The company has had problems with growing levels of work-in-process inventory. In addition, materials handling costs have become excessively high. As a result of these problems, management is considering reconfiguring the plant as a product-oriented facility. The process includes cutting, milling, assembly, and testing.

Required

A. Draw a diagram of Millworks' existing production processes. Assume the production facility has a square floorplan. Each process requires one-fourth of the floorspace. The first process begins in the top left corner. Products move clockwise around the facility, exiting at the bottom left corner of the building.

B. Draw a diagram that represents how Millworks might rearrange its processes consistent with cellular manufacturing concepts.

C. Explain how your two drawings differ. What are the benefits of a product-oriented plant layout?

P11-9   Push vs. Pull Inventory Systems

Objs. 2, 3, 4   Lamar Manufacturing produces radio alarm clocks. The company offers three clock models with various features. Each clock is assembled in a single plant that is laid out in a functional format. Each worker has been highly trained to perform a particular function in the manufacturing process.

In Department 1, circuit boards are combined with electrical components and attached to a "base." When a batch is completed, the base units are forwarded to Department 3, where they are shelved in work-in-process bins until needed.

In Department 2, speakers are attached to the radio cabinet, and buttons and knobs are attached. Each batch of cabinets is then forwarded to Department 3, where the units are also stored until needed in production.

Department 3 is the finishing department. In this area, the radio cabinets are attached to the base unit and the clock is packaged. The work-in-process area of Department 3 is always full. If a completed batch from an earlier department is found to be defective, Department 3 workers will automatically stop work on that particular model and work on another while the error is corrected.

Completed units are stored in the company's finished goods warehouse. On average, clocks are stored in the warehouse for 45 days before shipment.

Required

A. Is the company operating a push or a pull system of inventory management? Explain your answer.

B. What changes would be necessary to adapt the plant layout to a product-oriented facility? What benefits would the company realize from such changes?

C. Assume that the company implements total quality management by arranging the plant into a product-oriented facility and is successful in reducing work-in-process and finished goods inventories. What further actions should the company take to achieve total quality?

P11-10 Continuous Improvements, Behavioral Implications

Objs. 2, 4

Franklin Berm & Company is a manufacturer of sporting goods. The company employs over 700 workers who are organized under a labor union contract. Management at Franklin plans to implement total quality management and to reorganize the company's operations into a product-oriented layout. The company's plans include the restructuring of production so teams of 15 employees will work on specific product lines. The company wants to eliminate several layers of factory supervisors and place responsibility for production quality on the team leaders.

The company's plan will result in fewer job classifications by reducing the number of employee job descriptions and pay rates. The new job classifications will require broader employee knowledge and ability. In order for an employee to receive a raise under the plan, the employee will be required to learn additional skills and advance to a new job level. Compensation also will be tied to the quality of employee output.

Union leaders have reviewed the plan and are concerned that the restructuring is an attempt to eliminate jobs and to limit employee pay. They argue the plan will discriminate against slow learners and will require workers to dilute their technical skills by spreading their time among more activities. They are concerned that quality will not improve without new machinery and equipment, and that failure to achieve improved quality will be blamed on the workers.

Required

A. Why might the labor union constrain the successful implementation of quality-oriented programs?

B. What ethical obligations does management have toward workers implementing quality programs?

C. What role do employees have in implementing quality programs and continuous improvement?

P11-11 Plant Layout and Work-in-Process

Objs. 3, 4

Brown and Pickens manufactures a variety of battery-operated hand tools, including a cordless screwdriver, drill, and hand saw. The company produces these items in a plant organized in a process-oriented layout in two separate buildings. Batteries are outsourced to a dependable, high-quality supplier who makes deliveries to Brown and Pickens on a daily basis.

The main components of the tools are a motor, gears, and a casing. The company winds motors in one area of the plant, using coil-winding machines. The casings are manufactured in another area of the plant, using an injection molding machine. The gears are milled in the machine shop, using computer-controlled milling machines. All of the component parts are moved to the assembly area, where they are combined to form a finished product. Setup time on these machines is significant. To change any of these machines from one product to another takes over an hour.

The manufactured motors are moved to the assembly area by forklift every other day. The casings are produced in large batches and stored in a warehouse adjacent to the assembly area. The gears are manufactured in a separate building, across the street, and are held in that building until needed by assembly. The assembly area maintains just enough gears to meet production needs for a single day. Gears are delivered to the assembly department in small batches as needed to keep production flowing.

(Continued)

Required

A. How would having a manufacturing cell for each of the products differ from the current plant layout? What changes would this create in the product flow? How would work-in-process inventory be affected?

B. How could changes in the plant layout improve material handling and storage practices at Brown and Pickens? What effect would a change in plant layout have on the value of work-in-process? Explain your answer.

C. The gears are delivered in small batches just as needed by production. Would you consider this proper use of JIT? Why or why not?

P11-12 Performance Evaluation, Constraints

Obj. 5

Corsair Window Company manufactures custom-insulated windows and screens for residential and commercial uses. Each window is manufactured to specific building measurements. Corsair utilizes a JIT approach to manufacturing and plans each production run so that it can be shipped as soon as it is completed. Shipping dates are very important to Corsair, as most sales contracts contain a monetary penalty for late delivery.

All windows pass through a finishing station. At this station, hardware is installed, screens are attached, and an inspection is performed to ensure the windows meet specifications. The company has only one finishing station in its plant. Managers have long talked about adding a second finishing station. However, a second station is not warranted because the amount of processing time is so small. On average, a window is in the finishing station for 15 minutes, which is the least amount of time a window spends in any single process.

Recently, a large shipment of windows was not delivered on time, and the company incurred a significant penalty. After review of the manufacturing logs for these windows, it was determined that the shipment was late because all 48 windows in the order were delivered to the finishing station on the afternoon the windows were to be shipped. In addition, several of the windows had to be returned to other stations in the plant for minor rework and adjustments.

Required

A. How does the finishing station impose a constraint on production?

B. How does the finishing station constraint affect the utilization of other workstations and the amount of work in process in the other areas of production?

C. Should the inspection process be placed ahead of the finishing station? Where should the inspection process occur? Explain your answer.

P11-13 Bottlenecks, Value-Added Activities, and Process Improvement in a Service Organization

Obj. 6

Second Mortgage Lenders (SML) was established in 1985 for the purpose of writing home equity loans, often referred to as second mortgages. For example, if a homeowner's property has a market value of $250,000 with a mortgage balance of $180,000, the homeowner would have $70,000 in equity ($250,000 − $180,000). Second Mortgage Lenders would lend a homeowner up to 85% of the equity value for home improvements, college costs, or other personal needs.

The process of writing second mortgages involves an interview, credit history evaluation, financial analysis, property appraisal, loan committee meeting, and closing. At the interview, an SML loan officer would initially screen potential clients and provide a loan application packet. Upon receipt of the loan application, the loan officer would conduct a credit check and analyze the financial information provided by the applicant. Variables such as annual salary and employment history are considered. Next, a real estate appraiser is hired to estimate the property value. Following the appraisal, the loan committee meets to make a decision after considering all of the inputs. If the loan is approved, a meeting is scheduled to sign papers that close the loan agreement.

A typical loan package requires approximately two weeks from the initial interview until closing. SML wants to be more responsive to its customers by providing more rapid loan decisions. The following times are estimates based on past transactions.

Activity	Time Required
Interview	20 minutes
Credit history evaluation	$\frac{1}{2}$ hour
Financial analysis	$1\frac{1}{2}$ hours
Property appraisal	5 business days*
Loan committee meeting	10 minutes
Closing	35 minutes

*The actual appraisal requires approximately 4 hours.

Required

A. Why does SML want to reduce the time required to approve (or reject) a loan application?
B. Where is the bottleneck process?
C. What is the value-added time required to produce and to close a mortgage?
D. What is the non-value-added time associated with the loan process?   42 ⁹
E. What recommendations would you make to SML?

P11-14   TQM in a Service Environment

Objs. 2, 6

Olympic Insurance provides home and auto coverage to policyholders in six states. Olympic has agents in many cities, but has a central office in Atlanta, Georgia. This office issues policies and settles all claims.

If policyholders wish to file a claim, they contact their local agent. The agent gathers information, prepares a report on the damage, and submits the claim to the home office for processing. Managers at Olympic have determined that three weeks are required from the filing of the agent's report to the issuance of a check. Many customers have complained about the three-week delay, and Olympic would like to speed up the processing time.

Managers have determined that the delay in issuing checks occurs in the accounting department. The average claim is held in the accounting department for more than one week before it is processed and a check is prepared. Accounting personnel insist that weekly check runs are adequate to settle claims in a timely manner. The main reason for delays, they say, is incomplete files submitted by the claims processors that must be sent back to the processors for further work.

Required

A. How could Olympic utilize total quality management techniques to improve claims processing?
B. What does the information related to the accounting department suggest about processing time and product quality?

P11-15   Excel in Action

SPREADSHEET

Music Makers currently has the capacity to produce 500,000 CDs per month. It produces 400,000 data CDs and sells these for $2.50 per unit. It produces 100,000 music CDs and sells these for $3.10 per unit. Demand for the company's products is sufficient that it could sell more CDs if it could produce more.

CDs are produced in two departments. The copying department includes six work cells, one for each of six copying machines. Each cell can produce 150 units per hour and is capable of operating 600 hours per month under normal conditions. The packaging department includes 12 work cells. Each cell can produce $66\frac{2}{3}$ units per hour and is capable of operating 625 hours per month under normal conditions.

The company is considering the acquisition of new packaging equipment. The equipment would permit each cell to produce 75 units per hour. Each cell would operate only 600 hours per month because of the need for extra maintenance of the equipment. The equipment would require an additional investment in assets of $1,200,000 and would result in additional fixed manufacturing costs of $18,000 per month. Variable manufacturing costs would be reduced from 50% of sales dollars to 49%. The company could sell all the additional units it produced. Half of this additional production would be for data CDs and half for music CDs. The CDs could be sold at current sales prices.

(Continued)

Current fixed manufacturing costs are $326,000 per month, and current fixed general and administrative costs are $210,000 per month. The general and administrative costs would not be affected by the purchase. The company's current investment in assets is $6,550,000.

Required Determine the current production capacity of Music Makers' copying and packaging departments using a spreadsheet. What would the capacity be if the equipment is purchased? Calculate the company's sales, variable costs, fixed costs, and profits for the current and revised options. Also calculate the company's annual profit margin, asset turnover, and return on assets for each option. Annual asset turnover and return on assets is 12 times the monthly amount. Should Music Makers invest in the equipment?

Your analysis should use cell references and formulas where possible. Use appropriate formatting throughout.

Suppose the equipment required an investment of $1,600,000 and resulted in an increase in fixed manufacturing costs of $24,000 per month. Should Music Makers invest in the equipment?

P11-16   Multiple-Choice Overview of the Chapter

1. A key concept of the JIT inventory system is to:
   a. utilize work-in-process as a cushion for production when material deliveries are late or a department is unable to operate.
   b. purchase raw materials from many suppliers.
   c. keep large stocks of raw materials in order to maintain a high rate of productivity.
   d. keep inventories to minimum levels, or eliminate them entirely, through careful planning.

2. The flow of goods through a JIT system is based on:
   a. a department completing a batch of units as quickly as possible so that the units can be pushed to the next department.
   b. processing goods in large batches rather than less economical small batches.
   c. maintaining a stockpile of raw materials in anticipation of errors in production.
   d. meeting customer demand by pulling inventory through production, with no buildup of inventory at any point in the production process.

3. A successful JIT system is based upon which of the following concepts?
   a. A large number of suppliers ensures frequent deliveries of small lots.
   b. Suppliers offering the lowest prices should always be accepted.
   c. Long-term contracts with suppliers should be avoided.
   d. Suppliers make frequent deliveries, thus avoiding the buildup of material inventories on hand.

4. The plant layout under the JIT concept emphasizes a:
   a. functional approach, in which machines performing the same function are grouped together.
   b. product approach, in which all machines needed in the production of a particular product are grouped together.
   c. facilities approach, in which all machines of a similar nature are located in one plant building.
   d. contractual approach, in which the processing of certain subassemblies is performed by a small number of independent machine shops under contract to the manufacturing company.

5. The term *throughput* means:
   a. the length of time required to turn materials into products.
   b. the total volume of production.
   c. the time involved to prepare a machine for the production of a different item.
   d. production of goods without the accumulation of raw materials or work-in-process inventories.

6. A cluster of two or more related machines at a single workstation is referred to as a(n):
   a. manufacturing cell.
   b. activity center.
   c. functional layout.
   d. bottleneck.

7. Which of the following statements regarding total quality management is *not* correct?
   a. Inspection of finished goods is performed by quality control inspectors.
   b. Total quality demands that suppliers provide prompt delivery of goods that are free of defects.
   c. Defective components can halt the entire manufacturing process.
   d. The inspection function for incoming goods is shifted from the company to its suppliers.

8. Production rate refers to the:
   a. total amount of time to move a unit from raw materials inventory to finished goods.
   b. number of units completed by a process in a given period of time.
   c. number of minutes that pass between units completed.
   d. amount of time needed to prepare a machine for its next operation.

9. Under a total quality management system:
   a. understanding customer needs is critical.
   b. once a popular product has been perfected, a company can be assured that customers will continue to buy it.
   c. the primary focus is on accumulating quality accounting information.
   d. always having a lot of inventory available is critical.

10. Under JIT, the plant floor is:
    a. laid out in a functional format, with similar types of machines grouped together.
    b. laid out in a product-oriented flow.
    c. laid out in a single line through which all products must pass.
    d. usually cluttered with excessive work-in-process.

CASES

C11-1   **Reducing Process Time**

Objs. 3, 5

Many companies have made shortening the production rate of various processes their primary goal. Most of these companies have reviewed costs and eliminated as much product cost as feasible. Now the focus is on speed. The commitment to speed affects every phase of a company's business. Administration, sales, engineering, and production are all expected to complete tasks faster and more efficiently than ever before. Improved computer technologies have allowed companies to organize, synthesize, and analyze information, giving firms that can operate faster a competitive advantage.

Required

A. Explain how faster processes can be applied in areas such as engineering and administration. How can reduced process times in these areas help a company be more competitive?
B. Explain why improved quality is essential to a company that is able to work faster and reduce process times.
C. Teamwork is essential to any successful effort to reduce process time and speed up processes. Do you agree? Why or why not?
D. What are potential problems that may arise from the increased speed of processes?

C11-2   **Bottleneck Identification and Management at Perma-Clear Glass**
Obj. 5   **Company**

Perma-Clear Glass Company was founded in 1980 by Rob Samson and enjoyed rapid growth as demand for new construction materials exceeded supply. The company became efficient at

(Continued)

converting large sheets of glass into various smaller dimensions demanded by residential and commercial builders. In recent years, Perma-Clear diversified its product line to include specialty glass items, such as tempered glass tabletops and shower doors. More recently, large vertically integrated competitors have captured market share from Perma-Clear because these companies efficiently produce standard products in very large volumes.

In response to shrinking profit margins on standard high-volume architectural products, the marketing department at Perma-Clear identified a low-volume, high-margin niche in the sports/recreational vehicle industry. Because builders of specialty boats, custom vans, and travel trailers often require small orders of tempered glass cut in unusual shapes, these glass products command a market premium. Managers at Perma-Clear believe they can obtain a significant portion of this market because their competitors are not equipped to make small-volume, complex glass shapes efficiently.

Managers at Perma-Clear are analyzing the potential impact on existing production processes using a computer-based factory simulation package. They wonder whether the introduction of a new product line may adversely affect existing manufacturing processes. Specifically, they are concerned that introducing many small-batch production orders may reduce the plant's total throughput in units and profitability.

The production process for the standard architectural product consists of four steps: cutting, shape edging, tempering, and packaging. The cutting process utilizes a computer numerically-controlled cutting machine to produce various sizes and shapes from a large piece of glass. Following cutting, the glass pieces advance to the shape-edging area where workers fasten each piece onto a jig and grind the edges to meet engineering specifications. Following the shape-edging process, the piece is tempered. In the tempering process, glass passes through a heated oven for a specified period of time. Heat from the tempering process causes irreversible structural changes in the glass. If broken, a sheet of tempered glass should shatter harmlessly into many tiny pieces. Following the tempering process, individual orders are carefully packaged and attached to pallets for shipping.

Management has asked the industrial engineering department to compile relevant information about the process. A summary of the report is shown in Exhibit A. The report identified several key characteristics of the production process. Changeover times in the cutting area are rapid because of computer numerically-controlled equipment. Data from the shape-edging area present a different story. Long setups in the shape-edging area are required as jigs are changed between batches. Tempering setup requires adjusting the temperature controls and loading the racks for processing. The packaging area requires very little setup time, and the process is fast and reliable. An engineer noted that a major problem associated with packaging is the time required to bundle orders consisting of many different items.

Exhibit A
Processing Time and
Setup Time by Process

	Cutting	Shape Edging	Tempering	Packaging
Processing time (average per unit)	3 minutes	6 minutes	4 minutes	2 minutes
Setup time (average per batch)	2 minutes	10 minutes	3 minutes	1 minute

Managers are unsure how introducing a new product into the mix will affect existing processes. They would like the simulation model to help management identify the process constraint and to understand how the new marketing strategy will impact day-to-day operations at Perma-Clear.

Required
A. Discuss the competitive environment of Perma-Clear. What are its competitive strengths?
B. What is the nature of the new proposal?
C. Prepare a sketch of the manufacturing process at Perma-Clear. Include processing times in your sketch.

D. Where is the bottleneck located? Explain.
E. Using the information presented in Exhibit A, determine the number of products that can be produced in an eight-hour shift.
F. Can throughput increase if the cutting area is given increased capacity? Explain.
G. What do you think will happen to production volume (throughput) as a result of introducing a variety of new small-volume products? Why?
H. Are there additional factors that management should consider before adding new items to the product line?

CAPITAL INVESTMENT DECISIONS

How can managerial accounting help in choosing new manufacturing facilities?

Erin and Seth are debating whether to invest in new, largely automated, equipment for sealing and varnishing furniture parts. Young Designs, Inc., has been sealing and varnishing manually. At present, employees place furniture parts on racks and spray them by hand. After that, the racks are moved into a drying room and then into parts inventory until used in production.

Seth believes production volume will increase enough during the next year to justify investing in an automated system. Under the new system, furniture parts will travel on a conveyer belt. The parts will be dipped into a tank containing sealant and varnish, then continue along the conveyer belt through an automatic dryer, and move directly into the parts inventory.

FOOD FOR THOUGHT

What is the primary risk Erin and Seth face in making this decision? What type of financial model do you think would be appropriate for making this type of decision? Suppose the new system would reduce manufacturing throughput time by two-thirds. Based upon what you have learned about manufacturing so far, how might this influence the decision? Let's listen as Seth, Erin, and Roberta discuss the issues regarding the new manufacturing process.

Seth:	The new system will save a great deal on our cost of labor by cutting total labor hours by 20 percent.
Erin:	That assumes we are operating at practical capacity. Currently, we are operating well below capacity.
Seth:	Agreed. But over the last six months our sales have been increasing steadily. Based on that, we will be close to capacity by the beginning of next year. It will take that long to purchase and install the new system.
Erin:	Even so, our fixed costs will go up. We will have to pay more for maintenance in addition to the purchase and installation costs. We will also have a one-time training cost to teach our finishers how to use the system. Plus, we will have depreciation cost to consider. Will the lower operating cost of the new system really justify the cost of the investment?
Seth:	That depends upon the volume we expect to produce, and how certain we are that we can achieve that volume. Also, Roberta tells me depreciation is not a cost. It is an expensing of a cost that has already been incurred—the cost of purchasing and installing the new system. If we count both depreciation and the cost of the investment in our analysis, we will be double counting.
Erin:	What about the cost of the varnish?
Seth:	The cost of the varnish is the same using either the manual or automated system. I don't think it's relevant. We should consider only those costs that differ if we use one system or the other.
Erin:	Well, it sounds to me like we need to put all the relevant data into a model that will help us decide if we should make the investment.
Roberta:	I agree. You should be concerned about the risks of making such an investment. Consider fixed costs, breakeven point, and operating risk. If you make this investment, your operating risk will increase.

Seth: *So if we believe making the investment has the potential to reduce labor costs, we have to be willing to accept the risk that our breakeven point will increase.*

Erin: *Even if we are willing to accept the higher operating risk, how do we determine if this investment will pay for itself?*

Roberta: *Well, one way is to compare the value of the expected cash inflows from the investment to the value of the expected cash outflows. Since these inflows and outflows are likely to occur at different times, you need to adjust the value of the flows to a common point in time. This method is called discounted cash flow.*

Seth: *I can see that money has a time value. Certainly, money received sooner is more valuable than money received later. But, I'm a little concerned that we haven't considered all the benefits of making this investment. For example, I've read that decreasing the amount of time products spend in the manufacturing process—throughput time—can reduce the overall cost of manufacturing. The new system we're considering will reduce throughput time. How do we try to capture this benefit?*

Roberta: *We will need to identify benefits from the faster throughput, such as lower inventory levels, and attempt to quantify these benefits so that they can be included in the financial model.*

Erin: *Let's get some of this information together. Once we look it over, we can talk further about this investment.*

OBJECTIVES

Once you have completed this chapter, you should be able to:

1 Identify factors that affect capital investment decisions and explain why these decisions are important to companies.

2 Calculate net present value, internal rate of return, payback, and accounting rate of return.

3 Describe the effect of the new manufacturing environment on capital investment decisions.

4 Identify factors that are important for strategic capital investment decisions.

5 Describe the factors affecting capital investment decisions in service organizations.

FACTORS AFFECTING CAPITAL INVESTMENT DECISIONS

OBJECTIVE 1

Identify factors that affect capital investment decisions and explain why these decisions are important to companies.

When a company makes a decision to invest in long-term assets such as plant and equipment, it is making a *capital investment decision.* These decisions often involve large outlays of cash for long periods. **The process of making these decisions is known as** *capital budgeting.*

Capital investment decisions can be classified in various ways. One way is to view these decisions as either operational or strategic. *Operational capital investment decisions* **are those that affect only a part of a company's operations, have easily predictable lives, and represent relatively small capital outlays for a business.** An example is the purchase of several new personal computers to track operating data on a production line of a printer manufacturer. *Strategic capital investment decisions* **affect all or a considerable part of a company's operations, have uncertain lives, and require large investments.** A new computer-assisted, robotic production facility to manufacture transmissions is an example. Another example of a strategic capital investment decision is Young Designs, Inc.'s, decision regarding the automated varnishing system. Although this might be considered an operational capital investment decision for a large manufacturer, Erin and Seth would likely consider it a strategic decision because Young Designs is a small manufacturer, and the risks are likely to be considerable. The risks associated with strategic capital investment decisions are different from and considerably greater than those associated with operational capital investment decisions.

Capital investments affect a company's profits and cash flows as well as its assets. For example, Exhibit 1 illustrates that the purchase of new equipment, such as a computer, results in:

- A payment of cash for the equipment
- A payment of wages for employees
- Additional interest on money borrowed to finance the purchase
- Additional depreciation expense
- Additional revenues from the sale of goods or services

Exhibit 1

Financial Effects of Capital Investment Decisions

Activity	Cash Flow	Assets	Profits
Increased sales	+ Cash		+ Revenue
Purchase equipment	– Cash	Equipment	– Depreciation expense
Labor costs	– Cash		– Wages expense
Interest costs	– Cash		– Interest expense

Risk

Exhibit 2 depicts several factors that affect the risk associated with capital investment decisions. The outcomes of most investment decisions are uncertain. In addition to the effect of a decision on expected cash flows, risk is an important factor in determining the value of an investment. Erin and Seth are concerned about a particular type of risk—operating risk, which is the risk associated with a company becoming unprofitable because it cannot cover its fixed costs. In the following discussion we will learn that there are many other types of risk that are present in capital investment decisions.

Exhibit 2

Factors Affecting the Risk of Capital Investments

Factors that *Increase* Risk	Factors that *Decrease* Risk
1. Large investment size relative to the company's total investment (assets)	1. Large potential for recovery of investment through resale of the investment asset
2. Long-term recovery of the cost of the investment	2. Recovery of the investment in a short time period
3. Management inexperience with similar investments	3. Management experience with similar investments
4. Difficulty in reversing the investment decision	
5. High uncertainty about whether the asset will perform as expected	

A company is at greater risk if an investment fails when the investment is large relative to the company's size. For instance, a company that invests all of its investment funds in one large project is accepting greater risk than a similar company that invests its funds in five different projects. In addition, the longer it takes to recover the cost of an investment, the greater the risk of the investment because the opportunity for the investment to fail is greater. When the expected performance of the asset is uncertain, prior experience with similar investments can help reduce risk.

Companies typically invest large amounts of money in capital investments. Usually, a company cannot recover the amount it has invested if a project is unsuccessful. For example, consider the construction of a new bank branch. The bank must acquire land and have a building designed, constructed, and landscaped. Specialized construction is necessary, such as installation of a vault. A sign with the bank's logo must be erected, and drive-in windows must be installed. If the branch is unprofitable, other banks may be unwilling to purchase it for an amount close to its original cost. A non-bank purchaser would not need or pay for the specialized assets. As a result, banks are careful in making decisions about construction of branches so that they can avoid losses from unsuccessful investments.

Another factor that increases the risk associated with capital investments is uncertainty about performance, such as that associated with new technology. In general, the newer the technology, the greater the uncertainty about its performance. In addition, there is the risk that competitors will develop newer technology that will make a company's existing technology out of date and result in the loss of business. Often, it takes time to make new technology work correctly.

Case in Point

http://albright.
swlearning.com

Visit Intel's home page
to learn more about the
company.

A Concern About Accuracy

Intel experienced a problem with the accuracy of calculations made by its Pentium® processor, which **IBM** and other companies installed in their personal computers. New versions of the processor corrected this problem. However, the problem was an embarrassment to the company and required the costly replacement of many processors.

Generally, the greater the amount of the original investment that can be recaptured through the sale of the assets, the lower the risk. In the case of a branch bank, it is unlikely that a significant portion of the initial cost could be recovered unless the branch were sold to another bank. Likewise, the greater the value of the asset at the end of its service to a company, the smaller the portion of the investment that must be recovered in cash flows during its service to the company. For example, suppose computers purchased by a software development company can be sold at the end of their service lives for 50 percent of their cost. In this case, only half of the investment in the computers will have to be recovered during their operation at the software company. The rest will be recovered by their sale.

Finally, the more experience management has with a particular type of investment, the less likely the company is to develop problems. For example, if a company's usual business is making corrugated cardboard boxes for packaging, purchase of equipment to improve the efficiency of the business is less risky than purchase of equipment to enter a new line of business, such as making specialty gift boxes. The new line will require management to gain experience with a new manufacturing process and new markets.

Competing for Capital Investment Funds

Large capital investment decisions often involve company politics. Different divisions of companies compete for investment funds. Capital investment projects usually must meet a minimum rate of return on investment requirement before a company will commit funds. Often managers have a strong interest in having their projects funded. This means they are more likely to make favorable assumptions about the projects. However, since some of these projects actually will deliver lower rates of return than were estimated, key decision makers in companies tend to be very careful when they evaluate projects. They try to determine if assumptions are realistic.

Capital investment decisions often involve cash outflows over more than one period. Therefore, these projects must be monitored over time. Monitoring helps ensure that projects are developing satisfactorily and that continued investment is justified. Companies often use a milestone approach to monitoring.

Milestones, **which are major decision points,** are established at the beginning of a capital investment project. At each milestone, the project is reevaluated and a continue or discontinue decision is made. These decisions may be difficult because investments often do not produce positive returns for some time after an initial investment is made. The absence of positive returns during the developmental stage of projects increases investment risk. (Recall that the longer it takes to recover the cost of the investment, the higher the investment risk.)

Consider the decision by **General Electric** to produce a new model of refrigerator. This new model requires additional plant space, equipment, and tools. Considerable cost will be incurred before production can begin. If the model is unsuccessful, much of this cost will not be recovered. However, General Electric may be better off accepting its losses rather than continuing to invest in the product in an effort to make it successful. *Sunk costs* **are costs associated with decisions that have already been made.** For example, the costs of designing and making specific tools that are useful only in producing the new model of refrigerator are sunk costs. Sunk costs are not relevant for future decisions because future decisions cannot alter these costs.

[handwritten margin note: can increase loses]

Monitoring the progress of investment projects can be difficult, as can evaluation of the managers responsible for the projects. To develop forecasts about the amount and timing of returns on these projects, assumptions are necessary. It is frequently difficult to forecast the amount of time it will take to develop and market a new product. For example, Food and Drug Administration approval is required for new pharmaceutical products. In developing a new pharmaceutical product, there is often a long approval process during which the product is tested. In the meantime, the life span of the patent on the product is passing. This means that the pharmaceutical company will have fewer years in which it can market the product exclusively before its patent expires and generic brands begin to erode its sales. If delays occur, they may not be the fault of project managers. It is difficult to assess performance accurately because of uncertainty about what the performance should be.

TRADITIONAL APPROACHES TO CAPITAL INVESTMENT DECISIONS

OBJECTIVE 2

Calculate net present value, internal rate of return, payback, and accounting rate of return.

As discussed in the previous section, capital investments often involve long-term cash outlays. Consequently, the time value of money is an important consideration in making capital investment decisions. There are several tools that can assist managers in deciding whether or not to make a capital investment and in choosing between competing projects. Traditional tools can be divided into discounting and nondiscounting methods. *Discounting methods* **are those that rely on the time value of money.** *Nondiscounting methods* **ignore the time value of money.** Each method has advantages and disadvantages. Nondiscounting methods are less reliable than discounting methods, though some companies use them because they are easier to use. Roberta recommended that Erin and Seth use discounted cash flow analysis, which compares the expected cash inflows and outflows resulting from a capital investment. She said this method considers how the value of cash flows is affected based on *when* cash flows are received.

An important point to remember about the application of discounting methods to capital investment decisions is that they can be misleading when used improperly. This section describes how these methods are used in making capital investment decisions. Subsequent sections will discuss some of their shortcomings, especially in the new manufacturing environment. Also, it is important to keep in mind that these methods require long-term revenue and cost estimates, which often are uncertain. The most difficult task in using these methods is developing reasonable forecasts of revenues and costs.

Net Present Value

Recall that an important attribute of money is that it can be invested to earn interest. A dollar today is not worth the same as a dollar a year from now. **The translation of** future dollars into current dollars is known as *discounting.* The *net present value (NPV)* of an investment is the difference between the present value of expected cash inflows and the present value of expected cash outflows from the investment.

The net present value compares the present value of expected cash inflows and cash outflows associated with a project as shown in the following equation:

$$\text{NPV} = \sum \frac{C}{1 + R^t} - I$$

where NPV = net present value
I = amount invested at the beginning of the project
C = net cash inflow expected in period t
R = required rate of return
t = time period
Σ = summation for all periods

Thus, the net present value of an investment is the difference between the present value of expected future cash flows and the amount invested. Exhibit 3 illustrates an example. Assume that Stockdale Company has an opportunity to invest $60,000 in new equipment. Management expects the company to receive cash inflows of approximately $25,000 per year from sales of goods produced from the equipment. The equipment is expected to have a useful life of three years. In considering the investment, Stockdale's managers determine that the company has $30,000 available in an investment account that earns 8 percent interest per year. It would have to borrow the remaining $30,000 at 12 percent per year. Should Stockdale invest in the equipment?

Exhibit 3

An Illustration of Net Present Value

Time					
Present			**Year 1**	**Year 2**	**Year 3**
Expected future cash flows			$25,000	$25,000	$25,000
Discounted to present value at 10%					
	$22,727	← $25,000 ÷ 1.10¹			
	20,661	← $25,000 ÷ 1.10²			
	18,783	← $25,000 ÷ 1.10³			
	$62,171				
Less:					
Amount invested	60,000				
Net present value	$ 2,171				

To answer this question, consider the rate of return Stockdale will require. If the company uses the $30,000 from its investments, it will forgo the 8 percent interest on the invested funds for the coming year, or $2,400 (0.08 × $30,000). The $2,400 of lost interest is an opportunity cost that should be considered in the decision. *Opportunity costs* **are the costs associated with not taking a particular course of action.** Also, the cost to borrow $30,000 is $3,600 (0.12 × $30,000) for the next year. Thus, to break even on the investment, Stockdale will need to recover the $60,000 invested and earn an additional $6,000 ($2,400 + $3,600) per year. Any amount earned over $6,000 will increase company value and make the investment desirable. The $6,000 represents Stockdale's *cost of capital,* **which is the cost of funds that can be used to finance a project.** The rate of return necessary to earn $6,000 is considered Stockdale's *required rate of return.* **This rate sometimes is referred to as a** *hurdle rate* **because it is the rate that must be earned before an investment is made.** It is also known as the **discount rate** because it is the rate used to discount (reduce) future cash flows to their present value. In this case, Stockdale requires a 10 percent rate of return ($6,000 ÷ $60,000 = 10%).

Using the discount rate of 10 percent, we can compute the present value of the cash flows expected from the investment at the end of each of the three years.

$$PV = \frac{\$25{,}000}{(1.10)^1} + \frac{\$25{,}000}{(1.10)^2} + \frac{\$25{,}000}{(1.10)^3}$$
$$= \$22{,}727 + \$20{,}661 + \$18{,}783$$
$$= \$62{,}171$$

Alternatively, we can use the interest factor for an annuity from Table 4 (inside back cover) for three periods at 10 percent: $25,000 × 2.48685 = $62,171. Recall that an annuity results when the same amount is received each period over the life of an investment. The net present value, then, is the difference between the present value of the expected net cash inflows and the amount invested.

$$NPV = \sum \frac{C}{1 + R^t} - I$$
$$= \$62{,}171 - \$60{,}000$$
$$= \$2{,}171$$

A positive net present value indicates that the initial investment has been recovered and a return greater than the initial investment and cost of capital has been received. Thus, if the net present value is zero or greater than zero, the investment is expected to earn an acceptable return. If the net present value is less than zero, the investment should be rejected because it will earn less than the required rate of return.

To use net present value analysis, an organization must identify an appropriate discount rate. Usually, the discount rate is the company's average cost of capital, the average cost of all sources of financing available to a company, such as bank loans and expected returns to stockholders. Generally, managers should select those projects that promise the highest net present value.

In calculating the present value of cash flows, it is important to include all relevant cash flows. For example, if a capital investment is in property or equipment that has an expected disposal value, that value should be included. Suppose Stockdale invested in equipment that it expects to sell at the end of year 3 for $5,000. The net cash inflow in year 3 would be $30,000 ($25,000 of annual cash flows plus the $5,000 disposal value of the equipment).

If additional cash outflows were required each year as a result of the purchase of the equipment, those cash outflows also should be considered. For example, assume the equipment purchased by Stockdale would require additional insurance costs of $1,000 per year. The net cash flow each year would be $24,000 ($25,000 from sales minus $1,000 of additional insurance).

Also, observe that cash flows should be used in determining the net present value of a capital investment. Revenues and expenses are relevant only if they are consistent with cash flows. Depreciation, for example, is not relevant for a capital investment decision. The cost associated with the purchase of property and equipment occurs at the time the purchase is made. Depreciation is a noncash expense and is not relevant to the determination of net present value.

A cost savings is treated the same as a cash inflow. If the acquisition of equipment by Stockdale reduces annual operating costs (lower labor costs, for example) by $2,000 per year, those cost reductions can be treated as additional cash inflows because the company's cash flow increases by $2,000 per year.

1   SELF-STUDY PROBLEM

WebTUTOR Advantage

The management of Joyful Car, Inc., is considering replacing the company's current semiautomated car washing equipment with a fully-automated system that would eliminate all labor except that required to clean car interiors. Though the new system will reduce labor costs, it represents a substantial capital investment for the small company. Management has developed the following data regarding the investment:

Cost of the new system	$100,000
Sales value of the old system	$ 40,000
Sales value of the new system at the end of its five-year life	0
Required rate of return	10%
Net decrease in annual operating costs	$ 15,000

Assume that Joyful has the cash to pay for the new equipment, and ignore any tax effects.

Required Evaluate the investment using the NPV method. Assess the factors that increase or reduce the risk associated with the capital investment decision in this case. Explain whether you consider the investment to be an operational or a strategic decision for the company, and why.

The solution to Self-Study Problem 1 appears at the end of the chapter.

Internal Rate of Return

Another discounting method that sometimes is used in addition to or instead of net present value is the internal rate of return. **The** *internal rate of return (IRR)* **is the interest rate that results in the present value of cash outflows being equal to the present value of cash inflows from an investment.** In other words, it is the interest rate that results in a net present value of zero. The following equation can be used to determine a project's IRR:

$$PV = \sum \frac{C}{1 + R^t}$$

where PV = present value of the project

C = cash inflow to be received in period *t*

R = required rate of return

t = time period

Σ = summation for all periods

Let's consider Stockdale Company's investment decision using the internal rate of return method. Recall that an investment of $60,000 is estimated to return $25,000 each year for three years. The cost to Stockdale of the $60,000 it will invest is $6,000, or 10 percent, which is the hurdle rate.

Using the internal rate of return method, the investment would be accepted if its internal rate of return is greater than 10 percent. The internal rate of return is the interest rate that equates $25,000 each year for three years with $60,000 today. The IRR would be calculated as follows:

$$PV = \sum \frac{C}{1 + R^t}$$

$$\$60,000 = \frac{\$25,000}{(1 + R)^1} + \frac{\$25,000}{(1 + R)^2} + \frac{\$25,000}{(1 + R)^3}$$

We can find R by trial and error, or we can approximate the value using Table 4 from the back of the book. Table 4 provides an interest factor that associates the present value of an annuity with expected future cash flows:

$$PV = C \times IF$$

where PV = present value

C = expected cash flow each period

IF = interest factor

Therefore,

$$PV = C \times IF$$
$$\$60,000 = \$25,000 \times IF$$
$$\$60,000 \div \$25,000 = IF$$
$$2.4 = IF$$

Look at the third row of Table 4. (The investment is for three years.) Note that an interest factor of 2.4 is the approximate value in the 12 percent column.

Thus, the internal rate of return is 12 percent. Because the internal rate of return is greater than the required rate of return of 10 percent, the investment should be accepted. The internal rate of return is higher than the cost of capital; thus, accepting the investment would add value to the company.

The internal rate of return for a multiyear project where the net cash inflows are not the same each year is the interest rate that will make the present value of the cash flows equal to the initial cash investment. Consider a project with an initial investment of $15,403 that is estimated to return cash flows of $4,000, $4,000, $5,000, and $8,000 for years 1 through 4 of the project, respectively. Again, the interest rate that will make the cash flows from operations equal to the initial cash outlay can be found by trial and error. Exhibit 4 calculates the present value of cash flows from operations using a discount rate of 10 percent and the interest factor from Table 3 (inside back cover). (Table 4 cannot be used because the expected net cash inflows are not the same amount each year.)

Exhibit 4
Present Value
Calculation

Year	Expected Cash Flow		Interest Factor for 10% from Table 3		Present Value
1	$4,000	×	0.90909	=	$ 3,636
2	4,000	×	0.82645	=	3,306
3	5,000	×	0.75131	=	3,757
4	8,000	×	0.68301	=	5,464
					$16,163

The present value of the project is $16,163. This amount is greater than the initial investment of $15,403; therefore, 10 percent is *not* the IRR. A different interest rate must be tried. Should a higher or a lower rate be used? **The higher the interest rate, the lower the present value.** Since $16,163 is greater than $15,403, a higher interest rate must be used so that a lower present value is obtained. The present value using a rate of 12 percent is shown in Exhibit 5.

At 12 percent the present value of future cash flows from operations is exactly equal to the initial investment.

Exhibit 5
Present Value
Calculation

Year	Expected Cash Flow		Interest Factor for 12% from Table 3		Present Value
1	$4,000	×	0.89286	=	$ 3,571
2	4,000	×	0.79719	=	3,189
3	5,000	×	0.71178	=	3,559
4	8,000	×	0.63552	=	5,084
					$15,403

Since the interest rate that makes the cash flow from operations equal the initial investment is 12 percent, this is the IRR for the investment. A trial-and-error procedure must be used to determine the IRR when the cash flows from operations are not the same each year. Computer programs, such as Excel®, contain functions that simplify the calculation. Even these programs begin with an estimated rate of return and use trial and error to find the internal rate of return.

Although the internal rate of return is easily understood by managers, a major disadvantage is that it does not differentiate between two projects that have identical rates of return but that differ in some other important way. For example, consider a $100 investment and a $100,000 investment, both of which have a 15 percent rate of return. Using the IRR method, both investments would be equally desirable, since they have identical returns. However, these investments are not equal because of the substantial difference in the cash outlays required.

Another disadvantage of the IRR method is that it assumes cash flows from operations can be reinvested at the internal rate of return. For example, if a project is expected to have an IRR of 20 percent, it is assumed that each time a cash flow from operations is received, the company will be able to reinvest the cash and earn 20 percent over the remaining life of the investment. This assumption is not always true and is a weakness of the IRR method. If the reinvested cash flow earns only a 15 percent return, the overall return on the investment will be less than 20 percent.

Using Excel to Calculate NPV and IRR

Exhibit 6 illustrates how Excel can be used to determine NPV and IRR using the values shown in Exhibit 5. The NPV or IRR functions can be selected by clicking the insert function button or command and selecting NPV or IRR from the financial category. The cash flows are entered in the spreadsheet.

The NPV calculation in panel A includes the cash flows for each year from Exhibit 5. For example, the initial investment ($15,403) represents a negative cash flow and is entered into cell A1. The annual cash inflows for the following four years are entered into cells A2 through A5. The NPV function is entered in cell A6. The rate of return is entered as .12 and the values are referenced as cells A1:A5. The function returns a value of 0.22317, which is $0.22 or approximately 0, indicating that the NPV of the investment is $0.

In panel B, the IRR function is entered in cell A6. The values field in the dialog box refers to the values in A1 to A5 and an IRR guess is entered into the guess field. The value of the guess is not particularly important, but Excel will take longer to calculate the answer when the guess is not close the final answer. Excel reports the IRR as 12 percent.

Payback Period

An approach to capital investment decision making that does not involve discounting is based on the payback period. **The** *payback period* **is the time required to recover an original investment from expected future cash flows.** For example, if the original investment is $60,000 and the estimated cash inflows are $25,000 per year, then the payback period is 2.4 years ($60,000 ÷ $25,000 per year). When the future cash flows for each period are expected to be equal, the payback period can be computed as follows:

Payback period = Original investment ÷ Periodic cash inflow

If the periodic cash inflows are not the same, the payback period is computed by adding each cash inflow until the sum equals the invested amount. Management decides on a time period in which the invested amount is to be recovered. A project that does not pay back its original investment within this period is rejected. There are shortcomings to such an approach, however. Consider the following cash flows for two projects, each requiring an initial investment of $100,000.

Exhibit 6

Using Excel to Solve an
NPV or IRR Problem

Panel A

Panel B

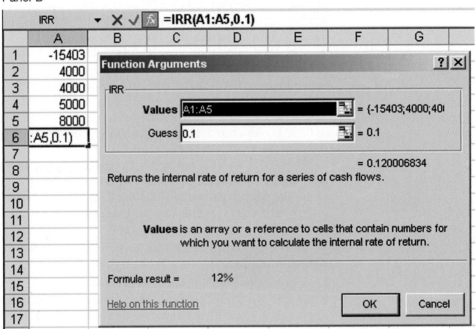

	Investment A	Investment B
Year 1	$20,000	$90,000
Year 2	80,000	10,000
Year 3	5,000	10,000

Both investments have payback periods of two years ($20,000 + $80,000 = $100,000, and $90,000 + $10,000 = $100,000). Thus, if a manager uses the payback period method, both would be equally desirable. In reality, however, B should be preferred over A. Project B returns $90,000 in the first year, compared to $20,000 for project A. The extra $70,000 can be invested in other projects during year 2. In addition, project B continues to return greater cash flows after year 2. Accordingly, the payback method ignores total profitability and the time value of money.

Many companies use the payback period as one of several criteria when making investment decisions. In addition, managers may use the payback method to choose among projects when other attributes, such as NPV, are similar.

Accounting Rate of Return

The accounting rate of return is another commonly used decision-making method that does not require discounting. **The** *accounting rate of return (ARR)* **is the average accounting income a project generates per period divided by the amount of the investment in the project.** ARR differs from discounting methods in that it uses income rather than cash flows to measure return. ARR is computed as follows:

Accounting rate of return = Average income ÷ Investment

The average income of a project is obtained by adding the net income for each period of the project and dividing by the number of periods over which the project will produce income. To illustrate the computation of accounting rate of return, assume that an investment requires an initial outlay of $100,000. The life of the investment is five years, and it is expected to produce net income as follows:

Year	Net Income
1	$10,000
2	10,000
3	20,000
4	15,000
5	25,000
Total	$80,000

Payback period [handwritten]

The average net income is $16,000 ($80,000 ÷ 5), and the accounting rate of return is 16 percent ($16,000 ÷ $100,000). *where DID this come from* [handwritten]

Unlike the payback method, the accounting rate of return considers a project's profitability. Like the payback method, the accounting rate of return ignores the time value of money. Failure to consider the time value of money may lead a manager to select a project that does not maximize company value. However, future cash flows are not always easy to determine. Many investments involve combinations of resources such as plant assets, working capital, and labor, making cash flow from a project difficult to estimate. ARR, therefore, may be used instead of cash flows to approximate the return on investment. *include dep exp.* [handwritten]

Other Considerations

In addition to the considerations discussed in the prior section, there are other considerations that affect the use of discounting models. Three of these considerations are (1) the service lives and residual values of investments, (2) the effects of income taxes on cash flows, and (3) the risk associated with capital investment decisions.

The trade-in or *residual value* **of an investment refers to its market value at the end of its useful life or service life to a company.** *Service life* **refers to the period during which an investment is expected to be used.** A residual value must be estimated in order to make net present value and internal rate of return calculations. Failing to include the residual value understates the cash flows from an investment and could lead to rejection of an acceptable investment. Residual values can be difficult to estimate for an investment in equipment that has an uncertain life.

Sometimes managers overestimate the service lives of assets such as computers because they fail to consider the rate of change of technology. When new technology becomes available (for example, new computer technology), management must decide whether to continue to operate with old assets or to purchase new assets sooner than expected.

Recall that depreciation is a noncash expense. However, depreciation reduces a corporation's taxable income because it is a tax-deductible expense. This reduction in taxes is cash that the company will not have to pay out. Therefore, although depreciation itself does not affect cash flows, its effect on taxes does. As a result, it is important to include the income tax benefits of depreciation when calculating the net present value or internal rate of return of capital investment projects. The following example illustrates how service life, residual values, and depreciation can affect investment decisions.

Merchants' Bank is considering an investment in a new computer system to replace the old computer that is used to process deposits, loans, and other customer transactions. The bank uses the net present value method in its analysis of investment decisions.

The new system, including workstations, a network, and software, will cost $450,000 and will have an estimated useful life of five years. The expected residual value at the end of five years is $50,000. Straight-line depreciation is used for accounting and tax purposes. The old computer system, which has been depreciated to its residual value, can be sold for $20,000. The bank's income tax rate is 35 percent, and its required rate of return is 10 percent. Bank managers believe that the bank can save $100,000 net of any income tax effects each year if the new system is purchased. Should the bank invest in the new computer system?

Exhibit 7 provides an analysis of the investment to answer this question. The analysis involves a series of steps. In step 1, the amount to be invested ($430,000) is determined. In step 2, the amount of depreciation ($80,000 per year) and the effect of depreciation on taxes (savings of $28,000 per year) are calculated. In step 3, the expected cash flows associated with the investment each year are identified. Step 4 involves calculating the present value of the expected cash flows ($516,267). Finally, in step 5, the net present value of the investment ($86,267) is determined.

Because the net present value of $86,267 is greater than zero, the bank should invest in the new computer. In this analysis, the effect of tax savings is important. It adds $106,142 to the present value of the investment (step 4). Without these savings, the present value would be $410,125 ($516,267 − $106,142), and the investment would be unacceptable. Thus, it is important to consider all of the financial consequences of an investment in making a capital budgeting decision.

When managers are unsure about the accuracy of assumptions used in making investment decisions, they often test the sensitivity of their decisions to these assumptions. For example, suppose the managers of Merchants' Bank are unsure about the cost savings they expect from investing in the new computer system. They believe that the savings are most likely to be $100,000 per year, but that they could be as low as $75,000 per year. What effect would the lower level of savings have on the decision? The present value of an annuity of $75,000 per year for five years at 10 percent is $284,309 ($75,000 × 3.79079). Therefore, the total present value of expected cash flows (step 4) would be $421,497 ($284,309 + $106,142 + $31,046), and the net present value (step 5) would be −$8,503 ($421,497 − $430,000). At the lower cost savings, the project would be rejected. The managers now must decide whether they believe the lower cost savings are likely to occur or whether they are confident that the higher savings are likely. Net present value analysis, like other decision tools, does not make decisions for managers. It provides them with information to help them with their decisions.

Exhibit 7

Net Present Value Analysis of Computer Purchase

Go over

Step 1: Amount of Investment

Cost of new computer	$450,000
Less: Sale price of old computer	20,000
Amount to be invested	$430,000

Step 2: Tax Savings per Year

Cost of computer	$450,000
Less: Residual value ~~trade in value~~	50,000
Amount to depreciate	$400,000 *sales*
Expected life	÷ 5
Depreciation per year	$ 80,000
Income tax rate	× 0.35
Tax savings per year	$ 28,000

Step 3: Expected Future Cash Flows

Year	Cost Savings*	Tax Savings	Residual Value
1	$100,000	$28,000	
2	100,000	28,000	
3	100,000	28,000	
4	100,000	28,000	
5	100,000	28,000	$50,000

Step 4: Computation of Present Value of Expected Future Cash Flows

Present value of annuity of $100,000 per year for 5 years at 10%:	
$100,000 × 3.79079 (interest factor from Table 4) =	$379,079
Present value of annuity of $28,000 per year for 5 years at 10%:	
$28,000 × 3.79079 =	106,142
Present value of single amount of $50,000 at the end of 5 years at 10%:	
$50,000 × 0.62092 (interest factor from Table 3) =	31,046
Total present value of expected future cash flows	$516,267

Step 5: Computation of Net Present Value of Investment

Total present value	$516,267
Amount to be invested	430,000
Net present value	$ 86,267

*Assume this cost savings is net of any tax effect due to an increase in income from the capital investment.

done better than 12% greater 10

THE NEW MANUFACTURING ENVIRONMENT

OBJECTIVE 3

Describe the effect of the new manufacturing environment on capital investment decisions.

The new manufacturing environment has changed the way capital investment decisions are viewed. Before the new manufacturing environment, many companies relied heavily on methods such as net present value to justify capital investments. Traditional capital investment analysis focused mainly on the immediate direct benefits, such as labor savings, reduced waste, lower inventories, and improved capacity. Less tangible benefits such as improved quality often were not considered. In the 1980s, foreign companies that produced high-quality products began to compete with U.S. companies. This competition increased the pressure on U.S. companies to improve the quality of their products, which, in turn, increased the need to consider quality improvements when making capital investments.

Increased automation is a major feature of many production processes in the new manufacturing environment. Automation has become a priority for many companies as they replace older equipment. Much of the older U.S. equipment is not computer-controlled, in contrast to that used in countries like Japan.

Another example of the association between the new manufacturing environment and capital investment decisions surfaced in the chapter opening scenario. Many companies embrace the notion of reducing throughput time as a means of reducing costs. Reduction of throughput time can be one objective of reorganizing plant layout and automating production processes.

Automation and Modern Manufacturing

The objective of automation often is not only to increase capacity but also to produce high-quality goods in a consistent, rapid, and economical manner. Used effectively, automation can improve a company's ability to deliver high-quality products, to create value for customers. Automation can help eliminate variation from production standards due to human error. The new manufacturing environment requires a fresh look at the ways capital investment decisions are made. The costs of quality and efficiency are important to many capital investment decisions. These costs are especially relevant when companies automate their production processes.

Frequently, automation is part of a plan to redesign the value chain. Redesigning the value chain can involve many activities, from changing a company's production process to eliminating activities such as inventory storage, material handling, and excessive rework.

In the new manufacturing environment, capital investments involving automation can be classified into four categories, as illustrated in Exhibit 8.

1. *Stand-alone tools*, such as robots used to weld steel, are commonly controlled by computers. Stand-alone tools are the most common form of automation. They can improve quality, speed, or capacity. The amount invested is relatively small compared to that needed for other types of automation. Also, the payback period is relatively short.
2. *Cells of machines* consist of multiple pieces of isolated equipment grouped closely together. An example of a cell is a computer-controlled machine for materials handling grouped with computer-controlled molding equipment to manufacture automobile body parts. These machines have a short setup time and can be quickly changed from the manufacture of one part to another. The amount of the investment often is much higher and the payback period much longer than for stand-alone tools.
3. *Linked islands* consist of cells of machines connected through computerized information networks. Islands give a company the ability to respond rapidly to developing markets by creating new, custom-designed products. Investments are large, and payback periods are long. Also, if one component of an island fails, the entire island is likely to fail.
4. *Computer-integrated manufacturing* links an entire manufacturing process through an extensive information network. For example, **Monsanto Plastics Division** manufactures plastics for use in automobiles, computers, and other products. In its old manufacturing process, changing from one type of plastic to another took hours. The division installed a computer-integrated manufacturing system that permits much faster changeover times, improved quality, and less waste.

Automated production can give a company a powerful competitive advantage in the global marketplace because it allows improved product innovation and quality, shorter delivery time, efficient production scheduling, and lower cost. Computer-integrated manufacturing can involve what are sometimes referred to as "greenfield factories" because virtually the entire factory is redesigned. This type of capital investment has been referred to as a "you bet your company" decision because of the high level of risk involved. Failure of the strategy often means failure of the company.

These capital investment categories in the new manufacturing environment involve different levels of decisions, ranging from lower-level, operational decisions for stand-alone tools to very costly strategic decisions for computer-integrated manufacturing.

Exhibit 8
Categories of
Automation

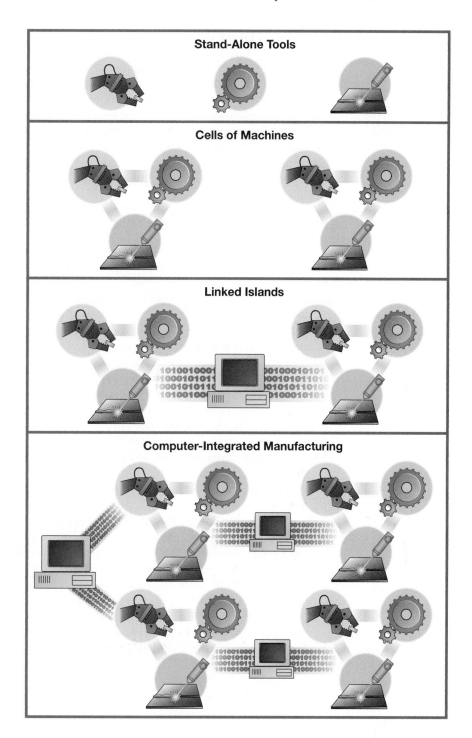

The new manufacturing environment has changed the way many companies make capital investment decisions:

- Investments are becoming more significant. Automation can be large in scope and affect an entire company.
- Equipment is more complex and expensive than the equipment that was the focus of traditional investment decisions.
- The cash flows required to justify capital investments are received over a longer period of time.

In short, capital investment decisions have become longer-term and riskier. The next section examines how managers make capital investment decisions in this new strategic environment.

MAKING STRATEGIC CAPITAL INVESTMENT DECISIONS

Managers making capital investment decisions in the new manufacturing environment do not rely solely on traditional methods, such as net present value. This section highlights problems in making capital investment decisions and provides guidance on how these decisions should be made in the new manufacturing environment to avoid such problems. These problems have led some companies to underestimate the value of strategic investments that would improve their ability to compete in the new manufacturing environment. In some cases these investments are necessary for the survival of companies in intensely competitive markets.

Problems in Making Decisions

What are these problems? First, residual values often are critical to investment decisions. Estimating residual values can require managers to forecast technological, economic, operational, strategic, and market developments over several years. Residual values are especially difficult to estimate because they come at the end of the investment's expected service life. For example, a company may have difficulty estimating the residual value of a computer system in five years because the value depends on new systems introduced by manufacturers during the five-year period. Managers sometimes ignore the residual value of an asset because of uncertainty about its value. However, because strategic decisions usually involve high residual values, the failure to include estimates of residual values in discounting models biases decisions against strategic investments.

Second, because strategic investments in the new manufacturing environment often are long term, the discount rate has a major effect on capital investment decisions. Many companies use discount rates that are higher than their current cost of capital. Setting discount rates too high biases decisions against strategic investments by decreasing the present value of the future cash flows.

Third, managers often fail to include the opportunity costs associated with not making a strategic investment. In the new manufacturing environment, these opportunity costs usually consist of the loss of future potential sales as a result of inferior quality, slower and less reliable delivery, and the inability to respond rapidly to customer demands for new products. These typical customer concerns in the new manufacturing environment often require strategic investments. Unfortunately, difficulty in estimating these opportunity costs often leads managers to omit them from their discounting models. Yet, consideration of the opportunity costs of not investing can be critical, not only to a single investment decision but also to the future of a company or a division.

As an example of a case in which opportunity costs are important, consider the following Case in Point, the World Transmission Project at the **Allison Transmission Division of General Motors.**

Case in Point

http://albright.
swlearning.com

Learn more about Allison Transmission.

Opportunity Costs

Allison Transmission is a world leader in making transmissions for heavy trucks. Allison has long been a very successful division of General Motors Corporation, with a reputation for consistently generating good cash flows.

During the 1980s, existing technology for making heavy transmissions was becoming obsolete. Further, foreign competitors threatened to build state-of-the-art facilities to manufacture a new generation of transmissions if Allison chose not to take this step. At the same time, General Motors was experiencing a financial downturn that made Allison's positive cash flows important to the company.

The facility that Allison needed if it was to continue to dominate the truck transmission market required an investment of over $500 million in robotics and built-in quality controls such as cameras that detected incorrectly assembled parts. Production scheduling and operations would be governed by a computer system that would integrate virtually all aspects of manufacturing.

Allison drew up plans for the new plant, called the World Transmission (WT) Project. It would take years to build the facility, to develop a new generation of transmissions, to train the workforce that would operate the new equipment, and to establish the products in the marketplace. Consequently, it would be some time before the new facility would begin to show positive cash flows. This presented a dilemma for General Motors. If Allison did not go forward with the WT Project, one of several foreign competitors probably would build a similar plant, and Allison would lose its edge in the market. If Allison built the plant, it would no longer produce positive cash flows for some time to come. After some delay, the project was approved. The opportunity cost of not modernizing the production process was too high not to make the investment.

Avoiding Problems

How should managers avoid the pitfalls associated with making capital investments in the new manufacturing environment? First, in applying traditional techniques for making capital investments, managers need to be careful in estimating residual values and discount rates. Second, managers need to include the opportunity costs of not investing in their strategic decisions. Third, managers should recognize the uncertainty of cash flows in many strategic investment situations.

Moving Baseline Concept

Traditional capital investment techniques compare the expected results of new investments with the company's current operating results. This comparison assumes that the company's current operating results will continue indefinitely and will not be hurt by the decision not to make an investment. If this assumption is wrong, the company will experience an opportunity cost by not investing in assets that will allow it to maintain its market share.

One method that addresses this issue is the *moving baseline concept.* **Instead of assuming that current operating cash flows will continue indefinitely, this concept assumes that if the investment is not made the cash flows will decrease because of the competition's superior quality.** For example, assume that Sandy States Insurance Company is considering upgrading its automated customer service system to lower costs and improve service. The lower costs will result in an improved net cash flow from operations of $75 million each year as shown in the table in Exhibit 9. The system will cost $450 million to purchase at the present time, but it will permit Sandy States to recover $525 million in three years when part of the present customer service facility is sold. After seven years, Sandy States expects to build an entirely new facility, with the selling price offsetting any residual value of the remaining old facility. New investments in software and hardware upgrades costing $50 million each year are expected in years 5–7.

If Sandy States does not switch to the new system it will likely begin to lose some business each year as a result of customer dissatisfaction. These losses are expected to accumulate to $435 million by the end of year 7 as the old system becomes increasingly obsolete, leading to greater and greater dissatisfaction. Including the losses due to customer dissatisfaction is what is meant by the moving baseline approach. Management has two choices: to assume that the current cash flows will continue or to assume that cash flows will decrease if the investment is not made.

Exhibit 9 compares the cash flows with the moving baseline (line a) to those without the moving baseline (line b). The moving baseline approach (line a) includes the benefits of improved customer service from investing in the new system, both in terms of reaching breakeven point sooner (c versus d) and in terms of total cash flows over the life of the investment. Including the cash flows that are preserved by the improved customer service could make the difference between Sandy States investing and not investing.

Exhibit 9
Comparison of
Cumulative Cash Flows
With and Without
Moving Baseline

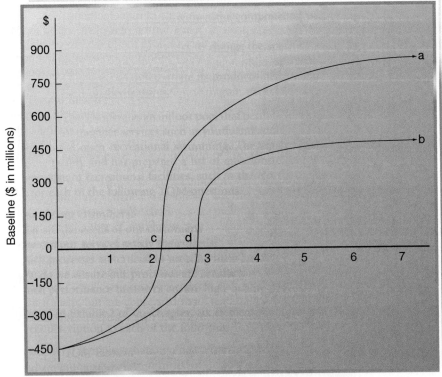

a = investment cash flows including the moving baseline
b = investment cash flows not including the moving baseline

Year	0	1	2	3	4	5	6	7
Investment cash in(out) flows	$(450)	$ 0	$ 0	$525	$ 0	$ (50)	$ (50)	$ (50)
Annual improvement in net cash flow from operations		75	75	75	75	75	75	75
Cumulative cash flow without moving baseline (line b)	$(450)	$(375)	$(300)	$300	$375	$400	$425	$450
Cumulative loss of business avoided with new system		25	300	350	375	400	425	435
Cumulative cash flow with moving baseline (line a)	$(450)	$(350)	$ 0	$650	$750	$800	$850	$885

Uncertain and Hidden Costs

Strategic investments often involve uncertain costs that are difficult to measure but that are extremely important to the decision. An example is a decision by a company to develop a new product line for unfamiliar markets. For example, **Pennzoil** made the mistake of underestimating warranty costs when it decided to invest in quick-change oil facilities. The failure of employees to remove and properly reinsert plugs in oil pans led to engine failures and unexpectedly high warranty costs. The company's lack of experience in the automobile maintenance business resulted in its failure to include adequate warranty costs in its investment decision.

The problems associated with strategic capital investments are not limited to manufacturing companies. Service companies can face similar decisions that have far-reaching consequences. Furthermore, marketing assumptions often are critical to the success of a strategic capital investment project, regardless of whether a company is a manufacturing or service business. Self-Study Problem 2 provides examples of two banks that made strategic capital investment decisions. In both cases, subjective marketing considerations were instrumental in the banks' decisions to fund the project. In analyzing this problem, keep the following points in mind:

- Capital investment decisions sometimes are made for reasons other than return on investment. For example, management may believe that being in a particular market improves the company's image. Image may be important to a company's marketing strategy. If return on investment is much lower than expected, however, any marketing advantage may be more than offset by the cost of the investment.
- Where uncertainty about future cash flows is high because of uncertainty about revenues and costs, managers should consider a range of possible outcomes resulting from the capital investment.
- In situations where cash flows are uncertain, managers should be careful that their assumptions regarding factors that could affect future cash flows are realistic.

2 SELF-STUDY PROBLEM

In the middle 1970s, the **National Bank of Georgia** (NBG) seized an opportunity to establish a branch in a major office complex that was being built in downtown Atlanta. The facility represented a new concept in urban office space for the city. It was to contain its own shops, restaurants, and branch banks. Workers in the office space could work, shop, eat, and bank without ever leaving the complex. Some were touting this approach as the wave of the future. The complex attracted a great deal of attention, and branch banks located in it were expected to be high-profile signals of the banks' presence in the downtown Atlanta market. At the time, NBG was the fifth largest bank in the city. NBG's management was trying to make a major push to become larger and more visible. Although the lease expenses and costs of improvements would be very high, the new office complex seemed to afford the type of opportunity the bank wanted.

At about the same time NBG was considering its branching decision, **Home Federal Savings** of Rome, Georgia, was considering a strategic branching decision of its own. Rome was a small city of approximately 40,000 people. Home Federal was a small, independent S&L that was totally oriented toward making home loans and accepting savings deposits from individuals. It had long had a conservative banking philosophy. Despite its retail orientation, it operated from only one downtown location, unlike most of its competitors, which long ago had embraced branch banking. Home Federal's management, however, had come to the conclusion that the city's growth was headed in a westerly direction and that it had to establish a branch on that side of town or lose customers who considered the drive into town too inconvenient. Home Federal had the opportunity to acquire and remodel a vacant facility that had been used as a fast-food restaurant at a cost that, although significant, was considerably lower than the cost of building a new branch. The facility was in a highly visible location. Home Federal's logo would be seen by thousands of motorists driving by each week.

Both banks elected to make the capital investments in branching. NBG's investment failed. The branch was closed within two years because the new office concept failed to generate enough customers. Leasing of office space in the complex was slower than expected, and far fewer customers than expected used the shops and restaurants. Conversely, Home Federal's branch was a great success. The branch was profitable within months after opening and continued to show good growth and profitability thereafter.

Required What factors could account for the difference between these two strategic investment decisions? Why are marketing assumptions often critical to the success or failure of strategic capital investment decisions?

The solution to Self-Study Problem 2 appears at the end of the chapter.

RESPONDING TO BAD CAPITAL INVESTMENT DECISIONS

Capital investment projects sometimes are funded in stages. Decisions are made at each stage about whether to continue to fund a project. Once it becomes apparent that the project has failed, these decisions pose serious difficulties because a decision to continue can be very costly. This problem occurs in a bank when a loan officer continues to lend money to a failing customer to delay recognizing a loss. Managers should know that there is a tendency to continue funding failed projects and be able to recognize the causes of this tendency.

Costs of a project that cannot be recovered are sunk costs. Decision makers should ignore these costs when deciding whether to invest additional money in a project. Unfortunately, they often fall into a sunk cost trap, as shown in Exhibit 10.

Exhibit 10 The Escalation Cycle

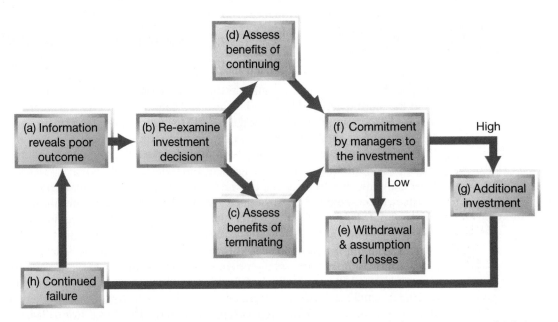

Adapted from Staw, Barry M. and Jerry Ross. 1987. Behavior in Escalation Situations: Antecedents, Prototypes, and Solutions, *Research in Organizational Behavior*: 39–78.

When decision makers become aware that an investment is failing (a), they reexamine the investment (b) and weigh the benefits of terminating the investment (c) against the benefits of continuing (d). If the estimated costs of terminating the project are less than the benefits, decision makers should withdraw from the project and accept the losses associated with withdrawal (e). However, if their commitment to the project is high (f), decision makers may continue to fund it (g) even though it is failing (h).

For example, suppose that a bank loaned money to a remanufacturer of automobile parts to buy raw materials for inventory production. Because of bad management practices, the remanufacturer used these funds to make inventory it could not sell. The remanufacturer then asked the bank for more money to buy raw materials to manufacture more inventory. The bank, fearing that the remanufacturer would fail if it did not loan the funds, made the second loan. The remanufacturer repeated its first mistake and ultimately failed. The bank lost considerably more money than it would have lost if it had recognized its first mistake and not loaned the additional funds. The bank focused on the sunk cost of the first loan and loaned additional money instead of cutting its losses.

In this cycle, information about a project's performance causes a reexamination of the project. If managers are committed to a project, they often fund the project until additional information is received.

Why do they do this? The reasons can be divided into four categories:

- *Project determinants:* These are objective features of a project. For instance, large sunk costs that cannot be recovered if the project is discontinued or the fact that there are no competing projects that provide higher returns are both features that may contribute to the decision to continue.
- *Psychological determinants:* These are forces that can introduce error into managers' estimates of the gains and losses. Such forces influence the decision to continue or discontinue a project and can lead to greater investment. Examples: (1) Managers may have made the earlier decision to invest in the project and may feel a strong desire to continue investing because of their earlier decision. (2) Decision makers may believe withdrawing from the project will mean a loss of money already sunk instead of viewing the withdrawal as saving money not yet spent.
- *Social determinants:* These are pressures within the organizational environment. The need to save face, the desire to beat a competitor, the support of others for a project, and attitudes such as "never quit no matter what" encourage increased investment.
- *Structural determinants:* These are features of the organization itself. For example, the absence of appropriate project controls and a desperate need for a company to show progress can lead to continuing a project.

To avoid these problems, a company periodically may replace some members of the project management team with new members to bring fresh insights and to prevent too much personal identification with the project. Also, initial investment decisions can be separated from later investment decisions by requiring rejustification of a project with every funding decision. Companies can reduce the threat of failure for decision makers by acknowledging that well-managed projects are sometimes unsuccessful. For example, many banks encourage aggressive lending by loan officers. Loan officers who never generate loan losses are not sufficiently aggressive.

Identifying the opportunity costs associated with continuing to invest in failing projects may help managers make termination decisions. Also, it may be helpful to identify the potential costs of terminating a project before initial funding of the project, so that these costs will be more obvious from the beginning. Some risk of failure is associated with any project, and some failures must be expected. Managers should learn to evaluate and accept some failures.

CAPITAL INVESTMENT DECISIONS IN SERVICE COMPANIES

OBJECTIVE 5

Describe the factors affecting capital investment decisions in service organizations.

Like manufacturing companies, service companies must make capital investment decisions. A service company must invest in those fixed assets that are necessary if it is to provide a service to its customers. This may mean investment in long-term construction projects such as railroad tracks, telephone lines, and even telecommunication satellites.

When making capital investment decisions, managers in service companies must take the same factors into consideration as managers in manufacturing companies. In addition, service companies such as railroads, telecommunication companies, and power companies often are government-regulated. Regulators frequently set the rates that service companies can charge their customers. They become concerned if they believe that the customers are being charged too much or are not being given good service. Regulators monitor regulated service companies' capital investments to determine whether they will lead to requests for higher rates and how they will affect customer service.

Remember that investment capital usually is scarce, so managers must put it to the best possible use. Managers in regulated service companies sometimes must choose between capital investments that will provide better service to different sets of customers. In such cases, regulators may exert pressure on the company to limit capital investment of one type in order to be sure that enough capital is invested in other services. This may be true even if the investment that the regulators limit has the potential to provide greater cash flows.

3 SELF-STUDY PROBLEM

Refer to the Case in Point involving General Motors' decision to fund the Allison Transmission "World Transmission Project." GM originally expected to spend approximately $500 million on the WT Project. After the project had been underway for several years, it became obvious that cost overruns would result in the project costing in excess of $600 million. By the time the overruns became known, GM already had spent over $250 million on the project. Further, Allison experienced some production problems with the new transmissions. The division's cash flows were negative.

Required Assume you are part of GM management. What factors would you consider in deciding whether to invest the additional $100 million to complete the WT Project? Discuss the factors in terms of the four categories of reasons for continuing to fund unsuccessful investments. What alternative(s) to abandoning the project might GM consider?

The solution to Self-Study Problem 3 appears at the end of the chapter.

REVIEW

SUMMARY of INFORMATION CONCEPTS

1. Capital investment decisions are important decisions about acquiring long-term assets.
   a. Operational decisions are those decisions that affect the day-to-day operations of the company and the short-run outcomes of those operations.
   b. Strategic decisions are those decisions that affect the major directions the company is taking and the long-run outcome of those directions.

2. Capital investment decisions often involve large outlays of cash for long periods of time.
   a. Several factors affect the risk associated with capital investments.
   b. Capital investment decisions can be difficult to reverse without large losses.
   c. Capital investment decisions often are political because different divisions compete for funds.

3. Traditional approaches to justifying capital investments are of two types, discounting and nondiscounting.
   a. Discounting methods take into account the time value of money.
      1. The net present value method compares the net present value of expected cash inflows and outflows associated with the investment.
      2. The internal rate of return method involves determining the interest rate that results in the present values of cash inflows and outflows being equal.
   b. Nondiscounting methods do not consider the time value of money.
      1. The payback period method involves determining the amount of time required to recover the initial investment.
      2. The accounting rate of return method uses the average accounting income a project generates per period divided by the amount of the investment.

4. Several additional factors should enter into capital investment decisions.
   a. The service life is the period during which an investment is expected to be used.
   b. Residual value is the market value of an investment at the end of its useful life.
   c. The income tax effects of depreciation on cash flows must be considered, because although depreciation is a noncash expense, it is tax-deductible.
   d. When there is uncertainty about future cash flows, managers should test the sensitivity of their decision to their assumptions.

5. The new manufacturing environment has changed capital investment decision making for many companies.
   a. Capital investment decisions have become more strategic.
   b. The costs of capital investments are increasing, and the payback periods are becoming longer.

6. Making sound strategic capital investment decisions requires managers to avoid several pitfalls.
   a. Managers should carefully consider salvage values and use appropriate discount rates.
   b. Managers should consider in their decisions the opportunity cost of not making a capital investment.

7. Managers often are reluctant to terminate a failing project.
   a. Reasons for this reluctance can be divided into project, psychological, social, and structural determinants.
   b. Managers can reduce this reluctance by being aware of the problem and taking steps to prevent it.

DEFINE

TERMS and CONCEPTS DEFINED in this CHAPTER

accounting rate of return (ARR) (M383)	nondiscounting methods (M376)
capital budgeting (M373)	operational capital investment
capital investment decision (M373)	decision (M373)
cost of capital (M377)	opportunity costs (M377)
discounting (M377)	payback period (M381)
discounting methods (M376)	required rate of return (M377)
hurdle rate (M377)	residual value (M383)
internal rate of return (IRR) (M379)	service life (M383)
milestones (M376)	strategic capital investment
moving baseline concept (M389)	decision (M373)
net present value (NPV) (M377)	sunk costs (M376)

SELF-STUDY PROBLEM SOLUTIONS

SSP12-1 Evaluation using net present value method:

Year Cash Flow	0 Present Value	
Purchase of new system	$(100,000)	
Net decrease in operating costs	56,862	$15,000 × 3.79079 from Table 4.
Sales value of old equipment	40,000	
Net present value	$ (3,138)	

In this case, the net present value analysis indicates that the new investment should be rejected because the net present value is negative.

Joyful Car is already in the car washing business, so this is an investment in a business in which management has experience. This tends to reduce the risk. On the other hand, this would seem to be a large investment for a small company, increasing the risk. It is likely that part of the $100,000 total investment cost is installation cost for the new system, which probably would not be recaptured if the system had to be sold before the end of its useful life. This also increases the risk. Overall, this would appear to be a strategic investment for Joyful Car. Even though a car washing system may not seem like a major investment for many companies, it is for Joyful Car.

SSP12-2 The difference in the outcomes of the two branching decisions can be explained by the fact that Home Federal appears to have been much more careful to reduce its risk than NBG. Home Federal kept its costs down by buying a building at a reduced cost and renovating it. Home Federal also appears to have a better understanding of its market. While NBG was inexperienced in dealing with the marketing environment of its new branch, Home Federal's management had observed the population movement in the area of its new branch for some time and was confident that the trade would support the branch.

Capital investment decisions often depend greatly on marketing assumptions. NBG's branch was inside a large office complex and not visible from the street. People driving by might not be aware of its existence. NBG gambled on a new concept in self-contained office space and hoped that the stores and restaurants would bring in enough outside clientele to support the branch. This did not happen—at least not in time to save the branch. In contrast, Home Federal's branch was in a visible location seen by many potential customers. NBG took a significant risk and lost, partly encouraged by the hope that being in a prestigious location would enhance its image. Home Federal took the safe road and was successful.

SSP12-3   GM should reconsider the costs and benefits of the WT Project. Among the factors to be reconsidered probably would be (1) the future stream of cash inflows and outflows based on revised marketing and production forecasts, (2) the likelihood of resolving the production difficulties with the new transmissions, and (3) any costs associated with abandoning the project, such as contract cancellation costs.

The WT Project falls into the category of computer-integrated manufacturing in terms of the level of automation. Virtually the entire manufacturing operation is controlled by computers.

It is difficult to determine at this point whether the WT Project is an escalation situation. After several years and over $500 million invested in the WT Project, it is unlikely that GM would abandon the project for several reasons. Some of these, categorized in terms of Staw and Ross's four determinants of escalation, are:

Project determinant: There is the possibility that the setback in the WT Project is only temporary and that it still might succeed in the long run.

Psychological determinant: There is a very large sunk cost in the WT Project that GM management would be reluctant to write off.

Social determinant: GM might naturally be reluctant to admit to a high-profile mistake such as the failure of a project like the WT Project.

Structural determinant: GM is in a battle with foreign competitors in many of its markets. Maintaining its position as the leading manufacturer of high-quality transmissions for heavy equipment could be important to GM's image.

GM did continue to fund the WT Project. However, it attempted to sell Allison Transmission to other corporations in the hope of eliminating the negative cash flows associated with the WT Project.

Thinking Beyond the Question

How can managerial accounting help in choosing new manufacturing facilities?

Currently, Young Designs, Inc., has been unable to sell to certain retailers that demand exceptionally high-quality finishes on their products. Suppose that by purchasing the new system discussed in the chapter opening scenario, the overall quality of the finish on the company's products is improved to such an extent that it would permit the company to enter the high-quality markets. If the company does not invest in the new system, it will continue to be excluded from the high-quality market. How would you analyze this cost of *not* investing in the new system? How should this cost affect the investment decision? What difficulties do you foresee in being able to forecast this cost?

QUESTIONS

Q12-1
Obj. 1
Managers at Precision Products are considering a change in the method used to apply paint to the company's products. The new method represents the newest technology. Instead of traditional "wet" painting, it uses electromagnetics to make powdered paint adhere to product surfaces. Precision's major competitors already have adopted the new paint method. The new method would require replacement of the paint booths currently being used, resulting in a $250,000 capital expenditure. Nearly all of Precision's products require painting. The new paint method is expected to improve the paint quality, reduce the product rejects, and enhance customer satisfaction. Is the decision to change painting methods an operational or strategic capital investment decision? Explain your answer.

Q12-2
Obj. 1
A local manufacturing company is planning to purchase a new computer software system that will affect the entire company. The new system will allow the receptionist to log all incoming calls and messages on the company's electronic mail system so that users will have immediate notice of incoming calls. The cost of the new system will be $20,000, and it is estimated that the investment will have a useful service life of five years. Would this investment be considered operational or strategic? Explain your answer.

Q12-3
Obj. 1
Tim and Tom are brothers who split a large inheritance. Tim used all of his money to buy a company that manufactures a single product used in high-tech industries. Tom used his money to lease two small retail stores in a nearby mall, one that sells candles and another that sells yogurt. He also purchased inventory and equipment to start the businesses. Assuming that neither of the brothers has any experience in his new endeavor, which of the brothers has the greater investment risk, and why?

Q12-4
Obj. 1
Caltron Enterprises operates a multimillion-dollar plant and is considering an expansion of its facilities to support a new product line. Should the cost of the company's existing plant and equipment affect the expansion decision? Explain your answer.

Q12-5
Obj. 1
Classify each of the following capital investment decisions as either operational or strategic. Briefly justify your answers.

1. A bank decides to build a new branch in the same town where it has 15 other branches. The new branch will cost $200,000 and will have an estimated service life of 25 years with a $150,000 residual value.
2. A bank decides to add automatic teller machines (ATMs) in the lobby of each of its 15 branches. The bank has never offered ATMs to customers in the past. The machines will have an estimated service life of 15 years with no residual value.
3. A company automates an entire production process that had not previously been automated. The automation includes computer-controlled equipment linked together in work cells. The machines will improve quality and increase the number of products offered, and they are expected to head off entry into the market by a major competitor. The machines will have an estimated useful life of nine years with a residual value of $350,000.
4. A company updates several pieces of factory equipment with new models. The new models have increased safety features and can operate faster than the older models. The new machines also have new features that will allow workers to perform tasks that the old machines could not perform. The estimated service life of the new machines is 10 years, and they will have a residual value of $75,000.

Q12-6
Obj. 2
Assume that a friend has asked to borrow $100 from you. You agree, as long as your friend pays you 6% annual interest to provide for the time value of money. Your friend wants to know what is meant by "time value of money." How would you explain this concept?

Q12-7
Obj. 2
Erin Brady won a $500 prize in a raffle. The winning ticket states, "Prizes are payable in six months from contest date, or may be discounted at 10% for immediate payment." Erin has asked you what is meant by the term "discounted." What will you tell her?

Q12-8
Obj. 2
Douglas Wright has calculated the net present value of a proposed project investment and has obtained a negative amount. Assuming that Douglas calculated the net present value properly, what does the negative amount indicate about this investment?

Q12-9
Obj. 2
Julie Russo attended a company meeting to discuss a potential investment in new machinery. The company uses the payback method to analyze potential investments. After reviewing the figures, Julie commented, "These figures are not reliable. They have not been discounted." Do you agree with Julie? Why or why not?

Q12-10
Obj. 2
Bill Rubble, president of Melinco Company, reviewed a proposal for a project investment that was submitted by the vice president of production. Bill attached a note to the proposal that said, "Please recalculate this proposal—adjust the rate of return by 2% to compensate for the higher risk involved." Should the vice president increase or decrease the rate of return when recalculating the proposal?

Q12-11
Obj. 2
Samuel Sanchez is a project manager for Johnson Industries. Samuel wants to analyze a potential investment. He seeks a method that considers the project's profitability but is not affected by the time value of money. What method would you suggest Samuel utilize?

Q12-12
Obj. 2
Capital budgeting models such as NPV, internal rate of return, payback, and accounting rate of return make managing easier, because future projects can be approved immediately if target values are obtained. Do you agree or disagree? Why?

Q12-13
Obj. 2
Paul Bruce, controller of Chief Industries, performs investment analysis for all of the company's capital projects. Paul has complained that investment analysis is difficult because there are so many estimates that must be made. What are some of the variables that typically must be estimated in a capital budgeting decision?

Q12-14
Obj. 2
Assume that the internal rate of return on a particular capital investment project has been calculated and is exactly equal to the target rate a company has established for such projects. If tax rates are expected to increase in the future, would the investment become more or less desirable from an internal rate of return standpoint?

Q12-15
Obj. 2
Woodcrest, Inc., a textile manufacturer, is considering purchasing a new type of technology that is advertised to improve the efficiency and lower the cost of its cloth dyeing process. What factors should be considered in making the decision to acquire this equipment?

Q12-16
Obj. 3
Auto Parts, Inc., uses traditional manufacturing assembly lines to manufacture starters and alternators. Much of Auto Parts' equipment is wearing out, and company management is considering what type of production facilities to invest in. Several factors have been changing in the industry. Over the past two decades the number of different automobile models has increased substantially. Because of this, customers are demanding many more models of alternators and starters but in smaller quantities. Labor costs have increased substantially. Customers are much less willing to accept problems with quality and frequently desire just-in-time deliveries. How should these changes affect management's decisions regarding investment in the new capital equipment?

Q12-17
Obj. 3
Tanguchi Equipment Company manufactures cabs and chassis for fire trucks, ambulances, and other emergency vehicles. Parts manufactured by Tanguchi require precision and quality. The company employs a highly trained workforce that produces most parts by hand and has maintained a moderate level of production quality. How would quality affect capital decisions at Tanguchi?

Q12-18
Obj. 3
Newhart Company is planning a major capital investment program to automate its production processes, which are currently labor-intensive. What impact on its cost structure should the company expect from its factory automation program?

Q12-19
Obj. 4
Everyday Plastics Corporation wants to invest in new machinery that will allow the company to be more responsive to changes in customer demand. The company has an excellent credit rating and can borrow funds at the prevailing prime interest rate. To be on the "safe" side, however, the company has analyzed the potential investment using a discount rate that is 3% above the prevailing prime interest rate. Why would the company want to increase the discount rate to be on the safe side, and what is the likely effect of using a rate higher than the available borrowing rate on the company's analysis of the investment decision?

Q12-20
Obj. 4
In an effort to convince the president of Utah Instruments to expand the company's product lines, Lynnette Peters, vice president of marketing, inflated potential future sales figures on a proposed product. Lynnette believed that without the inflated marketing estimates, the new

product would not be pursued. If the new product is undertaken, extensive capital investment will be required. How could improper or poor estimates of market conditions adversely affect a capital investment decision?

Q12-21
Objs. 2, 4

Chambers Industries manufactures copper tubing used in many mechanical applications. The company believes that it must invest in a new facility if it is to remain competitive with foreign manufacturers. A preliminary analysis of the proposed investment indicates that property, plant, and equipment costing more than $50 million will be needed to bring the facility into operation. The residual value of the investment would be $1.5 million at the end of 15 years. Failure to commit to the new investment will cause the company to realize an estimated $250,000 a year in lost income. What are the relevant costs that Chambers should include in its capital investment decision, and why?

Q12-22
Objs. 2, 4

Westco, Inc., is considering a capital investment project. Explain how each of the following situations would affect the capital investment decision Westco is considering. Explain whether each situation would make the project more or less likely to be accepted. Consider each situation independently.

1. The net present value of the proposed investment is zero.
2. The estimated service life used to evaluate the investment was 10 years, when in reality the actual service life is 12 years. The investment was analyzed using the accounting rate of return model.
3. The company desires a 12% return on the investment but inadvertently used a 14% factor in its analysis. The company utilizes the net present value method of investment analysis.
4. In its original internal rate of return analysis of the investment Westco failed to consider the income tax effects of depreciation on the investment. The net present value model was used in the analysis.
5. The residual value of the project under consideration was estimated at $30,000, when in reality the actual residual value of the project is $20,000. The company utilized the net present value method of investment analysis.

Q12-23
Obj. 4

Allen Hardaway is president of Fly High Shoes. Allen recently approved the purchase of several acres of land near the company factory to build a retail shoe outlet. Allen's plan to sell shoes directly to the public at the factory store was met with immediate disapproval by several of Fly High's largest customers, who have threatened to take their business to a competitor if the factory outlet is opened. "Never mind them," said Allen. "This project is a great idea. Besides, we already bought the land and paid an architect for store plans. We can't stop now!" Do you think Allen is throwing good money after bad if he pursues the factory outlet investment? What advice would you give Allen?

Q12-24
Obj. 4

JetPak, Inc., delivers overnight business letters internationally and very recently began building a new capital investment in an airport distribution center in Cincinnati. The project has been touted as the most significant investment decision in JetPak's history. Indianapolis had been considered as an alternate site, but Bob Smith, project manager, argued strongly in favor of Cincinnati on the basis of better airport facilities. Smith stated that the better facilities would allow JetPak's planes to arrive and depart much more efficiently with less time lost to airport delays. Smith is evaluated on the cost of building the facility compared to its budgeted cost and previously announced that he would ". . . bring the project in on time and under budgeted cost." Just after ground was broken on the new facility, a major airline announced that it would begin using Cincinnati as a regional hub. This decision is expected to increase the traffic at the airport by 30%. Further, the Indianapolis Airport just announced that it intends to build two new runways to expedite arrivals and departures. Despite these changes and a buyer that wants to purchase the land on which the Cincinnati facility is being built, Smith is adamantly opposed to reconsidering the location decision. Can you explain Smith's opposition?

Q12-25
Obj. 5

Home First Bank must invest in a new computer system to handle banking transactions. Management has considered buying from one of two vendors. National Computers, Inc., offers higher-priced equipment that has a higher residual value and a lower-priced contract service. American Computers, Inc., offers lower-priced equipment with a lower residual value and a more expensive contract service package. Both systems have the same expected useful life, and both have an established record of performing satisfactorily. It has been determined that there is no impact on customer service or operating costs other than service regardless of which vendor is chosen. Home First Bank's president, Jane Greene, has asked her chief financial officer, John Warren, how the decision should be made. Assume you are the CFO. How would you respond?

Q12-26
Obj. 5

Central European Telephone Service (CETS) wants to expand its cellular operations in a developing country. The country currently has a penetration rate of cable telephone service to only one in forty households. CETS would prefer to spend its funds available for capital investment on expanding cellular service since the company believes that cellular is more profitable than cable given the way rates have been set by the country's government. The government is opposing this approach, insisting that CETS raise the cable penetration rate to one in twenty before further expanding cellular service. Can you think of possible reasons why CETS and the government are taking these positions?

EXERCISES

If your instructor is using Personal Trainer® in this course, you may complete your assignments online.

E12-1
Write a short definition of each of the terms listed in the *Terms and Concepts Defined in this Chapter* section.

E12-2
Obj. 2

Audrey buys a new tanning bed for her salon. The tanning bed costs $6,000. The tanning bed generates cash flows of $2,500 the first year, $3,500 the second year, and $5,000 the third year. What is the payback period?

E12-3
Obj. 2

Alison Mayer, owner of a sports complex, is considering adding a climbing wall. The climbing wall costs $30,000. Alison estimates the climbing wall will generate cash flows of $8,000 the first year, $10,000 the second year, and $12,000 the third year. What is the payback period?

E12-4
Obj. 2

Shannon bought an ice cream truck for $20,000. Her net income was $3,500 the first year, $5,000 the second year, and $6,500 the third year of business. Calculate the accounting rate of return.

E12-5
Obj. 2

Stephanie bought a stereo system for her DJ service for $4,000. Her net income was $500 the first year, $900 the second year, and $1,000 the third year of business. Calculate the accounting rate of return.

E12-6
Obj. 2

Gerrish Corporation bought a new machine for $50,000. The net income from this machine is $8,000 in year 1 and $10,000 in year 2. In order to obtain an accounting rate of return of 20%, what would Gerrish have to make in the third and final year of this machine's life?

E12-7
Obj. 2

Kelly Sloan, purchasing manager at an Internet service provider, bought a new server for $4,000. The net income from this machine is $700 in year 1 and $900 in year 2. In order to obtain an accounting rate of return of 25%, what will they have to make in the third and final year of this machine's life?

E12-8
Obj. 2

Amy Sims runs an advertisement firm. She estimates that a $7,000 high-resolution printer will result in increased cash inflows of $2,000 in year 1, $4,000 in year 2, and $4,500 in year 3. Amy's cost of capital is 10%. Calculate the net present value. What is the internal rate of return at this price?

E12-9
Obj. 2

Ryan, owner of a furniture business, currently leases a small building for $20,000 per year. He is considering leasing a large store for his furniture business. He estimates the new store will result in increased net cash inflows (inflows − outflows) of $10,000 in year 1, $12,000 in year 2, and $13,500 in year 3. Ryan's cost of capital is 8%. Calculate the net present value.

E12-10
Obj. 2

Bill, owner of a video arcade, is considering buying a new game. The game would cost $5,000. He estimates the new game will result in increased cash inflows of $2,000 in year 1, $2,000 in year 2, and $2,000 in year 3. Calculate the internal rate of return.

E12-11
Obj. 2

Mike Gallager, owner of a bowling alley, is considering buying a new pool table. The pool table would cost $3,000. He estimates the pool table will result in increased cash inflows of $750 per year for five years. Calculate the internal rate of return.

E12-12
Obj. 2
Geory, general manager at a water park, installed a new waterslide with an estimated useful life of 10 years. The waterslide will generate cash inflows of $10,000 each year over the next 10 years. The waterslide has no salvage value at the end of 10 years, and the company's discount rate is 12%. Geory calculates the NPV of the investment to be $20,000. What is the cost of the waterslide? Assuming the waterslide costs $50,000, what is the payback period?

E12-13
Obj. 2
Henry, manager of a widget factory, bought a new machine with an estimated useful life of five years. The machine will generate cash inflows of $12,000 each year over the next five years. The machine has no salvage value at the end of five years, and the company's discount rate is 10%. Henry calculates the NPV of the investment to be $10,000. What is the cost of the machine? What is the payback period?

E12-14
Obj. 2
Briggs Corporation, a lawn mowing service, bought a new commercial lawn mower. The mower costs $12,000 and is expected to have a service life of five years. At the end of five years, the lawn mower can be sold for $2,000. Briggs has a 30% tax rate. What is the annual depreciation expense? What is the annual tax savings from depreciation?

E12-15
Obj. 2
Fix-It-Yourself, a rental equipment store, bought a jackhammer. The jackhammer costs $8,000 and is expected to have a service life of six years. At the end of six years, the jackhammer can be sold for $2,000. Fix-It-Yourself has a 30% tax rate. What is the annual depreciation expense? What is the annual tax savings from depreciation?

E12-16
Obj. 2
Matt invested $100,000 to open Steakhouse. He withdrew $10,000 at the end of each year for three years. At the end of the third year, Matt sold the restaurant for $120,000 cash. His discount rate is 15%. What is the net present value of Matt's investment? What is the internal rate of return on this business?

E12-17
Obj. 2
Elizabeth Ann invested $80,000 to start a business at the beginning of 2004. She withdrew $5,000 at the end of each year for three years. At the end of the third year, Elizabeth sold the business for $100,000 cash. Her discount rate is 10%. What is the net present value of Elizabeth's business investment? What is the internal rate of return on this business?

E12-18
Obj. 2
The Wild Side Bowling Alley is planning to invest in pinball machines and pool tables for use by its patrons. The equipment will cost $3,896 to acquire and will have an estimated service life of seven years with a $100 residual value. Based on estimates by the owner, the tables and games will generate approximately $800 a year of cash inflow after all expenses have been met. Compute the internal rate of return promised by the table and games. Assume that the owner will not invest in the equipment unless it has a 12% internal rate of return. Compute the amount of annual cash inflows that would be required on the initial investment to obtain this rate of return.

E12-19
Obj. 2
John's Arcade is planning on purchasing a virtual reality simulator for $210,000. The simulator's estimated service life is seven years with a residual value of $25,000. The simulator is expected to bring in $40,000 per year after expenses. Compute the internal rate of return on the simulator. If John wanted to get a 13% internal rate of return, what would the annual cash flows need to be in order generate this rate of return?

E12-20
Obj. 2
Alice owns a tow truck company. She is considering buying a new tow truck for $55,000. The service life of the truck is five years. At the end of the five years, Alice estimates she can sell the truck for $5,000. She estimates her revenues from the truck will be $15,000 per year. The tax rate of the company is 30% and its discount rate is 10%. What is the depreciation expense for the truck? How much tax will Alice owe each year? (*Hint:* Include savings from depreciation.) What will the annual cash flows be for the truck? What is the NPV of the truck?

E12-21
Obj. 2
Jim owns an ice cream store. He is considering buying a new waffle cone machine for $600. The service life of the machine is five years. At the end of the five years, Jim estimates he can sell the machine for $100. He estimates his net contribution from the machine will be $300 per year. The tax rate of the company is 20% and its discount rate is 10%. What is the depreciation expense for the machine? How much tax will Jim owe each year? (*Hint:* Include savings from depreciation.) What will the annual cash flows be for the machine? What is the NPV of the machine?

PROBLEMS

If your instructor is using Personal Trainer® in this course, you may complete your assignments online.

P12-1
Obj. 2

Calculating Accounting Rate of Return

A machine was purchased for $10,000. The net income from the machine is as follows:

Year 1	$3,000
Year 2	2,000
Year 3	1,000

Required

A. Calculate the accounting rate of return.
B. What are the drawbacks to using the accounting rate of return as a method of selecting projects?

P12-2
Obj. 2

Payback versus NPV

The cash flows from two capital expenditure projects follow. The discount rate is 10%.

	Project A	Project B
Initial cost	$(10,000)	$(10,000)
Year 1	6,000	2,000
Year 2	5,000	4,000
Year 3	1,000	8,000
Year 4	0	16,000

Required

A. What are the payback periods for both projects?
B. What is the NPV for both projects?
C. What are the drawbacks from using payback as a method for selecting projects?

P12-3
Obj. 2

Internal Rate of Return versus NPV

John is considering two capital expenditure projects; however, he has only enough money to do one project. The cash flows follow and the discount rate is 12%.

	Project A	Project B
Initial cost	$(50,000)	$(100,000)
Year 1	30,000	55,000
Year 2	30,000	55,000
Year 3	30,000	55,000

Required

A. What is the internal rate of return for each project?
B. What is the NPV for each project?
C. Which project should John choose?
D. What are the drawbacks to using internal rate of return?

P12-4
Obj. 2

Accounting Rate of Return and Payback

Mark Brown has an opportunity to invest in a bicycle franchise shop under a nationally recognized brand name. Mark has assembled the following information and estimates relating to this opportunity:

1. Rent on an operating facility would total $4,000 per month.
2. Estimated sales income would total $800,000 per year, and the variable cost of goods sold would be 70% of sales revenue.
3. Costs to operate the shop would include $87,000 per year for salaries and benefits, $4,000 per year for insurance, $15,000 per year for utilities, and $10,000 per year for office expenses.

4. Display racks, repair equipment, and other fixed assets would cost $270,000 and have an estimated service life of 15 years, with no salvage value at the end of the service life. Mark would use the straight-line depreciation method.
5. Mark must pay a commission of 5% of sales to the bicycle supplier.

If Mark does not invest in the bicycle shop, he could invest his funds in long-term bonds that would pay 8% annual interest.

Required

A. Determine the net annual income that Mark would realize from the franchise, ignoring income taxes. (Use the contribution approach format income statement.)
B. Compute the accounting rate of return that would be obtained by the franchise. Based on the accounting rate of return, would Mark be better off financially by investing in the franchise or the long-term securities?
C. Compute the payback period on the franchise. If Mark wants a payback period of five years or less, should he invest in the franchise? (Ignore income taxes.)

P12-5 **Accounting Rate of Return and Payback**

Obj. 2

Billy Boehm has a chance to invest in a company that manufactures televisions. Billy obtained the following information for his investment analysis:

1. Rent on the manufacturing facility is $5,000 per month.
2. Estimated sales income would be $1,000,000 per year, and the variable cost of goods sold would be 65% of sales revenue.
3. Costs to operate the facility would include $150,000 per year for salaries and benefits, *FC* $10,000 per year for insurance, $12,000 per year for utilities, and $8,000 per year for office expenses.
4. Storage racks, repair equipment, and other fixed assets would cost $400,000 and have an estimated service life of 20 years, with no salvage value at the end of the service life.

If Billy does not invest in the television manufacturer, he could invest in bonds that would pay a 10% interest rate.

Required

A. Determine the net annual income that Billy would realize from the company, ignoring income taxes. (Use the contribution approach format income statement.)
B. Compute the accounting rate of return that would be obtained by Billy. Based on the accounting rate of return, would Billy be better off financially by investing in the bonds?
C. Compute the payback period on the company. If Billy wants a payback period of six years or less, should he invest in the franchise? 1:5+ '✓✓ (-432,000, ᴸ 5)

P12-6 **Payback, Internal Rate of Return**

Obj. 2

A piece of labor-saving equipment is available to Armtech Company that could be used to reduce costs at one of its plants. Relevant data related to this particular equipment are as follows:

Purchase price of equipment	$432,000
Net annual cash savings provided by the new equipment	$90,000
Estimated service life of equipment	12 years
Required rate of return	14%

Required

A. Compute the payback period for the new equipment. If the company requires a payback period of four years or less, would you recommend purchase of the equipment? Explain your answer.
B. Compute the internal rate of return on the equipment. Use straight-line depreciation based on the equipment's estimated service life. Would you recommend that the equipment be purchased? Explain your answer.

P12-7 Payback, Internal Rate of Return

Obj. 2

Automation of the shipping department at Computer Mart would save labor costs. Details about the automation equipment are as follows:

Purchase price of automation equipment	$1,200,000
Net annual cash savings provided by the new equipment	$200,000
Estimated service life of equipment	10 years
Required rate of return	12%

Required

A. Compute the payback period for the automation equipment. If Computer Mart requires a payback of five years or less, would you recommend purchase of the equipment? Explain your answer.

B. Compute the internal rate of return on the equipment. Use straight-line depreciation based on the equipment's estimated service life. Would you recommend that the equipment be purchased? Explain your answer.

P12-8 Basic Net Present Value Analysis

Obj. 2

Community Drycleaning would like to purchase a new machine for cleaning large quilts and comforters. The current cleaning operation on quilts and comforters is done by hand. The new machine would cost $12,500. The estimated service life is 12 years, at which time it is estimated that the machine could be sold for $500.

The company estimates that it would cost $700 per year to operate the machine. The current cost of manual cleaning is $3,000 per year. In addition to reducing costs, the new machine would increase the drycleaner's ability to clean quilts and comforters by 600 per year. The company realizes a net contribution margin after tax effects of $1.50 per quilt or comforter. A 10% rate of return is required on all investments. Community expects its tax rate to be 30%.

Required

A. What are the annual net cash inflows that would be realized from the new machine?

B. Compute the net present value of the investment (round to the nearest dollar). Use straight-line depreciation based on the machine's estimated service life. Would you recommend that the machine be purchased? Explain your answer.

P12-9 Basic Net Present Value Analysis

Obj. 2

Ice Cream Galore, a manufacturer of gourmet ice cream, is considering purchasing a new, energy-efficient machine that will mix ice cream for a cost of $110,000. The estimated service life is 15 years, at which time the machine could be sold for $5,000. Ice Cream Galore expects the machine will cost $5,000 per year to operate. The current machine costs $10,000 per year to operate. The new machine will also be able to handle chunkier mixes, of which the company estimates they can sell 10,000 gallons per year. The company's contribution margin is $2 per gallon. A 12% rate of return is required on all investments, and the company's tax rate is 30%.

Required

A. What are the annual net cash inflows that would be realized from the new machine?

B. Compute the net present value of the investment. Use straight-line depreciation based on the machine's estimated service life. Would you recommend that the machine be purchased? Explain your answer.

P12-10 Analysis of Investment Decision

Obj. 2

John bought stock valued at $10,000. He received a cash dividend of $300 in year 1, $350 in year 2, and $400 in year 3. The cash dividends were not reinvested. At the end of year 3, John sold the stock for $12,000. If John didn't invest in stock, he would have invested in bonds that had an 8% return.

Required

A. What was the rate of return on John's stock?
B. Assuming the stock and bonds had equal risk, did John make the right decision to invest in the stock?

P12-11 Net Present Value and Automation Decision

Objs. 2, 3

Tony Setimi, president of Solidex Machinery, is considering the purchase of an automated stamping machine. In reviewing the figures prepared by the production department, Tony has noted that the machine would cost $500,000 plus another $80,000 for controls and programming. In addition, the production department estimates that the machine would cost $3,000 a month to maintain. Further, the production department estimates that repairs totaling $45,000 would be required at the end of seven years.

Tony gave the figures to Becky Roberts, the controller, and asked her to analyze the situation and be prepared to offer her opinion in the morning. Becky determined that the new machine would replace six workers and save $108,000 a year in labor costs. She also determined that $6,500 a year in scrap costs could be avoided and that the current equipment being replaced could be sold for $12,000. She then calculated depreciation on the new machine, assuming it would last 12 years and have a residual value of $20,000. She noted that the company's current cost of capital is 11%.

Required

A. Compute the net annual cost savings that would be realized from the new machine. (Ignore income taxes.)
B. Using the data from requirement (A) and information from the problem, compute the new machine's net present value. (Ignore income taxes.)
C. Assume that there are intangible benefits such as reduced setup time, improved quality, and greater flexibility of production. What annual dollar value would the company have to assign to these intangible factors in order to make the new machine an acceptable investment?

P12-12 Net Present Value and Automation Decision

Objs. 2, 3

A local printing company is trying to decide if it should install an automated job sorter. The details of the sorter are as follows:

Original cost	$53,000
Maintenance costs per month	$1,000
Labor expense savings	$20,000 per year
Depreciable life	10 years
Residual value	$3,000
Cost of capital	11%

Required

A. Compute the net annual cost savings that would be realized from the sorter. (Ignore income taxes.)
B. Compute the net present value of the sorter.
C. Assume that there are intangible benefits such as improved quality and efficiency. What annual dollar value would the printing company have to assign to these intangible factors in order to make the new machine an acceptable investment?

P12-13 Strategic Capital Investment Decisions

Objs. 2, 4

Feldman Cages manufactures cages for pets. Joe, the VP of operations at Feldman Cages, is considering a major capital investment decision. It would cost $2,000,000 to put new, highly automated machines in the factory. The equipment would last about 20 years and would have no salvage value at the end of that period. The equipment will replace eight workers, saving Feldman $200,000 per year in direct labor. Operating and maintenance costs on the machines are expected to cost $100,000 per year. The automated equipment is expected to improve quality. Feldman's main competitors are installing similar equipment. If Feldman installs the

(Continued)

equipment, its revenues are expected to remain steady. If Feldman chooses not to install the equipment, its contribution margin is expected to fall by $200,000 per year as a result of lower quality compared to its competitors. Feldman's discount rate is 10% and its tax rate is 30%.

Required

A. How much is Feldman expected to save each year if it installs the equipment (including tax effects)?
B. How much will Feldman lose each year if it does not install the equipment (including tax effects)?
C. Describe the moving baseline concept and how you would apply it to this problem.
D. Should Feldman purchase the new machines?

P12-14   Strategic Capital Investment Decisions

Objs. 2, 4

Smith Electronics manufactures portable CD players. Lillian Perez, the VP of operations at Smith Electronics, is considering a major capital investment decision. It would cost $2,500,000 to put new, highly automated machines in the factory. The equipment would last about 15 years and would have no salvage value at the end of that period. The equipment will replace 10 workers, saving Smith $300,000 per year in direct labor. Operating and maintenance costs on the machines are expected to cost $100,000 per year. The automated equipment is expected to improve quality. Smith's main competitors are installing similar equipment. If Smith installs the equipment, its revenues are expected to remain steady. If Smith chooses not to install the equipment, its contribution margin is expected to fall by $200,000 per year as a result of lower quality compared to its competitors. Smith's discount rate is 10% and its tax rate is 30%.

Required

A. How much is Smith expected to save each year if it installs the equipment (including tax effects)?
B. How much will Smith lose each year if it does not install the equipment (including tax effects)?
C. Explain how you would analyze this problem in order to determine if Smith should purchase the new machines.
D. Should Smith purchase the new machines?
E. Assume that programming and maintenance costs turn out to be much higher than Lillian's estimates. However, despite the fact that the automation equipment increased costs, Lillian still wants to continue with the project. Explain why Lillian might not want to scrap the equipment.

P12-15   Ethics and Investment Decisions

Objs. 2, 4

Ally Kat is the manager of the continuing education division of Rayford Enterprises, a large financial services firm. The division provides seminars and workshops for Rayford employees to keep them up to date with current economic events that affect their responsibilities in servicing customers and marketing products. Ally attended a trade show recently, where she saw the latest technology in computer learning systems. She wants to acquire this technology for her division and has prepared the following information:

Initial cost of hardware and software	$400,000
Cost to maintain system	$130,000 annually
Expected useful life of system	5 years
Residual value at end of five years	$50,000
Reduction in training costs	$30,000 annually
Increase in sales from improved services	$200,000 annually
Required rate of return	10%

You are responsible for approving the request. In researching the request, you collect the following additional information. The expected useful life of this type of system has historically been closer to three years than to five. Ally argues that she will use the system for five years regardless of future changes in technology. The required rate of return for other projects approved in the last year has been 12%. Ally argues that 10% is adequate because borrowing costs have decreased in the past year. The residual value estimated by Ally is based on the residual value of other equipment used in the continuing education division. The estimated reduction in training costs and increases in sales are based on estimates provided by the vendor of the learning system.

Required

A. Do you see any ethical problems with Ally's request?
B. Prepare a NPV analysis of the request using the data provided by Ally.
C. Provide a comparative NPV analysis using data that you believe are appropriate.
D. Explain how you would respond to Ally's request.

P12-16 ### Net Present Value Decisions in the Service Industry

Objs. 2, 5   A phone company with a discount rate of 8% is considering two investments.

	Residential Service	Commercial Service
Initial cost	$(50,000)	$(100,000)
Year 1	20,000	50,000
Year 2	20,000	50,000
Year 3	20,000	50,000

Required

A. Calculate the NPV for both services.
B. If the phone company can provide only one service currently, which project should it choose?
C. If this is a regulated service industry, explain why the phone company may have to invest in the residential service.

P12-17 ### Excel in Action

SPREADSHEET

As an additional cost savings measure, Music Makers is considering the purchase of a computerized office management system. The system would cost $98,000. It would have an expected life of 48 months and would be depreciated for tax purposes using the sum-of-the-years-digits' method. The company's tax rate is 30%. The company expects to save $2,500 per month from the system in addition to the tax savings. It requires at least a 12% return on investment (annual interest rate) for the project.

Required Use a spreadsheet to prepare a net present value and internal rate of return analysis for Music Makers. Use the format provided below as an example. Enter the data or use formulas to calculate data in column B, rows 1 through 7. Use references to these data to prepare the analysis beginning in row 10. Computations for month 0 (the date of the investment) and month 1 (the date the first cost savings are incurred) are provided as examples.

	A	B	C	D	E	F
1	Annual interest rate					
2	Monthly interest rate					
3	Investment					
4	Life (months)					
5	Tax rate					
6	Cost savings					
7	Internal rate of return					
8						
9	Month	Depreciation	Tax Savings	Cost Savings	Net Cash Flow	Present Value
10	0				(98,000.00)	(98,000.00)
11	1	4,000.00	1,200.00	2,500.00	3,700.00	3,663.37

(Continued)

In the Month column, enter each month for the computation, from 0 to 48. If you enter data in A10 and A11, you can select these two cells and drag them downward to automatically enter the remaining months (12 to 48). To calculate depreciation in column B, use the function button f_x and select Financial, SYD for sum-of-the-years-digits. In the pop-up box, enter references to the Cost (B3), Salvage (0), Life (B4), and Period (Per) (A11). Use absolute references for those cells that will not change in the calculation. Tax savings are the amount of depreciation each month times the tax rate. Cost savings are $2,500 per month. Net cash flow is the sum of tax savings and cost savings. Present value is calculated from the formula $PV = C/(1 + R)^t$, where C is the net cash flow for the month from column E, R is the monthly interest rate (B2), and t is the month from column A. The net cash flow in month 0 is the amount of the investment and is negative because it is a cash outflow. Once data are entered in row 11, you can select the cells in the row and drag them down to copy the formulas for the remaining months.

To calculate the net present value of the investment, sum the data in column F. Evaluate whether Music Makers should make the investment based on its net present value.

To calculate the internal rate of return in cell A7, select the cell, then click on the function button and select Financial, IRR. In the pop-up box, enter the Values by selecting the net cash flow cells (E10:E58). You can leave the Guess box empty or enter an estimate of the IRR (0.12, for example). The function uses this guess as a starting point to estimate the internal rate of return. Evaluate whether Music Makers should make the investment based on its internal rate of return.

Suppose Music Makers' annual required return is 25%. Would the investment still be justified? Recompute the net present value.

P12-18   **Multiple-Choice Overview of the Chapter**

1. In which of the following situations would it be appropriate to accept a project under the net present value method?
    I. Net present value is positive.
    II. Net present value is zero.
    III. Net present value is negative.
    a. Only I.
    b. Only II.
    c. Both I and II.
    d. Both II and III.

2. An investment for which the net present value is $300 would result in which of the following conclusions?
    a. The net present value is too small, so the project should be rejected.
    b. The investment project promises more than the required rate of return.
    c. The net present value method is not suitable for evaluating this project.
    d. The investment project should be accepted only if the net present value is zero.

3. Which of the following statements regarding investments in automated equipment is correct?
    a. The cost of automating a process is always minor compared to other alternatives.
    b. The total cost to automate a process consists of outlays for machinery and equipment.
    c. The benefits of automation are always tangible, direct, and easy to quantify.
    d. A decision to automate often results from a commitment to quality and customer satisfaction.

4. When a company considers an investment in automated equipment, it should:
    a. focus primarily on ways to reduce direct labor cost.
    b. select only automation projects with positive net present values.
    c. consider both the tangible and intangible benefits of automation.
    d. automate the entire process rather than take a piecemeal approach to automation.

5. Wilson Company purchased a machine with an estimated useful life of seven years. The machine will generate cash inflows of $8,000 each year over the next seven years. If the machine has no salvage value at the end of seven years and the company's discount rate is 10%, what is the purchase price of the machine if the net present value of the investment is $12,000? (Round to the nearest dollar.)
   a. $38,947
   b. $26,947
   c. $12,000
   d. $50,947

6. Elizabeth Rankin invested $60,000 to start a business at the beginning of 2005. She withdrew $10,000 at the end of each year for the next five years. At the end of the fifth year, Elizabeth sold the business for $100,000 cash. At a 12% discount rate, what is the net present value of Elizabeth's business investment? (Round to the nearest dollar.)
   a. $60,000
   b. $36,048
   c. $56,743
   d. $32,791

7. Anthony operates a part-time auto repair service. He estimates that a new diagnostic computer system will result in increased cash inflows of $1,200 in year 1, $2,300 in year 2, and $3,500 in 3. If Anthony's cost of capital is 10%, then the most he would be willing to pay for the new computer system would be (rounded to the nearest dollar):
   a. $4,599.
   b. $5,502.
   c. $5,621.
   d. $5,107.

8. The moving baseline concept is based on the assumption that:
   a. current cash flows can continue indefinitely into the future.
   b. customer dissatisfaction can be avoided with increased quality.
   c. a competitor will adversely affect a company's cash flows if an investment is not made.
   d. investment in new equipment is an opportunity cost.

9. A manager who fails to terminate a failing capital investment project:
   a. is probably unaware that the investment is failing.
   b. may do so because sunk costs are not being ignored.
   c. may be reacting to pressures within the organizational environment.
   d. All of the above are correct.

10. Which of the following items must be estimated when a capital investment decision is made?
   a. Service life of investment
   b. Residual value of investment
   c. Both a and b are correct.
   d. Neither a nor b is correct.

(Continued)

CASES

C12-1
Obj. 2

Capital Investment Decision, Discounting and Nondiscounting Methods of Analysis

Leroy Mandel is investigating the possibility of starting a hardware business. Leroy would sell home products, supplies, and maintenance materials. He has determined that the initial cost of the store would be $400,000 to acquire a suitable lease, obtain store fixtures, and fund working capital requirements. To obtain the needed funds, Leroy intends to sell $300,000 of stock and borrow $100,000 from a bank. The stock would pay annual dividends of 8%, and the bank loan will carry interest of 16%.

Leroy also has estimated that the store will generate an annual cash inflow of $50,000. For purposes of analysis, Leroy expects to operate the business for 20 years and then retire. Leroy does not want to invest unless he can fully recover his investment within nine years. There will be no residual value at the end of the 20 years, as the lease will expire, the inventory will be sold through normal operations, and store fixtures will be scrapped.

Required

A. Compute Leroy's cost of capital.
B. Calculate the payback period.
C. Assuming that depreciation is $10,000 per year, compute the accounting rate of return. (Ignore income taxes.)
D. Compute the net present value of the investment.
E. Compute the internal rate of return of the investment.
F. If you were Leroy, would you invest in the store? Why or why not?

C12-2
Objs. 2, 4

Investment Analysis, NPV, Payback, Uncertainty

Perfect Chef Company is constantly developing and marketing new cooking accessories. Based on past experience in forecasting cash flows for a new product, Perfect Chef has been able to predict cash flows within 10% of actual results. The longer the estimated life of a particular product, the greater the uncertainty surrounding future cash flows. The company currently is evaluating a project that is expected to have a five-year service life.

Accordingly, in performing net present value analysis of new product offerings, the company computes three different net present value figures: most likely, optimistic, and pessimistic. On a five-year project, the pessimistic computation assumes that the cash flows are overstated by 10% in the first three years of the project and by 50% in the last two years. The optimistic computation assumes that the estimates are understated by 10% in the first three years and 50% during the last two years. The most likely computations use the estimates without adjustment.

Perfect Chef is developing a new pressure cooker. To produce the pressure cooker, $625,000 must be invested in special equipment. The following are estimated net annual cash inflows that have been developed to analyze the potential product:

Year	Projected Net Annual Cash Inflows
1	$200,000
2	250,000
3	200,000
4	150,000
5	100,000

The company's cost of capital is 8%.

Required

A. Prepare a schedule of cash flows for five years based on the three methods described.
B. Compute the net present value for each of the three methods.
C. Compute the payback period for each of the three methods.
D. Based on your calculations in requirements (B) and (C), would you advise Perfect Chef to produce the cooker? Explain your answer.
E. Explain why Perfect Chef might not want to invest in a product that has a payback period greater than three years.

A Closer Look at Service Organizations

What's different about a service business?

Erin and Seth are considering whether to expand their business to include interior design consulting. Currently, they sell their furniture directly to retail stores. The retail stores then market the juvenile furniture to consumers. After purchasing a product or products, consumers may be referred to Erin and Seth's agency for assistance in creating innovative juvenile spaces within their homes. Thus, no conflict of interest exists, as Erin and Seth would not make recommendations about furniture purchases. The consulting business will produce additional sources of revenue. However, Erin and Seth are unsure about how to set prices for their services and how to determine the cost of providing the service.

FOOD FOR THOUGHT

Assume you are advising Seth and Erin. Do service companies, such as law firms, accounting firms, architecture firms, and hospitals, face different cost accounting problems than do manufacturing companies? What are the primary differences between service companies and manufacturing companies? Let's listen to Seth and Erin's discussion about expanding their business.

Seth: Erin, I think your idea to expand our company to include interior design consulting is a good one. It will help ensure that our customers get the maximum benefit from their purchases. Also, it helps us to establish a direct relationship with the end user of our products.

Erin: There's no doubt that the new service will provide a strategically important advantage to our business. However, I'm still not sure how we go about attaching costs to each consulting engagement and determing the appropriate amount to charge for each service. Unlike our furniture business, each consulting engagement will be different. Some engagements will be simple, while others will be lengthy and complex; no two will be the same!

Seth: I see your point. It seems to me our consultants must record the time they spend on each engagement, just as accountants and attorneys do. We will bill clients as a function of time.

Erin: I understand how professional time would be used to calculate the labor cost of a consulting engagement. But, there must be other costs as well.

Seth: Our consultants will use supplies, but I doubt the cost will be significant. Consulting supplies used will be on a much smaller scale than materials used in furniture production. Overhead costs, however, will be more important to understand.

Erin: I've been thinking about how to allocate overhead costs from various departments. The consulting business will use indirect resources that must be considered when determining the total cost of a job. For example, our accounting department will provide services to the consulting business; however, we cannot bill our customers directly for these accounting activities. Also, you and I will provide our time to help the manager of the consulting company establish and run the business. We need to make sure the job cost includes these indirect support costs.

Seth: We can think of our accounting, human resources, and systems support departments as service departments that assist the revenue-producing departments, such as furniture production or interior design consulting. *The costs incurred in these departments may be seen as indirect costs. The cost of making furniture or providing consulting services must include both direct and indirect costs.*

Erin: *The prices we charge for our products and services must be sufficient to cover both direct and indirect costs if our company is to be profitable. Also, we need to develop methods to accurately trace indirect costs to revenue-producing departments. Otherwise, our product costs will be distorted and not representative of resources consumed.*

OBJECTIVES

Once you have completed this chapter, you should be able to:

1 Explain how costs are classified within service organizations.

2 Allocate support department costs to revenue-producing departments.

3 Calculate costs of providing various services to customers and discuss how service costs may be used to make better decisions.

4 Describe various strategies used by service organizations to improve quality and reduce costs.

STONEBROOK MEDICAL CENTER: BACKGROUND AND ENVIRONMENT

A major insurer asked us to bid on performing all of its open-heart surgeries in the southeast United States. We prepared a bid by pulling cost information from our old cost system on all open-heart surgery patients we had treated. We did not get the contract, and we had no idea whether to be disappointed or relieved. From talks with third-party payers and major employers, we believed that we would be bidding for portions of business, like open-heart surgeries, on a regular basis. We realized that we needed a much better understanding of our costs if we were to be able to compete effectively.
—Jay Williams, Administrative Leader, Stonebrook Medical Center

Stonebrook Medical Center is a for-profit medical facility that offers a wide range of health-care services, including extended outpatient surgery, labor and delivery, psychiatry, and heart surgery. In addition, Stonebrook has initiated a number of programs to promote knowledge and wellness in the community. These programs include health and fitness courses, a cancer program, and a diabetes program.

The health-care industry currently is receiving more and more attention by the media, government, and public as a result of increasing health-care costs. In order to survive, providers must cope with constantly changing conditions. They must deliver high-quality health-care services in a time of intense competition.

The market for health-care services includes both patients and insurance companies. Thus, medical facilities are expected to deliver high-quality health-care services, while controlling health-care costs. Stonebrook and many other medical facilities are taking steps to improve their cost-reporting systems. In addition, hospitals are redesigning health-care delivery processes to reduce costs and improve quality.

Jay Williams, an administrative leader at Stonebrook Medical Center, selected a group of individuals with diverse professional backgrounds to serve on a committee to improve the clinical and financial outcomes at Stonebrook. The team consisted of Beth Rogers, the cost accounting manager; Linda Reynolds, a specialty nurse; and Tim Harris, a clinical case manager. Linda and Tim were asked to join the team because they have clinical and managerial experience. Beth and Jay brought accounting and business systems knowledge to the group.

Jay and his team had to find ways to improve the health-care delivery processes within the hospital. In addition, because of pressure from insurance companies, they had to reduce costs and at the same time improve the quality of care delivered to patients at Stonebrook. The health-care environment is changing rapidly because of managed-care systems. Employers often contract with insurance companies to provide health-care coverage for their employees at a fixed annual rate per employee. The insurance companies then contract with health-care providers, such as Stonebrook, to provide care at predetermined rates. Thus, hospitals that offer lower costs while providing quality care are more successful in securing contracts with managed-care systems. As a result, hospital cost systems have become increasingly important to managers as they attempt to understand the cost of providing services such as open-heart surgery and cancer treatment.

As indicated by Jay's quote at the beginning of this section, Stonebrook is facing a rapidly changing environment. The existing cost management system is inadequate for the decisions that managers must make. Of growing concern is the unexplained variation in physicians' practice patterns. As administrators attempt to control costs and modify physicians' behavior, accurate information on resource use by physicians would prove very useful. It is difficult to improve processes without accurate cost data.

An analysis of the effectiveness of care also would permit decisions about the types of clinical procedures Stonebrook and member physicians performed. Evaluating the effectiveness of a medical procedure involves clinical understanding. Thus, to be adequate for decision making in tomorrow's health-care environment, an information system must include the ability to gather and distribute information about the results of clinical procedures.

Other decisions that administrators face include cost versus value of care. For example, new medical technologies are developing continually. The decision to make investments in new technology is a complex process that compares existing clinical results with those promised by the new technology. Often, cost information can be a key factor in decisions about purchasing new technology.

Cost management systems for hospital use are evolving. Until recently, many hospitals used a facility-wide cost-to-charge ratio to estimate the cost of a medical procedure. This ratio is similar in principle to manufacturers using a facility-wide predetermined overhead rate to apply overhead to products. Thus, total annual facility-wide costs were divided by total annual facility-wide charges (billings) to determine a facility-wide cost-to-charge ratio. To estimate the cost of a procedure, the charge (amount billed) was multiplied by the facility-wide cost-to-charge ratio. For example, assume the following costs and charges for Stonebrook:

Cost and Revenue Data for 12 Months Ending December 31, 2005 (build patients)

Revenue Center	Total Costs	Total Charges
Radiology	$ 7,000,000	$ 7,000,000
Psychiatric care	5,000,000	6,000,000
Intensive care	9,000,000	9,200,000
Chemotherapy	5,000,000	7,000,000
Coronary care	7,200,000	7,400,000
Nursing/surgical	8,000,000	9,000,000
Emergency room	6,300,000	6,800,000
Operating room	26,000,000	45,800,000
Labor and delivery	9,000,000	11,200,000
Laboratory	5,000,000	15,000,000
Diabetes center	500,000	600,000
Total	$88,000,000	$125,000,000

The facility-wide cost-to-charge ratio is calculated as follows:

$$\frac{\text{Total costs}}{\text{Total charges}} = \frac{\$88,000,000}{\$125,000,000} = 0.704$$

If Stonebrook charged $5,000 for an appendectomy procedure, the estimated cost would be $3,520 ($5,000 × 0.704). Also, if charges for an open-heart surgery were

$30,000, the estimated cost would be $21,120 ($30,000 × 0.704). The system was adequate for determining the average cost of all procedures; however, it was not useful in helping managers determine the cost of a specific procedure. Unfortunately, many hospitals continue to use the cost-to-charge ratio to estimate costs. However, better cost management systems are becoming a necessity for survival as hospitals submit bids to insurance companies to acquire managed-care contracts.

MODERN COST MANAGEMENT SYSTEMS FOR SERVICE ORGANIZATIONS

OBJECTIVE 1

Explain how costs are classified within service organizations.

As you read earlier, Seth and Erin know they must allocate indirect costs to their new service business. They understand the consulting company will incur direct and indirect costs. This chapter uses Stonebrook Medical Center to illustrate the mechanics of indirect cost allocation to revenue-producing departments.

Jay and Beth sat at a table and sketched the structure of a cost system that would accurately trace costs to revenue-producing departments. Their sketch is reproduced in Exhibit 1. The system had to be one that could be understood easily because cost management systems for health-care decisions must be accessible by everyone in the organization. They began by classifying departments as either support departments or revenue-producing departments.

Exhibit 1 Conceptual Design of the Stonebrook Medical Center Cost Accounting System

Support Departments

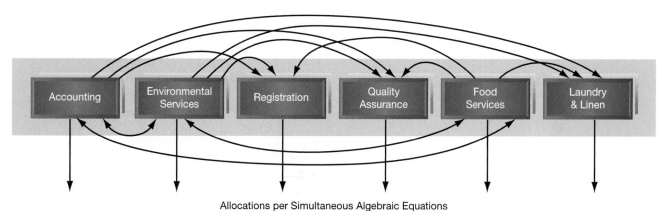

Allocations per Simultaneous Algebraic Equations

Revenue-Producing Departments

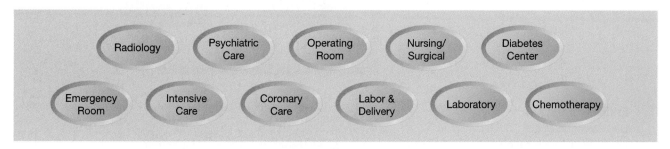

Revenue-producing departments at Stonebrook include the operating room, psychiatric care, radiology, the diabetes center, and coronary care. Each revenue-producing department incurred direct costs, such as supplies and salaries. Departments such as accounting, environmental services (janitorial and maintenance), registration, and quality assurance support the revenue-producing departments. Jay and Beth reasoned that the total cost of providing operating room services should include direct operating room costs plus part of the support department costs. Thus, allocations were necessary to transfer support department costs to revenue-producing departments.

In addition to providing services to revenue-producing departments, support departments often provide services to other support departments. For example, the environmental services department cleans the accounting department offices. Likewise, the accounting department provides payroll functions for the environmental services department. A *reciprocal service arrangement* **exists when support departments exchange services.** Health-care cost systems commonly use either a step-down or a simultaneous algebraic equation method to allocate costs among support departments. Simultaneous equations for real organizations are too complex to be solved manually. However, the following simple example illustrates key principles found in complex computer-based cost systems.

Step-Down and Simultaneous Algebraic Equation Methods for Allocating Reciprocal Support Costs

OBJECTIVE 2

Allocate support department costs to revenue-producing departments.

For illustration purposes, assume that Stonebrook has only two support departments, accounting and environmental services. In addition, assume that Stonebrook has only two revenue-producing departments, operating room and psychiatric care. A study conducted by the accounting department revealed that its efforts were distributed among the other three departments as follows: environmental services, 5 percent; operating room, 45 percent; and psychiatric care, 50 percent. A manager of the environmental services department estimated that the department's efforts and resources were consumed as follows: accounting, 10 percent; operating room, 60 percent; and psychiatric care, 30 percent. Exhibit 2 illustrates the relationships among the support departments and revenue-producing departments. Direct costs (before allocations have been performed) for each department are shown in Exhibit 3.

Exhibit 2
Reciprocal Service
Relationships
(Chart of %)

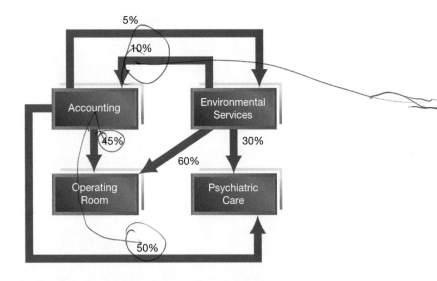

Exhibit 3
Departmental Direct
Costs Prior to Allocation

Accounting	$ 100,000
Environmental services	300,000
Operating room	1,600,000
Psychiatric care	1,000,000
Total	$3,000,000

This section considers two methods for allocating service department costs to revenue-producing departments: step-down and simultaneous algebraic equations. Allocations of service department costs using the step-down method recognize reciprocal relationships to only a limited extent because cost allocations flow in only one direction. Once costs are transferred out of a department, they do not flow back into it. Typically, departments that provide the most resources to other departments are allocated first. Using Stonebrook as an example, the step-down method first allocates the costs of environmental services to accounting, operating room, and psychiatric services. Next, the accounting department's costs (beginning costs and those transferred from environmental services) are allocated to the operating room and psychiatric care departments. Exhibit 4 illustrates the cost flows using the step-down method.

Exhibit 4

Graph of Cost Flows Using Step-Down Method

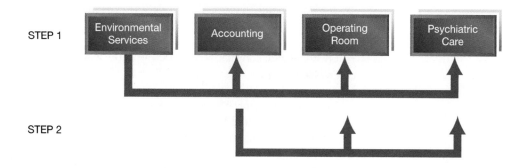

As indicated earlier, environmental services department costs were allocated as follows: accounting, 10 percent; operating room, 60 percent; and psychiatric care, 30 percent. Thus, to allocate the costs of the environmental services department, $300,000 is multiplied by the service percentages ($300,000 × 0.10 = $30,000; $300,000 × 0.60 = $180,000; $300,000 × 0.30 = $90,000).

After the costs of environmental services are allocated, the next step is to allocate the accounting department's costs. Although the accounting department provides resources to environmental services, the step-down method does not permit costs to be allocated into a department whose costs already have been allocated. Thus, the accounting department costs are allocated to the operating room and psychiatric care. From Exhibit 2 we know that the operating room and psychiatric care departments consume 45 and 50 percent of the accounting department's services, respectively. As a result, the allocation base is 95 percent (45% + 50%) rather than 100 percent. Thus, the operating room receives $61,579 ($130,000 × 0.45 ÷ 0.95), and the psychiatric services department receives $68,421 ($130,000 × 0.50 ÷ 0.95) from the accounting department. Exhibit 5 summarizes the allocation process for the step-down method.

Exhibit 5 Cost Allocation from Service to Revenue-Producing Departments, Step-Down Method

	Environmental Services	Accounting	Operating Room	Psychiatric Care	Total
Beginning	$ 300,000	$ 100,000	$1,600,000	$1,000,000	$3,000,000
Environmental services distribution	(300,000)	30,000	180,000	90,000	
Accounting distribution		(130,000)	61,579	68,421	
Ending	$ 0	$ 0	$1,841,579	$1,158,421	$3,000,000

The step-down method was commonly used in health-care organizations before sophisticated computer packages became generally available. This method recognizes reciprocal transfers among service departments to only a limited degree because costs flow in only one direction. The primary advantage of the step-down method is the ease of calculation. Also, because simultaneous equations or matrix algebra is not required, users of information easily understand how costs are allocated. However, the team at Stonebrook decided to use a computerized system to perform allocations based on simultaneous algebraic equations. Before the system could crunch the numbers, mathematical models of departmental relationships had to be constructed. The group asked Jay to develop these mathematical relationships.

Jay began to define the relationships among departments in mathematical terms. For example, the cost of providing environmental services equals $300,000 plus 5 percent of the costs incurred by the accounting department. The cost of providing accounting services equals the direct costs of $100,000 plus 10 percent of the cost incurred by environmental services. These relationships may be expressed mathematically as follows:

Environmental services = $300,000 + (0.05 × accounting)
Accounting = $100,000 + (0.10 × environmental services)

Because of reciprocal service arrangements, the cost of the environmental services department is affected by the cost of the accounting department, and the cost of the accounting department is affected by the cost of the environmental services department. Thus, simultaneous equations are used to arrive at a solution. First, solve the equation for the environmental services department as follows:

Step 1. *Define the mathematical relationship.*

Environmental services = $300,000 + (0.05 × accounting)

Step 2. *Substitute the mathematical definition of accounting.*

Environmental services = $300,000 + 0.05 [$100,000 + (0.10 × environmental services)]

Step 3. *Distribute 0.05 across both terms in parentheses.*

Environmental services = $300,000 + $5,000 + (0.005 × environmental services)

Step 4. *Subtract 0.005 × environmental services from each side of the equation.*

Environmental services − (0.005 × environmental services) = $300,000 + $5,000

Step 5. *Combine terms.*

0.995 × environmental services = $305,000

Step 6. *Divide each side of the equation by 0.995.*

Environmental services = $306,533

Therefore, the cost of operating the environmental services department is $306,533 after considering costs allocated from the accounting department. Next, solve the accounting equation by substituting $306,533 for the environmental services term in the equation.

Step 1. *Define the mathematical relationship.*

Accounting = $100,000 + (0.10 × environmental services)

Step 2. *Substitute the value from the previous step 6 into the accounting equation.*

Accounting = $100,000 + (0.10 × $306,533)

Step 3. *Multiply terms within parentheses.*

Accounting = $100,000 + $30,653

Step 4. *Combine terms.*

Accounting = $130,653

The simultaneous equations produce values for environmental services and accounting that are allocated among each of the four departments according to the percentages identified in Exhibit 2. This method commonly is used by hospitals to allocate the costs of service departments to other service departments and finally to revenue-producing departments. Though a computer routine performs the complex algebraic calculations, managers should understand the underlying concepts.

Having determined service department costs, Jay prepared the allocation schedule shown in Exhibit 6. He prepared a column for each department and placed the direct costs from Exhibit 3 into the columns to represent beginning balances before allocations. He noted the total cost of $3,000,000.

Exhibit 6 Cost Allocation from Service to Revenue-Producing Departments

	Accounting	Environmental Services	Operating Room	Psychiatric Care	Total
Beginning	$100,000	$300,000	$1,600,000	$1,000,000	$3,000,000
Accounting distribution	(130,653)	6,533	58,794	65,326	
Environmental services distribution	30,653	(306,533)	183,920	91,960	
Ending	$ 0	$ 0	$1,842,714	$1,157,286	$3,000,000

Jay began by allocating the accounting department's costs. In step 4 above, the algebraic solution stated that $130,653 was incurred by the accounting department. Thus, Jay subtracted $130,653 from the accounting department to distribute among environmental services, operating room, and psychiatric care using the percentages from Exhibit 2 ($130,653 × 0.05 = $6,533; $130,653 × 0.45 = $58,794; $130,653 × 0.50 = $65,326).

Next Jay subtracted $306,533 (from step 6 above) from the environmental services column to distribute among accounting, operating room, and psychiatric services using the percentages identified in Exhibit 2 ($306,533 × 0.10 = $30,653; $306,533 × 0.60 = $183,920; $306,533 × 0.30 = $91,960).

As shown in Exhibit 6, after the service department costs are distributed, both the accounting and the environmental services columns contain zero balances, while the revenue-producing departments, operating room and psychiatric care, contain all the costs from the service departments. Notice also that the total costs before and after allocation equal $3,000,000.

Managers use cost reports containing allocations to make various kinds of decisions. An objective of support department cost allocation is to understand the revenue-producing departments' total cost of providing services. To make pricing decisions, managers must understand how total resource consumption rates vary across revenue-producing departments. For example, in a hospital, the operating room and the psychiatric department consume support department resources differently because each has its unique function. Thus, the cost system must trace support department costs to revenue-producing departments accurately to allow managers to understand the cost of providing different types of services. When reciprocal service arrangements occur among service departments, cost allocation among these departments is necessary to determine each service department's total cost.

To improve processes and reduce costs, managers must understand cost drivers, the activities that cause costs. Choosing appropriate cost drivers, or allocation bases, helps managers understand the sources of costs and where to look for clues as to how to reduce costs. For example, managers may look at the allocated cost of lab services and consider whether the value of the services received equals the cost. If costs are thought to be excessive, consumption patterns may change, or a manager may decide to purchase these services from an independent laboratory. Finally, accurate allocations are necessary to reduce cross-subsidy among services provided. The cost-to-charge ratio averages many types of costs across various services. As a result, some services are reported at a cost greater than the actual, while other services are reported at a cost less than the actual. This is known as *cross-subsidy*. Eliminating cross-subsidy is important because managers using costs based on averages may make poor pricing decisions.

1 SELF-STUDY PROBLEM

WebTUTOR Advantage

Liberty School is a private institution offering preschool and kindergarten classes. All teachers are experts in the field of early childhood education. To support the primary function of classroom instruction, Liberty maintains a personnel department and an administrative department. The manager of the administrative department estimates that her department provides services to other departments as follows:

Personnel	15%
Preschool instruction	50
Kindergarten instruction	35
	100%

The manager of the personnel department estimates that his department provides services to other departments as follows:

Administrative	30%
Preschool instruction	45
Kindergarten instruction	25
	100%

The departmental direct costs are as follows:

Administrative	$100,000
Personnel	75,000
Preschool instruction	300,000
Kindergarten instruction	500,000
Total	$975,000

Required

A. Discuss the circumstances that create reciprocal relationships among service departments.
B. Draw a chart of the relationships among the four departments.
C. Allocate the service department costs to revenue-producing departments using the step-down method.
D. Set up the equations to mathematically explain the costs of providing administrative and personnel services.

E. Determine the costs of maintaining the administrative and personnel departments using simultaneous algebraic equations.

F. Allocate the costs from the administrative and personnel departments to the preschool and kindergarten departments.

The solution to Self-Study Problem 1 appears at the end of the chapter.

Cost Management Systems for Service Companies

OBJECTIVE 3

Calculate costs of providing various services to customers and discuss how service costs may be used to make better decisions.

Erin and Seth discussed the importance of understanding the cost of each consulting engagement in their new consulting business. Unlike their furniture business, each consulting engagement will require different amounts of resources. Managers of all types of service organizations, like their counterparts in manufacturing, need to understand the cost of providing goods or services to their customers. They must understand how costs change with activity levels if they are to determine appropriate prices for their services. Additionally, managers may use cost accounting information to help them identify expensive, inefficient processes that are candidates for improvement. Finally, having accurate cost information may permit managers to compare the cost of their services with those of competitors. The cost structure of most service organizations presents interesting challenges for managers. This section illustrates the design and use of a cost system in a service environment.

A Health-Care Cost Report for an Appendectomy Procedure. A cost system for attaching costs to services may use a two-stage process. In the first stage, support department costs are allocated to revenue-producing departments. In the second stage, costs are attached to a specific product, service, or customer.

Jay and Beth continued to work on their drawing of a new cost system for Stonebrook. Their final objective was to design a cost system that would attach costs to each patient based on resources consumed while treating the patient. Thus far, their model allocated costs among support departments and to revenue-producing departments. These support-related costs were added to the direct costs of the revenue-producing department, as illustrated in Exhibit 6. Their next step was to ensure that costs from revenue-producing departments were allocated to the patient, based on the resources consumed. Exhibit 7 illustrates the model designed by Jay and Beth.

Exhibit 7 extends the model shown in Exhibit 1 by adding allocations from revenue-producing departments to patients. As in manufacturing cost systems, a variety of allocation bases are used to attach costs to patient procedures. For example, from discussions with the clinical members of their team, Jay and Beth knew that some costs are incurred as a function of hours, whereas others are incurred at a daily rate. Finally, other costs should be applied to procedures using the actual cost, such as supplies.

Jay and Beth pulled data on a patient who recently received care at Stonebrook. Their cost analysis is shown in Exhibit 8. The patient was admitted to the emergency room for an appendectomy procedure. Jay and Beth identified departments and the description of services provided. Linda Reynolds, the specialty nurse, said that patients could receive various levels of nursing attention. Thus, when designing the system, Jay and Beth allocated nursing costs to patients based on a daily rate at various acuity levels. **Acuity levels** identify the amount of care required; higher acuity levels indicate sicker patients. The patient in their report required one day at acuity level 1 and two days at acuity level 2.

Jay and Beth used an hourly charge to allocate costs from the operating room. As shown in Exhibit 8, the patient spent one hour in the operating room. In the cost model, operating room supplies and central stores supplies are assigned to the patient using the items' actual costs. For example, five sutures costing $24 each were required for the appendectomy procedure.

Food services and laundry/linen costs were attached to the patient using a daily rate because costs of meals and laundry service typically do not vary significantly by the type

Exhibit 7 Design of the Cost Allocation System

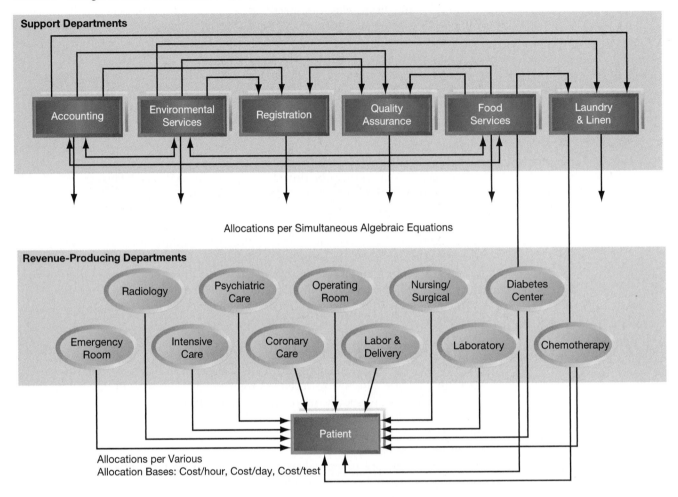

Exhibit 8 Appendectomy Cost Report

Department Description	Product Description	Cost	Quantity	Total Cost
Nursing—surgical	Acuity level 1—daily rate	$313.00	1	$ 313.00
	Acuity level 2—daily rate	369.00	2	738.00
Operating room (OR)	Major surgery—1 hour	449.00	1	449.00
Operating room supplies	Sutures	24.00	5	120.00
	Basic surgical pack	23.00	1	23.00
	Additional OR supplies	251.50	1	251.50
Food services	Daily hospital service	42.00	3	126.00
Laundry/linen	Daily hospital service	15.00	3	45.00
Emergency room (ER)	ER visit level II—intensive	222.00	1	222.00
				$2,287.50

of patient or procedure. Finally, emergency room costs of $222 were associated with the patient.

By way of comparison, Jay calculated the cost of the appendectomy procedure using the cost-to-charge ratio and compared the result with that found using his new cost system. Pulling data on the appendectomy patient, he found that the charge was $8,100. Thus, using the facility-wide cost-to-charge ratio of 0.704, Jay calculated the cost as follows: $8,100 \times 0.704 = \$5,702$. The cost-to-charge ratio had greatly overestimated the cost of this patient's appendectomy procedure. How could Stonebrook possibly use information based on the cost-to-charge ratio to submit bids? No wonder it had been unsuccessful in winning bids for procedures. Using this case as an example, Stonebrook would have overestimated its costs by \$3,414 (\$5,702 − \$2,288). Jay then had a frightening thought. If Stonebrook overestimated its costs (and bids), the worst that would happen was that another hospital would win the contract. What if the cost-to-charge ratio caused Stonebrook to underestimate its costs, thereby winning long-term contracts for procedures whose actual costs exceeded contract revenue!

Clinical Decisions Using Cost Information. The cost system designed by Jay and Beth as shown in Exhibit 7 is far superior to systems that estimate costs using a facility-wide cost-to-charge ratio. Like managers of manufacturing companies, managers of health-care facilities can use cost reports to understand the way in which clinical procedures consume resources. Opportunities for both cost control and quality improvement may be identified by careful analysis. For example, physicians can make decisions about the cost/benefit relationship of laboratory tests. They may reduce the number of unnecessary lab tests performed by specifying only required tests, rather than ordering an entire list of tests. Physicians may order lab tests every other day, rather than daily, if this is consistent with proper clinical practice. Where appropriate, physicians also may consider early discharge. In addition, carefully selecting the level of care may have a positive impact on costs. In the appendectomy example, the patient received two days of care at acuity level 2 and one day at acuity level 1. The physician can evaluate whether the additional clinical attention at acuity level 2 (\$369 per day) rather than acuity level 1 (\$313 per day) is necessary. Thus, better cost systems assist managers in making various types of operational decisions.

Case in Point

Cost Systems: Differences between Manufacturing and Nonmanufacturing Firms

A survey published by the Cost Management Group of the Institute of Management Accountants found differences in cost system design between manufacturing and non-manufacturing firms. For example, approximately 78 percent of manufacturing firms responding to the survey use a standard costing system (as discussed in Chapter M9). Thus, these companies routinely compute materials and labor variances. Alternatively, only 34 percent of non-manufacturing firms use standard costing systems. Managers indicated that standard costs are difficult to develop in service organizations because of unique services offered to clients.

Source: Krumwiede, Kip R. 2000. Results of 1999 Cost Management Survey: The Use of Standard Costing and Other Costing Practices, *Cost Management Update* (December/January).

The next section considers various ways service organizations may evaluate processes to reduce waste. While many factors are important to the delivery of health-care services, the cost system may highlight areas for improvement. However, many decisions and clinical assessments must be made by those who have medical, rather than financial, knowledge. Once again, a team approach to cost management is an effective management tool.

2 SELF-STUDY PROBLEM

WebTUTOR Advantage

Paradise Air is a small airline company located in the Florida Keys. The company provides transportation services to various Caribbean islands. Because Paradise Air competes directly with major carriers, controlling costs and setting appropriate fares are vital to the company's survival. Thus, management is preparing an analysis to assist it in understanding the cost of providing various services to customers. Five categories of costs have been identified:

1. Ticketing
2. Fuel, wages, maintenance, and operating expenses
3. First-class on-board services
4. Coach-class on-board services
5. Baggage handling

Managers at Paradise predicted the following costs and activity levels for the next month:

Ticketing	$10,000
Passengers	1,500 coach-class
	500 first-class
Fuel, wages, maintenance, operating expenses	$1.50 per passenger mile*
Baggage handling	$9,000
Number of baggage transfers	3,000
First-class in-flight service	$25,000
Coach-class in-flight service	$15,000

*Assume that management at Paradise had conducted a long-term study and determined the cost to be $1.50 per passenger mile. Therefore, to determine the fuel, wages, maintenance, and operating expenses cost of each ticket, $1.50 was multiplied by the number of miles traveled.

Ticketing costs are assigned using a cost per passenger basis. Fuel, wages, maintenance, and other operating expenses are assigned using cost per mile as a basis. Baggage handling costs are assigned using the number of times baggage is transferred. Finally, costs of in-flight services, including food, beverages, and other amenities, were estimated for each class of service.

Required

A. Describe the "product" delivered by Paradise Air.
B. Calculate the cost of providing first-class service to a passenger who requires two baggage transfers and travels 200 miles.

The solution to Self-Study Problem 2 appears at the end of the chapter.

PERFORMANCE MEASUREMENT AND COST MANAGEMENT STRATEGIES IN THE SERVICE ENVIRONMENT

OBJECTIVE 4

Describe various strategies used by service organizations to improve quality and reduce costs.

Jay and the team understood that developing a new management information system was only part of the plan to improve quality and reduce costs at Stonebrook. He and Beth had relied heavily on various clinical experts when designing the new cost system. Once again, a team orientation would be required to make the organizational changes that were necessary if Stonebrook was to become competitive in a managed-care environment.

In reaction to changes in the reimbursement policies of health-care payers, many health-care providers are making strategic changes in the way they deliver services. Though this chapter uses a health-care organization as an example, the same principles apply to other service (and manufacturing) organizations. Three strategies for improving the health-care delivery process are illustrated.

The team had gathered to consider the next step in restructuring the clinical-care delivery system at Stonebrook. *Operations restructuring* **involves a complete evaluation of the relationships among multiple processes and is conducted to improve the quality and efficiency of services provided to customers.** After months of design and implementation effort by Jay and Beth, the new cost system was in place. Armed with better cost information, the team considered the next step in the restructuring process.

While the cost system was under development, the clinical team members, Linda and Tim, had pursued another aspect of the restructuring effort.

Linda began, "As you know, the purpose of our restructuring effort is to improve efficiency and reduce the costs of our clinical delivery process. The result should be increased customer satisfaction and improved patient outcomes."

"We used the blood specimen procurement system as a trial process," continued Tim. "It was a very complex system, consisting of over 100 steps and requiring 10 employees. Everyone from the patients to the clinicians was dissatisfied with it."

"We studied the process and made recommendations for changes," Linda went on. "The new system is far less inconvenient for patients because the number of steps has been drastically reduced. Clinical staff members also appreciate the efficiency."

"The new process is less costly, too," added Beth.

"That's right. Beth helped clinicians see their processes from a financial perspective. She was a great help as clinicians struggled to let go of old ways of providing care," Tim said.

"Operations restructuring is the first strategy for becoming more competitive," said Linda. "Our new blood procurement system is an example. We think two other strategies are crucial to successfully changing the way we deliver care. The first is outcomes data dissemination, and the second is critical path utilization. Outcomes data dissemination involves communicating financial and clinical data to physicians and others who make clinical and resource decisions at Stonebrook."

Tim added, "Critical path utilization standardizes treatment routines for various medical procedures."

Outcomes Data Dissemination

The Stonebrook team decided that a key component of successfully improving clinical and financial outcomes involved communicating and acting on relevant data. *Outcomes data dissemination* **is the practice of sharing process and outcomes information with those who make resource decisions.** As with manufacturing processes, the people involved in the delivery of services must understand key process variables. Thus, Linda and Tim collected cost and outcomes data to help physicians improve their practice patterns so that they resulted in better outcomes and lower costs. An example of Linda and Tim's data is shown in Exhibit 9, which summarizes the cost per case for six physicians (A through F).

Exhibit 9

Outcomes Data Dissemination: Cost per Case

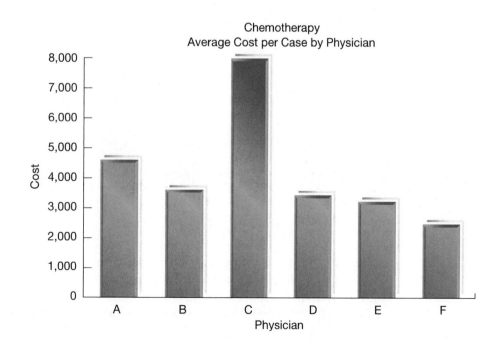

Linda pointed out that Physician C appears to have a high cost per case relative to other physicians in the group. In addition, Exhibit 10 suggests that Physician C's patients remain in the hospital longer than the patients of other physicians. At first, the team thought that Physician C's patients were sicker than those of other physicians. However, Exhibit 11 identifies AWAS (average weighted admission severity) scores for each physician. An AWAS score is a measure of patients' clinical conditions at the time of admission to the hospital; higher scores indicate sicker patients. Physician C's average patient AWAS score is lower than those of almost all of the other physicians in the group. Thus, upon admission to the hospital, Physician C's chemotherapy patients are not as sick as other chemotherapy patients in the sample, but they stay longer and have a higher average cost per case.

Exhibit 10

Outcomes Data
Dissemination: LOS Data

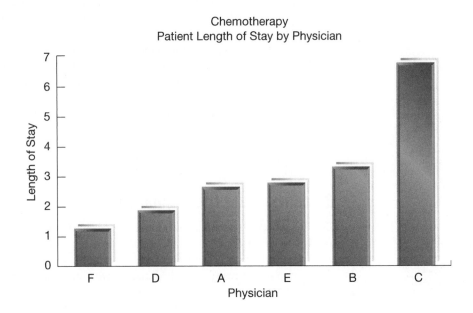

Exhibit 11

Outcomes Data
Dissemination: AWAS

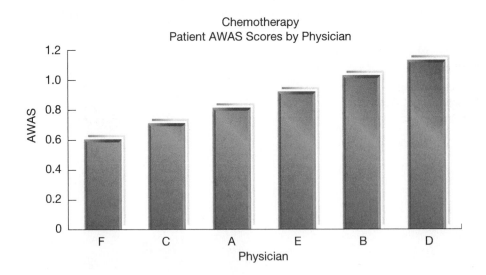

"Physician C contacted us for assistance," noted Tim. "He was interested in reducing his cost per case in order to be attractive to a managed-care company."

"We looked at his practice patterns. Using the new cost system, we made clinical recommendations for reducing waste. We also estimated the resulting cost savings," continued Linda. "For example, Physician C typically asks for a full list of lab work on all admissions. We recommended ordering lab work only for specific tests."

"In addition, most of the electrocardiograms and chest x-rays could be eliminated or completed on an outpatient basis. Full labwork would be completed only on selective groups as needed," said Tim.

Jay and his team borrowed numerous techniques traditionally used by manufacturing organizations. For example, they viewed each service as a process. To determine whether these processes were in a state of statistical control, the team used SPC (statistical process control) charts. One such process, called hydration, involves administering fluids to chemotherapy patients prior to treatment. As shown in Exhibit 12, the elapsed time from admission to the beginning of hydration for chemotherapy patients is plotted to determine if the process is in a state of statistical control. The average time from admission to the beginning of hydration is 89 minutes. However, significant variation in time exists among patients. As indicated by the point above the upper control limit, the chemotherapy administration process is not in a state of statistical control. Using their clinical expertise, Tim and Linda evaluated the process to discover underlying causes of variability and to make recommendations for improvement. They understood that reducing waiting time is important for patient satisfaction and continuous process improvement.

Exhibit 12 Statistical Process Control Chart for Hydration Data

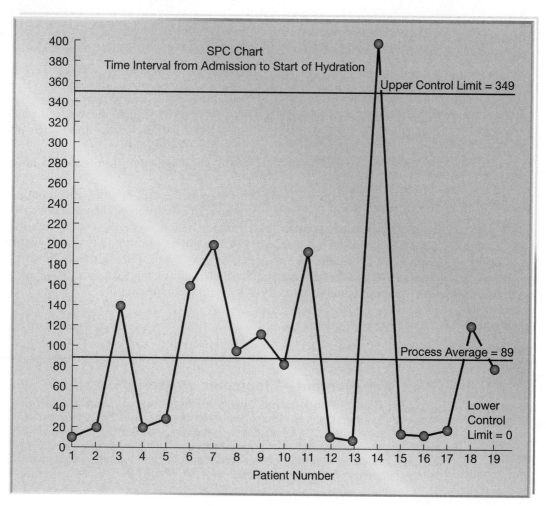

Critical Path Utilization

Before further improvements could be made in delivering clinical care to patients, the team found it necessary to develop standard treatment protocols. Thus, they developed critical paths for various clinical procedures. **A** *critical path* **outlines the steps needed to complete a process.** In the case of a health-care organization, this could be the sequence of tests, treatments, and medication provided to patients. The quantity and type of all procedures, tests, and labwork needed by patients were specified by the critical path. Cost data were evaluated to choose procedures that presented opportunities for cost and quality improvement.

This text has illustrated manufacturing processes that use concepts similar to a critical path. For example, as described in an earlier chapter, Tuff Cut's products were manufactured according to a "critical path" consisting of cutting, welding, painting, and assembly. Exhibit 13 illustrates a critical path for chemotherapy treatment.

Exhibit 13 Critical Path Chemotherapy Treatment

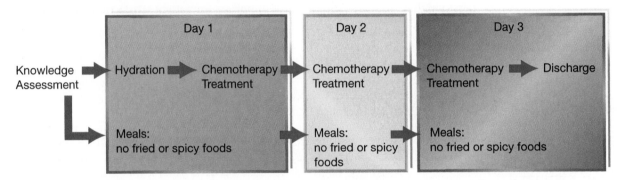

"The use of critical paths helps standardize and improve the delivery of care," said Linda. "Critical paths help everyone—patients, family, nurses, and physicians—understand the order and sequencing of care. Communication and understanding are improved."

"At the same time, adopting the best clinical practices for procedures improves the average quality of care," added Jay.

"We have evidence that suggests that costs decline, as well," added Beth.

Jay said, "We should be very pleased with our progress. Having redesigned the cost system and restructured many of the clinical delivery systems, we are preparing to meet the challenges of providing health care into this new century. I'm certain that next time we are asked to submit a bid for services, we'll have the information to make an informed analysis. We have better clinical delivery systems than most of our competitors, and we understand our costs. Let's keep up the momentum."

Case in Point

http://albright.
swlearning.com

Learn more about
Rhode Island Quality
Institute.

Cost Management—Electronic Prescriptions

A nonprofit group, **Rhode Island Quality Institute**, is implementing a pilot program that will allow physicians to communicate electronically with most pharmacies in the state of Rhode Island. The e-subscription program is expected to reduce subscription costs for patients, physicians, insurance companies, and pharmacies. As shown in this chapter, innovative cost management programs are an important aspect of providing quality, affordable health-care services.

Source: 2003. *The Wall Street Journal* (February 25).

3 SELF-STUDY PROBLEM

Refer to Self-Study Problem 2 for an introduction to Paradise Air.

Required

A. Discuss various strategies Paradise Air can use to improve quality and reduce the cost of performing maintenance services on aircraft. Use the techniques discussed in connection with Stonebrook to direct your answer.

B. Identify appropriate team members to analyze costs and recommend improvements in maintenance service.

The solution to Self-Study Problem 3 appears at the end of the chapter.

REVIEW

SUMMARY of IMPORTANT CONCEPTS

1. Service organizations deliver intangible products (or services) to their customers.
   a. Though their products are intangible, service organizations have processes for delivering their services.
   b. Service companies may use tools developed by manufacturing companies to help them evaluate and improve processes.

2. Support department costs must be allocated to revenue-producing departments for a full understanding of the cost of delivering services.
   a. Reciprocal service arrangements exist among support departments when support departments provide (and consume) services of other support departments.
   b. The step-down and simultaneous algebraic equation methods are commonly used to allocate support department costs to revenue-producing departments.

3. Service companies need high-quality cost management systems to understand the cost of providing services to their customers.

4. Like manufacturing companies, service companies monitor their operations and seek ways to improve their processes to promote efficiency and improve quality.
   a. Operations restructuring involves evaluating the relationships among multiple processes.
   b. Outcomes data dissemination is used to communicate important financial and operating information to decision makers.
   c. Critical paths are used to standardize the processes for cost reduction and quality enhancement.

DEFINE

TERMS and CONCEPTS DEFINED in this CHAPTER

critical path   (M428)   outcomes data dissemination   (M425)
operations restructuring   (M424)   reciprocal service arrangement   (M416)

SELF-STUDY PROBLEM SOLUTIONS

SSP13-1   A. Reciprocal service arrangements occur when support departments provide services to other support departments, as well as to revenue-producing departments. To recognize properly the cost of maintaining a support department, all costs must be recognized, including those provided by other support departments.

B.

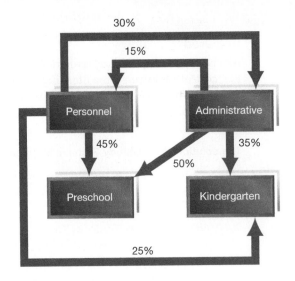

C.

	Administrative	Personnel	Preschool Instruction	Kindergarten Instruction	Total
Beginning	$100,000	$75,000	$300,000	$500,000	$975,000
Administrative	(100,000)	15,000*	50,000	35,000	
Personnel		(90,000)	57,857†	32,143	
Ending	$　　0	$　　0	$407,857	$567,143	$975,000

*$100,000 × 0.15 = $15,000
†($90,000 × 0.45) ÷ (0.45 + 0.25) = $57,857

D. Personnel　　　= $75,000 + (0.15 × administrative)
　　Administrative = $100,000 + (0.30 × personnel)

E. Step 1. Personnel = $75,000 + (0.15 × administrative)
　　Step 2. Personnel = $75,000 + {0.15 × [$100,000 + (0.30 × personnel)]}
　　Step 3. Personnel = $75,000 + $15,000 + (0.045 × personnel)
　　Step 4. Personnel − (0.045 × personnel) = $75,000 + $15,000
　　Step 5. 0.955 × personnel = $90,000
　　Step 6. Personnel = $94,241
　　Step 1. Administrative = $100,000 + (0.30 × personnel)
　　Step 2. Administrative = $100,000 + (0.30 × $94,241)
　　Step 3. Administrative = $100,000 + $28,272
　　Step 4. Administrative = $128,272

F.

	Administrative	Personnel	Preschool Instruction	Kindergarten Instruction	Total
Beginning	$100,000	$75,000	$300,000	$500,000	$975,000
Administrative	(128,272)	19,241	64,136	44,895	
Personnel	28,272	(94,241)	42,408	23,561	
Ending	$　　0	$　　0	$406,544	$568,456	$975,000

SSP13-2 A. The product delivered by Paradise Air is airline transportation. In addition to safe and timely travel, the company must provide dependable baggage handling and high-quality in-flight cabin service.

B.

Ticketing cost: $10,000 ÷ 2,000 passengers	$ 5
Fuel, wages, maintenance, operating expenses:	
$1.50 × 200 miles	300
Baggage handling: $9,000 ÷ 3,000 transfers = $3 per transfer;	
$3 × 2 transfers	6
First-class cabin service: $25,000 ÷ 500 first-class passengers	50
Total cost	$361

SSP13-3   A. Maintenance is one of the many processes required to provide airline services to customers. Using the Stonebrook techniques of outcomes data dissemination and critical path utilization, one may consider the following:

Outcomes data dissemination—Information regarding costs for routine maintenance may be distributed to the aircraft mechanics.
Critical path utilization—The team may develop a critical path for performing maintenance services. As with a critical path in a hospital, aircraft maintenance may be specified according to the number of hours of operation and other variables. Various tests and preventive maintenance may be routinely performed according to a schedule.

B. Teams consisting of mechanics, cost accountants, and managers should be formed to analyze processes. Presumably, mechanics have the necessary technical skills to recommend improvement in maintenance processes. Managers may add insights about forecasting passenger demand and FAA regulations. Accountants may assist with analyzing and interpreting financial information.

Thinking Beyond the Question

What's different about a service business?

Seth and Erin are considering expanding their company to provide consulting services. As a result, they face new challenges because service organizations differ from manufacturing companies. As they consider the opportunity, they realize a variety of costing and performance measurement issues will emerge. What are some of the primary differences in service and manufacturing organizations?

QUESTIONS

Q13-1
Obj. 1
Big Al's Car Care provides auto repairs such as tune-ups, brake work, and engine overhauls on all models of cars. Over 60% of the revenue generated by Big Al's is from the sale of parts. Would you consider Big Al's a service organization? Explain your answer.

Q13-2
Obj. 1
Nickles Consulting Services is a nonprofit organization that provides free legal assistance to clients who meet certain income criteria. The company's funding is obtained by means of fund-raising activities conducted by the board of directors. The directors are not compensated for their time, but Nickles does reimburse them for any out-of-pocket expenses that they incur in conducting company activities. Would the board of directors be classified as a cost center? Why or why not?

Q13-3
Obj. 2
Estella Rodriquez is a staff accountant for Baylor Software. Baylor has two separate departments, programming and consultation. The programming department provides services for

(Continued)

small manufacturing companies that are not large enough to employ their own programmers. The consultation department designs special software that is marketed under the Baylor logo. The president of Baylor has asked Estella to prepare an allocation of the company's in-house computer costs, dividing the costs of operating the company's large mainframe computer between the two departments. What is meant by cost allocation, and how can cost allocation be used by managers?

Q13-4
Obj. 2
What information must be known or estimated in order to allocate support department costs to revenue-producing departments?

Q13-5
Obj. 2
Trans Comm Airline flies domestic routes among several large regional airports. What information would management need in order to allocate the costs of services such as baggage handling, ticketing, and customer service among revenue-producing departments?

Q13-6
Obj. 2
Would you consider the step-down method of cost allocation to be more accurate than the simultaneous algebraic equation method of allocating service costs? Why or why not? What are the limitations or weaknesses of the step-down method?

Q13-7
Obj. 3
Service industries do not deliver a product to their customers; therefore, product costing concerns are limited to manufacturing organizations. Do you agree or disagree? Explain your answer.

Q13-8
Obj. 4
Southern Technical College is an accredited university that grants two- and four-year degrees. The registration process at Southern requires students to stand in long lines to obtain forms for the courses they desire, then take the forms to a service window where they are processed. Could operations restructuring assist Southern in improving the quality or efficiency of the service provided to customers? Explain your answer.

Q13-9
Obj. 4
A-1 Appliance Repair provides in-home service for major brands of household appliances. The company has six trucks staffed by service technicians, which it dispatches based on phone orders. Mark Maddox, owner of A-1, has noted a wide range of charges from his different technicians for similar repair work. He is worried that certain technicians may be performing excess repairs, or that others may be failing to identify problems that should be considered. How could A-1 use data dissemination to improve its service process?

EXERCISES

If your instructor is using Personal Trainer® in this course, you may complete your assignments online.

E13-1
Write a short definition of each of the terms listed in the *Terms and Concepts Defined in this Chapter* section.

E13-2
Obj. 1
Complete the following statements:

a. A _____ exists when support departments exchange services.
b. The _____ or _____ method could be used to allocate costs from service departments to revenue-producing departments.
c. Examples of _____ departments in a hospital include accounting, food services, and registration.
d. Examples of _____ departments in a hospital include the operating room, radiology, intensive care, and coronary care.
e. Service department costs must be _____ to revenue-producing departments to understand the full cost of providing products or services to customers.

E13-3
Obj. 1
Support department costs are allocated to revenue-producing departments. Often a reciprocal relationship exists among the support departments.

a. Prepare a sketch to illustrate how costs would flow among three support departments and two revenue-producing departments if a reciprocal support department relationship exists. Base your sketch on Exhibit 1 in this chapter.
b. Using your chart, describe how costs flow among the departments. Include a brief explanation of how allocation percentages are determined.

E13-4
Obj. 1
Following are various departments that may be found in an organization. Classify each department as a support or revenue-producing department. Explain.

Cafeteria (in a manufacturing organization)	Painting
Welding	Quality control
Tax department (in a CPA firm)	Accounting (in a manufacturing organization)
Assembly	Labor and delivery (in a hospital)
Personnel	Cafeteria (in a food services chain)

E13-5
Obj. 1
Sandy Lodges Hospital historically has used a facility-wide cost-to-charge ratio to determine the cost of various procedures. Cost and revenue data for a 12-month period are as follows:

Revenue Center	Costs	Charges
Nursing	$ 600,000	$ 750,000
Coronary care	1,500,000	2,300,000
Radiology	750,000	1,500,000
Laboratory	300,000	800,000
Emergency room	500,000	950,000

a. Calculate the facility-wide cost-to-charge ratio for Sandy Lodges Hospital.
b. Using the cost-to-charge ratio from part (a), calculate the cost of an emergency room visit that resulted in a charge of $7,500.
c. Why is the cost-to-charge ratio inadequate for making cost-based decisions in a hospital setting?

E13-6
Obj. 2
Assume Rockton Bank has two revenue-producing departments: mortgage lending and small business lending. To support the activities of these departments, Rockton uses three departments: financial research, account management, and personnel. The company uses the step-down method for allocating support department costs to revenue-producing departments.

Prepare a sketch to illustrate the cost flows among the five departments at Rockton. Assume support department costs are allocated in the same order as listed above. Identify potential allocation bases Rockton's management could use to allocate support department costs to revenue-producing departments.

E13-7
Obj. 2
Phillip Technologies has two support departments, A and B, that provide services to producing departments, C and D. Direct costs for service departments A and B are $250,000 and $300,000, respectively. The cost accountant estimates the proportion of services provided by the support departments as follows:

Service Department A	Service Department B
25% to Department B	40% to Department A
40% to Department C	35% to Department C
35% to Department D	25% to Department D

a. Draw a sketch of the reciprocal relationships among the various departments. Indicate the percentage of services provided by each support department to other departments.
b. Prepare the algebraic equation that describes the cost of operating each service department. (You do not have to solve the equation.)

E13-8
Obj. 2
Samson Enterprises uses the step-down method to allocate service department costs to revenue-producing departments. The support departments, personnel and janitorial, allocate their costs based on the number of employees and departmental square footage, respectively. Relevant data are presented as follows:

			Revenue Producing	
	Personnel	**Janitorial**	**Department 1**	**Department 2**
Employees	7	10	20	25
Square feet	3,000	1,000	10,000	15,000
Direct costs	$400,000	$500,000	$1,500,000	$2,000,000

Allocate the personnel and janitorial costs to the revenue-producing departments using the step-down method. Explain how service department allocation bases are selected.

E13-9
Obj. 2

The algebraic method for allocating service department costs recognizes reciprocity among various departments. In the real world, computer programs solve complex allocations when a company must allocate costs among many (more than two) departments. However, the same logic is applied for simple models having only two service departments.

Assume a company has two service departments, 1 and 2, and two revenue-producing departments, A and B. The direct costs of operating Service Department 1 and Service Department 2 are $500,000 and $600,000, respectively.

Allocation percentages are as follows:

Service Department 1	**Service Department 2**
35% to Department 2	40% to Department 1
30% to Department A	40% to Department A
35% to Department B	20% to Department B

a. Prepare the algebraic equations that express the cost of operating each service department.
b. Solving the equations you prepared in part (a), determine the total cost to be allocated to other departments within the company.
c. Explain why simultaneous algebraic equations are necessary to fully capture the reciprocal agreements among departments.

E13-10
Obj. 2

The following illustration shows reciprocal service relationships expressed in percentages of effort provided.

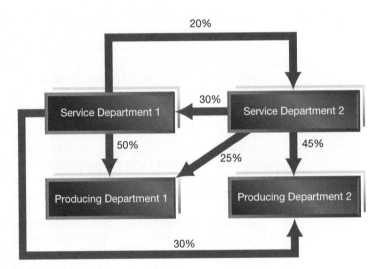

a. Explain the relationships shown in the illustration.
b. Express the reciprocal service relationships in mathematical terms. Assume Service Department 1 has direct costs of $250,000 and Service Department 2 has direct costs of $400,000.

E13-11
Obj. 2

Mary Taylor fell and broke her clavicle while on a university-sponsored weekend rock-climbing expedition. Mary was transported to the emergency room at a local hospital where she received services from emergency room physicians, the laboratory technicians, and radiologists. When she received her bill for services, Mary was surprised by the large amount of charges. The accounts receivable clerk explained how indirect charges in the form of overhead from support departments such as accounting, food services, and education are included in the cost of delivering emergency room, laboratory, and radiology services.

Assuming the hospital uses algebraic equations to allocate service department costs, prepare a sketch to illustrate how costs would flow among the departments and to a patient. Identify reasonable cost drivers (or allocation bases) that may be used to attach emergency room, laboratory, and radiology costs to a patient. Defend your choices.

E13-12
Obj. 3

Bill Watts awoke with intense pain in his side. After a 911 call, he was transported to the emergency room at Lodi Community Hospital, where he underwent surgery for a ruptured appendix. The surgical procedure required 30 minutes. His hospital stay lasted three days, one of which was classified as acuity level 2.

The following information has been retrieved from Lodi Community Hospital's cost information system:

Nursing:

Acuity level 1	$350 per day
Acuity level 2	$400 per day
Food services	$65 per day
Operating room	$450 per half hour
Laundry	$35 per day
Emergency room admission	$250 per admission
Emergency medical transportation	$300

Calculate the cost incurred by Lodi Community Hospital to care for Bill. Assume Lodi Community Hospital invoices clients on a cost-plus basis. If the markup percentage is 20%, what is the amount of Bill's invoice?

E13-13
Obj. 3

Jack Turner was reviewing his hospital bill upon returning to his home following a five-day stay in Stockton Community Hospital. He required two hours of surgery upon admission to the hospital's intensive care facility. He was classified as an acuity level 1 patient for two days and an acuity level 2 patient for three days. The hospital incurred a cost of $600 for surgical supplies associated with Jack's visit.

The following information has been retrieved from Stockton Community Hospital's cost information system. Calculate the cost incurred by the hospital to provide Jack's care.

Nursing:

Acuity level 1	$325 per day
Acuity level 2	$400 per day
Food services	$75 per day
Laundry	$20 per day
Emergency room admission	$200 per admission
Operating room	$550 per half hour

E13-14
Obj. 3

Glendale City Hospital uses a facility-wide cost-to-charge ratio to estimate the cost of providing a variety of medical services. The hospital has the following departments and associated financial information:

	Costs	Charges
Emergency	$2,000,000	$3,750,000
Labor and delivery	3,000,000	4,000,000
Laboratory	750,000	900,000
Cardiology	4,000,000	6,000,000
Radiology	1,000,000	1,500,000

a. Calculate the facility-wide cost-to-charge ratio for Glendale City Hospital.
b. Assume a cardiology patient is charged $75,000 for a procedure. Using the cost-to-charge ratio, calculate the cost to Glendale of performing the procedure.
c. Assume a family is charged $10,000 for the normal delivery of an infant. Using the cost-to-charge ratio, calculate the cost to Glendale of delivering the infant.
d. Compare your answers from parts (b) and (c). What is your impression of the cost-to-charge ratio as a tool to help hospitals understand costs?

E13-15
Obj. 3

Zippy Shipping Lines transports high-value freight across the Gulf of Mexico from New Orleans, Louisiana, to Miami, Florida. The company competes directly with trucking lines and air carriers. Service companies often use multiple activity drivers based on hours, days, voyages, and so on, in determining the cost of providing services to clients.

A cost summary to deliver a load of cargo for a client is as follows:

(Continued)

Service	Cost	Quantity	Total Cost
Freight handling—loading	$300 per hour	10 hours	
Fuel	$0.33 per gallon		$50,000
Crew costs	_____	1.5 days	$ 3,000
Freight handling—unloading	_____	12 hours	$ 4,200
Total			

a. Calculate the *total* cost of freight handling—loading.
b. Calculate the quantity of fuel consumed per *voyage*.
c. Calculate the crew cost per *day*.
d. Calculate the freight handling—unloading cost per *hour*.
e. Calculate the total cost of delivering the load of cargo.
f. Explain why a variety of rates were necessary to calculate the cost of providing shipping services.

E13-16   Complete the following definitions.

Obj. 4

a. _____ involves a complete evaluation of the relationships among multiple processes and is conducted to improve the quality and efficiency of services provided to customers.
b. _____ is the practice of sharing process and outcomes information with those who make resource decisions.
c. A _____ outlines steps needed to complete a process.
d. The strategy used by a hospital when changing the procedures for acquiring and analyzing blood samples is referred to as _____.
e. Standard treatment protocols are identified in a _____.

E13-17   Operations restructuring, outcomes data dissemination, and critical path are three strategies used by service (as well as manufacturing) organizations to improve efficiency and to reduce costs. Listed below are a variety of characteristics. Match each characteristic with the appropriate strategy.

Obj. 4

Strategy
Operations restructuring
Outcomes data dissemination
Critical path

Characteristic
a. This strategy may involve the use of statistical process control charts to determine whether a process is in a state of statistical control.
b. The purpose of this strategy is to improve efficiency and to reduce the costs of delivering products or services to customers.
c. In the case of a hospital, this could be the sequence of tests, treatments, and medication provided to patients.
d. This strategy involves sharing process and outcomes information with those who make resource decisions.
e. Team members would conduct a complete evaluation of the relationships among multiple processes to improve the quality and efficiency of services provided.
f. The use of this strategy helps standardize and improve the delivery of care.

E13-18   Minneapolis Physician Partners (MPP) is considering adding laboratory equipment to permit restructure of the clinical process of gathering and analyzing blood samples. Currently the process is as follows:

Obj. 4

- Physician orders blood test.
- Nurse informs office staff to schedule appointment with patient.
- Office staff telephones patient to schedule appointment.
- Laboratory assistant gathers specimen.
- Laboratory assistant collects a batch of 10 blood specimens before contacting medical courier.
- Courier transports batch of specimens to laboratory across town.
- Lab conducts lab tests requiring 20 minutes and contacts courier.

- Courier returns batch of specimens to MPP after tests are complete.
- Laboratory assistant receives test results, places reports into patients' files, and notifies nurse that reports have returned from lab.
- Nurse gives patient reports to physician for analysis and informs office staff to schedule appointment with patient.
- Office staff telephones patient to schedule appointment.
- Physician meets with patient to discuss report and treatments, if necessary.

Using your understanding of operations restructuring, explain how MPP could simplify the process by purchasing equipment to process blood samples. Explain why operations restructuring may result in more efficient, cost-effective care. Might operations restructuring also benefit the patient? Explain your reasoning.

E13-19 Dr. Walston is an accounting professor in a major state university. As part of the reaccredi-
Obj. 4 tation process, the college is systematically evaluating the quality and rigor of teaching within the various departments. A committee that Dr. Walston chairs is reviewing instructional data, including course grade distributions, course syllabi, student teaching evaluation scores and comments, and peer evaluation reports, for each professor in the college. Dr. Walston's committee will prepare a variety of charts and tables that summarize information by faculty member and department and will distribute the information to each faculty member for consideration. The anonymity of the faculty member and department is ensured. All parties will be identified as faculty A, B, or C, and department A, B, or C.

Using the terms in this chapter, what strategy is the college using to improve operations? How might this strategy be used in a university setting to improve teaching effectiveness? Explain your answer.

PROBLEMS   *If your instructor is using Personal Trainer® in this course, you may complete your assignments online.*

P13-1 ## Cost Allocation and Performance Evaluation
Obj. 1
William Davidson, departmental manager for an engineering consulting firm, recently attended a meeting to discuss a proposal for a new firm-wide cost accounting system. The proposal would change the method of allocating support department costs to producing departments. Management wants to better understand how resources are consumed across all departments. Currently, the step-down method is used; however, the proposed accounting system will require the company to redefine support department relationships to better capture reciprocal service arrangements.

William manages a revenue-producing department and is very interested in how costs flow into his department, as his bonuses are based on ROI. However, he sees the project as little more than a smoke-and-mirrors exercise—all form and no substance. "I can't see how a different allocation process will change the way in which I acquire services from internal departments such as information technology, accounting, personnel, and others. Will the new system really lead to better decision making, or are we simply rearranging the same accounting numbers?"

Required
A. Explain how the algebraic method of support department cost allocation might do a better job than the step-down method of capturing reciprocal service arrangements.
B. Do you agree, or disagree, with William? Explain.
C. Are allocated costs irrelevant to the decision-making process of departmental managers? Explain.

P13-2 ## Service Departments in a Manufacturing Environment
Obj. 2
Omega Manufacturing Company has two production divisions, industrial products and consumer electronics, and three service departments, administration, personnel, and maintenance. Budgeted costs for each service department are as follows:

(Continued)

Administration	$600,000
Personnel	280,000
Maintenance	320,000

Management has decided that administration and personnel service costs should be directly allocated based on the number of employees in each revenue-producing department, and maintenance should be directly allocated based on the dollar amount of assets employed in each revenue-producing department. The number of employees and dollar value of assets employed by each revenue-producing department are as follows:

	Number of Employees	Dollar Value of Assets Employed
Industrial products	225	$4,000,000
Consumer electronics	275	6,000,000

Required

A. Calculate the amount of service costs that should be allocated based on number of employees.
B. Determine the allocation percentages based on both number of employees and dollar value of assets employed.
C. Calculate the amount of service costs that would be allocated to industrial products and consumer electronics using the direct method.

P13-3   Service Department Cost Allocation

Obj. 2

First State Bank has two revenue-producing departments, demand deposits and loans. The bank also has three service areas, administration, personnel, and accounting. The direct costs per month and the interdepartmental service relationships are reflected below. The bank allocates costs in the following order:

1. Administration   *Personnel*
2. Personnel   *Admin*
3. Accounting   *Acc*

	Direct	Percent of Service Used By				
Department	Costs	Administration	Personnel	Accounting	Deposits	Loans
Administration	$40,000		10	10	30	50
Personnel	60,000	10		20	40	30
Accounting	60,000	10	10		40	40
Demand deposits	50,000					
Loans	80,000					

Required

A. Compute the total cost for each revenue-producing department using the step-down method.
B. Define the algebraic equations reflecting the reciprocal service cost functions for the personnel, administration, and accounting departments.

P13-4   Service Department Cost Allocation

Obj. 2

Med Alert is a 24-hour walk-in medical service provider that has two revenue-producing departments, laboratory and patient care. It also has two service departments, administration and custodial services. Service costs for the most recent year of operation were as follows:

Service costs:	
Administration	$ 340,000
Custodial services	100,000
Laboratory	250,000
Patient care	739,000
Total costs	$1,429,000

Med Alert utilizes two different allocation bases, labor hours worked and service space occupied, in assigning service department costs. Information on these allocation bases for the most recent year was as follows:

Labor hours worked:
Administration   12,000
Custodial services   6,000
Laboratory   18,000
Patient care   30,000

Service space occupied (square feet):
Administration   10,000
Custodial services   0
Laboratory   5,000
Patient care   45,000

Administration costs are allocated to revenue-producing departments based on labor hours. Custodial services costs are allocated based on service space occupied.

Required

A. Assume that Med Alert currently allocates costs to the revenue-producing departments individually and without regard to any reciprocal service arrangements. Determine the service costs that would be allocated to the revenue-producing departments using this approach.
B. Compute the costs of the revenue-producing departments using the step-down method to allocate service costs. Allocate administration costs first.
C. Which method of allocation provides a more accurate indication of service costs in the revenue-producing departments?

P13-5 Budgeted versus Actual Allocation Costs

Obj. 2

Dempsey Manufacturing operates a cafeteria for the benefit of all employees. The cost of operating the cafeteria is allocated to the operating departments on the basis of number of employees in the respective departments. Budgeted and actual data for operating the cafeteria during the previous month are shown as follows:

	Budgeted	**Actual**
Cafeteria services	$60 per employee	$72 per employee

The budgeted and actual number of employees in each operating department during the previous month are as follows:

	Departments			
	Receiving	Assembly	Machining	Administration
Budgeted number of employees	12	240	175	44
Actual number of employees	11	243	173	43

Required

A. For purposes of allocating cafeteria service costs, should budgeted or actual cost be used? Explain your answer.
B. Determine the amount of cafeteria service costs that should be allocated to each of the four operating departments.
C. How should cafeteria service costs be treated when evaluating the costs of each of the four operating departments for purposes of comparing actual to planned performance?
D. How should cafeteria service costs be treated by receiving and administration if these service department costs are also allocated to assembly and machining?

P13-6

Obj. 2

SPREADSHEET

Cost Allocation, Simultaneous Algebraic Equation Method

Rivercity Mortgage Company provides mortgage servicing for financial institutions. As a mortgage servicer, Rivercity collects mortgage payments from homeowners on behalf of banks and other mortgage lenders. The bank, or lender, pays Rivercity half of 1% of all funds collected as a fee for performing this service. The department that generates these revenues is called the mortgage service center.

Rivercity also coordinates escrow accounting, collecting funds from mortgagees that are used to pay real estate owners' taxes and insurance. Twice a year, Rivercity sends a report to each homeowner explaining the amount of escrow funds that have been collected and disbursed. Each time Rivercity processes an escrow analysis, it charges the lending bank a flat rate of $2.50. This revenue is generated by the escrow analysis department.

Rivercity maintains two departments that support mortgage servicing and escrow analysis: financial administration and computer services. The financial administration department provides accounting and auditing services for each department (mortgage servicing, escrow analysis, and computer services). Computer services provides the necessary computer hardware and programming for each department (mortgage servicing, escrow analysis, and financial administration). The computer services department also supports the financial administration department.

It is estimated that computer services dedicates approximately 70% of its efforts to support mortgage servicing, 20% to support escrow analysis, and 10% to support financial administration. The financial administration department has determined that approximately 60% of its efforts support mortgage servicing, 25% support escrow analysis, and 15% support computer services.

The direct costs to operate each department for the most recent year, prior to any cost allocation, were as follows:

Mortgage servicing	$360,000
Escrow analysis	284,000
Financial administration	235,000
Computer services	315,000

Required

A. Calculate the cost of mortgage servicing and escrow analysis using simultaneous algebraic equations.
B. How might managers of Rivercity Mortgage Company use the results of cost allocation to help make operating decisions?
C. Assume the mortgage servicing and escrow analysis departments had revenues of $800,000 and $475,000, respectively. Calculate costs as a percentage of revenues. What is your assessment?

P13-7

Obj. 3

Service Activities

Public Airlines provides low-cost commuter flight service between 10 cities in the northwest United States. During a recent stop in Seattle, the plane for Flight 107 had 4,000 pounds of passenger baggage and 2,000 pounds of commercial freight unloaded. Similar amounts of baggage and freight then were loaded onto the plane in preparation for the next leg of its flight. During this stopover, airline custodial personnel boarded the plane to clean the lavatories, seat pockets, and floors. The airline catering crew performed an inventory of drinks and restocked the refreshments. The catering crew loaded in-flight meals into the plane's galley. Laundry personnel exchanged soiled pillows, blankets, and first class linens with clean supplies. While all this activity was occurring, ground crew mechanics were busy inspecting and refueling the plane. Ticket agents issued seat assignments, and flight attendants checked passengers onto the aircraft.

Required

A. Why must management at Public understand all of the activities that occur on a plane during layover? What impact do these activities have on the cost of the flight?
B. How will the cost of these activities be recovered by Public? What can Public do in order to reduce some of the cost associated with providing these activities?

C. Airlines such as Public desire to minimize the amount of time it takes to prepare an aircraft for service. Why do you believe it is important for an airline to decrease a plane's "turnaround" time?

P13-8 Costing and Pricing Service Activities

Obj. 3

Ace Auto Repair Shop provides service repairs for most domestic car models. Ace charges customers based on the time and materials that are used for service repairs. At the beginning of each year, the shop calculates a standard labor rate that is based on estimated costs plus a per hour markup. The markup is based on the competitive environment that management must assess each year. For the coming year, management believes that a $5 per labor hour markup would be acceptable based on current market conditions. Any parts that are used during service repairs are billed to the customer at cost plus 15%. The 15% markup is expected to cover the cost of ordering parts, providing a parts manager, and other carrying costs. Estimated operating costs for the coming year are as follows:

Mechanic wages	$320,000
Employee benefits	36,000
Supervision	40,000
Supplies	2,400
Utilities	42,000
Property taxes	9,200
Depreciation	88,400
Environmental	12,000
Total	$550,000

Management estimates that there will be 25,000 mechanic hours charged during the coming year.

Required

A. Calculate the billing rate that should be used during the coming year.
B. Assume a customer service job results in the following: Labor time = 4 hours; Parts (at cost) = $200. Calculate the total cost for this particular service job.

P13-9 Product Costing in a Service Environment

Obj. 3

SPREADSHEET

Linus Railway operates a freight line connecting the southeast United States with ports located in Texas, New York, New Jersey, and South Carolina. Cost accounting data are used to help management understand the activities required for transporting a specific freight car. Linus Railway uses three factors to capture service costs:

- Costs per ton-mile
- Number of switches (number of times a freight car is connected to a different locomotive)
- Hazardous substance classification

Railroad engineers have long used cost per ton-mile as a cost estimate for moving a ton of freight over a one-mile distance. Freight cars often must be switched from one locomotive to another, just as airline passengers often change planes to reach their final destinations. Thus, the number of switches often is used to capture the costs of delivering a specific freight car to its final destination. Finally, if a freight car contains a hazardous substance, additional handling and equipment are required. These costs are attached to the shipments demanding the extra services.

Estimated costs based on ton-miles	$12,000,000
Estimated ton-miles	100,000,000
Estimated switching costs	$1,500,000
Estimated number of switches	60,000
Estimated hazardous substance costs	$200,000
Estimated hazardous substance shipments	5,000

(Continued)

Assume a client wishes to transport a three-ton container for 3,000 miles (9,000 ton-miles). The scheduler at Linus has determined the shipment will require three switches. In addition, the freight car will contain material considered hazardous.

Required

A. Calculate the cost to Linus for providing the transportation service.
B. How does the cost accounting system for a service company, such as Linus, compare to those of manufacturing companies? Explain.
C. In addition to pricing decisions, how might managers at Linus Railway use cost information? Explain.

P13-10   Cost Driver Selection and Policy Implications

Obj. 3

Use the cost information presented in Exhibit 8 of this chapter to assist you in preparing your responses to this problem.

Various stakeholder groups are interested in the cost and quality of health care. As evidenced by the national debate over health-care reform, patients, hospitals, physicians, employers, traditional insurance companies, pharmaceutical companies, and health maintenance organizations often have goals and objectives that seem incompatible. Though cost accounting information is one source of input for decision makers, many factors, including clinical and political, affect decisions made by health-care providers.

Required

A. Evaluating Exhibit 8, identify a key cost driver that a physician may control as a result of his or her orders. This particular driver affects nursing, food services, and laundry/linen costs.
B. Though pharmaceutical costs are not included in Exhibit 8, many health maintenance organizations encourage patients to request generic, rather than name brand, medications. What are the ethical issues associated with hospital length of stay and medication decisions?
C. In your opinion, should legislators and others who make health-care decisions consider cost when determining the amount and availability of care? Why or why not?

P13-11   Service Provider, Ethical Dilemma

Obj. 4

Ted Macintosh is a computer programmer for Warsaw Products. The computer programming department at Warsaw provides service support to every other department within the company, including other service departments such as accounting and human resources. The gossip at Warsaw is that upper management is considering the elimination of the programming department and outsourcing of programming requirements to a third-party consulting firm. According to the rumors that Ted has heard, the main reason for this possible change is the high cost of maintaining an in-house programming staff.

In response to these rumors, Ted has begun making unauthorized changes to many programs in an effort to "hide" certain programming costs and to make special-use programs too difficult for third parties to understand. Ted hopes that his actions will keep the programming staff from being eliminated.

Required

A. Many services that are provided within an organization can be obtained from outside sources. What are some of the main concerns management should consider before outsourcing a particular service?
B. If the programming staff at Warsaw is eliminated, would the allocation of service costs to other departments be eliminated as well? Explain your answer.
C. What are some arguments for and against Ted's actions? What is the ethical dilemma raised here?

P13-12   Cost and Quality Control

Obj. 4

Medic Delivery provides transportation services between doctors' offices and a hospital laboratory. The company owns three small cars and a minivan. Each morning the company runs specific routes to the offices of various physicians and collects lab specimens that are then delivered to the hospital for testing. Upon reaching the laboratory, the driver collects the previous day's examination results, if any, and delivers the results back to the physician offices in the afternoon. Every route covers over 100 miles each morning and afternoon. The drivers take the company vehicles home at night and begin their respective routes directly from home.

When a driver picks up either a lab specimen or test result, he or she records the pickup in a log book. Physicians are charged a fixed fee for each lab specimen or exam result that is handled by Medic personnel. If a physician has no specimens to be transported, or lab results to be delivered, there is no charge for the day.

Required

A. What data do the managers at Medic need to properly operate and control the business? How would this information improve quality or reduce operating costs?
B. How could the route drivers assist in improving the company's service and profitability?

P13-13 ### Operations Restructuring in Service Organizations

Obj. 4

A major airline is interested in restructuring its service operations to become more efficient, competitive, and customer-oriented. Management has identified the following areas to investigate:

- Ticketing
- On-board meal services

The ticketing process traditionally has been very labor intensive, requiring many customer representatives to individually assist customers in selecting flight schedules and then to issue tickets. Likewise, on-board meal services have been very labor intensive and expensive. On many routes, additional flight attendants were needed to help serve meals.

Two ideas have been suggested to help the company restructure its ticketing and on-board meal services operations:

1. The use of Internet web sites for flight selection and ticket processing
2. Using external suppliers to provide bag lunches that customers can select when boarding a flight

Required

A. Discuss the inefficiencies of traditional customer service representatives for ticketing and the problems associated with serving hot meals aboard aircraft.
B. How will Internet sites and self-serve lunches provided by suppliers help the airline reduce costs and improve service? Explain.

P13-14 ### Outcomes Data Dissemination and Decision Making

Obj. 4

Wild Bill's Muffler Shop employs mechanics to replace automobile muffler and exhaust systems for customers. The exhaust systems of certain vehicles are more complex than others and require more time to replace. Bill currently employs four mechanics. Their names have been disguised in this problem for confidentiality reasons.

Bill has been working on a program to improve the efficiency of his repair process. He would like to identify the best mechanics and help the others learn a few "tricks of the trade" from them.

Following are performance data collected by Bill:

SPREADSHEET

	Average Labor Cost	Average Parts Cost	Average Repair Difficulty
Tom	$80	$155	33
June	65	135	30
Sam	90	180	25
Kate	78	165	40

Required

A. Prepare three bar graphs similar to Exhibits 9, 10, and 11 in this chapter. Assume larger numbers in the average repair difficulty column indicate more difficult repairs.

(Continued)

B. Evaluate your graphs.

C. What decisions might Bill make as a result of your analysis?

P13-15 Excel in Action

SPREADSHEET

James Academy is a private school providing K-12 education. The academy operates three divisions: Lower, Middle, and Upper Schools. Two additional divisions provide support to these operating divisions: Administration and Human Resources. Direct cost data for each division are provided in the following partial spreadsheet. The percentage of costs that should be allocated from each support division to each of the other divisions also is reported in the spreadsheet.

	A	B	C	D	E	F	G
1	Cost and Allocation Data						
2		Administration	Human Resources	Lower School	Middle School	Upper School	Total
3	Direct Costs	560,000.00	325,000.00	1,300,000.00	1,200,000.00	1,486,500.00	4,871,500.00
4	Administration %		10%	30%	30%	30%	
5	Human Resources %	20%		20%	25%	35%	

Required Use the data provided to determine the total cost of each of the school divisions after allocation of support costs. Accomplish this task as follows: (1) Copy the data into a spreadsheet. (2) Use the simultaneous equations method to determine the costs of the support divisions that need to be allocated to the operating divisions. You will need to make these calculations and enter them in the spreadsheet. (3) Below the data and calculations you have entered, prepare a cost allocation schedule similar to Exhibit 6 in this chapter. Use cell references and formulas where possible. Use appropriate formatting throughout.

P13-16 Multiple-Choice Overview of the Chapter

1. Service department costs must be allocated to revenue-producing departments in order to:
   a. determine the proper value of services provided.
   b. assist in determining the profitability of services provided.
   c. provide managers with information to assist in planning and control.
   d. do all of the above.

2. The use of statistical process control in a service industry:
   a. is not possible, since services do not result in the fixed, measurable activities on which statistical process control is based.
   b. is impractical, since the outcome of services cannot be measured on a control chart.
   c. can be an effective management tool.
   d. will not reveal common cause exceptions.

3. Which of the following reflects a similarity between manufacturing and service companies in the use of accounting information?
   a. Both manufacturing companies and service companies use accounting information to value inventories.
   b. Both manufacturing companies and service companies can utilize just-in-time theories to control inventory purchases.
   c. Both manufacturing companies and service companies utilize processes that require accounting information to analyze and control.
   d. There are no similarities between manufacturing and service companies.

4. The allocation of service department costs to revenue-producing departments is necessary:
   a. only in service organizations.
   b. to accurately reflect the total cost of providing a particular product or service.
   c. unless reciprocal service relationships exist.
   d. only in manufacturing organizations.

5. The basic difference between a service department and an operating department is that:
   a. operating departments can have no reciprocal relationships with other departments.
   b. service departments have no identifiable customers.
   c. operating departments generate revenues, whereas service departments do not.
   d. service departments are not essential to the organization's product or service.

6. Which of the following would *not* be considered a service organization?
   a. A mortuary
   b. An airline company
   c. An advertising agency
   d. All of the above are service organizations.

7. In order for services to be delivered in a more efficient and cost-effective manner:
   a. service managers must receive information regarding process outcomes.
   b. interrelated services must be evaluated in order to improve quality.
   c. the critical service path must be identified by service providers.
   d. All of the above are true.

CASES

C13-1 Service Cost Allocation, Multiple Departments and Bases

Obj. 2

Majestic Manufacturing Company has three service departments: maintenance, cafeteria, and material handling. The company also has two operating departments: fabrication and assembly. The service departments provide services to each other as well as to the operating departments. The bases for service department cost allocation are as follows:

Department	Allocation Base
Maintenance	Square footage occupied
Cafeteria	Number of employees
Material handling	Direct labor hours

Service costs are assigned using the step-down method in the following department order:

1. Maintenance
2. Cafeteria
3. Material handling

The following costs were incurred during the most recent quarter of operations:

Maintenance	$130,000
Cafeteria	74,000
Material handling	42,000

The following operating data relate to the most recent quarter of operations:

Department	Number of Employees	Square Footage of Space Occupied	Direct Labor Hours
Maintenance	6	3,000	
Cafeteria	9	4,000	
Material handling	30	1,000	
Fabrication	190	8,000	300,000
Assembly	250	13,000	500,000

In addition to the above, the fabrication department incurred $1,240,000 of manufacturing overhead, and the assembly department incurred $1,536,000 of manufacturing overhead during the most recent quarter.

(Continued)

Required

A. Determine the amounts that should be used as a basis for allocating service costs to each of the operating departments, assuming the step-down method is used.
B. Prepare a cost allocation schedule for the most recent quarter using the step-down method.
C. Determine the total costs of operating the fabrication and assembly departments for the most recent quarter.
D. Which operating department consumes more indirect resources?
E. How would you respond to complaints from the assembly department manager who believes his/her department received a disproportionate share of indirect overhead cost?

C13-2 Strategic Planning and Cost Management in a Competitive
Obj. 4 **Environment: Brookwood Medical Center**

C. Everett Koop, former Surgeon General of the United States, said:

> The goal of healthcare reform should be a healthy society. People must take charge of their own health, should choose lifestyles so that they won't get sick, and should use the healthcare system less often. Healthcare providers must remember that the ethical imperative for healthcare reform is most important and must not focus only on cutting costs. In addition, we should all remember that it is healthcare, not healthcure. Caring is cheap and always ethical; curing costs billions of dollars and isn't always necessary or ethical.

Brookwood Medical Center (BMC) opened in March 1973 with 288 beds and immediately began its expansion program. BMC continued to grow during the 1980s by adding a heart catheterization laboratory, a detoxification unit (for both drug and alcohol abuse), intensive care units, additional surgical facilities, and an on-site motel. BMC also modernized its original hospital facilities through an extensive renovation program.

By the mid-1990s, BMC offered a wide range of health-care services including extended outpatient surgery and ancillary services, nuclear medicine, advanced radiological technology, CT scan, labor and delivery, neurosurgery, and heart surgery. BMC also initiated a wide range of service programs to promote knowledge and wellness in the community. These programs included health and fitness courses, a cancer program, a diabetes program, and medical education programs.

Technology was exerting upward pressure on health delivery costs, while payers, such as health maintenance organizations (HMOs) and preferred provider organizations (PPOs), simultaneously made demands for cost containment and reduction. Hospitals not associated with a university or governmental organization must generate revenues sufficient to cover costs in the long run. Hospitals unable to contain costs faced decreasing profitability, and ultimately, financial failure. Thus, Brookwood Medical Center executives designed a program to help develop a cost-effective, coordinated health-care delivery system that was designed for growth.

In a capitated environment, hospitals charge an annual fee per person for medical care and accept the risk that the costs of care will exceed a predetermined contract rate. Success in a capitated environment requires an increased level of cost sophistication and actuarial skills on the part of the provider. Employer coalitions require capitated contracts that provide complete coverage for their employees' families at a cost that is competitive with plans offered by other insurers. Under capitation, a provider assumes all risk of providing health-care services. Administrators at BMC are considering possible consequences of capitation for highly unprofitable procedures.

Three conditions were causing trouble for health-care providers and were making it necessary to consider economic-based decisions. The conditions are as follows:

1. Fixed fee per service
2. Competition leading to lower fees
3. Technology leading to higher costs

Fixed fee reimbursement policies were limiting the abilities of hospitals to pass along costs to payers. In addition, excess capacity resulted in competition among providers to secure contracts with HMOs and PPOs. The result often led to a decline in revenue per service. Finally, improvements in medical technology led to increased costs as providers acquired newer, modern equipment. Thus, hospitals found themselves in the middle of a big squeeze; revenues were declining while costs were increasing. Potential reactions by providers include implementing wellness programs and health-care rationing.

Capitation, soon to be a reality at BMC, required changes in the delivery of health-care services. The focus of health care changed from treatment to early detection and prevention. In order to survive in a capitated environment, BMC had to assume responsibility for the long-term health of its patients. Before capitation, hospital revenues increased as patient volumes increased; however, under capitation, hospital profitability increased only if capitated patient volumes decreased. Thus, it was necessary for BMC to help its patients take charge of their own health, choose healthy lifestyles, and use the health-care system less often. If BMC could find effective methods of caring for its patients before disease or complications developed, it could increase profitability by avoiding the need to provide high-cost cures and treatments.

The Diabetes Project: BMC's Outcome Management (OM) division compiled clinical and financial outcomes data for specific patient groups. This information was used to design, implement, and improve health-care processes. With the move to capitation, the OM division identified specific Diagnostic Related Groups (DRGs) that would benefit from early hospital intervention. One such group included patients admitted under Diagnostic Related Group (DRG) 294, Diabetes Out of Control. This patient group was targeted for a clinical study at BMC to determine if early intervention and patient education would improve clinical and financial outcomes. An interdisciplinary team, the Diabetes Quality Improvement Team (DQIT), was formed to review existing literature relating to clinical outcomes and compliance behaviors, to study BMC outcomes data, and to develop an intervention program for improving outcomes for BMC's diabetic patients.

Clinical Factors: Diabetes is a progressive and chronic illness with the potential for severe complications. The DQIT found that patients admitted under DRG 294 had high readmission rates and high costs per case. The DQIT found the incidence of strokes twice as common in diabetic populations compared to the general population. In addition, coronary artery disease was more severe in the diabetic patient and is responsible for as many as 60% of the deaths in diabetics. The team concluded that both illness and mortality rates were much higher for the diabetic patient than for the general patient population. However, the team also found evidence that negative outcomes can be altered by early and consistent patient education, support, and intervention. Thus, both physician and community groups supported the establishment of a diabetes education program. In addition, BMC could realize significant gains in profitability under capitation if the program was a success because of the high volume of diabetics treated.

Compliance Behaviors: The next step for the DQIT was to determine how to intervene in the treatment of diabetic patients. Team members found that research on diabetic compliance was inconclusive. However, the studies suggest that diabetic patients who receive education about diabetes and self-care tasks will be more likely to take better care of themselves and to experience positive clinical outcomes.

BMC's Intervention Program: The DQIT developed an intervention program to improve clinical outcomes of patients admitted to BMC with diabetes. DQIT members attempted to increase patient compliance and outcomes by providing patient education, social support, and increased medical support. First, diabetic patients were identified and recruited into the program. Next, patients took a pretest to measure their knowledge of diabetes and self-care processes. Team members found that patients had extremely low levels of knowledge about their disease before the education process despite the length of time since their original diagnosis as diabetics. In fact, the long-term diabetics suffered worse outcomes and consumed more resources than those who had been recently diagnosed. Diabetic patients received extensive education and were instructed about appropriate self-care tasks. BMC set up an outpatient support team so patients would have a source of support and information after hospital discharge. Patients were encouraged to take advantage of BMC's outpatient support team and to comply with physician recommendations regarding future care.

The DQIT measured changes associated with the diabetes intervention program by collecting data from patients at discharge, and at three months, six months, and 12 months postdischarge. The team obtained measures of clinical variables to evaluate the effects of the training program. Selected information appears in Exhibit A.

(Continued)

Outcome: Patients who participated in the Diabetes Outcomes Project have achieved enhanced quality of both care and life, decreased physical consequences of the debilitating disease, and improved self-care abilities. The diabetic patients in the study were not the only group to benefit. External payors experienced financial benefits from the decreased costs per case and the maintenance of stable lengths of stay. Although the diabetes project temporarily reduced BMC's revenue stream, the project has shown that appropriate intervention and proper education of patient populations can positively affect its bottom line when the hospital moves to a capitated environment.

Exhibit A

Compliance Behavior Percentages at Discharge, Three Months, and Six Months Following Discharge

	Compliance Percentages		
	At Discharge	Three Months	Six Months
Compliance Behavior			
Blood glucose monitoring	78	88	92
Calories	29	84	83
Follow doctor's advice	90	100	92
Blood pressure monitoring	90	100	100
Weight control	33	74	85

Required

A. Discuss the competitive environment and financial pressures facing BMC.
B. How is BMC responding to the new competitive environment?
C. Using the outcomes dissemination techniques discussed in the chapter, prepare informative graphs based on the data provided in Exhibit A.
D. What conclusions can you draw from your analysis of the data?
E. Do preventive measures, such as the diabetes intervention program, make sense (both clinically and financially) in a capitated environment? Explain.

GLOSSARY

A

absorption costing
Costing method that assigns costs by function, separating the costs of manufacturing products from the costs of selling, administration, and other nonmanufacturing activities. (M7)

accounting rate of return (ARR)
The average accounting income a project generates per period divided by the amount of the investment in the project. (M12)

activity base
A production activity (such as direct labor hours or machine hours) or a measure of the cost of production activity (direct labor cost, for example). (M3)

activity pools
Collections of costs that relate to an activity. (M5)

activity-based costing (ABC)
Costing method that allocates overhead costs to a product based on the cost of the activities that are required to produce the product. (M1, M5)

actual costing
Costing method that measures unit costs based on the actual costs of direct materials, direct labor, and overhead incurred in producing the units. (M3)

agents
People hired by owners who are expected to manage the company in a way consistent with the owners' interests. (M10)

application software
Software that includes the computer programs that permit data to be recorded and processed. (M8)

B

balanced scorecard
An approach to evaluation that uses key performance criteria in four categories: financial, customer satisfaction, learning and growth, and internal business processes. (M10)

batch processing
Process that combines elements of individual-job and continuous-flow processing. (M4)

bottlenecks
Processes that work at slow rates and restrict the flow of goods or services. (M11)

breakeven point
The level of sales at which all variable and fixed expenses are covered, but no profit is generated. (M7)

budget
A detailed plan describing the use of financial and operating resources over a specific period. (M8)

budgetary slack
The difference between a less demanding budget value and a value managers believe they realistically can achieve. (M8)

C

capital budgeting
The process of making capital investment decisions. (M12)

capital investment decision
A decision to invest in long-term assets such as plant and equipment. (M12)

cash budget
A budget that describes cash requirements for the budget period. (M8)

committed fixed costs
Costs that cannot be eliminated in the relatively short term. (M7)

common cause variation
A variation that is the result of randomness inherent in a process. (M9)

computer network
A network that includes the cables that connect the clients and servers and the hardware and software needed to make the networks function properly. (M8)

contribution margin
The difference between sales revenue and variable costs over an accounting period. (M7)

contribution margin ratio
The ratio (expressed as a percentage) of contribution margin to total sales. (M7)

conversion costs
The costs required to convert materials into products. (M2) The direct labor and manufacturing overhead costs required to convert raw materials into finished goods. (M4)

core activities
The primary activities a service organization carries out. (M5)

cost center
A division of an organization that consumes resources while performing its responsibilities, yet has no direct involvement in generating sales or acquiring property. (M10)

cost drivers
Activities that create costs. (M1)

cost of capital
The cost of funds that can be used to finance a project. (M12)

cost-based transfer pricing policy
A policy that uses either full cost or variable cost as a basis for determining a transfer price. (M10)

cost-volume-profit (CVP) analysis
The use of an understanding of the relationship among costs, volume, and profits to make managerial decisions. (M7)

critical path
The steps needed to complete a process. (M13)

cycle time
The total time required to move a unit from raw materials inventory to finished goods inventory. (M11)

D

database
A set of computerized files in which company data are stored in a form that facilitates retrieval and updating of the data. (M8)

database management system
A system that controals database functions to ensure data are recorded properly and can be accessed only by those authorized to record, update, or retrieve the data. (M8)

departmental production reports
Reports that describe the materials, labor, and overhead used by each department during a given accounting period. (M4)

direct labor costs
The costs of workers who add value to a product through their direct involvement in the production process. (M2)

direct material costs
The costs of the significant raw materials from which a product is manufactured. (M2)

discounting
The translation of future dollars into current dollars. (M12)

discounting methods
Methods of evaluating capital investments that rely on the time value of money. (M12)

discretionary fixed costs
Fixed costs that can be eliminated in the relatively short term. (M7)

E

e-business
Using computer networks, such as the Internet, to make customer sales. (M8)

economies of scale
The savings a company realizes in unit costs by spreading fixed overhead costs over a larger number of units. (M5)

enterprise resource planning (ERP) systems
Systems that integrate most of the business information functions as a basis for management decisions. (M8)

equivalent units
The number of units that would have been produced during a period if all of the department's efforts had resulted in completed units. (M4)

F

favorable variance
A variance that results when the actual price (or quantity) is less than the standard price (or quantity) for materials or labor. (M9)

fixed costs
Costs that do not change in total with volume but vary on a per-unit basis. (M7)

H

hurdle rate
The rate that must be earned before an investment is made; also called required rate of return. (M12)

I

initial department
The department that begins producing a product. (M3)

internal rate of return (IRR)
The interest rate that results in the present value of cash outflows being equal to the present value of cash inflows from an investment. (M12)

investment center
A level within an organization that has the strategic responsibility for generating profits and managing assets. (M10)

J

job cost sheet
A record used to identify each job and to accumulate the costs of manufacturing associated with that job. (M3)

job-order costing
A practice that assigns the cost associated with a particular job to the units produced in that job. (M3)

just-in-time (JIT)
A manufacturing philosophy that attempts to eliminate activities that do not add value by reducing inventory levels. (M2)

just-in-time manufacturing
A production system that pulls products through the manufacturing process on the basis of market demand. (M11)

L

labor budget
A budget that identifies labor resources required to meet production needs. (M8)

M

management accountant
An accountant who produces managerial accounting information for a specific company. (M1)

managerial accounting (management accounting)
The process of preparing, reporting, and interpreting accounting information for use by an organization's internal decision makers. (M1)

manufacturing cell
A group of related machines, typically arranged in the shape of a U. (M11)

manufacturing overhead costs
Usually produced by activities that support a process but often are not directly related to any specific product. (M2)

margin
For ROI, operating income expressed as a percentage of sales. (M10)

market share
That portion of sales a particular brand or company has of the total sales for all similar products. (M3)

market-based transfer pricing policy
A policy that requires buyers and sellers to transfer goods based on externally verifiable market prices. (M10)

master budget
A one-year financial plan for a company. (M1) A collection of related operating budgets covering sales, production, purchasing, labor, manufacturing overhead, administrative expenses, and financing activities. (M8)

materials purchases budget
A budget that identifies the amount of materials that will be required to support a company's total production needs. (M8)

milestones
Major decision points. (M12)

mixed costs
A combination of variable and fixed costs. (M7)

moving baseline concept
The assumption that if the investment is not made, cash flows will decrease because of the competition's superior quality. (M12)

N

negotiated transfer pricing policies
Policies that permit managers to consider factors such as cost and external market prices when negotiating a mutually acceptable transfer price between two business units. (M10)

net present value (NPV)
The difference between the present value of expected future cash inflows from the investment and the present value of expected cash outflows invested. (M12)

nondiscounting methods
Methods of evaluating capital investments that ignore the time value of money. (M12)

normal costing
Measures unit costs by adding the actual costs of direct materials and direct labor to an estimated overhead cost incurred in producing the units. (M3)

O

operating assets
Those assets controlled by the division; they include investments in cash, accounts receivable, inventory, and plant assets used in production. (M10)

operating income
Sales − (cost of goods sold + other operating expenses). (M10)

operating risk
The risk that a drop in sales volume will cause a company not to break even. (M7)

operational capital investment decision
A capital investment decision that affects only part of a company's operations, has an easily predictable life, and represents a relatively small capital outlay for a business. (M12)

operational planning
Identifying objectives for day-to-day activities. (M1)

operations restructuring
A complete evaluation of the relationships among multiple processes, conducted to improve the quality and efficiency of services provided to customers. (M13)

opportunity costs
Costs associated with not taking a particular course of action. (M2, M12)

outcomes data dissemination
The practice of sharing process and outcomes information with those who make resource decisions. (M13)

overhead budget
A budget that provides a schedule of all costs of production other than materials and labor. (M8)

overhead hierarchy
A framework that explains how overhead costs change with various activities. (M5)

P

payback period
The time required to recover an initial investment from expected future cash flows. (M12)

predetermined overhead rate
An estimate of the amount of overhead that management believes should be assigned to a unit of product. (M3)

process costing
Costing method that totals the costs of all units produced in a given accounting period and divides by the total units produced to develop a unit cost. (M4)

process-oriented plant layout
A plant arranged according to machine function, with machines that perform similar functions placed together. (M11)

product cost-subsidy
Term used to describe a situation in which one product subsidizes (supports) the reported costs of another. (M5)

production budget
A budget that identifies the amount of a product that must be produced to meet the company's needs for sales and inventory. (M8)

production rate
The number of units a manufacturing system is capable of producing in a given period of time. (M11)

product-oriented plant layout
A plant based on manufacturing cells that meet the production requirements of products or product families (products that have similar characteristics). (M11)

profit center
A division of an organization that is responsible for both generating sales and controlling costs and expenses. (M10)

Q

quality costs
Costs incurred because poor quality can or does exist in a particular product, function, or business. (M9)

quality loss function
A measure of the loss to society from a product that does not perform satisfactorily. (M9)

R

reciprocal service arrangement
An arrangement whereby support departments exchange services. (M13)

relational database
A set of related files that are linked together so that the files can be updated and information can be retrieved from the files efficiently. (M8)

relevant costs
Costs that change under two or more decision alternatives. (M7)

required rate of return
The rate that must be earned before an investment is made (also called hurdle rate). (M12)

residual value
The market value of an investment at the end of its useful life or service life to a company. (M12)

return on investment (ROI)
A performance indicator calculated by dividing operating income by operating assets. (M10)

revenue center
A division of an organization that has responsibility for generating sales. (M10)

S

sales budget
A budget that projects revenues from sales of a company's products or services. (M8)

schedule of cash collections
A schedule that identifies the timing of cash inflows from sales. (M8)

schedule of cash payments
A schedule that identifies the timing and amount of cash outflows related to production and administrative activities. (M8)

selling and administrative expense budget
A budget containing a list of anticipated expenses for the period for activities other than manufacturing. (M8)

semivariable costs
A combination of variable and fixed costs. (M7)

service life
The period during which an investment is expected to be used. (M12)

special cause variation
A variation with an identifiable source, such as faulty equipment or processes. (M9)

standard costs
The cost of the material and labor that should have been used to achieve actual production levels. (M9)

standards
A cost reporting system based on engineering studies to determine the amount of a resource (such as labor hours or pounds of material) necessary to manufacture a product. (M9)

step-pattern costs
Costs that increase or decrease in total over a wide range of activity levels. (M7)

strategic capital investment decision
A capital investment decision that affects all or a considerable part of a company's operations, has an uncertain life, and requires a large investment. (M12)

subsequent department
A department that continues production on a product. (M4)

sunk costs
Costs associated with decisions that have already been made. (M12)

T

table
A file that contains data represented as rows and columns. (M8)

target profit
The profit that a company wants to make over a given period. (M7)

theory of constraints (TOC)
A theory that states that by identifying a constraint, such as a bottleneck, that exists in the processing of a good or service and taking corrective steps, the process will be improved. (M11)

throughput
The number of units completed by a process in a given period of time. (M11)

total quality management (TQM)
A management philosophy that attempts to eliminate all waste, defects, and activities that do not add value to a company's products. (M1); A management system that seeks continual improvement by asking everyone in an organization to understand, meet, and exceed the needs of customers. (M11)

transfer pricing
A decision involving setting appropriate selling prices for goods or services when both buyer and seller are within the same company. (M10)

transferred-in costs
Costs that have been transferred from an earlier department to a later department in the production process. (M4)

turnover
For ROI, sales divided by average operating assets employed. (M10)

U

unfavorable variance
A variance that results when the actual price (or quantity) exceeds the standard. (M9)

unit cost
The cost of producing one unit of a specific product. (M3)

unit profit margin
The difference between the selling price per unit of a product and the unit cost. (M3)

V

value chain
The set of value-creating activities that extends from the production of raw materials to the sale and servicing of finished goods. (M2)

variable costing
Costing method that assigns costs by their behavior, separating them into variable and fixed components. (M7)

variable costs
Costs that change in total with volume but remain fixed on a per-unit basis. (M7)

variable-costing income statement
A managerial decision-making tool that measures net income by subtracting variable expenses from sales and then subtracting fixed expenses from the difference. (M7)

Appendix A

Future and Present Value

Present and future value concepts are based on the simple idea that a dollar received today is worth more than a dollar received at some future time. If you received a dollar today, you could invest it in a savings account or other investment to earn interest. At the end of a month, a year, or five years, the value of the investment would be greater than it is today because you would have earned interest for the period of investment.

Future Value of a Single Amount. As an example, if you invest $100 on January 1, 2005, in a savings account that earns 6% interest, your investment will be worth $106 on December 31, 2005. The value of the investment on January 1 is the present value of the investment. The value of the investment on December 31 is the future value of the investment. Thus, we can express the relationship as:

Future Value = Present Value $\times$ (1 + R)
$106 = $100 $\times$ 1.06

where R is the rate of return earned on the investment.

If an investment is made for more than one period in which interest is paid and the interest is not withdrawn, the investment earns compound interest. For example, if you leave your money in the savings account for a second year and it earns 6% in the second year, your investment will be worth $112.36 at the end of two years:

Future Value = Present Value $\times$ (1 + R) $\times$ (1 + R)
$112.36 = $100 $\times$ 1.06 $\times$ 1.06
$112.36 = $100 $\times$ $(1.06)^2$

Then, we can write the general equation for the future value of an investment as:

Future Value = Present Value $\times$ $(1 + R)^t$

where t is the number of periods of the investment.

The last term in this equation, $(1 + R)^t$, is referred to as an interest factor. Tables are available that provide the interest factor for various interest rates (R) and time periods (t). Table 1 at the back of this book provides this type of table. For example, the interest factor for 6% interest and two periods is 1.12360. Therefore, the future value of an investment of $100 that earns 6% for two periods is $112.36 = $100 $\times$ 1.12360. You can use the table rather than calculating the interest factor.

Present Value of a Single Amount. If we know the future value of an investment, we can solve for the present value using the same approach as in the previous section. For example, if we know an investment is worth $112.36 at the end of two years and earns 6% interest, we can solve for the present value as follows:

$$\text{Present Value} = \text{Future Value} \times \frac{1}{(1 + R)^t}$$

$$\$100 = \$112.36 \times \frac{1}{(1.06)^2}$$

Again, the last term in this equation is referred to as an interest factor. Table 3 at the back of this book contains this type of table. For example, the interest factor for 6% and two periods is 0.89000. Therefore, the present value of $112.36 received at the end of two years at 6% interest is $100 = $112.36 × 0.89000.

Future Value of an Annuity. In some situations, an investment consists of a series of payments. For example, you might invest $100 each year for three years in a savings account that earns 6%. This type of investment is an annuity because it consists of an equal payment ($100) during each period for a fixed number of periods (3) at a constant rate of return (6%). To calculate the future value of this series of payments, you could calculate the future value of each payment and add these amounts together:

$$\text{Future Value of Annuity} = \$100 \times [(1.06)^2 + (1.06)^1 + (1.06)^0] = \$318.36$$

Or, you could substitute the interest factors from Table 1:

$$\text{Future Value of Annuity} = \$100 \times (1.12360 + 1.06000 + 1.0) = \$318.36$$

We assume in these calculations that payments are made at the end of the period.

Another option is to use the interest factor from a table like Table 2 at the back of this book. This table provides interest factors for computing the future value of an annuity. For example, the interest factor for an annuity of three periods at 6% is 3.18360. Therefore, the future value of an annuity of $100 per period for three periods at 6% is $318.36 = $100 × 3.18360.

Present Value of an Annuity. We can use the same procedure as in the previous section to determine the present value of an annuity. For example, if you made an investment that paid you $100 at the end of each year for three years and earned a 6% rate of return, how much would the investment be worth at the beginning of the three-year period? You could solve for the present value of the annuity by determining the present value of each payment:

$$\text{Present Value of Annuity} = \$100 \left[\frac{1}{(1.06)^3} + \frac{1}{(1.06)^2} + \frac{1}{(1.06)^1} \right] = \$267.30$$

Or, you could substitute interest factors from Table 3 in the equation:

$$\text{Present Value of Annuity} = \$100 \times (0.83962 + 0.89000 + 0.94340) = \$267.30$$

Another alternative is to use the interest factor from a present value of an annuity table such as Table 4 at the back of this book. The interest factor for three periods at 6% is 2.67301 from Table 4. Therefore,

$$\text{Present Value of Annuity} = \$100 \times 2.67301 = \$267.301$$

Future and present value calculations are common in business decisions. Interest factor tables can make these calculations simpler. To use the tables, you must determine whether you are calculating a future or present value and whether you are dealing with a simple (one) amount or a series of equal amounts (an annuity). Also, you must know the number of periods and interest rate for the investment.

APPENDIX B

A Short Introduction to Excel™

SPREADSHEET

This introduction summarizes some of the primary operations and functions of a spreadsheet. It is intended to get you started if you have not had previous experience with Excel. There are many operations and functions in addition to those mentioned here.

Identifying and Selecting Cells

A spreadsheet consists of rows and columns. Rows are identified by numbers, and columns are identified by letters. An intersection of a row and column is a cell. A cell is identified by the column letter and row number that intersect at that cell.

To select a cell, click on the cell using the left mouse button. A cell must be selected before you can enter data or format the cell. Enter data by typing numbers, words, or characters. Enter numbers without commas. Commas can be added using formatting procedures described later. An entire row or column can be selected by clicking on the row or column header. The row header is the leftmost cell in a row that contains the row number. A column header is the topmost cell in a column that contains the cell letter. A group of neighboring cells can be selected by clicking with the left mouse button on the cell in the upper left corner of the group and then dragging the cursor over all the cells to be selected.

Referencing and Mathematical Operations

The contents of one or more cells can be referenced in another cell. To reference a cell, enter the equal sign followed by the cell being referenced. For example, entering =A1 in cell B1 will copy the contents of cell A1 in cell B1. If the contents of cell A1 are changed, these changes also will appear in cell B1. A common use of cell referencing is to calculate totals from data in a series of cells. For example, the following spreadsheet contains sales data for the first three months of a year. The total appears in cell B5. To calculate the total, you would enter a formula in cell B5. The formula would be =B2+B3+B4.

	A	B
1		Sales
2	January	3,457.38
3	February	3,892.90
4	March	3,204.07
5	Total	10,554.35

Normal mathematical operations can be entered in a cell:

=B2+B3 adds the contents of cells B2 and B3.
=B2−B3 subtracts the contents of cell B3 from cell B2.
=B2*B3 multiplies the contents of cell B2 by the contents of cell B3.
=B2/B3 divides the contents of cell B2 by the contents of cell B3.
=B2^B3 raises the number in cell B2 to the power of the number in cell B3.

Copying Cell Contents

The contents (including a formula) can be copied from one cell or group of cells to another cell or group of cells. To copy the contents, select the cells containing the data to be copied and click on Edit/Copy. Then select the cell you want to copy to (or the upper left cell of a group of cells) and click Edit/Paste.

The contents of a cell also can be copied to a neighboring cell using a shortcut procedure. In the following example, we want to copy the contents of cell B4 to cell C4. Cell B4 contains the formula =B2+B3. To copy the contents, we select cell B4 and drag the cursor over the box in the lower right corner of cell B4. The cursor changes shape and appears as crosshairs (+). If we click on the left mouse button while the cursor is in this shape, we can drag the contents of cell B4 to cell C4. The formula =B2+B3 is copied to cell C4, except that the references are automatically adjusted for the new column, and the formula appears as =C2+C3.

	A	B	C
1		Cash	Merchandise
2	Store 1	1,543.02	16,794.23
3	Store 2	4,587.45	24,586.50
4	Total	6,130.47	

Box

When you enter a formula in a cell, such as =B2+B3, the cell addresses are relative addresses. When the formula is copied to another cell, the relative addresses change. Copying the contents of cell B4 above to cell C4 results in an adjustment in the formula so that =B2+B3 is changed to =C2+C3. You can also enter absolute addresses. An absolute address results from entering a dollar sign ($) before a cell address. For example, if you enter =$B2+$B3 in cell B4 and then copy cell B4 to cell C4, the formula in C4 remains =$B2+$B3. You can use absolute addresses for the column (=$B2), the row (=B$2), or both (=B2).

Changing Column Widths

You can make a column wider or narrower using the Format/Column/Width menu. A simpler approach is to move the cursor to the right-hand side of the column header of the column you wish to adjust. The cursor changes to appear as ↔. Click and drag the cursor to the right or left to adjust the column width. The same procedure can be used for row height adjustments.

Menus

The top of an Excel spreadsheet contains menus. A brief description of the menu items you are likely to use on a regular basis follows.

File. Use the File menu to open a **New** spreadsheet, to **Open** an existing spreadsheet, to **Save** a spreadsheet, to **Print** a spreadsheet, and to **Close** the Excel program.

Edit. Use the Edit menu to **Delete** a row, column, or cell. Select the row, column, or cell and click Edit/Delete. You can delete the contents of a particular cell by selecting the cell and pressing the Backspace or Delete key.

View. Use the View menu to select which Toolbars appear on the spreadsheet. The Header and Footer command permits you to add titles and comments to spreadsheets that will appear on printed output. The Zoom command allows spreadsheets to be resized as they appear on the monitor to make them easier to see. This command does not affect printed output.

Insert. Use the Insert menu to insert **Rows, Columns,** and **Cells.** To enter a new row, select the row *above* the row you wish to add and click on Insert/Row. To enter a new column, select the column to the *left* of the column you want to add and click on Insert/Column. To enter a new cell, click on the cell where you want to add a new cell and click on Insert/Cell. A dialog box will ask whether you want the existing cell moved to the right or down. When you enter a new cell, all existing cells to the right or below the entered cell will be moved to make room for the new cell.

Format. Use the Format menu to format **Cells.** Select the cells and click on Format/Cells. A dialog box provides options. The **Number** tab provides various formatting options. The **Alignment** tab provides options for how numbers or text will be aligned. The Wrap text box can be checked (click on the box) to allow for more than one line of text to appear in a particular cell.

Tools. Use the Tools menu to check your **Spelling.**

Data. Use the Data menu to **Sort** data. To sort, select all the columns in the spreadsheet and click Data/Sort. A dialog box lets you select the column or columns you want to use to sort the data.

Help. Use the Help menu to get additional directions about using Excel. Click on Help/Contents and Index. Select a topic from the **Contents** tab or click on the **Index** tab. Type the keyword for an item to get additional information and click on the Display button.

Buttons

Several of the buttons under the menu are particularly useful. The identity of each button and its use are described below.

Save. Click to save your spreadsheet. **Save your work often.**

Copy. Copies the contents of a selected cell or group of cells.

Paste. Pastes the contents of a copied cell or group of cells into a selected cell or group.

Format Painter. Copies the format of a selected cell into another cell or group of cells. Select the cell with the format to be copied and click the button. Then click on the cell or click and drag over the cells where the format will be copied.

Σ AutoSum. Select a cell to contain the sum of a neighboring set of cells (above or to the left of the selected cell). For example, we want to sum the contents of cells E10 and E11 into cell E12. Select cell E12 and click on the AutoSum button. The =Sum formula appears in cell E12 as shown below. You can change the cells to be included in the sum by clicking on the top cell to be included and dragging the cursor over the cells to be added as part of the sum.

Once the sum formula is correct, click on the checkmark in the selection box at the top of the spreadsheet:

| ✕ | ✓ | ❘ = | | =SUM(E10:E11) |

Click on the green checkmark to accept the cell contents. Click on the red X to remove the cell contents.

B *I* <u>U</u>   **Format.** Select a cell or group of cells and click on B for bold, I for italics, and U for underline.

≣ ≣ ≣   **Align.** Select a cell or group of cells and click on a button to align the cell contents to the left, center, or right of the cell.

▦   **Merge and Center.** Select two or more neighboring cells in a row and click on the button to merge the cells into a single cell and center the cell contents. For example, the caption (The Book Wermz) in the following example was created by selecting cells B1 and C1 and clicking on the Merge and Center button.

	A	B	C
1		The Book Wermz	
2	Store 1	1,543.0	Merchandise
3	January	4,528.23	145,360.98

$ % ,   **Number Formatting.** Select a cell or group of cells and click on a button to include a dollar sign in the cell(s), to convert from decimals to percentages, or to add comma separators between thousands' digits in numbers.

+.0 .00   **Decimal Places.** Select a cell or group of cells and click on a button to increase or decrease the number of decimal places showing in the cell(s).

⇥ ⇤   **Indent.** Select a cell or group of cells and click on a button to indent the cell contents or to remove the indentation.

▦ ▾   **Borders.** Select a cell or group of cells and click on the down arrow. Select the type of border you want for the cell(s) from the options provided. If the option you want is already showing on the button, click on the button to select that option.

INDEX

TABLE 1
FUTURE VALUE OF SINGLE AMOUNT

Interest Rate

Period	0.01	0.02	0.03	0.04	0.05	0.06	0.07	0.08	0.09	0.10	0.11	0.12
1	1.01000	1.02000	1.03000	1.04000	1.05000	1.06000	1.07000	1.08000	1.09000	1.10000	1.11000	1.12000
2	1.02010	1.04040	1.06090	1.08160	1.10250	1.12360	1.14490	1.16640	1.18810	1.21000	1.23210	1.25440
3	1.03030	1.06121	1.09273	1.12486	1.15763	1.19102	1.22504	1.25971	1.29503	1.33100	1.36763	1.40493
4	1.04060	1.08243	1.12551	1.16986	1.21551	1.26248	1.31080	1.36049	1.41158	1.46410	1.51807	1.57352
5	1.05101	1.10408	1.15927	1.21665	1.27628	1.33823	1.40255	1.46933	1.53862	1.61051	1.68506	1.76234
6	1.06152	1.12616	1.19405	1.26532	1.34010	1.41852	1.50073	1.58687	1.67710	1.77156	1.87041	1.97382
7	1.07214	1.14869	1.22987	1.31593	1.40710	1.50363	1.60578	1.71382	1.82804	1.94872	2.07616	2.21068
8	1.08286	1.17166	1.26677	1.36857	1.47746	1.59385	1.71819	1.85093	1.99256	2.14359	2.30454	2.47596
9	1.09369	1.19509	1.30477	1.42331	1.55133	1.68948	1.83846	1.99900	2.17189	2.35795	2.55804	2.77308
10	1.10462	1.21899	1.34392	1.48024	1.62889	1.79085	1.96715	2.15892	2.36736	2.59374	2.83942	3.10585
11	1.11567	1.24337	1.38423	1.53945	1.71034	1.89830	2.10485	2.33164	2.58043	2.85312	3.15176	3.47855
12	1.12683	1.26824	1.42576	1.60103	1.79586	2.01220	2.25219	2.51817	2.81266	3.13843	3.49845	3.89598
13	1.13809	1.29361	1.46853	1.66507	1.88565	2.13293	2.40985	2.71962	3.06580	3.45227	3.88328	4.36349
14	1.14947	1.31948	1.51259	1.73168	1.97993	2.26090	2.57853	2.93719	3.34173	3.79750	4.31044	4.88711
15	1.16097	1.34587	1.55797	1.80094	2.07893	2.39656	2.75903	3.17217	3.64248	4.17725	4.78459	5.47357
16	1.17258	1.37279	1.60471	1.87298	2.18287	2.54035	2.95216	3.42594	3.97031	4.59497	5.31089	6.13039
17	1.18430	1.40024	1.65285	1.94790	2.29202	2.69277	3.15882	3.70002	4.32763	5.05447	5.89509	6.86604
18	1.19615	1.42825	1.70243	2.02582	2.40662	2.85434	3.37993	3.99602	4.71712	5.55992	6.54355	7.68997
19	1.20811	1.45681	1.75351	2.10685	2.52695	3.02560	3.61653	4.31570	5.14166	6.11591	7.26334	8.61276
20	1.22019	1.48595	1.80611	2.19112	2.65330	3.20714	3.86968	4.66096	5.60441	6.72750	8.06231	9.64629
21	1.23239	1.51567	1.86029	2.27877	2.78596	3.39956	4.14056	5.03383	6.10881	7.40025	8.94917	10.80385
22	1.24472	1.54598	1.91610	2.36992	2.92526	3.60354	4.43040	5.43654	6.65860	8.14027	9.93357	12.10031
23	1.25716	1.57690	1.97359	2.46472	3.07152	3.81975	4.74053	5.87146	7.25787	8.95430	11.02627	13.55235
24	1.26973	1.60844	2.03279	2.56330	3.22510	4.04893	5.07237	6.34118	7.91108	9.84973	12.23916	15.17863
25	1.28243	1.64061	2.09378	2.66584	3.38635	4.29187	5.42743	6.84848	8.62308	10.83471	13.58546	17.00006

TABLE 2
FUTURE VALUE OF ANNUITY (AMOUNTS PAID OR RECEIVED AT END OF PERIOD)

Interest Rate

Period	0.01	0.02	0.03	0.04	0.05	0.06	0.07	0.08	0.09	0.10	0.11	0.12
1	1.00000	1.00000	1.00000	1.00000	1.00000	1.00000	1.00000	1.00000	1.00000	1.00000	1.00000	1.00000
2	2.01000	2.02000	2.03000	2.04000	2.05000	2.06000	2.07000	2.08000	2.09000	2.10000	2.11000	2.12000
3	3.03010	3.06040	3.09090	3.12160	3.15250	3.18360	3.21490	3.24640	3.27810	3.31000	3.34210	3.37440
4	4.06040	4.12161	4.18363	4.24646	4.31013	4.37462	4.43994	4.50611	4.57313	4.64100	4.70973	4.77933
5	5.10101	5.20404	5.30914	5.41632	5.52563	5.63709	5.75074	5.86660	5.98471	6.10510	6.22780	6.35285
6	6.15202	6.30812	6.46841	6.63298	6.80191	6.97532	7.15329	7.33593	7.52333	7.71561	7.91286	8.11519
7	7.21354	7.43428	7.66246	7.89829	8.14201	8.39384	8.65402	8.92280	9.20043	9.48717	9.78327	10.08901
8	8.28567	8.58297	8.89234	9.21423	9.54911	9.89747	10.25980	10.63663	11.02847	11.43589	11.85943	12.29969
9	9.36853	9.75463	10.15911	10.58280	11.02656	11.49132	11.97799	12.48756	13.02104	13.57948	14.16397	14.77566
10	10.46221	10.94972	11.46388	12.00611	12.57789	13.18079	13.81645	14.48656	15.19293	15.93742	16.72201	17.54874
11	11.56683	12.16872	12.80780	13.48635	14.20679	14.97164	15.78360	16.64549	17.56029	18.53117	19.56143	20.65458
12	12.68250	13.41209	14.19203	15.02581	15.91713	16.86994	17.88845	18.97713	20.14072	21.38428	22.71319	24.13313
13	13.80933	14.68033	15.61779	16.62684	17.71298	18.88214	20.14064	21.49530	22.95338	24.52271	26.21164	28.02911
14	14.94742	15.97394	17.08632	18.29191	19.59863	21.01507	22.55049	24.21492	26.01919	27.97498	30.09492	32.39260
15	16.09690	17.29342	18.59891	20.02359	21.57856	23.27597	25.12902	27.15211	29.36092	31.77248	34.40536	37.27971
16	17.25786	18.63929	20.15688	21.82453	23.65749	25.67253	27.88805	30.32428	33.00340	35.94973	39.18995	42.75328
17	18.43044	20.01207	21.76159	23.69751	25.84037	28.21288	30.84022	33.75023	36.97370	40.54470	44.50084	48.88367
18	19.61475	21.41231	23.41444	25.64541	28.13238	30.90565	33.99903	37.45024	41.30134	45.59917	50.39594	55.74971
19	20.81090	22.84056	25.11687	27.67123	30.53900	33.75999	37.37896	41.44626	46.01846	51.15909	56.93949	63.43968
20	22.01900	24.29737	26.87037	29.77808	33.06595	36.78559	40.99549	45.76196	51.16012	57.27500	64.20283	72.05244
21	23.23919	25.78332	28.67649	31.96920	35.71925	39.99273	44.86518	50.42292	56.76453	64.00250	72.26514	81.69874
22	24.47159	27.29898	30.53678	34.24797	38.50521	43.39229	49.00574	55.45676	62.87334	71.40275	81.21431	92.50258
23	25.71630	28.84496	32.45288	36.61789	41.43048	46.99586	53.43614	60.89330	69.53194	79.54302	91.14788	104.60289
24	26.97346	30.42186	34.42647	39.08260	44.50200	50.81558	58.17667	66.76476	76.78981	88.49733	102.17415	118.15524
25	28.24320	32.03030	36.45926	41.64591	47.72710	54.86451	63.24904	73.10594	84.70090	98.34706	114.41331	133.33387

TABLE 4
PRESENT VALUE OF ANNUITY

Interest Rate

Period	0.01	0.02	0.03	0.04	0.05	0.06	0.07	0.08	0.09	0.10	0.11	0.12
1	0.99010	0.98039	0.97087	0.96154	0.95238	0.94340	0.93458	0.92593	0.91743	0.90909	0.90090	0.89286
2	1.97040	1.94156	1.91347	1.88609	1.85941	1.83339	1.80802	1.78326	1.75911	1.73554	1.71252	1.69005
3	2.94099	2.88388	2.82861	2.77509	2.72325	2.67301	2.62432	2.57710	2.53129	2.48685	2.44371	2.40183
4	3.90197	3.80773	3.71710	3.62990	3.54595	3.46511	3.38721	3.31213	3.23972	3.16987	3.10245	3.03735
5	4.85343	4.71346	4.57971	4.45182	4.32948	4.21236	4.10020	3.99271	3.88965	3.79079	3.69590	3.60478
6	5.79548	5.60143	5.41719	5.24214	5.07569	4.91732	4.76654	4.62288	4.48592	4.35526	4.23054	4.11141
7	6.72819	6.47199	6.23028	6.00205	5.78637	5.58238	5.38929	5.20637	5.03295	4.86842	4.71220	4.56376
8	7.65168	7.32548	7.01969	6.73274	6.46321	6.20979	5.97130	5.74664	5.53482	5.33493	5.14612	4.96764
9	8.56602	8.16224	7.78611	7.43533	7.10782	6.80169	6.51523	6.24689	5.99525	5.75902	5.53705	5.32825
10	9.47130	8.98259	8.53020	8.11090	7.72173	7.36009	7.02358	6.71008	6.41766	6.14457	5.88923	5.65022
11	10.36763	9.78685	9.25262	8.76048	8.30641	7.88687	7.49867	7.13896	6.80519	6.49506	6.20652	5.93770
12	11.25508	10.57534	9.95400	9.38507	8.86325	8.38384	7.94269	7.53608	7.16073	6.81369	6.49236	6.19437
13	12.13374	11.34837	10.63496	9.98565	9.39357	8.85268	8.35765	7.90378	7.48690	7.10336	6.74987	6.42355
14	13.00370	12.10625	11.29607	10.56312	9.89864	9.29498	8.74547	8.24424	7.78615	7.36669	6.98187	6.62817
15	13.86505	12.84926	11.93794	11.11839	10.37966	9.71225	9.10791	8.55948	8.06069	7.60608	7.19087	6.81086
16	14.71787	13.57771	12.56110	11.65230	10.83777	10.10590	9.44665	8.85137	8.31256	7.82371	7.37916	6.97399
17	15.56225	14.29187	13.16612	12.16567	11.27407	10.47726	9.76322	9.12164	8.54363	8.02155	7.54879	7.11963
18	16.39827	14.99203	13.75351	12.65930	11.68959	10.82760	10.05909	9.37189	8.75563	8.20141	7.70162	7.24967
19	17.22601	15.67846	14.32380	13.13394	12.08532	11.15812	10.33560	9.60360	8.95011	8.36492	7.83929	7.36578
20	18.04555	16.35143	14.87747	13.59033	12.46221	11.46992	10.59401	9.81815	9.12855	8.51356	7.96333	7.46944
21	18.85698	17.01121	15.41502	14.02916	12.82115	11.76408	10.83553	10.01680	9.29224	8.64869	8.07507	7.56200
22	19.66038	17.65805	15.93692	14.45112	13.16300	12.04158	11.06124	10.20074	9.44243	8.77154	8.17574	7.64465
23	20.45582	18.29220	16.44361	14.85684	13.48857	12.30338	11.27219	10.37106	9.58021	8.88322	8.26643	7.71843
24	21.24339	18.91393	16.93554	15.24696	13.79864	12.55036	11.46933	10.52876	9.70661	8.98474	8.34814	7.78432
25	22.02316	19.52346	17.41315	15.62208	14.09394	12.78336	11.65358	10.67478	9.82258	9.07704	8.42174	7.84314

TABLE 3
PRESENT VALUE OF SINGLE AMOUNT

Interest Rate

Period	0.01	0.02	0.03	0.04	0.05	0.06	0.07	0.08	0.09	0.10	0.11	0.12
1	0.99010	0.98039	0.97087	0.96154	0.95238	0.94340	0.93458	0.92593	0.91743	0.90909	0.90090	0.89286
2	0.98030	0.96117	0.94260	0.92456	0.90703	0.89000	0.87344	0.85734	0.84168	0.82645	0.81162	0.79719
3	0.97059	0.94232	0.91514	0.88900	0.86384	0.83962	0.81630	0.79383	0.77218	0.75131	0.73119	0.71178
4	0.96098	0.92385	0.88849	0.85480	0.82270	0.79209	0.76290	0.73503	0.70843	0.68301	0.65873	0.63552
5	0.95147	0.90573	0.86261	0.82193	0.78353	0.74726	0.71299	0.68058	0.64993	0.62092	0.59345	0.56743
6	0.94205	0.88797	0.83748	0.79031	0.74622	0.70496	0.66634	0.63017	0.59627	0.56447	0.53464	0.50663
7	0.93272	0.87056	0.81309	0.75992	0.71068	0.66506	0.62275	0.58349	0.54703	0.51316	0.48166	0.45235
8	0.92348	0.85349	0.78941	0.73069	0.67684	0.62741	0.58201	0.54027	0.50187	0.46651	0.43393	0.40388
9	0.91434	0.83676	0.76642	0.70259	0.64461	0.59190	0.54393	0.50025	0.46043	0.42410	0.39092	0.36061
10	0.90529	0.82035	0.74409	0.67556	0.61391	0.55839	0.50835	0.46319	0.42241	0.38554	0.35218	0.32197
11	0.89632	0.80426	0.72242	0.64958	0.58468	0.52679	0.47509	0.42888	0.38753	0.35049	0.31728	0.28748
12	0.88745	0.78849	0.70138	0.62460	0.55684	0.49697	0.44401	0.39711	0.35553	0.31863	0.28584	0.25668
13	0.87866	0.77303	0.68095	0.60057	0.53032	0.46884	0.41496	0.36770	0.32618	0.28966	0.25751	0.22917
14	0.86996	0.75788	0.66112	0.57748	0.50507	0.44230	0.38782	0.34046	0.29925	0.26333	0.23199	0.20462
15	0.86135	0.74301	0.64186	0.55526	0.48102	0.41727	0.36245	0.31524	0.27454	0.23939	0.20900	0.18270
16	0.85282	0.72845	0.62317	0.53391	0.45811	0.39365	0.33873	0.29189	0.25187	0.21763	0.18829	0.16312
17	0.84438	0.71416	0.60502	0.51337	0.43630	0.37136	0.31657	0.27027	0.23107	0.19784	0.16963	0.14564
18	0.83602	0.70016	0.58739	0.49363	0.41552	0.35034	0.29586	0.25025	0.21199	0.17986	0.15282	0.13004
19	0.82774	0.68643	0.57029	0.47464	0.39573	0.33051	0.27651	0.23171	0.19449	0.16351	0.13768	0.11611
20	0.81954	0.67297	0.55368	0.45639	0.37689	0.31180	0.25842	0.21455	0.17843	0.14864	0.12403	0.10367
21	0.81143	0.65978	0.53755	0.43883	0.35894	0.29416	0.24151	0.19866	0.16370	0.13513	0.11174	0.09256
22	0.80340	0.64684	0.52189	0.42196	0.34185	0.27751	0.22571	0.18394	0.15018	0.12285	0.10067	0.08264
23	0.79544	0.63416	0.50669	0.40573	0.32557	0.26180	0.21095	0.17032	0.13778	0.11168	0.09069	0.07379
24	0.78757	0.62172	0.49193	0.39012	0.31007	0.24698	0.19715	0.15770	0.12640	0.10153	0.08170	0.06588
25	0.77977	0.60953	0.47761	0.37512	0.29530	0.23300	0.18425	0.14602	0.11597	0.09230	0.07361	0.05882